FOUNDATION

PRESS

TRIAL STORIES

Edited By

MICHAEL E. TIGAR
Research Professor of Law
American University Washington College of Law
Visiting Professor of Law, Duke Law School

ANGELA J. DAVIS
Professor of Law
American University Washington College of Law

FOUNDATION PRESS
75TH ANNIVERSARY

THOMSON

WEST

Cover Design: Keith Stout

© 2008 By FOUNDATION PRESS
        395 Hudson Street
        New York, NY 10014
        Phone Toll Free 1–877–888–1330
        Fax (212) 367–6799
        foundation–press.com
Printed in the United States of America

ISBN 978–1–59941–119–4

TEXT IS PRINTED ON 10% POST CONSUMER RECYCLED PAPER

For Jane, the love of my life
M.E.T.

For my mother, Sara Harris Jordan (1917 - 2003)
A.J.D.

*

ACKNOWLEDGMENTS

Michael E. Tigar gratefully acknowledges the help of Natalie Hirt at Duke Law School, and Jennifer Dodenhoff at the Washington College of Law.

Angela J. Davis thanks Timothy Harris, Molly Hostetler and Elizabeth Janelle for their research assistance and Professor Gerald Uelman for his extremely helpful comments and advice. She also thanks Vanessa Martin, Rita Montoya, and Kendra Mullin for editorial assistance with all chapters.

"Treason, Aaron Burr, and the National Imagination" is (c) The University of Chicago Press, and is used by permission of the Press and the author, Prof. Robert Ferguson. It originally appeared as a chapter in Robert A. Ferguson, The Trial in American Life (2007).

Paul Bergman gratefully acknowledges June Kim, UCLA School of Law librarian, and his co-author Mimi Wesson for their marvelous research assistance. He also thanks Mimi for making the preparation of the essay such a wonderfully positive experience.

Space does not permit Marianne Wesson to acknowledge everyone who has helped her unearth the truth about the Hillmon case, but she would like to record her special gratitude towards her colleagues Jane Thompson and Dennis Van Gerven, the staff of the National Archives and Records Administration in Kansas City, and remarkable and generous attorneys Mark Thornhill and Mackenzie Murphy-Wilfong for achieving permission for disinterment of John Hillmon's remains.

Carol Steiker thanks Angela J. Davis, Jordan Steiker, and Michael Tigar for helpful comments, and Allen O'Rourke for extremely able research assistance.

Robert M. Lloyd thanks the staff of the Center for American History and the staff of the Tarleton Law Library at the University of Texas, particularly Jeanne Price, for the help they provided during his research.

Ellen Yaroshefsky thanks Jo Ann Harris for her thoughtful, careful editorial pen and unflagging friendship and Jill Mullins, a Seattle student, for her factual research. She dedicates her essay to Sherrie and Toni Allery.

*

TRIAL STORIES

*

FOUNDATION PRESS

TRIAL STORIES

*

Introduction

Trials—and particularly jury trials—capture the American imagination as do few other public events. Long before people eagerly scanned the sports pages for news of their favorite, or detested, teams, great trials were front page news and the subject of intense debate. Trials, when the advocates are worthy of their task, are forums in which themes of justice and human emotion are played out before the body of community representatives known as the jury.

The 1735 trial of newspaper editor John Peter Zenger was, according to Governeur Morris, who signed the Declaration of Independence, "the morning star of that liberty which subsequently revolutionized America." The trials challenging British search and seizure of colonists' property in the 1760s triggered events of which John Adams later wrote, "Then and there was the child Independence born." The trial and acquittal of Aaron Burr for treason raised issues that echoed in the public consciousness for decades. The advocacy of Clarence Darrow, in cases involving labor rights, race relations, and homicide, is studied today for what it teaches us about lawyering and the role of law in society. Civil cases raise significant issues about allocation of power, the social and legal responsibility of powerful entities and individuals, social relations, and allocation of risks in a complex society. They, too, have been front page news.

There is not, or rather should not be, any such thing as an "ordinary" or prosaic trial. If you are an advocate and you treat your trial as "just another day at work," you will fail to inspire the jurors and the judge. The jurors have taken time off from their daily lives. They are compensated at or below the minimum wage. They are told that their function lies at the heart of participatory democracy. It is often difficult for them to believe this adjuration, as they see and hear lawyers, parties and court officials going about their business in an uninspired way. Lawyers who awaken the jurors' sense of justice, and who put the case as a story that can have a just outcome if the jurors will make it so, succeed in their work. More broadly, they help redeem the public perception that justice is sometimes possible to achieve.

The reader may ask, "What purpose is this book intended to serve?" Understanding advocacy has for centuries involved two distinct, but related, aspects. The first has to do with the techniques and tools of advocacy—examining witnesses, arguing to judges and juries. These elements have been taught since Greek and Roman times under the rubric of "rhetoric" and today form the major part of trial advocacy simulation courses taught in law schools and in seminars. However, learning to use the advocate's tools is only the beginning. For observers of courts and trials, seeing these tools at work is only a part of experiencing and understanding what is going on.

The second aspect of learning is to see the advocate take up a client's claim for justice and understand that client and that claim so fully that he or she is able to use the techniques and tools to advance the claim. The stories in this book show us advocates doing that work, and how—and often why—they did it. The advocate's understanding begins with knowing the client, a process that involves empathy tinged with enough skepticism to preserve independent judgment. It continues with tireless research into facts and law. Every advocate in these stories displays a thorough command of complex and sometimes contradictory evidence. The advocate also brings to the process a way of telling the story that awakens the audience's sense of justice. This second aspect cannot be "taught" from case files; it must be learned by observing advocates and then by experience.

Trial advocacy stories differ from other stories in significant ways. There is an old image of two people each telling their "stories" to someone who must decide which is most persuasive. In conversation, we tell each other stories about past events. In this book, we have chosen trials in which the competing stories are compelling. However, the chapter authors have gone beyond retelling. They reveal how the story was told, and in that way teach us about advocacy and advocates. A trial story is highly structured. The substantive law—of contracts, civil wrongs or criminal law—defines what claims will be heard and what defenses allowed. The story cannot be told as narrative. Witnesses must appear, perhaps with documents and objects; their telling must take place within rules of evidence and trial procedure. Lawyers argue to the judge or jury, seeking to put the evidence in some kind of persuasive pattern.

This complex process does not take place in the abstract. Trials occur at moments of historical time. Advocate decisions about how to tell the story must be based on knowing what is likely to catch the attention of, and eventually persuade, the jurors chosen from the community and the judge who is presiding. So although this is a book about story-telling, it is not, and could not be, about making up tales. You will see made-up tales in these pages, but always there will be a lawyer tearing them down and exposing them for what they are, using the powerful tool known as cross-examination or the other means of contradiction in the adversary process.

The stories in this book are real, in at least three senses of that word. First, these stories are drawn from the records of actual cases. Second, every one of these cases is iconic because it tells us something important about the important social role of advocates and advocacy in the search for justice. Third, these cases illustrate techniques and skills that every advocate should learn: examination of prospective jurors—voir dire, opening statement, direct examination, cross-examination, use of expert testimony, closing argument, and argument to the judge.

The cases span more than two centuries. You will see, as you would expect, that rhetorical styles have changed. You will also see, and perhaps be surprised, that the basic themes of story-telling have hardly changed at all. At the dawn of the Republic, jury service was limited to white men of property. Until the last quarter of the 20th Century, it was constitutionally permissible to discriminate against women in jury selection. Racial discrimination in peremptory challenges was not held unconstitutional until 1986. These constitution-based changes are coupled with the increasing social and ethnic diversity of a society now numbering 300 million. Jurors today are not all one color, or one cast of mind.

Despite the change in jury composition, themes remain relatively constant. We will return to this point later in this introduction. What has changed? In 1800, lawyers and jurors, in addition to being white men, were more or less of the same social class. Today, a broader spectrum of people has the chance to go to law school, and a broader spectrum are jurors. It is difficult sometimes for advocates to understand and to bridge the gap between their own social situation and the varying situations of the jurors they are addressing. As you read the stories in this book, keep in mind the idea of bridge-building and see how advocates deal with it.

Some chapters discuss the advocacy on both sides. Other chapters take on the perspective of the plaintiff or defense, so that you the reader can deconstruct and evaluate the advocates' work. For example, you will see the prosecution perspective in the Burr case, and the defense view in the Leopold—Loeb and Nichols cases.

It is characteristic of American society that great social issues find their way to the courthouse. In a historic trial, one concern is that the verdict be seen as fair and fairly arrived at. Such a verdict commands community approval. It places beyond the reach of all but the most captious critic any claim that the events portrayed did not occur. A most dramatic example of this point is the Nuremburg trials at the close of World War Two. Some Allied leaders wanted to round up the Nazi leaders and shoot them. The decision to hold a trial was a commitment to display evidence of Nazi crimes to the world and to show how eleven million people died in the Holocaust. In this book, many if not most of the trials have achieved historical significance because they teach more than how a story is told; they teach how a story fits in the pattern of historical and social thought.

The Trial of Aaron Burr

The arrest and trial of Aaron Burr has many parallels to modern high-stakes, high-visibility trials. Burr's guilt was publicly avowed by President Jefferson. The trial judge, John Marshall, knew that his performance of duty would draw criticism from the President's allies and opponents, and might even lead to his impeachment. Defense counsel attacked the prosecution's alleged political motivation at every opportunity. Burr served as his own co-counsel. The prosecution sought to expand the definition of a political offense—in this case treason—by seeking to have advocacy, preparation for action, and planning included in the substantive offense that was charged. Lawyers on both sides knew that when they spoke in court they were addressing three distinct audiences: the jury, the presiding judge, and the public.

The defense eventually convinced the presiding judge that there was no case to answer. They did this through cross-examination and able argument. The prosecutors, though denied a conviction, seem to have convinced the jurors that Burr was guilty of something if not of the offense in the indictment. They certainly convinced the public, or at least important persons of the time, of Burr's guilt. The verdict of historians was unfavorable to Burr until the 20th century historical and fictional works that Professor Ferguson discusses. Aaron Burr served with distinction in the Revolutionary War. He was Thomas Jefferson's Vice President, 1801–05, though his own and Jefferson's stated reasons for his not being asked to serve a second term differ. John Adams, who despised Jefferson, thought that Burr's presence on the ticket had ensured Adams' electoral defeat and Jefferson's electoral victory in the 1800 election.

After Burr left the United States Senate on March 2, 1805, he set about organizing the political and military campaign that led to his being tried for treason. After a number of pretrial proceedings in different venues, he was indicted in Virginia on August 17, 1807. The indictment, in the form that such pleadings took at the time, began:

> The grand inquest of the United States of America, for the Virginia district, upon their oath, do present, that Aaron Burr, late of the city of New York, and state of New York, attorney at law, being an inhabitant of, and residing within the United States, and under the protection of the laws of the United States, and owing allegiance and fidelity to the same United States, not having the fear of God before his eyes, nor weighing the duty of his said allegiance, but being

moved and seduced by the instigation of the devil, wickedly devising and intending the peace and tranquility of the same United States to disturb and to stir, move, and excite insurrection, rebellion and war against the said United States, on the tenth day of December, in the year of Christ, one thousand eight hundred and six, at a certain place called and known by the name of "Blennerhassett's Island," in the county of Wood, and district of Virginia aforesaid, and within the jurisdiction of this court, with force and arms, unlawfully, falsely, maliciously and traitorously did compass, imagine and intend to raise and levy war, insurrection and rebellion against the said United States, and in order to fulfil and bring to effect the said traitorous compassings, imaginations and intentions of him the said Aaron Burr, he, the said Aaron Burr, afterwards, to wit, on the said tenth day of December, in the year one thousand eight hundred and six, aforesaid, at the said island called "Blennerhassett's Island" as aforesaid, in the county of Wood aforesaid, in the district of Virginia aforesaid, and within the jurisdiction of this court, with a great multitude of persons whose names at present are unknown to the grand inquest aforesaid, to a great number, to wit: to the number of thirty persons and upwards, armed and arrayed in a warlike manner, that is to say, with guns, swords and dirks, and other warlike weapons, as well offensive as defensive, being then and there unlawfully, maliciously and traitorously assembled and gathered together, did falsely and traitorously assemble and join themselves together against the said United States, and then and there with force and arms did falsely and traitorously, and in a warlike and hostile manner, array and dispose themselves against the said United States. . . .

Professor Robert Ferguson has focused on prosecutor William Wirt's construction and delivery of a story about Burr that portrays the defendant as dishonorable seducer, heedless of any sense of obligation to people or his country.

The Burr case has come to symbolize many important aspects of fair criminal trials in the United States. It is well-known that Chief Justice Marshall held that a criminal defendant might have compulsory process to subpoena even the President of the United States. Less well-known is Marshall's opinion from the bench on the purposes of jury trial and the need for impartial jurors.

The prosecution had argued that a juror who had "mere impressions" that Burr was guilty could still be qualified to serve, because such a juror would not have a fixed opinion of Burr's guilt. The defense argued that such a person was not impartial, but rather someone who had likely been influenced unduly by press comments and the prosecutors' public statements. These arguments are, the reader will appreciate, remarkably similar to those that are made in high-profile cases even today. Chief Justice Marshall's views are worth quoting at some length, for they too have a distinctly modern relevance, even though made in a time when only white men of property were eligible for jury service:

> The great value of the trial by jury certainly consists in its fairness and impartiality.... The jury should enter upon the trial with minds open to those impressions which the testimony and the law of the case ought to make, not with those preconceived opinions which will resist those impressions. All the provisions of the law are calculated to obtain this end. Why is it that the most distant relative of a party cannot serve upon his jury? Certainly the single circumstance of relationship, taken in itself, unconnected with its consequences, would furnish no objection. The real reason of the rule is, that the law suspects the relative of partiality; suspects his mind to be under a bias, which will prevent his fairly hearing and fairly deciding on the testimony which may be offered to him. The end to be obtained is an impartial jury; to secure this end, a man is prohibited from serving on it whose connection with a party is such as to induce a suspicion of partiality. The relationship may be remote; the person may never have seen the party; he may declare that he feels no prejudice in the case; and yet the law cautiously incapacitates him from serving on the jury because it suspects prejudice, because in general persons in a similar situation would feel prejudice.
>
> It would be strange if the law was chargeable with the inconsistency of thus carefully protecting the end from being defeated by particular means, and leaving it to be defeated by other means. It would be strange if the law would be so solicitous to secure a fair trial as to exclude a distant, unknown relative from the jury, and yet be totally regardless of those in whose minds feelings existed much more unfavorable to an impartial decision of the case.... Why do personal prejudices constitute a just cause of challenge? Solely because the individual who is under their influence is presumed to have a bias on is mind which will prevent an impartial decision of the case, according to the testimony. He may declare that notwithstanding these prejudices he is determined to listen to the evidence, and be governed by it; but the law will not trust him. Is there less reason to suspect him who has prejudged the case, and has deliberately formed and delivered an opinion upon it? Such a person may believe that he will be regulated by testimony, but the law suspects him, and certainly not without reason. He will listen with more favor to that testimony which confirms, than to that which would change his opinion; it is not to be expected that he will weigh

evidence or argument as fairly as a man whose judgment is not made up in the case. . . .

Were it possible to obtain a jury without any prepossessions whatever respecting the guilt or innocence of the accused, it would be extremely desirable to obtain such a jury; but this is perhaps impossible, and therefore will not be required. The opinion which has been avowed by the court is, that light impressions which may fairly be supposed to yield to the testimony that may be offered, which may leave the mind open to a fair consideration of that testimony, constitute no sufficient objection to a juror; but that those strong and deep impressions which will close the mind against the testimony that may be offered in opposition to them, which will combat that testimony, and resist its force, do constitute a sufficient objection to him.

The Hillmon Case

In 1879, a man died of a bullet wound to the head near Crooked Creek, Kansas. This unknown unfortunate left behind a legacy of mystery and landmark jurisprudence. From his death sprang six lawsuits between Mrs. Sallie Hillmon, who claimed the man was her husband, and the insurance companies that underwrote his life insurance policy, all of which suspected fraud. In addition, this man's death gave birth to a new hearsay exception: the "state of mind" exception, now codified as Federal Rule of Evidence 803(3). The insurance companies asserted that the dead man was not Mr. Hillmon, but rather an unsuspecting Mr. Walter, who was murdered by Mr. Hillmon so that the Hillmons could take advantage of their lucrative life insurance policies. As proof of their claim, the insurance companies offered a letter sent from Mr. Walter to his fiancée before the murder, stating that he would soon be traveling with a "man by the name of Hillmon" on a well-paid venture. He was never heard from again. The Supreme Court would eventually rule that this letter was admissible, because it declared his intent to take action in the future, and such declarations made the fact that he then took such action more likely.

In this essay, Professors Paul Bergman and Marianne Wesson channel the attorneys for Mrs. Sallie Hillmon and Connecticut Mutual Life Insurance Company. In order to harvest the truth from the fertile factual landscape, the spirits of these lawyers plow through the legal and social terrain of the Hillmon trials. They lay bare for a contemporary jury their knowledge, beliefs, and strategies. They compile the evidence and arguments presented throughout the serial Hillmon trial and seek to persuade a twentieth century audience of the justice of their cause and the legitimacy (or lack thereof) of the new hearsay exception. The authors' approach permits the modern reader to deconstruct the Hillmon story and see how the pieces of it may be made to fit.

Leopold and Loeb

On May 21, 1924, Nathan Leopold and Richard Loeb murdered Bobby Franks in Chicago. They were indicted and pleaded guilty to murder. Clarence Darrow defended them in a penalty trial. They waived a jury. The trial judge gave the defendants a life sentence. The Leopold and Loeb case is the only one in this book not tried to a jury. It is not difficult to fathom the reasons why Darrow chose to make his arguments to a judge. Opinion in Chicago was so inflamed against the defendants that selecting jurors who would swear to be impartial and be truthful in doing so was impossible. Darrow's first major contribution to the law was his advocacy of a pardon for the defendants unjustly convicted in the Haymarket case, an example of juror prejudice in the context of a high-profile trial.

The Leopold–Loeb case has been the subject of books, motion pictures and television plays. Professor Carol Steiker explains at the beginning of her chapter why she believes that the case deserves "yet another look." The editors agree. In any discussion of advocacy, Darrow's presentation and marshalling of the evidence represents the very best of 20th Century lawyering. Professor Steiker shows us how Darrow anticipated the issue that has become central in capital trials—the "reasoned moral response" to evidence not only about the crime but about the defendant's individual characteristics.

Dr. Ossian Sweet

In 1925, Dr. Ossian Sweet, who was African American, moved into an all-white neighborhood in Detroit with his wife and child. A white mob surrounded his home on September 9th of that year. A member of the mob was shot and killed, and Dr. Sweet was charged with his murder, along with his wife, brothers and numerous friends who were in his home that night. The story of how Clarence Darrow came to represent Dr. Sweet and his co-defendants is an interesting account of the development of the NAACP and racial dynamics in the north in the 1920's.

The first trial ended in a mistrial, and Professor Barbara Bergman compares Darrow's advocacy in the two trials, explaining why the result was different the second time around. Darrow's power of persuasion with a jury of twelve white men in this racially charged case was extraordinary. The fact that he represented Leopold and Loeb just one year before Sweet and tried the John Scopes case in the very same year explains why Clarence Darrow deserves to be called the trial lawyer of the century.

Pennzoil v. Texaco

On November 19, 1985, a Houston, Texas, jury made history when it returned a verdict for 10.53 *billion* dollars. That verdict was more than five times larger than the largest one ever before rendered. This verdict was not for a case involving any grievous bodily injury. It didn't involve wrongful death. It didn't involve medical malpractice. The verdict was rendered in a trial over a business practice that many in the corporate world found to be common place. The case was *Pennzoil v. Texaco,* and it involved a single business transaction. Prof. Robert Lloyd dissects and examines all of the case's manifold parties, events and details, making the complex lawsuit accessible to the lay reader. He explains a commercial maneuver that was, by corporate standards, rather typical. Then Prof. Lloyd explains how personal injury lawyer Joe Jamail was able to use simplicity, story-telling and appeals to a good versus evil mentality to persuade a jury that Texaco's behavior was egregious enough to warrant the staggering verdict.

State v. Allery

Sherrie Allery killed her husband in self-defense after years of extreme physical and mental abuse. As in most cases involving women who kill their batterers, Allery's behavior just before she killed her husband did not fit squarely within the law of self-defense, especially regarding the need to show an imminent threat of death or serious bodily injury. Hence, the trial lawyer in this case, Ellen Yaroshevsky, attempted to introduce the testimony of an expert on the Battered Woman Syndrome.

In one of the chapters that presents the perspective of the trial lawyer herself, Ms. Yaroshevsky describes the trial in riveting detail and provides the reader with unique insight into the strategic decisions that she made with her client. The Allery case is a fascinating account of the facts and circumstances that lead a woman to kill her batterer. It also ultimately resulted in a very significant change in the law in the state of Washington regarding the admissibility of expert testimony on the Battered Woman Syndrome and the law of self-defense.

People v. Orenthal James Simpson

Few cases have been written about as much as the Simpson case. Although it certainly does not deserve to be called "The Trial of the Century" as some have suggested, the Simpson case was much more than just another celebrity trial. As Professor Angela J. Davis points out, the Simpson case focused attention on some of the most important issues in the criminal justice system, including class and race disparities, DNA evidence, and police perjury.

In this essay, Professor Davis focuses on the issue of race—its significance in the trial and how it affected the advocacy of the lawyers. She discusses the emotional conflicts over race within the defense and prosecution teams and compares and contrasts the approaches that each side ultimately decided to take. Professor Davis examines how race affected the choice of lawyers, venue and jury selection, the direct and cross-examination of the trial's most controversial witness and the closing arguments. She suggests that the strategic decisions about race made by both sides may have largely determined the outcome of the case.

Terry Nichols and the Oklahoma Bombing Case

The Oklahoma City bombing on April 19, 1995, in which 168 people were killed, was big news all over the world. Timothy McVeigh and Terry Nichols were arrested and tried in federal court for conspiracy to bomb the Murrah Federal Building, two substantive offenses of bombing and arson, and eight counts of first degree murder of federal employees within the building. Judge Richard Matsch, of the United States District Court for the District of Colorado, moved the case from Oklahoma City to Denver and granted a motion to sever the two defendants for trial.

Judge Matsch's opinion on change of venue reflects the same views about implied bias as expressed almost 200 years earlier by Chief Justice Marshall in the Burr case—even though Judge Matsch did not cite those views.

McVeigh was convicted on all counts, sentenced to death, and after his appeals was executed in 2001. Nichols was convicted of the conspiracy count, acquitted of the substantive bombing offenses, and acquitted of first-degree and second-degree murder. The jury convicted him of eight counts of involuntary manslaughter. The jury declined to find that he was eligible for the death penalty and Judge Matsch sentenced him to life imprisonment. In a later trial, Nichols was convicted of murder in an Oklahoma state court. The jury declined to sentence him to death and he was again sentenced to life imprisonment.

Like the Allery essay, this essay provides the first-hand perspective of the trial lawyer. It is co-authored by Professor Michael E. Tigar, who was lead counsel for Mr. Nichols. Professor James Coleman of Duke Law School co-authored the chapter to provide the perspective that only an outsider can bring. The chapter authors' goal is to provide insight into the primary aspect of the advocate's job, which is to understand the client's claim for justice.

The authors have included material about venue and jury selection in addition to trial excerpts. These materials are designed to illustrate some of the same points as in Professor Ferguson's essay on Aaron Burr and Professor Steiker's discussion of the Leopold–Loeb case. One tells a story to an audience, whose readiness to accept is conditioned by the values they bring to court. Sometimes, community sentiment or the nature of the issues will make it impossible for one or more—or all— jurors to view the evidence and the legal principles with any degree of objectivity. In such a case, the lawyer has options that include waiving a jury or change of venue. Sometimes, as in the Burr case, the lawyer may sense that the judge or jurors will not accept his or her position, and in that case will speak to a broader audience outside the courtroom.

Two Episodes in the Vioxx Litigation

Vioxx is a drug designed to treat pain from arthritis and related conditions. The pharmaceutical company Merck marked Vioxx between 1999 and 2004, when Merck withdrew Vioxx from the market after clinical studies showed an increased incidence of heart attacks and strokes among patients who had taken the drug. In the chapter on Vioxx litigation, Michael Tigar has chosen two Vioxx jury trials from among the more than 10,000 cases that have been filed and the dozen that had been tried as of the time the chapter was written. One case was tried in state court in Brazoria County, Texas, and resulted in a verdict for the plaintiff for compensatory and punitive damages. The other was tried in federal court in Houston, Texas, where the judicial district includes Brazoria County, but where jurors are drawn from a larger area. The Houston trial resulted in a hung jury and on retrial a verdict for Merck.

The Vioxx litigation merits study because the cases involve the same aspects as any large-scale product liability litigation, whatever the challenged product might be. In such a case, a manufacturer has made a decision, in the light of legal and regulatory norms and controls, to market a product that has certain provable benefits. However, as with almost any product, there are risks. For example, a small car has the benefit of high gas mileage and a low price, but may be less safe in the event of a crash. A chemical substance may get the stove clean, but be harsh on the skin and may in the long run prove to be carcinogenic.

Jurors are therefore asked to examine and judge the manufacturer's decision to market the product, and to evaluate whatever warnings the manufacturer may have given and the sales "pitch" that was made in the marketing process. The Vioxx cases came to trial at a time when a television program called "CSI" was very popular; in that program, forensic science solves major crimes. In the Vioxx litigation, lawyers asked jurors to "do a CSI" and examine the scientific basis for Merck's decision that the benefits of Vioxx outweighed all the risks. Jurors were also asked to examine whether Merck had been candid about the known risks, and diligent enough in looking for unknown ones.

Of course, the root issue in these cases is whether Vioxx caused the heart attack or stroke at issue. However, jurors' feelings about whether Merck was a credible developer and marketer of this drug inevitably influenced their view whether its witnesses were credible when they said that causation had not been proved.

Professor Tigar chose two cases in order to contrast lawyer decision-making and advocacy, as well as the very different sets of controls on the process by the federal judge and the state judge.

1

Ellen Yaroshefsky[1]

State of Washington v. Sherrie Lynn Allery: Victory Despite Conviction

"Guilty. Second degree murder."

Sherrie Allery flinched, then tears welled up in her eyes as she slumped forward at the defense table; I reached over, tried to comfort her. It was 1980. She was not the first woman to be convicted of killing her batterer in what, on the surface, appeared to be a cold blooded act.

She was not the first to be deprived by a court of expert testimony explaining how she perceived grave danger and why she finally took action to protect herself from her batterer's imminent deadly force. *But, in Washington State she was the last.*

Four years after her conviction, the Washington State Supreme Court sitting en banc, reversed and established the admissibility of expert testimony on the "Battered Woman's Syndrome."[2]

Sherrie Allery was never retried. The case not only resulted in her freedom after conviction, it remains an important victory for justice in self-defense cases.[3]

The History of Violence

In the late night of November 1, 1980, Sherrie Lynn Allery, a 36

---

[1] Clinical Professor of Law, Benjamin N. Cardozo Law School.

[2] *State of Washington v. Sherrie Lynn Allery*, 101 Wash.2d 591, 682 P.2d 312 (1984).

[3] Years ago, Sherrie Allery gave me permission to use confidential information and to write the story of her case.

year old woman shot and killed her husband Wayne Allery in their home in Tacoma, Washington. It was the tragic end of five years of brutal physical, psychological and emotional battering that led Sherrie Allery, in fear for her life, to call the police repeatedly. There were beatings, punchings and kickings; threats with a knife held to her side and to her throat. Once she was hospitalized after Wayne hit her over the head with a tire iron, requiring 35 stitches. In early October 1980, she marshaled the courage to file for divorce and obtained a restraining order requiring Wayne to leave the home and refrain from contact with her. About the time Wayne was served with the papers, in a drunken state, he punched Sherrie and broke her nose. The police would not enforce the order. She went back to court and obtained another restraining order. It was served on him November 1, 1980.

She recounted that she was afraid he would try to find her after service of the papers. He did. He called her at work and wanted to get together. Fear mounted.

Sherrie left her job at a local bar early to avoid him, went to a tavern and waited a few hours. She then went home. The house was dark. She did not see his car so she felt safe entering the home. She brought with her possessions that had been stored with her friend, Scooter, including a camera and a shotgun. After she went in, dead bolted the door behind her and moved toward the kitchen, a light came on in the living room. He was on the couch. He looked up, cursed her and made repeated threats to kill her. She went to the bedroom and loaded the shotgun with one shell to defend herself. She heard metallic sounds in the kitchen and thought he was in there getting a knife. She moved slowly with the gun raised toward the back door, hoping to escape. She thought he was behind her. She turned and saw him pivot on the couch toward her. She shot once. It killed him.

Sherrie ran next door to her friends and neighbors, police officer William Holmes and his girlfriend, Tamara McDonald. She had sought refuge at their home on numerous occasions after Wayne's beatings and drunken rages. William was not home but Tamara was. Sherrie told her what happened and they both went back to her house. Sherrie thought, but was not sure, that Wayne was dead. He was. Tamara advised Sherrie to call her divorce lawyer, Ralph Baldwin. Many hours later, she reached Baldwin who called the prosecutor. In the meantime, in a fog, Sherrie returned to work and told two people what she had done.

Four days later Baldwin, apparently laboring under the mistaken belief that Sherrie might not be charged with murder if he brought her to be questioned by the prosecutor, appeared with Sherrie for a unique four hour recorded interview. The transcript of the interview was fifty two pages. In the first sixteen pages, Sherrie described the night of the shooting. The rest of the interview was about the five year history of violence in the marriage.

A few days later Sherrie was arraigned on a charge of murder in the first degree. Bail was initially set at $50,000 and reduced to $10,000. Sherrie was released when a friend posted bail. The case was followed by the Tacoma News.

First Steps

The police began their investigation quickly, obtaining statements from friends, acquaintances, co-workers, Wayne's family and former friends of Sherrie. It was a small community. Some friends of Sherrie remained steadfast. Others were angry. People quickly took sides. Gossip abounded. Stories became hardened.

Weeks later, Sherrie found her way to our office. I was a former public defender and transplanted New Yorker who was one of the few women criminal defense lawyers in Washington State in 1980. My law partner and I had worked on two "women's self-defense cases" in Washington, a relatively new legal phenomenon in 1980. The concept that a women who shot her abuser would claim justification (self-defense) instead of excuse (some form of mental irresponsibility) was relatively novel. The unspoken bias in the law and the culture discounted the view that a woman who kills could possibly be engaged in such behavior as a result of reasonable fear instead of rage and hysteria.

We began our investigation immediately, talking to scores of people in the community. A review of the early discovery, our factual investigation and lengthy discussions with Sherrie made clear that this was a self-defense case and that, if the case went to trial, we would present many witnesses, hospital records and photographs documenting the lengthy history of abuse. Sherrie would testify. The physical evidence would be contested. We would have to employ a number of experts—a criminalist[4], a firearms expert and notably, experts who worked with battered women. It would be an uphill battle. In 1980, the claim of self-defense in a case where the aggressor was not in the act of attacking the woman was regarded as simply not viable.

Unlike the usual criminal defense which more often than not relies on cross-examination of the state's witnesses to support the defense theory of the case, self-defense is always risky because the jury has to believe the defendant. It matters little that the ultimate instruction to the jury places the burden on the prosecution and requires it to disprove

---

[4] A criminalist employs scientific tools and training to analyze, compare, identify and interpret physical evidence. Examination may include hair, fibers, blood, and other stains, smeared or smudged markings, and foot prints. This case was tried long before DNA analysis was a staple of the criminal justice system.

self-defense beyond a reasonable doubt. As a practical matter, as soon as a defendant testifies, the jurors focus on whether they believe that she is truthful. We knew this burden to be daunting where a woman has shot her husband, and the jury could easily be swayed to think she killed him in revenge.

We, of course, tried to discuss the case with the prosecutor to no avail. Ellsworth Connelly, Tacoma's noted homicide prosecutor in his 60's was dapper, crusty and colorful. Connelly was legendary, notably for rousing summations. He loved trying homicides and, reputedly, rarely lost one. He had "no time" for this "battered woman business." For Connelly, this was an open and shut case of premeditated murder. From his viewpoint, Allery was a hard drinking, cussing, woman who was out to kill her husband. She wanted to get rid of him. She was a bad wife and bad mother. She threatened to kill him the night before and did it exactly as she said she would. She yelled about how glad she was that he was dead. Open and shut. It was starkly evident that he would imply to a jury that she deserved to spend her life in prison. No amount of discussion or plea bargaining was effective. This was first degree murder or nothing. And, he apparently relished the idea of trying the case against a thirty-something Seattle woman lawyer. He chided that he "didn't know women tried homicide cases" and "now you just want to beat up on this poor dead man." I knew I would be "home-towned."

Tacoma was a forty-five minutes drive from Seattle, but in 1980 its culture was light years distant. The Allery case was a working class, small town soap opera. It took place on the wrong side of the tracks and was replete with cursing, drinking, guns and violence. Sherrie was a stolid white woman of Montana stock with a wicked sense of humor and a mouth that could make one blush. On the surface, there was nothing passive, meek or vulnerable about her. No one who met her briefly would characterize her as a "victim." Her humor masked her vulnerability. It had gotten her through a tough life and a violent marriage. Our job was to convince the jury that Sherrie Allery reasonably perceived herself to be in danger of great bodily harm at the time she shot and killed Wayne and that her actions were subjectively and objectively reasonable.

This was a challenge for many reasons. First, Wayne did not have a weapon. Sherrie thought she heard him with something metallic but did not see one. Second, the physical evidence placed the muzzle of her shotgun three to five feet from his head and there would be conflicting expert testimony as to whether he was lying on the couch or whether he was turning toward her to get off the couch when she shot him. In either event, he was on the couch. Third, the long history of violence, if believed, could give her a motive to kill; if not believed, it would undercut the battered woman's defense. In addition, the prosecution had witnesses who quoted Sherrie as saying "I am going to kill him. I am going to blow his fucking head off" the day before the shooting. They had witnesses who said that hours after the shooting Sherrie said she was glad he was dead. We could argue all we wanted that the statements did not demonstrate anything other than anger, frustration and sarcasm, but the jury had to understand Sherrie, her relationship with Wayne and the effect of the history of violence on her perception of imminent danger on November 1, 1980.

A jury from these parts was not likely to be hospitable to our client or our view of self-defense, especially given the misconceptions and myths in the community about battered women. We needed an expert witness to help the jury understand her fear and her behavior.

Battered Women and Self–Defense

The battered woman syndrome and other forms of syndrome testimony have been well considered by courts, scholars, lawyers, psychologists, and social workers. The syndrome itself has been revised and refined by psychologists. Nearly thirty years after the first case discussing battered woman syndrome, the courts have well-developed and often contradictory views on the subject. Most importantly, there has been increased public awareness of domestic violence in the past thirty years. The media have presented countless stories and programs about domestic violence. Federal, state and local governments have enacted wide-ranging programs in an attempt to cope with battering and its effects. Private organizations, battered women's shelters, legal defense organizations and many social service groups work to enhance public awareness. While these efforts have not translated into a depth of understanding about causes and effects of violence against women, at least the myths and misconceptions that existed in 1980 are somewhat different today. The issue is openly discussed and the fact of such violence is no longer hidden behind closed doors.

But, in 1980, only three courts in the country had decided that testimony about the battered woman syndrome was admissible in a self-defense case. Washington was not one of them. Myths and misconceptions pervaded the culture and the law. A jury could not fairly judge the actions of a battered woman charged with murder unless it could overcome commonly held ideas that:

—Battered women are responsible for the beating and that they either deserve or ask for the violence;

—Battered women are masochistic;

—A woman who is a "good wife" will not be battered (in other words, "she deserved it.");

—Men who batter are violent in all of their relationships;

—Police can protect a battered woman

Significantly, most battered women will have to explain why, if the beatings were as extensive and frightening as she claimed, she did not leave the relationship and why she perceived herself to be in danger of losing her life when she killed. In other words, she must explain why this time was different than the previous times she had been beaten.

Sherrie's Case

Sherrie's case raised these issues, and more. We needed expert testimony to place the act of shooting within the context of the relationship. Only then could a jury fairly assess whether Sherrie had acted in reasonable fear of imminent danger when she shot and killed her husband. And we had to provide a basis for the jury to fairly assess Sherrie's incriminating statements before and after the shooting.

What was the likelihood that the court would admit testimony about the battered woman syndrome in Sherrie's case? The judge, Stanley Worswick, was thoughtful and knowledgeable about the law. Although there was no Washington case considering the admissibility of expert testimony, the Washington Supreme Court had issued a significant opinion in *State v. Wanrow*, 88 Wash.2d 221, 559 P.2d 548 (1977). The court recognized that sex bias permeates the legal doctrine of self-defense because it assumes that the attacker and victim have equal capacities; it found that there is sex bias in the law of self-defense because a woman who kills is viewed as inherently unreasonable.

Thus, the court approved a unique and detailed instruction to a jury in cases in which a woman argued that her actions were in self-defense:

> In judging Yvonne Wanrow's actions you should attempt to place yourself as a reasonable person in her position at the time of the incident. You should therefore consider her past and present knowledge, her beliefs, the relative size and strength of the participants, aggressor's words and actions prior to the shooting, the history of their relationship and all other factors bearing on the reasonableness of her actions and her apprehensions at the time as they appear to her.

The *Wanrow* decision, recognizing that equal protection required the jury to assess the action from a woman's perspective in light of all of her experiences, gave us hope that the Allery trial court would admit expert testimony about the battered woman syndrome.

In addition to the principle established in *Wanrow*, at other public policy levels, the State of Washington was enlightened, even if Tacoma was not. It was one of the first states to develop programs for women victims of violence, notably in prosecutor offices. Seattle, the city to the north of sleepy Tacoma, had a sexual assault unit in the prosecutor's office. Harborview Hospital in Seattle had one of the country's few sexual assault centers. It was a good bet that the director of Harborview's program, Karil Kleingbeil, would testify as an impressive expert.

Our plan was to educate the judge about the necessity for the testimony, so crucial to place Sherrie Allery's actions, thoughts, behavior, in context. We would be very specific as to reasons the testimony was proffered and would repeatedly answer clearly the question "Are you saying that that a history of battering is a defense to murder?" The answer is "no," but we knew that it was difficult for lawyers, judges and the public to understand. We would offer battered woman syndrome testimony to overcome myths and misconceptions and to establish that her behavior at the time of the shooting was reasonable.

The Client

Significant trial preparation is essential in all homicide cases, but there are added dimensions in cases involving women who kill. Lawyers are called upon to serve as support systems for the woman and her family. This was "team defense" dealing not only with legal issues, but with matters of heart and soul. We found social workers to assist Sherrie and her daughter Toni, investigators to interact with welfare offices, and social service agencies and hospitals to get the care necessary. She had no financial resources; thus most of the services were provided by public organizations or volunteers. Women's organizations supported her case and helped her care for her child.

Sherrie was suffering. However violent Wayne's behavior, she had killed the man she loved. Even though relieved that she was no longer in danger, she was guilty, angry, sad, depressed, and overwhelmed. She was grieving and in personal crisis. Many friends deserted her. Wayne's family and friends were saying horrible things about her and press accounts of the case did not help. Sherrie was vulnerable. She worried about the daughter that she had deprived of a father. She knew she might go to prison and leave her daughter without any parent.

It was apparent that it would be beneficial for Sherrie to begin psychological counseling to begin to cope with the enormity of her loss and her actions. Therapy would help. She had spent a lifetime coping and surviving in difficult circumstances and needed a developed understanding to move forward in life.

This certainly was a good long term goal but it could undermine our short term one—to maximize her credibility at trial. One goes through stages in therapy. The worst case scenario would be that Sherrie's therapy would be at the stage of anger at Wayne at the time she took the

stand or that she would appear to be too sophisticated in her understanding of the battered woman syndrome by the time she testified. She
might present as less vulnerable than she was. It was too risky. We
talked with her about setting up a support system short of therapy until
she testified at trial. She agreed.

Legal and Factual Preparation

The Witnesses

Trial preparation was far reaching and intensive, extending to
factual investigations, examination of physical evidence, retention of
experts and forensic preparation. We, of course, wished we had gotten
this case on November 1, 1980. By the time we could contact them,
attitudes were rigid and stories however shaky in fact, were firm.
Former friends of Sherrie no longer "liked" her. Statements were wildly
conflicting. Statements that some "former friends" made to others were
now denied. Rumors were flying. Everyone seemed to have an unbending
opinion about Sherrie's and Wayne's personalities, behaviors and what
happened on November 1, 1980. Now that Wayne was dead, sympathies
ran in his favor.

Memories were dredged up. It was not at all clear whether the
memories bore resemblance to the actual events. For many of the events,
there was no independent corroboration. Witness statements seemed the
product of self importance and improved memories for this newsworthy
case. Some prosecution witnesses barely spoke with the defense. Our
investigation dug deep to discover the background of Wayne Allery and
the various witnesses that the prosecution planned to call.

As we came closer to trial, it was apparent that there was little
factual dispute as to what Sherrie said before or after Wayne's death.
The defense would not contest that she made certain angry, sarcastic
statements, but we would contend that fear was the context in which the
statements must be understood. Her attitude, her intent, and her
perception were the focus of our preparation for cross-examination of the
state's witnesses. There would be few destructive cross-examinations
exploring bias, impeaching the state's witnesses or trolling for inconsistencies. Rather, during most of the cross- examinations we would use the
facts to bolster our theme and theory and to build up the credibility of
our witnesses.

Pretrial Motions

Pretrial motions practice was extensive and contentious. Some of
the motions were ruled on pretrial. Others would, of course, be reserved
until the issues arose in trial or during the instruction conference.

Nonetheless, these motions were filed early in pretrial proceedings. It was important to educate the court about the unique issues in the case.

We won some. An important and contested aspect of the defense was the physical evidence and what it demonstrated about Wayne's movements prior to the shooting. We needed to retain a criminalist and had to provide the court with extensive information to support the request for public funds to do so. We were successful.

We were not equally successful in our motion to secure an expert to testify on the battered woman syndrome. We submitted a lengthy memorandum providing case law and explaining the necessity for such testimony. The court approved only the services of an expert to make an offer of proof. Dealing a further blow to the defense, the court ordered that this expert proffer would not be heard until after Sherrie testified. Our strategy had been to present the expert testimony on the battered woman syndrome before Sherrie testified, so the jury would learn about myths and misconceptions and have context for understanding Sherrie's behavior.

We hoped to persuade the court to use the self-defense charge to the jury approved in *Wanrow* but it would be an uphill battle. The court, in response to our pretrial motions, commented that it considered most of the *Wanrow* opinion to be "dicta" and that it did not believe that *Wanrow* correctly stated the law. The judge offered no further insight on the self defense instruction. He would reserve ruling until the close of evidence.

Critical to the case were a myriad of evidentiary rulings, many of which were argued in motions in limine. Just as the defense sought to excise damaging, irrelevant and inadmissible hearsay, the prosecution repeatedly sought to introduce Sherrie's statements and statements of the deceased. The defense sought to preclude prosecution witnesses who would testify to Wayne's statements made months before his death that he feared his wife would shoot him. Ultimately, the court granted the defense motion to preclude such testimony in the prosecution's case in chief. We expected it would be excluded during any rebuttal case as well.

Upon the State's claim that it would only introduce the incriminating portions of Sherrie's statement to the police on November 4, the defense sought to offer the entire statement, including Sherrie's description of Wayne's violence toward her. In the end, the court denied our motion. The jury was to hear only the inculpatory portions.

We sought the admission of past acts of violence, destruction and bizarre behavior by Wayne Allery, known and unknown to Sherrie. The prosecution claimed that many of these acts were inadmissible as unduly prejudicial, too remote in time and not probative of her state of mind. The court reserved decision.

Most disturbingly, the prosecution sought and obtained sealed welfare records from the state of Montana. In a 1975 proceeding, Sherrie, who was in a common law marriage with an alcoholic, had been adjudged an unfit mother and lost custody of three children. The prosecution claimed the records had been sent to them by a concerned person. We sought discovery of these records. We lost. We moved to preclude the prosecution from mention of this former marriage and loss of three children. The prosecution could not articulate a theory of admissibility. The court reserved ruling.

Jury Selection

The "firm" trial date was delayed a week to permit the prosecution to attempt to secure the attendance of Sherrie's neighbors, William Holmes and Tamara McDonald, who had skipped town and reportedly were in Hawaii. Over defense objection, noting that the prosecution had months to subpoena them but had failed to do so, the court granted the adjournment. The consequence of the delay was that the jury pool was not a fresh one. Instead, it consisted of jurors who had not been chosen to sit on other cases during the first week of their jury term. Typically, this is not a good sign for the defense. New jurors begin service every two weeks. In general, defense lawyers want to seat jurors who have not served on a jury or who have been on juries that have not reached a verdict. The "best" jurors are often seated during the first week, leaving the least desirables for week two. We started on week two.

The court permitted wide ranging questions related to familiarity with women and violence, self-defense, guns and related subjects. We questioned jurors about attitudes toward the police, notably because Sherrie had been ridiculed by police officers when she had called for help. The only jurors with any knowledge or experience about the subject excused themselves. One prospective juror left the courtroom teary-eyed, having been excused after saying "there but for the grace of God go I." Shortly thereafter another prospective juror excused herself for the same reason. Why, we wondered once again, cannot the people who would understand the most, stay and serve? Instead, even after the use of all of our preemptory challenges, we had a jury with no knowledge about violence against women, many of whom were related to police officers and most of whom were blue collar workers. Nearly all of them had served on other juries that had reached a verdict. This was not a defense-friendly panel. Few if any of those prior verdicts were likely to be acquittals. The jury was sworn.

The Trial
Opening Statements

The opening statements offered a stark contrast. The prosecution painted a picture of premeditated murder by a woman who sought revenge against her husband, planned to kill him, and did. The night before the shooting Sherrie said to friends that she was going to blow his head off. The next day she retrieved a shotgun from her friend, went home and found him on the couch. Her gun was in the car. He was drunk on the couch asking her to bring him a pan. She went outside, got the gun, came in, loaded it, and shot him in the head from three feet away and went next door to her friend. No one called the police. Rather she and a friend tried to find her a lawyer. Sherrie then confessed to shooting and killing her husband, but distorted the facts and claimed somehow that she was entitled to do so because she he had beaten her in the past. Even if most of that was true, claimed the prosecutor, "domestic disputes" do not give anyone a right to kill someone. This was the first time the prosecution played the "domestic disputes" theme, but surely not the last; they wove it throughout direct and cross-examination and summation.

By contrast, the defense opening, evoking the history of violence throughout the marriage, described incidents of the physical, psychological and emotional battering that led Sherrie Allery to fear for her life when she shot and killed her husband. She did not intend to kill; she intended to protect herself. Challenging various myths and the sex bias that surround battering, the defense openly attacked the prosecution's theme which diminished violent beatings to mere "domestic disputes." Focusing on the day and night before the killing, the defense portrayed a frightened woman who had filed for divorce and sought two restraining orders to keep her batterer [or Wayne Allery] away. These measures did not protect her. On November 1, she was terrified that he was coming again, this time to kill her. Describing the chilling events, the defense argued that this time she thought she would be dead. Thinking he was about to kill her, she shot in an instant. It was self defense. Challenging the prosecution's rendition of events, the defense contended that Sherrie Allery's statement to the police on November 4 was the true story of what happened on November 1, not the version that others made up after the fact.

The Prosecution's Case

"I am going to kill him. I am going to blow his fucking head off."

Wayne died from a shotgun blast, to his head, within 24 hours of Sherrie's threat. And just hours after his death she was quoted as boasting that he was gone. There was no doubt about who fired the shot. The issue was Sherrie's state of mind when she fired the shot and these statements standing alone were devastating to her case.

The prosecution called a number of witnesses who had heard one or the other of Sherrie's statements. The defense could not and did not challenge the fact that the statements were made. Instead we set out to neutralize the damning content with cross-examinations designed to establish the all-important context in which the statements were made— the history of violence and threats and Sherrie's full-blown fear. Sherrie often made sarcastic comments; she used biting humor to cope with circumstances. In every instance, on cross- examination, no matter how hostile to Sherrie, the prosecution's witnesses conceded facts which supported this defense argument.

The cross, redirect and re-cross of each witness was a running battle between the prosecutor and the defense as to the meaning of Sherrie's statements. The prosecutor portrayed them as evidence of cold-blooded intent. The defense established that Sherrie and Wayne made statements like this in the past. It was not intent, only momentary anger. Sherrie was just blowing off steam.

Mary Kerr, a friend of Sherrie's, was called by the prosecution apparently because they thought she would establish that the disputes between Sherrie and Wayne were just "domestic arguing." Kerr would have none of it. To the contrary, she provided the first evidentiary glimpse of Wayne's threats and wild accusations directed at Sherrie.

Mary was the foundation for Sherrie's self-defense defense. She provided the context for the statements. She testified that the restraining orders did not work; told the jury about Sherrie's black eye the week before the shooting; and provided detail about an October 28 incident where Sherrie called the police, to no avail. A sympathetic neighbor who had repeatedly sheltered Sherrie, Mary knew about the extent of the beatings.

The prosecution then turned to Sherrie's comments after the shooting, calling two witnesses who were at the bar when Sherrie, distraught, disoriented, and in shock, went to work. Norma Jean Lindgren, the manager of the bar testified that Sherrie told her "there would be no more problems because he was gone."

The testimony of Carmen Conzatti was markedly negative. Conzatti was Sherrie's friend until the week after the shooting when she was befriended by Wayne's family. She admitted to Sherrie's love for her child, but minimized Wayne's violence. Inexplicably, she had come to believe that Sherrie acted in revenge.

Contrary to the testimony of Lindgren, Conzatti said that when Wayne showed up and Sherrie left work early on October 31 "Wayne seemed fine." She also was at the tavern when Sherrie came in on November 1. She said that Sherrie had glasses on, and was sniffling like she had a cold. One of the customers said "You must have had a hard night." Sherrie ran off to the restroom. Conzatti followed. Conzatti testified that Sherrie said "I really have hurt Wayne. I've done a horrible thing. I have shot Wayne." Sherrie's main concern was her daughter. Conzatti then reported that the next day, November 2, Sherrie called and asked Conzatti whether she had told anyone about what Sherrie said the day before. When Conzatti answered "yes," Sherrie said "oh fuck."

Our challenge was to minimize the negative impact of Conzatti's testimony. On cross she acknowledged nights when Sherrie, in fear, slept in her car with her daughter while Wayne went home. She confirmed Sherrie's fear after Wayne was served with the court order but still would not leave the home. She knew of Wayne's prior threats. Conzatti, obviously not sympathetic to Sherrie's suffering in the marriage, did acknowledge Sherrie's complaints about beatings and her concern about her child.

After the prosecution had framed Wayne's death with damning statements by Sherrie before and after the shooting, it turned to the physical evidence from which they would argue that Sherrie was lying about the way the tragedy unfolded the night of November 1.

The physical evidence was contested. The prosecution witnesses— the pathologist and a criminalist—testified, over objection, that Wayne was shot from three to five feet from the muzzle of the gun while lying down on the couch. Blood spatter analysis, in its early stages in 1980, was challenged unsuccessfully. Test firings, simulations of the shotgun firing, were admitted over objection.

With its last witness, the prosecution returned to Sherrie's statements after the shooting. Claudellen Edge ("Scooter"), another "ex-friend," was our biggest concern. Scooter painted the background portrait of Sherrie running around to bars with her friends and taking her young daughter with her. She testified that about ten days before the shooting, Sherrie asked her to store a camera, gun, jar of change, blanket and pillows. Scooter said that the day before the shooting, Sherrie asked Scooter to return the items. Scooter did so by taking them to Sherrie's work and putting them in her car. Scooter saw her at work the night of the shooting. Her testimony delivered one blow after another:

She said that she had something to tell me and that—she didn't want me to say anything to anybody else

What did you say?

You know. I said "okay". And just something flashed and I said you know—"is it something about Wayne?" And she said "yes". I said "is it criminal?" And she said "yes". And I said, "did you shoot him?" . . . .

What did she say?

She said "yes". And I said, "Is he dead?" And she said "yes" . . . .

Did you ask her what had happened?

Yes.

What did she say?

She said that—she had gone home and Wayne was there and he was getting sick and he was laying on the couch. And he said "mom get me a pan. I'm getting sick." And Sherrie said she went and got him a pan. And went out to the car and got the gun and came back in and shot him. . . . I asked her if there was a lot of blood and she said "no, that just his eye was hanging out."

How did she seem to you at this time?

Very perky.

Pardon me?

Happy. You know.

The prosecution, in its zeal to emphasize Sherrie's unrepentant mood, led Scooter to inadvertently set herself up for impeachment. Describing Sherrie as "perky" and "happy" was a direct contradiction to other witnesses who also disliked Sherrie but described her as wearing dark glasses and crying during the exact time frame. The cross-examination hammered on Scooter's insistence that Sherrie was "perky," "just fine," and "not upset" the morning after the shooting. Scooter began to get nervous on the stand. She had refused to talk to the defense and told this story to the police for the first time just days before the trial. Although her testimony about the shooting lent credence to the prosecution's theory, Scooter's credibility was severely damaged. The prosecution rested.

The Defense Case

We made the tactical decision to begin the defense case with a literal reading of the transcript of Sherrie's description of the shooting. There were several reasons for this unusual move. First, the prosecution was permitted to have a detective paraphrase the statement, casting it in the worst light. Second, we intended to call Sherrie to the stand and we wanted to make clear that her story had never varied. Third, and most significant, the description of the events on November 1, 1980, was detailed and chilling.

The defense then marshaled a powerful, unassailable presentation vividly re-creating the abuse Sherrie suffered at the hands of Wayne. Witness after witness described specific vicious attacks on Sherrie; personality changes in Wayne when drinking; and, on the other hand, those moments when Wayne appeared to be a good guy. The portrayal of Wayne as "Jekyll and Hyde" was important for jury understanding of why Sherrie stayed with him in spite of the spikes of violence. Wayne's sudden shifts in mood and focus were also important to understand Sherrie's growing apprehension and fear.

Duane Rader, a boilermaker who worked with Wayne, described personality changes two weeks before he died. Rader also testified that Wayne said "When I drink whiskey I beat the hell out of Sherry."

Detective Curt Benson then described in vivid detail the beating in December 1979. The detectives had responded to a call that her husband was intoxicated and threatening her with a gun and then a knife. Sherrie wanted to leave with her daughter, Toni. Wayne would allow her to leave but not take Toni. The police escorted her out the door with her daughter.

Sara Jane Holmes, a former neighbor testified about a number of instances when she observed Wayne hit Sherrie. She said Sherrie slept in her car in the driveway many times because she was afraid. Sara described one event when Sherrie came to her back door screaming. Wayne had torn off her clothing except her underpants and was chasing her to Holmes' door, kicking her and trying to drag her away. This was one of many times when Sherrie slept on her couch.

Mary Kerr, recalled by the defense, talked about an incident the week before Wayne died. Sherrie came over wearing dark glasses. Mary asked what had happened to Sherrie's face, but was not permitted to testify to Sherrie's answer, that Wayne had broken her nose.

Sherrie's sister and best friend, Linda Smith, who was "always there to clean up" after an attack on Sherrie, described a number of occasions where she went to Sherrie's home and took Toni with her because Sherrie had been "beat up" and could not lift her arms and hold the baby. When Linda started to testify to an incident in September 1979, that was a clear example of Wayne's bizarre and frightening behavior, the prosecution objected, the jury was excused, and lengthy argument followed. Linda was going to.testify that Wayne came in drunk

> took all his clothes off and sat down and spread his legs out and scooted way down in the chair and sat there with his arms crossed and smiled that stiff smile and then he got up and pulled the fuse out so the lights went out in the house and said: we are going to have a family discussion. . . . it was scary.

This sign of unpredictability underlined Sherrie's reason for being fearful of him. The prosecution objected loudly:

> To draw in out of the weeds all manner of things that a man has done in the past which might be disreputable or obscene or uncivilized or gross isn't really part of a legitimate defense. It is simply to prejudice the deceased in the eyes of the jury for no legitimate

purpose except to show he is a no good rotter of some kind who probably deserves to be shot.

Unfortunately the judge missed the fact that this is precisely what the prosecution was trying to do to Sherrie with its evidence of ancient history in Montana where Sherrie's three children had been removed from her. The court admitted that testimony against Sherrie. Argument that the stripping incident and Wayne's unpredictability added to Sherrie's perception of lurking trouble was not successful. The court struck the testimony.

Steve Hozan, Linda Smith's husband, spent a lot of time with Wayne because Wayne was building a boat and Steve did carpentry and mechanical work. He testified to their July 4th party when all four of them were on a boat and Steve heard Wayne's plans and threats to kill Sherrie. Wayne said he wanted to make sure that Sherrie got up to San Juan Island on a future boat trip because he was "going to get rid of Sherrie". He thought nobody would find her in the water and the crabs would eat her "right up." After testifying to his observations of bruises on Sherrie's face and arms many occasions, Steve talked about his conversation with Wayne the night before he died. He kept calling Steve telling him to hurry up and get his boat fixed. He offered to buy Steve a rifle if he'd hurry. He told Steve he planned to take his daughter to California.

Were you fearful?

Yes—fearful for everyone which is why I deliberately destroyed the ignition.

The judge excluded testimony about Wayne's reputation for violence when drinking. We made offers of proof including statements that "Wayne was a very high strung person when drinking." "He thought he was king of the road." "He was two people." "When he was drinking he was entirely different." "I have never seen anybody change like hitting a switch." The jury didn't hear any of these statements.

The arguments about the admissibility of such evidence, however, resulted in the court permitting some testimony about specific instances of behavior that had the same result. The defense elicited instances of Wayne's behavior when sober. It was important that jury could understand good qualities in Wayne so they could comprehend why she would stay in the relationship: "When not drinking he was a wonderful guy." "You couldn't believe it." "You could almost—he would almost be in the priesthood if you want to put it that way." "He was an entirely different person." "He was for his family."

Did you ever observe sudden switches in his personality?

Yeah.

One drink is all it took but he had four or five.

Five other witnesses, including the manager of an apartment building, co-workers, police and family testified to Wayne's acts of violence. Co-workers saw him come into the restaurant drunk, yelling, screaming, and grabbing Sherrie. Once he "held a knife to her ribs and talked through his teeth." "She was black and blue, she had black eyes, her leg was black and blue and her ankle was swollen." The witnesses knew that Sherrie left and slept in her car sometimes with her daughter, and that she stayed with friends and her sister.

Police officers and hospital personnel testified to a brutal incident in 1976 when Wayne hit Sherrie over the head with a tire iron. Admitted to the hospital with a four inch laceration requiring 35 stitches, Sherrie was told by Patrolman Jay Layton "don't you understand lady, he was trying to put you away?" The patrolman testified that Wayne's mood and attitude changed several times during their contact with him. The incident was over Wayne's accusations that Sherrie was having an affair with "a colored man down the hall." It was patently untrue, but the prosecution emphasized Wayne's accusation to sow seeds of doubt during summation—Wayne had suspicions and reasons to be angry. An expert would have testified that these kinds of accusations are consistent with the behavior of batterers.

The cross-examination repeatedly pointed out that witnesses did not see bruises each time she claimed to have been hurt, that Wayne was not as bad as the violent incidents portrayed him ("did not always come in drunk or yelling"), that she must have caused the violence. Her behavior—drinking at saloons around town—must have been a cause of Wayne's anger, according to cross-examination. "What did she say to make him angry?" Significantly, the prosecution emphasized that she was a bad mother for leaving her child and going to a friend's house.

In the face of overwhelming evidence of awful abuse, in its cross-examinations, the prosecution continued to play its tired and now wholly discredited theme that these were domestic spats, part of the ups and downs of marriage. Clinging to its position, the prosecution tried to support its argument that Sherrie was exaggerating the abuse, perhaps unmindful that the direct case had reduced this position to an absurdity.

One witness was asked: "Wayne did not always beat her, did he?"

Another, who just testified to Sherrie's bruised body and black eye was confronted with an equally outrageous question: "You never saw Wayne actually strike Sherrie, did you?"

And yet with others: "You didn't see bruises each time she claimed to have been hurt." "He did not always come in drunk or yelling". The prosecution also deliberately played into one of the most damaging myths about battered women, that she must have caused the violence: "What did she say to make him angry?" he asked other witnesses. The prosecution repeatedly attempted to establish that her behavior—drinking at saloons around town—must have been a cause of Wayne's anger.

The prosecution never missed an opportunity to ask whether Sherrie had been drinking. She had not, but objections were consistently overruled. Missing the irony, the prosecution emphasized that she was a bad mother for leaving her child with Wayne and going to a friend's house; and also for placing Toni with her sister when Wayne's violence peaked.

The defense then contested the physical evidence with its expert, crime scene reconstructionist Raymond Davis, who examined all reports and photographs, reviewed the test firing in the prosecution laboratory, and visited the scene. He testified that the flow of blood conclusively demonstrated that Wayne Allery could not have been shot while lying back on the couch. The evidence demonstrated that his head had to have been at an angle other than that in the prosecution's photo at the time of shooting. Photographs he had taken illustrated the position that Wayne Allery was in at the time of the shot were admitted, over prosecution objection, for illustrative purposes. The photographs were consistent with Sherrie's statement that Wayne appeared to be getting up to move toward her. Davis also testified that the trigger pull of the gun used by Sherrie (pounds of pressure) was less than other guns and he concluded:

> Based on blood on face, direction of blood spatter, presence of blood spatter behind victim, it would have been impossible for him to be shot in position found in police photos (meaning he was not shot when asleep)

His opinion on the direction of the shot was consistent with Sherrie's statement:

> It was unlikely that the shot could have come from an area other than near the kitchen in the hallway near archway, where Sherrie said she turned and saw him appearing to rise. It did not, as claimed by the prosecution, occur perpendicular to the couch.

Sherrie Allery's Testimony

After the parade of witnesses telling one harrowing story after another of Wayne's violence against Sherrie, the defense strategy had been to call an expert on the Battered Woman's Syndrome. Before Sherrie testified, we wanted the jury to understand the effects of this constant fear and physical assault on a woman's view of herself, her batterer, and her world. The expert would have provided the information that would help the jurors to fairly judge Sherri's actions. She would have explained her affect and behavior before and after the shooting and helped the jurors to put aside the myths and misconceptions about battered women and their batterers.

Again the judge would go no further than to permit an expert's offer of proof and would not hear it until *after* Sherrie testified. We then moved, once again, to preclude cross-examination about her prior common law marriage and the Montana court ruling that she was an unfit mother. (YES, it is accurate according to the transcript. I never saw the records). The prosecution refused to disclose the welfare records from Montana. Again, the court reserved ruling.

We called Sherrie to the stand, mindful of the several inexplicable aspects of her conduct she would have to explain without the benefit of an expert. We would have to explain why she kept returning to Wayne after each beating; we'd have to walk the fine line created by past incidents of violence which, while powerful evidence of her growing fear of him, also provided the prosecution with powerful evidence of a motive to kill him. The jury had to understand that she acted out of terror, not rage or anger. In this connection, we had to explain her threats to kill Wayne the night before the shooting.

Sherrie was nervous, respectful and surprisingly soft spoken. She became more comfortable on the stand after describing her background. The examination then turned to her marriage to Wayne in 1975. She told of an idyllic relationship. "He made me laugh. He understood my feelings. I understood his. It seemed too good to be true. We did everything together." Their daughter Toni was born two years after the marriage.

Sherrie then described early threatening incidents that were not violent, but disclosed a very different side of Wayne. Within a short time, especially when he was drinking, these threats escalated into serious physical abuse. One time he:

> Took out a pistol from his pocket—a 22 and he hit me with it. I fell with it and it knocked me onto the bed. Then he hit me a couple of times and he was holding the pistol in my face, like that, and he was shaking. The bed was bouncing he was shaking so hard. And then I remember looking at him and his face. And when I looked up in his face his eyes clicked like a shutter on a camera.... then he just fell down on the bed and he started holding me and he was crying. And he told me how sorry he was and nothing like that would ever happen again.

But the violence continued, at the most unexpected times.

Sherrie talked about Wayne's behavior after his heartfelt apologies for the violent episodes and his "Jekyll and Hyde" personality.

I called him Fuzzy. Fuzzy was the gentle person who loved me and everything. He was the person that I first met.

When I called him Wayne, Wayne was the person who acted ugly. Ugly was hitting, beating and accusing me of awful things. Oh lord you cannot believe all of the things.

She talked of the petty, bizarre things Wayne did to control her.

He'd check on the car mileage to see how far I had gone that day. He always asked where I was going and knew where my friends lived and stores were so he'd check to see if I'd driven further than that.

After we started managing the apartments there were a lot of black people that lived there. Tenants would come by and say hello how are you and things like that. And he started on me like things with black people. None of the things were true.

Then he accused me of stealing money from the checking account, which was not true, so we got separate accounts.

Detail about the savage attacks was vivid. She testified about the "tire iron" incident that resulted in 35 stitches in her scalp.

He (Wayne) was drinking whiskey—firewater we used to call it. All of a sudden I just couldn't see. My head was dripping.

The next thing I knew the paramedics were there screaming at me; screaming "don't you understand lady he tried to put you away? Don't you understand?"

Did you?

I don't know. I don't know if I did or not at the time. I don't know what I thought at the time.

The police took him to jail. Friends convinced her to visit him there and yet another expression of contrition persuaded her to lie to get him released. She took him back. After a peaceful period, the violence, once again, escalated.

Sherrie described other terrifying incidents; she described several instances where she called the police and was treated to "a man's home is his castle" mentality. It was an attitude exhibited by far too many police officers, and which powered the prosecutor's theme of just another "domestic dispute". She recalled a time she called the police, that they came and said that

I could pack up stuff for Toni and leave. I said "why do we have to leave?" The officer, placing his hands on his hips, feet spread apart, said "we don't like to put a man out of his house."

Hour after hour from the witness stand Sherrie recounted the brutality of her life with Wayne. He drank heavily. He was "odd, scary" because she "did not know what he was doing." This contributed to her fear of him because when "someone acts different than you know—things change and there's different behavior, it's scary."

She testified about the times that he held a knife at her throat, chopped up all the Christmas gifts with an axe, pointed rifles directly at her. She told of the many times she slept in the car and on neighbors' couches to escape him; of the time she tried to escape to her father's home in Montana, but returned to Wayne when he showed up and "told me everything I wanted to hear."

Thus, the defense confronted the question hanging over every courtroom where a battered woman stays with her batterer, giving rise to issues of credibility: Why stay? Sherrie answered as best she could. First she said she really didn't know; she said she was hampered because they had his two kids from a previous marriage. She didn't have a job. She simply did not know anything else. Later she attempted to address the question more fully:

Why didn't you leave?

I left him many times. I stayed at peoples' houses.

Why did you go back?

I think in the beginning it was because I had listened enough and believed myself at that time that I couldn't live without him; that I couldn't handle it on my own; that I wouldn't . . . I'd just go straight down the tube. And then later it was because I would believe what he would tell me. I think it's mostly because I wanted to. I don't know if I really did believe it or it was just because I wanted to believe it.

It was a classic answer for many women in these circumstances. But, without the help of an expert, the jury was likely to find it inexplicable.

Sherrie described substantial changes in the summer of 1980 with Wayne's behavior becoming increasingly disturbing. He took her out on a boat "and had that scary smile across his face." She never went with him on the boat again. The abusive, violent behavior continued.

She decided to file for divorce and got a restraining order.

He changed so much I could not tell what he was about. I couldn't read him anymore. I couldn't—I didn't understand him at all. And there was no more necessarily beating up on me when he was drunk, it was just anytime that he got mad . . . so I knew I was going to have to go. I knew things weren't ever going to be any different but I knew the only way was . . . to have a job and I needed some money. So I went to apply for a bartending job because I could make more money than as a cook.

Sherrie went to tell him that he would be served with divorce papers. Before she could do so, "he grabbed me by throat squeezing really hard and said 'I'm going to tear your throat out.' And I said, 'why?' And then he said, 'No, I am going to chop your nose up in your fucking brain.' He hit me. My glasses went flying; there was blood all over the place."

Wayne was served with a restraining order to stay out of the house. He showed up. She called the police. Once again, the police let her down. The officer said "just what do you want me to do?" Sherrie said, "What you do to people who have criminal restraining orders on them." The officer asked again, seeming bored. He left. Wayne stayed but was calm. She went to sleep on a neighbor's couch. The next morning when asked by Kathryn Fechter, a friend of Mary Kerr's, what she was going to do she repeated what Wayne often said about her: "I'm going to blow his f—ing head off?"

Why?

It's what Wayne would say around our house—what he would say he was going to do to me.

What was going through your mind?

I didn't know what he was doing—I was afraid—I didn't want to be out on the street. I had taken Toni to Seattle to be with my sister because I was staying in the car, and he could not take care of her because he was drunk and the back and forth bickering and the running and hiding and all that is not good for her.

The next day a second restraining order was served on Wayne. Ignoring it, he called and asked her if he could to come to the house. She was shocked. She testified:

Drastic change in behavior scares me to death. I didn't understand I didn't know what he was doing. It was very very scary to me.

Instead of going home, she stayed at work.

Later that day he walked into the tavern where Sherrie worked. She blanched. Sherrie described how Wayne "started talking ugly" and "I was very scared that he would hit me. He'd never done this in front of others before and now he was going to. I went and called the divorce attorney. He said there was nothing we could do because it was a public place. And I said 'Why? That means I can't die in a public place?' " He said "yes."

She stayed on Mary Kerr's couch that night.

Sherrie then turned to the next day, November 1. Wayne had scared her to death when he showed up at her job again. She left through a back door and escaped, spending time at several taverns where he could not find her. Hours later she returned home thinking she was safe. She was not.

The house was dark; Wayne's car was no where to be seen. Sherrie was relieved. Believing Wayne was not there, she was emboldened to take items from the car, including a shotgun, that she had kept out of the house, fearing he would use them. She had collected them from a friend earlier that day.

Sherrie dead bolted the door behind her. It would prevent him entering and, although she did not intend it, it made it difficult for her to get out fast. Only then did the light come on near the couch in the living room. Wayne was stretched out there and started cursing her. As he cursed, he was looking over his glasses, an expression she recognized as menacing from her long history with Wayne's violence. "I knew that meant I was in a lot of trouble." She told of dashing to the bedroom, and heard him say:

"I guess I'm just going to have to kill you sonofabitch. Did you hear me that time?"

Sherrie heard a metallic noise in the kitchen and thought he was getting a knife. Then footsteps. She told of putting a shell in the shotgun to cover her retreat and heading through the kitchen so she could leave through the back door. She then told of the shot she fired at Wayne.

As I was coming out of there and I was just past through my hallway and I was into the kitchen and he was not saying anything. I was thinking he was going to sneak up behind me because he had done it so many times. I could only hear the noise in my ears—a pushing noise. I lifted up the shotgun to go past the stove to the door.

I asked him why he did not leave because I did not want any more trouble. He said something about me and it was his house and why didn't I call the police because there was no point because they never did anything. I was trying not to move. I did not know where he was. I said why don't I just leave then?

Then suddenly he yelled at her, "You are not going anywhere." The sound came from every direction as it reverberated off the walls.

I couldn't tell where it came from. ... And it startled me and I jumped. I came out from the stove and turned and fired the gun.

She told of standing there for a long time; said she knew then what had happened but couldn't believe it. To the jury, she said: "I don't know the right words to say."

Sherrie went next door to neighbors who had given her refuge time and again from Wayne's violence. Stunned, she returned with her friend to her home and confirmed that Wayne was dead. She described her shock and that she wasn't really thinking. While the neighbor tried to make contact with the divorce lawyer, inexplicably Sherrie announced that she needed to go to work. And she did, telling two of her co-workers what had happened. Although she did not remember detail, she did not deny that she said something like "there would be no more problems because he was gone;" and "Wayne was gone." An expert could have explained that she was a woman in shock who was also relieved that she no longer was in danger. She left work as soon as her neighbor found her divorce lawyer, who agreed to see her.

We ended the direct examination with "Did you ever plan to kill your husband?" She answered, "No, I just wanted to get away from him. I wanted to be left alone." As she walked off the witness stand, I wondered whether the jury understood that her terror led her to the sincere, even if mistaken, view that she had to act to protect herself from death at her abuser's hand.

The Prosecution's Cross-Examination of Sherrie

The prosecution's cross-examination of Sherrie relied upon every stereotype, myth and misconception about women who have been savaged by their batterers. She was confronted with questions about her returns to him, her failures to press charges against him, and her lies to protect him. Drumming on the "just a domestic dispute" theme, the prosecution recast conversations where she perceived threat into normal husband and wife conversation, for example, on the night of his death when he talked about spuds and tomato sauce. Just after being served with a second restraining order following a vicious attack, the prosecution attempted to turn the whole matter into a picture of domestic tranquility:

He said he wanted to have dinner with you?

That's not what he said.

Well, it was about cooking and eating, wasn't it?

The prosecution presented the case as beleaguered husband versus bad mother, all delivered in a dismissive, denigrating tone with flourishes of sarcasm. Playing his theme relentlessly, the prosecutor tried to paint a picture of Wayne Allery, who had unmercifully beaten his wife, as a husband who just wanted to have a conversation about "mutual domestic problems." Over repeated defense objections, the court permitted the prosecutor to exploit a proceeding in Montana years before when Sherrie had lost custody of her three children having been found unfit. The prosecution bore in on the "bad mother" image, pointing out that she left their child behind with Wayne when she left him to stay with her father for a short time in Montana.

The cross careened from trying to make it look as if Wayne was illiterate and couldn't read the restraining order, to the contention that staying in other people's homes was impulsive, bad mothering, rather than the product of fear. Presumably the prosecution could not marshal the straight face necessary to accuse Sherrie of bad mothering when she and her daughter escaped and slept in the car.

Sherrie did not let the prosecutor intimidate her. As the he tried to put words in her mouth, she was clear on facts, and constantly corrected him. Explaining her state of mind when she loaded the gun:

> All I knew is that I had to get out of that house and it was to protect myself; if that's what need be. I really had not thought about firing it.

After his implication that she sat around and drank coffee for hours after she killed her husband, she let him have it. She said loudly, firmly, credibly through clenched teeth:

> I have been listening to the things you have said about me for four days and now I can't believe you refuse to allow me to say my side of the story.

As with many aspects of the case, Sherrie's strength on the witness stand was a two-edged sword. One of the important insights an expert could have given the jury was how a woman, so strong on the stand, could behave so docilely when taunted and attacked by her husband.

The Expert's Proffer

After Sherrie's testimony, the jury was excused and the court heard the offer of proof as to the expert testimony of Karil Klingbeil. As Dr. Klingbeil testified before the judge, it was clear that her credentials were impeccable; there was no question as to her expertise. Professor of Social Work at the University of Washington and Director of Social Work at Harborview Medical Center, she founded the sex assault program at the hospital. The Center was nationally recognized for its work with victims of violent crime, notably rape and incest victims, and women who are battered by intimate partners. Widely regarded as a pioneer in the area, Dr. Klingbeil worked for 15 years developing diagnostic criteria. She published in peer-reviewed journals, lectured around the country and testified before Congress on the Battered Woman's Syndrome. She had seen thousands of battered women over of the course of 15 years. In preparation for the trial, she had examined Sherrie for five hours.

Dr. Klingbeil's testimony first addressed the identifiable indices of the Battered Woman's Syndrome. She discussed the mentality and behavior of battered women that appear to be at variance with how lay people are likely to react to a spouse who batters. She provided a basis from which a jury could understand why a person suffering from the Battered Woman Syndrome would not leave her mate, would not inform police or friends, and would fear increased aggression. Professor Klingbeil further explained why Sherrie Allery perceived herself to be in imminent danger when she pulled the trigger. We argued that expert testimony on these critical issues would be helpful to a jury in understanding a phenomenon not within the competence of an ordinary lay person.

In the words of the Washington Supreme Court, reversing this trial court and holding expert testimony admissible:

> Professor Klingbeil testified that the battered woman syndrome is a recognized phenomenon in the psychiatric profession and is defined as a technical term of art in professional diagnostic textbooks. The syndrome is comprised of three distinct phases. In the first phase, tension mounts between the woman and her partner and minor abuse occurs.

> More serious violence follows and the woman experiences a sense of powerlessness to do anything to stop her husband. Psychologists describe a phenomenon known as "learned helplessness," a condition in which the woman is psychologically locked into her situation due to economic dependence on the man, an abiding attachment to him, and the failure of the legal system to adequately respond to the problem.

> Finally, there is a temporary lull in the physical abuse inflicted on the battered woman, and she forgives her assailant, hoping that the abuse will not reoccur.

We claimed and the appellate court eventually agreed that this evidence may have a substantial bearing on the woman's perceptions and behavior at the time of the killing and is central to her claim of self-defense.[5]

Characteristics of batterers

Moving from an overview of the syndrome, Professor Klingbeil turned to an outline of a batterer's characteristics. Her guidelines

---

[5] In reversing the trial court's refusal to admit expert testimony, the appellate court said: ". . . the jury must consider all the facts and circumstances known to the woman at the time of the killing in evaluating her claim of self-defense." To effectively present the situation as perceived by the defendant, and the reasonableness of her fear, the defense has the option to explain her feelings to enable the jury to overcome stereotyped impressions about women who remain in abusive relationships. It is appropriate that the jury be given a professional explanation of the battering syndrome and its effects on the woman through the use of expert testimony. *See* Comment, *The Expert as Educator: A Proposed Approach to the Use of Battered Woman Syndrome Expert Testimony,* 35 VAND.L.REV. 741 (1982).

described Wayne Allery precisely. She testified that batterers frequently are drinkers; have low self esteem and poor impulse control; and that they lump all emotions together and become angry and strike out physically.

Professor Klingbeil also described espionage-like tactics used by batterers to contain and control the partner or wife. She testified that early on in a relationship this insistence on control is seen as "caring that he loves me so much that he takes me to work or he comes home for lunch and we do all of our activities together." But slowly, Professor Klingbeil noted, this kind of activity increases until she becomes a prisoner in her own marriage. This leads to despair and a real wearing down of the woman, which is probably the hopelessness that is frequently characterized in these relationships. At this point, the batterer is insanely jealous and is frequently accusatory about all kinds of situations, including accusations of adultery. It may be the paper boy or it may involve someone like the grocery check-out person, or in Sherrie's case "the midget niggers" in the neighborhood.

Characteristics of Battered Women

Similarly, Professor Klingbeil's outline of the characteristics of battered women described Sherrie Allery. She explained why battered women don't leave, noting that they constantly cling to tiny pieces of reinforcement that the situation is going to get better. They frequently describe their partners as explosive and unpredictable. They are constantly walking on eggshells, not knowing when the next minor incident will kick off a major eruption of violence.

Professor Klingbeil explained the "Cycle theory of violence," providing insight into the puzzling reasons why women do not leave. She said that in a battering relationship, episodes of violence are typically followed by remorse. The batterer says he will never do it again and that he simply lost his temper. He begs her to stay with him and forgive him and declares they will work it out together. Because the woman wants so desperately to believe him, she stays. She also stays because research shows the woman suffers from:

1. tremendous fear which is an immobilizing factor that keeps women from looking at options
2. learned helplessness
3. economic dependency
4. fear that if they leave they will be killed

Gradually the women tend to lose sight of their personal boundaries or to assess the dangerous of their situation. They begin to accept blame and all responsibility for the situation; wondering what it is they have done to cause it.[6] This loss of perspective, of course, feeds directly into one of the major myths about the syndrome, that the woman deserves the violence because even she thinks she caused it and therefore deserves the beating. Professor Klingbeil also addressed the myth that women lie about beatings and make up stories. She discussed the established science and the predictability and reliability of research examining the accuracy of responses of battered women after violent incidents. Crisis literature, she testified, demonstrates that it is common to get a variety of twists on a story depending on how many people the traumatized person talks with and who gets her reports. For example, they may tell different details to police than to friends. Professor Klingbeil testified that because jurors do not have an understanding of the research and knowledge on these subjects, and many indices of violence are counter-intuitive, it is particularly important for lay juries to understand these concepts in cases involving battering.

Careful not to ask whether Sherrie was telling the truth, we asked Dr. Klingbeil about the type of statements Sherrie made just before and after the shooting. She said that statements such as "I'm going to blow his fucking head off" were not unusual when obtaining the history of a case. "It has turned up frequently in these kinds of situations. It becomes part of these violent relationships." Asked about expressions of relief after the battered woman kills her batterer, Dr. Klingbeil said that these expressions of relief are a post-trauma reaction. They reflect relief, reduction and the elimination of the source of fear that is no longer there.

After the offer of proof and testimonial proffer, we presented our arguments to the court. We urged the court to permit the testimony because the defense was self-defense, and within that context, the jury was entitled to have expert testimony from which they might evaluate the subjective and objective reasonableness of the defendant's perceptions. The defense relied upon three other state courts which had held that exclusion of testimony on Battered Woman's Syndrome undermines

---

[6] Put another way, this is called "learned helplessness," a theory widely accepted in 1984 as a consequence of work by Dr. Lenore Walker and others. They described a phenomenon where the women "tend to feel boxed in and unable to look at the options that they might have in order to get out of the relationship." They are depressed and subject to a lot of stress, constant badgering, harassment. They are essentially worn down by the constant psychological and physical abuse until they are simply unable to determine what is best for them or, in some instances, for their children. So they end up staying in the relationship and according to many researchers around the country and in England, it's probably this phenomenon that best describes why women stay in such a horribly dangerous and devastating kind of relationships. The "learned helplessness" theory was subject to intensive criticism because many of these women were not "helpless." This theory has been substantially modified to explain the woman's behavior as "survival instinct." *See e.g.*, Julie Blackman, INTIMATE VIOLENCE Columbia University Press, 1989.

a defendant's 14th amendment right to present her theory of the case. Ohio courts opined that where self-defense is justification for homicide, the defense is entitled to present expert testimony on the unique state of mind of the battered women because the subject of the battered woman, and especially her unique psychological characteristics and differences in reaction and perception, is not one within the knowledge and comprehension of the average person.

We argued this that expert testimony was critical to Sherrie's defense. We pointed out that the prosecution's theory was that Sherrie was lying about the number of times she was battered and the extent of the beatings. Instead, the prosecution had characterized the attacks as part of the normal ups and downs of a relationship. The prosecution further argued that Sherrie's statements before and after the shooting demonstrated that she planned to kill Wayne and was happy he was dead. The expert's testimony would give the jury the basis for considering the reasonableness of Sherrie's conduct. We reminded the court that during voir dire the prosecution excused all of the people who said they knew anything about battered women, leaving a jury vulnerable to all of the myths and misperceptions the prosecutor was peddling.

The prosecution's argument reinforced the stereotypes and myths. Ignoring the case law and distorting the offer of proof, the prosecutor belittled the research, the science, and the witness. He said the State would resist the expert testimony on its lack of relevancy:

> The woman (Professor Klingbeil) speaks of this syndrome which seems to be a collection of complaints that women who have been assaulted utter. It doesn't seem to me that there is anything in there that one might hear in any prosecutor's office on any given Monday. I don't care how many doctoral theses are written that say that's it a common myth that a marriage license is a license to beat your wife or the mythical belief that the woman had it coming. I don't see anything to that at all. I have been around people all of my life. I simply don't believe it. I have not experienced it. It's a lot of malarkey.

The court concluded:

> These jurors understand obvious things and they don't need any esoteria (sic) to explain the obvious. The question here is whether we are talking about something beyond the ability of the ordinary juror to understand. The question about the myth of whether somebody deserves a beating. I don't believe it and I don't believe the jury believes it. The myth [the expert] talks about simply does not exist.

A written offer of proof of Dr. Vicki Boyd, Clinical Psychologist, who administered a specialized program in family violence was also submitted to the court—and rejected.

The Rebuttal and Surrebuttal Cases

After Sherrie testified, there was a bitter argument about the permissible scope of the state's rebuttal case. They sought to elicit testimony from a few witnesses, including Wayne's sister, who said she never saw Sherrie exhibit fear of Wayne and observed no animosity right up to the eve of the shooting. The prosecution argued, with characteristic hyperbole:

> She gets on the stand and recites the day after day and week after week of torture, humiliation and so on and so forth which intensifies in degree into the last year of this sort of thing in 1980 until she finally can't stand this anymore and it's so horrible and ghastly that she finally serves papers on him. I am here to show by these people that they didn't seem to be having any problems at all, at least as she exhibited at late as October 27, 1980, four days before he was shot... I think it's relevant in light of her testimony and the positive that she leaves this thing, or attempts to leave this thing.

Although the defense disputed the admission of this testimony, the court permitted it, saying:

> Mrs. Allery did testify to the long history of the marriage, that Wayne Allery changed in a certain interval just before the incident; that his demeanor was different, his speech was different, the things he called her were different, what he called the house was different—called it a house instead of a home. I suppose all of this was to suggest that he was undergoing a change and it is therefore proper rebuttal to present evidence that he was not undergoing a change.

In our judgment, this testimony was not particularly harmful, especially in light of the strength of the defense case and the fact that even the defense did not claim the violence was unremitting.

The next two prosecution rebuttal witnesses dealt a terrible blow. The court permitted testimony addressing the prosecution's wildly improbable argument that Wayne was afraid of Sherrie. To support this argument they called Michael Richmond who testified that twice, once in 1979, and again four months before the shooting, Wayne brought two or three of his guns to Richmond's house and asked Richmond to hold them. Richmond testified that Wayne said he was concerned that Sherrie and he were fighting, and he was afraid she might do bodily harm to him or Toni. Richmond said he never saw Sherrie exhibit fear of Wayne and that he heard Sherrie curse Wayne out, sounding "like a construction worker."

The state's case ended with the recall to the witness stand of Robert Kerr who had not been permitted to testify about Sherrie's unfortunate but clearly sarcastic boasts months after Wayne's death. Now, on rebuttal. Kerr was permitted to testify about Robert's alleged fear of Sherrie, stating that Wayne told him that he was ready to move out because "I don't know if she wants a divorce, or I don't know if she wants to kill me."

Kerr's major assignment in the prosecution's rebuttal case was to describe in graphic detail a confrontation he had with Sherrie six months after the shooting:

> She jumped up and she said "you want to know the truth"? And then she commenced snapping her fingers, gyrating her hips and she said "I killed the sonofabitch. I enjoyed it. I enjoyed seeing his brains dripping out the side of his head. I enjoyed seeing his eyeball hanging down on his face".
>
> "Is that what you want to hear"?

Cross-examination effectively explored his bias toward Sherrie, his disagreements and arguments with his wife about Sherrie. He reluctantly admitted he "didn't care for her" and that he argued with his wife about Sherrie and Wayne and what occurred on November 1. However, the testimony could not help but further impugn Sherrie's character and provide the prosecution with more facts with which to argue she had acted with intent to kill.

It was essential that the defense attempt to demonstrate that Sherrie's outburst had been sarcastic and the result of her deep dislike of Kerr. To try to counter the effect of Kerr's testimony, the defense called William Holmes, a next door neighbor. in surrebuttal. Holmes was present during Sherrie's flare-up with Kerr. His detailed account of the words exchanged between Sherrie and Kerr was not as bad as the picture conjured up by Kerr, but it was bad enough. Holmes said Sherrie spoke with dripping sarcasm because she knew Kerr hated her and believed that she killed her husband in cold blood. In either case, the admission contained in her statement did its damage. Even if the jury accepted that Sherrie was sarcastic and recognized the poisoned relationship between Robert Kerr and Sherrie, they could not help but be prejudiced by either version of her words. The jury either understood her sarcasm and anger at Kerr or they did not. We rested. No further words were going to convert any one.

Jury Instructions

The jury instructions were critical. Despite the fact that in Washington there is no duty to retreat from one's home when one is feloniously assaulted, the court refused to give a "no duty to retreat instruction" because, the court said, Sherrie Allery was not in danger when she shot her husband.

After extended argument, the court refused to give the *Wanrow*[7] self-defense instruction that would make "manifestly apparent to the average juror" that it must judge Sherrie's actions from her the "conditions as they appeared to her at the time" taking into consideration all the facts and circumstances know to her at the time and prior to the incident.[8] Instead, Judge Worswick said that the requested language from *Wanrow* was only an opinion of minority, not majority of the court on issue of self-defense and that "my brothers [sic] upstairs if they are going to write some law on the subject, ought to write clearly and ought to remember not only what they write but read what other people write."

Summations

The passionate summations presented stark contrasts. As Sherrie Allery cringed and seethed, the prosecution wove a tale of a foulmouthed woman who did not learn her lessons from the loss of her children in 1975. She was a hot tempered wife who provoked her husband by her drinking and "carousing around" bars in saloons in Tacoma. She did not take care of him or her daughter. She exaggerated the physical abuse and certainly did not act as a victim of physical, psychological or emotional abuse. She was tired of him, planned to kill him, and told others she would. She did so and bragged about it afterwards. The inflammatory comments were powerful and the court sustained only a few of the objections during the prosecutor's summation. He effectively relied on every stereotype about battered women to damage Sherrie Allery and emphasized the bad mother and bad wife theme throughout. Sherrie was demoralized.

Her spirits lifted as the defense summed up. I portrayed the marriage, the violence and the personalities so that Sherrie felt present and alive in the courtroom. I attacked the idea that the violence was the result of "domestic disputes" and demonstrated that the violence was

---

[7] *State v. Wanrow*, 88 Wash.2d 221, 559 P.2d 548 (1977) was the watershed opinion that acknowledged gender bias in the law of self-defense and "squarely raised the issue of the different circumstances in which women killed in self-defense, the different means by which they killed and the different factual contexts, as well as the history and experience of sex-discrimination." Elizabeth M Schneider, *Describing and Changing: Women's Self-Defense Work and the Problem of Expert Testimony on Battering*, 9 WOMEN'S RIGHTS LAW REPORTER 195, 213 (1986). *Wanrow* required a trial court to provide instructions on the law of self-defense that take into account the historical, unique and individual circumstances facing the woman defendant at the time she killed. The work on *Wanrow* led to a field of work termed "women's self-defense." *Id.*

[8] *State v. Allery*, 101 Wash.2d 591, 682 P.2d 312, 314 (1984).

cyclical—sometimes the relationship was loving. I talked about the times she tried to leave and the dangers in doing so and about the build up of fear and those "looks"—the hints and signs that she was in danger. I talked about her tough exterior masking her feelings of fright and vulnerability. She had learned how to survive in that relationship. And of course, the bonds of love and care for her daughter, Toni were central to an understanding of Sherrie's life and motivation.

I wove the history of violence, the hospitalizations, and the calls for help to police, friends, family and coworkers into an understanding of Sherrie's mental state on November 1, 1980. I then recounted the events of that night in slow detail—Sherrie entering the darkened home, the startling light that signaled Wayne was there, the threats to kill, and the metallic sound. We hoped the jury could place themselves in Sherrie's shoes and perceive the fear as she stood in her home on November 1, 1980. We hoped the jury would not fall prey to myths about battering.

The jury retired and many hours later asked questions about the definition of self-defense and manslaughter. We were hopeful. Five minutes before they were to retire for the weekend, they sent a note that they had reached a verdict. As the foreman announced "Not Guilty of Murder in the first degree," I took a deep breath. Sherrie did not appear to move. Next the foreman said "We the jury find Sherrie Lynn Allery Guilty of murder in the second degree." Several spectators gasped. Someone said "Oh No." "Please be quiet," said the judge.

Talking later with several jurors who had obvious sympathy for Sherrie's plight, they thought they had done her a favor by the decision not to convict of premeditated murder. They said many jurors could not understand why she would not leave Wayne Allery if the history of violence was as bad as she said. They also thought she was a bad mother and a bad wife.

Even before she composed herself, Sherrie's main concern was her daughter Toni. She had to take care of her. Fortunately, the court permitted Sherrie to remain on bail pending sentence.

Women's groups organized around the case. They wrote articles, sent letters to the court, and held various programs to educate the public about battered woman's syndrome. In Washington, the court had the power to impose a sentence without incarceration. After a lengthy presentation, the court sentenced her to twenty years in prison but allowed her to remain on bond pending appeal. The appeal was supported by many organizations. The Northwest Women's Law Center became active in the case, writing an amicus brief for the appeal.

After oral argument, the Court of Appeals, stating that the case raised "issues of broad public import," certified the case to the Washington Supreme Court. On May 17, 1984, the Washington Supreme Court did what Judge Worswick suggested—it wrote clearly on the subject. In no uncertain terms, the court reversed the conviction, holding that (1) testimony on the battered woman syndrome is admissible because it "may have a substantial bearing on the woman's perceptions and behavior at the time of the killing and is central to her claim of self-defense"; (2) the court erred in failing to give a no duty to retreat instruction; and (3) the admission of the 1975 custody hearing in Montana where Sherrie Allery lost custody of her children was prejudicial error because her "prior misconduct as a mother was irrelevant" to the case. The court made plain that *Wanrow* was the standard to be applied and that, despite the fact that the court's instruction on self-defense "on its face adequately conveys the subjective self-defense standard," it did not make this standard "manifestly apparent to the average juror." Moreover, the court noted that Klingbeil had "well-established" credentials and that the scientific understanding of the battered woman syndrome was sufficiently developed to allow its admission at trial for a variety of purposes, including why a woman would not leave her mate, would not inform police or friends, and would fear increased aggression.

The decision was hailed by women's groups. We were relieved, but Sherrie Allery faced retrial. Four years had passed, and there was a new prosecutor and a somewhat more enlightened climate. Despite the fact that the prosecutor's office had repeatedly said that a polygraph would be of no moment to its decision, Allery took and passed a lie detector test on the crucial issues in the case. We met with the prosecutors again, presenting them with the polygraph results. We waited.

On July 31, 1984, the Tacoma prosecutor's office announced that it would not retry Sherrie Allery. After such a long struggle, she finally felt somewhat vindicated. Even thought she would have preferred to hear the words "not guilty," from a jury, she was relieved that the long ordeal was over. With only a day to breathe sighs of relief, she began to receive hate mail and angry phone messages for several weeks. She retreated to the warmth and support of her daughter and her friends. Slowly she was able to move on in life. Within a short time, she realized she would be taunted if she remained in Tacoma. She and Toni left for Montana. Glad that she was no longer in fear, she quietly admitted that she was so sad that Toni would not have her dad in her life. Through her tears, she cracked a joke I no longer remember except for its sarcasm.

2

Robert A. Ferguson[1]

Treason, Aaron Burr, and the National Imagination

A PERSONAGE IN THE DOCK

Unresolved communal anxieties magnify courtroom events, and no trial illustrates this phenomenon better than the first one to capture the national imagination, the trial of Aaron Burr for high misdemeanor and treason in 1807. Held in the Circuit Court of the United States in the District of Virginia, the trial would have been notorious anyway given the personalities involved. Aaron Burr, fifty-one years old, had been a Revolutionary war hero, the leader of a political party, a New York lawyer of note, a senator of the United States, and, three years before, the country's third vice-president. Presiding over the trial was none other than John Marshall, Chief Justice of the United States Supreme Court, an embattled figure in 1807. Around him, arguing the case, were the leading lawyers of the Virginia Bar, men with national reputations and connections that would allow Virginia to dominate the executive branch of the federal government for a quarter of a century, an unprecedented span of control in U.S. history. An even greater personality loomed just beyond the courtroom. Burr's prime accuser and the man who orchestrated the prosecution was the President of the United States, Thomas Jefferson.

Magnified personalities count for much in a controversial trial, but they become locked in conflict for reasons beyond their control. No one wants to be in court, and the underlying reasons for being there in 1807 were so many, so vexed, and so complicated that the trial remains a subject of controversy today. The specific question—Was Aaron Burr guilty of treason against the United States?—raised a series of problems

---

[1] George Edward Woodberry Professor of Law, Literature, and Criticism, Columbia University.

that the country was not ready to cope with, and the range of those problems pitted region against region. This spread in areas of uncertainty and conflict created a new phenomenon, the first high profile trial to capture national attention.

The politics of the time were controlling elements. Burr used his leadership role in the new republic to further his own agenda and wealth, and his naked ambition defied established norms. A governing elite wanted to believe that civic virtue could maintain a disinterested mien at the highest levels of the republican experiment.[2] It was a losing battle, but those who fought it took the goal seriously. Burr, who didn't, already had stepped over the line in 1804 when he killed Alexander Hamilton in a duel over political differences. Dueling remained a practice in a society where concepts of honor still dominated much of behavior, but it was against unspoken rules, as well as a crime, for one political leader to kill another on the dueling ground.[3] Burr had called Hamilton out with single-minded ruthlessness. As he would boast later, "[I] was sure of being able to kill him," an admission that made the duel "little better than murder" in the eyes of others.[4] Burr was also a known sexual predator. In a question still asked in American politics, what was the proper relation between private and public virtue in an official elected to guide the people?

Other transgressions by the man in the dock turned on questions of status. Burr fought in the Revolutionary army and could legitimately call himself a founder of the Republic. The extravagant welcomes he received during travels in the communities of the west in 1805 and 1806 were based on that heroic reputation, but what restraints were expected of a founder in the pursuit of personal business? No one knew exactly, but Burr flouted voluntary restrictions that others accepted. Imperiously aristocratic in bearing, Burr owed his original standing to an exalted birthright; for unlike other founders, he was the grandson and son of celebrated men. His immediate forebears, Jonathan Edwards and Aaron Burr Senior, were famous religious figures in colonial America, and both had been presidents of Princeton (the College of New Jersey). So

---

[2] For an account that sees this issue as "the real treason," see Gordon S. Wood, "The Real Treason of Aaron Burr," *Proceedings of the American Philosophical Society*, 143 (June 1999), 280–293.

[3] Joanne B. Freeman, "Dueling as Politics: Reinterpreting the Burr–Hamilton Duel," *The William and Mary Quarterly*, 3d series, 53 (April 1996), 289–318. The involved rituals around a challenge usually led to an accommodation. Hamilton, for example, had been involved in ten previous affairs of honor without engaging in combat.

[4] One witness of Burr's frequent boast—a witness who then called it murder—was Jeremy Bentham in 1808. See Milton Lomask, *Aaron Burr*, two vols. (New York: Farrar, Straus, Giroux, 1979–1982), II: 309. I rely on this standard biography when there are conflicts about the life and surrounding events.

significant were these credentials that John Adams would later complain
that Jefferson had won the Presidency from him in 1800 because Burr
had been Jefferson's running mate, bringing "100,000 Votes from the
single Circumstance of his descent."[5]

Filled with a sense of entitlement, Burr pushed the limits of acceptable behavior in early republican society even as he embodied its
conflicting understandings. The bible culture of early America and the
emerging secular enlightenment were both in him, and they clashed in
the wake of those 100,000 votes from 1800. No one knew the appropriate
answers when religious and secular spheres met in one person, nor
where aristocratic place ended and republican worth began. Living
imperiously on the cusp of these issues, Burr always knew that trouble
would follow him. "The Fates never decreed that I should go anywhere
but that someone should be the worse for it," he wrote early in life.[6]

The events for which Burr was on trial aggravated uncertainties of
another kind. Between 1805 and 1807, Burr schemed as a private citizen
to gain power in the western territories, and each scheme tweaked a
different growing pain of the new nation. His plans included vague but
related alternatives: secret expeditions of armed men into the western
territories to appropriate land, the expansion of American holdings at
the expense of Spanish claims, the outright conquest of Mexico for the
United States, and the conceivable creation of a separate western empire
to be financed by England or Spain. The anxieties these plans touched
off cannot be fully appreciated today because the circumstances no
longer exist. No one in 1807 could more than guess at the ultimate
dimensions of the United States, and those who did guess divided over
what the inclusion of additional territory meant for the existing arrangement. These debates grew fierce, and they pitted region against region
depending on where annexation would take place. Local identifications
and disputed borders still dominated the new states in their loose idea of
union.[7]

The questions raised by Burr's behavior thus extended well beyond
him. Numbers of Americans, some with only peripheral identifications to
the nation, were venturing westward in search of new lives on independent terms. Few knew or cared when personal actions taken to improve
one's lot within uncharted and disputed territories might constitute

---

[5] John Adams to Thomas Jefferson, November 15, 1813, in Lester J. Cappon, ed., 2
vols., *The Complete Correspondence Between Thomas Jefferson & Abigail & John Adams*
(Chapel Hill: The University of North Carolina Press, 1959), II.

[6] Aaron Burr to Sally Burr Reeve, January 17, 1774, Lomask, "Preface" *Aaron Burr*, I,
xix.

[7] Seymour Martin Lipset, *The First New Nation: The United States in Historical and
Comparative Perspective* (New York: Basic Books, 1963).

treason against the United States. What was treason, anyway, in a country where every American had faced the charge in embellished rhetorical terms during the Revolution? Western adventurers eagerly contested Spanish and French claims to territory with little concern for the crisis in international relations that an aggressive pursuit of new territory might bring. Jefferson himself had absorbed criticism when he unilaterally purchased huge tracts in the Louisiana territory from the French as president in 1803. What were the limits of executive authority in adding new regions beyond the official union, and how were such lands to be distributed? These questions led to another. Foreign claims over large western tracts were facts as well as threats in 1807. How dangerous was it for a recognized founder of the republic to involve foreign powers in his own design for advancement in those claimed territories?

These uncertainties, together with Burr's notorious behavior, meant that arguments in court over the defendant's guilt or innocence spilled into the public domain where they took on a life of their own. In effect, unbridled use of collateral arguments would undo Aaron Burr in a way that the trial itself could not sanction. Most Americans ignored the "not guilty" verdict reached in court, choosing a prosecutorial narrative instead to decide what had happened. Their selective interest had little to do with the law, and everything to do with ideological needs, and this was true even though Marshall's controlling opinion the other way held great national import. Indeed, the extent of this discrepancy between legal result and communal effect encourages a larger premise: when the public emphasizes aspects at trial that either ignore or reject a court's official decision, it is safe to assume that something more than crime and punishment are at work.

Countless newspaper articles, thirty-three plays, twice as many works of fiction, and numerous poems take up the life of Aaron Burr in some way, and they rely on a curious juxtaposition. The feckless adventurer and ineffective traitor emerges in popular lore as a capacious figure, a master of disguise, and the seducer of every woman in sight. Edmund Stedman's poem, "Aaron Burr's Wooing," catches the essence of this trend: "Where's the widow or maid with a mouth to be kist,/When Burr comes a wooing, that long would resist?"[8] These refashionings of Burr make seduction his primary attribute with special attention addressed to vulnerable elements in society. The historical figure's political opportunism melts into a sinister capacity to commit any despicable act; unaided virtue is particularly susceptible to the

---

[8] "Aaron Burr's Wooing," *The Poems of Edmund Clarence Stedman* (Boston: Houghton Mifflin, 1908), 389–390. [Stedman wrote the poem in 1887.]

traitor's charms unless communal vigilance responds. In victory, this fictional Burr plays on American fears; in defeat, he purges doubt.[9]

The puzzle in these representations deepens in the twentieth century. Starting with Gore Vidal's novel *Burr* in 1973, revisionist accounts have wanted "to restore Aaron Burr to the Pantheon of the Founders." Not treason but circumstance and party politics explain this new protagonist. The myth of history rather than patriotism is the modern novelist's controlling theme, and recent biographers have followed suit. This postmodern Burr is the victim of events and a proto-abolitionist who resists slaveholding Virginians on principle. A "jackal pack" of politicians engineers Burr's "fall from power," and Jefferson deteriorates as "the first President to make to the people assertions he later admitted were not true."[10] The basis for this shift in trajectories is not hard to find. Nineteenth-century Americans who feared foreign encroachment in the western territories have given way to twenty-first century counterparts who worry more about executive power, malfeasance in office, and the manipulation of truth by those in authority. There is, nonetheless, a similarity. Whether for or against the historical figure, all accounts make Aaron Burr the linchpin of communal anxieties.

THE POWER OF STORY

Anxiety and advocacy naturally embrace hyperbole, one reason why controversial trials are barometers of ideological concern. The example of Burr is of interest in this regard because it demonstrates how debate in the adversarial process marks a path of communal explanation. A trial presents contrasting stories of guilt and innocence for legal determination, and when the community accepts a story *against* legal resolution, it is an indicator of general thought; it tells us how a community thinks about its problems and even more about how it identifies and regards its enemies.

The argument that controlled communal perceptions in *United States v. Aaron Burr* was given by William Wirt, a protégé of Thomas Jefferson and junior counsel for the prosecution in 1807. Every later account of the trial agrees that Wirt's vivid speech in condemnation of Burr on August 25th "dazzled his audience—and posterity."[11] But what

---

[9] For the shifts in Aaron Burr's reputation and depiction of them, see Charles F. Nolan, Jr., *Aaron Burr and the American Literary Imagination* (Westport, Conn., Greenwood Press, 1980).

[10] Gore Vidal, *Burr, A Novel* (New York: Random House, 1973) and Roger G. Kennedy, *Burr, Hamilton, and Jefferson, A Study in Character* (Oxford: Oxford University Press, 2000), pp. 87–110, 353, 377. The quotations in the text are from Kennedy. See, as well, Thomas Fleming, *Duel: Alexander Hamilton, Aaron Burr, and the future of America* (New York: Basic Books, 1999).

[11] Lomask, *Aaron Burr*, II, 235–36, 275. See, as well, Herbert S. Parmet and Marie B. Hecht, *Aaron Burr: Portrait Of An Ambitious Man* (New York: Macmillan, 1967), pp. 299–

made Wirt so memorable? Most explanations simply allude to the speaker's towering eloquence. Wirt used the familiar tools of the early republican lawyer: oratorical profusion, literary reference, and a balance of secular and religious explanation.[12] The biographer of Patrick Henry and the longest sitting attorney general in the country's history, Wirt solidified his reputation for eloquence across subsequent decades, but other lawyers, especially Luther Martin for the defense, were at least as eloquent at the time, and John Wickham, Burr's main defense counsel, gave an address five days earlier that professional observers called "the greatest forensic performance of the American bar". It was Wickham's argument, not Wirt's, that Chief Justice Marshall would accept when instructing the jury as a matter of law (Burr could not be found guilty of treason on the evidence presented), and it was Wickham's argument that was admired in court.[13]

Wirt's capacity to control perceptions belongs to another level of understanding. He turned the concerns about Burr into a familiar story that alleviated those concerns. The charge of treason depended on whether Burr could be shown to have been "levying War" against the United States or to have been "adhering" to the enemies of the United States, "giving them aid or comfort," and it required the sworn testimony of two witnesses to the same overt act.[14] In practical terms, the prosecution had to prove an overt act of treason had been committed on Blennerhassett's Island, the part of Virginia in the middle of the Ohio River that gave the federal court in Richmond control of the case. Jurisdiction in the East was crucial. Burr had been acquitted of all wrong doing by three sympathetic grand juries in the West, two in the state of Kentucky and a third held in the Mississippi territory. The West had been generous to Burr because it, too, wanted war with Spain. It cared little about Burr's schemes of advancement except to acknowledge

---

300; Nolan, *Aaron Burr and the American Literary Imagination*, p. 35–36; and, most recently, Buckner F. Melton, Jr., *Aaron Burr: Conspiracy to Treason* (New York: John Wiley & Sons, 2002), pp. 210–213.

[12] Robert A. Ferguson, "The Configuration of Law and Letters," *Law and Letters in American Culture* (Cambridge: Harvard University Press, 1985), pp. 1–83.

[13] For the controlling importance of Wickham's argument, the quotation cited (from Littleton W. Tazewell, a respected lawyer but also a member of the grand jury responsible for the indictment of Burr), and Luther Martin's eloquence, see Lomack, *Aaron Burr*, II, 270–272, 245–46, 277–279. The trial transcript reveals Wickham's dominance as well. Case reporter David Robertson placed Wickham's decisive argument at the end of volume one of his *Reports*; much of the advocacy in volume two revolves around Wickham's argument.

[14] Article three, section three, part one, of the Constitution of the United States reads, "Treason against the United States shall consist only in levying War against them, or in adhering to their Enemies, giving them Aid and Comfort. No Person shall be convicted of Treason unless on the Testimony of two Witnesses to the same overt Act, or on Confession in open Court."

that he was a war hero who would adopt more heroic measures in opening western lands to further settlement.

The government's fourth attempt to prosecute Burr—in the East, where the defendant and war with Spain were viewed with suspicion and alarm—depended on whether or not a given fact could be tied to two controversial premises. Thirty to forty armed men had gathered on Blennerhassett's Island at Aaron Burr's behest to sail down the Ohio River into the Mississippi territory to Louisiana and Spanish territory. But had an overt act of rebellion taken place on the island on December 10, 1806 and had Aaron Burr conducted it? The main flaw in the charge lay in an undisputed detail. Burr had been two hundred miles away in Kentucky on December 10th. Everything hinged on the prosecution's ability to prove that Burr and one of his financial backers on the island, Harman Blennerhassett, had conspired together to commit treason and then acted upon that plan *on* the island.

Blennerhassett emigrated with his wife from Ireland in 1796 and had spent a fortune carving a plantation out of the wilderness. He turned what had been called Backus Island (near what is now Marietta, Ohio) into a personal haven dignified by his own name. Burr had been attracted by the refined setting, Blennerhassett's money, and some said by Blennerhassett's wife, and he had used his expertise and wiles on all three. His high social status and political fame allowed him to play upon his Irish backer's dreams of even greater possessions. Burr had convinced Blennerhassett that unlimited opportunities would materialize when the United States declared war on Spain, which seemed likely in 1806, but he carefully left the rest of his plans in vague terms.

When William Wirt attacked for the prosecution on August 25th, he had to counter difficulties in both aspects of the proof against Burr. John Marshall for the court had indicated clear reluctance to accept the available evidence as proof that an overt act of treason had taken place before two reliable witnesses on Blennerhassett's Island, and he had openly questioned whether Aaron Burr's *constructive* presence on the Island could be established as a matter of law. One long paragraph will be sufficient to demonstrate Wirt's rhetorical acumen in response to these difficulties:

> Who is Blannerhassett? A native of Ireland, a man of letters, who fled from the storms of his own country to find quiet in ours. His history shows that war is not the natural element of his mind. If it had, he never would have exchanged Ireland for America. So far is an army from furnishing the society natural and proper to Mr. Blannerhassett's character, that on his arrival in America, he retired even from the population of the Atlantic States and sought quiet and solitude in the bosom of our western forests. But he carried with

him taste and science and wealth; and lo, the desert smiled! Possessing himself of a beautiful island in the Ohio, he rears upon it a place and decorates it with every romantic embellishment of fancy. A shrubbery, that Shenstone might have envied, blooms around him. Music, that might have charmed Calypso and her nymphs, is his. An extensive library spreads its treasures before him. A philosophical apparatus offers him all the secrets and mysteries of nature. Peace, tranquillity, and innocence shed their mingled delights around him. And to crown the enchantment of the scene, a wife, who is said to be lovely even beyond her sex and graced with every accomplishment that can render it irresistible, had blessed him with her love and made him the father of several children. The evidence would convince you, that this is but a faint picture of the real life.[15]

If the attractions in the passage are obvious, they worked on the nineteenth-century imagination in a particular way. Blennerhassett appears as every romantic adventurer's wish fulfilled. He has managed to start life over, transforming a new world, one entirely of his own choosing, into paradise by retreating from a noxious world and by rendering nature mediate to his every need. His wealth, his taste, his technical knowledge ("philosophical apparatus"), and the ideal wife ("lovely even beyond her sex and graced with every accomplishment") provide the "mingled delights" of the virtuous man. Family values and a nation dedicated to "peace" and "quiet" guarantee continuing "tranquillity." Brief references to antiquity ("Calypso and her nymphs") and to English pastoral traditions (William Shenstone) cap the Horatian ideal of retreat born again as the American dream.

Hardly a "picture of the real life," Wirt's scene of wish-fulfillment illustrated a well-known Johnsonian adage: "the natural flights of the human mind are not from pleasure to pleasure, but from hope to hope."[16] Wirt gave the dream such scope because he wanted to shatter it with power for every auditor with similar aspirations. The paragraph turns even as it lingers on what can be hoped for:

In the midst of all this peace, this innocent simplicity and this tranquillity, this feast of the mind, this pure banquet of the heart, the destroyer comes; he comes to change this paradise into a hell. No monitory shuddering through the bosom of their unfortunate

---

[15] David Robertson, *Reports of the Trials of Colonel Aaron Burr, Late Vice President of the United States, for Treason and for A Misdemeanor ... in the Circuit Court of the United States Held at the City of Richmond, in the district of Virginia, in the Summer Term of the year 1807*, 2 vols. (Philadelphia: Hopkins and Earle, 1808) II: 96–97. All further reference to Robertson's *Reports* will be to this edition in parenthetical reference in the text.

[16] Samuel Johnson, "Rambler 2," *Essays From the Rambler, Adventurer, and Idler*, ed. W.J. Bate (New Haven: Yale University Press, 1968), p. 4.

possessor warns him of the ruin that is coming upon him. A stranger presents himself. Introduced to their civilization by the high rank which he had lately held in his country, he soon finds his way to their hearts, by the dignity and elegance of his demeanor, the light and beauty of his conversation, and the seductive and fascinating power of his address. The conquest was not difficult. Innocence is very simple and credulous. Conscious of no design itself, it suspects none in others. It wears no guard before its breast. Every door and portal and avenue of the heart is thrown open, and all who choose enter it. Such was the state of Eden when the serpent entered its bowers. . . . In a short time the whole man [the unfortunate Blennerhassett] is changed, and every object of his former delight is relinquished. No more he enjoys the tranquil scene; it has become flat and insipid to his taste. His books are abandoned. His retort and crucible are thrown aside. His shrubbery blooms and breathes its fragrance upon the air in vain; he likes it not. . . . His enchanted island is destined soon to relapse into a wilderness; and in a few months we find the beautiful and tender partner of his bosom, whom he lately 'permitted not the winds of' summer 'to visit too roughly,' we find her shivering at midnight, on the winter banks of the Ohio and mingling her tears with the torrents, that froze as they fell (II: 96–97).

The intertext in this passage is *Paradise Lost*, a familiar work in this Richmond courtroom and the model for epic poetry in America at the beginning of the nineteenth century. Wirt held to the theme of loss, though in his version the biblical story had secular dimensions. He emphasized what Blennerhassett gave up materially to Burr as Satan rather than what Adam lost spiritually in the sight of God. The modern accents left Wirt's auditors with a very different set of questions. How had Blennerhassett managed to lose the material happiness that he had pursued so eagerly and gained so completely through his own labor and intellectual planning? Was Blennerhassett typical in his vulnerability? Was everyone as susceptible to destruction? Wirt answered by playing upon the anxieties that made the trial so sensational. In his attack on Burr, the shift from paradise to wilderness comes in the blink of an eye, and the promise of the West gives way to the fearful possibility of an unyielding and inhospitable wasteland. Wirt incorporated another threat to explain matters. The welcome solitude gained in bucolic retreat left every possessor vulnerable to the appearance of a stranger ("every door and portal and avenue . . . is thrown open"). The suddenly "unfortunate possessor" is all too easily dispossessed! Wirt turns the ideal of prosperous possession into the uncertainty that it actually was.

Wirt's Blennerhassett qualified as an intelligent and educated man, but it didn't matter in his case, and it might not in another. The apparition of the stranger in Burr was particularly frightening. The Revolutionary hero gone amuck possessed insidious powers that could not be matched. Burr had taken unfair advantage through the sources of seduction at his disposal. He exploited the exalted role of founder, misusing "high rank" to undermine the patriotism and civic balance of "the unfortunate Blannerhassett." What is the role of a founder, Wirt asked, when the act of founding is complete? The biblical serpent lurking elsewhere in the paragraph represented "the poison of [Burr's] own ambition," and it had been loosed upon the newly created republic. Thinly veiled allusions to class also applied. The self-made man in the Irish immigrant naturally fell to the born aristocrat in Aaron Burr, who possessed a more innate elegance of demeanor and address.

The questions raised by Wirt do not end there. How had Blennerhassett, the man of peace, turned so suddenly and completely into a man of war? (In the same paragraph, we learn that Blennerhassett "no longer drinks the rich melody of music" but "longs for the trumpet's clangor and the cannon's roar.") Thirst for territory, a besetting vice in the rampant land speculation of the early republic, supplied one answer, and the imperialism in this mentality challenged the complacent image of a quiet, peace-loving nation. Wirt led his auditors to the edge of even deeper waters. Long before Satan engineers the fall in the Garden of Eden in book nine of *Paradise Lost*, we know in book one that "The mind is its own place and in its self/Can make a Heav'n of Hell, a Hell of Heav'n."[17]

Prosperity becomes its own trap in Wirt's fable of the fall. Blennerhassett's wealth draws Burr inexorably to him. The charm in the victim's innocence and ease robs him of vigilance. As the leading moralist of the age put the matter in *The Vanity of Human Wishes*, "Wealth heap'd on Wealth, nor Truth nor Safety buys/The Dangers gather as the Treasures rise." What kept Blennerhassett from being satisfied with his ideal lot? "With listless Eyes the Dotard views the store/He views, and wonders that they please no more."[18] Easily threatened, the reality of possession soon grows insipid to the holder of it. Wirt toys here with a

---

[17] John Milton, *Paradise Lost*, book 1, lines 254–55.

[18] Samuel Johnson, *The Vanity of Human Wishes*, lines 27–28, 263–264, in E.L. McAdam, Jr., and George Milne, eds., *The Works of Samuel Johnson* 12 vols. (New Haven: Yale University Press, 1964), VI: 90–109. Samuel Johnson was "by far the most widely available author, English or American, in the American book trade" and maintained "an astonishing dominance of the American periodical press throughout the late eighteenth and early nineteenth centuries," exceeding reference to even George Washington and Benjamin Franklin in the periodical press by 1810. See James Basker, "Samuel Johnson and the American Common Reader," in Paul J. Korshin, ed., *The Age of Johnson: A Scholarly Annual* (New York: AMS Press, 1994), pp. 6–13.

massive cultural predicament. In a country dedicated to the pursuit of
happiness, what if mere wealth failed to satisfy?

Another and more obscure intertext compounds these issues but
with a psychological escape route in mind. Virtue, it seems, is even more
difficult to maintain than satisfaction in wealth. The buried quotation at
the end of Wirt's passage—"whom he lately 'permitted not the winds of'
summer 'to visit too roughly' "—comes from Hamlet's speech "frailty,
thy name is woman!" Hamlet's mother, the symbol of happiness in
Denmark as Queen Gertrude, has re-married within two months of the
king's death to the king's own brother, Claudius, soon to be exposed as a
regicide. In the most famous speech in all of Shakespeare, Hamlet's
realization of this fallen state has caused him to lose all interest in his
surroundings in much the same way as Blennerhassett. "How weary,
stale, flat and unprofitable,/ Seem to me all the uses of this world!,"
Hamlet complains as he gazes on "an unweeded garden that grows to
seed." The parallels carry a further message. By implication, Blennerhassett's wife succumbs to "the seductive and fascinating power" of
Aaron Burr much as Gertrude falls into the "incestuous sheets" of
Claudius.[19] The real problem, in other words, is not the psychology of
Blennerhassett but the triggering depredations of Aaron Burr. It is the
seducer who has destroyed the fabric of happiness.

The spice of sexual connotation heightens the passage and gives the
full answer that Wirt wanted. Through such innuendo, his speech frees
his contemporaries from too much self-examination. Every problem
could be explained through the untoward presence and actions of Aaron
Burr. Could Burr be made to carry the weight of so many contradictions
within the American dream and could he be stretched even further to
cover the intrinsic maladies of the human condition? Yes, he could. As
long as the expanded frame of reference that Wirt sought to create in the
courtroom could be taken for granted, Burr symbolized "the destroyer"
on multiple levels of reference. By inverting the spiritual associations
that adhered to Burr's name from high to low, Wirt made his subject the
obverse of his famous forebears. Politics and religion together confirmed
the negative agency in Burr.

What had Aaron Burr ultimately been guilty of? In Wirt's pivotal
description, Burr went to Blennerhassett Island "to change this paradise
into hell." Crime and sin, seduction and evil, human endeavor and
cosmic design merge in Wirt's account, allowing his audience to fall back
on familiar typologies. These conflations between the human and spiritual worlds proved that Burr was condemned even if his guilt remained
mysterious. Could anyone plumb the ultimate depths of Burr's intentions? No, but it didn't matter as long as one knew that the intentions

19 William Shakespeare, *Hamlet, Prince of Denmark*, Act I, scene ii, lines 129–159.

were there. "They can be known only to the man himself," Wirt intoned, while calling on higher authority, "and to that Being whose eye can pierce the gloom of midnight and the still deeper gloom that shrouds the traitor's heart" (II: 104).

A modern reader finds mostly wretched excess in such posturing, but the legal mores of the time willingly gave Wirt the "picture of life" that he painted in such lurid tones. Language used in court is always subject to manipulation. Wirt looked around him and found ready material. The formal indictment read that Burr acted "not having the fear of God before his eyes"; that instead he had been "moved and seduced by the instigation of the devil" to commit treason against the United States (I: 430, 431). It was a short step to find the devil *in* Aaron Burr. Nor was Wirt the first to invoke the fall in the garden or *Paradise Lost* at trial. Luther Martin for the defense gathered that honor early on, castigating Thomas Jefferson for not divulging papers under court subpoena. Trials like this one usually turn on the cooperation of a co-conspirator who turns state's evidence. Martin, seeking to impugn the informers against Burr, argued that they had "instilled as much poison into the ear of the president, as Satan himself breathed into the ear of Eve" (I: 129).

What did it mean that both sides of the case drew on spiritual categories and patterns of Miltonic reference for expressing them? Pretty language? Certainly, but it also showed that a religious stamp of approval would convince early republicans that they were hearing the whole story.[20] The age embraced Wirt's account at trial through reigning verisimilitudes, the means of making the story told at trial believable. The legal designation of crimes of a certain dimension in early America followed English Common Law procedures in assigning theological terms to explain the level of depravity understood to have been reached. Since treason constituted "the highest civil crime which (considered as a member of a community) any man can possibly commit," it bespoke the gravest depravity, the hardest crime to explain. Wirt conveyed immeasurable evil as measured crime when he claimed only God could pierce the gloom of the traitor's heart.[21]

---

[20] "[D]eciders perceive whole stories" and "the way you tell it makes all the difference." Michael E. Tigar, "The Theory of the Case," *Examining Witnesses* (Chicago: American Bar Association, 1993), pp. 4–16. See, as well, Anthony G. Amsterdam and Jerome Bruner, "On Narrative," *Minding the Law* (Cambridge: Harvard University Press, 2000), pp. 110–142.

[21] William Blackstone, *Commentaries on the Laws of England*, 4 vols. (Oxford: Clarendon Press, 1765–1769), IV: 74–75. See, as well, Karen Halttunen, "The Murderer as Common Sinner," *Murder Most Foul: The Killer and the American Gothic Imagination* (Cambridge: Harvard University Press, 1998), pp. 7–32.

A conception of country was also at work in the Miltonic references employed by Martin and Wirt, as ready acceptance of it in later accounts of Aaron Burr would confirm. John Adams, a very interested observer in 1807, put the matter this way to Benjamin Rush: "I think something must come out on the trial, which will strengthen or weaken our confidence in the general union." The significance that both men attached to the trial as a national test appeared in a detail that would prove to be at odds with history. Adams and Rush were among the most perceptive observers of their age; yet both believed if Burr gained an acquittal in 1807 that his popularity would soar, that his escape could redefine the unfolding republican experiment, and that he might still become President of the United States.[22] The conception of the country itself was on display in this trial of a national figure for treason, and conflicting articulations of the defendant's reputation spoke to elements of it. For those who were afraid, it would be absolutely necessary to demonize Burr.

A MAN HERETOFORE DISTINGUISHED

Stabilizing the new nation required celebrations of its achievements, and the earliest celebrations turned on the "transcendent meaning" of its leaders. The apotheosis of figures like George Washington and Benjamin Franklin contributed to an emerging civil religion.[23] Even today, chronicles of the early republic foreground the stories of founders, and the respective roles of each. While they lived, the founders jockeyed for position as part of their quest for the one selfish object that most of them were willing to publicly condone, "the love of fame, the ruling passion of the noblest minds." Who belonged and in what place in the pantheon of the founders? Who was overrated? Who did *not* belong at all? These questions were food for thought among the survivors of the Revolution. "You rank Colonel Hamilton among the Revolutionary characters," ran a typical letter from John Adams to Benjamin Rush. "But why? The Revolution had its beginning, its middle, and its end before he had anything to do in public affairs."[24] It was, of course, one thing to be

---

[22] John Adams to Benjamin Rush, September 1, 1807 and Benjamin Rush to John Adams, July 9, 1807, in John A. Schultz and Douglass Adair, eds., *The Spur of Fame: Dialogues of John Adams and Benjamin Rush, 1805–1813* (San Marino, Ca.: Huntington Library, 1966), pp. 98–99.

[23] Robert Middlekauff, "The Ritualization of the American Revolution," in Stanley Coben and Lorman Ratner, eds., *The Development of an American Culture* (Englewood Cliff, N.J.: Prenctice–Hall, 1970), pp. 31–44, and Robert N. Bellah, "Civil Religion in America," *Daedalus*, 96 (Winter, 1967), 1–21. The quotation is from Middlekauff, p. 41.

[24] Alexander Hamilton, "The Federalist No. 72." *The Federalist: A Commentary on the Constitution of the United States*, ed., Edward Mead Earle (New York: Modern Library, 1937), p. 470; John Adams to Benjamin Rush, August 23, 1805, *The Spur of Fame*, p. 34;

diminished in these calculations; quite another to be excluded from them altogether.

Aaron Burr found himself falling out of this pantheon of the founders in 1805. Dropped from the vice-presidency for Jefferson's second term, Burr presumed a continuing right to high public rank and took little definition from success as a brilliant lawyer; he was all too suddenly a private citizen without portfolio. All of Burr's schemes in the West can be read as attempts to re-gain a former footing. His last discussion with Thomas Jefferson, a year after he had been pushed out of the vice-presidency, opens a window into his predicament. The report of the meeting comes from the President's pen, but even allowing for animus, the interview meant humiliation for Burr in the role of supplicant. Jefferson wrote his account of the interview in his daybook, or *Anas*, on April 15, 1806, a month after the fact:

> Colo. Burr called on me, & entered into a conversation in which he mentioned that little before my coming into the office I had written to him a letter intimating that I had destined him for a high employ, had he not been placed by the people in a different one; that he had signified his willingness to resign as V[ice] President to give aid to the adm[inistratio]n in any other place; that he had never asked an office however; he asked aid of nobody, but could walk on his own legs, & take care of himself: that I had always used him with politeness, but nothing more: that he had aided in bringing on the present order of things, that he had supported the adm[inistratio]n, & that he could do me much harm: he wished however to be on a differ[en]t ground: he was now disengaged from all particular business, willing to engage in something; should be in town for some days, if I should have any thing to propose to him.[25]

Jefferson's condensation of the meeting surely made the contradictions more blatant than they would have been in conversation, but the passive-aggressive stance ascribed to Burr rings true. Burr admitted rejection by the people even as he claimed a significant role in the present order; he insisted that he had never solicited an office while in the act of asking for one; he claimed to have been loyal to Jefferson while openly threatening him; and he argued for his own importance within the disclosure that he had nothing to do and found himself at loose ends. His great need was "high employ." Jefferson may have exaggerated

---

and John A. Schultz and Douglass Adair, "The Love of Fame, the Ruling Passion of the Noblest Minds," *The Spur of Fame*, pp. 1–18.

[25] "Thomas Jefferson: Memorandum of a Conversation with Burr," in Mary–Jo Kline and Joanne Wood Ryan, eds., *Political Correspondence and Public Papers of Aaron Burr*, 2 vols. (Princeton: Princeton University Press, 1983), II: 962–963. All further quotations in the next two paragraphs are from this source.

Burr's desperation, but the desperation was there. The former vice-president seemed to say "help me, or I must help myself, and I can do that now only by harming you." Jefferson certainly saw the danger, and his account must be read with that realization in mind.

The President didn't hesitate to twist the knife in response. Burr, Jefferson told him, had "lost the public confidence" not in the newspapers, as Burr believed, but through "the late presidential election; when tho' in poss[essio]n of the office of V[ice] P[resident], there was not a single voice heard for his retaining it." Burr had failed either because of a lack of support or because of his incompetence while vice-president. His political peers had condemned him. Jefferson used the opportunity to read Burr out of any alliance structure, adding in passing that he "feared no injury which any man could do me." Always the pedagogue, the President could not resist the temptation to lecture: "I observed to him ... that he must be sensible the public had withdrawn their confidence from him, & that in a government like ours it was necessary to embrace in its adm[inistratio]n as great a mass of public confid[en]ce as possible, by employing those who had a character with the public, of their own, & not merely a secondary one through the Ex[ecuti]ve." The insertion of the adverb *"merely"*—"merely a secondary" reputation— must have cut deeply.

Jefferson, the most powerful man in America with no end in sight to his power, had dismissed Burr's assumed importance against Burr's own experience of personal popularity in the western territories. Left with only that popularity, Burr decided to use it. His armed recruits never numbered more than one hundred men, though rumor would run it to a legion of 20,000! (a stupendous number for the times). Whatever their number, Burr's men were the focal point for a groundswell that would wrest territories from Spain as the United States declared war on that country. If Burr's own actions precipitated such a war, he knew that many westerners would celebrate his initiative, and the result would be the same. Both outcomes served the former vice-president's purposes. Either way, Burr would be the hero with a new base in the western United States or just beyond it, but everything depended on war with Spain, and there the schemer's miscalculation began and ended with Jefferson.

Tensions between Spain and the United States were high enough for war in 1806, but Jefferson foiled Burr's expectations by hanging fire for many months and avoiding open conflict at the last moment. His decision left Burr dangling—a private citizen, on an unlawful military venture, against a peaceful neighbor. Thus far, however, Burr's plan could not be characterized as a treasonous plot against the United States, and so Jefferson waited. The President moved to have Burr arrested only after receiving a letter ostensibly from Burr to General

James Wilkinson, military governor of the northern portion of the Louisiana Territory. The letter delivered to Jefferson by Wilkinson urged in cipher that Wilkinson join his official forces to Burr's volunteers under Burr's command in an armed expedition.

The articulated version of Burr's intentions in the Wilkinson letter came much closer to the line of treason, and Burr clearly *spoke* like a traitor at times in 1805 and 1806. Still, by definition, the crime of treason required an overt act *against* the United States, and for that purpose it had been useful to keep Burr from all semblance of official representation in the West. From the moment of their interview in March of 1806, Jefferson's purpose had been to lock Burr out of a formal capacity. The nature of Burr's fallen rank would come up again and again in the Richmond courtroom, and to that extent the trial for treason, like *Paradise Lost*, revolved around the theme of lost status.

Burr's grandiose behavior in the West had been possible as a personage in the early republic extending the Revolution. Only such a figure could have hoped to gather a meaningful force around him to take Mexico or build a separate empire. But which way did the claims of personage cut at trial? They cut in every direction, and each claim led to a further magnification of Burr for good or ill. Even insignificant defendants appear larger than life at trial because of the intense focus placed upon their behavior. In Burr's case, the liminality of the defendant in abeyance between guilt and innocence yielded unusual extremes in narrative projection. The one-time Revolutionary hero was either a complete knave in 1807 or the truest champion of the moment, depending on whom you asked. No one could ignore who he had been or what his previous status as a Revolutionary icon meant. He was, as the prosecution liked to claim "a man heretofore distinguished" (I: 402).

Another variable brought the problem home to everyone. Burr was at once the defendant and a defense attorney in his own trial, a vexed circumstance that the trial transcript recognized in a curious detail. Burr the subject at trial took regular title through the lore of his Revolutionary past. He was "Colonel Burr" as the defendant, but when speaking as his own counsel, he was simply "Mr. Burr." The awkwardness of dealing with both identities came up with frequency in the trial, most famously in Burr's sensational attempt to drag Jefferson into court with him by asking the court to issue a subpoena against the President (I: 113–114ff). The prosecution complained loud and long about "Mr. Burr's" legalistic adventurism. The man in the dock but also out of it had "with unexampled dexterity contrived from the very start, almost invariably, to quit his situation as an accused" with "the purpose of escaping the effect of the prosecution carrying on against him." Through some "strange manner," Burr had seized "the high ground of public accuser and assailing others" (II: 28). There was, everyone seemed to agree, a mysterious and dangerous brand of magic in the make-up of the defendant as defense counsel in his own case.

There was no way around the enlarged figure for either side. Prosecuting attorneys had the difficult task of proving that Burr was the principal actor and not merely an accessory in the events with which he was charged. Burr's absence from Blennerhassett island during those events compounded the difficulty and encouraged a magnification in capacities that would obviate the distance between man and event. Burr, after all, had been more than two hundred miles away in geographical terms (II: 209). To cover that distance, the prosecution made him "first mover of the plot," "the *Alpha* and *Omega* of this treasonable scheme," "the very life of this treason," "the abominable instigator," "the daring, aspiring elevated genius who devises the whole plot," "the great actor," and, in a more clever response to the problem of distance, "the sun to the planets which surround him" (II: 39, 66, 95). These efforts joined physical prowess ("a soldier, bold, ardent, restless, and aspiring"), to intellectual cunning beyond the norm ("for no man has a more comprehensive knowledge of human nature"), and on to Burr's overreaching sense of entitlement ("no man's talents are more competent to distinguish and assert his rights, than those of the accused") (II: 39, 33, 28).

The same traits could be found readily enough in the image of the Revolutionary hero, and the prosecution relied on that characterization to argue for Burr's prowess in conducting the conspiracy from afar. There was, however, a better way to convey Burr's absent presence on Blennerhassett's Island, and the prosecution was not at a loss for words. If shining presence at the scene of conflict defined the Revolutionary hero, subterfuge and evasion were the stock and trade of a traitor who would act in secret and, therefore, logically from afar. The prosecution raised this possibility through the negative imagery of cunning that would forever stick to Burr as a personage who had embraced diabolical means. How did one measure the presence of an absence? Once again, the spiritual world could be made to serve for an ordinary understanding. Freed of mere physical presence as the Alpha and Omega, Burr could be everywhere at once. He could, the prosecution argued, "secretly wander, like a demon of darkness, from one end of the continent to the other" (II: 65).

The defense worked even harder to inflate Burr's identity. Their client was a leader of men as his record in the Revolution proved. Luther Martin dared to compare Burr in the West to the greatest warrior of all, George Washington. In both men "plans were most meritorious, predicated on principles of an honourable war." (I: 467). Edmund Randolph raised another dimension, that of the stellar politician. The "censure and obloquy" heaped on Burr could be accounted for without any explanation of crime. False accusations came upon every leader, and Burr was no different than Jefferson or Washington in this regard: "many other great and eminent characters have been in like manner assailed." Randolph knew a noble figure when he saw one, and this one had been sacrificed "at the shrine of faction and persecution" (II: 391, 397).

Everyone was embarrassed to find a founder of the republic and a recent vice-president of the United States in the dock. Caesar Rodney, attorney general of the United States, said so in court. He pointed to the man "whom he once considered as his friend, and treated as such in his own house," lamenting the contradiction between "transcendent talents" and "the most heinous crime" (I: 8). The prosecution openly admitted that the former vice-president lived "perhaps the second in the confidence and affection of the people." It eschewed the intrusion of these facts as prejudicial popularity at trial and, in an awkward reversal, then used them to insist that Burr's "circumstances rather aggravate than extenuate his guilt" (I: 450–451). The defense played its own cards with equally feigned gestures of regret. Why had the President of the United States "let slip the dogs of war, the hell-hounds of persecution to hunt down" an innocent man and virtuous ally? (I: 128). Accusations of prejudice, general alarm, and danger for the country came frequently from both sides (I: 62, 78, 163, 233, 239–40, 409, 411), and, as frequently happens in a high profile trial, insults grew sharp between opposing counsel (I: 232. 263, 331, 386, 585).

Courtroom conflict notwithstanding, three things became clear to both sides and received confirmation from neutral observers. Everyone agreed that neither the larger situation nor the reputation of Aaron Burr could remain where events had left them. More positively but also ominously, they also assumed that the decision reached in Richmond would have national repercussions that no one could fathom, and finally, all eagerly awaited the outcome on these terms. Consensus on this last point entered the communal imagination in a special way and beyond the event itself. For the first time and as something of a precedent, Americans conceded and then welcomed the larger impact of a courtroom event as a legitimate barometer for gauging their collective situation. Whatever happened, early republicans accepted that the trial would shape communal perceptions and perhaps the direction of the country. Here, without anyone quite realizing it, was the birth of a ritual in the republic of laws.

After over a thousand pages of printed transcription of argument, the formal decision proved to be the simplest part of the case. John Marshall followed the lead that John Wickham had handed him on August 20th and 21st and gave the country a sharply restrictive definition of treason, partially reversing himself on an earlier decision in the process. It would be the longest opinion and the most detailed scholarly presentation that Marshall would ever write as a judge, and it took three hours for him to deliver. The gist can be given in a sentence. "In conformity with principle and authority then," Marshall announced, "the prisoner at the bar was neither legally nor actually present at Blennerhassett's Island; and the court is strongly inclined to the opinion that without proving an actual or legal presence by two witnesses, the overt act laid in this indictment cannot be proved" (II: 432).

With the answer predetermined, Marshall then instructed the jury to apply his finding in law to the facts, and the jury, after a brief retirement, returned with its verdict on September 1, 1807. "We of the jury say that Aaron Burr is not proved to be guilty under this indictment by any evidence submitted to us. We therefore find him not guilty" (II: 446). There was a last flurry. Burr and his attorneys struggled to remove the deliberately grudging tones in this statement, but the Chief Justice refused them the simpler verdict of "not guilty," perhaps in recognition of something else that had transpired in court.

Burr may not have committed treason, but his behavior had been unacceptable, and the more it was talked of in court the more unacceptable it became. The demonic image remained in place because it exorcised a national threat. Not for the last time, a high profile trial brought an inchoate problem into sharp focus. The possibility of a hostile nation rising in the western part of the North American continent worried many in 1807. Separate nations might duplicate the patterns of bloodshed then ravaging Europe. As late as 1804, Jefferson as President had faced the prospect of a separate empire with equanimity. "Whether we remain in one confederacy or form into Atlantic and Mississippi confederacies," he wrote to Joseph Priestley in triumph over the Louisiana Purchase, "I believe not very important to the happiness of either part."[26] The specter of Aaron Burr loose in the West changed this complacency into alarm. Jefferson would denounce the decisions in Richmond and predicted dire consequences from them. "They are equivalent to a proclamation of impunity to every traitorous combination which may be formed to destroy the Union," he wrote of the court's actions.[27]

Burr had shown how a bold leader with attractive credentials might delude others into forming a competitor nation. The trial raised frightening prospects for all to see. As one of those who claimed to have been misled by Burr said of him in court, "the distinguished rank he held in society, and the strong marks of confidence which he had received from

[26] Thomas Jefferson to Dr. Joseph Priestley, January 29, 1804, in Merrill Peterson, ed., *Thomas Jefferson: Writings* (New York: The Library of America, 1984), p. 1142.

[27] Thomas Jefferson to General James Wilkinson, September 20, 1807 in Albert Ellery Bergh, ed., *The Writings of Thomas Jefferson*, 20 vols. (Washington, D.C.: The Thomas Jefferson Memorial Association, 1907), XI: 375.

his fellow citizens did not permit me to doubt of his patriotism." In a disquieting moment for the listening nation, the speaker, an armed and ready veteran, asserted that he could find "none within the United States, under whose direction a soldier might with greater security confide his honour than colonel Burr." (I: 474).

The overblown image of Burr had its impact on communal thinking. Some of those involved recognized the process at work. Speaking of Harman Blennerhassett at trial, Edmund Randolph complained "he is to be called small in guilt because that of Mr. Burr is to be magnified" (II: 387). Each side exaggerated the figure of Aaron Burr for argumentative purposes, and everyone was left with its enlarged scope and no clear sense of what to do with its puzzling dimensions. In the end, hyperbole would clarify the pantheon of the founders through counter example. Burr as Satan was a fallen angel subject to parallel distortions in appearance and intention. The negative contrast reinforced what it meant in other founders to have acted correctly. The now misshapened figure of Burr would frighten early republicans into a tighter conception of civic identity. The seduction of the Blennerhassetts had given a timely warning for all to heed.

The concept of evil in a culture identifies the blamable other, imprisons it, and holds it up as a spectacle for all to see. Aaron Burr, like the Miltonic Satan, had conscripted followers into a false cause.[28] As more and more Americans envisaged a providential continental republic, the trial of 1807 dramatized where fault could be assigned if the preordained expansion of the United States went awry. Early republicans worried a great deal about how they should behave as public citizens in a changing nation.[29] Burr provided the object lesson in how *not* to behave—a lesson that brought new urgency and definition to westward expansion. The ultimate accusation leveled at Burr in his trial for treason charged him with dividing East against West in sectional strife (I: 447–48). The demonic image of him at trial, a representation of communal danger, would continue to flourish as the risk of a divided nation grew more likely across the antebellum period. In the most graphic account of him ever written, Aaron Burr would come to stand for the horrors of civil war.

THE MAN WITHOUT A COUNTRY

Most Americans first encounter Aaron Burr through a short story entitled *The Man Without a Country* written by Edward Everett Hale in 1863. Hale's biographer notes that the "combination of immediate

---

[28] Andrew Delbanco, *The Death of Satan: How Americans Have Lost The Sense of Evil* (New York: Farrar, Straus and Giroux, 1995), pp. 44, 234.

[29] Joyce Appleby, *Inheriting the Revolution: The First Generation of Americans* (Cambridge: Harvard University Press, 2000), pp. 1–55.

success and enduring emotional relevance" made the story "unique among American stories written for magazines," and he doesn't exaggerate by much when he places its protagonist, Philip Nolan, alongside Rip Van Winkle as a recognizable character in American literature. At Hale's death in 1909, *The Nation* would call *The Man Without a Country* "probably the most popular short story written in America." Within a year of its first appearance the story sold half a million copies, a stupendous figure for the times. It has been frequently re-published and anthologized ever since.[30]

Hale's parable on patriotism can be summarized in four sentences. Aaron Burr and other indicted "big flies" escape conviction in 1807, but the youthful Philip Nolan, a minor U.S. Army officer seduced by Burr, is found guilty, and in frustration, he shouts out at his trial "D—n the United States! I wish I may never hear of the United States again!" His judges, Revolutionary war veterans all, decide to grant this wish and sentence the defendant to spend the rest of his life at sea on government ships under the singular injunction that he "never hear the name of the United States again." A lifetime of penance in total ignorance of his country gradually teaches Nolan the lesson of patriotism. Still under sentence after more than half a century at sea, he dies in the middle of the Civil War but only after developing the deepest devotion to his country and its meaning.[31]

Hale wrote his story in 1863, the darkest moment of the war for the Union cause, and his stated purpose was to teach Americans, particularly the young, "what the word 'Patriotism' means,—or what one's Country is." When he saw that his story was "copied everywhere," he felt justified: "It met the taste of the patriotic public at the moment." He also revealed what he expected in his reader through his own recorded reaction. Hale engaged in careful research to surround his fiction with accurate historical detail, but he wrote the actual story "almost without a break," pausing only to check with his editor and finishing it in one sitting. He would argue that spontaneity in the act of writing should control the act of reading. "The sentimental reader may be interested to know," Hale revealed, "that my own tears blotted the paper of the original manuscript."[32]

[30] John R. Adams, *Edward Everett Hale* (Boston: Twayne Publishers, 1977), pp. 27, 111. "Edward Everett Hale, 1822–1909," *Nation*, 83 (June 17, 1909), 604–5.

[31] Edward Everett Hale, "The Man Without A Country," *The Atlantic Monthly*, 12 (December, 1863), 665–679. All further references to the story in the text are to this original version and will be noted parenthetically by page number in the text. [Hale made minor adjustments in later versions of the story to increase its narrative claims to authenticity as history.]

[32] Edward Everett Hale, "Editor's Note To Edition of 1897," *The Man Without a Country and Other Stories* (Boston: Little, Brown, and Company, 1899), pp. 4, 11–13.

The image of Aaron Burr in *The Man Without a Country* flows from the one that William Wirt created. Burr is a "gay deceiver," "a disguised conqueror," the clever lawyer who "had defeated I know not how many district attorneys," and finally the mythic figure of fantastic rumor with "an army behind him and an empire before him." When he meets "little Nolan," it is "as the Devil would have it," and to "seduce him." A first encounter leaves the "fascinated" Nolan bored and restless with ordinary life, much like Blennerhassett before him; the second meeting binds Nolan "body and soul" to Burr, and from that moment "though he did not know it, [Nolan] lived as A MAN WITHOUT A COUNTRY" (p. 666). As in Wirt's account, Burr conquers through the magnetism of his rank and personality. He possesses mysterious powers. Notably, Hale's fictional narrator, a retired naval officer, condemns Burr while admitting that he has no idea what Burr intended to accomplish or did in his western jaunts. "What Burr meant to do I know no more than you, dear reader," this narrator admits, in one of many direct addresses that control the emotional timbre of the narrative. "It is none of our business just now" (p. 666).

Why can the narrator say with such confidence that Burr's guilt or innocence is none of our business? Burr, a cameo figure in *The Man Without a Country*, functions as a stage prop in support of a familiar lesson. The prop works so well because Hale duplicates the picture that the trial of Aaron Burr has already imprinted on republican culture. The narrator must confess his ignorance of Burr's intentions because every court that tried Burr came to the conclusion that it could not convict him of anything, and so the phrase used over and over again in the narrator's description of Burr is "I know not" (666). The refrain repeats the jury's finding in Richmond while the pejorative connotations of the trial remain in place. The combination means the narrator need not explain the connotation of "gay deceiver" in league with the devil. Aaron Burr, the mythic figure with "an army behind him and an empire before him," has betrayed the future vision of America—more than enough to condemn him outright. The image of Burr is less clarified than fixed in Hale's story, and it serves a particular purpose. A confederacy of republics defined by the right of revolution in the eighteenth century has been replaced by a modern nation state in which the test of membership is going to be loyalty. Its explicit goal by 1863 is complete continental union.

The Man Without a Country facilitates the shift from early republic to modern nation state for those caught in the crucible of civil war. The story, while simple, unfolds with this ideological shift in mind. Philip Nolan's disastrous cry against the United States occurs because he has kept to himself in his feelings of outrage (not an infrequent impulse in the early republic) instead of accepting a national identity or his assigned place in his military unit, where a greater sense of membership might have saved him from his mistake (666). Poorly educated in citizenry as a boy by "an Englishman" in the then disputed territory of Texas, Nolan chooses affiliation incorrectly, "body and soul," when the need for membership takes hold of him. He is undone by his ignorance and failure to recognize national values: "to him 'United States' was scarcely a reality" (667). That reality hardly existed in its full definition by 1807. The Burr conspiracy is useful to Hale precisely because it hastens a shift in perspective on the national question. Hale would admit the chronological problems in this evolving conception of the nation but only in a much later comment on his story:

> The Civil War has taught its lesson so well that the average American of the year 1896 hardly understands that any such lesson was ever needed. The United States *is* a nation now. And there is not left any one, living in the Northern, Middle, Western, or Pacific States, who ever thinks that the United States *are* a confederacy. The War settled that.[33]

Plurality was a dangerous conception for the fighting Union in 1863. Hale wrote to demonstrate the need for cohesion and to offer dramatic proof that his own definition should never have been in doubt.

The story pulls the reader into its claim of national unity in three ways, only one of which has been firmly identified. The first and frequently noted means of control involves Hale's use of vraisemblance to establish authentication. The fictive narrator of the story, a retired captain in the American navy named Fred Ingham, speaks in sailor's jargon but with high literary tones as well. Although the story appeared anonymously, this speaker secretly identifies the author by bearing parallel initials once removed: Officer *Fred Ingham* follows author *Edward Hale*. The story works through Ingham's "half-confidence" with Nolan. Narrator and character learn from each other; they grow "confidentially intimate" and are "very kind" to each other (675, 677). As symbiotic creations, Ingham, the boy midshipman, first learns from the adult Nolan's example in a series of sea adventures. Now as an old man from the sea, this narrator writes to warn the American youth of 1863 "of what it is to throw away a country" (666, 677).

Ingham is a partially unknowing but thoroughly reliable narrator who must piece his story together from many accounts: "from one and another officer I have learned, in thirty years, what I am telling" (675). Just as sea voyages would have been regularly spaced, so each successive officer in the story informs the reader of another pattern in shipboard

---

[33] Hale, "Editor's Note to Edition of 1897," p. 3. For scholarly confirmation of this point, see Carl Van Doren, "Introduction" *The Man Without a Country*, limited editions club edition (New York: Marchbanks Press, 1936), ix.

custom, which, in turn, connects with the history of the American navy. The clincher in this series comes when a final officer, named Danforth, writes to Ingham of Nolan's repentance and death. The internal narrative of this letter is festooned with the name of the writer's ship and its longitude and latitude as Nolan dies (677–79). Hale succeeds so skillfully with these authentications that some nineteenth-century readers would write to him with confirmations and corrections on the life of his fictional protagonist![34]

Hale's second device in unifying the nation reaches back to the jumble of rumor and fact that defined Aaron Burr in the early republic. Like the first historian Herodotus, the narrator distinguishes between what he saw and what he heard, between conjecture and fact, between the reliability of one source and the fallibility of another, and he is similarly quick to confess an uncertainty. These gestures guard an inner truth where all before has been mystery. Many sentences in the story begin with phrases like "I have reason to think," "I have always supposed," "It may have been,." They allow Ingham to step forward at other times with the firmer claim "But this I do know." These assurances culminate in absolute certainty over Nolan's final and utter repentance (665, 666, 667, 670, 675).

The narrator clarifies Nolan's life beyond "the mysteries that we boys used to invent" and wields this new precision to define the nation. "These are the traditions," he tells us, "which I sort out, as I believe them, from the myths which have been told about this man for forty years. The lies that have been told about him are legion" (677, 671). The biblical reference—Jesus casts "an unclean spirit" in the form of "devils" out of a madman and its "name *is* Legion"—reaches obliquely toward the demonic, but this time in elimination of confusion.[35] The narrator's careful distinctions between his previous ignorance and current knowledge parallel the ideal of education that the good citizen must undergo.

The same mystery and confusion apply to accounts of Aaron Burr. Hale draws the connection by dismissing a rumor that Nolan later met Burr on one of his cruises. There was no fortuitous meeting, no "tremendous blowing-up." Nolan never gets to ask Burr "how he liked to be 'without a country.'" The narrator's dismissal of this fantasy allows

---

[34] Hale, "Author's Note To Edition of 1897," pp. 16–19. Hale's compulsive desire to authenticate his story is shown in his minor corrections of historical fact in later editions. I am indebted for the full extent of Hale's compulsive authentications in later editions to John Seckinger, " 'The Man Without A Country': Its Moment of Production, Moment of Representation, Reception History, and Adaptations" [course essay submitted in the graduate program of the Department of English and Comparative Literature, University of California at Irvine.] See, as well, Adams, *Edward Everett Hale*, p. 30.

[35] The Gospel According to St. Mark, 5: 1–15.

Hale to secure the rest of his imagined account as fact. Ingham first calls the meeting with Burr "a lie" but immediately corrects himself, turning it more deftly into "a myth, *been tomato*," one so well said that people will believe it (675). Hale wants his readers to know that the dangerous self-interests in history welcome exaggeration and distortion. The problem, of course, is that similar fabrications now threaten the nation. The Southern Confederacy has adopted a false narrative of national origins to break up the union, and its leaders, in their ignorance, deserve "all the agony of Nolan's" (676). Accuracy becomes the prime virtue of correct national identity. Hale's sequential storytellers replace exaggerations with negative truths, a device that guards their reliability for the positive truth of defining the nation.

A third authenticating device secures the psychological dimension. The plot line of *The Man Without a Country* is highly sentimental. Reader after nineteenth-century reader followed Hale's example in weeping over his pages. We must look to an emotional progression to explain these reactions. Too harshly punished, Nolan undergoes six formative crises during a half century of captivity aboard ship, and they gradually lead him to *accept* his incredible sentence as just. Each incident teaches a different part of the lesson to be learned and imbibed vicariously by "the sentimental reader."

In the first lesson, Nolan breaks down in public while reading aloud from Sir Walter Scott's "Lay of the Last Minstrel." Scott, an early symbol of literary nationalism, reminds Nolan of his isolation. Dispossessed of "my own, my native land," Nolan has become a "wretch, concentrated all in self" (670). A second incident, in which "a celebrated Southern beauty of those days," "a splendid creature," refuses to talk of home to Nolan during a ball held aboard ship, completes his isolation, this time in social terms. It also gives an image of the true South through a potent symbol of that culture, the Southern belle (670–71). The third crisis, Nolan's heroic participation in a battle at sea during the War of 1812, teaches him and everyone else that courage has never been the issue; it therefore brings no change in punishment (671–72). The fourth incident, which begins at the center of the story and is by far the longest, requires more careful treatment. Set in the 1820's, it entails the capture of a slave ship, the freeing of the slaves on it, Philip Nolan's first public repentance, and the definition of citizenship that Hale wants to impose (673–75).

Brought aboard the slave ship as an interpreter, Nolan experiences "the horrors of the Middle Passage," a "Nastiness beyond account." "Nolan's agony" develops as he translates for the freed slaves who plead "Take us home, take us to our own country, take us to our own house." These events trigger a confession to Midshipman Ingham as they return by boat to their own ship. "Youngster," Nolan begins, "let that show you what it is to be without a family, without a home, and without a country." Family, home, country are all one in Nolan's new conception of country. Ingham hears "forget you have a self, while you do everything for them!" By the end of this soliloquy the conflation is complete: "Remember, boy, that behind all these men ... there is the Country Herself, your Country, and that you belong to Her as you belong to your own mother. Stand by Her, boy, as you would stand by your mother" (675). Becoming "a sort of lay chaplain" of nationalism, Nolan realizes in the fifth lesson that his previous home, Texas, must have joined the Union. In a phrase that will come to mean everything, he learns "Texas is out of the map" (676).

The sixth and concluding vignette reveals that the dying Nolan has built "a little shrine" to country in his stateroom aboard ship (677–79). His place of worship is complete with the stars and stripes, a picture of Washington, and the American eagle. "Here, you see," he explains, "I have a country!" This profession, if nineteenth-century accounts are to be trusted, brought endless tears.[36] "There cannot be a man who loves the old flag as I do, or prays for it as I do, or hopes for it as I do," adds Nolan, and he means it quite literally. In a ritual performed twice a day, he has knelt to thank God "that there has never been any successful Burr" and prayed that God will "behold and bless Thy servant, the President of the United States, and all others in authority."

The truly striking discovery in the cabin is Nolan's empty map. Early republicans lived with the iconographic anxiety of territory beyond their definition and grasp. Nolan in his ignorance in 1863 remains an early republican held in suspension, and he has tried to fill the emptiness with imaginary categories. The first thing he asks for, the gesture that means the most to him, comes when Danforth agrees to "take down his beautiful map and draw [the new states] in as I best could with my pencil." Nolan turns "wild with delight." His shock of recognition reveals in emblematic form the trial of Aaron Burr better than any narrative. The problem is not just a question of boundaries. The uncertainty in unboundedness and the ensuing inability to imagine a satisfying spatial coherence led the first republicans to behave in ways and beyond the ken of later Americans.

The legal implications of Nolan's cabin take shape in an epitaph that he has left for his tombstone. These last words, also the final words of Hale's story, are "He loved his country as no other man has loved her; but no man deserved less at her hands" (679). Trials want a defendant to accept punishment while enduring it. When a defendant actively refuses the legitimacy of a court's finding, uneasiness lingers over the

---

[36] For readers' reactions, see Jean Holloway, *Edward Everett Hale, A Biography* (Austin: University of Texas Press, 1956), pp. 139ff.

process like a bad smell. Nolan has been too severely dealt with, no question, but his love of country overcomes whatever hesitation he may have felt on that score. As he says of country, "never dream a dream but of serving her as she bids you, though the service carry you through a thousand hells" (675).

A defendant overly punished deserves sympathy; one that rises above the fact receives admiration. The nobility of Nolan comes through his growth in punishment, just as the presumed ignobility of Aaron Burr lies in his unwarranted escape. Nolan's one moment of anger in death comes when he learns that Burr was never tried again. The narrator tells us that Nolan "ground his teeth" over this travesty. The moment leaves us with two questions that Edward Everett Hale expected his reader to take for granted (678). Did Aaron Burr deserve punishment? What is more, did he really escape it?

JUDGMENT AT RICHMOND

The continuum of publication around a trial is of particular use in gauging what is called "public justice," the compensatory reaction when a community acts through its own conclusions about what has taken place in a trial. Public justice develops into a serious matter when a discrepancy exists between official findings and communal perception. It becomes acute when a verdict of "not guilty" fails to convince a community that the defendant has deserved the benefit of the doubt just received.[37]

A verdict of "not guilty" may be entirely appropriate. The legal system assumes that defendants do not have to prove their innocence; they need only raise a reasonable doubt to avoid a determination of guilt. But "not guilty" leaves serious questions unanswered in a legal contest that has attracted great attention. If the defendant is not guilty when a crime has been committed, then who *is* guilty? The question invariably becomes an angry one. Communities expect the clarification that a trial can bring them, and grow annoyed when a crime or other form of deviance remains unresolved. When negative decisions are reached, perspectives about a courtroom event still change. Reputations are made and lost. All of these conditions applied in the trial of Aaron Burr, and they can be used to delineate a larger shift in historical understanding.

Of the reputations involved in the Burr trial, only that of John Marshall emerged fully intact. The Chief Justice, acting as a circuit judge, was criticized at the time, but the opinion that he delivered in Richmond on August 31, 1807, represents one of the finest hours in an illustrious career. Marshall conducted the trial under enormous pressure

---

[37] David Richard Kasserman, "Public Justice," *Fall River Outrage: Life, Murder, and Justice in Early Industrial New England* (Philadelphia: University of Pennsylvania Press, 1986), pp. 213–245.

from all sides, and the greatest pressure came from above. Marshall presided under a threat of impeachment from his chief political enemy, The President of the United States. Jefferson oversaw the prosecution of Burr from Washington. He justified every expense, sent scores of letters with suggestions about strategy, and offered blanket pardons to co-conspirators who would cooperate as witnesses. Six months before the trial, Jefferson had declared that Aaron Burr was "the principal actor, whose guilt is placed beyond question."[38] He needed a conviction. Threats of impeachment against Marshall for an unfavorable decision were first raised obliquely in court but then explicitly by both sides, and the threats had substance. Attempts to intimidate Federalists who sat on the bench during Jefferson's administrations included impeachment proceedings as well as legislative plans to curtail the judiciary.[39]

Worried by the government's tactics, the defense added to Marshall's discomfort by hinting that he had slipped in the temple of justice. "The floor of that temple is slippery," observed Edmund Randolph, questioning Marshall's resolve: "He who means to stand firm in that temple must place his hand on the statue of wisdom; the pedestal of which is a lion." Randolph wondered whether Marshall had the courage, symbolized by the lion since antiquity, to act appropriately, and he left none of the negative implications to chance. "In the conflicts of political animosity justice is sometimes forgotten or sacrificed to mistaken zeal and prejudice," Randolph concluded (II: 400). This rather pompous lecture on professional courage included the last words that Marshall would hear before sitting down to write his opinion on whether or not the prosecution would be allowed to proceed with what amounted to a constructive theory of the crime of treason.

Strain is unavoidable in a high profile case. The population of Richmond doubled during the trial, and newspaper coverage exploited every moment of the proceedings with speculation about individual performances and particular scrutiny given to Marshall. The Chief Justice faced serious procedural challenges over the fairness of his proceedings. He had to make crucial distinctions between questions of

---

[38] Lomask, *Aaron Burr*, II: 232–235, 251,199. For the direct source of Jefferson's comment and other public statements regarding Burr's guilt, see *American State Papers: Miscellaneous*, (Washington, D.C.: Government Printing Office, 1835), I: 472; also James Richardson, ed., *A Compilation of Messages and Papers of the Presidents, 1789–1897*, 10 vols. (Washington, D.C.: Government Printing Office, 1896–99), I: 406, 412–17.

[39] Implied and direct threats of impeachment against Marshall appear in Robertson's *Report* at II: 193, 200, 205, 238 and Raymond E. Fitch, ed., *Breaking With Burr: Harman Blennerhassett's Journal, 1807* (Athens, Ohio: Ohio University Press, 1988), p. 61. See, as well, Lomask, *Aaron Burr*, II: 276–77 and Samuel H. Smith and Thomas Lloyd, eds., *The Trial of Samuel Chase, an Associate Justice of the Supreme Court of the United States, Impeached b the House of Representatives, for High Crimes and Misdemeanors, before the Senate of the United States*, 2 vols. (Washington, D.C.: Samuel H. Smith, 1805), I: 8ff.

fact, which should be given to the jury for decision, and questions of law, which the court would decide. How, in the first place, could one come up with an impartial jury in Richmond, where most potential members of the *voir dire* pool admitted some prejudice against Burr through newspaper commentary and their acceptance of the President's comments against Burr? Jefferson, after all, was a fellow Virginian complaining about a New Yorker. When the jurors finally took their assigned places on August 17th, it was only after two weeks of wrangling and an analysis by Marshall of the reasonable limits on jury impartiality (I: 414–20). Everyone understood that the twelve men selected would lean against the defendant (I: 427–430).

The legal contest depended absolutely on the choices that Marshall would make. The prosecution wanted as many issues as possible before the favorably inclined jury, while the defense asked for judicial decisions out of jurors' hands. What did it mean to "levy war"? Was this a question of fact for the jury or of law for the bench? Was Aaron Burr's constructive presence at Blennerhassett's Island, a question of fact or of law? Was Burr an accessory or a principal in the events that took place on the island, and was this question, too, one of fact or of law? Marshall found himself in the uncomfortable position of having to deal with his own loose words about treason from just a year before. In *Ex Parte Bollman*, a case that touched on others in the Burr conspiracy, he had declared that "if war be actually levied, that is, if a body of men be actually assembled for the purpose of effecting by force a treasonable purpose, all those who perform any part, however minute, or however remote from the scene of action, and who are actually leagued in the general conspiracy, are to be considered traitors."[40] Did this seemingly broad construction of treason decide the issues of principal versus accessory and the degree of activity for war to be levied? The legal questions were far more complicated than the public discourse on Burr's behavior wanted to allow.

In rendering his opinion, the Chief Justice knew better than to follow his customary reliance on broad principles. He took up the same tangle of arcane cases and statutes in English and American law that counsel had argued before him, citing more authorities than in any other opinion that he would ever write.[41] Then, after claiming "the most temperate and the most deliberate consideration," he came down hard on the side of a strict construction of treason, one that held the Government to the literal meaning of Article three, section three, of the

---

[40] *Ex Parte Bollman*, 4 Cranch 75, 115, 125–27 (1807).

[41] G. Edward White, *The American Judicial Tradition: Profiles of Leading American Judges* (New York: Oxford University Press, 1976), pp. 11–15, and Albert J. Beveridge, *The Life of John Marshall*, 3 vols. (Boston: Houghton Mifflin Co., 1919), III: 504.

Constitution (II: 401, 443). Marshall noted "there must be a war or the crime of levying it cannot exist," and he found that there had *been* no war by the evidence shown (II: 402). An "assemblage of force" to which the defendant could be tied directly by two witnesses were indispensable conditions in an assessment of guilt (II: 421–22).

Marshall also found that English doctrines of constructive treason were "inapplicable to the United States," which meant that the overt act of treason could not be stretched to include one "who counsels and advises it," as Burr seemed to have done (II: 405, 439). Not content with the theory of the matter, Marshall came close to questions of fact in a final crushing blow against the prosecution's case: "in conformity with principle and authority, then, the prisoner at the bar was neither legally nor actually present at Blannerhassett's island" (II: 432). It seemed hardly necessary to add more, but Marshall did: "the court is strongly inclined to the opinion that without proving an actual or legal presence by two witnesses, the overt act laid in this indictment cannot be proved" (II: 432).

Leaving the jury with nothing to decide, Marshall turned next to his tormentors at the Bar. The final words of his opinion established a touchstone of judicial independence against the intrusions of executive and legislative authority. Earlier, when defense counsel "plainly insinuated the possibility of danger to the court" through threats of an impeachment proceeding against him, Marshall blandly refused to find "any personal allusion" in the language cited (II: 238–39). Now, with the case decided, he demonstrated just how solid his footing had been on the floor of justice that counsel had so glibly derided as too "slippery" for him. His opinion had been carefully prosaic up to this point, even matter-of-fact, in careful contrast to the "degree of eloquence" that he already had thanked counsel for exhibiting (II: 401). At the very end, though, he lifted his own language, choosing cannily but quietly from the same registers of religiosity that the lawyers before him had wielded with such bombast. "That this court dares not usurp power is most true," Marshall began. "That this court dares not shrink from its duty is not less true" (II: 444).

Marshall gently chided the lawyers in front of him. His stance had never deviated "to the one side or the other from the line prescribed by duty and by law." He reminded them that "on each side" they had tried to "press their arguments too far"; they had been "impatient at any deliberation in the court" and had come to "suspect or fear the operation of motives." These tendencies were "perhaps a frailty incident to human nature," but a judge had to operate above such fears while also controlling them. These references to frailty took a compelling form. Marshall had been hurt by the veiled accusations bandied about him, and he said so, not hesitating to use the language of Christ to present his situation. He had not enjoyed finding himself "in a disagreeable situation." What person would? "No man is desirous of becoming the peculiar subject of calumny," he reminded those who had abused him, including the President of the United States. "No man, might he let the bitter cup pass from him without self reproach, would drain it to the bottom." Marshall had persevered after being forced to drink deeply. A conception of duty beyond the view of those around him had sustained him and guided his conduct throughout (II: 444–45).

The Chief Justice saw what an expansive definition of treason could mean. "As this is the most atrocious offence which can be committed against the political body," he observed when committing Burr for trial, "so it is the charge which is most capable of being employed as the instrument of those malignant and vindictive passions which may rage in the bosoms of contending parties struggling for power." Sensibly, the American people had "refused to trust the national legislature with the definition," fixing it instead in the body of the Constitution (I: 13–14). Only a restricted definition could possibly hold unwarranted passions in check. *United States v. Burr* would secure that result but at a price. Soon there would be an ugly stepchild to circumvent the difficulties in a charge of treason: the crime of conspiracy. Marshall would even show the way as, once again, Aaron Burr served as a catalyst in thought.

The arch conspirator in the Burr conspiracy was clearly identified in Marshall's opinion. The Chief Justice made the connection repeatedly but with a vital distinction in mind. "However flagitious may be the crime of conspiracy to subvert by force the government of our country," he reasoned, "such conspiracy is not treason" (II: 416). The plotter of a crime could be a "blacker criminal" than the physical actor, but "moral guilt" could not convict Burr of treason by reason or authority (II: 440–41). If Burr had been up to something, it was nonetheless true that "the law does not expect a man to be prepared to defend every act of his life" (II: 424). Could one who procured a treason be found guilty under the Constitution? Possibly, but the Supreme Court had not yet said so; Marshall distinguished all earlier cases on the subject, including *Ex Parte Bollman* (II: 439). Had Burr been an accessory to treason? Marshall handled the question tongue in cheek:

> pleading to an indictment, in which a man is charged as having committed an act, cannot be construed to waive a right which he would have possessed had he been charged as having advised the act. No person indicted as a principal can be expected to say I am not a principal. I am an accessory. I did not commit, I only advised the act (II: 442).

No one could miss the schemer in these descriptions of Burr. Marshall seemed to say that the Government had bungled its case more than Burr had won it. Timing and precise wording were everything in his view of the matter. It was only "the present indictment" that had failed (II: 443). Could there be others? Marshall implied that was possible (II: 444) If Jefferson had been listening carefully, he might have realized that Marshall was fulfilling the basic goal of the prosecution. Everything in the Chief Justice's demeanor toward the man he frequently called "the prisoner" implied unacceptable behavior at the source. The implication though muted would carry the day. It was not necessary to convict and execute Aaron Burr to punish him. Better far to avoid even the hint of martyrdom. The personage who still carried a political threat would suffer more from his release.

PUBLIC JUSTICE

The subsequent life of Aaron Burr would prove the point. His career in American politics was over the moment he left the courtroom, and Marshall's handling of the trial had much to do with that result. The restraint shown in letting a seeming rascal go enhanced the dignity of the legal process and left Burr with none. No longer a founder who had shared in the creation of the republic, Burr was now and forever the conniver who tried to tear it down: "the destroyer comes" (II: 97). He was also what no success story in America could ever tolerate: a bungler. Nothing that Burr had attempted had worked. Long before the creation of Philip Nolan, Burr was the man without a country. For the four years following his trial he wandered in exile through Europe, where his moods would swing between grandiose plans and realization of what he had become. As his journal from those years indicates, he led an aimless life organized around constant travel, frustrated ambitions, shallow acquaintances, compulsive womanizing, and grinding poverty. He described it once as "too long a story to tell, and worth nothing when told."[42]

Always resilient, he struggled against a fate that he could not change. Burr went to Europe with major ambitions, and, as always, he made friends easily. In Europe, those friends would include Jeremy Bentham, Charles Lamb, William Godwin, and Johann Wolfgang von Goethe, but the former vice-president was shunned everywhere by Americans abroad, and every attempt to re-establish himself as a personage led to further humiliation. Burr's dreams bore no relation to his new reality. "I sit down to recollect the trifling incidents of the last six days," he wrote from Stockholm in 1809. "Trifling indeed. But if the operations of my head and heart could be delineated, each day would fill a volume." Final realization would come in Paris in 1810, where he

---

[42] Matthew L. Davis, ed., *The Private Journal of Aaron Burr, During His Residence Of Four Years In Europe; with Selections From His Correspondence*, 2 vols. (New York: Harper and Brothers, 1838), I: 382.

grandly "hoped to do the emperor [Napoleon] and myself so much good." Once there, however, and spurned when not harassed by officialdom, he found "no prospect but that of starving in Paris."[43]

Social slights of all kinds came thick and fast. Dining at the Baron d'Albey's in Paris, Burr discovered that he "was of so small account that neither chair nor plate was provided" and "he stood a minute after all were seated." At another noble house, he was denied admission altogether, "not being on the list of receivables." With the Duke of Rovigo he was one of forty-seven beseechers in a semi-circle; the Duke kept him waiting for hours before a thirty second interview that accomplished nothing. Poverty would eventually drive Burr completely "out of society." Toward the end of his European sojourn, he found himself too poor to keep a fire in the dead of winter or to reclaim his boots from repair. Hunger was now a reality instead of a metaphor, and it led to new levels and kinds of degradation. "Better than starving," he turned translator. "[T]he book in question," he discovered on one occasion, "contains a quantity of abuse and libels on A. Burr."[44]

The journal became the record of a man fighting depression. Burr complained of "great torpor." He slept too much and remembered no dreams from his prolonged slumbers. "Home at six," ran an early entry, "a little stupid or so." "I had to go sauntering about the streets of a strange place, alone and unarmed, on Christmas Eve," ran another from Birmingham. "It is no easy matter to determine how to dispose of myself," he wrote from Stockholm in 1809. "Why stay here? The summary is that I am resolved to go without knowing exactly why or where." A sojourner in Europe, Burr had no word from home for years at a time. By his own admission, he grew rude and irritable.[45] When he did hear from his beloved daughter, Theodosia, to whom he addressed his journal, it could not have helped that she expected some great thing of him. "Tell me," she wrote in October of 1808, "that you are engaged in some pursuit worthy of you." Reading the newspapers from America he looked for "some consequence to me, if, indeed, anything be of any consequence." This was punishment indeed for a fastidious socialite driven by ambition and the quest for fame.[46]

Rarely reflective, Burr knew what had happened to him. His experience in Europe became a pointless and prolonged exercise in misery. Early on he described the consequences. His life had become a "sort of non-existence." The founder's fall had been from a great height, and like

---

[43] *Private Journal*, I: 228. 411; II: 53.

[44] *Private Journal*, I: 435, 428, 413, 441; II: 32–33, 82, 108.

[45] *Private Journal*, I: 431, 124, 412, 434, 127, 228, 333, 300; II: 27, 72, 80, 95.

[46] *Private Journal*, I: 72–73,114; II: 10.

his accusers, he described it in religious though mocking terms. "I have often heard that great sinners have relieved their consciences in full confession," he wrote late in 1808. "Let us try." In Paris, the military man toured the Hotel des Invalides, the hospital and memorial to France's own military heroes. As Colonel Burr he naturally went to pay his respects to the fallen Duke of Montebello, a hero mortally wounded in battle the year before as one of Napoleon's valiant field marshals. Honored in every way, the Duke, in Burr's description, "lies in state" amongst "lamps innumerable hung with black." The American outcast admitted that he went for personal reasons: "what I was most desirous of seeing was the process of getting a soul out of purgatory."[47] Even as a joke, the contrast to his own situation could not have been without recognition and pain.

Another sacred building in Paris brought full-fledged despair. Burr visited the Panthéon early in 1811. He was impoverished and in hiding from his creditors as well as the French authorities at the time. All of his vaunted projects lay in ruins, and he was without either the means or the official papers to leave France. The account from his journal is worth quoting in full:

> thinking of other things as I walked; got to the Panthéon without thinking whither I was going. I then stood some minutes to discover who I was. In what country I was. What business I had there. For what I came abroad. And where I intended to go.[48]

The symbol of French national glory, the Panthéon stood for everything that Burr had tried to achieve and failed to accomplish. It, too, contained the honored dead, and the motto above its portico read "Aux Grands Hommes La Patrie Reconnaissante." The impoverished translator would have had no trouble rendering the English: "To Great Men the Grateful Country."[49] Burr was no longer great and his country was certainly no longer grateful. No similar arrangement awaited him. The scene so represented lost status and absent prospects that he wondered who he was and where he could possibly go from there. Burr was an eighteenth-century man. His life as an ostracized exile lacked all meaning before the monument of civic coherence before him. Here, if anywhere, was the man's recognition and acceptance that he no longer belonged in the story of American formations and receptions. None of Aaron Burr's enemies could possibly have wished for more.

---

[47] *Private Journal*, I: 94, 227; II: 10.

[48] *Private Journal*, II: 128.

[49] For the symbolism and cultural importance of the Panthéon, see Priscilla Parkhurst Ferguson, *Literary France: The Making of a Culture* (Berkeley: University of California Press, 1987), pp. 1–7.

Lingering over Burr's descent serves a purpose. The grip of a high profile trial can lead to permanent change when the circumstances are right, and there are lessons to learn from the phenomenon. This trial stripped a prominent figure and successful defendant of all identity—even in his own mind. Burr would return to America in the middle of 1812 to live out a long private life of legal practice, but nothing changed in the way that his country regarded him. It made no difference when Texas broke from Mexico in 1836 and declared itself a separate empire as the conspirator had wished many years before. *"There!,"* Burr is supposed to have claimed, "you see? I was right! I was only thirty years too soon! What was treason in me thirty years ago, is patriotism now!!"[50] Not so. The charge of treason held mud that stuck. National understanding would never entertain another conception. Burr's trial for treason had formed a permanent niche in the conception of national formations. He remained too valuable an example of forbidden behavior for the still expanding United States to revise its opinions of the man who lived on and on but never beyond his fixed moment in history.

One cannot lose caste; only status. Permanently enlarged but ignored, Burr sought a return to respectability in one final act that reached back in principle to the Panthéon and the Hotel des Invalides. He asked, as a matter of right, to be buried with honor in the President's Plot of the college burial ground at Princeton beside the graves of his forebears, President Jonathan Edwards and President Aaron Burr, Sr. Would Princeton deny him that right? In a final twist of negative mythology, the College granted the wish while thwarting the desire. On September 16, 1836, Aaron Burr received burial with full ceremony in the appropriate place, but the grave itself went unmarked for decades. Today, a simple marker identifies the deceased as "colonel in the army of the Revolution" and "vice-president of the United States," Burr's primary patriotic identifications.[51]

The graveyard is worth the trip. To see Burr's marker you must search for it. Princeton has shrouded the tombstone on three sides with a bush that separates it from the other graves in the President's Plot. The separation is complete. The bush around the stone obscures Burr's grave from every position except straight on. To take up that position, to see the inscription, you must stand outside of the President's Plot and look within. No other headstone in the plot is surrounded in this manner. Aaron Burr, not guilty of treason, is still damned for it into the twenty-first century.

---

[50] Quoted in James Parton, *The Life and Times of Aaron Burr* (New York: Mason Brothers, 1858), p. 670.

[51] Lomask, *Aaron Burr*, II: 405–6.

*

3

Paul Bergman[1]
Marianne Wesson[2]

"I Am Going With a Man by the Name of Hillmon"

1. Statement of the Case

In March of 1879, a man died of a bullet wound in the head at a campsite near Crooked Creek, in a remote area of southwest Kansas. The decedent may have been John W. Hillmon, and he may have been shot accidentally by his traveling companion John Brown. If it was Hillmon's body, three life insurance companies should have honored Hillmon's widow Sallie's claims for a total of $25,000, the combined sum for which Hillmon had only very recently insured his life.[3] After some investigation, the life insurance companies decided that the man who was shot was Frederick Walters, whose family had reported him missing around the time of the shooting. Believing that Hillmon had conspired with others to fraudulently pass Walters' body off as Hillmon's in order to collect the policies' proceeds, the insurance companies denied Sallie's claims.

Sallie sued for the proceeds in 1880, and her three lawsuits (later consolidated for trial) against the Mutual Life Insurance Company of New York, the New York Life Insurance Company and the Connecticut Mutual Life Insurance Company set off one of the most protracted civil cases in American courtroom history. The case was tried six times, to six

---

[1] Professor of Law Emeritus, UCLA School of Law.

[2] Professor of Law, Wolf–Nichol Fellow and President's Teaching Scholar, University of Colorado.

[3] Averaging the results of using two common measures for estimating how much $25,000 1879 dollars would be worth in 2005, the figure is around $480,000. See http://www.eh.net/hmit.

different judges and juries, and it produced two U.S. Supreme Court decisions, separated by over a decade. The pattern of outcomes was remarkably consistent, and was reminiscent of the fates of the six wives of Henry the Eighth ("Divorced, Beheaded, Died, Divorced, Beheaded, Survived."). In Sallie Hillmon's case, the less poetic fates were Hung Jury, Hung Jury, Judgment for Sallie Reversed, Hung Jury, Hung Jury, Judgment for Sallie Reversed.

The first reversal resulted from the Supreme Court's opinion in *Mutual Life Insurance Co. of New York v. Hillmon,* 145 U.S. 285 (1892). The Court ruled that the trial judge in Trial No. 3 committed reversible error by allowing the insurance companies only a total of three peremptory challenges to potential jurors, rather than three challenges each. Much more significantly for the development of the law of Evidence, the Court also ruled that the judge erred by excluding evidence of letters written by Frederick Walters to his fiancée and various relatives. The letters to the relatives were never produced, but the letter to Walters' fiancée Alvina Kasten was. This letter stated that Walters intended to travel with "a man by the name of Hillmon" who would pay him "more wages than I could make at anything else." This opinion is the genesis of the "state of mind" exception to the hearsay rule, now codified as Federal Rule of Evidence 803(3).

The second reversal resulted from the Supreme Court's opinion in *Conn. Mutual Life Ins. Co. v. Hillmon,* 188 U.S. 208 (1903). The Court's second opinion in the case created no novel legal doctrine, but it did create the possibility of a 7th trial. However, the case ended with a whimper rather than a bang, as Connecticut Mutual, the one insurance company that had remained in the case to the bitter end, agreed to pay the face amounts of the policies plus interest. As a result, no judicial resolution as to whether the dead person by the side of Crooked Creek was John Hillmon or Frederick Walters was reached. Moreover, neither Hillmon nor Walters was officially seen or heard from after 1879.[4]

This essay focuses on Trial No. 6, which took place in 1899. Trial No. 6 lasted for about five weeks, and over 100 witnesses testified. The testimony of many witnesses made its way into the record via the reading of a deposition or a transcript of their testimony from an earlier trial. Sixteen witnesses who had testified in earlier trials had died by the time of the 6th trial, and others had left the state or simply could not be found. Surprisingly, some of the witnesses in Trial No. 6 had never

---

[4] Popular media anointed various 20th century U.S. trials as the Trial of the Century. Included were the murder prosecutions of O.J. Simpson (1995) and Leopold and Loeb (1924), and the prosecution of John Scopes for teaching evolution (1925). Perhaps *Hillmon* deserves a place as the Trials of Two Centuries, since the case spanned the years 1880 to 1903.

testified previously. Judge William Hook presided over the trial; he was a law student when Trial No. 1 took place.

The lawyers for both sides poured a tremendous amount of time, energy and creative advocacy into a case that failed to produce a final judicial resolution. We therefore think it quite likely that the lawyers' "states of mind" have been so restless ever since that wherever they ended up, their spirits have continued to argue their clients' positions. In an effort to allow their souls to rest in peace once and for all, we have channeled back John Atwood and James Green, two of the lead lawyers for Sallie Hillmon and the Connecticut Mutual Life Insurance Company respectively. We have given Atwood and Green a chance to present their arguments to 21st century readers, who form truly a Court of Last Resort. In return, Atwood and Green have promised to share and reflect on their trial strategies. Dedicated to the legal profession and the jury system, they hope that their experiences will benefit new generations of lawyers.*

2. Initial Strategies

May It Please the Court, my name is John Atwood and I represent Sallie Hillmon. Sallie was a plucky woman who stood up to the wealth and power of three Wall Street insurance companies for a quarter of a century before they finally gave up their implausible claims that the man who died at Crooked Creek was not her husband but another, and paid her claims in full, with interest. Mr. Green is going to tell you that the money all went to her lawyers, and that is not far from the truth, but at whose feet may that misfortune be laid? A young widow, a waitress—how was she to find the funds to finance the extensive investigation, arduous preparation, six trials, and three appeals (one to a then newly-created intermediate court of appeals) occasioned by the recalcitrance of her opponents, if not by pledging her expectancy?

---

* The arguments the lawyers will present here are all based on documents and other historical evidence, although of course in many instances the witnesses contradicted one another. The authors have taken the liberty of attributing various thoughts and strategies to the lawyers; no documentation of these mental events exists. The imagined reminiscences are, however, entirely compatible with the historical record known to the authors. The authors relied on contemporaneous articles about the trial (which often included excerpts of testimony and arguments) in the following newspapers: the TOPEKA DAILY CAPITAL, the LAWRENCE DAILY TRIBUNE, the LEAVENWORTH EVENING STANDARD, and the LEAVENWORTH TIMES. These newspapers can be accessed in archives maintained at the Kansas State Historical Society in Topeka. We also based the essay on the record on appeal pertaining to the 1903 U.S. Supreme Court opinion, including the arguments of counsel and excerpts of trial testimony. In addition, we consulted various documents available in the Hillmon case file at the National Archives and Records Administration, Central Plains Region, Kansas City, Missouri.

I admit that when first approached about representing Sallie Hillmon, my co-counsel and I had our doubts. First, there was the knowledge that we would be taking on ruthless and well-financed opponents. We were all aware of the extent to which the insurance companies had managed the inquest in Lawrence. There had been quite an adequate inquest in Medicine Lodge, near the campsite where the body was found. John Brown described the accident that had resulted in the death of his friend John Hillmon. He explained how a rifle had accidentally fired as he unloaded it off a wagon, striking his friend Hillmon in the head. Quite properly, the coroner's jury brought back a verdict of death by misadventure.

The insurance companies sent their agents to insist that the body be brought back to Lawrence, where they arranged for a second inquest. We suspected that the companies paid off Assistant County Attorney George Barker, as well as the coroner himself and every one of the jurors, although it was not until the fifth trial that we were able to get one of their agents to admit to this underhanded conduct. (Barker and his boss, County Attorney James W. Green, were indignant when it was suggested at the time of the inquest that they were working for the insurance companies, but they lost no time in appearing as counsel of record for the defendants when our suits were first filed, and you will have noticed that they remained in that status throughout—even until now!) Nor did we doubt that the verdict arrived at by the Lawrence coroner's jury—that the corpse was a "person unknown" killed feloniously by "J.H. Brown"—was composed by the companies' officers in order to protect their coffers and facilitate the intimidation of Mr. Brown by another attorney of unstable loyalties, Mr. W.H. Buchan.

Buchan employed the threat of arrest and prosecution appurtenant to this verdict, together with the mendacious claim that he had been hired by Brown's aged father to represent his son, to procure a false affidavit. Brown swore in this coerced statement that the dead man was not Hillmon, but a fellow traveler named "Joe Berkley" or "Joe Burgis" whom Hillmon had recruited to their party for the purpose of killing him at a remote spot and leaving his body behind to be passed off as Hillmon's. We knew all of this when we filed Mrs. Hillmon's lawsuit—or suits, for at first there were three, one against each insurance company. (I will have more to say about this presently.)

Perhaps our reluctance had another cause as well, for I would not want you to think we are timid advocates, easily discouraged by powerful opposition. There was this: we could not be altogether certain that Mrs. Hillmon's claims were just. Mrs. Hillmon, John Hillmon's friend Levi Baldwin and the Hillmons' landlord Arthur Judson all swore that the dead body brought to Lawrence for the inquest belonged to John Hillmon. But many citizens of Lawrence, including those with no obvious motive to lie, viewed the body (for it was displayed for this purpose at the Bailey and Smith's undertaking establishment) and said that it was not he. Disputes arose about teeth, height, and scars. Those who claimed that John Hillmon was shorter in life than the corpse, which was near six feet, were numerous, as were those who claimed that Hillmon had a mouth marred by at least one black or missing tooth. As the corpse had a nearly perfect smile, this could not be overlooked. Moreover, Sallie's, Baldwin's, and Judson's claims that Hillmon's teeth were unremarkable lacked the specificity of those who claimed to remember the blackened or absent tooth.

Sallie's cause had other troubling aspects. It cannot be denied that it was unusual, to say the least, for a cowhand like John Hillmon to have insured his life for such a large amount, and such a short time before his death. And Levi Baldwin (who was Sallie's cousin) had undoubtedly furnished some of the money that Hillmon employed to pay the first premium, and we learned that the companies had found a witness who would say that Levi Baldwin had talked of a scheme to make money by taking out a sum of life insurance and then faking one's death. Too, John Brown's description of the accident at Crooked Creek—the trigger of the rifle catching on a blanket as he unloaded it from the wagon—was not altogether convincing (perhaps because he was an unlettered fellow and not used to having to give an account of himself).

Yet Mrs. Hillmon was determined and stuck to her identification of her husband, never once being caught in a contradiction. Hounded by Buchan, John Brown defected to sign the wretched affidavit in September of 1879, but he could not live with this lie for very many days before he repudiated it in favor of his original story. Brown even went so far as to throw the paper into a stove in Buchan's office, although that perfidious lawyer rescued it in order that it might be used to impeach Mr. Brown at the trials, thereby showing where Buchan's true loyalties lay. Buchan then displayed Brown's affidavit to Mrs. Hillmon, who agreed to read it in Buchan's office unaccompanied by a legal representative. No doubt Buchan believed that he could in this way frighten the young widow into renouncing her claims. When shown the affidavit, however, Sallie said calmly to Mr. Brown: "Do you think I would not recognize the body of my own husband?" Many years later, Buchan admitted that his only pay in the Hillmon matter came from the insurance companies, but we were sure of this all along.

These events convinced me that the companies would do their best to persuade witnesses to falsify matters, as they perhaps already had in the matter of Levi Baldwin's alleged loose talk about insurance fraud. Such chicanery by the defendants made us doubt their bona fides, just as Mrs. Hillmon's steadfastness won us to her cause. We agreed to take on her case, though perhaps we were over-confident that a jury would resolve these disputes in her favor. We had not, at that time, ever heard of Frederick Adolph Walters, nor of his fiancée Alvina Kasten and the letter he wrote to her.

With that same discerning hindsight I can now see that the defendants were, as far back as the inquest of April 1879, casting about for an identity, other than Hillmon's of course, to attach to the dead man. In this effort they had no difficulty enlisting various newspapers (no doubt aided by the efforts of Mr. Charles Gleed, a young journalist who had just finished a year of law instruction under—who else?—Mr. Green). Thus it was suggested in the papers at various points during the inquest that the body belonged to the truant brother of a Mrs. Lowell of Lawrence, a missing "young man of Indiana," and a man named Frank Nichols, known as "Arkansaw." All of these rumors were false, of course. When the body was dug up for her inspection, Mrs. Lowell said it was no one she knew; the Indiana suggestion was dropped; and "Arkansaw" turned up alive and kicking not long after the Lawrence inquest concluded. But these machinations should perhaps have made us more wary about what we would be hearing after receiving, not long after we filed the Hillmon lawsuits, a notice to attend the deposition of a Miss Alvina Kasten. But I digress.

It may arouse the curiosity of some that we filed the cases in federal court, rather than in the local courts, where it might have been anticipated that a local citizen would fare better in a suit against large out-of-state entities. We considered this matter at length, but decided in the end to save ourselves some time by filing in federal court. We never doubted for a moment that the companies would remove the suits thence, as the rules permitted, had we begun in state court. Much later the state Insurance Commissioner tried to limit out-of-state insurance companies' resort to the federal courts by requiring them to foreswear that privilege as a condition of doing business in the state, but these efforts were unsuccessful, and in any event came too late to affect our case. In 1897, however, Commissioner McNall courageously tried to revoke the business license of Mr. Green's client for the bad faith implicit in its long-time refusal to pay Mrs. Hillmon's just claims, an effort that contributed to the settlement of Mrs. Hillmon's suit against the New York Life Insurance Company on the eve of Trial No. 6. So as you may appreciate, over the years we were working in the interest of our client on several fronts, not only in the main litigation. And as always, we believed we were serving not only Mrs. Hillmon, but all citizens of Kansas who were vulnerable to sharp dealing and unethical practices by large, out-of-state insurance companies (and other companies too!).

Another matter about which I am sometimes asked is why we filed three separate lawsuits, rather than one against all three defendants.

The answer is that we thought perhaps one suit might settle, and provide funds to finance the prosecution of the others. Judge Foster, however, consolidated the cases before Trial No. 1, in the interest of judicial efficiency. In this decision we acquiesced, for by that time the companies' intransigence was evident. But perhaps we would not have done so had we realized the trouble it would later cause. (Hindsight is always sharp-eyed, is it not?) For when the consolidated cases came to trial for the third time, in 1888 before Judge Shiras, the question of peremptory challenges became a matter of dispute. The defendants, although their interests and positions were quite identical, maintained that they should each have the same number of challenges that each would have been entitled to in a separate trial. We argued successfully to Judge Shiras that they ought to be required to exercise their strikes jointly, and so they were able to remove only three veniremen, the same number we were permitted to exclude. In retrospect, perhaps we ought not to have argued this point so strenuously. As you may recall (although few do), it was this ruling that became the main ground of appeal when the companies lost Trial No. 3. The Supreme Court then decided for the companies, ruling that they should have been afforded three strikes apiece, instead of three altogether.

Thus the Court's remarkable invention of the "state of mind" exception to the hearsay rule might appear to have been merely an afterthought, even dictum, despite the significance this decision held for the law of evidence. To us, however, it appeared that the Court appreciated that no matter how many peremptory challenges they enjoyed, the companies would never prevail on retrial unless they were permitted to employ the Alvina Kasten letter as evidence. I think the Court would have reversed Mrs. Hillmon's initial victory on the ground of the letter's exclusion in any event—and on some other ground if Judge Shiras had not excluded the letter. For I have come to believe that the Supreme Court saw the case as one of fraud, and was determined that the Hillmons should not walk away with ill-gotten gains. For this perception—in which the Court is not alone, for almost all later students of the case have shared it—we have that d——d letter to thank.

* * *

May It Please the Court, my name is James Green and I had the honor of defending the rights of Connecticut Mutual, a company that did a lot of good for a lot of people at a time when early death was more common than I suspect it is today. Nevertheless, insurance companies and big businesses in general were whipping boys for Populist politicians and their newspaper allies late in the 19th century. A lot of hard-working farmers were suffering through hard times in the 1870's and 80's. The Populists figured that the easiest way to get elected was to blame the problems on banks, railroads and insurance companies, and

Kansas was a hotbed of Populism. At one point Kansas Superintendent of Insurance McCall denied my client a license to do business in the state because it had the audacity to defend itself in court against Sallie Hillmon's claim. So egregious was McCall's conduct that he was indicted for interfering with the rights of litigants and enjoined from interfering with the company's right to do business in Kansas. And all of this even though most of my client's policy holders were individuals and their families, no doubt many of them members of the Populist Party. From my short time back on earth it seems that many people continue to try to advance their own interests by demonizing successful corporations. I suspect that just as we defense counsel did, many lawyers today have to devise strategies for preventing the victimization of unpopular clients.

I know that many of you on the jury are law students, so you might be interested to know that I started the law school at Kansas University back in 1878. My first class had 13 students, each of whom paid me $25.00 for the privilege of attending. For awhile I served as the law school's Dean and only Professor, and I'm proud to say that my sister-in-law Kate Stephens was one of the law school's first female professors. Law school professors didn't earn much in those days, so I continued to practice law. *Hillmon* was the most memorable and certainly the most drawn-out case I was ever involved in.

The plaintiff's lawyers did everything they could to make sure that the jury decided the case based on emotion and prejudice rather than the evidence and the law. For example, during his portion of the plaintiff's closing argument in Trial No. 6, Hutchings called the defense evidence "a putrid heap of garbage." He stressed repeatedly that the case involved one poor lone widow against powerful, heartless and unfeeling companies. This was not only unfairly prejudicial but grossly inaccurate. Any money that was awarded to Sallie Hillmon was going to go right to her lawyers, so they were really fighting for their own pocketbooks.

Even more prejudicial were the closing argument remarks of Mr. Atwood. He referred to me and my colleagues as crawling, slimy serpents and jackals who have "no greater work than to gnaw with his senile, toothless jaw at the reputation of a woman." Judges would never allow such vituperative comments today, but over-the-top oratory was more common in my day. Proper or not, Sallie's lawyers obviously believed that the only way they could win was to appeal to prejudice and bigotry rather than reason and fairness.

Of course, we knew going in that no matter how much the jurors assured us during *voir dire* that they would be fair to both sides, Sallie had the psychological edge. Therefore, we developed a strategy that was directed both at the jury and at the appellate courts. Before the jury, we offered evidence from medical experts, neutral witnesses and witnesses from both the Walters and the Hillmon families showing that the body was not that of Hillmon and was in fact the body of Walters.

With an eye towards a possible appeal, we took exception to many of Judge Hook's adverse evidence rulings, thus preserving our right to raise them on appeal. (I understand that lawyers today don't have to rub trial judges' noses in the dirt by taking exception to adverse rulings in order to preserve the right to contest the rulings on appeal.) Most significantly we offered proposed jury instructions that if given would support our view of the case, while if denied would allow us to prevail on appeal. Constantly having to plead the cause of out-of-state businesses to local jurors whipped into a frenzy by strident adversaries, we always knew that our best chance for justice lay in the appellate courts. While appellate court judges could not explicitly substitute their factual conclusions for those of the jurors, we believed that the strength of our evidence would incline them to accept our legal arguments.

Let me give you three examples. As Mr. Atwood told you, John Brown is the man who claims to have accidentally shot Hillmon. On various occasions, Brown did testify under oath to an implausible account of the accidental shooting, and the plaintiff read his deposition containing this account to the jury in Trial No. 6. However, we contended that Brown was truthful only on one occasion, when he signed an affidavit admitting that Hillmon had gone looking for a man to pass off as himself and had in fact fired and not received the fatal shot. During Trial No. 6, the plaintiff *and not the defendants* read this affidavit to the jury. We therefore requested that Judge Hook instruct the jurors that they could consider the contents of Brown's affidavit for its truth, not just for impeachment of his deposition testimony. Judge Hook refused to give this instruction, thus making an error that we were confident would produce a reversal on appeal. We were correct; one ground of reversal in the Supreme Court's second opinion in the case in 1903 opinion was "the error in the instructions regarding Brown's affidavit."

My second example is, I readily admit, more devious. Yet it is an example of creative and zealous advocacy. The plaintiff's Complaint had alleged that Hillmon had died, and the companies' Answers denied that Hillmon had died and alleged a conspiracy to defraud them. These initial pleadings were never amended, and each trial basically revolved around the factual question of whether Hillmon or Walters had died at Crooked Creek. Before Trial No. 6, however, my co-counsel and I developed a brand new and alternative line of defense. Even if Hillmon did die at Crooked Creek, we planned to argue, the companies were not liable because the policies had been obtained with the intent of committing a fraud, and thus were void *ab initio.*

We based this line of defense on the language in each policy stating that "if this policy has been obtained by or through any fraud, misrepresentation, evasion or concealment, then the same shall be absolutely null and void." The beauty of this defense was that it provided us with a way to win even if the jurors believed that the conspiracy had gone awry and Brown had accidentally shot Hillmon. Moreover, we could surprise the plaintiff's lawyers with the argument because we did not have to amend the pleadings to make it. We had already pled that fraud had occurred, and we believed that the existing pleadings and the contract language provided sufficient notice to the plaintiff. Finally, if as we expected Judge Hook refused to give this instruction, we had a clean and appealable issue. The Supreme Court ultimately decided that it was "not called upon to express an opinion on the question whether the mere proof of conspiracy to defraud the defendant ... would be sufficient to avoid the policies." However, the Court did reverse the judgment partly on the basis of Judge Hook's improper exclusion of some of our evidence of the conspiracy, so I believe that our strategy on this issue was successful.

As my third example of our strategic approach, consider the insurance companies' attitude towards Sallie Hillmon. The companies were already suffering from an image that they were faceless, greedy, out-of-state monoliths bent on cheating a woman who her own attorney Atwood characterized in his opening statement as "a silly, green, unsophisticated country girl who knew little or nothing of the ways of lawyers." To attack Sallie directly in court, we believed, would only feed this prejudice. Therefore, from the very beginning of the case we made it clear to jurors that we did not believe that Sallie was part of the fraudulent scheme. In my opening statement in Trial No. 6, for instance, I said that "Levi Baldwin, John H. Brown and John Hillmon entered into a conspiracy to defraud the insurance companies. We have not claimed that Mrs. Hillmon was a party to that conspiracy."

The strategy of separating Sallie from the conspiracy was an effort to impress on the jurors that we were treating Sallie fairly while not interfering with our ability to offer evidence of the conspiracy. And if Judge Hook excluded evidence of the conspiracy based on Sallie's not being a party to it, we believed we would have grounds for reversal if the verdict went against us. Again, our strategy was successful. Judge Hook's exclusion of some of our conspiracy evidence was a primary basis on which the Supreme Court overturned the verdict in 1903. The Court held that "any fraud perpetrated by him [Hillmon] at the time the policies were taken out was available as a defence [sic] by the company in an action by her [Sallie]."

Yet on reflection, I wonder about the wisdom of treating Sallie with kid gloves. Admittedly we did not have evidence directly linking Sallie to the conspiracy. However, we had plenty of circumstantial evidence, consisting of the behavior of Sallie and the other conspirators, that but for our strategy we might have argued supported an inference that she was in on the conspiracy. Had we been more aggressive on this point, the jurors might not have felt so solicitous towards Sallie.

For instance, John Brown, who allegedly accidentally killed Hillmon, wrote a letter to Sallie informing her that her husband had been accidentally killed. Brown wrote the letter from Medicine Lodge, where he had taken the body. However, Sallie did not rush to Medicine Lodge to be with her husband's body. Instead Sallie asked the brothers Levi and Alva Baldwin to go to Medicine Lodge and bring the body back to Lawrence, where she lived. Sallie's behavior is contrary to human nature. Supposedly a loving newlywed, surely she would have gone with the Baldwin brothers to Medicine Lodge if she really thought that her sweetheart had been killed. Her behavior supports the inference that she stayed home because she knew that the letter was a ploy to fool the insurance companies and that her husband was still alive.

Moreover, the Baldwin brothers did not in fact return the body to Lawrence. Instead, before anyone from the insurance company could be present, they and Brown rushed to bury the body at Medicine Lodge and fence off the grave. They testified to a cock and bull story about not being able to get the metallic coffin which they needed if they were to transport a body back to Lawrence. Even if we accept the accuracy of this unverified claim, it would not explain why they wouldn't make every effort to bring Sallie to Medicine Lodge so that she could see her beloved one last time before burying the body. Again, the inference from this unlikely behavior is that they all knew that the body was not that of John Hillmon and that they needed to bury the evidence of their crime as quickly as possible.

Perhaps the most telling evidence supporting an argument that Sallie was in on the conspiracy was her behavior when an insurance company attorney named Buchan told her about the affidavit in which Brown admitted that his story that he had accidentally killed Hillmon was false. If she were not in on the conspiracy, wouldn't you reasonably expect Sallie to be thrilled and relieved to learn that her husband was alive? Might she not also have been furious at Brown and the Baldwin brothers because their false stories and perjured inquest testimony caused her such unnecessary grief? Yet Sallie did not behave that way. Instead, at Buchan's urging, she meekly signed releases formally relinquishing her claims to the policies.

Now, Judge Hook ruled that because Sallie gave no consideration for those releases, they did not bar her from going forward with the lawsuit. We disagreed with that ruling, but it does not detract from the point that Sallie's behavior was not that of a relieved wife, but rather that of a conspirator who had been found out. I think that her cross-examination testimony in response to my question will completely satisfy you that Sallie was not the grieving widow her attorneys made her out to be:

Q: Did you go to the funeral of your husband?

A: No sir, the Judsons went.

Strategies aside, you may wonder why the insurance companies paid us lawyers to fight Sallie Hillmon for close to a quarter of a century. Since I've been back I've seen what you pay for basics like food and transportation, so I know that $25,000 isn't worth anything close to what it was when we were trying this case. But $25,000 wasn't a king's ransom even then, and the insurance companies spent a lot more just on us lawyers alone than they would have spent had they just paid Sallie off. Not that any of us lawyers complained, you understand. However, good counselors that we were, often we advised settlement.

To understand the insurance companies' motivation, you have to realize that the *Hillmon* case arose during an era when insurance companies believed that fraud was a growing problem. You can read about some of the schemes in a colorful book written in 1896 by J.B. Lewis and C.C. Bombaugh, *Remarkable Stratagems and Conspiracies: An Authentic Record of Surprising Attempts to Defraud Life Insurance Companies.* Contesting Sallie Hillmon's false claims was the companies' way of drawing a line in the sand, indicating that they would not be easy marks for scammers.

I'm sure you could tell me about insurance fraud schemes that go on today, human nature hasn't changed much I suspect. But if I tell you about one of the most notorious attempted frauds of the 1870's, maybe you'll understand why the insurance companies believed it necessary to carry on the fight against John Hillmon and the other conspirators.

In 1872, two confederates, William Udderzook and Winfield Scott Goss, insured Goss's life for a total of $25,000 through three different companies. Sound familiar? The men obtained a corpse from a medical supplier and staged a kerosene lamp explosion after placing the cadaver in Goss's rented house. Udderzook claimed that the corpse was Goss and sought to collect the proceeds, but the insurance companies refused to pay. Again echoing *Hillmon,* the companies pointed to disparities between the corpse's teeth and those of Goss. However, Goss' "widow" successfully sued the life insurance companies.

Despite the successful outcome of the lawsuit, Udderzook apparently remained alarmed by the vigor of the companies' investigations. These included the widespread circulation of photographs of Goss inquiring whether anyone knew of his whereabouts. Udderzook decided that he could not trust Goss to remain in hiding, especially knowing that Goss had a weakness for liquor. So Udderzook lured Goss into a wooded area and murdered him. Udderzook didn't get away with it, and in 1874 he was convicted and hanged for murdering Goss. Mrs. Goss suffered a second loss—the verdict in her favor was overturned. I hope this illustration indicates what life insurance companies were up against in the latter part of the 19th century, and why my client and the other companies believed it necessary to resist Sallie Hillmon's claims.

John Atwood again here, Ladies and Gentlemen (forgive me my awkwardness, for I am unused to addressing ladies, as they did not serve on juries during my time in the courts of Kansas and elsewhere). Before I move on to recount some interesting aspects concerning the matter of Miss Alvina Kasten and her love letter, I will respond briefly to Mr. Green's points.

We felt we had no choice but to introduce the affidavit that Mr. John Brown signed at the behest of Buchan. Had we not done so, the defendants surely would have. Mr. Brown, never very fond of testifying under oath, became unavailable after his testimony in the first trial. We therefore had to acquaint the jury with his account of the accidental shooting at Crooked Creek through the medium of a transcript of his pretrial deposition. (The first trial having ended in a mistrial—like the second, fourth, and fifth—there was no transcript made of his testimony, but the transcript of his deposition survived.) The rule being at the time (as I believe it is still) that a hearsay account may be impeached in the same manner as live witness testimony, we knew of course that the affidavit would be offered by the companies as a prior inconsistent statement. I believe you may have heard of the technique of anticipating impeachment in order to rob it of its sting? We had this in mind a bit, as we wanted the jury to be aware during our case of the pressures that had been brought to bear on Mr. Brown in order to induce him to give the lying statement, rather than have the good jurors believe that we had tried to conceal from them the existence of the affidavit.

But there was more to this as well. Buchan had succeeded, after he coerced the affidavit from John Brown, in obtaining Mrs. Hillmon's signatures on three releases—promises not to sue the companies. She had executed them in despair after learning that Buchan had apparently recruited John Brown to perjure himself against her claims. (Almost immediately afterward Mr. Brown recanted the affidavit, but not in time to prevent her from signing the releases.) Fortunately, the law provided that these releases (having been given for no consideration) were of no binding effect unless accompanied by her surrender of the policies themselves. This surrender she was prevented from performing by her counselor at the time, Mr. Wheat, who was in possession of the documents. But the law would not prevent the jurors from being told that she had signed the releases, and we knew that Mr. Green and his colleagues would attempt to make it appear that our client had no faith in her own case. Mr. Brown's affidavit and its contents were the best proof that she had suffered this momentary loss of nerve only because of the shocking conduct of the companies and their agents.

Our mistake was to ask that the affidavit be given only limited effect (as impeachment and as an explanation for Mrs. Hillmon's conduct), rather than being taken as proof of the truth of its contents. We still think this limitation was quite proper, as did Judge Hook, who so instructed the jury. But it is well known that such instructions are not of much meaning to the jurors, and by obtaining it we gave the Supreme Court, which had once before robbed our client of a victory, another excuse to re-enact its hostility toward our client and her claims.

Mr. Green is correct that his clients' strategy (of shifting their ground from an insistence that John Hillmon had not died at Crooked Creek to the claim that even if he had, the policy was void because he had contemplated insurance fraud) was devious. I would like to say that this choice represented an uncharacteristic departure from the otherwise aboveboard conduct of the defense, but I find myself unable to say so in truth. As we are not here bound by the rules that govern courtroom conduct (especially those pertaining to the general inadmissibility of character evidence) perhaps I may also take the liberty of puncturing somewhat Dean Green's rather self-important description of his role in founding the University of Kansas Law School and his pride in the accomplishments of his sister-in-law Kate Stephens. Professor Stephens was no admirer of the man who married her sister. If you doubt me, I encourage you to look for a rare but instructive volume published by Professor Stephens in 1924, in which she reveals how Green (who was known to his students as "Uncle Jimmy") stole credit for being the founding member of the Law School faculty from his father-in-law, to whom it justly belonged. The book is rather colorfully titled: ***Truths Back of the Uncle Jimmy Myth in a State University of the Middle West.***

3.   The Crucial Letter

This is Mr. Atwood, still with you. I said I would tell you of our first acquaintance with Miss Alvina Kasten and her letter. So I shall, after a brief preface that may enable you to appreciate our situation in the months leading up to Trial No. 1. You will recall that despite our original misgivings, my co-counsel and I estimated our chances of prevailing before a jury as excellent. In our opinion John Brown's conflicting accounts rather cancelled each other out, as did the differences of opinion about whether the corpse that had been displayed at Bailey & Smith's resembled John Hillmon. Some of what we expected as defense evidence we deemed implausible. For example, John Hillmon had a recent smallpox vaccination scar, and so did the corpse, a point definitely in favor of Mrs. Hillmon's claims. But the insurance companies had procured a physician to opine that the scar on the corpse was too recent to be Hillmon's, and the Brown affidavit had given a highly unlikely account of the wayfarer "Joe Berkley" having consented to Hillmon's giving him a makeshift vaccination using a pocket knife and the virus from Hillmon's arm. We did not think the jurors would credit this story, especially once they learned that the insurance companies' doctors had removed the vaccination scar at the post-mortem and thereafter "lost" it, so it could not be examined by an expert of our choosing.

Another improbable piece of defense testimony would come, we expected, from Dr. Miller, who had given Hillmon a physical examination at the companies' request before they would issue the policies. Dr. Miller had to acknowledge in his testimony at the inquest that in the policy application form John Hillmon had filled out, Hillmon had written "5 feet, 11 inches" (the precise length of the corpse) as his height. The good doctor claimed however that Hillmon had come back a few days later to admit that he was only "5 feet, 9 inches," whereupon the physician, on this occasion carrying out an actual measurement and observing the shorter height, noted this unusual event in his ledger book (a book otherwise given over to recording his patients' payment accounts). This convoluted history, we thought, defied human experience, as none of us could conceive of any reason, consistent with either Hillmon's innocence or his guilt, that he should behave in the way attributed to him. An attempt by the doctor at perjury and fabrication of evidence was the far more believable explanation, and we looked forward to so arguing to the jury.

These calculations, alloyed with what we believed would be the jury's revulsion at the behavior of Buchan, and with the innate attractiveness of our client (for Mr. Green is quite correct that her status as poor widow was an asset to our labors), conspired to inflate our hopes. We had underestimated, once again, the ingenuity of our opponents.

Not many months after filing suit on behalf of our client, in June of 1881 we received a notice that the defendants intended to take the deposition of a Miss Alvina Kasten of Fort Madison, Iowa. We had no idea whatsoever what Miss Kasten might have to do with Mrs. Hillmon and the insurance companies, but of course we were curious to find out. We expected, if anything, that she might be the latest in what was becoming rather a long line of persons who claimed that their missing relative might belong to the corpse that was now far below ground in the Oak Hill Cemetery. She was that, or almost, but something much more dangerous as well: a correspondent.

We arrived at the Fort Madison courthouse, where the deposition was to be taken, and saw the companies' lawyers and agents surrounding a diminutive young woman, even younger in appearance than Mrs. Hillmon, and sweetly and modestly dressed. She took the oath, and began her deposition. After some preliminaries, she explained that she was the betrothed of a young man named Frederick Adolph Walters, who had left his home Fort Madison in March of 1878, to seek his fortune. He had written to her every two weeks during his absence, up until early March, 1879, when she received what she testified was her last communication from him. This last letter she said she had received from the postmaster's own hand on March 3, 1879. It was, she claimed, ummistakably in the handwriting of her absent fiancee, Frederick Adolph Walters. She never heard from him again.

The letter was thereupon produced, and made an exhibit to the deposition. I am afraid that all of us on Mrs. Hillmon's team rather crowded around the young lady in our eagerness to read this epistle. Here is what we saw:

Dearest Alvina:

Your kind and ever welcome letter was received yesterday afternoon about an hour before I left Emporia. I will stay here until the fore part of next week & then will leave here to see a part of the Country that I never expected to see when I left home as I am going with a man by the name of Hillmon who intends to start a sheep range and as he promised me more wages than I could make at anything else I Concluded to take it for a while at least until I strike something better. There is so many folks in this country as have the got the Leadville Fever, & if I would not have got the situation I have got now I would have went there myself but as it is at present I will get to see the best portion of Kansas Indian Territory Colorado & Mexico the route we intend to take would Cost a man to travel from $150 to $200. but it will not cost me a cent. Besides I get good Wages. I will drop you a letter occasionally until I get settled down then I want you to answer it. (You bet Honey.) Don't it? So you can see that I will not get home for a few months yet, but cannot tell you how soon I will get back, I am about as Anxious to see you as you are to see me. But I do not want to get back there without a sent of money for that is not what I left for (you know). When I get back you will get to see me in about the way we parted (You bet)!? If anyone asks what I am doing tell them that you were not Informed for it is none of their Business and an other thing don't ask me to write long letters for I would without being told if I could find the Words when I write as I am generally Busy when I receive a letter from my (Old Woman) Sweet Little Girl.

*But you know how that is without being told so I will not have to
waist any more paper on that subject (at present). I will have to
come to a close before long or I will have to do as that Other
Fellow write 2 Sheets & swindle the P. Master out of 3 cents and
you know that I don't like to do that. (Pet) Please give compliments to inquiring Friends and all that love that you can
embrace for yourself & no body else. I will close for this time
Love, to let you hear from me soon again.*

Yours as ever,

F.A. Walter

*P.S. Much obliged for that Poetry & I done as you said (thought
of you when I read it.)*

Poetry! My heart sank at once, for we had in a trice acquired several
formidable obstacles to success. First, a letter placed Mr. Hillmon in the
company of this missing young man, making him a suspicious offer of
"more wages than I could make at anything else," just before his
mysterious disappearance! But not only that, this demure young woman
was a near-widow herself and her appeal was scarce less than that of our
client (or possibly even greater). And a missing young swain whose heart
sought adventure but also cherished the memory of his awaiting betrothed by reading the poetry she had recommended! No longer was the
case one of the poor widow versus the heartless Eastern corporations; it
was now widow versus widow, and we had no doubt of the defendants'
intentions to play that theme to the hilt! It was a low moment indeed,
and perhaps robbed us not only of our optimism but of our wit, for a
time. For how else can one account for the rather mortifying circumstance that it did not dawn on any of us for nearly eight years that this
letter was hearsay? I am rather embarrassed to admit that we allowed
the letter to be placed into evidence in the first two trials without
objection.

Hello Friends, James Green back with you. Our ability to
attach a name and an identity to the unfortunate soul who had been
shot at Crooked Creek was vital to the defense. Mr. Atwood callously
implies that we were engaged in a battle of wits to produce a Battle of
Widows, but our only purpose was to tell the jurors what really happened.

Our strategy in this regard raises an important consideration for all
defense attorneys. We could have defended this case solely by contesting
the claim that the body was that of John Hillmon. The evidence that we
amassed and offered into the record was more than sufficient in our view
to prevent the plaintiff from carrying even the civil burden of proof,
preponderance of the evidence. Let me remind you of just some of the
evidence:

- The corpse had virtually perfect teeth, no small accomplishment in the era in which I lived. Yet the defense presented numerous witnesses, including some of Hillmon's relatives and his former fiancee, to testify that some of Hillmon's teeth were missing or blackened. Not all of our witnesses agreed as to the precise problems with Hillmon's teeth, but that they were not in as good a condition as those of the corpse could not be doubted. Moreover, while Mr. Atwood and his colleagues had no qualms about accusing me of knowingly presenting perjured testimony, my willingness to present testimony from witnesses whose recollections didn't precisely jibe certainly shows that I was willing to accept their best recollections and let the chips fall where they may.

- Alva Baldwin accompanied his brother Levi to Medicine Lodge, where the corpse had been quickly buried. Major Wiseman, an insurance company representative who helped make sure that the corpse was dug up so that it could be examined, testified that when the cloth was lifted from the corpse's face, Alva Baldwin immediately cried out, "What the hell, that's not Hillmon." Alva denied at trial that he said this, but though his whereabouts were at all times known to the plaintiff Alva never testified until Trial No. 6.

- We offered evidence that Hillmon had a large scar near the base of his thumb on his right hand, the result of a hunting accident that occurred when Hillmon's own gun exploded in his hand. The corpse had no such scar.

- The corpse was 5′11″ tall. Yet when Hillmon enlisted in the Union Army in 1864, the enlistment document recorded his height as 5′5″. The plaintiff admitted that the corpse was dressed in clothes that belonged to Levi Baldwin when he was shot, and Levi Baldwin testified and admitted that he was only 5′8″ tall. Hillmon might have grown a bit after he enlisted at age 16, but 6 inches of growth is unlikely and doesn't explain why if the body was that of Hillmon he would be wearing the clothes of a man who stands 5′8″. Lastly, Michael Mesh, a man in whose house Hillmon and Brown stayed for a couple of weeks before setting off for Crooked Creek, swore that he (Mesh) and Hillmon had measured each other and that Hillmon was only 5′9″ tall. Mesh had not known Hilllmon previously, and he had nothing to gain from testifying. Actually Mesh was lucky to survive long enough to testify. Hillmon and Brown had offered him a salary to join them on their supposed ranching quest, and had he accepted it might have been Mesh's body and not Walters' that was found by the side of Crooked Creek.

- Even setting aside John Brown's affidavit in which he recanted his story that he had accidentally killed Hillmon, his account of the killing was unbelievable. Is it plausible that his rifle fired accidentally while he was unloading a wagon? Doesn't this sound like a phony story that can account for Hillmon's death without implicating Brown in a murder? Moreover, Brown explained the fact that the corpse was burned by testifying that Hillmon danced around after being shot and finally fell into the campfire. Yet Dr. Stuart examined the head wound and testified for the defense that "the man would immediately fall to the ground, becoming paralyzed, death following instantly." The plaintiff failed to offer contradictory medical evidence though Dr. Stuart had testified at every previous trial. Finally, Brown testified that over the period of time that he and Hillmon were going through desolate and dangerous country, Hillmon never once mentioned all the insurance coverage that he had on his life. This even though even Mr. Atwood readily concedes that it was an extraordinary amount of insurance for a man in Hillmon's economic position to take out.

However, I did not think it sufficient merely to undermine the plaintiff's false claims. Understandably, many of the jurors would have wondered whether if the body were not that of Hillmon, then whose was it? The jurors would reasonably expect my client to answer this question, and if so might decide that the body was Hillmon's simply because I failed to offer them an alternative. Therefore I told the jurors that the body was that of Frederick Walters and offered substantial proof of this contention.

This strategy entailed a risk of my losing the benefit of the plaintiff having the burden of proof. Presenting jurors with a choice between two alternatives implies that they can choose the one they find more satisfactory regardless of who has the burden of proof. Thus, in my final argument I was careful to tell the jurors that "You are not to find whether it was Walters or whether it was not, but whether it was Hillmon." Nevertheless, insisting that the body was that of Walters may have resulted in our losing whatever benefit accrued to us by the plaintiff having the burden of proof.

I don't second guess the wisdom of my strategy for a moment, because the evidence supporting the Walters theory was emotionally powerful and factually strong. I'm a big believer in beginning and ending a case on strong points, and I followed that approach in this trial. Though I was forced to have much important testimony read into evidence, I made sure that I began and concluded with live witnesses. I began with Major Wiseman, who as mentioned above testified that Alva Baldwin, upon seeing the corpse dug up from the ground, immediately exclaimed, "Hell, that's not Hillmon."

I called my last witness in the hope of making a dramatic and lasting impression on the jurors. She was Fannie Walters, the youngest sister of Frederick Walters. Like her sister and brother, Fannie had seen photos of the corpse and she testified that the body was that of her brother Frederick. Fannie had also received letters from Frederick stating that he was going to go out west with a man by the name of Hillmon. Then I took her testimony a step farther.

Fannie and Frederick closely resembled each other. For example, the general contour of the faces was the same, and they both had prominent cheekbones and large Roman-type noses. Therefore, I asked that photographs of the cadaver be handed to the jurors. I then asked Fannie to stand up and face the jurors, and asked them to compare her face to that of the cadaver as depicted in the photographs. I asked Fannie to give a broad smile, because her teeth so closely matched the mold of the cadaver's teeth that had been admitted into evidence. The demonstration would, I hope, constitute silent but powerful evidence that the body was that of her brother, Frederick Walters. With that, I rested the defense case.

Now, Mr. Atwood attacks the Walters theory by arguing that the insurance companies fished around for a suitable victim, and in at least one case identified the corpse as a person who later proved to be very much alive and well. I do not apologize for these events and do not think that they undermine the Walters theory at all. Initially the insurance companies had no idea of the corpse's actual identity, and so circulated notices asking for people to come forward if they knew of someone who matched the general description who had recently gone missing. The companies acted responsibly by checking out the responses thoroughly. When possible matches failed to pan out, the companies moved on. If anything, the companies' careful behavior strengthens rather than detracts from their determination that the corpse was that of Walters.

You should also understand that the affidavit that John Brown gave to Buchan delayed the companies' quest to learn the corpse's true identity. In his affidavit, Brown stated that the victim was "Burgess or Francis ... a man that they called Joe." Brown's vague and misleading description was undoubtedly calculated to give himself some added protection from prosecution by throwing the insurance companies off the scent, and for a time he succeeded.

The letter from Walters to Alvina Kasten, along with the letters that he wrote to other relatives indicating his plan to accompany Hillmon, were crucial to our claim that the corpse was that of Walters. I also offered testimony from a number of Walters' relatives and acquaintances that based on seeing photos of the corpse, they were confident that the body was that of Walters. Physical evidence also linked the corpse to Walters. For example, we offered evidence that Walters, like the corpse, had a mole on his back, and that like the corpse, Walters' teeth were in excellent condition. Moreover, both Walters and the corpse measured out at 5'11".

However, Mr. Atwood was a formidable adversary who took advantage of his opportunities to attack this evidence. For example, defense witnesses who identified the corpse as that of Walters did so based only on photographs of the corpse. Most of the photos were taken after, shall we say to preserve delicacy for the ladies (as we did in my day), some deterioration in its condition had occurred. And there was some testimony to the effect that Walters had a bunion on one foot and a small scar on one hand, neither of which was found on the corpse. Thus, powerful as our evidence was, it could not banish all doubts about the corpse being that of Walters.

I believed that Walters' letters erased any remaining doubts by tying Walters directly to Hillmon. Mr. Atwood's efforts to undermine the letters' importance were tortuous and labored. Maybe Walters was referring to a different man by the name of Hillmon. In one or two of his earlier letters, Walters wrote of planning to go to Nebraska; since he didn't follow through with those plans, why should the jurors believe that he carried out his plans to accompany Hillmon? Most ill-founded was Mr. Atwood's argument that since Alvina Kasten never testified personally at a trial, her deposition testimony that was read into the trial records must have been perjured and the letter a phony. Alvina had seen the photos and knew that her sweetheart had been killed at Crooked Creek. She had already said all she had to under oath at her deposition. She was beyond the court's subpoena power and had nothing to gain from testifying except to relive her painful loss. I would also point out that Mr. Atwood had the same opportunity to persuade her to leave Iowa and testify in person that I did. Finally, in over two decades of litigation, Mr. Atwood never produced a scintilla of evidence casting doubt on the letter's authenticity. Walters was the undoubted author of the letters, and they are tangible proof of Hillmon's plan to defraud the insurance companies.

John Atwood here again, ladies and gents. It has taken quite a while to get as far as the sixth trial, has it not? If our reader is becoming weary, she may perhaps imagine how exhausted the attorneys were by the time the case reached its last encore. Mr. Green, as always, leaves me with a great deal of confusion (I was going to say obfuscation but would not want him to think me intemperate) to clear away.

- On the vexed question of the teeth, Mr. Green neglects to mention that even one of the companies' own physicians, pressed into service to perform the autopsy, acknowledged at the inquest that the corpse had one upper tooth that was shorter than the others, in a manner that would permit an acquaintance of the living man to gain the impression that the tooth was missing if the man were not wearing a broad grin. (No reason appears that Mr. Hillmon should have grinned while alive at any of these witnesses, as after his death they displayed an unmistakable hostility to him and his widow.)

- Mr. Alva Baldwin denied saying "Hell, it's not Hillmon" during his only appearance as a witness, in Trial No. 6. This disclaimer may have been a bit belated, but at least he addressed the matter during his first testimony in the case. By contrast, the witness who attributed this statement to him, Mr. Theo Wiseman, testified at each of the first three trials but never mentioned Alva Baldwin's very incriminating comment until the fourth. If this event that Mr. Green regards as so very convincing had really occurred, why would Wiseman have failed to describe it (or Mr. Green to elicit it) until his fourth witness appearance?

- As for the height recorded on John Hillmon's Army enlistment document, the lad was sixteen or seventeen years old at the time he enlisted. Surely he had not attained his full height by any means, nutrition at the time not being what you are accustomed to in your more fortunate century.

- Ah, yes, the interesting Mr. Mesh. When did you ever know grown men to entertain themselves of an evening by the expedient of measuring one another's height? It is true that we did not have your television or that—what do you call it? Internet?—in the nineteenth century, but we were not so desperate for entertainment as this account suggests. It may be true that Mr. Mesh was invited to join Hillmon and Brown on their journey, and now regards that invitation as sinister, and also as a badge of fame. I am afraid it is not unknown for insignificant persons to seek to attach themselves to notorious causes by reasoning that they narrowly escaped becoming enmeshed (pun intended, I am sorry) in them. The number of persons who decided at the last moment not to sail on the Titanic would be sufficient to populate a medium-sized island.

- If the companies' floating of supposed dead men as candidates for the identity of the corpse had been limited to their names and the circumstances of their disappearances, perhaps Mr. Green's defense of this dragnet would be persuasive, but I must remind you

that it was not so limited. One of this platoon of the disappeared—
Frank Nichols, nicknamed "Arkansaw"—was actually reported in
the newspapers to have told friends before disappearing that he
had "met a man named Hillmon" who had offered him large
wages to accompany him. I am sure Mr. Green will deny having
anything to do with this report, but he had many minions and
sympathizers in the press, and this account had the effect of
stirring up sentiment against Mrs. Hillmon—until "Arkansaw"
turned up quite alive. This notion of putting the words about a
man named Hillmon into a missing man's mouth (or on his page)
was too good to surrender, however, and that is why we see it
again in the Kasten letter.

That d——d letter!! Every time it comes up it makes me so hopping
mad I get ahead of myself!! But before, as you would say, "going there,"
I must remark on one other matter. It is handsome of Mr. Green to
acknowledge that the identification of photographs of a corpse (taken
after it has sustained considerable indignity) as one's missing son, or
brother, or fiancé is not reliable. The wisdom of this observation led us
to object in the last trial to one item of evidence: testimony that F.A.
Walters' mother, when shown these images, cried "That's my son!" and
then fainted. Judge Hook sustained our objection. "So far as the pictures
would affect the mother," he observed, "they would naturally have the
effect they did. She was aged and had long mourned her son as dead. The
picture of any cadaver would have much the same effect." We were
happy to enjoy this small victory, for despite the wisdom of the judge's
words, the emotional effect of any account of the mother's reaction
would have been considerable.

Mr. Green is quite right to note that neither I nor my colleagues on
Mrs. Hillmon's side of the courtroom ever produced a scintilla of evidence to question the authenticity of the Walters/Kasten letter. Until the
jury heard from Mr. Henry Simmons, that is. I see Mr. Green practically
dancing to address this matter with you, so I will yield to him, but please
remember that I will have more to say about it presently.

4. A Surprise Witness

Mr. Green back with you again. You might think that after five
trials spanning nearly two decades, every bit of evidence bearing on the
identity of the corpse would already have been offered by one party or
the other. Imagine my surprise, then, when on rebuttal Mr. Atwood
shocked the courtroom with the testimony of Arthur Simmons. Simmons
had never previously testified, even though as a resident of Leavenworth,
Kansas, he knew all about the case and claimed to have crucial information about Frederick Walters.

Please understand that my surprise at Simmons' appearance was not due to any lack of preparation by my defense team. Discovery didn't exist when I was trying cases, nor did we have extensive pre-trial conferences in which lawyers were expected to exchange witness lists. Pulling rabbits out of hats was a common technique back in the day.

In 1879, Simmons owned a cigar factory. Twenty years later, in Trial No. 6, he suddenly produced records of the business showing that in May of that year, some two months after someone died beside Crooked Creek, Frederick Walters was alive and working in the cigar factory. Simmons identified photographs of Walters as the man who had worked for him. Excerpts from his testimony are as follows:

Q: When did you first learn that this man Walters had worked for you?

A: My attention was called to it a short time ago by several persons.

Q: Did you, after your attention was called to the matter, look it up in your books?

A: Yes sir, I did.

Q: (The witness is handed the company's day book for 1879.) Is the memorandum in your own writing, and was it made at the time Walters was working for you?

A: Yes, sir.

Q: When was it that Walters worked for you?

A: I cannot remember the exact date without looking at my book.

Q: Have you any recollection of the man independent of the book?

A: Yes. I remembered the man distinctly as soon as I saw his picture.

Q: When you look at this book, does it refresh your memory?

A: Yes, sir, it does.

Q: What month was it that Walters worked for you?

A: I find from this book that it was in the month of May, 1879.

Comment: I think it plain that this testimony was hearsay, because the witness was simply testifying to the contents of the day book, not from present memory. However, Judge Hook had already overruled our objections to the use of the day book.

Q: What was his name in the book, and what name did he go by?

A: His name was F. Walters.

I'm sure you can imagine how stunned I was. Here was a local business owner who testified that Walters was alive, some two months after we claimed he died. Obviously we had to try to cast doubt on his testimony. We might have immediately charged at him like a bull at a matador and accused him of lying, but we didn't think that the jury would accept that argument. Simmons appeared to be a forthright citizen with no motive to commit perjury. Instead we asked for a brief recess, carefully examined Simmons' day book, and decided that my co-counsel Mr. Barker's cross-examination would emphasize the implausible aspects of Simmons' story. This is an important lesson for beginning lawyers. Unless you have nearly airtight proof, judges and jurors are loath to believe that witnesses are conscious liars. You'll usually accomplish more on cross-examination if you nibble around the edges and take what witnesses give you. Some excerpts from Mr. Barker's skillful cross-examination will demonstrate what I mean:

Q: This book is written in pencil?

A: Yes. Some of it was written in pen.

Q: A name has been erased and the name of Walters has been written above it?

A: Yes.

Q: What name was erased?

A: The name Anderson was erased and the other was written above it.

Q: You have lived here in Leavenworth ever since this occurred?

A: Yes, sir.

Q: You remember this case having been tried here before?

A: Yes, sir.

Q: Is this the first trial you have attended?

A: Yes.

Q: And after 20 years you remember the photograph of that man?

A: Yes, sir.

Q: You never saw the picture before?

A: No.

Q: Who else worked for you at the time this man Walters was working?

A: I don't remember.

Q: How many men did you have employed at that time?

A: About 25 I think, I don't know.

Q: How many have you had altogether from that time until now?

A: I could not say. They changed often.

Q: Do they travel around? Are they like lawyers?

A: Yes.

Q: Will you count the number of cigar makers who were working for you at the time Walters was?

A: I find there were 22. That was with the week ending April 28.

Q: How many times does the name Walters appear on your book?

A: Twice in three weeks.

Q: Did Walters work for you any other time?

A: No.

Q: What explanation have you to make of that erasure?

A: I was accustomed to keep account of the work which the men did by taking care of the cigars which they made and keeping an account for each man. I went around among the men to do this and took the cigars from their tables. When I came to the week ending April 18, 1879, a man by the name of Anderson quit with 900 cigars. As Walters took his place I simply erased Anderson's name and wrote Walters' above it in order to keep the column even. On May 4 Walters has to his credit 1200 cigars; on May 31, 900.

Q: Can you describe Walters?

A: Only slightly.

Q: Do you remember anything about his teeth, his eyes or his hair?

A: I cannot recollect.

If Mr. Barker were here, he'd no doubt apologize for asking Simmons to explain the erasure. To that point he had controlled the examination, limiting Simmons to short answers suggesting that the day book had plainly been tampered with. (I make no claim that Mr. Atwood had anything to do with that.) Simmons obviously had no recollection of Walters beyond what the day book said, and his claim to recognize a photo of one employee among hundreds who had worked for him briefly 20 years earlier is incredible on its face. By asking Simmons to explain how the erasure came about, however, Mr. Barker allowed the witness to determine the scope of the answer and account for the erasure. Nevertheless, we brought out the implausibility of a man living in the very city where this widely-reported case had been tried repeatedly, yet sitting idly by for two decades before suddenly rushing into court with crucial evidence. I believe that we completely neutralized Simmons' testimony.

John Atwood again, gentle readers. The delicious thing about Henry Simmons was that we heard about him through the defendants' old stalking horse, the newspapers. The *Leavenworth Times* was always seeking to put the defendants' case in a good light; it announced in its issue of October 25th, 1899, as we were close to concluding our case in chief, that the defendants' case would include testimony that F.A. Walters was in Leavenworth in 1878 and worked in the Staiger and Simmons tobacco house. We read this report with interest, for like all good trial lawyers, we read the papers every evening after court was adjourned to see how our efforts were being described and judge whether they required some alteration (although we knew better than to expect any flattery from the *Times*). The report mentioned a Mr. Arthur Simmons in connection with this prediction. It appeared to me that one of us ought to go to speak with this Mr. Simmons, for we had never heard of him before. It did not seem to us that his testimony, as described, would be very damaging to our case: what did it prove that Walters had worked in Leavenworth during the year preceding the important events? But one never knows, and so I equipped Mr. Hutchins of our legal team with some photographs of Walters that his family had supplied, and sent him round to find Mr. Simmons.

It developed that his name was not Arthur, but Henry, and that he was co-owner of the tobacco house, but this was not all the newspaper had gotten wrong. Never have I been happier to make the acquaintance of a witness, for as Mr. Green's account discloses, Henry Simmons' account was that he had employed the young cigar maker in May of **1879**—two months after the death at Crooked Creek! Not only that, he had documentary proof of these events.

We knew, of course, that the defendants would attack the regularity of his records. As you have read, he was well-prepared to meet this criticism. But best of all was Mr. Barker's falling into the trap of suggesting that his memory of these events twenty years in the past could not be very good, especially as he had employed many scores, perhaps hundreds, of cigar makers in the meantime. For this impeachment opened the door to a particularly satisfying bit of rehabilitation, which might otherwise have been excluded as improper character evidence.

Myself: What was there peculiar about that man that made you recognize him?

Mr. Simmons: He was a man who was all the time talking to the men about him and telling of his many travels. He had been in a large number of towns in different places and he also talked a great deal of his love scrapes and how he had gotten out of them.

Love scrapes!! You may be certain I was delighted to hear those words, as they not only accounted for Mr. Simmons' memory of the fellow but also put the braggart's relationship with Miss Alvina Kasten in rather a different light—don't you think? I did not spoil the moment by seeking to gild this lily, but merely paused for a moment and then thanked the witness for his testimony and sat down. The rest was formality; after arguments and instructions, the jury returned a verdict for Sallie Hillmon following only ten hours of deliberation (this may sound like a long time to you but we were accustomed to far longer sieges of consideration).

Now, back to the d——d letter, for that is what it always comes back to in my mind. I blame myself for not having given more thought to the genuineness of the letter's assertions, but after the Supreme Court's decision of 1892, we simply believed that it had to be explained away somehow. We knew the circumstance of a young man's writing such a letter—making mention of John Hillmon and Wichita and going west to start a ranch—and then never being seen again, and all this shortly before the Hillmon death, was too much to credit as coincidence. We tried to argue that "John Hillmon" was not such a common name and it might have been some other man with whom young Walters had taken up. I appreciate that it sounds rather feeble, but we could come up with nothing else. I do not wish to boast, but think it to our credit that even laboring under the handicap generated by the letter's admission, we staved off victory for the companies in the trials of 1895 and 1896.

You are no doubt thinking that we should have investigated the likelihood that the letter was a forgery. We thought of this, of course, and I was able early on, through some adroit investigation, to obtain some other specimens of the writing of young Walters. (Miss Kasten claimed that she had thrown away all of her swain's letters except for the last one—a claim I found unlikely—but we made a few friends in Fort Madison and were able to secure some exemplars.) To our great disappointment, every eye we consulted was of the opinion that the writing of the letter was identical to that in the exemplars. Although document science was not so advanced as it became in your day (though I understand there is some controversy about it even in the twenty-first century), we thought we would have little success in persuading a jury that the Kasten letter was not in Mr. Walters' hand. In the last trial, Mr. Walters' sister produced a great bundle of letters from her brother, claiming they had been mislaid until just then. A quick comparison with them confirmed our original opinion that the Kasten letter was no forgery. The matter was over and done, the last trial over, the appeal decided, the case negotiated to a close, before I ever reflected on the events of the Hillmon case sufficiently to realize that the words of the letter from Frederick Adolph Walters to Alvina Kasten were full of lies.

For it was Henry Simmons, I am certain, whose testimony led to our final victory. His identification of Walters as a man who was quite alive two months after the Lawrence inquest was so convincing that the jurors were able to put the letter aside somehow. But as I looked back over this monumental lawsuit, I was moved to wonder how the jurors explained the letter away, in their own minds I mean, well enough to arrive at a unanimous verdict for Mrs. Hillmon. The letter was not a forgery, of that I was certain, and I doubted that the jurors saw the matter differently. So if it was written in Frederick Adolph Walters' hand, and if (as seems to be the case) his friends and family and fiancee never heard from him again after its delivery, how could that be accounted for? It could not be a coincidence that the letter mentioned Hillmon and going west to start a ranch, and was dated and marked Wichita, March 1st, 1879.

I am sorry to say that as I have considered this matter for these long years I am unable to come to any conclusion but this: Mr. Green's clients (I do not say he was personally involved) located Mr. Walters not long after the inquest, some time during the fall of 1879 or early months of 1880. They quickly took his measure and saw that he was a young man enamored of himself and his adventures (and *love scrapes*). They realized that he would serve their purposes excellently, and contracted with him to pay him a generous sum monthly in exchange for his agreement to, as Mr. Huckleberry Finn might say, "light out for the territories," never to return to Kansas or Iowa. Oh yes, and before leaving, he must just write out a letter, the substance of which the companies' agents would describe for him (although he was encouraged to add embellishments if he wished to make it seem like his own style).

Yes, I realize the difficulties with this theory: the avarice it ascribes to the companies and their agents, the puzzle of why Miss Alvina Kasten would lie about when and how she received the letter, and the necessity of forging at least the postal cancellation. I have answers to all of these objections, but perhaps I ought to give Mr. Green the chance to say a few words, happy in the knowledge that like all who carry a burden of proof, I will have the last opportunity to address you.

5. Closing Remarks

James Green with a few final remarks, ladies and gentlemen. Mr. Atwood and I are very grateful for your careful attention to the evidence and our remarks. I hope that more than a century removed from the hostility and prejudice that faced the insurance companies every time we set foot in a Kansas courtroom, you'll rectify the erroneous outcome of Trial No. 6 and decide that the corpse was that of Frederick Walters.

I don't think I have to say much more about Arthur/Henry Simmons. Confronted by the numerous variances between the living Hillmon and the dead body, Mr. Atwood at the last asks you to place your confidence in a witness who kept silent while the news of this case swirled around him constantly, only to suddenly produce a doctored day book indicating that Walters had worked for him in the month of May, 20 years earlier. Simmons would have you believe that two decades after he last saw him, he recognized a photograph of Walters as one of the hundreds of employees who had worked for him. And this even though Simmons admitted that he had no recollection of Walters' eyes, teeth or hair.

I used to tell my students that implausible testimony often begets implausible explanations, and that's certainly true for Simmons' claim to remember Walters because he talked about love scrapes. Mr. Atwood thinks that this explanation unravels the defense case, but in fact it only further destroys Simmons' credibility. If Simmons had such a good reason to remember Walters, no way would Simmons have stayed silent over the course of five trials and 20 years. And how about the 20–25 other men who worked in the cigar factory supposedly at the same time as Walters (none of whom Simmons can recall, by the way, just Walters), the men to whom Walters was supposedly "all the time talking to?" Surely one of them at least would have remembered that Walters was making cigars with them when he was supposedly already dead. Yet none of them ever testified? Did the insurance companies buy all of their silence? Finally, Simmons is busy counting cigars by the hundreds, but he can remember what Walters talked about 20 years later? I'm sorry that Mr. Atwood has had to come from so far to try to foist this unbelievable story on you.

Mr. Atwood acknowledges the difficulties with his theory that insurance company agents found Walters and convinced him to write a phony "Dear Alvina" letter some two months after the body was found at Crooked Creek, then disappear. But the difficulties even he must acknowledge barely scratch the surface. Let me say explicitly that neither I nor anyone on the defense team had anything to do with the writing of that letter. Nor could we have. I remind you that Walters did not just write "a" letter, as Mr. Atwood claims. Walters wrote letters to various people mentioning that he was going off with Hillmon. Were all these letters phony as well, and did the insurance companies manage to forge the postal cancellations on all of them and inveigle all the recipients to commit perjury?

Now let's ignore for the moment all these problems with Mr. Atwood's theory and focus just on the "Dear Alvina" letter. I'll even concede, for the sake of argument, that as Mr. Atwood claims, Walters wasn't head over heels in love with Alvina; she was just a "love scrape."

But surely, everything we know suggests that Alvina was deeply in love with Frederick Walters. If she were handed a phony letter, can you imagine for a moment that she would have compliantly testified that a photograph of Hillmon was her beloved Frederick Walters, and that he was dead? Would Walters' father and sisters also swear falsely that the son and brother who they loved was dead? Would they all have agreed never to see Walters again, because of course they couldn't once they had said under oath that he was dead? People who would behave like that towards their loved ones would have to be monsters, and there's never been a hint of a suggestion (certainly none brought forward by Mr. Atwood) to show that Alvina's and Walters' relatives' feelings for him were anything other than caring and loving. They accurately believed that they had suffered a horrible loss. At the end of the day, defending their loving memories was far more important to me than the financial impact of an adverse verdict on my clients.

Thank you so much.

I thank you for your attention one last time, Ladies and Gentlemen. John Atwood would be a fool were he to stand here and declare that James Green's arguments have no force. Dean Green is a formidable advocate and I know you must be troubled by some of the points he raises. But in his zeal to redeem his losses before two juries, Mr. Green has misrepresented some matters, and omitted a couple of others. I must set them to rights as an obligation not only to my client, but to history and to the law of evidence.

It would be unprofessional for me not to accept Mr. Green's assurances that he and his co-counsel had no role in the dishonest creation of evidence. Perhaps he was unaware of what some of his clients' other representatives were up to. For example: on the same occasion when Mr. Buchan (who you may remember confessed to being solely in the pay of the companies) pressured Brown to sign the false affidavit, Buchan also dictated a letter, to be written from Brown and addressed to Sallie Hillmon. In it, Brown wrote "I would like to know where John is, and how that business is, and what I should do, if anything. Let me know through my father. Yours truly, John H. Brown." The letter was plainly designed to serve as evidence that Brown and the two Hillmons were united in a conspiracy, and for this purpose it was offered in each of the trials. But Brown said that he only wrote it to preserve himself from Buchan's threats of prosecution, and Buchan himself admitted that he never posted it to Mrs. Hillmon, but delivered it straight to the insurance companies. The companies were not strangers to the fabrication of evidence—epistolary evidence—that would serve their purposes.

I must also call your attention to the attempts of the defendants' lawyers, including Mr. Green, to explain the discrepancy between the name "Frederick Adolph Walters" and the name "Joe Burgis," the latter said to be the murder victim in the affidavit that Buchan coerced Brown into signing. In each trial until the last, Mr. Green and his co-counsel argued that Walters was simply traveling under an alias, and that Walters and "Joe" were one and the same. But in the last trial, the companies' agent Theodore Wiseman admitted that "Joe Burgess" was an actual person, another in the list of temporarily missing young men whose identities the defendants had sought to attach to the corpse. Moreover, Wiseman confessed that he had located this Joe Burgess quite alive not long after the affidavit was signed (and so notified his employers). Rather obviously, the defendants hoped at the time Buchan drafted the affidavit that young Mr. Burgess would remain missing. When he did not, and they later learned of the disappearance of Mr. Walters, they improvised the story of the "alias," and stuck to it for nearly twenty years even though they knew it to be false. What better proof could one hope for that the notorious affidavit was a product of Buchan's strategies, and not the truth? (Nor, I must say, must one look further for evidence that the defendants' lawyers were not all as saintly as Mr. Green would have you believe.)

Concerning the various Walters relatives who swore to the receipt of letters from Frederick Adolph mentioning John Hillmon—well, the human heart is not a scientific instrument and I will not pretend that I can explain these events with any certainty. I do know that not a single one of these "Hillmon" letters was ever produced except for the letter to Miss Kasten—they were all said to have been lost or mislaid (although many other letters from young Walters were found). And I am sure the companies persuaded the Walters family that the corpse photos did depict their lost loved one—as Judge Hook so wisely observed, this would not have been a difficult task (which is why the 20th century Supreme Court required that identifications in criminal prosecutions depend on lineups or photo arrays, not the manipulative display of a single photo to a group of distraught witnesses). Once thus persuaded, it would not be surprising if they began to remember that he had written to them something similar to the information he was claimed to have conveyed to his fiancée. And perhaps soon they became willing to say nearly anything if they thought it would succeed in denying the wicked Hillmons, whom they regarded as murderers, the proceeds of their terrible crime.

As for Miss Kasten, my heart goes out to her. It could not have been easy for her to acknowledge that she had been jilted by her betrothed, in favor of a life of travel and freedom. His murder by a scheming family of outlaws would have been a far less humiliating explanation. She was no doubt instructed that she would only have to lie once, harmlessly: she would say that she had received by post, shortly after the date of its postmark, a letter (unquestionably in her fiance's handwriting) that was in fact shown to her by the defendants' lawyers some months thereafter. Alvina may even have been told that the letter was intended for her, but that some mishap had prevented its timely delivery. A quick deposition given outside the presence of an intimidating judge, a modest refusal to travel to Kansas for any of the trials, and the deed was done: the criminals who had murdered her beloved would be thwarted. I do not blame her, but only those who, pretending sympathy, took advantage of her trusting nature.

I have imposed on your good nature for long enough, but before leaving you to deliberate on what you have learned, I ask that you take one further consideration into account. It is deplorable that the defendants in this matter succeeded for so long in depriving Sallie Hillmon of the funds her husband had taken pains to provide for her in the event of his death. But although they delayed this justice, she was victorious in the end. It is far more consequential that the companies' shenanigans, and the credulity of a Supreme Court that was easily misled into believing their version of the Hillmon affair, have left us with a highly questionable rule of evidence: the "state of mind" exception to hearsay rule. I believe you now refer to it as Federal Rule of Evidence 803(3). It represents a gravely misguided policy choice. Declarations of what one intends to do are notoriously unreliable guides to what one may actually do, as the fate of most New Year resolutions demonstrates. Moreover, this rule rests solely on the prestige of the *Hillmon* decision, which turned on the Court's desire to make the Alvina Kasten letter admissible: this is a frail foundation indeed. As for the letter for which this unwise rule was invented, it is full of lies from beginning to end, from the implicit declaration at its outset ("Today is March 1, 1879") to its professions of affection ("I am about as Anxious to see you as you are to see me") to its most important, and most prevaricating, words: "I am going with a man by the name of Hillmon." Frederick Adolph Walters never met John Hillmon, who was laying dead in Oak Hill Cemetery on the day those words were written.

Thank you for your attention.

6. The Verdict

Ladies and gentlemen of the jury, please retire to consider your verdict. Please let me know when you have decided whether the person who died by the side of Crooked Creek was John Hillmon or Frederick Walters.

7. Atwood's Contingent Motion for New Trial Based on Newly–Discovered Evidence

Plaintiff Sallie Hillmon, through her counsel of record John Atwood, hereby notifies the court and all counsel of her intention to move for a new trial based on newly-discovered evidence should the jury decide that the decedent was Frederick Walters. In support of the motion, plaintiff submits the following Declaration from Prof. Marianne Wesson:

With a colleague from the University of Colorado, in May of 2006 I undertook exhumation of the body buried in John Hillmon's grave in the Oak Hill Cemetery of Lawrence, Kansas. We had located a descendant in the direct male line of descent from John Hillmon's father; if DNA could be extracted from the remains, we hoped to be able to ascertain with some confidence whether the deceased was related to the descendant, Leray Hillmon. Unfortunately, deterioration related to the remains' long immersion in an underground stream has so far prevented the extraction of any human DNA from the bone fragment that we were permitted to retain from the exhumation.

After this disappointing outcome, my colleague Dennis Van Gerven, Professor of Anthropology, undertook a forensic examination of the facial features of the corpse and the two men, as displayed in photographs. The corpse was photographed in its coffin during the inquest in Lawrence, and photographs of the two men were also among the exhibits used in the trials. I was able to make digital copies of these photographs from the originals, located at the National Archives and Records Administration. Professor Van Gerven's full report is accessible at our website, www.thehillmoncase.com, but his conclusion can be briefly summarized: the dead man was not Walters, but there is a high likelihood that he was Hillmon.

4

Carol S. Steiker[1]

Darrow's Defense of Leopold and Loeb: The Seminal Sentencing of the Century

Nineteen-year-old Nathan ("Babe") Leopold, Jr., and eighteen-year-old Richard ("Dickie") Loeb brutally murdered fourteen-year-old Bobby Franks in Chicago in 1924. It is impossible, even in this media-saturated age, to overstate the attention lavished by the press—local, national, and even international—on the crime and the ensuing legal proceedings. The youth of the defendants and their victim, the great wealth and privilege of the defendants' families, the utter senselessness of the "thrill" killing, and the appearance of Clarence Darrow for the defense all conspired to earn the case the now familiar sobriquet of "the trial of the century." The Leopold–Loeb trial wasn't the first case of the 20th century to be considered a contender for this title (Sacco and Vanzetti had been tried three years earlier), and it certainly wasn't the last (think of the Lindberg baby kidnapping trial, or the trials of Julius and Ethel Rosenberg, Charles Manson, O.J. Simpson, or Timothy McVeigh, among many others). It wasn't even Clarence Darrow's only "trial of the century" or even of the decade—he went on to defend John Scopes in his "monkey trial" in Tennessee the very next year! But the hold of the case on the public's attention and imagination—then and now—cannot be gainsaid: it is testified to by the hordes who descended on the courtroom during the proceedings,[2] by the innumerable banner headlines that the case

---

[1] Howard J. and Katherine W. Aibel Professor of Law, Harvard Law School.

[2] *See* Orville Dwyer, *Riotous Crowds Battle Police to Hear Darrow*, Chi. Daily Tribune, Aug. 23, 1924, at 3.

produced in the newspapers,[3] and by the rich trove of books,[4] films,[5] plays,[6] websites,[7] and law review articles[8] produced in the 80–plus years since the case was resolved.

Despite its notoriety, the Leopold and Loeb case may seem an odd choice for inclusion in an edition of "Trial Stories," for two quite different reasons. First, given all the ink that has been spilled addressing various aspects of the case over the better part of a century, what is the point of revisiting it once more? Second, the case did not actually involve a trial—at least not in the conventional sense. Leopold and Loeb pled

---

[3] When Leopold and Loeb were arrested for the murder of Franks, the case made the front page of the New York Times three days in a row. *See Two Rich Students Confess to Killing Franks Boy in Car*, N.Y. Times, June 1, 1924, at § 1, at 1; *Student Slayers Accuse Each Other of Actual Killing*, N.Y. Times, June 2, 1924, at § 1, at 1; *Slayers of Franks Now Suspected in 2 More Crimes*, N.Y. Times, June 3, 1924, at § 1, at 1. Each phase of the trial yielded huge banner headlines in the Chicago Tribune. *See, e.g.,* Robert M. Lee, *Darrow Urges Life Terms*, Chi. Daily Tribune, Aug. 23, 1924, at 1; John Herrick, *Darrow Pleads for Parents*, Chi. Daily Tribune, Aug. 26, 1924, at 1; Orville Dwyer, *Slayers' Trial Ends Today*, Chi. Daily Tribune, Aug. 28, 1924, at 1.

[4] For some of the most thorough and frequently cited books about the case, see Clarence Darrow, The Story of My Life (1932); Hal Higdon, Leopold and Loeb: The Crime of the Century (1975); Maureen McKernan, The Amazing Crime and Trial of Leopold and Loeb (1924); Alvin V. Sellers, The Loeb–Leopold Case (1926); Kevin Tierney, Darrow: A Biography (1979); Arthur Weinberg & Lila Weinberg, Clarence Darrow: A Sentimental Rebel (1980).

[5] At least four feature-length films have been inspired by the case, some more factually based than others: Alfred Hitchcock's *Rope* (1948), Richard Fleischer's *Compulsion* (1959) (based on Meyer Levin's 1956 novel of the same name), Tom Kalin's *Swoon* (1992), and Barbara Schroeder's *Murder by Numbers* (2002).

[6] John Logan's play, *Never the Sinner: The Leopold & Loeb Story*, premiered in Chicago in 1985; Stephen Dolginoff's musical, *Thrill Me: The Leopold & Loeb Story*, premiered in New York in 2003.

[7] For some of the most complete websites, see Leigh Bienen, Homicide in Chicago, 1870–1930: Crimes of the Century: 1924: Leopold and Loeb, http://homicide.northwestern. edu/crimes/leopold/ (last visited March 28, 2007); Douglas Linder, Famous American Trials: Illinois v. Nathan Leopold and Richard Loeb, http://www.law.umkc.edu/faculty/projects/ ftrials/leoploeb/leopold.htm (last visited March 28, 2007); Scott A. Newman, The Leopold and Loeb Case of 1924, http://chicago.urban-history.org/scrapbks/leo_loeb/leo_loeb.htm (last visited March 28, 2007); Marianne Rackliffe, Leopold and Loeb, http://www.leopoldandloeb. com/ (last visited March 28, 2007).

[8] *See, e.g.,* Jonathan L. Entin, *Book Review: Using Great Cases to Think About the Criminal Justice System*, 89 J. Crim. L. & Criminology 1141 (1999) (reviewing Gilbert Geis & Leigh B. Bienen, Crimes of the Century: From Leopold and Loeb to O.J. Simpson (1998)); Scott W. Howe, *Reassessing the Individualization Mandate in Capital Sentencing: Darrow's Defense of Leopold and Loeb*, 79 Iowa L. Rev. 989 (1994); Gerald F. Uelman, *Symposium on Trials of the Century: Who is the Lawyer of the Century?*, 33 Loy. L.A. L. Rev. 613 (2000). The first treatment of the case in a law review was the publication of a symposium held just a few weeks after the sentencing of Leopold and Loeb, in which a panel of legal experts, including a judge, a death penalty prosecutor, and a criminal law scholar, commented on the case. See *A Symposium of Comments from the Legal Profession, in the Loeb–Leopold Murder of Franks in Chicago, May 21, 1924*, 15 J. Crim. L. & Criminology 347, 395–405 (1924).

guilty to the capital indictment, and Clarence Darrow focused all of his efforts on introducing evidence of the young men's backgrounds and mental states in order to plead for their lives before the sentencing judge. Yet it is precisely this latter feature of the case that answers the former question and calls for yet another look. On more recent reflection, Darrow's defense of Leopold and Loeb reveals itself not only as an exemplar of skillful legal strategy in a very difficult case, or as a masterful oratorical performance, but also as a stunning precursor of contemporary capital sentencing law and practice. Darrow's arguments about the relevance of his clients' youth to the judge's sentencing decision find themselves uncannily reproduced in the Supreme Court's recent decision declaring capital punishment for juvenile offenders unconstitutional under the Eighth Amendment.[9] Moreover, Darrow's insistence on the relevance of his clients' family backgrounds and mental states to the sentencing decision anticipated the Supreme Court's general constitutional insistence on individualized capital sentencing under the Eighth Amendment,[10] as well as its more particular recent holdings rejecting capital defense lawyers' decisions to forego careful investigation of their clients' social histories as "ineffective assistance of counsel" in violation of the Sixth Amendment.[11] Darrow's litigation and oratorical strategies in his defense of Leopold and Loeb now bear the imprimatur of the Supreme Court as constitutional *essentials* in capital cases. Moreover, the skills that Darrow applied to the case in his capacity as all-purpose criminal defense lawyer have become professionalized in the person of the "mitigation specialist" now routinely used in capital trials and, indeed, required by the ABA's Guidelines for the Appointment and Performance of Defense Counsel in Death Penalty Cases, most recently revised in 2003.[12]

If one measure of how "memorable" or "great" a long-ago trial was is its capacity to speak to the administration of justice today, then Darrow's performance in defense of Leopold and Loeb richly deserves such description. My goal here is to revisit the aspects of Darrow's defense that preview the development of modern death penalty law and practice. In doing so, I hope both to uncover the early roots of what is now accepted by the Supreme Court as mandated by "evolving standards

---

[9] *See* Roper v. Simmons, 543 U.S. 551 (2005).

[10] *See* Woodson v. North Carolina, 428 U.S. 280 (1976); Lockett v. Ohio, 438 U.S. 586 (1978); Eddings v. Oklahoma, 455 U.S. 104 (1982).

[11] *See* Williams v. Taylor, 529 U.S. 362 (2000); Wiggins v. Smith, 539 U.S. 510 (2003); Rompilla v. Beard, 545 U.S. 374 (2005).

[12] *See American Bar Association Guidelines for the Appointment and Performance of Defense Counsel in Death Penalty Cases*, 31 Hofstra L. Rev. 913 (2003).

of decency that mark the progress of a maturing society"[13] and to reflect upon Darrow's strategy and oratory in light of current understandings of the requirements of effective representation in capital cases. Lest we get too smugly celebratory—either of Darrow's brilliance and humanity or of our own "progress" as "a maturing society"—I will conclude with consideration of some of the substantial ironies that attend the apotheosis of Darrow's Leopold and Loeb strategy.

I. Darrow's Defense of Leopold and Loeb

A. The Crime, Investigation, and Guilty Plea[14]

Bobby Franks was murdered on May 21, 1924. At the time, Nathan Leopold was a nineteen-year-old recent graduate of University of Chicago, who was planning to study law at Harvard in the fall. Richard Loeb was an eighteen-year-old recent graduate of the University of Michigan—the youngest in its history—who was planning to study law at the University of Chicago in the fall. Both young men were from wealthy and prominent Jewish families who lived in impressive homes on the South Side of Chicago; both were academically gifted and precocious, having graduated from college at ages when it was more common for students to be graduating from high school. For several years before the murder, the two forged an intense friendship, as well as an episodic clandestine sexual relationship. Together they planned the commission of the kidnapping and murder over several months, debating the choice of victim (considering and discarding on practical grounds the possibility of killing one of their own family members), scouting for a place to dispose of the body, and even drafting and typing the ransom letter before the identity of the victim was chosen.

Eventually, the two decided to let the victim choose himself (it was definitely to be a "he," as girls were too closely watched to make easy targets): they decided to see who was available for quick snatching in the neighborhood on the afternoon of the planned crime. As it turned out, Bobby Franks—a fourteen-year-old distant cousin of Loeb—was on his way home from school (the same expensive private school that Leopold himself had attended) when he was lured into a rented car by Loeb and Leopold. Although the two defendants each insisted that the other did the actual killing, they both acknowledged and medical evidence confirmed that Bobby Franks was killed by some combination of repeated blows to the head with a chisel and suffocation (a gag was stuffed into the victim's mouth). Leopold and Loeb covered the bleeding body with a blanket brought along for that purpose, drove out into the country—

---

[13] See, e.g., Simmons, 543 U.S. at 561 (quoting Trop v. Dulles, 356 U.S. 86, 100–101 (1958)).

[14] The description of events that follows is a summary drawn from the detailed accounts of Hidgon, supra note 3, and McKernan, supra note 3.

stopping for dinner along the way—and then disposed of the body in a culvert previously selected on their scouting excursion.

Leopold and Loeb went to great lengths to prevent discovery. They stripped Bobby Franks' body and poured acid on it to impede identification, before secreting it in the culvert. They hid the blood-soaked blanket in some bushes, burned the bloody clothes in Loeb's basement, tried to wash the bloodstains out of the rented car in Leopold's garage, and tossed the chisel out of the car window. They called the Franks family on the evening of the murder and told them that their son was kidnapped but safe and that they should look for further news in the morning. In the morning, the typed ransom letter was delivered directing Mr. Franks to assemble $10,000 in ransom and to wait at home for further instructions by telephone. Later in the day, Leopold and Loeb called the Franks residence directing Mr. Franks to bring the ransom to a drugstore (where they planned to leave further directions for him that would eventually instruct him to throw the ransom money from a moving train). Before Franks could comply, Bobby's body had been found and identified. The hunt for the murderers began.

Despite the intelligence of its perpetrators and the care they took not to be caught, the case was solved quite quickly. Attention first focused on Leopold when he was identified as someone who frequented the area where the body was found (he was an avid bird watcher). Then, some eyeglasses that had been found near Bobby Franks' body were identified after careful inspection as one of only three such pairs sold in the Chicago area—one of which was purchased by a Nathan Leopold, Jr. The police brought in Leopold and his constant companion Loeb for questioning, and at first they gave conflicting accounts of what they had been doing on the day of the murder, now more than a week earlier. As police suspicions mounted, the typewritten ransom letter was found to match exactly—down to a twisted "i" key—the typing on "dope sheets" (law school study notes) prepared at Nathan Leopold's home. Finally, Leopold's chauffeur contradicted Leopold and Loeb's eventually convergent story that they had been out picking up girls in Leopold's car on the day of the murder; rather, the chauffeur stated unequivocally that Leopold's car had remained in the garage all afternoon, and that the young men had arrived at the house in a different, unfamiliar car (the rented one).

When confronted with the chauffeur's repudiation of a key piece of their alibi, Loeb broke first and offered a confession to the State's Attorney. Although Leopold remained steadfast when confronted with the chauffeur's statement, the revelation that Loeb had confessed and implicated him galvanized Leopold's own confession. The two confessions together established unequivocally the joint guilt of the two defendants in the kidnapping and murder scheme, though each continued to insist that it was the other who had actually killed Bobby Franks. On May 31, 1924, the Chicago papers reported the breaking news that Leopold and Loeb had confessed, and the Chicago *Herald and Examiner* reported the following day that it had distributed 100,000 copies of the confession "extra" in ten minutes flat in front of the Hearst building.[15]

The case moved as quickly as the news of it: Leopold and Loeb were indicted by a grand jury less than a week after their confessions and arraigned on June 11, represented jointly by Clarence Darrow and Benjamin Bachrach, two of most renowned criminal defense lawyers in Chicago.[16] At their very next court appearance, on July 21, Leopold and Loeb pled guilty to the indictment—that is, to murder and kidnapping, exposing themselves to a maximum punishment of death by hanging and to a minimum punishment of fourteen years of imprisonment. Although the guilty pleas apparently "were a great surprise to everyone,"[17] it seems hardly a surprising move in hindsight for the defense to forego a jury trial. The evidence against the defendants was overwhelming, and a jury was bound to find highly unsympathetic such rich and remorseless murderers, who killed so randomly and senselessly (even apart from their Jewishness and the sexual overtones of the case, which might have elicited even further contempt).

The only remotely plausible defense that could have been mounted was an insanity defense, which would have required demonstrating that the defendants either did not know the nature of their actions (that is, did not know what they were doing) or did not know that their actions were wrong. Given the defendants' intelligence, education, and extensive statements to the press and the police, such a defense would have been doomed, as Darrow knew from the outset.[18] Instead, Darrow had his clients plead guilty promptly in hopes of preventing the prosecution from severing the murder and kidnapping charges in order to seek two separate convictions and death sentences (each was independently a capital offense).[19] Then, Darrow sought to introduce evidence of his clients' backgrounds and psychological states to urge a life sentence from the judge for the single (though compound) guilty plea. Illinois law required both that the State prove the elements of the crime, even after the acceptance of a guilty plea, and that the judge consider evidence in aggravation or mitigation of the offense. It was in this trial-like proceed-

---

[15] Higdon, *supra* note 4, at 112 (citing Chicago *Herald and Examiner*, June 1, 1924).

[16] Benjamin Bachrach's brother, Walter, joined the defense team the following month; the Bachrach brothers were cousins of the Loebs, and Darrow was an old family friend.

[17] McKernan, *supra* note 4, at 76.

[18] See Darrow, *supra* note 4, at 234–37.

[19] *Id.* at 236–37.

ing that Darrow hoped to make his case for sparing the lives of Leopold and Loeb. He faced a formidable opponent in State's Attorney Robert Crowe, who gave a statement to the press immediately following the defendants' guilty plea: "There is but one punishment that will satisfy the prosecution—that they be hanged!"[20]

B. The Presentation of Evidence in Mitigation

The "trial" began only two days later, on July 23, 1924. Over the course of the following week, the State offered its proof of the crime through the examination of around eighty witnesses. Their detailed testimony overwhelmingly met the State's burden of proving the elements of the offense, and the defense engaged in very little cross-examination. On July 30, the State rested its case, and the defense began the introduction of its testimony. At this point, the novelty and brilliance of Darrow's strategy became clear: his plan was to introduce the kind of mental state evidence that might have been offered in support of an insanity defense before a jury, but to use it instead to urge the sentencing judge to return a sentence less than death.

Darrow's attempt to convert the all-or-nothing issue of sanity into a question of degree of culpability (or "mitigation") was entirely unprecedented[21] and immediately contested by the State. As Crowe, the State's Attorney, insisted: "[T]hey are attempting to show degrees of responsibility. There is nothing in law known as degrees of responsibility. You are either entirely responsible for all the consequences of your act, or you are not responsible at all."[22] Crowe demanded that evidence about the defendants' mental state could be relevant only to a defense of insanity "and ought to be submitted to the jury."[23] In response, Darrow insisted that he was not contesting his clients' legal sanity; rather, he was seeking to introduce evidence of their mental condition—indeed, of their "mental disease"—that would not be sufficient for an insanity defense but that was still relevant to the proper sentence. He argued: "[E]vidence falling short of a competent legal defense is a circumstance which this court may take into consideration and should, in determining the punishment to be meted out to these defendants in the exercise of the discretion conferred upon the court by the statute."[24]

---

[20] Higdon, *supra* note 4, at 167 (quoting Chicago *Tribune*, July 22, 1924).

[21] "Never before had evidence of a defendant's mental condition been offered to lessen a sentence. Such evidence had heretofore been used exclusively to show that a defendant was insane, not responsible for his actions, and thus not subject to punishment." Higdon, *supra* note 4, at 164.

[22] McKernan, *supra* note 4, at 79.

[23] *Id.*

[24] *Id.* at 80.

The argument between the prosecution and the defense over the relevance and admissibility of evidence of the defendants' mental condition continued for three days, culminating in the following ruling by the court:

> [U]nder that section of the statute which gives the court the right and says that it is his duty to hear evidence in mitigation as well as evidence in aggravation the court is of the opinion that it is his duty to hear any evidence that the defense may present, and it is not for the court to decide in advance what it may be.[25]

The judge didn't promise anything about what he might make of the defense evidence, stating only: "The court will hear it and give it such weight as he thinks it is entitled to."[26]

The defense had hired some of the most famous psychological experts (then referred to as "alienists") of the time to examine Leopold and Loeb. Anticipating an insanity defense, the prosecution had preemptively hired several of the best-known local experts to attest to the sanity of the defendants immediately after obtaining their confessions. Thus, for better or worse, the defense turned to national experts from Washington, New York, and Boston. The remainder of the Leopold and Loeb trial essentially became a contest between the defense alienists and the State's alienists.[27] Defense experts prepared two detailed reports on the defendants' backgrounds and mental states, reprinted in their entirety ("except for the unprintable matter") in McKernan's account of case.[28] One report was prepared jointly by Dr. William A. White, Superintendent of St. Elizabeth's Hospital in Washington, D.C.; Dr. William Healy, director of the Judge Baker Foundation in Boston, and former director of the Juvenile Psychopathic Institute in Chicago; Dr. Bernard Glueck, formerly director of the Psychopathic Clinic of Sing Sing prison, and of the Bureau of Children's Guidance in New York City; and Dr. Ralph C. Hamill, a neuropsychiatrist from Chicago. Three of these noted experts testified for the defense at trial, though their written report was not introduced into evidence. An earlier and even more exhaustively detailed report was prepared by two other experts, Dr. H.S. Hulbert, a neuropsychiatrist in private practice in Chicago, and Dr. Karl M. Bowman, chief

---

[25] *Id.*

[26] Higdon, *supra* note 4, at 193.

[27] Indeed, it was so clear from the outset that the mental state of the defendants would be the central issue in the case that the leading newspapers in Chicago had sought to bring Sigmund Freud himself from Europe to examine Leopold and Loeb. William Randolph Hearst personally approached Freud and offered him any amount to come to the United States, even volunteering to charter a special liner for his trip. Freud declined all such offers, citing his health. *Id.* at 139–40.

[28] McKernan, *supra* note 4, at 82 (quote), 83–163 (reports).

of staff of the Psychopathic Hospital in Boston and lecturer at Harvard Medical School. Dr. Hulbert also testified at the trial, and his report was entered into evidence—constituting nearly three hundred pages of official transcript and forming the centerpiece of Darrow's defense.[29]

The reports and the testimony of the defense alienists painted a portrait of two very disturbed young men, interweaving both medical and psychological observations in a striking mixture of "hard" and "soft" science. The doctors noted early head injuries sustained by "Dickie" Loeb and the repeated fainting spells that ensued; they went on to describe how Loeb reacted to an overly strict governess by becoming a skilled and pathological liar. Loeb also developed an intense fantasy life around detective stories, imagining himself as a criminal mastermind. Noted Dr. White at trial: "There is a tendency for the fantasy life, an abnormal fantasy life, to realize itself in reality."[30] Dr. White testified that Loeb was "still a little child emotionally" and estimated that his emotional age (and that of Leopold as well) is "anywhere from five to seven, perhaps."[31] Dr. Healey described Loeb's mental condition as decidedly abnormal: "To my mind the crime itself is the direct result of the diseased motivation of Loeb's mental life. The planning and commission was only possible because he was abnormal mentally, with a pathological split personality."[32] Dr. Glueck described himself as "amazed by the absolute absence of any signs of normal feelings" from Loeb in describing the crime and concluded that "the whole thing became incomprehensible to me except on the basis of a disordered personality."[33] Dr. Hulbert linked Loeb's mental disorder to what he observed be a disorder of the endocrine glands: "My opinion is that the man in not normal physically or mentally, and there is a close relation between his physical abnormalities . . . and his mental condition." The doctor concluded: "The discrepancy between his judgment and his emotions on the one hand, and his intellectual attainments on the other hand, is a greater discrepancy than we find in normal persons and therefore I am forced to conclude that he is mentally diseased."[34]

The defense alienists emphasized different aspects of "Babe" Leopold's upbringing and personality, noting his inappropriate sexual relationship with his governess as a child, his feelings of physical inferiority coupled with his strong sense of mental superiority, and the death of his

---

[29] Higdon, *supra* note 4, at 147.

[30] *Id.* at 208.

[31] *Id.* at 212.

[32] *Id.* at 217.

[33] *Id.*

[34] *Id.* at 224.

mother when he was teenager. Dr. White described Leopold's fascination with the philosophy of Friedrich Nietzsche, especially the idea of the Nietzschean "superman" or *Übermensch* standing above the rules and conventions that lesser beings must obey. White also noted Leopold's obsession with king-slave fantasies and described how he and Loeb played out these fantasies, with Leopold playing the role of Loeb's abject, though powerful slave. Dr. Healy described a sexual compact between the defendants, in which Leopold agreed to help Loeb carry out his criminal ideas in return for Loeb's submitting to Leopold's sexual advances. A long history of undetected joint criminal activity by the two defendants was detailed in the Hulbert and Bowman report, including incidents of theft, burglary, and arson. Dr. Healy concluded that Leopold, like Loeb, was "mentally diseased" and went on to explain that Leopold had "a paranoid personality . . . an established pathological personality before he met Loeb."[35] Dr. Glueck also emphasized the relationship between the two defendants as key to understanding their crime: "I think the Franks crime was perhaps the inevitable outcome of this curious coming together of two pathologically disordered personalities. . . ."[36] Dr. Hulbert emphasized the same theme: "The psychiatric cause for this [crime] is not to be found in either boy alone, but in the interplay or interweaving of their two personalities. . . ."[37]

The State's alienists, of course, presented a very different picture of the defendants' mental states. Within a day of Leopold and Loeb's confessions, the prosecution had the defendants examined by a trio of local specialists: Dr. Hugh T. Patrick, a past president of the American Neurological Association and professor emeritus at Northwestern University Medical School; Dr. Archibald Church, author of a well-know textbook on mental illness and head of the department of nervous and mental diseases at Northwestern; and Dr. William O. Krohn, also a published expert in private practice in Chicago. The three doctors testified after the defense alienists and expressed their opinions that the defendants showed no evidence of mental disease, notwithstanding the testimony and of the defense alienists and the report of Hulbert and Bowman. The doctors emphasized that the defendants were "entirely oriented"[38] and demonstrated good powers of memory and logic. They explained that having fantasies is entirely normal: "Phantasies are day dreams. Everybody has them."[39] As the State's first expert bluntly

---

[35] *Id.* at 216.

[36] *Id.* at 218.

[37] *Id.* at 225.

[38] *Id.* at 228 (meaning that they knew who they were, where they were, and when it was) (testimony of Dr. Church).

[39] McKernan, *supra* note 4, at 183 (testimony of Dr. Church).

concluded, one couldn't draw an inference of mental disease from the evidence presented

> unless we assume that every man who commits a deliberate, cold-blooded, planned murder, must, by that fact, be mentally diseased. There was no evidence of any mental disease ... in any of the statements the boys made regarding it, or their earlier experiences; there was nothing in the examination; there were no mental obliquities or peculiarities shown, except their lack of appreciation of the enormity of the deed which they had committed.[40]

C. The Plea for Life

After the State's rebuttal testimony of its alienists, the evidentiary portion of the trial was over, and it was time for arguments to the court. The State had the opportunity for both an opening argument and a rebuttal. Assistant State's Attorneys Thomas Marshall and Joseph Savage jointly made the State's opening, each one's speech spanning two days of court proceedings. Marshall argued that "there is but one penalty that is proportionate to the turpitude of this crime"[41] and cited numerous prior cases in which the death penalty had been imposed, even on teenagers, despite judicial discretion to grant mercy. Savage reviewed the facts of the case and argued that mercy was wholly inappropriate for such heinous murderers, exhorting the judge, "Hang them! Hang these heartless supermen!"[42] Walter Bachrach spoke first and quite briefly on behalf of the defendants, but it was Darrow from whom everyone was waiting to hear: a veritable "tidal wave of men and women" poured into Court on Friday, August 22, to hear his plea for his clients' lives.[43]

By all accounts, Darrow's two long days of oratory on behalf of Leopold and Loeb constituted a brilliant and moving performance, judged by many to be the best of his career.[44] Darrow wept as he

---

[40] *Id.* at 171–72 (testimony of Dr. Patrick).

[41] *Id.* at 306.

[42] Higdon, *supra* note 4, at 233.

[43] *Id.* at 234 (quoting Chicago *Daily News*, August 22, 1924). The full text of Darrow's argument is *available* in McKernan, *supra* note 4, at 213–305, and on line at Douglas Linder, Famous American Trials: Illinois v. Nathan Leopold and Richard Loeb, http://www. law.umkc.edu/faculty/projects/ftrials/leoploeb/darrowclosing.html (last visited March 28, 2007).

[44] *Id.* at 235. Alan Dershowitz describes the Leopold and Loeb case as Darrow's best achievement in his introduction to the 1996 edition of Darrow's autobiography. *See* Clarence Darrow, The Story of My Life xi (Da Capo Press 1996). Elsewhere, however, Dershowitz floats the possibility, without offering much evidence for this speculation, that Darrow paid off the judge: "Despite Darrow's brilliant and compelling advocacy, the distinct possibility remains that he enhanced its receptivity to this Chicago judge through bribery." Alan M. Dershowitz, America on Trial 261 (2004).

concluded his impassioned argument, and the judge's eyes were wet as well. Perhaps most astonishingly, Darrow's plea moved even Loeb himself to tears—he who had shown so little emotion during his confession and psychological evaluations and who had joked and snickered throughout much of the trial.[45] Darrow gestured and shouted, paced and whispered; he quoted poetry from A.E. Housman and from Omar Khayyám. But the core of Darrow's argument was two central points: Leopold and Loeb's youth and their disturbed mental state. As Darrow crisply put it, dismissing the prosecution's contention that the defendants were motivated by greed: "It was not money. It was the senseless act of immature and diseased children."[46]

Darrow began emphasizing the importance of the defendants' youth long before his closing argument. In arguing to the judge that he should be allowed latitude to introduce testimony in "mitigation" of the offense, Darrow asked rhetorically, "Is youth a mitigating circumstance?"[47] Yes, argued Darrow:

> Simply because the child has not the judgment of life that a grown person has. . . . [W]e have all been young, and we know that fantasies and vagaries haunt the daily life of a child. We know the dream world we live in. We know that nothing is real. We know the lack of appreciation. We know the condition of the mind of a child. Here are two boys who are minors. The law would forbid them making contracts, forbid them marrying without the consent of their parents, would not permit them to vote. Why? Because they haven't that judgment which only comes with years, because they are not fully responsible.[48]

Darrow returned repeatedly to the issue of his clients' youth in his closing argument, almost always describing them as "children," "boys," or "lads." First, he sought to establish that it was exceedingly rare for defendants as young as Leopold and Loeb to be sentenced to death, arguing that "never had there been a case in Chicago, where on a plea of guilty a boy under twenty-one had been sentenced to death."[49] Indeed, Darrow was willing hazard that no one under twenty-*three* had been executed on a guilty plea in the entire state of Illinois.[50] Darrow mocked the prosecutors and the State's alienists for supporting the execution of

---

[45] Robert M. Lee, *Darrow Urges Life Terms*, Chi. Daily Tribune, Aug. 23, 1924, at 1.

[46] Higdon, *supra* note 4, at 237.

[47] *Id.* at 191.

[48] *Id.*

[49] McKernan, *supra* note 4, at 214.

[50] *Id.*

"a child if he was barely out of his cradle" if "he knew the difference between right and wrong."[51] Darrow wished aloud for a "real" psychiatrist "who knows the misfortunes of youth, who knows the stress and the strain of adolescence which comes to every boy and overpowers so many, who knows the weird fantastic world that hedges around the life of a child...."[52] Darrow called upon the judge to remember his own childhood and asked, "What do we know about childhood?" He answered himself:

> The brain of the child is the home of dreams, of castles, of visions, of illusions and of delusions. In fact, there could be no childhood without delusions, for delusions are always more alluring than facts. Delusions, dreams and hallucinations are a part of the warp and woof of childhood. You know it and I know it.... Before I would tie a noose around the neck of a boy I would try to call back into my mind the emotions of youth.... I would try to remember how strong were these instinctive, persistent emotions that moved my life. I would try to remember how weak and inefficient was youth in the presence of the surging, controlling feelings of the child.[53]

Darrow addressed the powerful effect of adolescent sexuality, as well: "Both these boys ... are in the most trying period of the life of a child ... when the call of sex is new and strange."[54] Darrow explained: "From the age of fifteen to the age of twenty or twenty-one, the child has the burden of adolescence, of puberty and sex thrust upon him."[55]

Toward the end of his plea, Darrow insisted that "progress" and "humanity" were on his side, and predicted that "if there is any humanity that is working in the hearts of men, some day men would look back upon this as a barbarous age which deliberately set itself in the way of progress."[56] Darrow asserted confidently, "I know the future is on my side. Your Honor stands between the past and the future."[57]

Darrow spent even more time in his closing argument on Leopold and Loeb's backgrounds and mental conditions, and he emphasized how their diseased minds interacted with their youth to produce their senseless crime. Noting the irrationality of their plan, Darrow insisted: "[N]o one, unless he had an afflicted mind, together with youth, could possibly

---

[51] Id. at 215.

[52] Id. at 258.

[53] Id. at 263, 265.

[54] Id. at 266.

[55] Id. at 267.

[56] Id. at 298.

[57] Id. at 304.

have done it."[58] Long before his closing argument, during his argument
for the admissibility of the defense alienists' testimony on the issue of
mitigation, Darrow insisted to the judge that evidence of the defendants'
disturbed mental states was entirely relevant to the sentencing decision
"as a matter of humanity, as a matter of common justice."[59] Darrow
elaborated extensively on this theme in his plea.

He repeated in various ways his central contention that "[t]here is
not a single act in this case that is not the act of a diseased mind, not
one."[60] Darrow asked the judge to imagine whether a "normal" boy
could have committed the crime at issue: "I might just as well ask you
whether you thought the sun could shine at midnight in this latitude. It
is not a part of normality. Something was wrong."[61] Darrow painstaking-
ly called up the details of each defendant's upbringing and obsessions
and then defied the court to blame Loeb or Leopold for their ensuing
behavior. "Who is to blame?" asked Darrow, in his rhetorical mode. "He
did not make himself."[62]

Darrow dismissed the conclusions of the State's alienists that the
defendants were not mentally ill as biased, based on inadequate examinations of the defendants, and even insincere.[63] The defense alienists,
Darrow argued, had done thorough examinations and had put before the
court "the story, the sad, pitiful story, of the unfortunate minds of these
young lads."[64] This "pitiful story" lay at the root of the defendants'
crime, insisted Darrow, and it lessened—indeed, eradicated—their responsibility for it. "[H]umanity has been at work ... and intelligent
people now know that every human being is the product of the endless
heredity back of him and the infinite environment around him."[65] True
humanity and intelligence, according to Darrow, not only should lead us
to the conclusion that Leopold and Loeb did not deserve to hang for their
crime, but also should require us to give up trying to determine what
people deserve:

---

[58] *Id.* at 231.

[59] *Id.* at 192.

[60] *Id.* at 243.

[61] *Id.* at 255.

[62] *Id.* at 267, 266.

[63] "Could there be any doubt, your Honor, but what both those witnesses, Church and
Singer, or any doubt but what Patrick would have testified for us?" *Id.* at 287. Only Krohn
did Darrow dismiss as a bloodthirsty monster, who savored sending the defendants to the
gallows the way boys enjoy devouring watermelon. *Id.* at 257–58.

[64] *Id.* at 290.

[65] *Id.* at 254.

To hear young men talk glibly of justice. Well, it would make me smile if it did not make me sad. Who knows what it is? ... Does your Honor know? Is there any human machinery for finding it out? Is there any man can weigh me and say what I deserve? ... Let us be honest. Can your Honor appraise yourself and say what you deserve? Can your Honor appraise these two young men and say what they deserve?[66]

After Darrow's long and emotional appeal, Benjamin Bachrach spoke briefly on behalf of the defendants, breaking no new ground. The case concluded with a long and frenzied appeal in rebuttal argument from State's Attorney Crowe. Soaked with sweat as he shouted, Crowe derided the defense alienists as "three wise men from the east,"[67] disdained the concepts of "aggravation" and "mitigation" as "strange, foreign words,"[68] assailed the defendants as "perverts" who perhaps had raped Bobby Franks along with murdering him,[69] and attacked Darrow's "dangerous philosophy of life."[70] Innocent young men were sent to die on fields of Flanders, argued Crowe, so how could the court declare that Leopold and Loeb were too young to die for their crimes?

D.   The Sentencing

Judge John R. Caverly took the case under advisement until September 10. On that day, he rendered his judgment, sentencing Leopold and Loeb to life imprisonment for the murder of Bobby Franks and to ninety-nine years for the kidnapping. The court noted the "profound and unusual interest"[71] that the case had provoked and explained the reasons for his sentence. The sole reason that the judge offered for foregoing the death penalty was the youth of the defendants:

> ... In choosing imprisonment instead of death, the court is moved chiefly by the consideration of the ages of the defendants, boys of 18 and 19 years.
>
> It is not for the court to say that he will not, in any case, enforce capital punishment as an alternative, but the court believes that it is within his province to decline to impose the sentence of death on persons who are not of full age.

---

[66] *Id.* at 240

[67] *Id.* at 312.

[68] *Id.* at 318.

[69] Higdon, *supra* note 4, at 244–45. This racy speculation led the judge to temporarily clear the ladies from the courtroom. *Id.*

[70] *Id.* at 247.

[71] McKernan, *supra* note 4, at 376.

This determination appears to be in accordance with the progress of criminal law all over the world and with the dictates of
enlightened humanity. More than that, it seems to be in accordance
with the precedents hitherto observed in this State. . . .[72]

As for Darrow's elaborate psychiatric case in mitigation, the court
carefully acknowledged its persuasiveness and interest, but then put it
firmly aside:

The court . . . feels impelled to dwell briefly on the mass of data
produced as the physical, mental, and moral condition of the two
defendants. They have been shown in essential respects to abnormal; had they been normal they would not have committed the
crime. . . .

At the same time, the court is willing to recognize that the
careful analysis made of the life history of the defendants and of
their present mental, emotional and ethical condition has been of
extreme interest and is a valuable contribution to criminology. And
yet the court feels strong that similar analyses made of other
persons accused of crime will probably reveal similar or different
abnormalities. The value of such tests seems to lie in their applica-
bility to crime and criminals in general.

Since they concern the broad question of human responsibility
and legal punishment and are in no wise peculiar to the individual
defendants, they may be deserving of legislative but not of judicial
consideration. *For this reason the court is satisfied that his judgment
in the present case cannot be affected thereby.*[73]

The court went on to suggest that the parole board ensure that Leopold
and Loeb never be paroled for their crimes in order to "satisfy the ends
of justice and safeguard the interests of society."[74]

Darrow had won his battle for his clients' lives. He did so by
winning the battle about the significance of his clients' youth in the
sentencing decision. But Darrow lost the bigger battle about the significance of social background and mental condition to criminal culpability.
Indeed, according the judge, the entire contest of the alienists—as time-
consuming and expensive as it was—was nothing but a pointless diver-
sion. On the broader battlefield of legal doctrine and practice over time,

---

[72] *Id.* at 379. Later, Leopold wryly commented that "the herculean efforts of our
brilliant counsel were of no avail . . . we need only have introduced our birth certificates in
evidence!" Higdon, *supra* note 4 at 266 (quoting Nathan Leopold, Jr., Life Plus 99 Years
(1958) at 82).

[73] McKernan, *supra* note 4, at 378 (emphasis added).

[74] *Id.* at 380.

however, both of Darrow's arguments won decisively, at least within the special legal regime that governs capital punishment.

II. Modern Death Penalty Law and Practice

A. The Abolition of the Death Penalty for Juvenile Offenders

For years, Darrow's ringing invocation of Leopold and Loeb's youth as a reason to spare their lives was quoted by those who called for an end to the execution of juvenile offenders.[75] Such calls occasionally succeeded before individual sentencing judges and juries, and before state legislatures who raised the minimum age for execution, but the practice of executing juvenile offenders was not abolished until 2005, when the Supreme Court declared it unconstitutional under the Eighth Amendment's proscription of "cruel and unusual punishments." The terms of the Supreme Court's constitutional analysis were remarkably similar to the arguments Darrow had made 81 years previously. This victory is stunning, both in its national breadth and its absoluteness: constitutional law now mandates not only that capital sentencers in every jurisdiction must consider the youth of offenders in determining the appropriate sentence, but also that formal status as a juvenile (under 18 at the time of the offense) absolutely precludes the imposition of the death penalty.

Such a ruling was slow in coming. When the Supreme Court first "constitutionalized" the administration of capital punishment,[76] it required that a capital defendant's youth be considered by the sentencing judge or jury—but not that it be specifically identified as a relevant factor. The Court upheld, twice, the Texas capital punishment scheme[77] —responsible for the execution of most of the juvenile offenders executed in recent decades[78]—which asked the sentencing jury only whether the defendant acted "deliberately" and whether the defendant was likely to pose a "danger" in the future.[79] Answers of "yes" mandated the imposi-

---

[75] See, e.g., Lisa Kline Arnett, Death at an Early Age: International Law Arguments Against the Death Penalty for Juveniles, 57 U. Cin. L. Rev. 245, 245 (1988) (quoting Darrow's plea); Dershowitz, supra note 43, at 260 (quoting Darrow's plea and adding: "I wonder if we would still be executing 'boys and girls' if we had a Clarence Darrow today who could appeal with his eloquence to the evolving historical conscience of our Constitution, and not just to its dry words.").

[76] See infra Part II.B. The Constitutional Requirement of Individualized Sentencing.

[77] See Penry v. Lynaugh, 492 U.S. 302 (1989); Johnson v. Texas, 509 U.S. 350 (1993).

[78] Indeed, in the "modern era" of capital sentencing (from 1976 to the present), Texas has executed more juveniles than all the other states put together (13 in Texas, as compared to 9 in the rest of the states combined). See Death Penalty Information Center: Juvenile Offenders Executed, by State, 1976–2005, at http://www.deathpenaltyinfo.org/article.php? scid=27 & did=882 (last visited March 28, 2007).

[79] At one point, the statute also asked the jury to determine whether there had been any provocation from the victim. The current, revised version of the Texas statute does not

tion of the death penalty. The Court reasoned that consideration of a defendant's youth could be afforded adequate consideration under this "special issues" scheme, given that youthful offenders will inevitably outgrow their youth, thus rendering it relevant to the question of their future dangerousness.

Moreover, the Supreme Court twice rejected arguments that the execution of all juvenile offenders was constitutionally forbidden. In 1987 in Thompson v. Oklahoma,[80] a plurality of the Court concluded that "civilized standards of decency"[81] did not permit the execution of offenders aged 15 or younger, but the majority of the Court declined to extend that holding to offenders older than 15. Two years later, the Court held the line permitting executions of those over 15: in Stanford v. Kentucky,[82] a majority of the Court reasoned that executions of offenders aged 16 and 17 were neither as rare as those of offenders aged 15 or younger, nor rejected by anything that could be deemed a national consensus. The Justices of the *Thompson* plurality dissented vociferously in *Stanford*, urging that the juvenile death penalty had been rejected by legislatures, juries, expert organizations, and other nations. The dissenters invoked the lesser moral culpability of juveniles and the failure of the execution of juvenile offenders to make any measurable contribution to acceptable goals of punishment.

Thirteen years later, the tides shifted again, and a different majority of the Supreme Court in Roper v. Simmons[83] adopted and expanded the arguments of the *Stanford* dissenters—and Darrow—to reject the death penalty for any offender under the age of 18. Just as Darrow had argued that no other judges had sentenced youthful offenders to death in Chicago,[84] the Supreme Court looked to the sentencing decisions of juries and the age limits set by state legislators in order to determine whether a consensus existed against the practice of sentencing juveniles to death. Both arguments—Darrow's and the Court's—about "consensus" were rather tendentious and reveal the inherent contestability of the concept.

---

contain the provocation question but does contain a more general question asking whether "taking into consideration all of the evidence, including the circumstances of the offense, the defendant's character and background, and the personal moral culpability of the defendant, there is a sufficient mitigating circumstance or circumstances to warrant that a sentence of life imprisonment rather than a death sentence be imposed." Tex. Code Crim. Proc. art. 37.071 (2006).

[80] 487 U.S. 815 (1988).

[81] *Id.* at 830.

[82] 492 U.S. 361 (1989).

[83] 543 U.S. 551 (2005).

[84] "[N]ever had there been a case in Chicago, where on a plea of guilty a boy under twenty-one had been sentenced to death." McKernan, *supra* note 4, at 214.

Darrow sought to limit the universe of past practice to youthful offenders *who had pled guilty* and to the city of Chicago, thus enabling him to
lower the tally of youthful offenders executed to zero. The Court counted
the 12 jurisdictions that had abolished the death penalty entirely as
jurisdictions that rejected the death penalty for juveniles, thus making
the count 30 to 20 against the practice (rather than 20 to 18 in favor of
the practice among states that authorized the death penalty).[85] In his
scathing dissent, Scalia puckishly observed: "Consulting States that bar
the death penalty concerning the necessity of making an exception to the
penalty for offenders under 18 is rather like including old-order Amish-
men in a consumer-preference poll on the electric car. Of course they
don't like it, but that sheds no light whatever on the point at issue."[86]
Appeals to "objective" criteria like prior decisions of courts, juries, and
legislatures quickly devolve into bitter contention about what "counts"
in establishing an emerging consensus.

Particularly controversial was the *Simmons* Court's invocation of
international opinion regarding the execution of juveniles. In its prior
decision declaring unconstitutional the execution of offenders with mental retardation, the Court had noted—in a footnote and rather off-
handedly—that its finding of a national consensus was bolstered by the
fact that the "world community" (along with religious leaders and
psychological experts) overwhelming disapproved of the practice.[87] In
Simmons, this reliance on international opinion was elevated to text and
ringingly defended:

> Our determination that the death penalty is disproportionate pun-
> ishment for offenders under 18 finds confirmation in the stark
> reality that the United States is the only country in the world that
> continues to give official sanction to the juvenile death penalty. This
> reality does not become controlling, for the task of interpreting the
> Eighth Amendment remains our responsibility. Yet at least from the
> time of this Court's decision in Trop [v. Dulles, 356 U.S. 86 (1958)],
> the Court has referred to the laws of other countries and to
> international authorities as instructive for its interpretation of the
> Eighth Amendment's prohibition of "cruel and unusual punish-
> ments." . . . It does not lessen our fidelity to the Constitution or our
> pride in its origins to acknowledge that the express affirmation of
> certain fundamental rights by other nations and peoples simply
> underscores the centrality of those same rights within our own
> heritage of freedom.[88]

---

[85] *Simmons*, 543 U.S. at 564.

[86] *Id.* at 610–11 (Scalia, J., dissenting).

[87] *See* Atkins v. Virginia, 536 U.S. 304, 316 n.21 (2002).

[88] 543 U.S. at 575, 578.

Although Darrow himself had not pushed hard on international practice in his plea, (invoking instead vaguer notions of advances in "humanity"), Judge Caverly had pointedly remarked that his reliance on the defendants' youth in sparing them the death penalty was "in accordance with the progress in criminal law all over the world."[89]

Most notably, the central arguments made by Darrow about youthful offenders were echoed, almost eerily, by the Supreme Court, often citing expert "alienist" opinion from the many *amicus* briefs filed in *Simmons* on the capacities of juveniles. First, Darrow had insisted that the legal system's special treatment of juveniles in other contexts warranted their special treatment with regard to capital punishment: "The law would forbid them making contracts, forbid them marrying without the consent of their parents, would not permit them to vote. Why? Because they haven't that judgment which only comes with years, because they are not fully responsible."[90] Noted the *Simmons* Court in a virtual paraphrase: "In recognition of the comparative immaturity and irresponsibility of juveniles, almost every State prohibits those under 18 years of age from voting, serving on juries, or marrying without parental consent."[91]

Darrow's finest rhetoric poetically evoked the distinctive mental state of a child or youth. He urged the judge to remember his own youth and asked the entire courtroom, rhetorically, "What do we know about childhood?" In answering, Darrow described the "illusions and delusions" and "instinctive, persistent emotions" that impair the judgment of the young; he characterized the heart of a child as full of "its abundant life, its disregard for consequences, its living in the moment, its lack of responsibility, and its freedom from care."[92] More dryly, the *Simmons* Court concurred in this assessment, explaining "as any parent knows," that juveniles exhibit a "lack of maturity and an underdeveloped sense of responsibility."[93] While Darrow lamented "how weak and inefficient was youth,"[94] the *Simmons* Court noted how juveniles "have less control, or less experience with control, over their own environ-

---

[89] McKernan, *supra* note 4, at 379.

[90] Higdon, *supra* note 4, at 191.

[91] 543 U.S. at 569.

[92] McKernan, *supra* note 4, at 263, 265.

[93] *Id.* (internal quotations omitted). The *Simmons* Court was also able to draw on much more accumulated "hard" science to support its (and Darrow's) intuitions about juveniles' lack of responsibility: on the heels of the phrase "as every parent knows," the Court added the phrase "and as the scientific and sociological studies respondent and his *amici* cite tend to confirm...." *Id.*

[94] McKernan, *supra* note 4, at 265.

ment"[95] and thus are more subject to peer pressure. Darrow evoked the transience of the infirmities youth by asking, provocatively: "How many men are there today—lawyers and congressmen and judges, and even state's attorneys—who have not been guilty of some mad act in youth?"[96] The Court explained that "the personality traits of juveniles are more transitory, less fixed."[97]

It is true that Darrow had a broader conception of "youth" than is encompassed by the constitutional category of "juvenile." Leopold and Loeb, at ages 19 and 18 respectively, would not have been protected by the *Simmons* ruling.[98] But the Court's validation of the accuracy and the significance of Darrow's description of the mental condition of youth— even if the definition of youth is scaled back in years—can only be viewed as vindication for what must have seemed his breathtaking arrogance at the time: "I know the future is on my side."[99]

B. The Constitutional Requirement of Individualized Sentencing

The later constitutional vindication of Darrow's argument about the relevance of Leopold and Loeb's background and mental condition to the judge's sentencing decision is even more striking than the abolition of the juvenile death penalty. After all, arguments that youthful offenders should be spared the harshest punishments have been around for a long time; Darrow hardly invented them. But it is much fairer to claim that Darrow invented the idea that family background and mental state, as attested to by psychiatric specialists, could "mitigate" a crime for sentencing purposes.

It was well accepted at the time of the Leopold and Loeb case that psychiatric evidence was admissible only to negate criminal responsibility altogether; as State's Attorney Crowe indignantly protested: "[T]hey are attempting to show degrees of responsibility. There is nothing in law known as degrees of responsibility."[100] In his closing argument, Crowe would deride the terms "mitigating" and "aggravating" as "strange, foreign words."[101] Darrow had a hard time finding legal support for his

---

[95] 543 U.S. at 569.

[96] McKernan, *supra* note 4, at 265.

[97] 543 U.S. at 570.

[98] The consensus that 18 is the age of majority is the product of more recent times, both promoted by and reflected in the 26th Amendment to the Constitution, which was ratified by the states during the Vietnam War in 1971: "The right of citizens of the United States, who are eighteen years of age or older, to vote shall not be denied or abridged . . . on account of age." U.S. Const. amend. XXVI, § 1.

[99] McKernan, *supra* note 4, at 304.

[100] *Id.* at 79.

[101] *Id.* at 318.

"mitigation" argument: "Precedent for the introduction of psychiatric testimony as a mitigating defense was difficult to find; the decision in the Franks murder case would *establish* precedent. The United States Supreme Court had made no decisions, nor had any court in Illinois."[102] And we cannot forget that Darrow ultimately failed to convince Judge Caverly to actually consider any of the testimony that Darrow argued for three days to admit into evidence.

Half a century, later, however, the Supreme Court would hold not only that judges *may* consider evidence of a defendant's background and mental state in capital proceedings, but also that consideration of what the Court termed "mitigating evidence" was a constitutional *entitlement* of the capital defendant. This requirement came about in a rather backhanded way. The constitutional assault on the death penalty launched by the abolitionist NAACP Legal Defense Fund (LDF) in the 1960's focused primarily on the arbitrariness of the imposition of the death penalty and the lack of standards to guide its use. Many crimes— not only murder, but also rape, kidnapping, and even robbery—were death eligible crimes in many jurisdictions, and sentencing juries had wide discretion in choosing an appropriate sentence.[103] Yet only a handful of defendants, on average, were actually executed each year during the 1960s—and they seemed disproportionately poor and from minority groups. After considering and rejecting a due process challenge to "standardless" capital sentencing in 1971,[104] the Supreme Court accepted the same arguments under the Eighth Amendment's "cruel and unusual punishments" clause the very next year, and the Court thus invalidated capital punishment as it was then administered throughout the United States in its landmark decision in Furman v. Georgia.[105]

The *Furman* Court was closely divided—5 to 4—and deeply fractured. Each of the five Justices in the majority authored his own opinion, and none of the five joined any of the others' opinions.[106] Nonetheless, it was clear that the breadth of capital statutes combined with the lack of standards for imposing a death sentence was key to the crucial moderate votes of Justices Stewart and White. It was a line from Stewart's concurrence that epitomized what most took to be *Furman*'s holding:

---

[102] Higdon, *supra* note 4, at 190.

[103] As in Illinois at the time of the Leopold and Loeb case, it was common for juries to determine sentences in capital cases, even though judges generally determined sentences in non-capital cases. Darrow made his guilty plea decision in large part to avoid a jury sentencing for his clients.

[104] *See* McGautha v. California, 402 U.S. 183 (1971).

[105] 408 U.S. 238 (1972).

[106] The dissenters each wrote their own opinions as well, though some of them joined in other dissents.

"These death sentences are cruel and unusual in the same way that being struck by lightning is cruel and unusual."[107] There was a strong backlash of resistance to the *Furman* holding, especially in the South; within a few years, thirty-five states had redrafted their capital punishment statutes in an attempt to preserve the death penalty in the wake of the Court's ruling. Not surprisingly, in light of the "struck by lightning" concern, a number of states enacted *mandatory* capital statutes that required the imposition of the death penalty for certain crimes, with no discretion for the sentencer to impose a lesser sentence. Other states amended their capital sentencing schemes to try to limit or control the exercise of discretion in capital sentencing without eliminating it, by refining the offenses eligible for capital punishment and by directing capital sentencers to relevant considerations.

In 1976, the Supreme Court granted review to consider the constitutionality of five of the new breed of capital statutes. It upheld three statutes (from Georgia, Florida, and Texas), approving what it deemed their provision of "guided discretion" in capital sentencing.[108] Georgia and Florida's statutes were the norm among the new generation of capital statutes in their use of the terms "aggravating" and "mitigating" circumstances to describe the factors that capital sentencers must consider; these terms came from the Model Penal Code's proposed capital punishment system, to which state legislatures turned for inspiration in the wake of the *Furman* upheaval.[109] In contrast to its approval of such guided discretion schemes, the Supreme Court struck down the two mandatory statutes that it reviewed from North Carolina and Louisiana,[110] a decision the plurality explained in words that might have come from Darrow's closing plea: "[T]he fundamental respect for humanity underlying the Eighth Amendment requires consideration of the character and record of the individual offender and the circumstances of the particular offense as a constitutionally indispensable part of the process of inflicting the penalty of death."[111]

In the years immediately following its rejection of mandatory capital statutes, the Court strengthened and deepened its Eighth Amendment commitment to consideration of mitigating evidence. In an Ohio case, a

---

[107] 408 U.S. at 309 (Stewart, J., concurring).

[108] *See* Gregg v. Georgia, 428 U.S. 153 (1976); Proffitt v. Florida, 428 U.S. 242 (1976); Jurek v. Texas, 428 U.S. 262 (1976).

[109] *See* Model Penal Code § 210.6 (1962 Official Draft).

[110] *See* Woodson v. North Carolina, 428 U.S. 280 (1976); Roberts v. Louisiana, 428 U.S. 325 (1976).

[111] *Woodson*, 428 U.S. at 304 (opinion of Stewart, Powell, and Stevens, JJ.) (citation omitted).

young woman named Sandra Lockett was sentenced to death for her participation with her brother and some other men in the robbery of a pawnshop in which the shop owner was killed in a struggle over a gun. Lockett played only a minor role in planning the crime and waited in the car while the men entered the shop. The Court invalidated Lockett's death sentence because the Ohio statute limited mitigating circumstances to a short statutory list that allowed no consideration of Lockett's "character, prior record, age, lack of specific intent to cause death, and her relatively minor part in the crime."[112] The *Lockett* Court concluded that the Eighth Amendment requires that a capital sentencer "not be precluded from considering, as a mitigating factor, *any aspect of a defendant's character or record and any of the circumstances of the offense that the defendant proffers as a basis for a sentence less than death.*"[113]

Four years later, in a case with surprising echoes of Leopold and Loeb's trial, an Oklahoma judge imposed the death penalty on sixteen-year-old Monty Lee Eddings for shooting a police officer who had pulled over his car. As Darrow had done for Leopold and Loeb, Eddings' defense lawyer elicited psychiatric evidence detailing Eddings' background and mental state. Eddings had been raised in chaotic setting by his alcoholic mother and then handed off to his strict father, who beat him in an effort to control his behavior. He was emotionally disturbed and arrested in his mental and emotional development. Exactly as Judge Caverly had done, the trial judge agreed that Eddings' youth was relevant to the sentencing determination, but concluded that the law did not permit him to consider "this young man's violent background."[114] The Supreme Court disagreed, noting that at this point in death penalty practice, "[e]vidence of a difficult family history and of emotional disturbance is typically introduced by defendants in mitigation."[115] In a holding that directly repudiates Judge Caverly's reasoning in the Leopold and Loeb case, the Court ruled not only that judges must permit the *introduction* of such typical mitigating evidence, but also that "*Lockett* requires the sentencer to *listen.*"[116]

In recent years, the Supreme Court has gone even farther toward promoting Darrow-style advocacy in capital cases. It is one thing to permit defense lawyers to introduce mitigating evidence in capital cases, or even to require sentencers to consider such evidence if it is intro-

---

[112] Lockett v. Ohio, 438 U.S. 586, 597 (1978).

[113] *Id.* at 604 (emphasis added).

[114] Eddings v. Oklahoma, 455 U.S. 104, 109 (1982).

[115] *Id.* at 115.

[116] *Id.* at 115 n.10 (emphasis added).

duced. It is another thing entirely to require that capital defense lawyers unearth all possible mitigating evidence in capital cases, especially given the lack of funding for indigent capital defense services and the abysmally poor lawyering that often results.[117] Without changing the relevant standard for what constitutes "ineffective assistance of counsel" requiring reversal of a conviction or sentence under the Sixth Amendment, the Supreme Court has recently taken a much more demanding stance regarding acceptable investigative practices in capital cases. Since 2000, the Court has invalidated three capital sentences on "ineffective assistance" grounds for counsel's insufficient attention to mitigating evidence of precisely the sort that Darrow and his alienists unearthed for Leopold and Loeb.

In Williams v. Taylor,[118] the Court lambasted defense counsel for failing to prepare for the sentencing phase of the trial until a week before the trial date, and for failing to conduct an investigation that would have uncovered extensive records describing Williams' "nightmarish childhood" of violence and neglect, as well as evidence of his borderline mental retardation and good behavior in prison.[119] In Wiggins v. Smith,[120] the mitigating evidence that was not unearthed was similar—a terribly violent and neglected childhood that included severe sexual abuse, as well as evidence of the defendant's diminished mental capacities. However, Wiggins' public defenders were clearly diligent and able counsel who failed to extend their investigation beyond the presentence report and department of social services records and thus inadvertently, rather than grossly neglectfully, missed some potent mitigating evidence. The Court held that the defense lawyers' failure to conduct a "social history" of their client—as was customary in the state of Maryland and for which the Public Defenders' Office made funds available—was deficient lawyering that required reversal of Wiggins' death sentence when it failed to unearth powerful mitigating evidence that might have swayed the single juror necessary to say Wiggins' life. Finally, Rompilla v. Beard,[121] also involved diligent and able public defenders who made a single mistake; here, they failed to examine a public court file that the prosecution announced it would rely on to introduce evidence about a prior crime committed by Rompilla, similar to the capital crime with which he was currently charged. Had defense

---

[117] See generally Stephen B. Bright, Counsel for the Poor: The Death Sentence Not for the Worst Crime, but for the Worst Lawyer, 103 Yale L.J. 1835 (1994).

[118] 529 U.S. 362 (2000).

[119] Id. at 395–96.

[120] 539 U.S. 510 (2003).

[121] 545 U.S. 374 (2005).

counsel examined the file, they would have found as-yet undiscovered mitigating evidence of Rompilla's abused childhood, problems with alcoholism, and possible mental illness and cognitive impairment. The Court held that, as in *Wiggins*, the failure to unearth this potentially powerful mitigating evidence required reversal of the defendant's death sentence.

The willingness of a non-too-liberal Supreme Court to hold capital defense lawyers to a demanding standard of mitigation investigation shows just how far the law has developed since Darrow's time, when he was on the cutting edge of the "strange, foreign" concept of mitigation. State's Attorney Crowe, in his ferocious rebuttal argument, mocked the defense psychiatrists for their interest in the defendants' childhoods: "Dr. White took me by the hand and led me into the nursery...."[122] But today, there is even a term—"social history"—for the sort of deep investigation of his clients' lives that Darrow hired his alienists to conduct.[123] And, as the Supreme Court's recent decisions teach, capital defense lawyers who fail to pay a visit to the nursery by compiling a social history do so at their peril.

C. The Professionalization of Mitigation

Not only is there a professional *term* for the process of deep investigation into a defendant's background, there is a specialized professional *role* in capital trials for a person who conducts a social history and develops mitigating evidence—the "mitigation specialist." The Atlantic Online highlighted this designation in its *Word Watch* section[124] in 1999 and defined it as follows:

---

[122] McKernan, *supra* note 4, at 312.

[123] One expert (the Director of Investigation and Mitigation at the Capital Defender Office in New York City) gave this description of what goes into a social history:

> Mitigation investigation begins with the client, but it is inevitably a multi-generational inquiry aimed at identifying the genetic predispositions and environmental influences which molded the client's life and defined his or her range of choices.... A key element in social history investigation is the collection of reliable, objective documentation about the client and his or her family.... The search for records typically includes birth certificates and genealogical archives; prenatal, birth, and pediatric charts; physicians, hospitals and mental health records; school, social service agency, juvenile court, employment, Social Security, and workers compensation files; military records; marriage and divorce files; death and autopsy records; correctional, probation and parole records; court files and litigation records.

Russell Stetler, *Capital Cases: Mitigation Evidence in Death Penalty Cases*, 23 Champion 35, 38 (Jan./Feb. 1999).

[124] Anne H. Soukhanov, *Word Watch*, The Atlantic Online (Apr. 1999) (compiling a selection of terms that have newly been coined, have recently acquired new currency, or have taken on new meanings), *available* at http://www.theatlantic.com/issues/99apr/9904 wdwtch.htm (last visited March 28, 2007).

Mitigation specialist *noun*, a member of a criminal-defense team who gathers detailed background about the defendant in order to persuade a jury not to impose the death penalty: "Increasingly, lawyers defending death-penalty cases rely heavily on *mitigation specialists*" (*U.S. News & World Report*).

The need for such a specialist in capital cases has received the weighty imprimatur of the ABA in its Guidelines for the Appointment and Performance of Defense Counsel in Death Penalty Cases, recently revised in 2003. The ABA called the mitigation specialist "an indispensable member of the defense team throughout all capital proceedings."[125] In describing what mitigation specialists do that is so indispensable, the ABA might well have been describing what Darrow retained his alienists to do in the Leopold and Loeb case:

> Mitigation specialists possess clinical and information-gathering skills and training that most lawyers simply do not have. The have the time and the ability to elicit sensitive, embarrassing and often humiliating evidence (e.g., family sexual abuse) that the defendant may have never disclosed. They have the clinical skills to recognize such things as congenital, mental or neurological conditions [and] to understand how these conditions may have affected the defendant's development and behavior ... The mitigation specialist compiles a comprehensive and well-documented psycho-social history of the client based on an exhaustive investigation [and] analyzes the significance of the information in terms of impact on development, including effect on personality and behavior.[126]

Of course, the mitigation specialist need not be, and generally is not, trained as a psychologist or psychiatrist him-or herself. The ABA emphasizes that part of what the mitigation specialist does is identify the proper experts to examine the defendant and ensure that the defendant receives any necessary therapeutic services. But the role is so important to the outcome of capital cases and so specialized in its skills and tasks that the ABA is emphatic that every capital defense "team" (comprised of a minimum of four individuals) must have such a specialist. Moreover, the ABA is quite clear that its recommendation is not "aspirational" but rather embodies "the current consensus about what is required to provide effective defense representation in capital cases."[127]

The significance of the ABA's imprimatur has grown in recent years. When the Supreme Court first announced its currently prevailing standards for assessing constitutional claims of ineffective assistance of

---

[125] *ABA Guidelines, supra* note 12, at 959.

[126] *Id.*

[127] *Id.* at 920.

counsel, it gave a nod, but only a rather perfunctory one, to the ABA's role in setting the constitutional minimum:

> American Bar Association standards and the like are guides to determining what is reasonable [for defense lawyers to do], *but they are only guides.* No particular set of detailed rules for counsel's conduct can satisfactorily take account of the variety of circumstances faced by defense counsel or the range of legitimate decisions regarding how best to represent a criminal defendant.[128]

However, in each of its three recent reversals for inadequate investigation into mitigation, the Supreme Court cited general ABA standards in support of its conclusion that counsel's behavior was deficient,[129] and in the latter two cases, it specifically noted the relatively new death penalty-specific defense standards, first promulgated in 1989 and revised in 2003.[130]

The role of the mitigation specialist as articulated by the ABA is now well accepted as a "new profession,"[131] with its own training and funding issues. Arguments for the need for mitigation specialists in capital cases[132] now mingle with publications and organizations that assume the existence of such a role and offer training advice and tips for such professionals,[133] including tips for funding.[134]

---

[128] Strickland v. Washington, 466 U.S. 668, 688–89 (1984) (emphasis added).

[129] *See Williams*, 529 U.S. at 396; *Wiggins*, 539 U.S. at 522, 524–25; *Rompilla*, 545 U.S. at 387.

[130] *See Wiggins*, 539 U.S. at 524; *Rompilla*, 545 U.S. at 387.

[131] Pamela Blume Leonard, *A New Profession for an Old Need: Why a Mitigation Specialist Must be Included on the Capital Defense Team*, 31 Hofstra L. Rev. 1143 (2003).

[132] *See id.; see also* Craig M. Cooley, *Mapping the Monster's Mental Health and Social History: Why Capital Defense Attorney and Public Defender Death Penalty Units Require the Services of Mitigation Specialists*, 30 Okla. City U.L. Rev. 23 (2005); David D. Velloney, *Balancing the Scales of Justice: Expanding Access to Mitigation Specialists in Military Death Penalty Cases*, 170 Mil. L. Rev. 1 (2001).

[133] *See, e.g.*, Natman Schaye and Roseann Schaye–Glos, *Mitigation in the Death Belt—Twelve Steps to Saving Clients' Lives*, 29 Champion 18 (2005); Russell Stetler and Kathleen Wayland, *Capital Cases: Dimensions of Mitigation*, 28 Champion 31 (2004). The National Legal Aid & Defender Association just offered a training for capital defense lawyers and mitigation specialists entitle "Life in the Balance" in March, 2007. *See* NLADA Training and Conferences at http://www.nlada.org/Training/Train_Defender/Train_Defender_Balance (last visited March 28, 2007); Similarly, The National Association of Criminal Defense Lawyers, in conjunction with the well-known capital defense organization the Southern Center for Human Rights, list a similar "Making the Case for Life" training on its 2008 CLE calendar. *See* NACDL and Affiliate CLE Schedule, at http://www.nacdl.org/public.nsf/freeform/affiliate_cleschedule?OpenDocument (last visited March 28, 2007).

[134] *See, e.g.*, Chris Adams, *Death Watch: Securing the Funding for Your Mitigation Specialists*, 28 Champion 19 (2004).

It's fair to say that you know when a new idea or service or product has arrived when its name enters the lexicon of regular use. After all, many consumers say Kleenex for tissue, Jello for gelatin, and Xerox for photocopy. Although we do not today describe it as a "Darrow defense" or as a "Leopold and Loeb strategy," we now have "social history" and "mitigation specialist" to describe the radical—and, let us not forget, *rejected*—capital defense that Darrow offered on behalf of Leopold and Loeb. Clarence Darrow would no doubt be amazed—and I expect he would be pleased—if he were alive today to see his defense strategy triumph in such unequivocal fashion.

III. A Legacy of Irony and Hope

But Darrow, though thought to be a soft-hearted humanitarian, was not in the least soft-headed. I doubt that he would be blind to the many ironies that attended both his victory in the Leopold and Loeb case and the eventual victory of his strategy on the broader field of death penalty law and practice.

First, the case itself. Although Darrow won his plea for his clients' lives, Richard Loeb still died young—stabbed to death in prison at the age of 30.[135] Despite his life sentence, Loeb did not live much longer (if any longer at all) than he would have had he been sentenced to death today, when the average length of time spent on death row exceeds ten years.[136] On the other hand, Nathan Leopold did not end up serving his entire "life" sentence, despite Judge Caverly's stern admonition to the Parole Board to keep the defendants locked up forever. Rather, Leopold was released after serving 33 years in prison and soon thereafter published his memoirs, entitled *Life Plus 99 Years*.[137] He married and lived out the rest of his life quietly in Puerto Rico, dying there in 1971 at the age of 66.[138] Darrow lived to see Loeb murdered but not to see Leopold released: Darrow himself had died at the age of 81 on March 13, 1938.

Though Darrow might well have been surprised by his clients' unexpected ends, he could only have been astonished by the legal developments described above that enshrined his defense strategy

---

[135] Higdon, *supra* note 4, at 295. Despite overwhelming evidence against him, the inmate charged with Loeb's murder was acquitted at trial based on his extremely dubious claim of self-defense. *Id.* at 310.

[136] *See Time on Death Row*, Death Penalty Information Center, at http://www.death penaltyinfo.org/article.php? & did=1397#INTRODUCTION (last visited March 28, 2007) ("Death row inmates in the U.S. typically spend over a decade awaiting execution. Some prisoners have been on death row for well over 20 years.").

[137] *See supra* note 72.

[138] Higdon, *supra* note 4, at 340.

through constitutional fiat. But astonished is not necessarily the same thing as pleased, because Darrow's sharp eyes would not have missed the shadows amidst the progress.

First, Darrow's arguments about the relevance of mitigating evidence to his clients' culpability were far more thoroughgoing than the mitigation requirement adopted by the Supreme Court. Darrow was arguing for nothing less than determinism—the view that *no* wrongdoer has any real choice in his fate and therefore deserves no blame: "[I]ntelligent people now know that every human being is the product of the endless heredity back of him and the infinite environment around him."[139] But the Court's mitigation doctrine—though it would have allowed, even required, Darrow's defense of Leopold and Loeb—is based on a theory wholly antagonistic to determinism. According to the Court, some people *do* "deserve" the death penalty, and the job of the capital process is to sort those people from the others, who might be less culpable than the truly deserving by reason of background or experience. This kind of thinking is deeply retributivist and both reflects and reinforces what some have identified as a "retributivist revival"[140] in punishment theory in the contemporary United States—something Darrow would clearly have abhorred. This revival emphasizes personal accountability and the moral duty to tailor punishment to "just deserts." Under such a theory of punishment, mitigation is central to the task of doing a proper accounting and assessing the precise degree of each offender's "desert" in order to identify accurately the truly deathworthy. Darrow surely would have been chagrined to see that his energetic case for the relevance of mitigation was able to win the day only in an era of retributive penology, which utterly rejects the determinism that was the motivating engine of his impassioned plea.

Second, Darrow would be greatly disappointed to see the vigorous continued use of capital punishment in the United States, especially at a time when so many of our peer countries in the developed world have repudiated it. Darrow's opposition to the death penalty crystallized in his representation of Leopold and Loeb, and the very next year he founded the American League to Abolish the Death Penalty.[141] Though he would have been heartened by the constitutional rejection of capital punish-

---

[139] McKernan, *supra* note 4, at 254.

[140] *See, e.g.*, Jeffrey L. Kirchmeier, *A Tear in the Eye of the Law: Mitigating Factors and the Progression Toward a Disease Theory of Criminal Justice*, 83 Or. L. Rev. 631 (2004) ("During the last forty years in the United States, there has been a 'great philosophical revival of retributivism,' reintroducing 'ideas of moral agency and moral responsibility into the criminal law, abandoning the brute therapeutic psychologism of the mid-twentieth century.' ") (quoting James Q. Whitman, Harsh Justice: Criminal Punishment and the Widening Divide Between American and Europe, 23–24 (2003)).

[141] *See Death Penalty Debate*, 20 Champion 20, 23 (1996).

ment for juvenile offenders, I doubt he would be insensitive to the possibility that this narrowing of the death penalty, along with the constitutional regulation that led to the individualization requirement, may well have played a part in the ossification of our national practice of capital punishment. I have made this case more extensively elsewhere that the "reform" of the death penalty may very well not lie along the same track as its abolition: the narrowing of the scope of capital punishment and procedural improvements in the capital sentencing process may well help to entrench the practice, both by genuinely improving it and by creating the false impression that it is better regulated than it truly is.[142] Darrow would have understood this fear and worried himself that improving the capital process as a lawyer might delay the day when the process stops for good.

Despite these ironies and the legitimate worries they raise, I think Darrow would embrace and even celebrate his Leopold and Loeb legacy. Every criminal defense lawyer knows that victories are rarely total. Indeed, as he entered his clients' pleas to capital murder, Darrow knew that the only victory possible in the case was for Leopold and Loeb to escape the gallows. But Darrow saw himself not only as pleading for his clients' lives, but also as "plead[ing] for the future."[143] He saw the judge standing with him there on the bridge "between the past the future."[144] The distance we've come between the capital practices of 1924 and those of today gives us reason—small but real—to keep alive Darrow's evident faith in the future.

---

[142] *See* Carol S. Steiker & Jordan M. Steiker, *Sober Second Thoughts: Reflections on Two Decades of Constitutional Regulation of Capital Punishment*, 109 Harv. L. Rev. 355 (1995); Carol S. Steiker & Jordan M. Steiker, *Should Abolitionists Support Legislative "Reform" of the Death Penalty?* 63 Ohio St. L.J. 417 (2002).

[143] McKernan, *supra* note 4, at 304.

[144] *Id.*

*

5

Michael E. Tigar[1]
James E. Coleman, Jr.[2]

A Sanctuary in the Jungle: Terry Lynn Nichols and His Oklahoma City Bombing Trial[3]

FACTUAL BACKGROUND

On April 19, 1995, Timothy McVeigh, who was then 26 years old, stepped from the cab of a rented Ryder truck parked in front the Murrah Federal Building in Oklahoma City. The truck carried a 5000 pound bomb made of barrels of ammonium nitrate mixed with diesel fuel and nitromethane, with blasting caps rigged to set it off. Ammonium nitrate is a commercially-available fertilizer, whose explosive properties are well known. On a farm, ANFO (ammonium nitrate/fuel oil) charges often are used to blow stumps and for other benign purposes, and United States Department of Agriculture literature describes how to make them. McVeigh's purpose was much more sinister.

---

[1] Research Professor of Law, Washington College of Law, American University, Visiting Professor of Law, Duke Law School.

[2] Professor of the Practice of Law, Duke Law School.

[3] The entire trial transcript is on Westlaw in the database OKLA–TRANS. There are also DVDs of the pretrial and trial proceedings in the McVeigh and Nichols cases, published by PubNetics, Inc. of Denver, Colorado and available in law libraries, including the Pence Library at Washington College of Law. Michael Tigar's opening and closing arguments are in Volume XXV of the Classics of the Courtroom Series, published by Professional Education Group, www.proedgroup.com. In excerpting trial materials, the authors do not always used ellipses to indicate omissions. The phrase "sanctuary in the jungle" was used by Edward Bennett Williams, during oral argument in Alderman v. United States, 394 U.S. 165 (1969). *See* Michael E. Tigar, Persuasion: The Litigator's Art 281 (1999).

McVeigh ignited a timed fuse and walked away. The explosion devastated the building, killed 168 people, wounded hundreds more, and damaged many nearby buildings. McVeigh's motives were difficult to establish precisely, but he was a right-wing zealot convinced that the American government was the corrupt agent of an international conspiracy to deprive Americans of their liberties. He had ties to several armed militia groups.

McVeigh left Oklahoma City in his Mercury Marquis automobile, which he had parked near the Murrah Building as a getaway car. On his way North on Interstate 35, an Oklahoma trooper noticed that the Marquis had no license plate. During the routine stop, McVeigh revealed that he had a loaded pistol in his car. The trooper arrested him on the firearm and license plate charge. While McVeigh was in the Perry County, Oklahoma jail, the FBI search team in Oklahoma City found the Ryder truck rear axle and traced the truck to a rental agency in Junction City, Kansas. The agency employees described the two men who rented the truck, one of whom matched McVeigh's description. A local motel owner identified McVeigh from an FBI sketch. On April 22, 1995, FBI agents took McVeigh into custody in Perry County.

The FBI also discovered that McVeigh had a friend, Terry Nichols, whom he had first met in the Army and with whom he had lived for a time on the Nichols family farm in Michigan. Nichols' name and photograph were broadcast nationwide. Nichols was then living in Herrington, Kansas, with his wife Marife and their young daughter. On the afternoon of April 22, 1995, Terry Nichols—having heard of the news broadcasts—voluntarily went with his family to the Herrington police station. The local police notified the FBI and Nichols was taken into custody, first as a material witness and later as an alleged accomplice.

McVeigh and Nichols were jointly charged in Oklahoma federal court with conspiracy to use a weapon of mass destruction and to commit arson, use of a weapon of mass destruction, arson, and eight counts of first-degree murder of federal employees. Oklahoma authorities reserved the right to try the two in state court for an additional 160 homicides.

Stephen Jones of Enid, Oklahoma, was appointed counsel for McVeigh. Because of the difficulty in finding an Oklahoma lawyer who would accept appointment to represent Nichols, or who did not feel a conflict in the representation, Chief Judge David Russell of the Western District of Oklahoma appointed Professor Michael E. Tigar, then of The University of Texas School of Law, as Nichols' counsel. Because this was a capital case, Nichols was entitled to two experienced counsel.[4] The

---

[4] In a capital case, the court will also appoint additional lawyers to assist with the work, as well as paralegals and experts in relevant fields. *See, e.g.*, Ake v. Oklahoma, 470

court appointed Ronald G. Woods of Houston, Texas. Woods was a University of Texas law graduate who had served as an FBI agent, an assistant district attorney in Houston, Texas, and an assistant United States attorney before being appointed by President George H.W. Bush as United States Attorney for the Southern District of Texas. After he left government service, Woods went into private practice. He and Tigar had teamed up before as co-counsel—with Dick DeGuerin—in the defense of Senator Kay Bailey Hutchison. As the case developed, the court also appointed additional lawyers to assist with the work, as well as paralegals, experts and investigators.

THE IDEA OF SANCTUARY

The Oklahoma City bombing was world-wide news, billed as the worst act of domestic terrorism in American history. It so profoundly affected Oklahomans that it became the event by which time was measured: Newspaper articles about even unrelated events placed the date as occurring at a certain time after April 19, 1995. Tigar and Woods recoiled at the prospect of a trial in Oklahoma City, Oklahoma, presided over by a judge who had been affected in some way by the bombing and before jurors whose lives were interwoven with the important events. Regardless of where the trial was eventually held, the prosecution's case would inevitably recall, for the jurors as for all Americans, the devastation, fear and anger of the bombing and its aftermath. The government's theory of Terry Nichols' liability rested on his alleged complicity in McVeigh's actions of that morning and the preparation for them.

The overriding Nichols defense theme would have to be "sanctuary." The image of sanctuary is one of safety, reason, compassion, and redemption. Those were the human qualities on which Nichols' defense would rest. Sanctuary is a quiet place from which one could evaluate the evidence of Terry Nichols' alleged involvement, detached to the extent possible from the fear and anger that the bombing engendered. If he were convicted, this sanctuary would be a setting to consider the issue of punishment.

THE STORY OF THE CASE—A DUAL APPROACH

In a capital case, understanding the client's story is perhaps more significant than in other cases. The Eighth Amendment commands that the life-death decision be a "reasoned moral response:" The defense is entitled, indeed required, to find and present a complete possible picture of the accused and the offense. The accused is in turn entitled to have this evidence considered by the jury and given effect. A defense effort

---

U.S. 68 (1985); American Bar Association Guidelines for the Appointment and Performance of Counsel in Death Penalty Cases (1989), cited with approval in Rompilla v. Beard, 545 U.S. 374, 387 n.7 (2005).

that fails to explore all aspects of the defendant's life and character is not only likely to fail at trial, but it also constitutes constitutionally-deficient, ineffective assistance of counsel.[5]

A capital case is bifurcated. In the innocence-guilt phase, the jurors deal with evidence focused on the elements of the charged offenses. If the jury finds the defendant guilty of a capital offense, there is a penalty phase, a trial for life. In that phase, the rules of evidence may be relaxed, and the defense—and to perhaps a lesser extent, the prosecution—is entitled to broad latitude.[6] For example, on the issue of mitigation, the Eighth Amendment requires that evidence of a mental condition that is not a defense nonetheless must be received and considered during the penalty phase, and such evidence may come from expert or lay witnesses.

So, for these constitutionally-based reasons, the advocate must think about a capital trial from two quite different perspectives: first, presenting a story of the offense that contradicts the prosecution story enough to create a reasonable doubt; and second, presenting a picture of the defendant's life that provokes a life verdict.

This dual approach does not mean that trial preparation and presentation take place on two parallel tracks that never meet. To the contrary, the advocate must begin, in the first phase, to build a bridge to the second phase. For example, a defendant may be an aider and abettor or conspirator based on relatively minor participation, and therefore be guilty of an offense from which death has resulted.[7] He or she would therefore be constitutionally-eligible for the death penalty.[8] However, minor participation is a mitigating circumstance. The best opportunity to show minor participation, however, is in the trial phase, when confronting witnesses who come to testify about the defendant's alleged activity. This is particularly so if one or more of those witnesses is a plea-bargaining cooperator. In the discussion below, the cross-examination of cooperating witness Michael Fortier had a dual purpose—first to show that Terry Nichols was not guilty, and also to point out ways in which his alleged participation was certainly no greater than Fortier's own. Both had to be done during the innocence/guilt phase of the trial.

Initially, having been denied bail, Nichols was held at the federal prison on the outskirts of Oklahoma City. There was no particular

---

[5] *See generally* Rompilla v. Beard, *supra* (standards for effective counsel in capital case); Wiggins v. Smith, 539 U.S. 510 (2003) (duty to investigate).

[6] The federal death penalty statute used in the Nichols case is 18 U.S.C. §§ 3591-96.

[7] On the relationship between trial and penalty phases, *see* Oregon v. Guzek, 546 U.S. 517 (2006) (defendant does not have the right to reopen guilt/innocence phase issues with new evidence in penalty phase).

[8] *See* LaFave, Israel & King, CRIMINAL PROCEDURE § 3.5(f) (4th ed. 2004).

reason that he should trust appointed defense counsel. The sad statistics on the quality of appointed counsel would give him an objective basis for doubt.[9] His own distrust of government, and his real concern about his predicament, no doubt weighed on him. The advocate's job was to build trust and to know his story. The success of the team requires the defendant's cooperation and trust. One of the paralegal assistants' jobs was to spend as much time with Nichols and his family as possible. The defense also retained a consulting psychiatrist and Georgetown Medical School professor, Dr. James S. Gordon, founder and head of the Center for Mind–Body Medicine. Dr. Gordon spent hundreds of hours with Nichols and his family.

The defense worked hard to know the details of Nichols' life, with several goals in mind. First, in the details of his relationship with McVeigh, one could build a theory of innocence. Second, jurors are more ready to acquit someone they can understand, and see as a whole person; they can get such a picture from defendant testimony, character evidence, and the testimony of family members or experts. Third, if there were a penalty phase, this life story would form the basis of proof and argument.

The Nichols trial presented two competing stories. The government had its version, which had been leaked to the media: Timothy McVeigh had recruited his friend and old Army buddy Terry Nichols to assemble the ingredients of a bomb built of ammonium nitrate and diesel fuel, and ignited with blasting caps stolen from a quarry. McVeigh had rented a Ryder truck in Junction City, Kansas, using a false name. He and Terry had mixed the bomb. McVeigh drove the truck to Oklahoma City and set off the bomb. The Nichols team had a different version. Nichols and McVeigh had known each other since Army days, and had done business together selling items at gun shows. McVeigh had lived with the Nichols family for a time. But Nichols had never embraced McVeigh's overtly racist and violent set of social attitudes, and had taken care to distance himself from McVeigh. Nichols became focused on his marriage and his family.

From the beginning, this was fundamentally a conspiracy and accomplice case, in which the rules on inchoate and accessory liability would play a large role.[10] The Nichols team never doubted that McVeigh had planned and carried out the bombing, or one or more others helped him to do so. In view of this, two basic principles of advocacy were important: First, do not make yourself look bad to the jury by denying the obvious. Second, employ the theory of minimal contradiction; look for a case theory that shifts perspective just enough to require a

---

[9] *See, e.g.*, Stephen B. Bright, *Essay: Counsel for the Poor: The Death Sentence Not for the Worst Crime But For the Worst Lawyer*, 103 Yale L.J. 1835 (1994).

[10] *See generally* Wayne R. LaFave, Criminal Law, chs. 12–13 (4th ed. 2003).

different result. It is never enough, in a criminal case, simply to rest on reasonable doubt. Never assume a burden you do not have, but always provide the jurors a plausible alternative view of events.

The alternative view was that Terry Nichols was unlikely to have joined with McVeigh or anyone else to plant a bomb that would kill people indiscriminately. In fact, Nichols had severed his relationship with McVeigh months before the bombing. There was evidence that, as a result, McVeigh thereafter derided Nichols as "domesticated" and reached out to others to help him with his plot. In short, the defense would tell the complete story of McVeigh's search for the equipment and personnel he would use to do the crime. To that end, the defense called 92 witnesses in this case. Mr. Nichols did not testify.

In a relatively brief essay, it is not possible to reproduce all the evidence at this months-long trial. We can only sketch the themes and suggest how advocates deal with complex factual and legal issues. If Nichols' undeniable association with McVeigh was, as the defense would argue, innocent—unaccompanied by either the intention to further an unlawful plan or significant acts in furtherance of such a plan—how had McVeigh carried out his crime?

The government has an obligation in all cases, but particularly in major ones, to do a careful investigation. In a high-profile case, this obligation helps to ensure that the jury's verdict and the judgment of onlookers are reliable. Yes, one says to jurors, this is a terrible crime and an historic case. Precisely for these reasons, the government has a special obligation to get it right. Therefore, the defense focused on errors and omissions in the government's forensic evidence, and on its failure to pursue leads to other conspirators.

The first and most publicized lead had to do with "John Doe #2." The witnesses at the Ryder truck rental facility all agreed that McVeigh had been accompanied by someone who was not Terry Nichols. Other witnesses saw someone with McVeigh at a Junction City, Kansas Motel and at other locations. That person matched the same description as the person at the truck rental store. The FBI had used a sketch artist to make composite picture of John Doe. The media had published the picture.

As the investigation unfolded, the defense found other evidence of McVeigh reaching out to potential accomplices, and even uncovered some of McVeigh's statements that arguably acknowledged that Nichols was not going to help him.

THE TRIAL TEAM—PREPARATION

Advocacy skills are indispensable to success, but are worthless without thorough and thoughtful preparation on facts and law. That preparation involves investigation and legal research that in almost every case require that the advocate assemble a team. Eventually, the Nichols defense team included five lawyers, five paralegals, and five investigators, with contract services from experts in several key subjects, and the help of a dozen law students at various times. The team met regularly to discuss the entire case. Under a reciprocal discovery agreement with the prosecutors, the defense had access to more that 40,000 witness statements collected by the FBI, 100,000 items of physical evidence, and dozens of expert reports. The defense turned over thousands of statements from witnesses that its investigators had interviewed. The defense team catalogued the physical evidence and evaluated every item to see if it had potential relevance to the defense. The court allowed the defense to retain a computer expert to help scan the witness statements and other materials so that they could be searched electronically. Lawyers and law students prepared and filed dozens of pretrial motions. From April 1995, when Tigar was first appointed, until the Nichols trial began in September 1997, the team worked full-time.

TRIAL EVENTS IN THIS ESSAY

First, we introduce the idea of sanctuary through defense motions on recusal, change of venue, and severance of defendants.

Second, we illustrate voir dire techniques designed to probe potential jurors' ability and willingness to consider all the evidence and, if there were a penalty trial, to give full effect to the law and evidence about mitigation.

Third, we have reproduced some of the opening statements that set out the defense factual themes, and expressly deal with the need to create a space where reason and compassion can have a part.

Fourth, we reproduce excerpts from the cross-examination of Michael Fortier, to illustrate the dual purpose of creating doubt about Nichols' involvement in the crime but also showing that Nichols' involvement with McVeigh was no greater than Fortier's involvement, and that Fortier was not subjected to a possible death sentence. The excerpts also show how to weave defense themes into the examination of a key cooperating witness.

Fifth, after a brief look at closing argument themes, we present portions of the penalty phase argument, to show how the idea of sanctuary dominates the defense presentation of its mitigation ideas in a capital case.

RECUSAL AND VENUE AND JOINDER: WHERE AND TO WHOM TO TELL THE STORIES

Recusal

The bomb blast had fatally damaged the Murrah Federal Office Building, and had done significant harm to the federal courthouse behind it. Indeed, the Federal Defender office had been so hard hit that the defender declared a conflict in representing either McVeigh or Nichols. Despite national and international publicity, the attitude of potential jurors in Oklahoma especially was, the defense contended, not conducive to a fair trial. The defense sought recusal of the Oklahoma federal judges and a change of venue.

The trial judge in a capital case cannot simply be a referee. Every capital case is tried at the edge of Eighth Amendment jurisprudence. The Supreme Court repeatedly revisits the constitutional contours of death. Nichols and McVeigh were tried under a 1994 statute, the text of which raised many issues of constitutionality and interpretation.[11] There was the risk that any Oklahoma judge would feel he or she had a stake in the outcome. The Court of Appeals for the 10th Circuit agreed. In a ruling on mandamus that the Nichols team sought, it disqualified all Oklahoma federal judges.[12] Acting under a statute permitting the court of appeals chief judge to name a trial judge, Chief Judge Stephanie Seymour selected Richard P. Matsch, chief judge of the U.S. District Court for Colorado. This was a brilliant and logical selection. Judge Matsch was known to be solid and scholarly. He respected the adversary system.

Venue

The defense then filed a motion for change of venue. Judge Matsch granted it, and moved the case to Denver, Colorado. In his opinion, he accepted a defense theory regarding the special way that jurors perceive events that they believe affect their own lives and interests. Without doubt, publicity about the Oklahoma City bombing was pandemic. How could it be argued, then, that Denver was any "safer" a fair trial venue than, say, Tulsa? A poll can show that fixed attitudes about the case differ in those two cities. Comments by Oklahoma public officials favoring the death penalty in the event of a conviction were also relevant. But there was more.

Scott Armstrong, a respected journalist who worked for the Washington Post and has written several important books on aspects of the legal system,[13] provided important evidence in the venue hearing. Armstrong observed that media editors serve their readers and viewers. When a tragic event happens, it may be national or even international news. But the community immediately affected has a special interest in a

---

[11] Judge Matsch's consideration of constitutional and interpretation issues are reported at 940 F.Supp. 1571 (D.Colo.1996) and 944 F.Supp. 1478 (D.Colo. 1996).

[12] Nichols v. Alley, 71 F.3d 347 (10th Cir.1995)(granting mandamus, ordering recusal, and directing chief judge of the circuit to appoint a trial judge).

[13] He is co-author with Bob Woodward of THE BRETHREN: INSIDE THE SUPREME COURT (1979).

special kind of coverage. That community wants "justice" and "closure." Its members are more concerned than outsiders with the tragedy's effect on particular community members and groups. These special concerns can be seen in print and electronic media, as editors serve their local market. As a result of this kind of coverage, there is a high risk that community members develop attitudes that make fair and impartial consideration of trial evidence more difficult. In the language of lawyers, the sort of community sentiment that Armstrong identified is called "implied bias."

Tigar explored these themes in the following excerpts from his oral argument on the motion to change venue.[14]

> We looked, Your Honor, at the quantity of media coverage; the quality of media coverage; the content of that coverage. We looked, Your Honor, at a simple idea that undergirds all of our economic system, the idea of a market. Mr. Armstrong helped us see that the idea of the market has come to play a much bigger role in editorial decision-making than it used to do. That is, media moguls, editors, are much more sensitive to responding to the needs of their market.

> Now, the government says that, "Well, this is a national and an international story." Of course it's a national and an international story. It was on CNN for an hour. They have an exhibit like that. It was on CNN for one hour, one time. But, by the time the dust had settled, the national media dealt with aspects of the story as they happened, and the local media replicated the whole story, beginning to end, over and over and over again.

> This concept is the one that Dr. Vinson [government expert] and Dr. Bronson [defense expert] agreed is called, "salience." The media editors in this single Oklahoma market, that Mr. Armstrong found in his analysis, are doing this because they think that's what grabs their audience. That the sociologists call "salience," but it is, to trivialize it, like some darn song or jingle that you get in your head, driving down the road, and I start humming and I realize that it's that toothpaste commercial that my daughter listened to, or it's some other that I can't get it out of my head because the sheer force of repetition has put it there.

> The people of Oklahoma were told over and over again—this salience thing again—that they had a special relationship to these events, and they came to believe it. But it wasn't simply that the media told them; their leaders told them; they were told by their leaders to identify themselves in this way, by Governor Keating, by Senator Inhofe. They showed that they had this sense of identity by

---

[14] The complete arguments are at 1996 WL 45128 (2/02/96).

their purchase of the memorabilia; by their adoption, their embracing of slogans, that showed the entire state and the ribbon around the Heartland. They embraced that concept as a mechanism for their recovery.

Now, there's a second part of this media difference. It isn't just that there's more in Oklahoma City. It's what Dr. Bronson called, "thematic thinking." Why is it that a prospective mock-trial jury trying the Oswald case, with all the information that it had to bring to that task, would be influenced by seeing the motion picture "JFK"? The inference is that it's because that motion picture—and I think Dr. Vinson and Dr. Bronson agree about this—has a powerful theory of events, cogently argued, with what seems to the onlooker to be evidence that it is so.

After all, we teach—when we teach young lawyers to be trial lawyers—at least I do when I've taught lawyers—we teach them that deciders perceive whole stories. Dr. Vinson tells us that when prospective jurors come to the task of deciding and bring a set of attitudes and beliefs, that they have a whole story; that trying to present evidence that's contrary to the story they've got worked out induces cognitive dissonance and causes them to engage in coping behaviors that include nonrational ignoring of the evidence, trying to rationalize it, forgetting it, minimalizing it, and so on.

We're not saying that the local media set out to prejudice anyone; we are saying that it responded to this need. Thus, the contrast between not only the quantity but the nature of the local coverage and the national coverage is what counts.

Now, there's something that's more telling, I think, than all of this, and that's what the Supreme Court has said over and over, that death is different. Well, of course it is. That's a trivial statement. But the court, ever since Furman v. Georgia, has told us that death is different, and in a quite decisive way.

Why is death different? What's the procedural meaning of that? The Federal Death Penalty Act of 1994 is a weighing statute, and it places upon the jury the responsibility for assessing punishment. The jury doesn't simply find factors; it's makes an ultimate decision. That's the characteristic of this statute.

A lot of studies have been done, whether Furman versus Georgia has achieved its purpose. There's a recent article in the Harvard Law Review. Well, we're not here to debate that. What is clear is that sentencer discretion in jury sentencing cases, under weighing statutes, puts before the jury a huge quantity of highly emotionally-charged evidence and expressly invites the jury to do something that is unique to death cases, and, that is, to make a reasoned moral response, this free-floating decision, in which their sense of anguish, and anger, and sympathy, and so on, can expressly be considered.

Now, Your Honor stopped me yesterday because I had gone too far with Dr. Holden. I'm not sure just where I crossed the line but I hope that it was sometime after I asked him about the Bosnian Serbs, because Dr. Holden does know, as an expert, about how people identify with events: the them-versus-us. The them-versus-us here is Oklahoma versus these defendants.

Governor Keating has been quoted over and over again, repeating his mantra, "We will give these people a fair trial. Oklahomans are independent. We want to make sure we've got the right people, but, if we do, they should be executed," as though the Furman v. Georgia gene had dropped out of his legal chromosome makeup.

C.S. Lewis writes, in one of his letters, in that wonderful collection, that, "There are times, as for example on a dark mountain road at night, when we would give far more for a glimpse of the few feet ahead than for a vision of some far horizon." The few feet ahead that we can see tell us that in this time and place, that a jury, in this city, charged with that decision, would be one as to which one can confidently say there is this reasonable likelihood of prejudice.

Two roads, two roads, diverge before us, gathered as we are, with the decades of constitutional liberty piled so high, the anguish of the victims close at hand. To one of those roads we are beckoned, from sadness, to anger, to vengeance. Governor Keating beckons us along that road by what I suggest is deliberate design. The media have beckoned us along that road, simply by their desire to serve their market. The other road, I suggest to the Court, is the one the framers laid out for us while the memory of unfair trials in distant forums was fresh in their minds.

We neither dishonor nor deny the grief and anger of the victims, nor even their cry for vengeance. Your Honor, this is my 30th year in the law, and I believe, more than ever, that when we summon someone, anyone, Terry Nichols, into court, to find out whether he's going to live or die, that it is our job to construct, where we best can, a kind of sanctuary in the jungle.

One obvious question, and government counsel asked it rhetorically, is why voir dire is not an adequate remedy to explore juror attitudes and eliminate those whose minds are made up. Many cases deny change of venue motions on the theory that juror attitudes can be explored on voir dire. To this concern, which Judge Matsch expressed in a question, Tigar replied:

Nothing I have said, Your Honor, diminishes the power of advocacy nor the abilities of judges to ferret out bias and get at the truth, but my mother always told me not to eat my soup with a fork. Forks are good implements, but there are some things they're just not designed to do.

JOINDER AND SEVERANCE—A SEPARATE
TRIAL FOR A SEPARATE DEFENSE

Even in a forum not dominated by predetermined attitudes, it is often very difficult to tell your client's story in a multi-defendant case. The very fact that the parties are joined for trial and all sitting on the same side of the courtroom may lead jurors to think that they are all involved together in the challenged conduct. Having each party represented by separate counsel can help keep the issues and evidence separate. The judge will instruct the jury that each party's case is entitled to separate consideration. But where there are antagonistic trial positions, or contradictory trial stories, joinder is problematic. The Supreme Court has spoken favorably of prosecutors' preferences for multi-defendant trials.[15] Severance motions are hard to win, and denial of severance is reviewed on appeal for "abuse of discretion" and with an eye to upholding the district judge's ruling.

For Terry Nichols, the defense position was that McVeigh did the bombing acting together with others, some of whom were known and others of whom the FBI knew about but had not tried very hard to find; but Nichols was not one of them. The Nichols team view was that McVeigh was a racist and something of a fanatic.

Both McVeigh and Nichols moved for severance. The Nichols motion focused on the fact that in capital cases individual consideration of sentencing factors is the hallmark of Eighth Amendment jurisprudence. Such consideration becomes very difficult when two defendants with very different stories are joined for trial. In order to forestall an argument that one might cure this problem by having a single trial on liability and then two separate trials on punishment if that were necessary, the defense also pointed out the ways in which the defenses of the two defendants were different and in many ways contradictory. Judge Matsch granted the severance, again in a reported opinion.[16] McVeigh was tried first.

SELECTING A JURY

The court sent out more than 1,000 jury summonses for the Nichols trial. Those summoned came to the Denver fairgrounds, about 500 of

[15] Zafiro v. United States, 506 U.S. 534 (1993).

[16] 169 F.R.D. 362 (D. Colo. 1996)(focusing in large measure on the problems of inadmissible codefendant hearsay in any joint trial, and on antagonistic defenses).

them in the morning and about 500 in the afternoon, to hear instructions from Judge Matsch and to fill out lengthy questionnaires. Given that voir dire is often truncated, and often conducted only by the judge and not by counsel, the questionnaire has become an indispensable tool for helping find qualified jurors. Jurors provide information about their residence, employment, religious affiliation, military service, education, reading habits, exposure to media coverage of the case, and so on. A person who fills out a questionnaire, and is assured that it will be confidential, will often be more candid than in open court. Because the fairgrounds sessions were a critical trial stage, Mr. Nichols was present, dressed in normal clothes and not prison attire. There could not be any obtrusive security measures that would suggest an official judgment that he was dangerous.[17]

After several hundred jurors were eliminated from the pool based on the questionnaires, voir dire began in the federal courthouse. Jurors were summoned into the courtroom one at a time for questioning by the judge, prosecutor and defense counsel.

Voir dire is an opportunity to develop rapport with those who may be on the jury, and to provide a basis for exercising peremptory challenges, as well as establishing the basis for cause challenges. Although peremptory challenges are controversial, their utility in capital cases is obvious. Jurors are often reluctant to discuss deeply-held beliefs, and in a capital case this reluctance surely applies to their willingness to follow the law on mitigation in any penalty phase. Since at least the time of Blackstone, peremptory challenges have been said to be in favorem vitae—in favor of life—and therefore indispensable to the defendant.[18]

A newspaper article from the October 19, 1997, Daily Oklahoman captured the flavor of the defense approach to voir dire:[19]

> In the three weeks of jury selection, [Tigar has] quoted Latin to the Latin teacher, talked landmarks in Paris with a woman who went to college there and asked fans of the novel "The Horse Whisperer" if they support that gentle approach to breaking horses.[20]

---

[17] *See* Estelle v. Williams, 425 U.S. 501 (1976) (defendant cannot be made to wear jail apparel in presence of jury); Holbrook v. Flynn, 475 U.S. 560 (1986) (uniformed officers may be in the courtroom, provided that there is no suggestion that this is due to defendant's dangerousness).

[18] *See* 4 Blackstone, Commentaries 353 (15th ed. 1809).

[19] This material is adapted from Michael E. Tigar, PERSUASION: THE LITIGATOR'S ART 60–70 (1999), and is annotated with footnotes.

[20] This is not "making conversation"—it is a way to find out how these folks approach difficult issues. If you can find out what books jurors have read recently, you know that a

He sits next to Nichols at the defense table—which he had scooted over to get a better view of the candidates. He often puts his large right hand on Nichols' shoulder, as if to comfort his client.

Jury candidates are questioned one at a time, and U.S. District Judge Richard Matsch lets prosecutors go first.

So Tigar, waiting his turn, makes listening an interactive exchange. Leaning toward the candidate with shoulders slumped, he holds a firm grin and bobs his head in response to certain answers.

When his time comes, he carries his imposing figure to the podium, where his baritone voice commands the room.

"My name is Michael Tigar," he tells the candidate. "And Ron Woods, sitting right there, and I are lawyers. We were appointed . . . shortly after the bombing to help out Terry Nichols. And I'd like to follow up on some of the things that were asked and spend a little time with you."

Tigar's folksy manner often gets results—candidates respond more candidly. They are engaged by his knowledge as he sprinkles in references to bioenergetics, farming, birthing methods—whatever applies.

Tigar wants to know whether candidates choose spanking or time-outs with their children.[21]

He asked a study hall supervisor how he decides who is right when there is a classroom fight.[22] He asked a school bus driver how students would describe her.[23]

From No. 52, a nursing assistant who thought death was too easy for a criminal, Tigar wanted to know what she thought a crook should contemplate while in prison. "That they would regret what they've done and that they would know that they have committed a crime that is wrong," she replied.

---

given juror reads books, and you will find that a lot of them have read popular books about the legal system such as those by John Grisham or Scott Turow. "The Horse Whisperer" was a popular book at the time of this voir dire. It said something about an approach to people and issues.

[21] In a criminal case, this is a key question, particularly when the jury will decide punishment. It also illuminates juror attitudes in any case where punitive damages or a theory of deterrence may be in issue.

[22] The study hall supervisor decides "cases" all the time, such as when there is a fight in school. How does he do it? Does he listen to both sides? Does he find it hard to set aside some preconceived idea based on who is involved?

[23] Tough but fair? Caring? Safe driver? How?

He sometimes goes out of his way to not seem overbearing when he is getting unsatisfactory answers and has to ask more questions.[24] "Well, I hear you say, 'I think I would,' " he said softly to one candidate. "It's like if my wife said, 'Do you love me?' and I said, 'I think I do,' she'd want to ask another question."

Tigar impressed a Teamsters member by describing the logo on his union handbook. "You still get a little booklet there with the two pictures of the horses in front looking at each other?" Tigar asked him.

"Right," he said.[25]

Tigar even spoke the language of No. 763, a psychic and energy reading enthusiast who believed her karma would catch up with her if she sentenced someone to death.

"Now, much of your reading is about the energy in the human body. Is that right?" Tigar began.

"Right," she said.

"I mean, chakras are—well, how would you define a chakra?"

"I would say the chakras are points in the body, in the energy body that interact with the physical body; and they're data centers and energy centers where we're receiving and energy is leaving our bodies," she said.

"And in your view, do they occur along meridians?" Tigar asked.

"Yes."

---

[24] During individual voir dire, negative responses give the questioner a chance to emphasize that there are no right or wrong answers, only truthful and candid ones. In pursuing information about a prospective juror, open-ended questions are the norm. When counsel senses that a juror must be challenged for cause, then is the time to switch to closed-ended questions. If a juror doesn't answer questions directly, counsel should keep on asking. Then when you get a candid answer, you need to say "Thank you. I know this is difficult territory." If counsel gets a "bad" answer during group voir dire, thank the juror, "I appreciate your point of view." Then ask, "Does anybody have a different idea about this that you would like to share with us?" By this means, counsel is not only getting answers, but also watching people participate in something like a deliberative process.

[25] The questionnaire revealed that this juror was a loyal union member. He had been on strike with his union. Under his contract, he is paid his full wage during jury service. He had read his contract and knew his rights in this respect. He is therefore the kind of thoughtful intelligent juror one might want. It is important to show respect for somebody who goes to that trouble to prepare for jury service. As for knowing what is on the Teamster contract—the logo—that is old knowledge counsel happened to have, but if you needed to understand how union contracts provide for jury service, you should study that before you talk to this juror.

"So that there are meridians of energy that run in the body and along these are the chakras that are centers; is that—"he said.

"That's correct."

"And is that based on a study of Eastern medicine?" Tigar said.

"That's an ancient knowledge, yes," she replied.[26]

When No. 657 turned out to be a Latin teacher, prosecutors and reporters knew what to expect as Tigar approached the podium. He didn't disappoint.

"Have you ever heard the expression, 'Ubi societas ibi jus' "he said, then gave the translation. " 'Wherever there is society, there is this idea of justice.' ... My pronunciation is wrong, please don't grade my paper; but there's this social structure within which we all live that defines ... what the rules are?"

"Uh-huh," No. 657 said.[27]

Tigar sometimes slips in a point during his questioning—kind of to get potential jurors thinking ahead to his defense.

Jurors are expected to hear testimony that Nichols set off small explosives with his son in Kansas and a brother in Michigan. The defense will contend they were just having fun.

So, Tigar took special notice when a school bus driver wrote on her questionnaire that she had a friend with a homemade cannon.

"Made a big noise?" he asked.

"Yeah," she answered.

"Did everybody enjoy that?"

"Yeah," she said. "I guess so. Sometimes it was pretty loud."

"Well, you wouldn't jump to the conclusion that some fellow that wanted to set off things that made a noise on the Fourth of July was a bomber, would you?" the defense attorney said.

"No," she said.

"Wouldn't be logical?" he asked.

"No," she said again.

Point made.

---

[26] The defense is probing here to see how "grounded" this juror is. The prosecution had tended, in its questions, to dismiss her as a "flake." She was not.

[27] The Cicero quote is a potent observation on the rule of law, and can get the discussion started on that issue in a high-visibility trial. The aphorism is usually contrasted with another, inter arma silent leges, which means in time of war the laws are silent.

Another candidate, No. 848, complained, "I felt very uncomfortable with the defense. I would not want to be in a dark alley, a light alley, day or night with them."[28]

Tigar at first had no questions, but jumped to his feet as the candidate got ready to leave.

"Excuse me, your honor. May I just put one question?" he asked.

"Yes, you may," the judge said, then joked, "In self defense? Is that name-clearing?"

But Tigar was serious.

"Ma'am," he asked, "Have you shared your views—to which you are entitled—with any of the other jurors riding in the van or in any other context?"

"No, sir," she replied.

The judge turned serious, too, telling Tigar he appreciated that question "because I didn't think of it."

The judge is trying to find 64 acceptable potential jurors, weeding out those who could never vote for the death penalty and those who automatically would. Then he will let prosecutors and defense attorneys make cuts, until 12 jurors and six alternates are left. Each side gets to knock off 23. Defense attorneys try to save their cuts for the most objectionable candidates and try to force prosecutors to waste the government's strikes.

So, defense attorneys end up trying to persuade opponents of the death penalty to consider voting for the punishment. If that happens, the judge will accept the candidate and frustrated prosecutors will have to use a strike they might have saved for someone worse. Tigar has won admirers for his skill in swaying potential jurors to be open-minded.

It happened most dramatically with No. 474, who said, "I think that's something that should be left up to God and not for me."

Prosecutors didn't ask any questions—certain the judge would remove No. 474. But Tigar switched the business manager's opinion by first asking if she would defend herself if foreign troops invaded American soil. By the time he was finished, she agreed to consider both life and death sentences.

The Nichols defense team wanted jurors who would be willing to listen to the evidence and make a reasoned decision. The voir dire

---

[28] This juror will be off for cause, but counsel needed to make sure that she had not spread her ideas around the other panel members.

questions were designed to find out how jurors confronted and dealt with issues in their daily lives: that is the surest guide to how they will behave in the jury deliberative process.

OPENING STATEMENTS[29]

Judge Matsch did not limit the time for opening statement. Each side took about two hours. Judge Matsch forbade the use of demonstrative evidence such as charts and pictures in opening. An opening statement, he ruled, was counsel's time to address the jury directly.

Tigar and Woods agreed with the maxim: never waive the right to open at the beginning of the case. The defendant usually has the right to wait and open a the beginning of the defense case. However, waiting until then sacrifices the benefits of primacy, and lets the jury hear the government's evidence without any idea of how it might be contradicted. The defense does present evidence, in the form of cross-examination, during the government's case. It is important to give the jurors a road map to what they will hear. People tend to remember and retain information that relates to a story they have heard, particularly if the story is one they are inclined to believe.

In the Nichols case, the jurors had already read, heard, and seen a great deal about the Oklahoma City bombing before they came to court. They then heard the government theory of how Nichols allegedly helped McVeigh plan, prepare and carry out the bombing. It was important for the defense to acknowledge what the jurors had heard and would hear, but to put all of that into a different context.

In a criminal case, defense counsel starts with a certain reservoir of credibility with the jurors, and seeks to conserve that credibility and transfer it to the defendant. One way to exhibit credibility is to show a command of the relevant evidence. The Nichols team wanted to do this by confronting the government's evidence and theory of the case, and by presenting a plausible alternative reality based on the idea that the government's investigation had been slipshod.

The Government's Opening

The prosecution, led by an experienced trial lawyer named Larry Mackey, knew that a main theme of Nichols' defense would be that he was not present when the bomb went off. Mackey decided to confront that issue at the outset, in opening statement:

> May it please the Court. Ladies and gentlemen of the jury, good morning. April 19, 1995, fell on a Wednesday, the middle of the workweek. On that morning, Terry Nichols was home. He was home

---

[29] The full text of these openings is at 1997 WL 677907 (1997).

in Herington, Kansas, with his wife and his daughter. He was home and at a very safe distance from a truck bomb that exploded in downtown Oklahoma City in front of the federal building in Oklahoma City in the heartland of America. And Terry Nichols had planned it just that way.

There were others in Oklahoma City on that morning, and Terry Nichols had planned on that, too. Tim McVeigh was in Oklahoma City on the morning of April 19. He was one of those people. And on that day, Terry Nichols knew exactly where Tim McVeigh would be and knew exactly what he would be doing.

Tim McVeigh was there to do one thing, one thing only, the only thing left to do, the final act in a plan of terrorism that Terry Nichols and Tim McVeigh had embarked upon months and months before that date.

This is a case about two men who conspired to murder innocent people. Their plan succeeded when the bomb went off and people died.

On that day, at that moment, Terry Nichols was not in Oklahoma City; but during the months before that date, Terry Nichols had been side by side with Tim McVeigh, together in their plan of violence.

And true to that plan, on Wednesday, April 19, 1995, Terry Nichols knew that Tim McVeigh would be delivering a large Ryder truck as close as he could get it to the federal building in downtown Oklahoma City. And true to that plan, Tim McVeigh detonated that bomb.

When the bomb exploded at 9:02 that morning, it consumed the truck, it destroyed the building, and it changed the face of American history forever. And it killed 168 people, men, women, and children, the cross section of this country, whites, African–Americans, Hispanics, Native Americans, people of all ages, races, and backgrounds.

For just as Terry Nichols and Tim McVeigh had planned, there were others in Oklahoma City on April 19, innocent others. And at that moment, in fact, there were hundreds of people inside the Murrah Building. Most of those people were there as workers, men and women carrying out the business of the federal government. Others were there as citizens, seeking the assistance of that very same government. And still others were youngsters and toddlers and infants entrusted by their parents to the safekeeping of the day-care center in that building.

Those who died were there inside the building. Scores of people, including 19 children, died because they were there inside the building. They were inside a nine-story building as the floor below them gave way and the ceiling above them crashed down.

The Nichols Opening

The Nichols opening was in three parts. Michael Tigar began with an overview of the allegations and evidence, seeking to establish the main defense themes. Ron Woods then took apart the FBI investigation, noting all the leads that the FBI had overlooked as it decided to focus exclusively on the theory that Terry Nichols was Timothy McVeigh's only truly culpable accomplice. Tigar began this way:

> May it please the Court, Counsel, Mr. Nichols[30], members of the jury, on the 19th morning of April at 9:02 in the morning, or actually just a few minutes before, Timothy McVeigh parked in front of the Murrah Building in Oklahoma City. He was in a Ford F–700 truck from Ryder rentals with a 20–foot box. And Timothy McVeigh was not alone. With him in the cab of that truck were one or two other people. The driver parked the truck and set the bomb to go off.
>
> Yes, Terry Nichols was not there and did not know about the bombing until the next day. He was at home in Herington, Kansas, at 109 South 2d Street in a house he'd bought and moved into one month and six days before. He was at home. With him there were his pregnant wife, Marife; their infant daughter, Nicole; Marife Torres Nichols, born in the Philippines, who came to the United States as Terry Nichols' wife. Terry Nichols was building a life, not a bomb.[31]
>
> My name is Michael Tigar; and with our team, I represent Terry Nichols. We're here to gain respect for the undeniable fact that right now Terry Nichols is presumed innocent. We're here to help point out the hundreds of reasonable doubts that lurk in the evidence.
>
> In this opening statement, I want to introduce you first to our team members, the ones that are going to help us here; and then I want to outline for you the allegations, the charges, to point out what is not in dispute, what we agree with these prosecutors about, and what on the other hand we do contest, what the Government

---

[30] Always acknowledge your client by name in the opening. Let the jurors know that he or she is basic to the work you are about to do. Show respect to your client.

[31] This sentence, which expresses so well the theme of the Nichols case, was coined by Cathy Robertson, who was the mitigation specialist on the Nichols team. She is by profession a professor of English. She had worked with the defense team along with her husband, Adam Thurschwell. Tigar and Woods recruited her to be in charge of the mitigation evidence process. One day, in the team office, she stepped out of her cubicle and spoke this sentence aloud.

will try to prove and fail, and where you may find the reasonable doubts when the evidence is all in. Yes, when the evidence is all in.

Can you see my hand? You can't see my hand. Not until I've turned it over and showed you both sides could you say that you've seen my hand.

And just as in life, the last bit of evidence about an important thing may be the thing that lights up the whole picture, so we beg you to have open minds. We'll present evidence to you, beginning with our cross-examination of the very first witnesses that take that witness stand; but for the first few weeks of the trial, the Government has the choice of what witnesses to bring, what evidence to bring. He that pleadeth his cause first seemeth just, but the defendant come and searcheth it out.

Over and over again, you're going to hear about the presumption of innocence. That means we start with a clean page. That means that suspicion, prejudice, prejudgment, speculation have no place.

Now, when the Government rests, we are going to present our witnesses and exhibits. So after introductions and review of the allegations here, Ron Woods and I, my co-counsel, are going to do an opening statement in three parts so that you can have a perfect way of keeping track of the strands of proof.

First, I'm going to describe for you the results of our investigation into the Oklahoma City bombing. I'm going to describe for you how Timothy McVeigh planned this crime, who he planned it with, and who helped him commit it. I will tell you about the people that Timothy McVeigh used and lied to, the people he used in ways that he had to know would put them under unjustified suspicion.

Second, Ron Woods and I are going to tell you about Terry Lynn Nichols, born and raised in a farming community, married, the father of three children. Ron will tell you about what happened when Terry Nichols first heard on the radio that he was being sought as somebody who knew Timothy McVeigh, how he went right to the police station and spent nine-and-a-half hours telling the truth—yes, the truth—to the FBI, even as the FBI agents lied to him, lied to his family, and lied to the court.

And third, I'm going to talk very briefly about the FBI and its laboratory, its so-called "experts," some of whom are going to testify here, how those people ignored vital evidence, used junk science, did sloppy fieldwork, and rushed to a very wrong and quite early judgment. I say "briefly," because when their witnesses testify, we will cross-examine them fully and you'll have a chance to see who it is that's right and who is not.

So who's on the Nichols team? Well, the first member is Terry Lynn Nichols. Me, I'm Michael Tigar; and I am a school teacher. I teach at the University of Texas in Austin, Texas. My co-counsel is Ron Woods, solo practitioner from Houston, former United States Attorney for the Southern District of Texas and formerly special agent for the Federal Bureau of Investigation. We have some lawyers here, young lawyers helping: Reid Neureiter from Washington, Adam Thurschwell from New York, and Jane Tigar from Austin.

Now, handling the evidence—and you'll see these people working in the courtroom from time to time—we have Rose Haire, Tia Goodman, and Jan Halbert and Molly Ross from Oklahoma City and Stephanie White from Denver.

So let's begin by asking: What are those prosecutors charging that Terry Nichols did? What are they going to try to prove beyond a reasonable doubt? Well, you know there's an indictment, and there are 11 separate charges. When the case is all over, Judge Matsch will tell you what the formal, legal elements of each of these charges are; and he'll say to you, in effect, that if the Government fails to prove any element of a charge beyond a reasonable doubt, then it becomes your duty to acquit on that charge and to say "not guilty."[32]

Now, the first charge is that Timothy McVeigh, Terry Nichols, and others used—conspired to use a weapon of mass destruction against the Murrah Federal Building and the people in it. We do not contest that Timothy McVeigh did indeed conspire with several other people to blow up that building. We agree and understand and stipulate and concede that at least 168 people died from that crime, that the crime visited enormous harms on the hundreds of others. There's no dispute about that. The dispute is can they overcome the presumption in law that Terry Nichols had nothing whatever to do with it.

But I want to warn you: The prosecutors may choose not to accept the reality that we accept. They may choose to put before you graphic, emotional, tragic evidence of the devastation on April 19. These evidence—these events, I repeat, are—they're not in dispute. We understand that there's not a joy the world can give like that it takes away. The prosecutors may replay these terrible images over and over as if to say that somebody has to be punished for these things. That, of course, is not the question. The question for you at

---

[32] It is almost always a good idea to state clearly the elements of each claim and defense in opening, to help provide the jurors a framework within which to see the evidence. Tigar did this in detail for each of the counts of the indictment.

the end of the evidence will be who; and that is a question to be answered, we trust, in the light shed by the evidence and the law and not in flashes of anger.

If the prosecutors present this evidence, our concern will be to show how it fits the picture that we have drawn and not theirs. We will cross-examine all the witnesses who come here, even those who have lost so much. By doing that, we mean them no disrespect. To the living, we owe respect. To the dead, we owe the truth.

Now, there will be plenty of evidence that Timothy McVeigh promised to do violence and that he preached his gospel of hate, that he assembled the bomb materials. But there will not be any witness who will say that they heard Terry Nichols utter any threats of violence to anybody. The key to this case is the charge, the allegation that Terry Nichols knew there was a conspiracy to use a weapon of mass destruction against the building and the people in it and intentionally joined in that agreement. As to that, Terry Nichols says not guilty, and as to that, the evidence will show you plenty of reasonable doubts. Guilt by association is not conspiracy, knowing is not conspiracy, being associated is not conspiracy.

In saying what the evidence will show—by the way—we don't assume a burden we don't have. Terry Nichols is innocent. He's presumed innocent. If they want to change that, they've got to bring you evidence, to satisfy you beyond a reasonable doubt. We don't have any burden of proof here. And our job is simply to show the reasonable doubts; and to do that, we'll show you the hard evidence, the truthful alternatives to their theory. And from the first witnesses they present, we'll do that when we rise to cross-examine.

Ron Woods spoke next. He began by stating a major defense theme: the government's investigation had failed to follow evidence that would have led away from Terry Nichols. His opening illustrates a good way to put evidentiary detail in perspective.

If it please the Court, counsel, Mr. Nichols, members of the jury, the evidence will show that in conducting the investigation right after the bombing that the FBI did an excellent job—for a day and a half. The evidence will show that the FBI was able to find the rear axle of the Ryder rental truck which had been blown a block away from the site. And on that rear axle is a VIN number, a vehicle identification number. Each vehicle has a separate identification number so that it can be traced back to the manufacturer. By looking at that number, they were able to trace that Ryder truck back to a Ford manufacturer; and then the sale from Ford to Ryder rental.

They were able to go to Ryder rental's national headquarters in Miami and, through their computer records, find that that truck had been rented only two days before in Junction City, Kansas, by Robert Kling. They had that information on Wednesday, the 19th, that afternoon, quickly, by checking records and doing an efficient job.

They immediately sent the closest FBI agent they could find to Junction City, who was Scott Crabtree, in Salina, Kansas. They told him to call Eldon Elliott's Body Shop and get there right away.

Scott Crabtree will testify that he called Eldon Elliott's Body Shop, told them to keep the documents handy, don't talk about the case: I'm coming there right away to interview everybody involved in the rental.

Agent Crabtree got there that afternoon and separated Eldon Elliott, Vicki Beemer, and Tom Kessinger, and interviewed them in depth as to the description of Robert Kling and the second person that was with him.

He then had the FBI headquarters in Washington fly down that evening one of their forensic artists, who arrived in the early morning hours and met with Vicki Beemer, Tom Kessinger and Eldon Elliott separately; and by interviewing them and by getting descriptions, he was able to come up with sketches of Robert Kling and John Doe No. 2.

During this period of time, the FBI, utilizing the information on the contract, had determined that the name Robert Kling and the address in South Dakota was false, did not exist, there was no address.

So when the artist completed the sketches, they were designated as John Doe 1 and John Doe No. 2. This is early Thursday morning, the 20th. And you may have seen—you may recall having seen those on television, those two sketches.

That was done by talking to the three witnesses whose memory was fresh. This is on the 19th. Remember that the rental had only occurred two days earlier. Their memories are fresh. They can recall the details.

The FBI then took these sketches of John Doe 1 and 2 and dispersed their forces throughout the Junction City area and the surrounding area, taking these sketches around to all the businesses, the filling stations, the restaurants, the motels, attempting to find out who John Doe 1 and 2 were. They were also at that time released nationwide on television that you probably recall seeing.

They were very fortunate in arriving at the Dreamland Motel that afternoon, and the owner of the Dreamland, Lea McGown, told the FBI agents, this John Doe No. 1 sketch is Tim McVeigh, who was a renter in my motel from Friday, April 14, till Tuesday, April 18. The FBI looked at the registration records and found that Tim McVeigh had registered in his own name and had given North Van Dyke in Decker, Michigan.

Woods continued by showing the FBI's missteps and missed opportunities to locate those who were, the defense view, McVeigh's true accomplices.

CROSS–EXAMINING THE INFORMER—MICHAEL FORTIER

As noted above, Michael Fortier was a key government witness. He had known and lived with McVeigh, and had known Nichols. He had been essential to the case against McVeigh, who was tried before Nichols and sentenced to death. He recited many of McVeigh's out-of-court declarations, admitted as conspirator statements, inculpating Nichols. In opening statement, Tigar had reminded the jury that such statements, admissible as conspirator declarations, faced two hurdles. One had to believe first that Fortier was telling the truth that McVeigh said these things, and second that McVeigh was telling the truth if and when he said them. Consequently, Tigar was entitled under the rules to attack McVeigh's credibility as well as Fortier's, for a declarant such as McVeigh is subject to the same impeachment rules as if he or she had testified as a witness.[33] Fortier's unfavorable characterizations of McVeigh could therefore be used to undermine McVeigh's hearsay.

Fortier had traveled with McVeigh to "case" the Murrah building. Fortier lived with his wife Lori in Kingman, Arizona, where McVeigh had lived for a time. He knew of others to whom McVeigh had turned to help with the bombing, none of whom was ever prosecuted.

Fortier had given the FBI dozens of interviews, all of which were memorialized in FBI 302 reports that were not Fortier's prior statements, but rather the agent's impression of what Fortier had said. These 302s could be used to refresh recollection, but not admitted unless the agents testified.[34] Much of the cross-examination was devoted to tracking the way in which Fortier's testimony developed as he worked with the FBI and prosecutors, gradually adding more details that inculpated

---

[33] Fed. R. Evid. 806.

[34] An FBI "report of interview," known as a Form 302, is the FBI agent's "statement," and not that of the witness who was interviewed, except to the extent that he witness signs or otherwise adopts it. The Jencks Act, 18 U.S.C. § 3500. *See* LaFave, Israel & King, CRIMINAL PROCEDURE § 24.3(c) (4th ed. 2004).

Nichols. As Tigar said in summation of this process, "The Marine Corps builds men; the FBI builds witnesses."

The cross-examination also focused on Fortier's drug use, in part to show that he would not be prosecuted for it. More significantly, the defense was going to call a physician who would describe the adverse effects of methamphetamine on cognition and memory.

Fortier had reached a plea bargain with the government. He pled guilty to a conspiracy to sell stolen firearms, transporting stolen firearms in interstate commerce, making a false statement that he did not know of plans to blow up the Murrah Building, and misprision of felony. He was not asked to plead guilty to a conspiracy to blow up the building, nor to any offense directly connected with the bombing. In making as good a bargain for himself as possible, he had a powerful motive to tailor his testimony to the government's theory of the case. The cross-examination would focus on this theme.

Another goal of the cross-examination was to show that Fortier was more culpably involved with the bombing than Nichols. If the jurors believed this, they might acquit Nichols of at least the more serious charges against him. If there was a penalty phase, the jurors could consider as a mitigating circumstance that others as guilty as they had found Nichols to be would not be sentenced to death.

Fortier's direct examination consumed about a day of trial. The prosecutor led Fortier through his connection with McVeigh and through McVeigh with Nichols. The thrust of the direct was to show that McVeigh and Nichols were partners, and that McVeigh had often said that he and Nichols would act together. What follows are a number of brief excerpts from a lengthy cross-examination:[35]

Opening Theme—The Charges Against Fortier

Q. Good morning, sir.

A. Good morning.

Q. My name is Michael Tigar. I'm one of the lawyers appointed to represent Terry Nichols. You've told several different stories about what happened to you in April 1995, haven't you, sir?

A. Yes, I have.

Q. I want to ask you first about what you told us yesterday and today, and then I'm going to ask you about some of the things you said other times.[36] You have a written agreement with the

---

[35] The entire cross is at 1997 WL 703345 (morning session) and 1997 WL 703866 (afternoon session).

[36] The jury now has an idea of the order of topics in the cross-examination.

government. Is that right?[37]

A. Yes, I do.

Q. You are not charged with a conspiracy to blow up the Murrah Building, are you, sir?

A. That's correct.

Q. You did not plead guilty to that; is that correct, sir?

A. Yes, sir.

Q. And you did not plead guilty to blowing up the Murrah Building; correct?

A. That is true.

Q. You didn't plead guilty to murdering anybody inside it; is that correct?

A. Yes, sir.

Q. And didn't—the prosecutors told you, did they not, that you were being asked to plead guilty to everything that you did. Is that your understanding?

A. Yes, everything that I could be charged with.[38]

McVeigh the Racist—Fortier and Nichols Are Not

Q. Now, you mentioned that you first had a political discussion with Mr. McVeigh in the Army; is that correct? Did he share some literature with you?

A. Yes, he did.

Q. He gave you a copy of a book called The Turner Diaries; correct?

A. Yes.

Q. And is it fair to say, sir, that from that day down to the time when you last saw him, he often gave you political literature?

A. Yes, that is true.

Q. And is it fair to say, sir, that he made copies of political literature that he had and handed it out to others?

A. I believe he did.

* * *

---

[37] Introducing the first topic.

[38] He waffles a little in his response, but it is good enough not to require the examiner to pin it down further. Fortier has spent hundreds of hours preparing for this cross-examination. The cross-examiner must not try to get more out of it than it can possibly yield. This is the idea of immanence.

Q. And is it fair to say that this political literature that Mr. McVeigh began to share with you in the Army had a certain character?

A. Yes, I think that's fair.

Q. It was white supremacist literature; correct?

A. The book in the Army certainly was, yes.

Q. And—now, you did not agree with the white supremacist agenda, did you, sir?

A. I do not.

Q. You do not and you did not; correct?

A. That is correct.

Q. You were his friend all of these years, but you did not share his racism; is that right?

A. That is correct.

Q. Now, you mentioned that Mr. McVeigh's attitudes changed over time. Is that fair?

A. Yes.

Q. After the events in Waco in 1993, he became much more agitated; right?

A. He was upset about the events in Waco.[39]

McVeigh Untrustworthy

Q. Now, you know that [Mr. McVeigh]'s a thief; correct?[40]

A. What do you mean?

Q. Well, sir, you and Mr. McVeigh snuck into a National Guard yard and stole things together; correct?

A. Yes, sir, that is correct.

Q. So that's thieving, isn't it?

A. Yes, it is.

Q. And Mr. Nichols wasn't with you then, was he?

A. No, he was not.

---

[39] The "events in Waco" referred to the 1993 shootout between federal authorities and a religious group known as the Branch Davidians. The final and deadly day of the shootout was April 19, 1993, which was the reason McVeigh selected the April 19 date for the bombing. *See generally* ARMAGEDDON IN WACO: CRITICAL PERSPECTIVES ON THE BRANCH DAVIDIAN CONFLICT (Stuart A. Wright ed. 1995). This line of questions also helps to separate Fortier's and Nichols' views from those of McVeigh.

[40] We now begin to deal with McVeigh's lack of credibility.

Q. Didn't have anything to do with that; correct?

A. No, he did not.

Q. So you learned that Mr. McVeigh was a thief; right?

A. Yes.

Q. Now, in addition to that, you heard Mr. McVeigh on a number of occasions say that he was going to blow up a building; correct?

A. Yes.

Q. And he told you that he was going to blow up a building while it had people in it; correct?

A. Yes, he did say that.

Q. You learned that Mr. McVeigh uses narcotics; correct?

A. He has.

Q. On how many occasions have you seen Mr. McVeigh use controlled substances?

A. Two or three times.

Q. What controlled substances did you see Mr. McVeigh use on the occasions when you were with him?

A. He smoked a marijuana joint with me once; and on two or three other occasions, he used crystal meth.

* * *

Q. Now, you never saw Mr. Nichols steal anything; right?

A. Never.

Q. And you know that Mr. Nichols has two little kids; right?

A. At that time—now I do, yes.

Q. Yes. And as a matter of fact, his daughter is the same age as your Kayla; correct?

A. About a year—I think there is almost a year difference.

Fortier and McVeigh Do Things Nichols Did Not

Q. The first time after the Army that you saw Mr. Nichols was in the fall of '93. Is that right?

A. Yes, that's correct.

Q. You met him at a Wal–Mart and he came to your house and spent a little while. Right?

A. Yes.

Q. And that was the time you told us that he and your wife—or
    that Mrs. Nichols and your wife, Lori, talked about babies and
    you and Mr. Nichols talked about that he was going to get a job
    as a carpenter in Las Vegas. Is that fair?

A. Yes.

Q. Now, during that time—during that conversation, did Mr. Nich-
    ols—did you hear Mr. Nichols threaten anybody?

A. No.

Q. He didn't say that he was going to bomb anything; right?

A. No, he did not.

Q. He didn't express any political views to you, did he?

A. No. We didn't speak about political issues.

Q. Didn't give you any political literature; correct?

A. No, he did not.

* * *

Q. You didn't have any political conversation of any kind with him
    that evening, did you?

A. Not that I remember.

Q. Now, in—sometime in 1994 later on, Mr. McVeigh left King-
    man. Correct?

A. Yes.

Q. Now, when he left Kingman—and you told us that—he had
    some kind of a sale. Correct?

A. He did. He had a sale, but it wasn't when he left. It was prior to
    that.

Q. All right. When he had the sale, did you buy something from
    him?

A. Yes.

Q. What did you buy from him?

A. Among other items, I bought some explosive items from him.

Q. What explosive items did you buy from Mr. McVeigh there in
    1994 when he left Kingman?

A. I bought some cannon fuse.

Q. Some what? I'm sorry?[41]

A. Some cannon fuse.

---

[41] Tigar heard it the first time, but maybe the jury didn't.

Q. Cannon fuse. All right, sir.

A. Some blasting caps.

Q. Yes, sir?

A. Some aluminum powder that he said would blow up in some way. A can of gun powder. Possibly other items, but I can't remember.

Q. In addition to explosive items, did you buy fertilizer from him?

A. No, sir.

Q. Did you ever get fertilizer from Mr. McVeigh?

A. Yes.

Q. When did you get fertilizer from Mr. McVeigh?

A. That night he asked me to—if I wanted to buy the fertilizer also, ammonium nitrate in the bag.

Q. That's the same night as the garage-sale night?

A. Yes.

Q. And he asked you if you wanted to buy some ammonium nitrate. What did you say to him?

A. I told him no. I didn't know how to use the ammonium nitrate. And he asked me if I would just hold onto it for him then.

Q. Did you hold onto it for him then?

A. I took it home and put it in my shed.

* * *

Q. You also mentioned in talking to us yesterday something about a militia. Correct?

A. Yes.

Q. Did you all contact some individual or organization about the possibility of forming a militia?

A. We contacted an individual in Prescott, Arizona, and talked to him about what his militia consisted of and how myself and Tim could build one.

Q. And who was that person?

A. I believe his name is Walter Bassett.

Q. And is that the National Alliance?

A. I don't know about that.[42]

* * *

---

[42] Later evidence will tie Bassett to the National Alliance.

Q. Now, was there any time in your life when Mr. McVeigh and Mr. Nichols were standing so that everybody could hear when Mr. McVeigh said in words or substance: "This is my friend Terry. We're going to blow something up that belongs to somebody else, like a building"?

A. No, sir.

Q. Was there ever a time in your life where Mr. McVeigh and you and Mr. Nichols were standing side by side, where everybody could hear each other, when Mr. McVeigh said in words or substance: "My friend Terry and I are going to blow up a building with people in it and kill people"?

A. No, sir.

* * *

[Fortier describes a road trip with McVeigh during which they visited the Murrah Building in Oklahoma City.]

Fortier's Drug Use

Q. Now, you told us in direct examination that you had used methamphetamine; correct?

A. Yes.

Q. How did you use it?

A. I either smoked it, or I snorted it through my nose.

Q. And when you "smoked it," you smoked it in some kind of— how did you smoke it?[43]

A. We either put it on glass or on tinfoil, and you heat the bottom of it and it will smoke.

Q. And then what do you do with the smoke as it comes up off the glass or the tinfoil?

A. You inhale it.[44]

Q. Well, you can inhale it. One does inhale it. Is that what you do with it?

A. Yes.

Q. What does it do for you?

A. It makes you feel very excited.

---

[43] This is a non-leading question, asked on cross-examination. There is almost no potential downside to this question. *See* Michael E. Tigar, EXAMINING WITNESSES, Chapter 8 (2d Ed.2003).

[44] He says "you" inhale it. I do not accept this careless terminology. I am trying to make a point here.

* * *

Q. Now, you say also you snorted it; correct?

A. Yes.

Q. How would you do that?

A. One would form it into a line on some surface, and you take a straw—

Q. What do you mean "form it into a line"?

A. Well, sometimes it comes in a powder form, or sometimes it comes in a solid form. If it came in a solid form, you'd have to crush it up into a powder. Then you could form that into a line and snort it through a straw into your nose.

Q. And show the jury how you would do that.

A. What you do is you take a razor blade or a knife or some type of sharp instrument and you would just go like this [indicating] and it would form a line.

Q. And then to snort it, what would you do? Put the straw in your nose?

A. Yes.

Q. And then what, go, "Chnchnchnchcn"? Like that?

A. Just like that.

Q. Just like that. And then it would get up—what would it do to you when the stuff got into you?

A. Right off the bat, it would burn real bad; and then that would go away.

Q. You did this on purpose?

A. Yes. Many times.

Q. Okay. And then what would happen?

A. And then you would feel like—I'd describe it as an excitement. It feels as if you would just get off a roller coaster and you're just very excited.[45]

More on Fortier–McVeigh Contacts With Explosives and Charges Against Fortier

Q. Now, you said that Mr. McVeigh dropped some things by your house; correct?

---

[45] The judge's charge will describe a reasonable doubt as one that would cause a reasonable person to hesitate in making an important decision. In summation, Tigar could ask whether knowing Michael Fortier is a narcotics-using person who cooperated with McVeigh in so many ways, jurors would hesitate to let him baby-sit their children.

A. Yes.

Q. So you got some blasting caps from Mr. McVeigh. We talked about that. Correct?

A. Yes.

Q. You got some ammonium nitrate from Mr. McVeigh; correct?

A. Yes.

Q. You got some Primadet from Mr. McVeigh; correct?

A. I don't know what Primadet is.

Q. Oh. You got that stuff that—the orange tubing that you saw during your direct examination. You got that from him; correct?

A. Yes. Blasting caps, yes.

Q. Well, it's a blasting cap, but it has the orange stuff at the end of it; right?

A. Yes.

Q. You got some Kinepack or some Kinestik, some binary explosive from him?

A. Yes.

Q. You got both halves of it?

A. Yes.

Q. And your understanding is you can mix those together and you can make an explosive; right?

A. Yes.

Q. And you had all of these things at one time or another either in your house or your storage shed; correct?

A. The shed in my yard, yes.

Q. And you didn't conspire with Timothy McVeigh to blow up that building, did you?[46]

A. No, sir, I did not.

How Fortier's Story Originated and Developed

Q. Now, sir, I'd like to turn to the versions of events—the things that you said before you came here today. When is the first time that you were interviewed by the Federal Bureau of Investigation in connection with this case?[47]

---

[46] Again the theme: Fortier did more than Nichols and yet was not asked to plead guilty to conspiracy.

[47] Now the examination turns to an orderly development of how Fortier's story was built up over time.

A.   I believe it's April 22, 1995.

Q.   And do you remember on April 22, which would be a Saturday, being interviewed by Agents Williams, Petrie, and Mooney?

A.   Yes.

Q.   Now, they told you that they were investigating the bombing; correct?

A.   Yes, they did.

Q.   And you told them that you had not left Kingman, Arizona, for several months; right?

A.   That's what I told them.

Q.   According to you today, that was true; correct?

A.   No, that is not true.

* * *

[Tigar asked a series of questions concerning what was true and what was false about his story to the FBI.]

Q.   Well, where did this interview take place? At your house, or down at some sort of facility they had there?

A.   Both places.

Q.   So it started one place and then moved to another?

A.   Yes.

Q.   How did you decide what you were going to tell the truth about and what you were going to lie about?[48]

A.   The factor would be the legality of the issue. Anything that was illegal, I would lie about.

Q.   Well, why would you do that? What were you afraid of?

A.   Of getting in trouble.

Q.   What kind of trouble did you think you'd get into?

A.   Well, for one reason, I had a bunch of stolen weapons in my house. I did not want them to know that.

Q.   Right.

A.   I had prior knowledge of the bombing, and I didn't know—I wasn't sure if that was illegal or not, but it sure did seem like it should be; so I did not want to tell them about any prior knowledge.

---

[48] This is an open-ended question. It illustrates when and why such questions can be useful during cross-examination.

* * *

[Following up on his many talks with the FBI just after the bombing:]

Q. Okay. Did you then look at your wife and say: "Lori, let's tell them that we know Tim McVeigh. Let's tell them every time we saw him, and let's do the best we can to remember all these things that happened these last few months so that we can help"? Did you say that?

A. No, sir.

Q. Did you think that?

A. The first day of the bombing, the first morning?

Q. The 21st, sir?

A. Not on the 21st.

Q. Did you do that?

A. No, sir.

Q. In fact, sir, you were extremely proud of the confrontational approach that you took to the FBI. Isn't that a fact?

A. Yes.

* * *

[Tigar then played a series of excerpts from the electronic surveillance that the FBI put in place on Fortier's house trailer and telephone. During these conversations, he boasts that he is going to sell his story for a million dollars, rants at his mother for talking to the media without being paid, and boasts of his intended exploits as a potential witness. In one recorded conversation, Fortier says, among other things that he would pick his nose and flick the resulting material at the judge. He was, from his tone of voice, obviously high on something, probably methamphetamine, which can make one boastful. In one recording, he is overheard asking his wife to light a tinfoil pipe used to smoke meth. The government did not charge Fortier with any narcotics offenses.

Now the examination moves to the time when Fortier decides to become a cooperating witness.]

Q. Now, sir, there came a time when you got a grand jury subpoena; correct?

A. Yes.

Q. You and your wife, Lori, went to Oklahoma City?

A. Yes.

Q. Did you—you stayed in a motel?

A. Yes.

Q. And at 4:30 p.m. on the 17th of May, 1995, did you call the FBI?

A. I called a number that was on the subpoena. I don't know if it was the FBI or not.

Q. And did you later that day speak to some FBI agents?

A. Yes.

Q. Now, they got there at about 5:35 p.m.; correct?

A. That sounds right.

Q. And you told them you wanted to correct the statements that you had made to the FBI in Kingman, Arizona; is that right?

A. Yes. I said that to them.

Q. And Mrs.—your wife, Lori, what—how does she like to be referred to? Mrs. Fortier, Ms. Fortier? What—

A. Mrs.

Q. Mrs. Okay. Mrs. Fortier said that she wanted to correct her statements, as well; correct?

A. Yes. That was her intentions, also.

Q. Now, you also said that you were fearful of reprisals from the Aryan movement if you testified against Timothy McVeigh; correct?

* * *

Q. Well, isn't it the way it happened, sir, that the agents got there, you told them you wanted to correct your statement, you talked about reprisals and that you didn't want Mrs. Fortier to go before the grand jury and then they asked you do you still want to correct your statement?

A. Yes, sir.

Q. All right. And then the next thing that happened, sir, isn't it, is that you and Mrs. Fortier started to talk amongst yourselves about just exactly what you were going to do?

A. Yes.

Q. And then the next thing that happened, sir, was that the two FBI agents just left the room? Isn't that what happened?

A. Yes.

Q. And while the FBI agents were out of the room, you and Mrs. Fortier talked; correct?

A. Yes, sir.

* * *

Q. Then you stepped out of the room; correct?

A. Yes.

Q. Where did you go?

A. I went to speak with Special Agent Volz.

Q. Physically where was that?

A. Outside the room on the balcony.

Q. This is a balcony on the second floor?

A. Yes, sir.

* * *

Q. And you told the agents in effect, "I want immunity, and I'll give you Tim McVeigh"? Isn't that what you said?

A. In effect, that is what I said.

Q. And they told you that they didn't have the power to give you immunity, didn't they?

A. I don't remember them saying that.

Q. Did they tell you that they were going to give you immunity?

A. No, sir, they did not.

Q. Did they tell you that they weren't?

A. I don't remember them saying they weren't.

Q. Isn't it a fact, sir, that they told you that you would not and could not be granted immunity by the interviewing agents and that only prosecutors involved could do that?

A. I don't remember them saying that.

Q. Didn't they tell you, sir, that they didn't need you to make a case against Mr. McVeigh?

A. Yes, I do remember Special Agent Volz saying that.

Q. And after they told you that, you went back in the room; right?[49]

---

[49] This is a key portion of the examination. Fortier did not admit that the FBI agents said they could not give immunity, but the jury knows he did not in fact get immunity, only a plea bargain, and the FBI practices will be in evidence from other sources. The key here is that he offered only McVeigh, not Nichols, and was turned down flat with the assertion that they already had McVeigh and did not need Fortier to make that case. The clear inference is that he would have to give them somebody else, probably Nichols, who was already in custody. His statements to the government from that point on progressively expand his alleged knowledge about Nichols.

* * *

Fortier's Gun Transactions Come In Now and Will Be Used at the End

Q. I show you now, sir, what has been—. May I approach, your Honor?

THE COURT: Yes.

Q. [continuing]—what has been marked as Defendant's 397 for identification. And the first page is a government document. I'm asking you, please, to look at the second page and tell us whether you recognize the handwriting.

A. Yes, I do.

Q. And whose is that, sir?

A. That is my handwriting.

MR. TIGAR: Your Honor, we offer pages 1 and 2 of 397. 397 is a self-authenticating government document, and page 2 Mr. Fortier has just identified.

PROSECUTOR: No objection.

THE COURT: All right. D397 is received.

Q. I'm placing up on the [ELMO] here what has been received in evidence as government's 397, page 2.

Q. Mr. Fortier, this is a firearms transaction record; correct?

A. Yes, sir.

Q. And you filled it out, did you not? On July 17, 1993? Right?

A. Yes, sir.

Q. And you were asked are you an unlawful user or addicted to marijuana or any depressant, stimulant or narcotic drug or any other controlled substance; and you answered no. Correct?

A. That is true.

Q. And then you signed it; right?

A. Yes, I did.

Q. And before you signed it, did you read the part that says, "I hereby certify that the answers to the above are true and correct. I understand that a person who answers yes is prohibited from purchasing and/or possessing a firearm except as otherwise provided by federal law. I also understand that the making of any false oral or written statement or the exhibiting of any false or misrepresented identification with respect to this transaction is a crime punishable as a felony"? Did you read that?

A.   I do not recall. Most likely, I skipped that part.

Q.   Well, was the "no" true?

A.   No, the "no" was false.

Q.   Why did you put a false statement on a firearms record, sir?

A.   Because I knew that if you answered yes, they would not let you buy the weapon.

Q.   You committed a federal felony because you wanted to have a gun?

A.   Yes, sir.

*   *   *

Q.   I'm going to place this in front of you, sir; and I'll ask you, please, will you turn to Tab No. 484. Is that a—a gun purchase form dated December, 1993? Looking at page 2, D484.

A.   This is a firearms transaction record.

Q.   And whose is it?

A.   It is mine.

Q.   Did you sign it?

A.   Yes.

MR. TIGAR: Offer D484.

PROSECUTOR: No objection.

THE COURT: Received.

Q.   Did you make the same false statement, sir?

A.   Yes, I did.

Q.   And what—what gun was it that you told the lie to get there?

A.   This was a 10/22.

Q.   What's a 10/22?

A.   It's a small arms. It's a .22 caliber rifle.

Q.   Would you look at D485, sir. Is that a firearms transaction record?

A.   Yes, sir.

Q.   Whose is that?

A.   This is mine.

Q. We offer it, your Honor.

PROSECUTOR: No objection.

THE COURT: D485 is received.

Q. July, 1993?

A. Yes.

Q. Did you lie?

A. Yes, sir.

Q. Was it the same lie?

A. Yes, sir.

Q. What gun did you get for that lie?

A. Two guns, actually. A .38 pistol and a Mini–14 rifle.

Q. Now, under your plea agreement, you will not be prosecuted for any one of the lies you've told on these firearms forms; is that correct, sir?

A. I do not believe so.

THE COURT: I'm not sure of the answer. You don't believe it's correct—

THE WITNESS: I don't believe I'm going to be prosecuted for this.

THE COURT: All right.

Fortier's Plea Bargain

Q. Now, you testified on direct examination, sir, that you had spent some time with government lawyers discussing the matters you were going to present in court; is that correct, sir?

A. Yes.

Q. And you said you met with government lawyers about 25 times?

A. Yes. And each one of those times were for either one day or maybe two days.

* * *

Q. Now, I'm going to show you page 7 of the plea agreement portion of government's Exhibit 193 in evidence. That is entitled, "Breach of Agreement," isn't it, sir?

A. Yes, sir.

Q. And is that part of the deal that you have with the government?

A. Yes, it is.

Q. It says, "If further investigation discloses that Mr. Fortier conspired to bomb any federal building"—and then it continues on with some other things. It says, "... then the United States will have the right to characterize such conduct as a substantial breach of this agreement," and so on. Correct?

A. Yes.

Q. And it says, "... in which case the obligations of the United States under this agreement will be void, and the United States will have the right to prosecute Mr. Fortier for any and all offenses that can be charged against him in any district or state." Do you see that?

A. Yes.

Q. You have not been charged with conspiring to bomb a federal building, have you, sir?

A. No.

Q. And the United States is aware of everything, all the facts, that we have talked about today, are they not?

A. Yes.

Q. They're aware that you got ammonium nitrate from Mr. McVeigh; correct?

A. Yes.

Q. They're aware that Mr. McVeigh left explosives in your house; correct?

A. Yes.

Q. They're aware that Mr. McVeigh could—lived in your house and could use your tools; correct?

A. Yes.

Q. They're aware that Mr. McVeigh could use your phone?

A. Yes.

Q. They're aware that Mr. McVeigh borrowed your car?

A. Yes.

Q. They're aware that you went to Oklahoma City with Mr. McVeigh?

A. Yes.

Q. They're aware that you wrapped explosives for transport?

A. I was a part to that, yes.

Q. They're aware that you tried to get a storage shed in a different name than your own?

A. Yes.

Q. They're aware that you handled guns you thought were stolen?

A. Yes.

Q. They're aware you handled explosives you thought were stolen?

A. Yes.

Q. They're aware that you shared money with Mr. McVeigh in connection with the guns?

A. Yes.

Q. They're aware that you wanted to form a militia and took steps to that end?

A. Yes.

Q. They're aware that you had literature that you got from Mr. McVeigh that you had in your house; correct?

A. Yes, they are.

Q. And those are just—those aren't all of the things we talked about today but some of them; correct?

A. That is correct.

Q. As you sit there today, sir, are you fearful that the United States will decide to charge you with conspiring to bomb a federal building?

A. No, sir, I am not.

Q. Now, you testified in direct examination—excuse me. One moment. Let's look at more of the paragraph here, if we may. It also says that if further investigation discloses that you refused to answer any questions put to you—well, you haven't done that, have you?

A. No, sir, I have not.

Q. "... or makes any false or misleading statements to investigators or attorneys of the United States or makes any false or misleading statements or commits any perjury before any grand jury or court," do you see that, sir?

A. Yes.

Q. Now, who do you understand has the right to decide whether or not you have committed perjury and prosecute you for it?[50]

---

[50] This is a vital part of any cross-examination of a plea-bargaining informer. All such bargains recite that if the informer lies, he or she can be prosecuted. Prosecutors point to these terms as a guarantee of truthfulness, subject to the restrictions on "vouching." *See* QXR case on impermissible vouching. The cross-examiner must point out who makes the decision as to what is true or false.

A. I believe that would be the judge.

Q. Well, is it your understanding, sir, that it's prosecutors who decide whether to prosecute people?

A. Yes.

Q. You're aware that neither I nor Mr. Woods nor Mr. Nichols has any power to prosecute you if we should think that you're committing perjury?

A. I'm aware of that.

Q. Now, in your direct testimony, sir, you discussed the charges to which you have pleaded guilty and the maximum potential sentence that you might receive. Do you remember that?

A. Yes.

Q. And what do you understand to be the maximum potential sentence that you could receive?

A. 23 years in prison.

Q. Now, when—do you expect to do 23 years?

A. I think that's a distinct possibility.

Q. Now, Judge Matsch is not the judge who will sentence you; correct?

A. No, sir.

Q. That is, another judge has been appointed for that purpose; right?

A. That is right.

Q. And you understand that's a judge in Kansas; correct?

A. Yes.

Q. Now, at the time you are sentenced, which hasn't happened yet—correct?

A. That is correct.

Q. —your lawyer will have the right to present reasons why the sentence should be less than 23 years; correct?

A. Yes.

Q. Do you know what the guidelines' sentence is that—

A. Yes.

Q. Yes. What is it?

A. I believe it's 27 to 33 months.

Q. So if you were sentenced in accordance with the sentencing guidelines, you'd get 27 to 33 months; correct?

A. Yes.

Q. Now, your lawyer and you would have the right to argue for something less than that; correct?

A. I believe that's true.

Q. And a probation report would be prepared; correct?

A. Yes.

Q. In addition to that, the government will have the right to present evidence at that sentencing hearing; correct?

A. Yes.

Q. Now, is it your understanding that the government has the right but not the obligation to say to the judge, should it choose, that you have rendered substantial cooperation?

A. Yes.

Q. Are you aware that neither you nor I nor Mr. Nichols nor Mr. Woods would have any right to ask the judge to consider substantial cooperation? Is that your understanding?

A. Yes.

Q. Now, looking here at page 5 of your plea agreement, sir, do you see paragraph 65, Section 23—excuse me—Section 3553(e) motion. What do you understand a Section 3553(e) motion to be?

A. That if I fulfill my obligations with the United States prosecution, they under their sole discretion—they may file a—they may ask the judge to reduce my sentence.

Q. Let's read this: "If Mr. Fortier completely fulfills all of his obligations under this agreement"—that's the first part; correct?

A. Yes.

Q. One of your obligations is to tell the truth. Correct?

A. Yes, sir.

Q. But the decision as to whether you did or not is going to be made by the prosecutors—right—for these purposes?

A. Yes.

Q. "At the time of sentencing, the United States will advise the sentencing judge of the full nature, extent, and value of the cooperation provided by Mr. Fortier. In addition, the United

States will evaluate the information provided by Mr. Fortier pursuant to the preceding paragraph." Do you see that, sir?

A. Yes.

Q. And then it says, "If the government determines in its sole discretion that Mr. Fortier has rendered substantial assistance in the investigation and prosecution of others involved in criminal activities"—"others" includes others than yourself; correct?

A. Yes.

Q. ". . . then it will file a motion pursuant to"—and it cites some laws which will so advise the judge. And then it tells you the judge has the discretion to determine the sentence. Correct?

A. Yes.

Q. Now, we read here that the United States will evaluate the information provided by Mr. Fortier. Do you read that?

A. Yes.

Q. What does "evaluate" mean to you, sir? You worked at the True Value hardware store; right?

A. Yes.

Q. What does "evaluate" mean to you?

A. It means to me like they will grade my cooperation.

Q. Pardon me?[51]

A. "Evaluate" means grade or consider how helpful I was.

Q. Okay. And the United States prosecutors are the only ones under this agreement who have any power to grade or to consider your cooperation. Correct?

A. Yes.

Q. And then the judge will decide based on what they do or do not say; correct?

A. Yes.

Q. When you went into prison, sir, had your youngest child been born?

A. No, sir.

Q. Have you seen your youngest child?

A. Yes, I have.

Q. Is it your hope, sir, to be reunited with your children?

---

[51] Tigar probably heard the answer the first time, but wanted it repeated.

A. Yes.

Q. Of all of the things in the world, is being reunited with your family the most important to you?

A. Absolutely.

Q. And you want that to happen as soon as you can, don't you, sir?

A. Yes, I do.

Q. And you are a man who would lie just to have a gun, aren't you, sir?

A. I did do that, yes.

MR. TIGAR: No further questions.

TRIAL EVENTS AND RESULTS

The jury heard from more than 200 trial witnesses, and saw more than 2,000 physical exhibits. More than a dozen forensic experts testified on such things as bomb residue, plastic barrel composition, truck body construction, toolmark identification, fingerprints, and handwriting analysis. The defense called witnesses to establish its theme that McVeigh had reached out, independent of Nichols, to people who would help him with his plan. The prosecution focused on direct and circumstantial evidence of the Nichols–McVeigh connection.[52]

In the end, as noted, the jury's verdict—reached after more than a week of deliberation—was clearly a compromise—guilty only of conspiracy and involuntary manslaughter, not guilty of first degree murder, second degree murder, of arson and use of a weapon of mass destruction.

PENALTY PHASE

Judge Matsch rejected a defense contention that the verdict could not, consistent with the Eighth Amendment, lead to a penalty trial.[53]

The penalty phase was emotion-laden to an unusual degree. Groups of victims and their supporters decried the jury's initial verdict. They

---

[52] The summations of the prosecution and defense, which took many hours, are *available* at 1997 WL 765592 (first morning, government summation begins), 765971 (first afternoon, government summation concludes, defense summations begin), 769081 (defense summation concludes, government rebuttal summation).

[53] The offenses of conviction were involuntary manslaughter and conspiracy to commit arson and to use a weapon of mass destruction. The conspiracy count did not allege any culpable intent with respect to resulting death. The defense argued that major participation in intent to kill homicide—at least express malice second degree murder—is the minimum level of criminality that will support a death sentence, and that the conspiracy count did not provide that foundation. *See* LaFave, Israel & King, CRIMINAL PROCEDURE § 3.5(f) (4th ed. 2004). The government countered that the question of culpable intent would be dealt with in the penalty phase, under 18 U.S.C. § 3591(a)(2).

held public meetings around Denver in the ten-day recess between the two trial phases. In a capital case, the Supreme Court has permitted victim impact evidence. Therefore, it was expected that family members of victims would testify. The court permitted testimony from any relatives of any of the 168 victims, not only the eight federal officers named in the homicide counts. Witness after witness sobbed, and in some instances shouted. Judge Matsch intervened at some points, but interrupting this flow of painful recollection was a task that nobody in the courtroom relished undertaking.

Relatives of the federal officers displayed not only sadness but anger at the jury's finding that Nichols was guilty of involuntary manslaughter rather than murder. In addition, there was graphic testimony from medical and emergency personnel about the deaths and injuries. The defense called a number of Nichols' friends and family members attesting to his personal qualities.

In a federal death penalty case, the jurors are told to proceed in three stages. They must first decide whether the defendant had a culpable role in the death of another, under applicable intent and participation standards.[54] Next, they must decide if the prosecution has established one or more aggravating factors beyond a reasonable doubt. Finally, if they get past those two stages, they weigh mitigating and aggravating factors on which the judge has instructed them based on the statutory factors and items submitted by the parties.

In this weighing process, each juror is sovereign, in the sense that she may assign to any factor such weight as she believes it should have. Thus, a juror may think that one mitigating factor outweighs everything else, and vote for life. A death verdict requires that all twelve jurors concur at each of the three stages. A disagreement at any stage is a life verdict under the law. This point had not yet been established by the Supreme Court[55] at the time of the Nichols trial. Therefore, when the jurors announced failure to agree on the first phase issues, the government moved for a mistrial with an eye to having another penalty trial. Judge Matsch considered the matter overnight and held that the jury's disagreement was a verdict. Under that interpretation, the sentencing decision lay with the judge. Judge Matsch sentenced Nichols to life imprisonment.[56]

The prosecution's penalty phase argument focused on what the government claimed the jury had necessarily decided by finding Mr.

---

[54] 18 U.S.C. § 3591(a)(2).

[55] Jones v. United States, 527 U.S. 373 (1999).

[56] Later, Nichols was tried for murder in Oklahoma state court, and that jury also did not vote for a death penalty.

Nichols guilty of conspiracy, and on the destruction and loss of life in Oklahoma City. The defense took a different tack. Early on, the defense team had decided that all the testimony and argument would be conducted as calmly as possible, seeking to create an atmosphere of reason to counter the anger and sadness that pervaded the courtroom.

With respect to the first issue, culpable participation, the defense had to go back and look again at trial phase evidence. This is an example of that "bridge building" discussed above. In addition, evidence about Nichols' character and conduct from the trial phase was once again open for consideration.

The defense summation returned to the idea of sanctuary. In a sanctuary, all the people are part of the group, and of equal dignity. The argument for death must always deny those propositions that portray the defendant as "the other," or as somehow without those human qualities that entitle him to live.[57] The defense must also focus on the process by which the jurors decide, and the responsibility of each juror for the ultimate result:

> Counsel, Mr. Nichols, members of the jury, just shy of two weeks ago—it was in the afternoon—you came in and you rendered a verdict in this case. And since that time, it would come as no surprise to you to know that pundits and hired lawyers and TV talk-show hosts and lawyers and everybody has tried to figure it out. But the Judge is going to tell you in a few minutes when we're all done that all of that figuring and all of that posturing and all of that parading can't change a fact and it can't change the law. The verdict that you rendered is your verdict. It is final. It is binding on everybody in this courtroom, including the jurors who reached it.

> And I am not going to spend any time at all trying to tell you what you decided. I think that would be arrogance for me to tell you what you decided. Rather, I'm going to talk about the things that the Judge, when we're all done here, will tell you [in his instructions] are yet to be decided, keeping in mind that there is no going back on what's been done.

> I won't take long. When we're done here, this time that we've spent together, which has represented an enormous sacrifice, I know, for all of you, will be done and you'll go back to your jobs and back to the community. We'll all go back to our jobs, the prosecutors to other cases, me back to teaching school, Mr. Nichols to a prison, which is the result of the verdict that you already reached, not a pretrial detention facility but a prison. And one of the things we're here to decide today is whether or not in addition to that, beyond

---

[57] The entire argument is at 1998 WL 1057.

that, over and above that, 12 of you should sign a piece of paper that authorizes a sentence of death to be carried out with respect to Mr. Nichols; that authorizes somebody to come get him one day and carry out a sentence that he be put to death.

What you won't see when you go back, by the way, is any of us on this side joining the parade of talk-show hosts and as-told-to books. I think those things are a disgrace to a profession that tolerates them, and I think they are a disgrace to lawyers who do that.

* * *

Your verdict was that Mr. Nichols was guilty of the crime of conspiracy to carry out—use a weapon of mass destruction; that he was not guilty of use of the weapon of mass destruction; that he was not guilty on Count Three, and then with respect to those eight counts, an acquittal on the first-degree and second-degree murder charges and a conviction on the involuntary manslaughter.

Now, the Judge gave instructions at that time. And as I say, I can't describe for you what it is that you decided, and I don't think it's right for anybody to try to tell you what it is that you decided. The Judge did permit you to convict Mr. Nichols of the crime of conspiracy even if he did not know all the details of the agreement or understanding or even if he played only a minor role so long as he understood the unlawful nature of the plan and voluntarily and intentionally participated in it.

I ask you when you look at the effect of what you decided on what you're going to do now to look back at the instructions that the Court gave you at that time because it was clear to us, although we might be wrong, that you had read those instructions with extraordinary care and discussed amongst yourselves what those words meant as you were making a decision.

Well, as you discussed what the words meant and then applied them in your decision, that's the decision you made. So you'll have them again so that you can go back and refresh your mind about what it is that was involved in the things that you did and what was involved in the things that you didn't do.

And if you do that, I suggest that you will avoid an error such as the one made no doubt unintentionally by the prosecutor in summing up: "The crime he agreed to commit happened." Well, the happening of it, I had always thought, was Count Two and the agreeing part was Count One. But that, as I say, will be before you to decide.

Now, why does the Government want you to reach a verdict of death in this case? Well, they say it is to vindicate some vision of the law. They say it is because of certain facts that they have shown to you.

* * *

The process that you'll get into when you go back into the jury room to deliberate is in three stages. The first stage, as Counsel said, requires you to look at two findings. And unless you are unanimous beyond a reasonable doubt as to these, the process is over—if you answer no; that is, there is a reasonable doubt. You come back and the Judge sentences on Counts One as he will on Counts Four through Eleven in accordance with the law.

[Tigar reviewed the judge's charge, element by element, recalling evidence from the trial phase as well as from the penalty phase. A guiding theme was that only the jurors knew what they had decided, and that their conspiracy verdict could lawfully have rested on Nichols' minor participation. Tigar then reviewed the aggravating circumstances alleged by the government, noting that many of them required the jurors to place their trust in Michael Fortier's version of events, again harking back to the trial phase evidence.]

* * *

I feel now when I think about that evidence as though I'm standing before you and trying to sweep back a tide of anger and grief and vengeance. And I'm given pause by the fact that I feel that way, and I wonder if sometimes you might feel that way. But when I think that, then I think also of the instructions that the Judge is going to give you, because those instructions, as we contemplate this tide of anger and grief and vengeance, can get us all to higher ground, because the instructions will tell you that neither anger nor grief nor vengeance can ever be a part of a decision reached in a case of this kind.

I am, when I say this, not attacking these victims. We know their sacrifice. But we know that with the centuries of our civilization piled so high that we have come a very long way from justice based on vengeance and blood feuds.

This trial was moved from Oklahoma City because, I submit to you, it was thought that even the neighbors of those who lost so much would not do to sit in judgment. And to them, therefore, we can only say when we hear their grief and their anger and their desire for vengeance, "Bless those in need of healing."

But when I talk about this process, I want to say that I believe something else. And I don't want to say it in an effort to reach into a

place that I'm not entitled to be but to share with you some
thoughts about a concept of justice, to share with you some thoughts
that suggest that if you come to this point you would turn your face
towards the future and not towards the past.

We presented to you only nine witnesses. We could, as I suppose
the other side could for theirs, have presented to you many, many
more. But they told you about Terry Nichols, the son of Robert and
Joyce, the brother of Susie and James and Les, the father of
Christian and Nicole and Joshua, the husband of Marife, the friend
who had helped save the farm of Lyle Rauh. Each of these witnesses
lives in a community. And we were trying to give you a picture of
what Terry Nichols was like, this—his life that we're presenting to
you.

And I was interested to see the reaction of the prosecutors to
that, because I respectfully submit to you that it really wasn't fair.
[Tigar analyzed some of the prosecution's attacks on defense mitigation evidence, and some of the prosecution's characterizations of
Nichols's actions and motives.]

* * *

Why is it necessary if you're going to ask 12 people to sign a
piece of paper that says go get him someday and take him and put
him on a gurney and put poison in his veins—why do they have to
exaggerate? Why do they have to do that?

* * *

[Tigar then turned to the mitigating factors that the defense had
proposed and on which the judge instructed.]

Now, if you get there, you're going to find a list of mitigators at
page 5 of your jury form and then after that, a place to consider all
of these things, each individually, and then a place to sign that says
do you think it's death, life without possibility of parole, or some
lesser sentence to be decided by the Court, which sends it back to
Judge Matsch to consider in accordance with the law which binds us
all here, and along with those counts on which you found him guilty
of involuntary manslaughter.

Mitigator 1: That Terry Nichols' participation in the offense
was relatively minor. The term "relatively" is for you to define. I've
already read out the excerpt from the Judge's instruction on Count
One, which permitted you to find him guilty of conspiracy even if
you found he only played a minor role. That's for you.

Second, that another defendant or defendants equally culpable
in the crime will not be punished by death. Michael Fortier—
Michael Fortier was not asked to take a count that would carry a

death sentence. He wasn't even asked to do that. His wife, Lori, is home with the kids. You heard what Michael Fortier did. You heard his relationship with Timothy McVeigh; and without suggesting for a moment that you should decide, try to dictate to you one way or another, because again this is bound up with what you did before— you know what you thought about that. That mitigator is in there for your consideration.

Duress. Why is that in there? Well, that's in there because at one time Michael Fortier (sic) said, "I'm going to force Terry Nichols to do it." I don't know what you thought about that statement of Michael Fortier's made at a time when he himself was carrying a gun because he was frightened, but it's in there for your consideration.

No prior criminal record. Of course.

A concerned and loving son.

A concerned and loving father.

A devoted and loving husband.

These are by a preponderance, by the way. No one is requiring you to find or asking you to find that he was a perfect any of these. That is a standard, I suggest, that none of us could meet.

Concern for the welfare of his family, even in difficult circumstances, to the point where when his mother would send him money to buy things that they don't give you when you're in the prison, his commissary money, he would turn right around and send that to [his wife] in the Philippines.

That he's a caretaker for others including those not related to him by blood. . . .

A creative person, who has tried to use his creativity for the benefit of others.

A positive impact on the lives of many people.

Committed to self-improvement.

Served honorably in the United States Army.

And then one that may give you pause, if you get there, No. 14: That Terry Nichols is a human being.[58] Well, you'll find it, I suggest; but this emphasizes the individuality of the decision that you're to reach, the decision that says that for each individual deliberating juror, the weighing, how much of it goes into this process of decision is for you; that ultimately, when the matter is in your hands, you're

---

[58] Over the prosecution's objection, Judge Matsch included this as a mitigating factor.

going to decide what feels for you to be this conscientious response, this reasoned moral response.

Now, what if you get back there and somebody says: An eye for an eye? Well, you could start by saying: Wait a minute. Let's read the instructions. Shall we? Because there is no place for vengeance of that character in the decision that all of us here took an oath to administer.

You took an oath with respect to the questionnaire, another oath when we had you here to talk to you back and forth and asked all of those questions, and another oath to well and truly try. And all of those oaths dealt with the necessity and importance of following the Judge's instructions.

But, of course, even then, an eye for an eye, conscience of the community? Well, the words do appear, I know, in the Old Testament. They appear at a time when God is instructing the people of Israel about a system of blood feud and vengeance. But later on even at that time when a court was convened to decide who should live and who should die, called a Sanhedrin, it was decided that a judgment of death could only be pronounced in the Temple. And so the Sanhedrin stopped meeting in the Temple. And why? Because in the earliest stages of the development of our cultural tradition, it was recognized that when the law in its solemn majesty directs that life be taken, that can be crueler than deliberate vengeance because it teaches, because it is a voice that comes from a place that is at war with a reasoned and compassionate system of social organization.

I suggest to you that the Government wants to drag you back to a time of vengeance. I suggest to you that the FBI agent who said to Lana Padilla on the 21st of April, 1995, before a jot of evidence was in his hand, "Those two guys are going to fry," symbolized a rush to judgment that is at war with what the conscience of the community ought to do and ought to think about.

I submit to you that to surrender your deliberations to vengeance is to turn your back on lessons that we have all learned with great difficulty and a great deal of pain.

Nobody knows the depths of human suffering more than those who have been the systematic victims of terror; and yet in country after country, judicial systems are saying that in each case, the individual decision must triumph over our sense of anger. Even the Supreme Court of Israel freed from a death sentence a man found to have no direct participation in the deaths of people that he had been accused of killing.

In South Africa, when Mandela was released from prison, it was decided that it would be very, very difficult despite the record of violence against the black majority to obtain a death sentence and that a system would be put in place to make sure that acts of vengeance and anger were not carried out in the name of the law.

Well, I've gone through the form and I've gone through the instructions. And if I've said anything that makes you think that I'm trying to tell you what you already decided or what you ought to think in terms of your deepest convictions, please disregard it.

The last time I spoke to you in a closing argument, I said some things. Let me finish now by noting: The recommendation you're going to make, if you get to the point of choosing one of those three things, is binding on the Judge. If you get to that point, you've got those three choices and that's what's going to happen: death, life without parole, some other sentence.

When I concluded my earlier summation, I walked over to Terry Nichols and said, "This is my brother."[59] And the prosecutor got up and reminded all of us, thinking that he would remind me, that there were brothers and sisters and mothers and fathers all killed in Oklahoma City. Of course, when I said, "This is my brother," I wasn't denying the reality of that. I hope I was saying something else. I was talking about a tradition that goes back thousands of years, talking about a particular incident, as a matter of fact. You may remember—most of us learned it I think when we were young—the story of Joseph's older brothers, Joseph of the many-colored coat, now the "Technicolor Dream Coat" in the MTV version. And they were jealous of him, cast him into a pit thinking he would die, and then sold him into slavery. And years later, Joseph turns out to become a judicial officer of the pharaoh, and it happens that he is in a position to judge his brothers. And his brother Judah is pleading for the life or for the liberty of the younger brother, Benjamin; and Joseph sends all the other people out of the room and announces, "I am Joseph, your brother." That

---

[59] The earlier phase summation had ended with:

168 people died in Oklahoma City. We have never denied the reality of that. More than 30 years ago, I went to Washington, D.C., for the first time. And the very first public building I ever saw was the Supreme Court of the United States. And I saw where it said, "Equal Justice Under Law." And that means rich or poor, or neighbor or stranger, or a tax protester or not, or somebody who is different from us, or not. And wouldn't it be terrible if it was thought by anybody that a fitting memorial to the 168 who died would be to go there some dark night and chop those words off where they are on the lintel above the Supreme Court of the United States? Members of the jury, I don't envy you the job that you have. But I tell you this is my brother. He's in your hands. 1997 WL 769081.

was the story, that was the idea that I was trying to get across; that in that moment, in that moment of judgment, addressing the very human being, his older brother Judah, who had put his life at risk and then sold him into slavery, he reached out, because even in that moment of judgment he could understand that this is a human process and that what we all share looks to the future and not to the past.[60]

Members of the jury, we ask you, we suggest to you, that under the law, your judgment should be that this case go back to Judge Matsch and that he reach the just and appropriate sentence under the law and under the verdict that you've already reached.

I won't have a chance to respond to what the prosecutor says, but I know that after your 41 hours of deliberations on the earlier phase, you're all very, very accustomed to thinking up of everything that could be thought.

My brother is in your hands.

CONCLUSION

There was not even unanimity on the jury about Nichols' mental state with respect to resulting death. The jurors did not even get to weighing mitigating and aggravating factors. Juror interviews after the trial ranged wide. Many jurors professed that they lost faith in the government's competence and candor. Some of them thought that the government lawyers were prone to exaggerate. These interviews give reason to believe that the "sanctuary" idea and theme played an important role in defusing the emotion that was inherent in the case and leading the jurors to see the underlying issues.

---

[60] The story of Joseph is a part of a shared cultural tradition, known to Christian, Jewish and Muslim believers and, through its popularization in musical form, to a broad audience. The story is therefore suitable for jury argument, as a story with more limited cultural significance would not be. The imagery in William Wirt's arguments in the Burr case, discussed in Professor Ferguson's essay in this volume, are drawn from materials familiar to the jurors of that time and place.

6

Prof. Robert Lloyd[1]

Pennzoil v. Texaco

On November 19, 1985 a jury in Houston, Texas returned a verdict of $10.53 *billion* against Texaco, Inc., one of the nation's largest and most respected corporations. The size of the verdict shocked the business world. It was more than five times larger than the largest verdict in history, and that verdict, rendered in an antitrust treble damage suit, had been reversed on appeal.[2] The damages assessed against Texaco were more than the company was worth, whether that value was based on the net worth shown on Texaco's books or the total value of all the Texaco stock outstanding. Even more shocking was the fact that this verdict did not arise out of a mass tort or a treble-damages antitrust suit. It arose out of a single business transaction, a transaction in which most professionals in the field believed that Texaco had done nothing wrong.

Why then did the jury give the plaintiff so much money? The answer is that Joe Jamail, a personal injury lawyer, a self-styled "sore back lawyer," had been able to turn what appeared to be a complex business case into a simple melodrama. Like all melodramas, it was a case of good against evil. Jamail was able to paint the plaintiff as pure good and the defendant as pure evil. All the complexities of human nature were brushed aside. The story had the classic melodrama story line. The virtuous person was about to win the prize. (In this case it was not true love, but another oil company.) The evildoer stole it away. Then, in came the hero (in this case the jury) to right the wrong.

In his book, *Legal Blame*, Professor Neal Feigenson explains how good tort lawyers intuitively realize that jurors see accidents as melodra-

---

[1] Lindsay Young Distinguished Professor, University of Tennessee College of Law.

[2] *See* MCI Communications Corp. v. AT & T, 708 F.2d 1081 (7th Cir. 1982), *cert. denied*, 440 U.S. 971 (1983).

mas and how these lawyers present their cases as melodramas. The genius of Joe Jamail was that he was able to adapt this technique, which he mastered in decades of trying personal injury cases, to an entirely new situation. *Pennzoil v. Texaco* involved a complex series of business transactions. It had a large cast of characters who were themselves complex human beings. Yet, through four and half months of trial and 24,000 pages of transcript, Jamail was able to tie everything to a simple story line. Pennzoil had a deal. Texaco and its evil allies stole the deal. The jury had an opportunity to right the wrong and send corporate America the message that this behavior will not be tolerated.

Getty Oil Company

The source of all the trouble was Getty Oil Company, built by J. Paul Getty, one of the legendary figures in American business. Getty was a bizarre individual, and his personal peculiarities (idiosyncracies is too mild a word) would have an indirect effect on the deal that occurred years after his death.

J. Paul's father, an insurance company lawyer from Minneapolis, had gone to Oklahoma to collect a debt. He saw the possibilities in the infant oil business and moved his family to Oklahoma, where he became one of the first wildcatters and made several million dollars, a considerable fortune at the time. Growing up rich, J. Paul was for a time a wild and reckless playboy, but he soon became consumed by a passion to build an enormous fortune. He threw himself into the oil business, and through a combination of business acumen, drive, and ruthless greed, he became one of America's first billionaires. By the late 1950s, *Fortune* magazine was calling him the richest person in America. His continual womanizing was only secondary to his greed.

Unlike many of the other legendary figures of the oil industry who were portrayed (correctly or not) as big-hearted romantics who loved a good time, J. Paul Getty was cold, calculating and mean-spirited. He had five wives, all of whom he treated shabbily, and five sons, whom he treated worse. His oldest son, George, seemed destined to succeed in his father's business. George became the chief operating officer of Getty Oil and was so respected a businessman that Bank of America and Douglas Aircraft Company named him to their boards of directors. But J. Paul was so compulsive and controlling that the stress of working for him drove George to suicide. J. Paul disinherited his second son, Ronald, because Ronald's mother had won a divorce settlement J. Paul deemed too generous. The third son, Eugene Paul Getty, who later changed his name to J. Paul Getty, Jr., joined the international jet set, hobnobbed with Mick Jagger, and became a hopeless drug addict. Another son, Timothy, died in infancy all but ignored by his father.

The only son to escape relatively unscathed was Gordon Getty, a charming eccentric, who, after a disastrous career in his father's oil company, became a poet and composer. Whether Gordon was a hopeless innocent or whether his absent-minded-professor facade concealed a shrewd mind was to become a central issue in the trial.

Gordon was important because he was the trustee of the family trust. Early in his career, J. Paul needed to borrow money from his mother (his father had by that time died) to take over Tidewater Oil Company. Fearing that her son would lose the family fortune in reckless ventures, Sarah Getty conditioned the loan on J. Paul putting the family's money, his as well as hers, into a trust, which became known as the Sarah C. Getty Trust. In 1983, the trust owned 40% of the stock of Getty Oil Company, and Gordon was the sole trustee.

J. Paul hadn't intended Gordon to be the sole trustee. Before his death, he had amended the trust so that upon his death there would be three co-trustees: Security Pacific National Bank, then the second-largest bank in California, Lansing Hayes, J. Paul Getty's long-time attorney and confidant, and Gordon, whom J. Paul then considered the least-incompetent of his surviving sons. When J. Paul died, the bank refused to serve as trustee, calculating that the $3 million a year fee it would earn would not adequately compensate it for the risk inherent in managing so large a fortune.[3] So, when Lansing Hayes died, Gordon became the sole trustee.

Before J. Paul Getty died in 1976, he began erecting a monument to himself, the J. Paul Getty Museum. Getty became an art collector in the 1930s, pursuing depression-era bargains in art with the same ruthless determination he used in the oil business. Before his death, he commissioned the building of a museum to house his collection. It was said that he had it designed to resemble a Roman palace because he believed he was the reincarnation of the Emperor Hadrian. One writer called it "a garish $17 million monstrosity full of proto-Classical geegaws."[4] Getty organized the museum as a charitable foundation, and he left to it the part of his fortune that he had been able to keep out of the family trust, twelve per cent of the stock of Getty Oil Company. At the time Getty's estate was probated, the museum's share was worth $1.2 billion.

Trouble at Getty Oil

J. Paul Getty's death changed Getty Oil Company. During his last years, Getty lived in England, and had left the day-to-day operations to

---

[3] The bank's particular concern was the liability which might result if the trust were to sell its stake in Getty Oil. As it turned out, this concern was particularly well founded, because if the bank had become a trustee, it might well have been a defendant in the Pennzoil suit.

[4] THOMAS J. PETZINGER, JR., OIL AND HONOR: THE TEXACO–PENNZOIL WARS 88 (1988).

Harold Berg, a no-nonsense oilman of the old school. When Berg retired, two years after Getty's death, leadership of the company fell to a group of professional managers, headed by Sid Petersen, a finance man who liked the trappings of office so much that his subordinates referred to him as "the Imperial Chairman."

When Gordon Getty became the sole trustee of the family trust, he decided that Petersen and his management team were not running the company in a way that best served the interests of the trust, the holder of 40% of the company's stock. Gordon thought the stock price was lower than it should be, given the value of the oil reserves the company owned. Gordon studied the company's finances and approached a number of outsiders, soliciting ideas for improving the value of the trust's investment. This horrified Getty Oil management, for among those whom Gordon consulted were not only executives of rival oil companies, but a number of people who might use the information Gordon gave them to take over the company.[5] Even if the people Gordon talked to didn't launch hostile takeovers, the news of Gordon's conversations was sure to get out, leading others to see Getty Oil as a potential target. When Getty Oil management and directors, including Petersen, warned Gordon that these contacts were improper and dangerous, Gordon brushed them off.[6] Gordon even refused to listen to his own lawyers, causing them to hand deliver to him a strongly-worded letter warning him of his potential liability for disclosing inside information. But instead of heeding the warnings, Gordon continued as before, even meeting with the notorious corporate raider T. Boone Pickens, who proposed his own plan for taking over Getty Oil.

Finally, in an attempt to put a stop to Gordon's seemingly random schemes and to make it appear that Gordon and management were working in concert, Petersen agreed to hire the prestigious Goldman, Sachs investment bank to study ways to raise the depressed price of Getty Oil stock and to recommend to the board of directors a course of action. The Goldman, Sachs study, which took several months and cost Getty Oil more than a million dollars, explored many possibilities, including all the schemes proposed by Gordon and the people he consulted. Goldman, Sachs concluded that all these ideas were impractical. While many of these strategies had worked in other companies, the size of Getty Oil Company and the special tax problems of the trust rendered the ideas impractical for these entities. Goldman, Sachs presented its

---

[5] Some of the people Gordon talked to went so far as to present proposals for takeovers, and one, the oil-rich Cullen family, even lined up an eight billion dollar line of credit to fund such a takeover.

[6] As one writer put it: "To Petersen, Gordon was like an ancient Christian asking the hungry lions what kind of food they'd like for supper." STEVE COLL, THE TAKING OF GETTY OIL 49–50 (1987).

conclusions at a board meeting in July, 1983. At that meeting several members of the board expressed outrage at money spent simply to placate Gordon, and Gordon made things worse by saying he thought "additional alternatives should be considered." When one of the outside directors, John Teets, chairman of Greyhound Corporation, asked him what he wanted to accomplish he said: "What I really want to do is find the optimum way to optimize values."

This led Teets to respond: "Gordon, you may know what you just said, but nobody else in this room does." Other directors agreed, and they made it very clear that the studies and explorations, whether by Gordon or by management, had to end.

Gordon, however, was not dissuaded. He immediately began thinking up new schemes. One called for the trust to join forces with the J. Paul Getty Museum, which owned 12% of Getty Oil's stock. Together, they would acquire the rest of the corporation's stock through a leveraged buyout. Like all of Gordon's other schemes, this one would have resulted in Sid Petersen, the Getty Oil directors, and most of the Getty Oil's other senior management losing their jobs. The extent to which management's opposition to Gordon's schemes stemmed from this fact rather than from genuine concern for the company would become an issue in the trial. When investment bankers explained that a leveraged buyout would put the company's entire future (and the trust's entire fortune) at risk, Gordon backed off from this plan. But shortly thereafter he came up with another plan whereby the trust and the museum would join to use their combined 52% voting power to replace the entire Getty Oil board. Even Gordon's own lawyers opposed this plan, and the museum rejected it out of hand.

The museum was headed by its president, Harold Williams, a man with a considerable reputation. He had been a top corporate executive before becoming Dean of the Graduate School of Management at UCLA and later Chairman of the Securities and Exchange Commission. Williams realized that Gordon's maneuverings were likely to result in a battle between Gordon and the Getty Oil management, that inevitably would involve the museum. He knew the museum needed a lawyer, and he prevailed upon his friend Marty Lipton to represent him. Lipton was the world's leading mergers and acquisitions lawyer. He was the inventor of the "poison pill" takeover defense.[7] Lipton very quickly came to the conclusion that the best thing for all concerned would be for all parties to stop what they were doing and enter into a standstill agree-

---

[7] A poison pill is a shareholder rights plan that allows existing shareholders to acquire additional securities to dilute the holdings of an entity attempting to make a hostile takeover.

ment whereby they agreed that for a specified period none of them would take any action affecting control of Getty Oil.

In the meantime, Gordon's lawyers had decided that if Gordon was going to get involved in the sorts of deals he was thinking about, he needed an investment banker. They chose Marty Siegel of Kidder, Peabody & Company. Siegel would later go to jail for selling inside information to arbitrageur Ivan Boesky,[8] but in 1983 Siegel was considered one of the best and most aggressive investment bankers in the business. He was also a friend of Marty Lipton.

With Siegel on board, the three factions—the company, the trust, and the museum—met in the San Francisco offices of Gordon's lawyers. There, after much prodding by Williams, Siegel, Lipton, and even his own lawyers, Gordon reluctantly signed a handwritten standstill agreement that Siegel and Lipton had drafted on the plane trip from New York. In addition to providing that no major corporate changes could be undertaken for 12 months, it provided that Harold Williams, the museum's President, and Moses Lasky, Gordon's principal attorney, would become directors of Getty Oil. When Lipton presented the agreement, signed by Gordon and Harold Williams, to Getty Oil President Sid Petersen, the company's outside counsel, Bart Winokur, balked at having his client sign, objecting that the agreement was much too vague and left too much open to dispute. Lipton was adamant that it was the best they could hope to get from Gordon, so Petersen signed it, writing "Subject to approval of the board of directors" below his signature.

At the same time they were negotiating the standstill agreement, Getty Oil management was conspiring against Gordon on another front. When Gordon became the sole trustee of the family trust, other family members were concerned about Gordon's ability to manage the trust and began pushing for the appointment of a co-trustee. Gordon and his lawyers rebuffed their requests, and the family members didn't appear to be contemplating legal action. Sid Petersen, however, saw the appointment of a co-trustee, preferably a conservative financial institution, as a way to keep Gordon from pursuing his risky schemes. With the help of Bart Winokur, who had become Getty Oil's main outside lawyer after the death of Lansing Hays, Petersen concocted a plot to have a trust beneficiary file a lawsuit to force the appointment of a co-trustee. They first began working on this project in April, 1983, consulting several of California's leading trusts and estates lawyers, some of whom declined to get involved. Through intermediaries, Petersen and Winokur were able to get Seth Hufstedler, a respected Los Angeles attorney, to agree he would act as guardian ad litem to prosecute a suit on behalf of a trust

---

[8] Using information from Siegel, Boesky made more than $50 million from the Getty Oil takeover.

beneficiary if a suitable beneficiary could be found. Working with Gordon's brother J. Paul Getty, Jr. and Paul Jr.'s London solicitor, they decided that the appropriate plaintiff would be Paul Jr.'s 15–year–old son, who was living at a boarding school in England. The son, born during Paul, Jr.'s days as a hippie jet setter, bore the name Tara Gabriel Galaxy Gramaphone Getty. He knew virtually nothing about what was being done in his name.

On November 11, 1983, Getty Oil Company held its regularly-scheduled quarterly board meeting at its regional headquarters in Houston. What happened at that meeting did not directly affect the deal that was the subject of the lawsuit, but the way Jamail's legal team was able to use the events of that meeting to influence the jury may have been the decisive factor in their victory. The first action item on the agenda was the standstill agreement. Because the trust and the museum were parties to the standstill agreement, Gordon left the room. After he left, Bart Winokur came into the room. He was accompanied by Geoff Boisi, the head of Goldman, Sachs' mergers and acquisitions department, and Herb Galant, a Wall Street lawyer Getty Oil management hired when it became evident Gordon's maneuverings might make them a takeover target. The exact circumstances of how the three came into the room became an issue at trial. Pennzoil claimed that they clandestinely entered the room to hide from Gordon the fact that they were going to discuss the suit to have a co-trustee appointed. The Pennzoil lawyers referred to Winokur as "Back Door Bart." Winokur, however, claimed he and his companions were merely late for the meeting and entered through the same door as everyone else.

During Gordon's absence, the directors did discuss the standstill agreement, but they spent more time discussing whether Getty Oil Company should intervene the in the co-trustee suit. Some of the directors felt that intervention in the affairs of the family was improper and would subject the company to criticism. Petersen and Winokur, however, insisted that the company's intervention was necessary. Without that support, Hufstedler, who was to act as guardian ad litem, would not go ahead with the suit. The company, they said, had to get involved in the suit to protect to public shareholders (48% of the company's stock was in the hands of the public) from Gordon's irrational and high-handed actions. He had already attempted to take over the company, and it was only the museum's refusal to go along that had prevented it. Petersen and Winokur eventually persuaded the directors, and they approved the intervention.

When the directors called Gordon back into the meeting, they told him the standstill agreement had been approved, but they told him nothing about the suit against him.

The board meeting had taken place on a Friday. On Monday, Hufstedler filed the suit in Los Angeles, and on Tuesday, Getty Oil Company filed notice of its intervention in the suit. When he heard about the suit, Harold Williams, the museum's President was outraged. So was Marty Lipton, his attorney. They thought the Getty Oil management had behaved unethically and immorally, and were in fact so outraged that they decided to join forces with Gordon. Gordon wanted the museum to join with the trust to replace the board of directors, fire Petersen and his management team, and run the company themselves. Williams and Lipton weren't ready to go that far. They were, however, willing to take less drastic action. Early in December, the trust and the museum, which together owned 52% of Getty Oil's stock, used their power as holders of a majority of the corporation's stock to change its by-laws. Among other things, the amended by-laws required a supermajority of fourteen of the sixteen directors to approve any major corporate transaction. Because, under the standstill agreement, three of the directors were Gordon's nominees, the change to the by-laws meant Gordon could block any major corporate action. Unfortunately, the consent had another effect that Gordon did not intend. It told the world that there was trouble at Getty Oil and that the corporation was ripe for a takeover.

The Deals

When Hugh Liedtke, Chairman of the Pennzoil Company, heard about the consent, he saw an opportunity. He had been following the Getty Oil situation ever since the standstill agreement was announced in October, and the news about the consent told him it was time to act. Liedtke wanted to be a big player in the oil business, and being a big player meant expanding from lubricating oils to fuels: gasoline, diesel, aviation fuels, and the like. This required enormous amounts oil reserves. Pennzoil did not have those reserves, but Getty Oil did. Buying Getty Oil would make Pennzoil and Liedtke major players in the oil business.

To get control of Getty Oil at the least cost, Liedtke decided to make a tender offer for 20% of the company's stock. This would enable him to join with Gordon and do what Williams and Lipton had been unwilling to do—throw out the existing management. Liedtke's financial experts analyzed all the information he could get on Getty Oil. Their studies showed that Pennzoil would be getting a good deal if it bought Getty Oil for $120 a share, but Liedtke thought he could get 20% of the stock for a much lower price. The stock was then selling for $80, although it had been selling for as low as $50 before news of Gordon's activities had caused investors to buy the stock in the belief that there would be a takeover.

Pennzoil announced its tender offer to the Getty interests on on Tuesday, December 27th. It offered $100 per share. The announcement set off a fury of meetings in which various factions aimed at forming alliances or making side deals. Lipton met with Pennzoil's investment banker to discuss a sale of the museum's stock to Pennzoil. Gordon proposed to Harold Williams a plan whereby the trust and the museum would take over the company and Gordon would become CEO. This was another bad move on Gordon's part. Williams considered the plan so unrealistic that he decided he wanted the museum to sell its stock in Getty Oil if Gordon was to remain involved with the company. Williams' decision killed another plan that Marty Lipton, Williams' attorney, had been working on independently. Lipton's plan would have had the museum and the trust join forces with the company to oppose the Pennzoil takeover on the condition that Sid Petersen be forced to retire from his position as President of Getty Oil.

In the end, the proposal that had legs was one that Gordon and his advisors made to Liedtke's advisors. The trust and Pennzoil would acquire between them all of the stock of Getty Oil in an arrangement that would give the trust four-sevenths of the company and Pennzoil three-sevenths. Both the ownership of the stock and the seats on the board of directors would be divided in that ratio. The Pennzoil people said that Liedtke might be agreeable to the deal if it contained a divorce clause—if things were not working out after one year, the two parties would go their separate ways and split the assets of Getty Oil Company four-sevenths, three-sevenths. This was something Liedtke had already discussed with his advisors, and in a worst case, it would give Pennzoil a lot of oil reserves at a bargain price.

The Getty Oil Company board of directors scheduled an emergency meeting for January 2, 1984 to discuss the Pennzoil tender offer. Gordon Getty was in New York for the meeting, so Liedtke flew to New York to talk with Gordon about the deal Gordon's people had proposed. On New Year's Day, Gordon and Liedtke, along with their lawyers, investment bankers and other advisors, met at Gordon's suite in the Pierre Hotel. Liedtke was charming as he told Gordon about his company and about his past association with Gordon's father. They agreed that Gordon would become chairman of the company, and Liedtke would be chief executive officer and would run the day-to-day operations. Marty Siegel, Gordon's investment banker, insisted that Pennzoil increase the price to be paid the public shareholders to $110 per share, which Siegel maintained was the lowest price the board would accept. Liedtke was reluctant, but he ultimately agreed to $110 after they had run the deal by Marty Lipton, and Lipton had said that the museum would accept the deal at $110 but not at a lower price. During the night of January 1–2, Moulton Goodrum a partner in Baker Botts, Pennzoil's Houston law firm, drafted a five-page Memorandum of Agreement spelling out the terms of the agreement. The next day, Gordon Getty signed it on behalf of the trust and Hugh Liedtke signed it on behalf of Pennzoil. The memorandum stated "This Plan is subject to approval by the Board of Directors of [Getty Oil Company] at the meeting of the Board being held on January 2, 1984 and will expire if not approved by the Board."

To keep Gordon from changing his mind yet one more time, Arthur Liman, a New York lawyer Pennzoil had retained to assist on the deal, drafted a letter for Gordon to sign. In the letter, Gordon agreed not only that he would support the plan before the board of directors and oppose any competing plan, but that if the directors did not support the plan, he would execute a consent to replace them. The letter also obligated Gordon to use his best efforts to get the museum to execute a similar consent. Gordon signed the letter after writing in by hand the qualification that his undertakings were "Subject only to my fiduciary obligations."

The Getty Oil board meeting was scheduled for 6:00 P.M. that afternoon. Earlier in the day, the Pennzoil people had informed Petersen, Boisi and Winokur of the basic deal Gordon had struck with Liedtke (but not of the side letter in which Gordon agreed to replace the board if they didn't go along). In his book *The Taking of Getty Oil*, Steve Coll describes the atmosphere of the meeting:

> It would be difficult ... to comprehend the swirling anger and confusion which pervaded the Inter–Continental Hotel that night and well into the following day. So much had passed between the participants before the meeting began—an indelible, bitter poison had seeped into their relations. Gordon Getty's long, sometimes irrational bid for control of the company; the attempt by Sid Petersen and his advisors to instigate a family lawsuit against Gordon, the increasingly cantankerous negotiations between the plethora of lawyers and investment bankers; the shifting role of Harold Williams and the museum—all of this had infected the executives, directors, and advisors who gathered in Sutton Room II on the third floor of the Inter–Continental Hotel.

The meeting began with thirty people, the board members plus a variety of lawyers and investment bankers, squeezed inside a too-small conference room. Dave Copley, Getty Oil's General Counsel, was taking hand-written notes of all that was said. When the meeting began, the museum had not yet signed the Memorandum of Agreement. The directors waited while Marty Lipton made some changes it, and Harold Williams signed on behalf of the museum. The directors then discussed and rejected the original Pennzoil tender offer while they waited for the Memorandum of Agreement to be re-typed and copied.

When the Memorandum of Agreement was finally delivered and read aloud, there not being enough copies available for everyone present, most of the directors were indignant. Some thought the price was too low, but what really bothered them was the provision that the deal was good only as long as the board was in session. The directors were being forced to vote on a proposal involving billions of dollars, one likely to result in litigation, without time to study it.

Some of the directors felt that if they approved the price of $110 per share they would be failing in their duty to protect the public shareholders. Geoff Boisi, their Goldman, Sachs investment banker, made them even more uncomfortable when he refused to give an opinion that $110 was a fair price. In transactions of this sort, corporate boards customarily require their investment bank to give a "fairness opinion," in which the banker formally advises the board that the price being paid is fair to the shareholders. The primary purpose of these opinions is to give the directors some protection against suits alleging they failed to use their best efforts to get a fair price for the selling shareholders, and it is often alleged that fairness opinions are mere shams—that investment bankers will give whatever opinion is necessary to get the deal done. But that was not the way it happened here. Boisi said $110 a share was too low. When the Pennzoil proposal was put to a vote, the board rejected it by a vote of 10 to 5 or 9 to 6, depending on the way one ambiguous vote was counted.

As the meeting dragged on, the directors became more frustrated with Gordon Getty, who opposed, often without apparent reason, all of the alternatives others proposed. Shortly after 1:30 A.M., Harold Stuart, a long-time director, suspected there was something else going on. He asked Gordon point blank if there was any secret agreement with Pennzoil. Gordon said he would have to talk with his lawyers. Tim Cohler, one of Gordon's lawyers, then came into to the room from the hallway where he had been waiting and read aloud the letter in which Gordon had promised to try to replace the board if they failed to go along with the Pennzoil deal. (This letter was to become known during the trial as the "Dear Hugh" letter.) The directors, even those who had been named to the board by Gordon himself, were outraged.

By 2:30 A.M., however, tempers had cooled enough that the board was able to agree on a counteroffer. Under the terms worked out by the lawyers and investment bankers, the price per share would be determined by a complex formula dependent in part upon the price Getty Oil received when it sold its insurance subsidiary, which it would do as part of the deal. Those involved believed the formula would yield a price close to $120 a share. The board then adjourned until three the next afternoon to give Liedtke time to respond to the counteroffer and to give the directors time to get some sleep.

Their counter offer did not get the response the directors hoped for. Liedtke was furious. Getty Oil stock had been selling for $80 when he made his first offer, and he thought $110 was generous. His advisors, however, were calmer and they came up with a complex price formula that Liedtke could live with. Marty Lipton, who enjoyed the trust of all parties and thus was acting as a mediator of sorts, assured them that the proposal wouldn't fly. But Lipton and Liman, the New York lawyer who was acting as Liedtke's spokesman in the negotiations, came up with an alternative formula that Lipton thought he could sell to the board. This deal provided that Getty Oil would sell its insurance subsidiary, and all proceeds in excess of $1 billion after taxes would be distributed to the selling shareholders of Getty Oil. Pennzoil and the trust would guarantee that the payment to the shareholders would be at least $5 per share and that it would be received within five years. Because Liedtke was so angry, Liman refused to convey the proposal to Liedtke until it had been approved by the board.

While this was going on, Boisi, Getty Oil Company's investment banker, was looking for other buyers for the company. Among the other oil companies he contacted were Chevron, Shell, and, of course, Texaco.

When the directors reconvened, Lipton presented his proposal. Despite pressure from Lipton and others, Boisi still refused to give a fairness opinion. He mentioned that he had engaged in discussions with other buyers that might lead to a higher price. (Everyone seemed to assume that the "stub," as the amount above $110 per share was being called, was worth approximately $2.50 to $3.00 when discounted to present value.) After three more hours of discussion, the board voted 15 to 1 in favor of this counterproposal, even though they did not have a fairness opinion. The board then recessed to allow Liman to get Liedtke's acceptance of the proposal.

Lipton, the museum's attorney and the prime mover in putting together the deal, told Liman, who was acting as Pennzoil's liason to the board, of the board's action. Liman then telephoned Liedtke, who indicated he agreed with the counterproposal. When Liman passed this news to Lipton, Lipton told him the board would have to re-convene momentarily for Lipton to announce that Liedtke had accepted the counterproposal. Marty Siegel, the trust's investment banker, made the actual announcement and the meeting was adjourned. Bart Winokur, Getty Oil Company's outside counsel, asked whether a document containing the terms of the deal would come back to the board for approval, and Lipton told him that normally a final, written agreement would be presented to the directors for their ratification.

What happened next was to be hotly contested at the trial. Liman was waiting in the hall outside the room where the directors were meeting. He would testify that when the meeting ended and he entered the room, Marty Lipton, Marty Siegel and some of the other participants congratulated him on having made a deal and shook his hand. No one else recalled this. Lipton would testify that he had no memory of any such exchange and that, in any event, he was concerned about Boisi's refusal to issue a fairness opinion and was not in the mood to congratulate anyone. At trial, Siegel's memory was vague. *Wall Street Journal* writer Thomas Petzinger said of the testimony "Never ... would so many handshakes be remembered by only one-half of the clasp."

Later that evening, there was another seemingly unimportant social gesture that was to loom large in the trial. Liedtke telephoned Gordon's suite at the Pierre. Gordon wasn't in, but Ann Getty, Gordon's wife, invited Liedtke to a champagne party they were having to celebrate. Liedtke declined, having plans to dine with his company's top executives. Getty Oil director Larry Tisch did go to Gordon's suite and toasted the deal.

While the executives and directors were celebrating, the lawyers and investment bankers had work to do. The first priority was a press release. The securities laws required that the directors' action be quickly disclosed to the public. Ordinarily in a deal of this magnitude, several experienced lawyers from Marty Lipton's firm would have supervised the drafting of the press release. But Lipton's involvement in this deal was unusual. He had come in at the last minute as a personal favor to Harold Williams. Rather than having the usual battery of lawyers working with him on the deal, he was assisted only by Patricia Vlahakis, a second year associate. Lipton was tired and so he left Vlahakis to work with the public relations professionals. (Both Pennzoil and Getty Oil had hired New York public relations firms in anticipation of the need to issue a press release.) The PR people did the first draft of the press release. Their draft stated that the Getty Oil board had voted to "accept" a plan that would provide for the merger of Pennzoil and Getty Oil. Elsewhere, it stated: "The agreement provides...." Vlahakis found this unacceptable. She grabbed one of Gordon Getty's lawyers, and together they prepared a draft that used the word "agreed" without qualification. Instead, the press release said Getty Oil, Pennzoil, the museum and the trust "announced today that they had agreed in principle" to a merger.

The next morning, Geoff Boisi, who, like most mergers and acquisitions specialists, believed that an agreement in principle was not binding, continued his search for a buyer who would pay more for Getty Oil. He called a number of potential buyers, including the government of Saudi Arabia. Boisi considered Texaco a prime candidate because it was well known in the oil industry (an industry in which Boisi had become an expert in the course of representing Getty Oil), and Texaco was running out of reserves. In a conversation with Texaco president Al

DeCrane, Boisi assured DeCrane that there was no contract between Pennzoil and the Getty interests and that Getty Oil was still for sale.

DeCrane, well aware that Texaco had previously lost an opportunity to merge with reserve-rich Conoco because it had not moved aggressively, called his boss, Texaco chairman John McKinley, at his home in Alabama. DeCrane told McKinley of his conversations with Boisi. DeCrane said that if Texaco wanted to bid on Getty Oil, they needed to move quickly. McKinley, who was known for his caution, called Boisi's boss, Goldman, Sachs chairman John Weinberg and asked him to confirm what Boisi had told DeCrane, that there was no deal between Getty Oil and Pennzoil. Weinberg confirmed it, and McKinley was assured. He had known Weinberg for years and often played golf with him. McKinley flew to New York on a Texaco jet.

At about the same time, another investment banker, Bruce Wasserstein of First Boston Corporation, was getting involved. Wasserstein was famous (or infamous) for his aggressive tactics in corporate takeovers. For months, Wasserstein had been following the troubles at Getty Oil, expecting that there would be a takeover and hoping that he would be able to get involved and earn a large fee. If there was to be another deal, he wanted to find a client. But he was a Harvard Law School graduate, and before he got involved, he wanted to make sure he wasn't going to get in trouble by trying to bring his client into what was already a done deal. Marty Lipton was a friend of his, so Wasserstein called Lipton and asked whether there was in fact a deal. Lipton assured him there was not.

Then Wasserstein called another friend, Getty Oil director Larry Tisch, who had himself been a principal in some of America's largest takeovers. Tisch likewise assured Wasserstein that there was no deal. Tisch neglected to tell Wasserstein about the toast he had drunk to the deal the night before. He didn't think it was significant.

With that, Wasserstein began calling other potential buyers, assuring them that Getty Oil was still available, but warning them they needed to move quickly and aggressively. As it turned out, a buyer came to him. Texaco needed an investment bank. Normally, it would have used the conservative Morgan, Stanley & Company. But Chevron had already retained Morgan, Stanley to assist it in a potential bid for Getty Oil. Because the other leading investment banks were already representing parties involved in the deal, this left only First Boston and Drexel Burnham Lambert. Texaco considered Drexel Burnham out of the question because it had already developed a reputation for overly-aggressive (some said unsavory) practices. (The firm later folded when its leader, the junk bond king Michael Millken went to jail for securities law violations.) So Texaco was paired with First Boston, whose mergers and acquisitions department had an energy and aggressiveness that was foreign to the staid Texaco executives.

It was late in the evening when the Texaco executives were finally able to meet with Wasserstein's boss, Joseph Perella, head of First Boston's mergers and acquisitions department. Wasserstein himself was in a private jet on his way back from Houston where he had been working on another matter. Perella briefed the Texaco executives on the status of Getty Oil as they understood it, telling them not only about the Pennzoil deal, but also about other potential buyers who might make a bid. Al DeCrane took handwritten notes that would become key evidence at trial. Perella described a strategy whereby Texaco would make a deal first with the museum and the Getty Oil board so as to threaten to put Gordon Getty in the position of a minority shareholder who could be squeezed out. This might be necessary, Perella explained, because the terms of the trust provided that the trustee could sell the Getty Oil Company shares only to avoid a loss. Thus, in order to give Gordon the power to sell, it might be necessary to put him in a position where he had to sell to avoid a loss.

McKinley had called an emergency meeting of the Texaco board of directors for the next afternoon. He spent the morning making up his mind whether to go ahead with a bid for Getty Oil. After receiving assurances from Marty Lipton that there was no contract between Pennzoil and the Getty parties, he decided to go ahead. The board authorized him to offer up to $125 a share for the Getty Oil stock.

Meanwhile, the Pennzoil lawyers were working on the "definitive merger agreement" referred to in the press release and on all the necessary collateral documents. As was customary, Pennzoil, the acquirer, was to prepare the first draft. It was a bigger job than anticipated. The deal was especially complex, not only because of the amount of money involved but also because there were four parties instead of the usual two. The details of the stub (the future payment to be made to the shareholders from the sale of the insurance subsidiary) were an especially complex drafting problem. Baker Botts, Pennzoil's primary law firm, flew in additional lawyers from Houston. At 8:30 P.M. on Wednesday, January 4, a couple of hours before Perella met with the Texaco executives, the Pennzoil lawyers finally got the drafts to their Getty Oil counterparts, who had expected to have them twelve hours earlier. At this point, the Getty Oil lawyers decided it was too late to start work on them that night. They had been up most of the last two nights working on the deal, and they decided it would be best to go home and get a good night's sleep and start their review of the documents in the morning. They spent January 5th, the day McKinley was making up his mind and meeting with his board, reviewing the draft documents, and according to Winokur, studying a number of important issues that had not been addressed in the Pennzoil drafts. All the while, the Pennzoil lawyers, who were hearing rumors of other companies interested in Getty Oil, were telephoning, urging them to hurry up.

Finally, Winokur and his team agreed to a meeting at 6:00 P.M. at the offices of Liman's firm. Patricia Vlahakis, the associate assisting Marty Lipton on the deal, was planning to go because she had concerns about the draft agreement, but Lipton told her not attend. He told her there was a potential deal with Texaco and he needed her with him when he met with the Texaco people.

At the same time, another front was opening up. Claire Getty, a daughter of Gordon's deceased older brother George, had long had concerns about Gordon's management of the trust. She had not been willing to take part in litigation to have a co-trustee appointed, but now she wanted time to study the Pennzoil deal. On the afternoon of January 4th, her lawyers went to court in California and obtained a restraining order, prohibiting Gordon from signing "any legally binding documents" until a hearing was held the next day. Tim Cohler, a partner in Moses Lasky's firm, flew to California to deal with the suit.

At 9 P.M. on the fifth, McKinley arrived at Gordon's suite at the Pierre, accompanied by Wasserstein and two Texaco executives, Vice Chairman Jim Kinnear and General Counsel Bill Weitzel. McKinley had tried to arrange for an earlier meeting, but Gordon needed time to gather his advisors. All he could get on such short notice were investment banker Marty Siegel and Tom Woodhouse, another of Lasky's law partners. After some initial pleasantries, which McKinley, an introverted technocrat, handled awkwardly, they discussed whether Gordon was in fact free to accept an offer. Weitzel and Woodhouse discussed this issue, focusing on the "Dear Hugh" letter. In the presence of the Texaco negotiators, Woodhouse advised Gordon that he was free to receive higher offers and should.

No one recognized the significance of a phone call Woodhouse had taken just a few minutes before. He had spoken with Cohler, who was reporting from Los Angeles on the suit by Claire Getty. In fact, Cohler was calling from the offices of Pennzoil's lawyers. In his oral argument, Cohler had stated that there was "a transaction presently agreed upon" among Pennzoil, the trust and the museum. Moreover, he had filed an affidavit of Marty Siegel that had been faxed to him for that purpose. The affidavit was to become an important piece of evidence in the trial. While its main purpose was to convince the court that the Pennzoil deal was the best of the then-available alternatives for the trust, there was language in it that the Pennzoil lawyers were able to use as evidence that there was already a binding agreement among the parties. Cohler obviously didn't have that in mind at the time because the affidavit was focused on the business aspects of the deal, not whether there was a binding agreement. Siegel was an investment banker, not a lawyer.

The negotiations then stalled because neither Gordon nor McKinley would make the first offer. Marty Siegel tracked down Larry Tisch, who was at a restaurant celebrating a friend's birthday, and asked him to come to help move things along. Tisch began to mediate, but he wasn't having much success, so Siegel called Marty Lipton, who had been so successful in working out the Pennzoil deal. Lipton was able to get Gordon and Woodhouse to agree that if they could settle on a price, Gordon would sign a letter saying that he would sell to Texaco if the California restraining order were lifted.

While Gordon and his advisors waited in the suite, Tisch and Lipton caucused with the Texaco negotiators in the hotel lobby. Lipton and Tisch told McKinley that Gordon was not in a mood to bargain and that if he wanted to make a deal, he had to offer $125, the maximum Texaco's board had authorized. When they returned to Gordon's suite, McKinley told Gordon, "I am prepared to make an offer since you said you would be happy to receive one. I had been thinking of a price of about $122.50." He paused and smiled. "But I have gotten some indications here that there is another price that would be more agreeable to you, and so I am prepared to offer. . . ." Before McKinley could finish his sentence, Gordon said, "I accept." Then he added, "Oh! You're supposed to give the price first." Everyone laughed, and Gordon said "I think we can probably do business, if the courts okay it and the price is what I heard."

Lipton wrote out by hand the letter that Gordon was to sign saying he would sell to Texaco if the California restraining order were lifted. Woodhouse telephoned his partner Tim Cohler (the lawyer who had that day told the California court of the "transaction presently agreed upon")and explained what had happened. Woodhouse read Cohler the letter, and Cohler suggested a few changes. Lipton wrote a new copy. Then Gordon decided that because the deal was so important, he wanted to run it by Moses Lasky. He had been the family lawyer for many years and knew more about the trust than anyone alive. It took some time to track down Lasky, who was eating dinner in a Chinese restaurant, but when they finally reached him and read him the letter, he said he had no problems with it and that he thought Gordon was doing the right thing. With that, Gordon signed the letter shortly after midnight.

After they left the Pierre, the Texaco negotiators went to Lipton's offices, where they spent the rest of the night negotiating an agreement for Texaco to buy the museum's shares. Lipton insisted that the museum would sell only if Texaco indemnified it against suits arising out of the Pennzoil transaction. He assured them that the Memorandum of Agreement executed by Pennzoil, the trust and the museum was not a binding contract and that the Getty Oil board's vote was merely an authorization to negotiate. This of course gave rise to the question: if you're so sure why does your client need an indemnity? Lipton's response was that Harold Williams, his client's president, was a public figure, a former business school dean, and a former Chairman of the Securities and Exchange Commission. He had a reputation to protect and he could not risk being brought into a very public lawsuit. Then, Lipton insisted on another provision that was even more inconsistent with his assurances that the Getty interests were not bound. The agreement had to contain a disclaimer that "no representation is made with respect to ... the Pennzoil agreement." The Texaco executives went along with this, not only because they wanted to make the deal, but also because they respected Lipton.[9] It was not just that he was the best mergers and acquisitions lawyer in the country. Throughout the course of the deal, he had shown himself to be a fair and impartial mediator. At that point, it must have seemed like he could do no wrong. It was only later that Texaco would find out how wrong that perception was.

While the negotiation between Texaco and the museum was going on, the Getty Oil lawyers were meeting with the Pennzoil lawyers to work on the merger documents. Late in the evening, the Getty Oil lawyers began quietly leaving the meeting, one by one. At about one in the morning, the Pennzoil lawyers realized that even though there were a few more points to be covered, there was nobody from Getty Oil there to negotiate.

To make sure their deal didn't get undone the way Pennzoil's had, the Texaco team worked frantically to get the final documents prepared. DeCrane, Kinnear and Weitzel stayed personally involved in negotiating and drafting the final documents, which were much less complex than Pennzoil's because their deal was much less complex. Because the museum had been given an indemnity, the lawyers representing Gordon and the Getty Oil directors demanded that they be indemnified as well. Texaco gave these indemnities, little realizing how much the indemnities were to cost them in the future. At noon the next, day the Getty Oil directors held a meeting by conference call and voted to "withdraw" the $112.50 counteroffer they had made to Pennzoil and accept the Texaco deal.

The lawsuits began almost immediately. Liedtke sent a threatening telegram to the directors of Getty Oil Company. In response, Getty Oil filed a suit in Delaware seeking a declaratory judgment that they had no

---

[9] It should be noted that Lipton did not spring these conditions on the Texaco negotiators after they had reached an agreement with Gordon Getty. He had raised the indemnity with them before they met with Gordon.

contract with Pennzoil. Three days later, Pennzoil filed its own lawsuit, also in Delaware, asking for specific performance of the Getty Oil–Pennzoil contract.[10] There was a frantic round of accelerated discovery, and the Pennzoil lawyers quickly learned that Texaco had given the Getty interests indemnities. Seeing the indemnities as evidence that Texaco knew the Getty entities had a contract with Pennzoil, the Pennzoil lawyers amended their complaint to sue Texaco for interfering with that contract.

In the meantime, Liedtke and Texaco Chairman John McKinley met in Washington, D.C. to see if they could work out a deal. Unfortunately, what McKinley was willing to offer was so meager it only made Liedtke more angry.

The Delaware chancery court denied Pennzoil's request for a preliminary injunction. The ultimate decision on whether Texaco was liable for interfering with a contract was left for trial. While the court stated that Pennzoil had made a sufficient preliminary showing that there was a contract, it said there was not sufficient evidence that Texaco had knowledge of it.

Hugh Liedtke decided that the way to win the case was to get it to Texas, where his friend Joe Jamail could be lead counsel. Jamail was one of the great personal injury lawyers of all time.[11] He had won more than forty verdicts or settlements in excess of $1 million, more than anyone else in history.[12] He was famous not only for his courtroom theatrics, but also for his partying. He hung out with Willie Nelson, and it was said that Mr. Nelson's song about "a good-hearted woman in love with a good timin' man" had been inspired by Jamail's long-suffering wife. At first, Jamail resisted Liedtke's attempts get him involved, but Jamail finally agreed to take the case because his wife told him he should do it out of friendship.[13]

John Jeffers and Irv Terrell, the Baker Botts lawyers who were heading Pennzoil's litigation team, found a way to move the suit to Texas. As elsewhere, the rules in Delaware provided that a plaintiff could dismiss without prejudice at any time before a defendant answered. The lawyers representing Texaco in the suit were used to litigating injunctions against mergers. They didn't file answers because

---

[10] *See* PETZINGER, *supra* note 4, at 241.

[11] According to Jamail, he and Liedtke had "traveled the world together with our wives." JOE JAMAIL, LAWYER: MY TRIALS AND JUBILATIONS 138 (2003).

[12] When he published his memoir in 2003, Jamail claimed to "have served as lead counsel in over 200 personal injury cases where recovery was in excess of $1 million." JAMAIL, *id.* (dust jacket).

[13] *See id.* at 139–40.

it took time away from fighting the injunction. By the time the answer was due, the deal had either gone through or it hadn't. In either case the answer was moot. So they didn't file an answer in this suit. When Jeffers and Terrell realized the opening this gave them, they filed a dismissal in Delaware and 15 minutes later filed a complaint in Houston.[14] The Texaco lawyers' oversight became known as "the ten billion dollar boo-boo."

The Trial

When the Texaco executives learned they were going to have to try a case in Houston, they knew they needed local counsel. After an extensive search, they chose Dick Miller. Miller had grown up in Tulsa. He left high school to enlist in the Marine Corps during World War II, but he ultimately graduated from Harvard College and Harvard Law School. He had been the head of the litigation department at Baker Botts and had helped train Irv Terrell and John Jeffers. In fact he considered them his protégés. An intense, driven man, Miller had left Baker Botts to form his own boutique litigation firm, Miller, Keeton, Bristow & Brown.

As part of their trial preparation, Miller and his partners conducted three mock trials. Texaco won two of them. In the two that Texaco won, the jurors decided that Pennzoil had no contract because there were issues yet to be resolved and there was no definitive written agreement. The third mock jury decided that "a deal is a deal" and decided the case for Pennzoil.

There were three major elements to Miller's case. First, it was Texaco who was the good guy. They were the ones who had come in to rescue the Getty interests from Liedtke's attempt to steal the company. They had even saved Gordon from his own folly. Second, Pennzoil had no contract. However things might be done in the oilfields, in the world of corporate acquisitions there was no binding agreement until the details were hammered out and the final documents were signed and delivered. Finally, even if Pennzoil did have a contract, Texaco had not tortiously interfered with it. Texaco had taken every reasonable precaution to assure itself there was no contract.

Pennzoil's strategy was simpler. Jamail's memoir describes his strategic thinking:

> ... I would try this case not as a matter of securities law, or fiduciary duty, or any other issue of the takeover game, but as a matter of honor. I would ask the jury to send a message that the

---

[14] Lynn LoPucki and Walter Weyrauch have stated that the Pennzoil lawyers "deliberately ignor[ed] a local custom that required Pennzoil to give Texaco notice of its intent to dismiss and an opportunity to prevent dismissal by filing the answer." Lynn M. LoPucki & Walter O. Weyrauch, *A Theory of Legal Strategy*, 49 Duke L. J. 1404, 1417 (2000).

public demanded a higher standard of behavior from Wall Street and its giant corporations.... I planned to hammer the point that Texaco stole this oil from Pennzoil and that made the company no better than a thief.[15]

The trial began on Monday, July 1, 1985. Judge Anthony J.P. Farris, who had heard the pretrial issues, presided.[16] Administrative matters took up the first two days. While the parties did not agree on how long the trial would last, all the estimates turned out to be ridiculously optimistic. They ranged from four weeks to ten weeks.

The third day was devoted to motions in limine. Here Pennzoil won a major victory. Judge Farris denied Texaco's motion to exclude evidence of the internal struggles at Getty Oil. This was crucial to one of Jamail's major strategic objectives—lumping the Getty Oil management, the investment bankers, and the Wall Street lawyers together with the Texaco executives as one homogeneous set of melodrama villains.

Jury Selection

When jury selection began, it was, like all other aspects of the case, driven by the competing themes. Miller was looking for smarter and more sophisticated people. He believed that these people would be more in touch with business realities and less inclined to be swayed by the emotional arguments that were Jamail's forte.

Jamail, on the other hand was looking for jurors who would be receptive to his theme that the case was just a simple matter of honor. As he put it:

> There were two characteristics I was looking for, loyalty and honesty. Why? When you give your word, that brings in loyalty. I could prove that the Getty board was disloyal to J. Paul Getty, who had founded the company. I wanted jurors who had longevity in marriage, longevity in job, longevity in church.[17]

Voir dire lasted six days and, like many other aspects of the case, it was unusual. One observer called it "the broadest voir dire I had ever seen in Texas." This was saying something, because Texas is famous for wide-open voir dire.

Jamail began his voir dire by giving the jurors the essence of his case:

---

[15] JAMAIL, *supra* note 11, at 142–43.

[16] For a discussion of the controversy surrounding a contribution Jamail had made to the judge's re-election campaign, see PETZINGER, *supra* note 4, at 284–88; JAMAIL, *supra* note 11, at 141.

[17] JAMAIL, *supra* note 11, at 150.

There are going to be a lot of issues that you are going to hear, but
after you sift through all the issues, only one thing is going to be
clear to you. And that is this is a case of promises, and what those
promises meant to Pennzoil, what they ultimately meant to Texaco.
Pennzoil had a promise with Getty Oil and the Getty interest to
purchase three-sevenths of the assets of the Getty Oil Company.
That promise was not just your ordinary promise. It was made by
people, not companies.

He then proceeded to personalize it even more:

Hugh Liedtke, who I represent and who is my friend, who is seated
here today, was the chief executive officer and chairman of the board
of Pennzoil. Wasn't a building that made those promises, it was
people. And the question ultimately that you are going to have to
decide, those of you that get chosen to serve on this jury, is what a
promise is worth, what your word is worth, what a contract is
worth. Because that's what a contract is, a promise.

The reference to the building was one of the brilliant but subtle
strokes that made Jamail so persuasive. Pennzoil's headquarters, a pair
of 36-story trapezoidal towers built by architect Philip Johnson, had
been a source of civic pride in Houston. Its completion in 1976 announced that Houston was one of the world's major cities. Throughout
the trial, Jamail would remind the jurors that Pennzoil was a Houston
company and that Texaco (in spite of its name, which had originally been
The Texas Company) was now headquartered in New York and was
represented by "New York lawyers" and "New York investment bankers."

Jamail went on with his voir dire, taking advantage of the court's
license to make what was in effect an extended and repetitious opening
statement. In a speech that fills 90 pages of the trial transcript, he
outlined the evidence, hammering away at the morality theme in several
variations, making numerous references to promises and handshakes,
and telling the jury the case was about "whether there is morality in the
marketplace." He told the prospective jurors "it's—I think the most
important case ever brought in the history of America."

Jamail continued voir dire by giving the jurors a chronology of the
transaction from his point of view. Interspersed in the chronology were
questions ostensibly asked to explore the jurors' attitudes and preconcep-
tions, but that were in fact highly-charged summaries of Pennzoil's key
arguments, followed by hard-to-resist invitations to buy in to them. His
question about the indemnities is representative:

I want to ask each of you, and this is so vital, is there any member
of this panel who could not and would not accept that indemnity
that Texaco gave at the insistence of the Getty people, that indemni-

ty that Texaco gave to the Gettys as evidence of the fact that Texaco had knowledge of the Getty and Pennzoil agreement and binding contract? Is there anyone who would not accept that as that kind of evidence? If there is, I've got to know that now, obviously, because that is our proof. Raise your hands if there's anybody. I see no hands. I didn't expect any.

This type of questioning is allowed in voir dire so that counsel may weed out jurors who have prejudged the case, but it may not be used to make jurors commit to a particular position. The line between the two is hard to distinguish, and effective advocates will often skirt as close to the line as possible, as Jamail appears to be doing here.

Jamail went on to make similar, but usually more extended, arguments about such things as the press release, the warranty disclaimer concerning the Pennzoil claims, Texaco's failure to talk to Pennzoil prior to making its bid, the affidavit filed in the California lawsuit, Texaco's admission that they had read the press release, and the handwritten notes that the Texaco officers had made during the meeting with the First Boston investment bankers. The last of these he asked the jurors to accept as evidence of Texaco's intent to induce a breach of contract and as going to the issue of punitive damages.

In his book on the trial, juror James Shannon states that by the end of voir dire, "Jamail had secured a quasi-commitment that the jury would 'accept' as 'powerful evidence' the documents that bolstered his version of the facts."[18] He also got a commitment that they would reject Texaco's arguments, for instance, asking if there was anyone who would accept the words "subject to a definitive agreement" in the press release as "shutting the doors" to Pennzoil's claim or would accept Gordon's qualifier "subject to his fiduciary relationship" in the "Dear Hugh" letter "as an excuse to break the promise." In this part of his voir dire presentation, Jamail even used a chart showing the chronology of the transactions.

Jamail then resumed the process of getting the jurors to buy into his view of the case by explaining his theory of the damages: (1) that three-sevenths of the proven reserves of Pennzoil was 1.008 billion barrels of oil, (2) that Pennzoil's historical cost of finding and developing such reserves was $10.87 per barrel, (3) that under the breached contract, Pennzoil would have acquired Getty Oil's reserves for $3.40 per barrel, and (4) therefore that Pennzoil's damages were 1.08 billion times the difference between two costs, or $7.53 billion. Row by row, he asked any juror who had any feeling that they would not be able to assess such

---

[18] JAMES SHANNON, TEXACO AND THE $10 BILLION JURY 97 (1987).

damages to identify himself or herself. Nobody did.[19] Jamail then turned
things over to Irv Terrell, a Baker Botts litigator, who used the rest of
the third day of jury selection by not only giving the panel more of the
details of Pennzoil's damages argument, including the basis for its claim
for punitive damages, but also again bringing up the issue of the
indemnities.

On Friday morning, the fourth day of jury selection, Judge Farris
called the lawyers into his chambers and asked how long "this mara-
thon" was going to take. Jamail refused to commit to a time for
concluding his "questioning" of the jurors. Following the conference,
Terrell continued the voir dire by summarizing the testimony that each
of Pennzoil's expert witnesses would give and paying lip service to the
fact that it was still voir dire by asking if any of the potential jurors
knew the witnesses. Terrell then moved on to discuss Texaco's defenses.
Before the jurors had heard them from Texaco's attorneys, they heard
them from Terrell, who obviously characterized them in the least favorable light, and said of them, "These defenses are the after-the-fact
excuses that these people are raising to justify what they did." He then
returned to the Texaco officers' notes of their meeting with the investment bankers, asking the jurors if they would read these notes again
when they retired to deliberate.

When Terrell was finished, the jurors got to hear Jamail again.
Jamail summarized Pennzoil's case still another time, and he took one
more opportunity to let the jury know what truly awful people the
Texaco executives were. Although Terrell had just asked the jurors,
minutes before, if they would read the notes when they retired to
deliberate, Jamail read the most damning parts again to the jurors and
asked if they would consider the notes to be "evidence of reckless
disregard, callous, wanton, intentional evidence of Texaco's disregard for
the rights of Pennzoil."[20] He then asked several questions to make sure
the jurors would be willing to assess large punitive damages. Then it was
back to Texaco's wrongdoing. Dave Copely, Getty Oil General Counsel,
had been the secretary for the Getty Oil board meeting of January 2–3.
Copely had taken detailed handwritten minutes of the meeting. Copely
had dictated the final version of the minutes from his handwritten notes.
He later destroyed the handwritten notes. Jamail implied that this was
intentional destruction of evidence and that Texaco had played a part in
it.

It was Monday before Miller got his chance. Like Jamail, he used the
wide-open Texas rules to get his story in front of the prospective jurors.

---

[19] In the course of doing this, Jamail told the jurors he was not really comfortable with
numbers; he was just taking the number the experts had given him.

[20] SHANNON, *supra* note 18, at 131.

But his approach was different. Whereas Jamail gloried in showing the jury his street-fighter attitude, Miller, in the words of Thomas Petzinger, the *Wall Street Journal* reporter who wrote a book about the trial, "came off in the courtroom as a true Southern gentleman, like Gregory Peck as Atticus Finch in *To Kill a Mockingbird*."[21] His strategy immediately became apparent. Jamail had said the case was about honor; Miller said it was about money. It wasn't the most important case in the world; it was just a greedy corporation trying to get through the legal system what it had lost fair and square in business:

> Now, Mr. Jamail and Mr. Terrell have told you that this is the most important case that has ever been filed in the history of mankind. I take exception to that. I tried a case two months ago where a father was trying to get his children back. I consider that case considerably more important than I consider this case. This is a suit over money. Well, everybody needs a certain amount of money, but the idea that money turns this into the most important case that's ever been filed, I think, tells you something about the company that's bringing the case.

Where Jamail's story was that Texaco had come in and stolen the deal from Pennzoil, Miller's was that Texaco had come in at the request of the Getty Oil board to keep the predatory Pennzoil from taking advantage of Gordon Getty's naïveté:

> We did not crash this party. We did not butt into anything. The Getty Oil Company, its officers, and its directors through their representatives came to Texaco and asked us to make a bid on this company. Now, why did they ask us to bid: Very simple straightforward answer. The Pennzoil Company had prevailed upon Gordon Getty, who you will learn, is not and never will be a businessman, by making him a promise that he would head his father's company.

Miller accused Pennzoil of "relying first on [Gordon's] emotional desire to succeed his father" and of "relying not upon the best motives of human nature but the worst." The Getty board had asked Texaco to come in because they were "in the grasp of a tender offer that had been instituted by Pennzoil on the 27th day of December in the greatest secrecy that can be imagined, [Pennzoil] scheduling their offer between Christmas and New Year's when they knew Getty would be weakest and least able to defend itself."

Then Miller shifted gears, attempting to counter the Pennzoil team's demonization of Texaco's top executives. McKinley, Kinnear, and DeCrane were present in court, and Miller introduced them. McKinley, Miller said, was a "native son of Alabama. Been known to root for

---

[21] PETZINGER, *supra* note 4, at 300.

Alabama even when they played Texas." Pointing out that McKinley had been with Texaco all his life, Miller attempted to portray him as a solid, loyal company man, contrary to the picture of vicious opportunist that the Pennzoil team had already begun to paint.

Kinnear, Miller explained, was a graduate of the Naval Academy, something that could be expected to play well among patriotic Texans. He had "been with Texaco ever since the war was over" (more loyalty and patriotism). Kinnear, Miller introduced as "head of Texaco U.S.A., which has its offices here in Houston." Miller did not mention that, in addition to being the head of the Houston-based subsidiary, Kinnear was also Vice Chairman of the parent corporation, Texaco, Inc. and was under consideration for the top job.

Miller gave DeCrane, who was Kinnear's competition for the top job when McKinley retired, the shortest introduction. Miller said that he was a graduate of Notre Dame and Georgetown Law School and "the only one of the three who has a law degree." As Miller continued his voir dire presentation, he developed his own story of the transaction, quite different from Jamail's. He described Gordon Getty's conflicts with the Getty Oil management team and Pennzoil's interest in those conflicts as a vehicle for getting their hands on Getty Oil's reserves. Miller described the Pennzoil tender offer as an attempt "to dismantle[Getty Oil Company], to get the resources represented by the public shares and bring them back to Houston at a price that was unfair to the public." He explained the difference between friendly tender offers and hostile tender offers:

> The word "hostile" in and of itself suggests a kind of economic war. People who conduct these tender offers are frequently known in the trade as "raiders" or "sharks" or "predators".... [W]hen you make a hostile tender offer is always at a time when you think the target is not going to be able to fight back, and you conduct your own little economic Pearl Harbor.

After this, Miller produced large posters of the key documents (in his version of the story). The first was the Memorandum of Agreement. He pointed out that the last page called for a signature by Getty Oil Company. "Where's the signature? The Getty Oil Company never signed the agreement, never."

Next was the "Dear Hugh" letter, which Miller characterized in these terms:

> So Gordon Getty signed a secret agreement with Pennzoil that if the board of directors of the Getty Oil Company would not vote for this plan, by George, we will get us some more directors. And if those directors won't support it, we will get another bunch.

Without yet revealing the details of the way the directors had discovered the existence of the letter, Miller told the jury that it had created so much distrust that, to say the Getty board had later "entered into a handshake" with Pennzoil was "a little rough, [wa]sn't it?"

Counsel for Pennzoil has said "Hey we love competition." Yes, in a pig's eye. Everything they did from the beginning to the end, including the claim that they have a contract, is so anticompetitive, because they were only interested in this fantastic bargain. They didn't want to pay fair price.

Miller then tried to explain away the press release by saying it was an attempt to comply with a Securities and Exchange Commission requirement that Getty Oil management explain the reason they had removed the stock from trading on the day before. The handshake and the press release's use of the term "agreement in principle" were the next of Pennzoil's arguments that Miller tried to turn against them:

They say, "Well, we had a handshake."

We say, "Well, who was the handshake with?"

"Well, we shook hands with Gordon." Right. Did you ever shake hands with the museum?

"Well, no, but we waved to them."

"Well, how about the Getty Oil Company? Did anybody ever shake hands with the Getty Oil Company?"

"Hey, no, we never talked to them. We never talked to the Getty Oil Company."

So what is this handshake business that we've been hearing so much about. Did they ever shake hands with the Getty Oil Company? They didn't even speak to them, ever, So what does that press release say? The have "agreed in principle."

Now is that the same as an agreement? The answer is no.

This phrase "agreed in principle" in the context of what was going on in New York City means just the opposite. It means you have not agreed. You have reached an agreement on a concept.

And if "agreed" is the same as "agreed in principle," why did he use the extra words?

So it has the meaning that anybody involved in the takeover business knows about. And while Texaco has never, in the history of 80 years of its corporate existence, made a tender offer, Pennzoil has made seven. They made the first major tender offer ever made in this country. So they knew, they knew. They knew they didn't have a deal.

Miller began his second day of voir dire by trying to teach the prospective jurors (people of varying degrees on of intelligence, education, and interest) in a few minutes what contracts professors spend several weeks teaching first year law students—what it takes to form a contract. In connection with this, Miller discussed the press release again, this time pointing out the phrase "Subject to the execution of a definitive merger agreement." Having made his technical points, Miller shifted gears:

> Now, there's some things a lawyer ought not be willing to do to win, and I put at the top of the list the attempt to create prejudice for race or creed or geography or anything like that.

> And I'm suggesting to you, ladies and gentlemen, when they talk about these New York lawyers in the tone of voice they used, that they're really suggesting more than that to you. And you know what I mean; I want to be certain that we don't have anything like that in this case. If they can win, let them win fair and square.

> * * *

> Is there anybody who is going to decide this case on the basis of who is from where? I need to know that because if we can't look at a man and judge him on his merits and not his religion or his race or the place he comes from, then something is wrong with this case.

Many of the people who represented or advised Texaco in the transaction, or who would testify as witnesses on behalf of Texaco were not only New Yorkers, but were Jewish as well. Miller was extremely concerned that not only regional prejudice but anti-Semitism would play a part in the trial.[22] In his book about the trial, however, juror Jim Shannon states: "Throughout this case ... [anti-Semitism] was absolutely a non-issue." Moreover, Shannon says that he was "puzzled" at the time by Miller's remarks and he suggests that if Miller had wanted to raise the issue, he should have done so directly.[23] Miller obviously didn't want to make any more direct accusations against his opponents, making the conflict bitterer than it was already and possibly alienating the jurors, but by not doing so, he may have failed to make his point.

Opening Statements

On the morning of July 17, after six days of voir dire, the jurors were seated and the opening statements began. After the extensive voir dire presentations, there wasn't much left to say, but that didn't stop either side from making an extensive opening statement. As juror Jim

---

[22] SHANNON, *supra* note 18, at 148.

[23] *Id.* at 148.

Shannon put it: "Redundancy would remain a prominent feature of the case for both the plaintiff and the defendant."[24]

John Jeffers made the opening statement for Pennzoil. Because Jeffers had not addressed the jury in voir dire, he was a new face and a new voice. Because the voir dire presentations had explained the case to the jurors, his opening statement was more of a rebuttal of Miller's voir dire presentation, doing in detail what Jamail had already done with a very broad brush on the previous day. He attacked Miller's characterizations of the companies involved, pointing out that while "Getty Oil Company had almost $12 billion dollars [in 1983] when it was supposedly weak and defenseless," Pennzoil's annual revenues were "something over $2 billion." Texaco's revenues in 1984, with Getty Oil folded into it, he noted, were $47 billion.

Jeffers went on to attack Miller's characterization of J. Paul Getty as a money-grubber who didn't care for his family and Miller's characterization of the press release as a product only of the Getty Oil Company. After this, he gave a detailed history of the dealings, beginning with J. Paul Getty's founding of Getty Oil and Liedtke's of Pennzoil, the establishment of the Trust, a primer on corporate law, and a description of the maneuverings at Getty Oil—the meetings, the deals, everything. In the course of doing this, he spent a great deal of time trying to head off Texaco's arguments that there were many essential terms that Pennzoil and the Getty interests never agreed to. While he was doing this, he also tried to turn the jury against the people who would be Texaco's key witnesses. "Boisi again, remember his name, Geoff Boisi, the $18 million dollar man, Goldman, Sachs."

Jeffers concluded with a beautifully-developed argument that repeated Pennzoil's theme, while at the same time turning Texaco's main theme against it. As noted earlier, Jamail's strategy was to try the case as "a matter of honor" and to ask for large punitive damages to teach not only Texaco, but corporate America in general, to leave their devious ways and return to the basic notions of honor and keeping one's promises. Texaco, on the other hand, intended to educate the jury as to contract law, where "usage of trade" and other norms of the business world determine at what point an agreement becomes legally binding. Jeffers headed that off by characterizing investment bankers (and their lawyers), not as a group of experts who knew how to handle large, sophisticated corporate transactions better than anyone else, but instead as a small group of predators who shunned honest people's norms of decent behavior.

There are investment bankers who are going to testify at this trial that in their circles and by the way they practice their trade, an

---

[24] *Id.* at 155.

agreement in principle is an invitation to the world that you are open for bids. And we think that one of the things that has to be done in this case is to bring that circle of people square with the law.

That may be their tactics, but it's not right and it's not the law.

... The men from Texaco who have been here—Mr. McKinley, Mr. Kinnear, Mr. DeCrane—sit at the pinnacle of one of the largest corporations in the world.

But jurors like yourselves judge the rich and the powerful, the small and the weak, and that is what you are here for.

People from Texaco will tell you that what they did was right. But if they were wrong, who is to tell them that they were wrong if not this jury and this Court at this time?

We have a government of laws and not of men. We ask your patience and your indulgence as we tell our story. Thank you very much.

The afternoon session belonged to the Texaco team. Just as the Pennzoil team had brought in Jeffers as a fresh face after the prolonged voir dire presentation by Jamail and Terrell, Miller had his partner Richard Keeton deliver Texaco's opening statement.

Keeton, the number-two partner in Miller's firm, was known for his keen intellect. He was the son of Page Keeton, the legendary dean of the University of Texas Law School. Keeton emphasized that Texaco wasn't the only company that showed an interest in making a bid for Getty Oil after they heard of the Pennzoil deal.

Well, there are sure a lot of sophisticated people in companies that don't think the curtain is falling when they read that "agreement in principle" because this press release has been out.

Now it doesn't say "invitation to bid," but what this is is something that says, There is going to be, in all likelihood, not certainty, but in all likelihood, some sort of transaction is going to happen. If you want to get in, if you want something, put in your bid.

Now, that doesn't say that. I'm not going to fool you. It doesn't say that. I'm talking about to knowledgeable people. That may include some of you. That's what it means. It means we're working and there's a tender offer going on, so there's time pressure.

Keeton finally got to the key point in his opening statement—the need for the plaintiff to show intent.

You are going to be asked "Did Texaco tortiously interfere with some contract?"

I don't think you are going to find there is a contract. But in order to find that Texaco has done anything wrong, they are going to have tortiously interfered, and they're going to have to have known. Known not suspected. Known, not should have known. Known.

Pennzoil's Case

As its first witness, Pennzoil called Baine Kerr. Kerr, who had been severely wounded as a Marine on Guadalcanal, began his career as a Baker Botts lawyer working on Pennzoil matters. He attracted Liedtke's attention and became Pennzoil's general counsel and then its president. Kerr was Liedtke's number two man and his confidant.

The decision to call Kerr as the first witness was based not only on Jamail's many years of courtroom experience, but also on his intimate knowledge of the people involved. Although most people expected him to call Liedtke first, Jamail was afraid that on cross-examination Miller would be able to goad the combative Liedtke into a verbal brawl that would turn the jury against him and reinforce Miller's claim that Pennzoil was the predator in the case. So instead Jamail chose the imperturbable, mild-mannered Kerr. As Jamail later explained, "I wanted to set the tone. Here's Texaco and its bully lawyer and here's this nice, kindly gentleman simply trying to tell him what happened. But Miller is macho and I knew he'd try to intimidate Kerr." Jamail was confident Kerr was more than equal to the task. "Baine has insides of solid steel. He's one tough Marine."[25]

Kerr told the jury about Pennzoil as a company. He told a romanticized and idealized story about Hugh Liedtke and his dream of building a company. J. Paul Getty and George H.W. Bush came in, perhaps a little more prominently than history warranted. (The first President Bush had been Liedtke's partner in an oil company.) As told by Kerr, Liedtke's story became the quintessential American Dream. Juror Jim Shannon describes the story as "almost inspirational, lacking only thundering orchestration and shimmering visuals depicting the oilfield equivalent of amber waves of grain."[26] Jamail's set up was perfect. It was the classic story line: Boy gets girl; boy loses girl; boy gets girl back. But it was Liedtke building the American Dream; American Dream thwarted by Texaco and its band of New York lawyers and investment bankers;

---

[25] PETZINGER, *supra* note 4, at 304–05. In a post-trial interview with author-juror Jim Shannon, Jamail put it a different way:

Many people thought we ought to start out with Liedtke to make that big impression with the jury. I said bullshit. If I haven't impressed them enough when the voir dire's over, then we've got trouble anyway. We've got to start with the glue and facts man and the dull bullshit. But it has to be done for the record. Not only that, for appeal purposes you have to build your record. It's like building a house.

SHANNON, *supra* note 18, at 215.

[26] *Id.* at 200.

American Dream restored (and American business ethics along with it) by a jury of ordinary American citizens.

Kerr was also the vehicle through whom Pennzoil spelled out most of the details of the transactions and introduced into evidence the documents upon which Pennzoil based its case. Courtroom technology was still in its infancy, and Jeffers, who conducted the examination, used the classic tools. Blow-ups of the documents sat on a large easel, as did Pennzoil's chronology of the events. There was even a large map of midtown Manhattan on which Jeffers traced the dealmakers' movements with a pointer as Kerr told the story.

Even though the theme upon which Jamail and his team were basing their case was simple and elemental, the facts of the case were, as the reader is undoubtedly painfully aware, complex. For the jurors, already numbed by seven days of voir dire and opening statements, the story was hard to follow. Miller knew this, and when Kerr finished his background on Pennzoil and began recounting the story of the deal itself, Miller began making the story even harder to follow. With years of courtroom experience, he was able to make technical objections to even the most innocuous questions. Judge Farris was receptive to these, and Jeffers was constantly forced to re-phrase questions, breaking the flow of Kerr's story (if a story like this could ever have a flow). Even more distracting were the constant sidebars, some of which became so heated or extended that the jury was sent into the hall.[27]

After Jeffers led Kerr through four days of direct examination, Miller got his chance at cross-examination. It lasted three days. Throughout the examination, Miller tried to depict Pennzoil as the predator and Gordon Getty as the weak, naive, and insecure Getty Oil insider whom they were able to use as their stalking horse. He had some success. But Kerr scored some points as well. Particularly effective was Kerr's seemingly spontaneous emotional outburst in which he responded to Miller's badgering with an impassioned defense of Gordon Getty as a person standing up for his rights in the face of outrageous conduct, not only by the Getty Oil board, but also by members of his own family.

In his book, *Wall Street Journal* reporter Thomas Petzinger lauds the way Jamail used the Baker Botts lawyers, particularly Terrell and Jeffers, taking advantage of their strengths: business-like demeanor,

---

[27] SHANNON, *supra* note 18, at 202.

Miller used a variety of objections. He objected that the witness was giving a narrative and asked that the testimony be conducted in a question-and-answer format. When this was done he objected at crucial points to leading questions, while letting other leading questions pass without objection. He objected to hearsay and to legal conclusions. When Jeffers tried to tied together disjointed bits of testimony, Miller objected that the question was summarizing the witness's testimony.

experience in complex corporate cases, and the large number of attorneys, support staff and physical facilities needed to support a complex case with a lot of witnesses and documents. While Miller tried to do most of the key work himself, Jamail spread the load effectively, using the Baker Botts lawyers to examine many of the important witnesses and to make many of the important arguments.

After Kerr, Pennzoil was forced to put on two weeks of mind-numbing deposition testimony in order to get into evidence facts known first-hand only by unfriendly witnesses beyond the reach of subpoena. Videotaping depositions was much less common than it is today, so only 15 of the 63 depositions Pennzoil took were videotaped.[28] Other deposition testimony had to be read into the record. The videotaped depositions might have provided some entertainment for the jurors because they were rancorous affairs, with the lawyers objecting repeatedly and sometimes exchanging curses and even threats. But this only meant that the jurors had to spend more time in the hall while Judge Farris listened to the lawyers argue about which parts of the videos the jurors should be allowed to hear. And most of what they did hear was painfully boring. With the lights off, which made for better viewing on the monitors of the day, jurors fell asleep during the video testimony.

But it was through this deposition testimony that much of the most important evidence came in, including Dave Copley's minutes of the Getty Oil board meeting and Marty Siegel's affidavit in the California injunction hearing stating that "the Getty Oil board of directors approved a reorganization transaction." The deposition testimony also included the fee letter in which Goldman, Sachs billed Getty Oil for its services in the transaction the day after the Getty Oil board voted, treating the Pennzoil merger as a done deal, even as Goldman, Sachs partner Geoff Boisi was shopping Getty Oil to Texaco and others.

Jamail didn't show the depositions just to get in evidence. He also wanted to show the Texaco witnesses at their worst—under hostile questioning—before the jury could see them answering the easy questions served up by their own attorneys. While he was doing this, one particular bit of evidence became key. During discovery, Pennzoil sent Texaco an interrogatory that read: "Identify each Texaco individual who saw on January 5, 1984, the article entitled 'Pennzoil's Alliance with Trust Leads to Accord for Getty Oil Company,' that appeared in the *Wall Street Journal*, Eastern edition, issued that date." Texaco responded: "No one within the identified group remembers seeing this article on January 5, 1985." The article which Texaco fought bitterly to keep from being introduced as evidence described Pennzoil's deal with Gordon and used the word "agreement" *fourteen* times. The Baker Botts lawyers

---

[28] PETZINGER, *supra* note 4, at 311.

asked virtually every Texaco witness whether they usually read the *Wall Street Journal*. Most said they did. But when they were asked if they read it on January 5th, every single one of them said they had not. This was incredibly damaging. Shannon writes, "I suppose this was possible, however, I don't think one person in the jury box believed it."[29] This played right into Jamail's hands. It made it much harder for Miller to make the case that the Texaco people were just honest businesspeople doing their jobs.

There were a number of other things in the depositions that worked against Texaco in subtle ways. In fact, when taken together, they could have even allowed the jury to infer that there had been a cover-up. Sid Petersen testified that the 15 to 1 vote by the Getty Oil board was only an approval of the price. When the lawyer taking Petersen's deposition confronted him with an article from *Fortune* magazine in which he said,"We approved the deal but we didn't favor it," he claimed he didn't remember making that statement. Dave Copley's destruction of his handwritten notes after he dictated the final version gave rise to the interference that Texaco management (his new bosses) had ordered him to alter the record. Tim Cohler, who had acted as Gordon's lawyer in the California injunction hearing, had, after he learned of the Texaco offer, changed his affidavit in the California action. Pennzoil introduced both his original affidavit and the amended version. Of these, Shannon says: "Looking at the original affidavit, it was obvious that Cohler was telling the California court that the trust, at least, believed it had a deal with Pennzoil. The implications of the amended version of the affidavit were not lost on the jury."[30] Geoff Boisi's deposition answer that he would testify at the trial "if my schedule allows," reinforced Jamail's characterization of New York investment bankers as arrogant rich guys who needed to be taught a lesson in mainstream values. So did the evidence that Boisi's firm charged a fee of $18 million for a few days' work. This allowed the Pennzoil team to refer to Boisi as "the $18 million dollar man."[31] Bart Winokur, Getty Oil's outside counsel testified that he did not normally take notes during meetings, while at the same time holding a pen in his hand.

---

[29] *Id.* at 208.

[30] *Id.* at 219.

[31] This was an allusion to the then-popular television series "The Six Million Dollar Man," featuring a character with super-human abilities resulting from bionic body parts implanted in him at the then-fantastic cost of $6 million.

Miller had tried to take the bite out of this by saying in his opening statement that the Pennzoil lawyers would refer to Boisi as the "18 million dollar man," and that his efforts in getting a higher price for Getty Oil had earned the shareholders an extra $1.2 billion. In any event, his fee was tiny in comparison to what Jamail earned from the case.

To put life back into the case, Jamail chose Arthur Liman as Pennzoil's first live witness after the video depositions. Liman had been Pennzoil's negotiator when the Getty Oil board meeting was going on. Liman was partner in the New York firm of Paul, Weiss, Rifkind, Wharton & Garrison. In addition to being one of New York's leading trial lawyers, he had a distinguished career in public service, having served as chief investigator for a commission reporting on the Attica prison riot and chair of a commission investigating brutality in the New York City police department.

As the person to tell the story of Pennzoil's deal with the Getty interests, Liman was a perfect choice. In addition to having great credibility because of his distinguished background, he was a gifted storyteller. And his being a Jewish lawyer from New York took much of the force out of Miller's charges of geographical and religious bias. Liman gave an account of the initial steps in the negotiation of Pennzoil's deal with Gordon and the museum. Because there were many meetings and other exchanges among the various players that Liman had not been present for, much of his testimony was hearsay. Bob Brown, who was handling Liman for the Texaco team objected continually but was overruled.

Over Brown's objection,[32] Liman gave his impression of Gordon Getty:

My opinion of Gordon Getty is that Gordon Getty knew what he wanted; that Gordon Getty understood the strength of his bargaining position; that Gordon Getty was approaching the decisions that were made in a very businesslike way; that Gordon Getty was exceptionally methodical; that Gordon Getty was very careful about not being taken advantage of as a person of great wealth and was concerned that people might try to manipulate him and was on his guard about that; and that Gordon Getty went to lengths that I had never seen before in selecting his advisors to make sure that he was getting the best advice he could obtain.

After Miller had put so much emphasis on his argument that Gordon Getty was an impractical innocent, this assessment of him from a man

---

[32] Brown claimed the opinion was "totally irrelevant to anything at issue in this case."

Terrell responded that Texaco had put Gordon's competence into issue. This seems clearly right, given Miller's voir dire presentation, although Jamail may have overstated it a bit when he told the judge: "The impression that they've tried to give this jury is that Pennzoil took advantage of a nincompoop."

Brown also objected that Liman had very limited contact with Gordon, but the judge seemed to have been persuaded by Jamail's argument that this fact went to the weight of the evidence, rather than to its admissibility.

with Liman's credentials must have been a huge blow to Miller's credibility.

Next, Terrell led Liman through the intricate details of the negotiations that surrounded the Getty Oil board meeting. This was necessarily long and involved, but it allowed Pennzoil to get into evidence many of the details covered in their opening statement. As Pennzoil's representative, Liman had not been present for the board meeting. He had waited in a suite that Gordon had taken on the same floor of the Intercontinental Hotel where the Getty Oil board was meeting. He explained how he was informed that the board had rejected the Memorandum of Agreement, that the $110 a share price was not enough and that they wanted an additional $10 a share. Liman told of Liedtke's response to the counterproposal: "He thought it was outrageous...." He told of Pennzoil's new proposal and of Lipton's response that it was "too cute." Liman told of the development of the proposal for the "stub," of Liedtke's agreement to it, and of Lipton's counterproposal for a guarantee of $5.

To continue the story with the details of what happened when the. board meeting resumed and Liman was excluded, Terrell had Liman read from the Copely notes:

> Mr. Williams then moved that the Board accept the Pennzoil proposal provided that the amount being paid relating to ERC be $5 per share. The motion was seconded by Mr. Mitchell. The vote was taken with all directors voting "For" other than Mr. Medberry who voted "No."

When the board meeting adjourned, many of the participants came into Gordon's suite. Siegel and Lipton told Liman of the board's counterproposal. Liman telephoned Liedtke and got his acceptance of it. Then, according to Liman:

> [Lipton] and everyone else then went back into the board room. [Lipton] said, "You can come and wait outside. This is only going to take two seconds," and then he went in.

In response to Terrell's question as to what happened next, Liman testified:

> Then within a few minutes, Marty Lipton and Marty Siegel came out, the door opened and they said, "Congratulations, Arthur. You got a deal."

Liman went on, saying that, after compliments and thanks were exchanged,

> I said, "I'd like to ask permission to go into the board meeting and to shake hands with all of the directors because they've been at it for so many hours and I'd like to just shake hands with all of them."

And they said that would be okay. So, I was finally allowed into the board room.

* * *

Everyone was sort of milling around. I guess there were—there were probably twenty people because there were directors and lawyers, bankers, and I went around the room. . . . I went around the room and I introduced myself and I shook hands with everyone I could.

I said, "Congratulations."
They said, "Congratulations to you."
I said, "Thank you for—for putting in all these hours. I know that—that you were doing your best."

Terrell then went on to the Texaco purchase. Over an objection that Liman's reaction was immaterial, Liman testified that when he heard of it, his reaction was "disbelief." He went on to say that when he called Marty Siegel, he told him he [Siegel] should tell Liedtke of the Texaco purchase himself "and not just slink off."

This was another devastating blow to Miller's theory of the case. He had staked much on the idea that Texaco's conduct had been in perfect conformity with the way things were done among those who did this sort of thing all the time. Now, a pillar of the New York bar was telling the jury, more convincingly than if he had said so directly, that this was *not* the way things were done.

On cross, Brown got Liman to admit that Marty Lipton was "an honest gentleman," "a trustworthy gentleman," and "a man of his word." Liman did, however, add to the last two characterizations the qualifier "putting aside the dispute we're in here."

With respect to Lawrence Tisch, another key Texaco witness, Liman said: "He is a fine human being, He has been a close friend of mine and my family for a long time." Judge Farris sustained an objection when Brown asked Liman "can this jury, in your opinion, believe everything [Tisch] says?" But Liman did say:

I have no doubt that Larry Tisch will tell this jury the events as he remembers them just as I've tried to do. I have no doubt about that.

Liman, who had finished first in his class at Yale Law School, showed his brilliance by deftly turning Brown's questions against him. When Brown returned to Marty Lipton and tried to get Liman to admit that Lipton was too honest to advise a client to breach a contract, Liman explained that in our legal system a person is generally allowed to breach a contract as long as they are willing to pay the resulting damages. Lipton, Liman explained, had done "an extraordinary job" for his client (the museum) by getting it the extra money from the Texaco contract and getting an indemnity that made Texaco liable for the resulting damages.

If this wasn't enough, Texaco's subsequent efforts to discredit Liman only served to enhance his impact. Jim Shannon wrote:

> If we [the jury] had any doubts about [the] significance [of Liman's testimony], they were quickly laid to rest. For the remaining three months of the trial, Texaco attorneys went to great lengths trying to discredit Liman. Their efforts served to remind the jury repeatedly just how convincing Arthur Liman had been.[33]

Having put some excitement back into his case, Jamail returned to videotape depositions to secure the admission of some damaging documentary evidence—the handwritten notes of DeCrane and Texaco Deputy Controller Patrick Lynch.

Lynch's deposition was shown first. Lynch was the most junior Texaco officer present when Joseph Perella, the First Boston investment banker, made his presentation urging Texaco to move quickly to top the Pennzoil offer. Capturing Perella's colorful investment banker language, Lynch's notes used phrases like "Stop the train" and "Stop signing." These words, Pennzoil argued, were evidence of Texaco's intent to interfere with Pennzoil's deal.

DeCrane's notes were even more crucial. Jamail had referred to them in his voir dire presentation as a "smoking gun" and he would call them the same in his closing argument. They were, in Pennzoil's version of reality, damning evidence of Texaco's actual knowledge that there was a contract between Pennzoil and the Getty interests. The fact that they were made by Texaco's president, who was himself a lawyer, was icing on the cake.

In his videotaped deposition, DeCrane made a bad impression on the jury, and this may have been a factor in turning the jury away from Texaco. As a lawyer, DeCrane knew exactly what he was supposed to do in a deposition. He gave short answers, he didn't volunteer evidence, he asked for explanations when he didn't understand the question, and when he didn't recall, he said so. Unfortunately, this made him look evasive when the Pennzoil lawyers played the tape for the jury. All the jurors had undoubtedly seen the Watergate hearings, and the "I don't recall" answers of Nixon's advisors were still in the mind of everyone in America. It would be many years before a witness in any trial could say "I don't recall" without bringing to mind the image of the White House insiders sitting before the Congressional committees covering up the cover-up.

---

[33] SHANNON, *supra* note 18, at 236.

Next, Jamail's team began developing its evidence on damages. The jury's award of $7.47 billion in actual damages was the ultimate tribute to Jamail's skill. The calculation of damages in a business case, even a relatively simple one, is so difficult and confusing that most law professors don't even attempt to teach students how to do it. Explaining the numbers to the jury could easily have become a morass.

The Pennzoil team, however, came up with a very simple explanation. If Texaco had not interfered with their contract, Pennzoil would have obtained three-sevenths of the assets of Getty Oil. These assets consisted of 1.008 billion barrels of proved oil reserves i.e, oil discovered and owned but still in the ground. The price they would have had to pay for the 3/7 interest in Getty Oil divided out to $3.40 for each barrel of reserves they would have acquired. Pennzoil's historic cost for finding and acquiring such oil reserves was $10.87 per barrel. The difference was $7.47 per barrel. Multiplying that $7.47 per barrel by the 1.008 billion barrels of oil meant that Texaco's interfering in Pennzoil's purchase had cost Pennzoil $7.53 billion dollars. The formula was set out on an exhibit five feet high with bold black lettering.

It was a perfect theory for a jury trial. It was simple, logical, and easy to understand. It was also, according to *Wall Street Journal* reporter Thomas Petzinger, Jr., "utterly outrageous."[34] The theory could not withstand economic scrutiny. If Getty Oil's reserves had been worth $10.43 a barrel, then the total value of its reserves would have been $27.4 billion. If Getty Oil had been worth nothing more than the value of its reserves, it would have been worth $27.4 billion. With 79 million shares outstanding, this works out to $346 a share. At $115 a share, Pennzoil would have been stealing the company from the public shareholders, and the directors' negligence in approving such a deal would have bordered on criminal. But of course the company couldn't have been worth that. If it had been, Wall Streeters and oil barons would have been fighting to take it over long before Gordon put it into play. In short, Pennzoil's damage theory attributed to the markets a level of irrationality that even the most die-hard opponents of free markets would be embarrassed to claim. Still, Jamail and his team were able to sell it.

Pennzoil began its case on damages by proving its historical average finding and development costs through the testimony of Dr. Ron Lewis, head of its offshore division. Dr. Lewis's testimony was technical and dull. Jim Shannon seems to have thought that Richard Keeton could have been more effective on cross-examination if he had pressed the witness harder but that he chose not to do so to avoid confrontations

---

[34] PETZINGER, supra note 4, at 318.

with Judge Farris, who had been criticized in a recent bar association poll for not protecting witnesses.[35]

What gave Pennzoil's damages theory its credibility was the testimony of Thomas Barrow. Barrow had recently retired as vice chairman of Standard Oil Company. Irv Terrell had given Barrow a big build-up during Pennzoil's voir dire presentation. Terrell had pointed out that Barrow had also been chairman of Kennecott Copper and a member of the board of directors of Exxon. Terrell had further noted that Barrow was testifying as an expert witness without the compensation ordinarily required by expert witnesses. Nor was he, Terrell had argued, doing it out of friendship for Liedtke and Kerr. Barrow had no personal relationship with them. Terrell had told the jurors: "You may judge for yourself why he is testifying in this case."

For his part, Miller had attacked Barrow's motives in his voir dire presentation, pointing out that Barrow had for many years been a director of Texas Commerce Bank, which was a Baker Botts client. As Miller put it,

> As you all know, there is more than one way to receive compensation. It could certainly be in the form of money. It could be in the form of creating friendship and business opportunities. Compensation may take many forms.

Jim Shannon was not impressed. He described the theory as "[a]nother red herring Miller tossed into his voir dire presentation" and said: "This theory dwindled away without anything of substance being added."[36] But to allay any suspicions that Miller might have raised, Jeffers read Miller's statement and had Barrow refute it in detail. Barrow testified that Baker Botts was not Texas Commerce Bank's principal law firm, that he had never personally been represented by Baker Botts, and, most tellingly, that he had closer personal relationships with Texaco's top officers, McKinley and Kinnear, than with Liedtke and Kerr, their Pennzoil counterparts.

When Barrow was asked why he was testifying without compensation, he responded

> First, I was not interested in being a professional expert witness. Second, I felt that the issue of contract was a matter of principle as far as I was concerned and, therefore, I was willing to do it on that basis.

---

[35] SHANNON, *supra* note 18, at 244–47. Judge Farris indicated the he had been criticized for "being mean" to witnesses, but he apparently took it as meaning (at least in part) that he did not protect witnesses from badgering by opposing counsel.

[36] *Id.* at 148.

This was perfect—a man with experience on corporate boards in and out of the oil industry who was testifying out of the same sense of principle and honor that Pennzoil claimed motivated it to bring the case in the first place. Moreover, he was not a Houston good old boy. Early in his direct examination of Barrow, Jeffers subtly established Barrow as a member of the Eastern establishment. Not only did he testify that he had lived in New York City and in its exclusive suburb of Greenwich, Connecticut, but Judge Farris had asked him about his attendance at the Phillips Andover Academy.

Pennzoil tendered Barrow as an expert "on the issues of contract formation and damages." Over Keeton's objection that expert testimony on the issue of contract formation was invading the province of the jury, Judge Farris said that he would allow him to testify as to the meaning of the 15 to 1 vote of the Getty Oil Board. "I will allow this line of questioning based on his experience as having served on various boards," said Judge Farris, "not as a mind reader."

Jeffers then led Barrow through a series of carefully-phrased questions about the significance of the board's actions. With respect to the 15–to–1 vote in favor of making the counterproposal to Pennzoil, Jeffers asked: "And do you read any qualifications or any tentativeness into that board vote?"

Barrow answered: "I do not."

Jeffers then asked whether Barrow had in his extensive experience as a board member, dealt with motions and votes "of just that kind." When Barrow answered that he had, Jeffers had Barrow read the portion of the Texaco board minutes that said:

> The meeting was reconvened at 6:55 P.M. Eastern Standard Time, January 3, 1984, following which Mr. Siegel advised the directors that Pennzoil had indicated to him that it would accept the counterproposal presented by the board.

Jeffers then asked: "And what significance, based on your experience, did you attach to that portion of the minutes or notes?"

Barrow responded: "That the Getty Board had made an offer and that Pennzoil had accepted it."

In response to the next question, "In your experience, what is that confluence of events?" Barrow said:

> I would interpret that to mean that there was an agreement in principle that they would sell the company under the terms and conditions that are indicated in the—in their discussion. Price had been set. Form had been set.

After additional questioning and objections that the testimony was invading the province of the jury, Barrow testified:

> Based on the evidence that I have seen and only as an experienced executive who served on boards, I would come to the conclusion that the Getty board had reached an agreement with Pennzoil.

He then went on to testify that "Once an agreement has been reached, it's their [the board's] responsibility to see to it that the final written agreements are prepared and executed." He indicated that in the course of negotiating the final documents, the parties were bound by "the money terms" agreed upon. He never, however, said there was a "contract." He always used the term "agreement."

Barrow did, however, undercut, although not directly refute, one of Texaco's key points. Miller had emphasized in his voir dire presentation that "[t]his phrase 'agreed in principle' in the context of what was going on in New York City means just the opposite. It means you have not agreed."

But when asked what the term "agreement in principle" meant in his experience, Barrow testified: "I would interpret it to mean that they have agreed on the principal, substantial—substantial—substantive terms of the—and in this case, price and structure being the two most important and that they were proceeding to finish out the remainder of the agreement." He said that the use of the term "agreement in principle" in the press release in no way altered his conclusion that the parties had reached an "agreement." He also said that he "would not consider it proper in any case that I can think of" for a board that had "agreed" on a transaction to direct its investment bankers to shop for a better price.

Having dealt Texaco's case on contract formation a damaging blow, Jeffers took Barrow to the subject of damages. This was where his testimony had its most important effect. It gave credibility to Pennzoil's theory. But on this topic, Barrow was guarded in his testimony. He clearly knew that Pennzoil's theory had serious weaknesses. Jeffers led him through the model. Pennzoil's historical finding costs of $10.87 per barrel minus $3.40 per barrel, gives $7.47 per barrel. Three sevenths of Getty Oil's proven reserves was 1.08 billion barrels. Multiplying gives $7.53 billion. Then Jeffers got him to vouch for the model. His questions were carefully worded to keep from going farther than Barrow was willing to go.

Q. [I]n your opinion, based on experience in the oil business, does this replacement model of damages have any validity?

A. Yes, it would.

Q. Is it an acceptable method of measuring damages?

A. Yes.

* * *

Q. [I]f you were in Pennzoil's position or any company's position looking at Getty to see whether it were a desirable bargain, would you in fact look at this differential between your finding cost and what you would be able to buy these Getty barrels for?

A. That would certainly be one of the factors I would take into consideration.

On cross-examination, Keeton was able to make many good points that should have undercut the effectiveness of Barrow's testimony on damages. He got Barrow to admit that Pennzoil's cost of finding and developing reserves was not necessarily the measure of the value of the Getty Oil reserves, and that Pennzoil's theory had failed to take into consideration such factors as the quality of the oil, the location, and the production costs. Finally, Keeton got Barrow to admit that he did not attempt to equate the Getty oil to the oil that Pennzoil had found at a cost of $10.87 a barrel.

Ultimately, Keeton made a number of good points on cross-examination. And if Barrow had been the typical hired gun, it might have destroyed, or at least seriously damaged, his effectiveness. But Texaco had given the jury no credible basis for believing that he was anything other than what he purported to be, a disinterested leader of American business, seeking to uphold justice and honor in business dealings. If he said that there was "an agreement," why should the jury believe otherwise? And if he said Pennzoil's damage model was legitimate, who should doubt that? What may have been more important was the fact that the jurors had been sitting through seven weeks of mind-numbing testimony. It was hard for them to summon the mental energy to follow the points Keeton was making. The simple theory that Jamail had come up with and Barrow had now approved was much easier to follow.

After Barrow, the trial, as it had done so many times before, shifted gears. Pennzoil introduced the video deposition of Gordon Getty.[37]

Gordon came across as a strange figure, beyond eccentric. Under the careful tutelage of his lawyer, the 80–year–old Moses Lasky, he came across as evasive, but in a charming, innocent way. It was also clear, at least to the sophisticated observer, that he was very intelligent. One answer was particularly noteworthy. When asked about a conversation with Harold Williams, president of the Museum, he responded:

---

[37] Gordon Getty refused to testify at the trial because he was then involved in yet another intra-family lawsuit.

I recall a few things. Again, memory can be tricky. We recall some things that may not be the most important, but for some reason we remember them. I do recall him making the point that at $100 a share or higher, the museum was a definitely a seller and not a buyer, which was a rhyme. Put me in the circle of poets for that. That's the lowest circle in hell, by the way.

Remarks like this, coupled with Gordon's multitude of nervous mannerisms, gestures, and facial expressions made his video deposition much more entertaining than those that had preceded it.

With respect to the champagne toast, Gordon's testimony might seem to have favored Texaco. When asked what he was celebrating, he said: "Seemed to me there had been a lot of progress in my ambition to raise the value of the trust." When pressed to be more specific, he said: "I thought the 14–to–1 vote was progress; that would be specific. I wish I could tell you more clearly what the vote was for, but I can't. But I nonetheless thought it was progress."

It could be argued that Gordon hadn't seen it as an agreement, but merely as progress in getting more money for the trust. Jim Shannon saw it differently, however:

> The champagne was another piece in the evidentiary mosaic being assembled by Pennzoil. Like the handshakes, the champagne was not the turning point in the case. But these things did start to add up, especially when considered in light of the documentary evidence.[38]

Jeffers was also able to elicit insights into Gordon's thinking, which proved to be very helpful in building Pennzoil's story of the case. Gordon agreed, in response to Jeffers' leading question, that when Marty Lipton had announced that the museum was selling to Texaco, that he (Gordon) "felt that [the trust] had no choice but to do so [also]." Gordon also indicated that Bruce Wasserstein (Texaco's investment banker) made it clear to Gordon that if the trust didn't sell to Texaco, it would be a locked-out minority with no voice in the control of the company. In other words, Gordon's testimony was, at this point, buttressing Pennzoil's story that Texaco had come in as a bully, forcing Gordon to breach his contract with Pennzoil. At the same time, of course, it was undercutting Texaco's story that it came in as a rescuer, saving the naive Gordon from being taken advantage of by the fast-talking Liedtke.

Miller's cross-examination did little to further his argument that Gordon was an innocent being taken advantage of by the oil barons. Gordon did admit that before the deal began he had thought of Pennzoil primarily in terms of their television advertisements featuring golfer

---

[38] SHANNON, *supra* note 18, at 276.

Arnold Palmer, but he rejected Miller's suggestion that he might have been under the impression Mr. Palmer was Pennzoil's chief executive. Perhaps the best evidence that Gordon wasn't used to the rough and tumble of business came when Miller, seemingly for other reasons, asked Gordon what Pennzoil lawyer Arthur Liman had said about Getty Oil director Chauncey Medberry. Gordon refused to repeat Liman's characterization of Medberry as a "duplicitous prick," because there was a female court reporter present at the deposition. It was only after Miller had obtained the court reporter's permission that Gordon was willing to say the words, and even then he was obviously uncomfortable doing it.

Following Gordon, Jamail put on Hugh Liedtke. Jamail examined Liedtke himself, and he played him beautifully. Jamail had prepared his friend to testify by talking with him about the case over drinks, at his house or Liedtke's, for three or four evenings a week over a period of several weeks. Jamail had told Liedtke, "If we have any chance at all, you *have* to come across as the Hugh Liedtke who's sitting in my living room."

That was exactly the way Liedtke came across, not as the aggressive opportunist who had been a pioneer in hostile takeovers, but as the guy next door who just happened to be a successful businessman. He exuded the same folksy charm Jamail did. Jamail began his orchestration by having Liedtke answer the standard questions about age, family status, background and education, but Jamail explained, ostensibly for Liedtke's benefit, that this "gives the jury a better insight into you and what you are about and gives them a better opportunity to judge your credibility and analyze your testimony." Answering these questions, Liedtke came across as a sympathetic human being. He was embarrassed that he couldn't remember the birth dates of his five children.

From there, Jamail walked Liedtke through the story of how he had built his company. Along the way, Liedtke told of his partnership in the oil business with George H.W. Bush, then vice President of the United States, and of his association with Getty Oil Company and with J. Paul Getty and George Getty, Gordon's brother. By the end of the story, Liedtke had, through determination and hard work, transformed the little oil company he started, after serving in World War II and attending the University of Texas Law School, into a Fortune 500 company. But he was still the same down-home Hugh Liedtke who enjoyed the simple pleasures of family and friends and fishing. Left out, of course, were the stories of the back-room manipulations and cutthroat deals that characterized the independent oil operators of Liedtke's day. Liedtke had made it big without becoming like Jamail's villain, Corporate America.

In his description of the Pennzoil tender offer and the dealings that followed, Liedtke stuck to the same theme. He wasn't like the executives from Texaco or Getty Oil, who surrounded themselves with accountants, lawyers, and investment bankers. When he did a deal, he made back-of-the-envelope calculations to decide on a price and negotiated directly with the other person. He was still a Texas oilman at heart.

He described the strife at Getty Oil that had led him to come into the picture, not to take over the company, but to make peace among the warring factions. This gave him a chance to re-tell the story of "Back-Door Bart" and the other machinations of the Getty Oil board, reinforcing the idea that the Getty Oil managers were not only corporate connivers, but also allies of Texaco. He told this story with the air of one who was appalled and amazed that such things occurred. The jury apparently had no idea that he had taken part in plenty of corporate intrigues in his career. In fact, Judge Farris had ruled that Texaco could not make reference to Liedtke's previous problems with the Securities and Exchange Commission.

Jamail also asked Liedtke about the Getty family trust. Liedtke said that the trust was set up to avoid the family having to sell the Getty Oil stock, and that under the Pennzoil deal, the trust would not have had to sell the stock. But under the Texaco proposal, "the trust was forced to sell and frightened into selling." This was reinforced by the allusions to the threats that if Gordon didn't sell to Texaco, he would be left as a frozen-out minority shareholder.

Jamail used Liedtke to cover virtually every aspect of Pennzoil's case, repeating in a comprehensible and interesting fashion (and of course with a Pennzoil spin) the key testimony from the six boring weeks that had gone before. In addition, Jamail used Liedtke to undercut many of Texaco's strongest arguments. The open items in the deal with the Getty interests, Liedtke dismissed with comments such as, "Well, Mr. Jamail, you are dealing in minutiae now," or "If you look at it in terms of this deal, it's a fraction of one per cent."

Texaco's argument that the unresolved question of how the Getty Oil employees would be dealt with under the Pennzoil proposal was a major sticking point, but it was turned into a point in Pennzoil's favor, if not in legal effect, at least in jury sympathy. "It was our plan to build Getty Oil.... It is quite clear that Pennzoil is a company that builds rather than destroys and liquidates." Liedtke went on to talk about the way Texaco had laid off Getty Oil employees and diverted money from the Getty Oil pension fund.

Asked whether Texaco should have known that Getty Oil already had an agreement with Pennzoil, Liedtke replied: "People don't get to that place in a corporation without doing their homework." Asked whether he would have interfered with someone else's deal, he responded "Mr. Jamail, I would consider that about as arrogant and unethical a thing to do as I could possibly imagine."[39]

Shannon describes how well the Pennzoil story unfolded during Liedtke's testimony:

> This harmonizing between the chairman and his friend the lawyer was comparable to two jazz musicians exchanging leads. Jamail would blast a handful of staccato notes from his trumpet, to be answered by a towering riff from Liedtke's baritone sax.[40]

Elsewhere, Shannon describes it as "riveting theater," made more effective with the jurors because it followed so much dry and boring testimony.[41]

Miller's cross-examination lasted six days, but it did little to detract from Liedtke's effect. Liedtke conceded nothing and in fact scored some points of his own. It was obvious that Liedtke was well prepared for Miller's cross-examination. Petzinger quotes one piece of Jamail's preparation:

> Miller's going to try to bait you. I don't want you getting into any fishmonger fights with him, and if you do, it will make me mad.
> "How will I know if you're mad?"
> Because you'll see the back of my ass going right out the door.
> "You'll leave?"
> "You're goddamn right."[42]

As Pennzoil's final witness, Jamail called, of all people, *Texaco's* chairman, John McKinley. This was a most unconventional move, but Jamail, as usual, knew what he was doing. There are people who make good witnesses and there are people who make bad witnesses. Jamail knew that John McKinley, in spite of his great ability as a corporate executive, would make a bad witness. In fact, some of the traits that made him effective in running a huge, bureaucratic corporation made him a bad witness. What was more, Jamail knew that Miller knew this, and he suspected Miller would not call McKinley as a witness for Texaco. So Jamail called McKinley as a witness for Pennzoil. In addition to making sure that McKinley testified, it ensured that McKinley was attacked and, to the extent that Jamail could do it, destroyed, before Texaco got to tell its story.[43] To secure his presence, Jamail had him

---

[39] PETZINGER, *supra* note 4, at 332.

[40] SHANNON, *supra* note 18, at 294.

[41] *Id.* at 296.

[42] PETZINGER, *supra* note 4, at 33.

[43] Petzinger stated that Texaco had three other executives it could have used to tell its side of the story. Two were lawyers (DeCrane and General Counsel Bill Weitzel) and Kinnear had been sitting through every day of the trial. *Id.* at 340.

served with a subpoena during Texaco's voir dire presentation when
Miller had presented him along with Kinnear and DeCrane as the
human face of Texaco.

On a rational, intellectual level McKinley did a good job of testifying.
He avoided many of Jamail's traps. He qualified his answers when he
was allowed to. He named several people at Getty Oil who had had
assured him that they were not bound to any deal, as yet. When he
explained how the investment bankers had assured him that Getty Oil
was not bound, Jamail slipped in a bit of argument: "We been told about
the financial interests of investment bankers in these kinds of things."

But in spite of McKinley's determined efforts to protect himself, he
was clearly outmatched. He was playing against a master at the master's
game. Where Liedtke had come across as a straightforward builder of the
American dream with nothing to hide, McKinley came across as an
evasive bureaucrat, motivated solely by profit. According to Jim Shannon, Jamail had "attach[ed] an air of menace to the soft-spoken engineer"[44] Moreover, in the eyes of Jim Shannon at least, Jamail had made
the substantive point he intended. He had "solidif[ied] Pennzoil's claims
of Texaco's knowledge and interference."[45]

Miller, who was now in the position of having to use his cross-
examination to bring out what should have been direct examination
testimony, was unable to do much to rehabilitate McKinley. The job was
made that much harder by McKinley's lack, not only of a flair for the
dramatic, but even seemingly of humor.[46] When Miller made jokes,
McKinley failed to pick up on them. When Miller asked him to tell about
himself, he responses fell flat there as well:

Q. How about yourself, Mr. McKinley, your progress in the company.
    How did a guy from Alabama ever get to be the head of the Texas
    Company?

A. On a serious answer, I don't suppose anybody really knows how
    these things happen.

On redirect, Jamail was able to score some more points. He asked
Miller if when he decided to take over Getty Oil, he had expected there
would be layoffs of Getty Oil employees. McKinley answered, apparently
without considering its effect on a jury of Houston residents, "Yes. It

---

[44] SHANNON, *supra* note 18, at 312.

[45] *Id.* at 317.

[46] According to some reports, McKinley actually had a good sense of humor. But he was
a formal, introverted person, and Jamail knew that whatever humor and warmth he
possessed would not be evident to the jury. George Washington, who, according to
historians, had a personality much like McKinley's, would also have made a poor impression under questioning by Jamail.

was my hope that there would be some redundancy of personnel and they could be terminated. Yes."

It must have taken all of Jamail's acting talent to control his joy at having this gem thrown into his lap. But he did control himself and asked in mock horror: "That was your *hope?*"[47]

That concluded Pennzoil's case in chief. At that point, nine weeks had elapsed since the day when the jurors first came into the courthouse and were told they might be chosen to participate in a big case. The reporter's transcript filled 13,992 pages. Jamail's team thought they were ahead at that point. Miller's team thought they were at least even.

Texaco's Case

As its first witness, Texaco called Bart Winokur. Like Miller's other key decisions in the case, this one would be second-guessed. Texaco's management had suggested using a Texan, perhaps Getty Oil president Robert Miller, or Harold Berg, Getty Oil's board member and former chairman. Dick Miller had originally planned to start off with Sid Petersen, but he changed his mind and settled on Winokur.

The Pennzoil team had expected Miller to lead off with Al DeCrane, Texaco's articulate and unflappable president. For Miller, however, it was important to start of with a witness from Getty Oil, rather than a witness from Texaco. Texaco's case had two parts; convincing the jury of either of them would win the case. The first part was that there was no contract between Pennzoil and the Getty interests; the second was that, even if there was a contract, Texaco didn't know it. The witnesses from Getty Oil were primarily testifying as to the first part and the witnesses from Texaco as to the second. Miller felt that beginning with a witness from Texaco would give the appearance of conceding the first part of his argument. Moreover, Miller wanted someone who could make the jury understand the pressure that Gordon Getty and Hugh Liedtke had brought to bear on the board.

Miller had told Sid Petersen that he would be Texaco's first witness, but he later changed his mind. Winokur was more confidant and articulate. He was a great storyteller. He was an experienced mergers and acquisitions lawyer who could explain to the jury that the mergers and acquisitions business had its own language and its own culture and that it was a culture where people documented things carefully and didn't make deals on the basis of a handshake. Winokur could explain the significance of the issues that were still open between Pennzoil and Getty Oil when Texaco made its offer.

Miller was of course aware of that the Pennzoil team's attempt to make the jury hate "Back Door Bart," as the Pennzoil lawyers had been

---

[47] PETZINGER, *supra* note 4, at 343.

calling him, might already have succeeded. But given the advantages that Winokur's testimony offered, he was willing to take that risk.

Miller used Winokur for the same purpose that Pennzoil had used Baine Kerr, to give background and present an overall picture of the transaction. This time, however, it was to give a picture that fit Texaco's theory of the case. The picture he attempted to paint was that of a specialized type of transaction with its own language, its own customs and its own rules. It was a business where people did not make contracts casually. At one point Winokur said of the Getty Oil board's plan to hold a "controlled auction" in response to the arrangement that Gordon and Liedtke had worked out: "We're not talking about a five cent candy bar. We're talking about a ten-billion-dollar company."

In contrast to Liedtke's characterization of Pennzoil's approach to Getty Oil as friendly, Winokur implied that Pennzoil had lied when it stated in its tender offer documents that it intended to "participate in a constructive way" in the restructuring of Getty Oil:

> Well if somebody was interested in participating in a constructive way in restructuring a company, one would have thought they would have talked to the company about restructuring.

> What's more, I think that if you want to be constructive, you don't hold a gun to somebody's head. I mean if somebody came to your front door and had a paintbrush in one hand and gun in the other and said, "I heard your house needs painting," I mean, you might suspect he's there for something other than painting your house.

At this point, J.C. Nickens, the Miller, Keeton partner handling the direct examination had Winokur define some of the colorful terms of takeover jargon, like "in play," "bear hug," "shark," "blood in the water," "gun at the head." As he did so, a Texaco lawyer stood at a whiteboard, listing the terms one by one. Then Winokur wove the terms into his story. The infighting at Getty Oil put Getty Oil "in play" and put "blood in the water." The "shark" (Pennzoil) smelled it and put a "gun to the head" of the Getty Oil board to get the company in a "bear hug."

Next Nickens tried to get Winokur to give the details of the Getty Oil board meeting of January 2–3 and to explain the thinking of the Getty Oil board. Terrell objected vehemently on the ground that Winokur could not speak for Getty Oil Company because he was not a member of the board. Terrell also raised the issue of the Copley notes, arguing that Winokur could not testify as to facts not in the notes, raising still another time the implication that evidence had willfully been destroyed at the behest of Texaco, and suggesting that Winokur, or at least his firm, might have played a part:

I want to bring to the court's attention that Mr. Copely prepared these edited notes in this man's law office; and this man's partner was right there when Mr. Copley threw the original notes away; and further, this man's law firm filed a lawsuit against Pennzoil on January 6, before those notes were destroyed. It would be a total miscarriage of justice to let this man now get up and talk about something that's not even in his own edited notes with Mr. Copely, and I don't think he's got the right to do that.

Judge Farris, however, allowed Winokur to testify as to these matters, so long as his testimony did not include legal opinions.

From the beginning of his testimony, Winokur continually strayed beyond the facts into legal opinions. Judge Farris cautioned him about "slipping in" legal opinions, precipitating a rancorous exchange between Miller and the judge over the judge's use of the term "slipping in" in front of the jury. Whether Winokur was intentionally slipping legal opinions into his testimony or inadvertently straying across the fact-opinion line is not clear. Shannon thinks it was the latter.[48]

But, in fact, Judge Farris's "slipping in" remark was the least of the troubles with Winokur's testimony. Even though the story he told should have been devastating to Pennzoil's case, Winokur's attitude and his demeanor so offended the jury that they seem to have missed the substance of his testimony. Petzinger says he "seem[ed] sarcastic, distant and cold. Winokur was almost too smart, too glib for his own good—and for Texaco's."[49] Shannon concurs:

> The utter contempt he [Winokur] had for the plaintiff seemed to spill over to include the whole trial as well. As for the jury, he studiously avoided ever looking in our direction. It was as if we were scullery maids and field hands let in to the Great Manor to see the master's debating society. Winokur never deigned to even look at the jury.

* * *

I remember wondering how the Texaco lawyers could have possibly thought this guy would make a good witness.[50]

The answer is that in the right situation, Winokur could be charming and ingratiating. His law firm thought of him as a "client's man," a lawyer who could make a good impression with business clients. In fact, it had been his ability to ingratiate himself with clients that had brought him into the deal in the first place. His firm had acquired Getty Oil as a

---

[48] SHANNON, *supra* note 18, at 353.

[49] PETZINGER, *supra* note 4, at 347.

[50] SHANNON, *supra* note 18, at 359.

client when it merged with Lansing Hays' firm. The senior partners had been concerned that they might lose Getty Oil as a client when Hays died, so they looked for a lawyer who would get along well with management, one who could give the firm a good chance to keep Getty Oil as a client. They chose Winokur, and it had appeared to be a good choice. Sid Petersen found him to be a refreshing change from the abrasive Hays, and Dechert, Price kept the representation.

Unfortunately, there was also a cocky, arrogant side to Winokur's personality, and it was that side that the jury saw. Late in his book, when discussing the jury deliberations, Shannon describes its effect:

> Winokur's unbridled arrogance on the witness stand had altered the intended effect of his testimony. When he should have been scoring points for the defendant, his antipathy for the plaintiff was so apparent it colored his testimony.[51]

There was also the matter of his conduct at the Getty Oil board meeting, when he had come in while Gordon was absent to urge the directors to back a suit against Gordon. Before the jurors saw Barton Winokur in the flesh, they had come to know him as "Back Door Bart."

To make things worse, Winokur wanted to complete his testimony on a Friday afternoon so that he could return to Philadelphia to celebrate the Jewish holidays with his family. Normally this would not have been a problem, but with the trial in its tenth week, Judge Farris had been giving the jurors Friday afternoons off so that they could attend to those items of personal business that could not be conducted on the weekends. The jurors had been given no reason to believe they would not have this Friday afternoon free. Two of them had scheduled medical appointments and others had made plans as well. Ultimately, the problem was resolved, albeit unsatisfactorily, by giving the jurors Friday afternoon off, allowing Winokur to return to Philadelphia for Yom Kippur and conclude his testimony the following week.

When Winokur returned, he was no more likable, but he did continue to give testimony that showed the weaknesses in Pennzoil's case. Miller's partner, J.C. Nickens concluded his direct examination with this exchange:

Q. Mr. Winokur, in your role as a negotiator and advisor to the company, did the Getty Oil Company have an agreement with Pennzoil on January 3rd?

A. No.

Q. Did it have an agreement with Pennzoil on January 4th?

A. Absolutely not.

---

[51] SHANNON, *supra* note 18, at 479.

Q. Did it at any time, have an agreement with Pennzoil?

A. No.

Q. How many mergers and acquisitions have you been involved with?

A. Hundreds

Q. Are you familiar with the customs and practice with regard to whether such transactions are reflected in writing?

A. Yes.

Q. What is that custom and practice?

A. They are always reflected in writing.

Mr. Nickens: We pass the witness your honor.

On cross-examination, Terrell had two major objectives. One was to make the jury dislike Winokur even more than they did already. The second was to embarrass Winokur with the back-door board meeting. As Petzinger points out, on a strictly legal basis (and on a strictly rational basis), the suit to have a co-trustee appointed had no relationship to Pennzoil's claim that Texaco had interfered with its contract. But it was an important part of the story Jamail and his team were telling the jury. It showed why Liedtke had come in to rescue Gordon and the company his father had founded from the evil people who had taken over the company. Moreover, through the indemnities, Jamail's team was seeking (with considerable success, it turned out) to tie Texaco in the minds of the jurors to the wrongdoing of the Getty Oil management.

The cross-examination began late in the day and Terrell started off with the back-door incident. When Nickens objected that Terrell's questions were irrelevant, Terrell seized the opportunity not only to attack Winokur's ethics, but to try to make Texaco guilty by association:

> This man's credibility [is] before this jury. This man came in and did something that I think this jury ought to know about. There's been prior testimony about this. This man's credibility, he's sworn here, he's the lead witness for Texaco, they are vouching for his credibility, and I think the jury needs to know the facts; I think it's entirely relevant.

After indicating that this was a good stopping point, Judge Farris dismissed the jury for the day. When they were gone, he addressed Terrell:

> I don't want you or indeed any lawyer on either side to tell the jury what a bad guy somebody is. Just go ahead and question them. If they think you're a bad guy after they hear the answers, so be it. But don't again go ahead and start slicing on him.

Terrell found plenty of ways to slice Winokur without again incurring Judge Farris's wrath. One way was simply to develop the facts of the suit against Gordon. Winokur had encouraged the board to intervene in the suit at the same time they were entering into the standstill agreement that Winokur himself had helped negotiate. Winokur had helped lead the board to believe that Getty Oil was only intervening in a suit brought by someone else, when in fact Winokur and Sid Petersen were the prime movers in the suit. Winokur had left the board meeting before Gordon returned.

Winokur seemed oblivious to the impression these facts were making on the jury. Perhaps it was because he didn't think he had done anything wrong. Terrell beat on Winokur with the details of not only the back-door board meeting, but also the drafting session where the Getty Oil lawyers, knowing that a deal with Texaco was in the works, hindered and delayed the preparation of a definitive agreement that would have unquestionably sealed Pennzoil's deal.

Winokur tried to make it hard for Terrell, but, perhaps because he was so arrogant or perhaps just because he didn't have much litigation experience, he only made it easier. He not only attempted, rather transparently, to evade questions; he engaged in semantic quibbles that sometimes bordered on the ridiculous.

What Winokur failed to understand was that the jury didn't see his intellectual game as cute or clever or entertaining. They were infuriated.[52] They had already given up three months of their lives to the case, and there seemed no end in sight. Winokur's constant sparring with Terrell was pushing farther into the future the day when they could return to their lives. In addition, it made Winokur look like he had something to hide. As Jim Shannon put it, "that arrogant ass sat there and stonewalled like H.R. Haldeman," a reference to Richard Nixon's chief of staff in the Watergate hearings, which everyone in the courtroom still remembered.[53]

In addition to hammering Winokur with embarrassing facts, Terrell used non-verbal cues to reinforce the bad impression Winokur was making on the jury. Steve Coll describes it in his book:

> Terrell understood that he and the witness were not standing on level ground in the eyes of the jury. Here was Winokur, Harvard-educated, Jewish, boyish-looking, bright, brash, and articulate, at-

---

[52] Jim Shannon said: "the longer the Winokur testimony continued, the more it seemed like fingernails scratching on a blackboard." He described it as: "a prime example of the type of excruciating word play that gives lawyers a bad name with so many people." SHANNON, *supra* note 18, at 369.

[53] PETZINGER, *supra* note 4, at 354.

tacking the credibility of Hugh Liedtke, that dog-faced monument to everything that was good and right about the Texas oil business. The contempt on Terrell's face was chilling, and the gangly lawyer made it a point to communicate his feelings to the jury at every opportunity. So often did Terrel shake his head sarcastically or scrunch his face into an expression of extreme skepticism, it became a running objection by Texaco's attorneys.[54]

After Winokur, Texaco put on Geoff Boisi, the Goldman, Sachs investment banker who had refused to give an opinion that the Pennzoil tender offer was fair. Boisi offered powerful testimony in support of Texaco's story. Boisi explained how he had spent almost a year analyzing Getty Oil Company and how, on the basis of all he knew about it, he could not declare Liedtke's offer to be "fair." He described the pressure he was under to issue the fairness opinion and the pressure the board was under because of the side deal Liedtke and Gordon had made in the "Dear Hugh" letter. Boisi's picture of the board was not of men trying desperately to protect their jobs, but of men worried about their fiduciary duty to protect the public. Boisi described what he himself had done to help the board get the best possible price for the shareholders, shopping Getty Oil to a number of oil companies, of which Texaco was only one.

Boisi was unequivocal in his testimony that Pennzoil did not have a deal. The board vote reflected only the approval of the price. Not only did every other issue of the deal remain open, but there had been discussions of those issues at the board meeting, discussions that showed the difficulty of resolving these issues with Pennzoil. Boisi was adamant that these conversations had occurred, even though they weren't reflected in Copely's notes.

As a finale to his direct examination, Miller asked Boisi how the directors felt when they learned of the "Dear Hugh" letter.

> They felt under even more pressure. This was the first time true acknowledgment was made that they would be thrown out of their positions if they did not knuckle under to the proposal. There was a combination of outrage and a feeling of terrific pressure.

As helpful to Texaco as Boisi's direct testimony was, it would have been even more effective had it not suffered from some problems. First, it was clear to the jury that Boisi was being guarded in his testimony. He didn't open up as fully as he might have, apparently because he was afraid to say anything that might damage the reputation of his own firm, Goldman, Sachs. Early in his examination, Miller tried to hint this to the jury by noting the presence of a Goldman, Sachs lawyer, whom Miller

---

[54] COLL, *supra* note 6, at 432.

pointed out as the man sitting in back and "looking real serious." The jurors apparently failed to pick up the hint.

Also, Boisi was a New York investment banker, a group of whom Jamail and his team had already made the jury suspicious. Miller tried to rehabilitate Boisi by taking a humorous, folksy approach, but Boisi didn't seem to pick up on his cues and the attempt made Boisi seem even more foreign. To make things worse, the jury was getting tired. Miller felt he had to keep his examination short. Perhaps if he had had more time, he could have warmed Boisi up and allowed him to testify in a way that would ingratiate him more to the jury. Then there was Boisi's part in the back-door incident, something the jury was already aware of because Pennzoil had played Boisi's video deposition as part of their case in chief and something of which Terrell would, on cross-examination, make the jury even more aware.

Terrell began his cross-examination by attacking the very point that had so effectively closed Boisi's direct examination:

Q. Are you telling the jury that fifteen members of the board of directors, when they voted 15 to 1 on the evening of January 3rd, did not have the courage to stand up and say "No, you bullies, we won't do this," that only Chauncey Medberry could muster the courage to ward off Pennzoil?

A. I am not saying that.

Q. Okay.

Terrell continued to beat up on Boisi. Petzinger describes how he would "turn his back on Boisi, heave a sigh, stare at the ceiling, put his head on the table and jangle his pocket change whenever he felt it necessary to cast doubt on Boisi's responses."[55] In another context, this might have made the jury feel sympathy for the witness. But like Winokur, Boisi neglected to make eye contact with the jury. And he had a habit of fluttering his eyelids that made him seem arrogant. The jury had already seen him give evasive answers in his videotaped deposition, and instead of rehabilitating himself by giving direct and forceful answers to Terrell, he fell into the same sort of evasiveness that had turned the jury against Winokur. Terrell played on it beautifully, making Boisi seem even more evasive than he was. Leading Boisi into the back-door incident, Terrell began:

Q. You remember the November 11,1983 board meeting in Houston, don't you?

A. I remember the November meeting. I don't remember the day.

Q. And you remember it was in Houston?

---

[55] PETZINGER, *supra* note 4, at 359.

A. I remember it was in Houston.

In another context, it would have been a harmless exchange, but coming on the heels of Winokur's evasiveness and with the jury now tired and frustrated, it damaged Boisi irreparably. Petzinger wrote that "some of the jurors were now openly rolling their eyes and muttering to one another."[56]

Terrell intentionally put pressure on Boisi, hoping he could make the high-strung New Yorker sweat and stammer. It worked. When Terrell asked Boisi about his participation in the back-door meeting, Boisi could not muster a forceful answer.

Q. Do you feel that was an honest thing to do?

A. I guess I do.

In spite of Boisi's evasiveness (and perhaps in some cases because of it), Terrell also managed to extract some very useful testimony from him. Boisi admitted that under the Pennzoil deal Goldman's fee would have been $9 million, but with the Texaco deal, Goldman got $18 million. This was not only motive to kill the Pennzoil deal; it was a huge amount of money for a few days' work, making the New York investment banking crowd look even more like sharks.

On its third try, the Texaco team finally got a witness who was a clear success. Henry Wendt, the president and chief executive officer of SmithKline Beckman, had been a member of the Getty Oil board. He looked like a CEO sent over from central casting, and his demeanor was as good as his looks. Unlike Winokur and Boisi, he looked directly at the jurors and also unlike Winokur and Boisi, he spoke forcefully, so forcefully that Bob Brown, who was handling the direct, had to ask him to move back from the microphone. What was more, the jurors saw him as a relatively disinterested witness.

The substance of his testimony was as good as his demeanor. When asked if he would ever permit his own company to enter into a substantial transaction unless it was "evidenced by a written document signed by all the parties to be bound," he responded "I can't imagine such a thing." He said that the Pennzoil offer was a hostile offer and that the directors had unanimously believed it was "grossly inadequate," which, he volunteered was the phrase that Goldman, Sachs had used as well. When asked about his personal reaction to the "Dear Hugh" letter, he said: "I was absolutely outraged. I still am." He "saw it as an act [by Gordon Getty] to sell the other shareholders down the river." When asked for an explanation of this, he said he "saw Pennzoil trading off a lower value for the shares for the chairman's title for Gordon Getty" and he saw "the public shareholders getting less than full value for their shares from this transaction."

---

[56] *Id.*

At this point, the Texaco trial team was forced to make a major decision—whether or not to use Marty Lipton as a witness. This was not a decision they made lightly. Whether putting Lipton in front of this jury would help Texaco's case or hurt it had been debated extensively, not only within Miller's firm but at the highest levels of Texaco, Inc. Petzinger quotes Texaco in-house counsel Charlie Kazlauskas as saying "Everyone was torn." Keeton, who had known Lipton long before the case began, argued that Texaco had to call Lipton. Lipton had been a major player in the deal. Virtually every witness to date had emphasized Lipton's role in the deal. Not only was he in the best position to rebut the accounts of the Pennzoil witnesses, but if Texaco didn't call him, it would look like Texaco had something to hide. Moreover, Lipton was the arguably the world's leading mergers and acquisitions lawyer. Who was in a better position to explain to the jury that Pennzoil did not have a binding contract?[57]

On the other hand, many on the Texaco team worried that Lipton would not go over well with the jury. They sensed the jurors were hostile toward people from the East Coast. If no such hostility had been there at the beginning, Winokur and Boisi may have had a hand in creating it. Boisi had sensed so much hostility that he asked Lipton what arrangements he was making for his personal security if he traveled to Houston.

Miller was also suspicious because Pennzoil had not deposed Lipton. He suspected that Jamail had questions he wanted to spring on him for the first time when he had him before the jury.[58] Also arguing against calling Lipton was the fact that the jury was getting impatient. The trial had been dragging on too long.

On the Pennzoil side, Jamail and Terrell had each bet Jim Kronzer, the appellate practice consultant they had brought on board to make sure they made the most favorable record for appeal, $250 that Texaco would not call Lipton. Jamail and Terrell lost the bet.

In the end, Texaco probably had no choice in the matter. Shannon says that if Texaco had failed to call Lipton, he would have thought Texaco had something to hide.[59] Other jurors probably would have thought the same.

---

[57] Coll suggests that there was also pressure to call Lipton from Texaco board members who knew Lipton personally and that there was the concern that if Lipton were not called and Texaco lost, the decision would be second-guessed. COLL, *supra* note 6, at 441.

[58] *Id.* at 441. Jeffers later explained to Steve Coll that part of the reason Pennzoil chose not to depose Lipton was that they knew he would feel uncomfortable testifying in a Texas courtroom. They didn't want to give him a warm-up in a New York lawyer's office, a venue where he would feel much more comfortable. COLL, *supra* note 6, at 442.

[59] SHANNON, *supra* note 18, at 377.

Lipton arrived for his testimony wearing a bright red handkerchief in the pocket of his double-breasted suit. He had thick glasses and an accent that showed he had grown up in Jersey City. Keeton began his direct examination by having Lipton review his credentials. These made it clear Lipton was a New Yorker through and through. Keeton tried to make him more sympathetic by asking about his connections to Houston, but Lipton's response that he had represented a number of Houston companies may have backfired, given the fact that many of the mergers and takeovers engineered by Lipton and his fellow Wall Streeters had resulted in people being laid off in Houston.

There weren't many surprises in Lipton's direct testimony. He recounted the events that others had already described to the jury. His take on them was generally favorable to Texaco, but his delivery was so flat and dispassionate that it failed to make a strong impression. In some cases, his direct testimony may have even harmed Texaco. In the course of describing how he assured the Texaco executives that Pennzoil didn't have a binding contract, he recounted statements by the Texaco people that indicated they were worried that Pennzoil did have a binding contract.

Jamail was able to plant suspicion against Lipton even before Keeton finished his direct examination. Just as Winokur and Boisi had their testimony undercut by charges that they had engaged in double-dealing in the back-door incident, Lipton was vulnerable to the charge that he had kept his associate, Patricia Vlahakis, away from the Pennzoil–Getty drafting session to slow that deal. Keeton moved to head off that charge:

Q. Did you prevent her from going to the meeting or ask her not to go to the meeting in order to in some way delay or frustrate the negotiations with Pennzoil?

A. No.

Mr. Jamail: Your honor, I object. The answer he's going to give is obvious. It speaks for itself. He told the lady not go to the meeting and now to explain or alibi or make some self-serving statement by this witness as to why he did it, I object.

Mr. Keeton: Your Honor, the motivation which Pennzoil has put in issue on this question is certainly one that the man can state and that's the question I asked.

The Court: Mr. Jamail, you will, of course, have the opportunity on cross to correct that if you feel it needs correcting. The objection is overruled.

Mr. Jamail: And I will.

Jamail had told the jury that he was going to correct this bit of Lipton's testimony, and they must have wondered what other parts he would correct as well.

On cross-examination, Jamail had what he describes as "a field day" with Lipton.[60]

Q. Mr. Lipton, you seem to be a man who uses his words precisely—do you?

A. I try to.

Q. Did I understand you earlier to testify that not one of your clients ever intended to be bound prior to signing a definitive merger agreement? And you meant it when you said it?

A. Yes.

At this point, Jamail picked up a three-page document from the Pennzoil counsel table.

Q. Were you involved in the acquisition by Esmark of Norton Simon?

A. Yes.

Jamail showed Lipton the document he had in his hand. It was a copy of a preliminary acquisition agreement between Esmark and Norton Simon.

Q. Although there was not a definitive merger agreement this was a binding agreement. Isn't that correct?

A. Yes, sir

Q. Sir?

A. Yes, sir.

Q. All right, sir. Now let's talk for a minute about Mr. Siegel. Would you say Mr. Siegel is a man who uses words precisely, correctly?

A. Yes.

Q. And Mr. Siegel is a knowledgeable man in the mergers and acquisitions trade?

A. Yes.

Q. And a man who would not use words foolishly—if under oath, especially?

A. That's correct.

---

[60] JAMAIL, *supra* note 11, at 152.

At this point, Jamail handed Lipton a copy of Siegel's affidavit filed by Gordon's lawyers in opposition to his niece's attempt to enjoin him from going forward with the Pennzoil deal.

Q. Would you read it aloud please?

The jury had heard this several times before, but it had more impact now, being read by Marty Lipton, who had just vouched for it.

Q. Mr. Lipton, he used the words "transaction now agreed upon," didn't he?

A. Yes he did.

Q. Well, do you believe that he knew what he was saying?

A. No.

Q. You just disagree, is that it?

A. I disagree.

Q. You've never been shown this, have you?

A. I have not.

At this point, Miller told Keeton, "Tell Lipton to get rid of that fucking handkerchief."

When Lipton returned the next day, he seemed no more aware of the way Jamail was using him to make Pennzoil's case. Lipton continued to let Jamail maneuver him into positions where he had no alternative but to say things that devastated Texaco's theory of the case.

There was Texaco's argument that the Getty Oil board had voted for the Pennzoil deal only because they had caved under the pressure of the position in which Liedtke and Gordon had put them.

Q. When did you first become aware of the Pennzoil tender offer, Mr. Lipton? Did you feel threatened and under pressure at that time?

A. Yes, I did.

Q. Just a mere tender offer put you under pressure? Does it cause you to act irrationally?

A. Well, I sure hope not.

Q. You do know how to act under pressure, don't you?

A. I hope so.

Q. Well, you're paid large amounts of money to help people under pressure learn how to react, to do what they have to do to ward off tender offers, and to do all these things you've told us about. Isn't that correct?

A. Well, my professional life is basically one of advising targets of tender offer how to respond to them. That's correct.

Q. To make sure they don't act irrationally under pressure, right?

A. That's correct.

Q. To make sure they don't succumb to pressure?

A. That's correct

Q. You felt terribly pressured?

A. Yes, I did.

Q. You didn't crater, did you?

A. I hope not. . . .

Q. Are you telling this jury that you, who pride yourself on being the
leading takeover lawyer in the country, could not prevent that board
from cratering because of this assault by Pennzoil? Are you telling
us that these sixteen board members with their lawyers, their
advisors—all sophisticated people who have pressures every day—
succumbed to Pennzoil's pressure and voted fifteen-to-one on the
counterproposal that they themselves made?

A. No, I don't think the pressure by Pennzoil motivated them. I think
that [here Lipton was again cut off by Jamail].

Q. That answered the question.

On another occasion, Jamail was able to grab Lipton's correct, but
too complex, explanation of a legal principle and make Texaco's whole
theory of the case seem not only elitist, but ridiculous as well. Jamail
describes it this way:

> Any trial lawyer worth his fee is willing to abandon even the
> most carefully planned line of questioning to seize a small piece of
> testimony and enlarge it into something the jury will not forget.
> Just such an opportunity arose when Lipton testified that in his
> opinion Gordon Getty could never have completed the Pennzoil deal
> without hiring lawyers who specialized in complex oil and gas
> transactions.[61]

Jamail goes on to quote the following exchange:

Q. Are you saying that two people cannot agree unless they hire a
bunch of lawyers to *tell* them they've agreed?

A. I'm not saying that at all Mr. Jamail. I'm saying that two people
who are contemplating an agreement with respect to a ten-billion-
dollar transaction would be awfully foolish to do it on the basis of an
outline and the absence of a lawyer's advice . . .

Q. Mr. Lipton, are you saying that you have some distinctions between
just us ordinary people making contracts with each other, and

---

[61] JAMAIL, *supra* note 11, at 154.

whether or not it's a ten-billion-dollar deal? Is there a different standard in your mind?

A. Yes, indeed.

At this point, Jamail, with the sense of timing he had developed over years of trying jury cases, stopped to let the effect of Lipton's statement sink in.

And sink in it did. Shannon writes: "At that statement, my jaw dropped. Lipton had just affirmed Pennzoil's whole case, as I saw it."[62]

Jamail then led Lipton further down the same path:

Q. Oh, I see. So, if it wasn't a bunch of money involved in this Getty–Pennzoil thing, it could be an agreement?

Lipton failed to see that the jury didn't share his view of contract law. He answered: "Well, if there was five or ten dollars involved, I guess you might say that."

Jamail, however, understood what the jury was thinking: "As far as the jury was concerned, Marty Lipton had just made honor in business contingent on the number of dollars involved."[63]

Jamail concludes his recollection of Lipton's cross-examination with the following observation:

> He was a smart lawyer, but I will remember that cross-examination like a bullfight. Even while I was doing it, I felt that way, nicking him, nailing him. *I've got you bleeding now, Marty, and I can kill you any time I want.* It was fun.
>
> But, respectfully, I must say that Marty Lipton in my opinion is the best acquisition lawyer in America.[64]

It was during Lipton's testimony that Judge Farris learned he had cancer, an advanced case that gave him little time to live. Judge Solomon Casseb was appointed to take over the case. Texaco moved for a mistrial, claiming not only that a new judge could not acquaint himself properly with the record (which now included almost 18,000 pages of trial testimony), but also that a mistrial was necessary to correct the prejudice that Texaco had suffered as a result of the constant interruptions during its case necessitated by Judge Farris's medical problems. Judge Casseb overruled the motion from the bench and gave each side 90 minutes to summarize the case to date. Then he was ready to preside over the rest of the trial.

---

[62] SHANNON, *supra* note 18, at 381.

[63] JAMAIL, *supra* note 11, at 155.

[64] *Id.* (emphasis in original).

Judge Casseb immediately instituted new rules to speed up the trial. Court would begin at 8:30 rather than 9:00 and run until 5:00, rather than 4:15 as had been the custom under Judge Farris. Lunch breaks would be 60 minutes, rather than 90, and jurors would no longer have Monday mornings and Friday afternoons to attend to their personal business. Although he did not tell anyone else, Judge Casseb intended to have the case concluded in three weeks. Maybe he should have told the jury he intended to have them free in a short while, because his measures to expedite the trial exacerbated the strains the jurors were feeling.

Miller sensed these strains and resolved to cut his case to the bare minimum, deciding against calling many of the witnesses he would otherwise have used.

One witness he wasn't going to pass up was Chauncey Medberry III, the retired chairman of Bank of America. Medberry had been made a member of the Getty Oil board by J. Paul Getty, himself, and it had been Medberry who had cast the single vote dissenting from the Pennzoil deal. He forcefully made the point that was the linchpin of Texaco's case:

> You would not sell a ten-billion-dollar corporation based on a discussion that takes place in the middle of the night. There would have to be a document with all terms agreed upon, hammered out, negotiated. That's the way business is conducted in this country.

As former head of the largest bank in the United States, Medberry was an impressive person. He cast Gordon Getty as an incompetent, Liedtke as an evildoer taking advantage of Gordon, and himself as the person who had stood up for what was right.

> Here is a buyer, sensing an opportunity for a quick kill, hovering around, pressing. They had encamped two of the major shareholders, who, for different reasons, would have favored a quick deal with Pennzoil, and the other directors were sort of handcuffed.

On cross-examination, Terrell used a clever trap to undercut Medberry's testimony that Pennzoil's tender offer was not conducted in a totally above-the-board manner. He asked Medberry whether Bank of America financed unsolicited tender. Medberry said they financed them only after careful review, implying that not all unsolicited tender offers were bad. Terrell then sprung on Medberry a fact of which Medberry was unaware—that Bank of America had participated in the financing of Pennzoil's tender for Getty Oil.

Miller followed Medberry with deposition testimony. Unlike Pennzoil, Texaco had not videotaped its depositions, so they had to be read into the record. Although Miller had taken most of the depositions himself, he played the part of the witness, sitting in the witness chair and reading the witness's testimony, while his partner, Bob Brown, played the part of Miller and read the questions. The format was tedious, and the substance of the testimony was not particularly powerful. Miller tried to enhance the testimony by signifying with a vocal inflection when he had made a particularly important point and adding more emphasis by pausing and looking directly at the jury. Jamail tried to counter this by looking particularly unconcerned at such times.

After this, Miller brought in a live witness, another giant of corporate America, Laurence Tisch. Tisch had the most impressive credentials of any witness who appeared at the trial. He was chairman of Loew's Corporation, which owned many brands familiar to the jurors: Bulova Watch, CNA Insurance, Kent and Newport cigarettes, and many luxury hotels. He was chairman of the board of trustees of New York University. Tisch had additional credibility because he had been invited to join the board by Gordon Getty and had not been involved in the board's earlier disputes with Gordon.

Tisch's testimony for Texaco was forceful and direct.

Q. Mr. Tisch, will you express to this jury as accurately as you can, please, sir, what proposal you understood that you voted on when your board meeting resumed on the afternoon of the 3rd?

A. The proposal for Pennzoil to pay one hundred and ten dollars per share with a five-dollar stub that we estimated could be worth in the area of two-fifty or three dollars a share.

Q. Mr. Tisch, did you or did you not understand that the proposal included a vote on the Memorandum of Agreement?

A. It did not include a vote on the Memorandum of Agreement.

Q. How can you be certain of that, Mr. Tisch?

A. I know what I voted on.

Jamail cross-examined Tisch. In an apparently spontaneous response to an opening Tisch gave him, Jamail summarized very neatly his theme that the case was about oil patch honor.

Q. You're not friends with Gordon Getty?

A. No, sir.

Q. Did Gordon Getty think you were his friend?

A. Define friend and I'll answer the question.

Q. Sir, I can't define New York friendship.

A. There's no difference between a friend in Texas and a friend in New York, sir ... Mr. Getty is an acquaintance of mine.

Jamail is so proud of this exchange that in his memoirs it is set off by itself (with Tisch's final response omitted) on a page introducing the three chapters discussing the trial.[65]

Jamail also used Tisch to bolster Liman, whose credibility other Texaco witnesses had attacked. Using a series of yes or no questions, Jamail got Tisch, to affirm that he had known Liman for 20 years and that Liman was "a man of integrity," an "honorable man," a man "who will tell the truth." Tisch had testified that he did not remember Liman coming into the room where the directors had been meeting and shaking hands, but on cross-examination he admitted that he would not dispute it if Liman had said it happened. When Jamail asked what Ann Getty had invited Tisch to their home to celebrate, Tisch responded "I think it was the acceptance of a price that could lead to an agreement."

After Tisch, there was more reading of depositions. This was incredibly tedious for the jury. Judge Casseb's bench record of the trial refers to "tired, bored, and somewhat sleeping [sic] jurors."

Next, Miller put on three Texaco executives: Kinnear, DeCrane, and General Counsel Bill Weitzel. Up to this point, he had been presenting the story from the viewpoint of Getty Oil Company and the museum, both saying they didn't have a contract. Now it was the turn of Texaco's management to say, in effect, "Even if they had a contract, which of course they didn't, we had a good faith belief they had no contract."

Kinnear played well with the jury. He had sat through all of the testimony to date, and he sensed the jury's anger at the evasions of Winokur, Boisi and too many of the other Texaco witnesses. He was friendly and open. He told a straightforward and seemingly convincing story, emphasizing that Texaco understood all along that the trust and the museum were not legally bound to Pennzoil. Jamail took it easy on him, perhaps sensing that the jury was sympathetic to him because he had sat through the four months of boredom with them.

Weitzel, Texaco's general counsel, was a graduate of Harvard Law School and had himself been a trial lawyer at one time. He gave the most detailed account to date of the negotiations between Gordon and McKinley. He also gave what he thought was a very convincing account of Texaco's efforts to make sure that there was no binding contract between Pennzoil and the Getty interests.[66] On cross, Jeffers was able to provoke Weitzel into an angry outburst by implying that Texaco was

---

[65] JAMAIL, *supra* note 11, at 135. at 449. Interestingly, Steve Coll implies that with his final response (omitted in Jamail's book) Tisch got the better of the exchange. COLL, *supra* note 6, at 449. The jury verdict would seem to imply otherwise. Shannon is noncommital, merely describing it as "a curious exchange." SHANNON, *supra* note 18, at 394.

[66] PETZINGER, *supra* note 4, at quotes him as saying he thought the jury knew he was telling the truth.

desperate for the deal because it needed new oil reserves and that Weitzel wanted the deal to go through in order to further his own career in the company.

Miller then put DeCrane on the stand, spending four days going over with him virtually every aspect of the deal. Throughout the trial Pennzoil had constantly reminded the jurors of the notes that DeCrane had made during Texaco's initial meeting with the First Boston investment bankers, saying that the notes were (in the words of Jamail's voir dire presentation) "evidence that Texaco knowingly interfered with Pennzoil's agreement and contract" and "evidence of Texaco's bad faith and motive." Miller had DeCrane attempt to explain away all that he could. The "stop the train" and "key man—Marty Lipton" notes, DeCrane explained as his taking down more or less verbatim ideas that had been thrown out by the First Boston investment bankers. They were not his ideas. DeCrane explained that his note "only have an oral agreement" was his way of saying Texaco had been told that there was not a binding contract. DeCrane's testimony didn't have the desired effect on the jury. Jim Shannon describes it as "explanations and alibis . . . much too little, far too late."[67]

Whatever the jury thought of the substance of his testimony, DeCrane was smooth and controlled. On cross, Terrell was not able to trap him or obtain any damaging admissions, but he was able to work DeCrane into Pennzoil's story by portraying him as a cold, calculating businessman, quite the opposite of the romantic, idealistic Liedtke.

At this point, Miller rested his case. His decision not to put on a damages case has become one of the most second-guessed decisions in the history of American advocacy.

Refusing to dignify the plaintiff's case by not discussing damages is a well-accepted defense strategy, and it was one that had served Miller well in the past. In fact, it was part of his style. He liked to think of himself as a lawyer who was willing to take big risks where big risks needed to be taken.

In discussing whether or not to go to trial, Miller had told McKinley that it was unlikely that the jury would award more than $250 million to $500 million against Texaco, if it decided the liability issue against Texaco. His worst case, "runaway jury," scenario had been $2 billion. The largest civil verdict ever returned at that time had been $1.8 billion in MCI's antitrust case against AT & T. That had been an antitrust case where $600 million in compensatory damages had been trebled, and that damage award had been reversed on appeal.

---

[67] SHANNON, *supra* note 18, at 400.

Although the decision not to put on damages testimony was ultimately Miller's, he had consulted on it not only with his partners, but also with Texaco's management. John McKinley told writer Steve Coll that he had merely followed Miller's advice,[68] but other Texaco executives affirmatively supported the decision. They thought they had done nothing wrong and they thought the jury would understand that.

Miller did not commit himself to the decision until the last moment. He flew three damages witnesses to Houston and had them on standby. But in the end he felt that the case he had made was strong enough that he did not have to rebut Barrow's testimony on damages. He thought Barrow had failed to make a strong impression on the jury.

Miller would undoubtedly have done things differently had he known the jury instructions he was going to get. New York law governed the question of whether or not Pennzoil had a contract, but Judge Casseb decided not to have the parties brief the issue of contract formation. Priding himself on being a no-nonsense judge, he had them give him copies of the cases on which they relied. When the parties gave him a stack of cases and he saw that only three cases appeared in both stacks, he decided to rely only on those three cases.

As soon Texaco rested, Judge Casseb scheduled a conference for the next day to hammer out the jury charge. He told the lawyers they would be there until it was done. When it was done, it adopted almost verbatim Pennzoil's proposed language on the key issues. Rather than using the word "contract," it used the word "agreement." Thirty-two times in all, it used the word "agreement." "Contract" never appeared once. There were a host of special issues, with the most important of them using Pennzoil's word: "agreement." Special Issue Number One asked whether Pennzoil and the Getty entities had "intended to bind themselves to an agreement." Special Issue Number Two asked whether Texaco had "knowingly interfered with an agreement between Pennzoil and the Getty entities." And on it went.

Judge Casseb had apparently accepted Jamail's argument that "contract" and "agreement" are often used interchangeably. His charge ignored the fact that in both the parties' transactions and their trial testimony, the word "agreement" had many times been used in ways where it might or might not have indicated there was a contract. There were DeCrane's notes of the meeting with the investment bankers where he wrote "only have an oral agreement;" there was the "agreement in principle" announced in the press release; there was Barrow's testimony in which he talked of how a board makes "an agreement" and never used the word "contract."

---

[68] COLL, *supra* note 6, at 456.

What may have been even worse was that the charge did not include Texaco's theory on damages. Miller's decision not to present evidence on damages was based in part on his expectation that he would be able to get a jury instruction incorporating his damages theory, a theory based on the price of the stock rather than on Pennzoil's historical cost of finding oil. But Judge Casseb refused to include any of Miller's proposed instructions.

Superior preparation may have been the decisive factor in Pennzoil's success with the jury charge. While Pennzoil's other lawyers were trying the case, Mark Yudoff, dean of the University of Texas Law School and a former contracts professor, was hard at work on the charge, along with Randall Hopkins, a Baker Botts partner. They prepared ten drafts of the charge, and Hopkins spent countless hours familiarizing himself with New York contract law. This willingness to throw specialized legal talent at particular issues may have been important to the outcome of the case. While Miller later insisted that his firm's limited resources weren't a factor in the outcome, it's hard to believe Texaco wouldn't have been better off with more people to put to work when they needed them.[69]

After the cards fell against them with the charge, closing arguments became the Miller team's last chance to recover. Closing arguments began as soon as Judge Casseb had summarily disposed of Texaco's objections to the charge. Forty-eight hours had not yet elapsed since the jury heard the last witness.

Judge Casseb gave each side four and a half hours. Jamail stuck with the team approach. John Jeffers led off, and significantly, he began by discussing the testimony of Thomas Barrow. He reminded the jury of Barrow's stature in the business world and that he had volunteered to testify as an expert witness without compensation "because he believes the principles here in this case were important ones." Jeffers recounted Barrow's testimony in the strongest possible terms. "To him an agreement in principle signifies a meeting of the minds on essential terms and carries with it a duty of good faith to proceed towards consummation."

Early in his argument he brought in Pennzoil's dominant theme: "There is an opportunity here in this case to send a message which will preserve honor and integrity in the American business system." He went on for an hour and a half, savaging Texaco's witnesses, including "the eminent Mr. Martin Lipton" and the Getty Oil board, whom he accused of trying to sell the company twice. Subtly implying that Texaco was

---

[69] The Pennzoil trial team also included Jim Kronzer, a solo practitioner from Bay City, Texas, who was considered the foremost authority on Texas civil procedure. Kronzer sat through the entire trial, tasked with assuring that a proper record was being made for appeal. Miller had no similar backup.

responsible for the conduct of the people they had called as witnesses, he
concluded by telling the jury:

> In my humble opinion, the defenses to these issues have been
> an outrageous cover-up. If Texaco's witnesses can get away with the
> things they said here, if they can do what they did to Pennzoil in the
> marketplace, they can do it to someone else somewhere else.

> But they are here; we're four and a half months into it. It's time
> for an accounting.

Irv Terrell did the second half of the argument. Jim Shannon likens
his argument to that of "a criminal prosecutor who wanted to send
Texaco to the penitentiary for a long, long time."[70] He began his
argument in the same way Jeffers had concluded. He told the jurors they
were deciding a case of "tremendous importance." He told the jurors
they were sending a message to the entire business community:

> You will decide the ethics. You will decide whether you can go
> out and take someone else's deal just because you're bigger and
> stronger, you've got a lot of muscle, you've got a lot of lawyers,
> you've got a lot of investment bankers.

He went on for an hour and a half, arguing passionately that the
evidence, particularly the indemnities, showed that the Texaco executives were arrogant, irresponsible bullies—and liars to boot.

When Miller got his turn, it was 2:45 in the afternoon. Some
observers thought he looked exhausted. He should have been. He'd been
in trial for four and half months and working hard to prepare long
before that. His primary theme was that the Pennzoil people, Hugh
Liedtke in particular, were the bad guys. Texaco had saved the Getty Oil
shareholders from a bad deal that was being forced upon them. Pennzoil
had twisted the facts. Liedtke was the demon, not the Texaco executives.
It was Liedtke who had the history of doing hostile takeovers. Texaco
had never done one. Liedtke was the fabulously wealthy wheeler-dealer.
McKinley was just a professional manager doing the best he could for his
shareholders.

On the second day, Miller gave more emphasis to the legal argument
that there was no contract between Pennzoil and the Getty entities and
that even if there was, Texaco reasonably believed there was none.
Miller characterized DeCrane's notes as powerful evidence for *Texaco*.
"Stop the train," and "Stop the signing" meant there wasn't a contract
yet. Texaco wasn't trying to interfere with an existing contract, it was
trying to get in a better offer before the Getty interests committed
themselves.

---

[70] SHANNON, *supra* note 18, at 413.

Later he returned to another variation on the theme of the previous day. "We didn't crash this party. We were invited to this party. We didn't look them up. They looked us up.... [t]his has got to be the first case in history where the white knight got sued by the dragon."

Miller also tried to put Pennzoil's damage claim in perspective. He pointed out that the market value of all the outstanding stock of Texaco (which now owned all the assets of Getty Oil, not just the three-sevenths Pennzoil was complaining about) was less than $10 billion. In the entire 23 years Pennzoil had been in business it had only earned a little over $2 billion *total*. "My little grandchild has a little book that says 'How much is a billion?' And there is a little thing in the book, it says it would take you 95 years to count to a billion."

When Miller finished, the court recessed for lunch with everyone aware that after lunch Joe Jamail would have the last word.

Jamail spoke without notes. His argument was rambling but it was impassioned. He began by savaging Miller's argument:

> There were so many misstatements in what Mr. Miller told you that I'm not going to try to answer all of them. He starts out be giving you four hours of excuses for Texaco's conduct and he ends it by saying to you, "Don't take away our company, because if something went wrong, it was Getty that did it."

He heaped more abuse not only on Texaco's witnesses, but the mergers and acquisitions community as a whole. There was "Back Door Bart" who "snuck in the back door when they got Gordon Getty out of the room." There was Marty Lipton. "To him, money is the object. That's what it is." From this he generalized to "that specialized group you had to deal with that would have injected themselves into our business community and our law, calling themselves mergers and acquisitions lawyers, carving up corporate America to their liking. They get together. They're all within a couple of miles of each other. One wins one day and another wins another day—and the investment bankers win *all* the days and *they win with these indemnities*."

The indemnities were a major theme. In his closing argument, Miller had tried to explain away the indemnities, likening them (correctly) to an insurance policy and saying that just because you insure your car, it doesn't mean you expect to have an accident. But Jamail knew that Miller had not been able to make the jury understand that indemnities are a legitimate and important part of many business transactions. So Jamail stressed the indemnities, as he had ever since voir dire. Early in his closing argument he had told the jury Texaco "bought and paid for this lawsuit when they gave the indemnities." Over and over, Jamail hit on the indemnities. He said that Lipton, whom he characterized as "the engineer" whom Texaco got to stop the train, "slicked them with the indemnities."

As to the damages, he pointed out that the un-refuted testimony supported his theory. There was no evidence supporting Miller's theory. "There is no evidence that this is the measure of damages, and that would be insulting to you and to us. It would not be following our oaths."

He concluded as he often had before, telling the jury to "send a message to corporate America." Because he wanted it to be a message of unprecedented size, he gave them special encouragement:

I ask you to remember that you are in a once-in-a-lifetime situation. It won't happen again; it just won't happen. You have a chance to right a wrong, a grievous wrong, a serious wrong.

It's going to take some courage. You've got that.... You are people of conscience and morality and strength.

Don't let this opportunity pass you.

The Jury Verdict

The jury verdict was by no means a foregone conclusion. On Special Issue Number One, whether Pennzoil had an "agreement" with the Getty entities, the first vote was 7 to 5 in favor of finding that there was an agreement. Texas law required at least 10 votes. After a weekend break and more deliberation, the majority was able to get three more votes and the jury moved on the question of whether Texaco had knowingly interfered. On that special issue, the vote was 10 to 2 on the first ballot.

Special Issue Number Three was "What sum of money, if any, do you find from a preponderance of the evidence would compensate Pennzoil for its actual damages, if any, suffered as a direct and natural result of Texaco's knowingly interfering with the agreement between Pennzoil and the Getty entities, if any?" Some of the jurors were reluctant to award the damages Pennzoil had asked for and made arguments for awarding a lesser sum. Some were concerned about inflicting so much damage on Texaco, and some were concerned about the effect on Dick Miller, whom they had come to like during the course of the trial. But Jim Shannon read from the jury instructions: "You will not consider or discuss anything that is not represented by the evidence in this case." To this he added: "Look, it isn't our place to fabricate a case for Texaco. We have to decide the case on the evidence presented in court." With this the jury voted 10 to 2 for awarding Pennzoil compensatory damages of $7.53 billion.

On the issue of punitive damages, the jury split, with some favoring awarding the entire $7.53 billion that Pennzoil had asked for and some strongly opposed to giving any punitive damages at all. It became apparent that the proponents of punitive damages were not angry so much at Texaco and its executives as at the Getty Oil people, and in particular, at the outside advisors whom Texaco had called as witnesses. At one point, a juror suggested awarding three billion dollars in punitive damages, a billion each for Winokur, Boisi, and Lipton.

Jury foreman Rick Lawler became concerned about this, and he sent a note to the judge: "To what extent is Texaco liable for the actions of Lipton, Winokur, and Boisi?" Jamail immediately grasped what was going on in the jury room and told the judge he should tell the jurors to follow the evidence and the charge. At this point Miller made a huge mistake, one likely caused by exhaustion. He recalled, incorrectly, that the charge contained an instruction that a party is responsible only for the acts of its own agents. So he did not protest. It was not until that evening that he remembered the language he recalled had been in Texaco's draft, but Judge Casseb had refused to include it in the final jury instructions. In the morning, Miller requested that Judge Casseb re-instruct the jury. The judge denied his request. Ultimately, the jury agreed on three billion dollars in punitive damages—not a billion for each of the hated witnesses, but a billion for each of the indemnities that Texaco had given to Gordon, the museum, and the Getty Oil board.

The verdict was so large that Texaco did not have the resources to post an appeal bond. It went to a federal court in its home state of New York and obtained an injunction against the enforcement of the judgment pending appeal. The federal court ruled that under the circumstances the requirement for an appeal bond violated the Due Process Clause of the Fourteenth Amendment. Pennzoil took the case to the United States Supreme Court. When the Supreme Court ruled in favor of Pennzoil, Texaco filed a Chapter 11, the largest bankruptcy in history. Ultimately, the case was settled for $3 billion.

Jamail never revealed the amount of his contingency fee. One writer says it was $600 million;[71] another says it was only $300 million.[72]

Why Did Pennzoil Win?

Why did Pennzoil win? There are a number of reasons.

First, their case had a simple and comprehensible theme. It followed the classic melodrama format. Pennzoil made a deal with the Getty

---

[71] Harold A. Segall, *An Executive's Lesson in the Law From a Typical Business Encounter*, 23 FORDHAM URB. L.J. 257, 260 n. 18 (1996).

[72] Herbert M. Kritzer, *From Litigators of Ordinary Cases to Litigators of Extraordinary Cases: Stratification of the Plaintiff's Bar in the Twenty–First Century*, 51 DEPAUL L. REV. 219, 221 (2001).

interests, Texaco took it away, and it was up to the jury to give it back to Pennzoil. This was a theme the jury could understand and relate to.

Texaco's theme was complicated and unusual. On the moral level, Texaco was saying, "We were rescuing the Getty interests from the bad deal Pennzoil was forcing on them. The dragon is suing the white knight." On the legal level, they were making an either-or argument: Pennzoil didn't have a contract with the Getty interests, but if they did, we didn't know about it.

Legally, Texaco had the better argument on contract formation.[73] Every first-year law student learns that whether or not a contract has been formed depends on the totality of the circumstances. Specific words or acts that would result in a contract in some circumstances will not in others. The bigger the deal, the more likely it is that the parties are not bound until they sign a definitive agreement setting forth all the details. Customs and practices in the business *do* matter. Marty Lipton *was* correct when he said that what it takes to make a contract in a New York boardroom is not necessarily the same as what it takes to make a contract in a Texas oilfield. But this is something it takes law students a while to comprehend. It would have been hard enough to get a lay jury to comprehend this idea, but the Pennzoil legal team was able to make it nearly impossible. Beginning with Jamail's voir dire presentation, they repeated their "a deal is a deal" theme, so that when Lipton made his correct statement of the law, the jury not only refused to believe it; they saw it as a lie so crude as to be insulting. Judge Casseb's adoption of Pennzoil's cleverly-simple jury charge precluded any attempt to undo the damage.

In addition to being straightforward, Pennzoil's story was consistent. Nearly all of Pennzoil's evidence fit with the simple "we had a deal and they stole it" theme. Texaco's theme, on the other hand, was riddled with inconsistencies. Texaco portrayed the Getty board as the innocent victims of Pennzoil's predatory attack. But the Getty board didn't look so innocent when the back-door board meeting and the board's participation in the suit to oust Gordon came to light. And while a person familiar with the corporate lawyer's obsession to leave nothing to chance would not have seen the indemnities as inconsistent with a good faith belief that Pennzoil had no contract, it certainly appeared inconsistent to a lay jury.

The witnesses also had a lot to do with the verdict. While Pennzoil's came across almost without exception as human, sympathetic, likeable, and honest, many of Texaco's most important witnesses had problems.

---

[73] For an extended discussion of the contract formation issues in the case, see Michael Ansaldi, *Texaco, Pennzoil and the Revolt of the Masses: A Contracts Post–Mortem*, 27 Hous. L. Rev. 733 (1990).

Winokur, in addition to coming across as arrogant and evasive, was tainted by the back door incident. Boisi should have come across as extremely credible, given that he was one of the few investment bankers in history to fail to give a fairness opinion. But he, too, seemed evasive and had off-putting mannerisms. Moreover, the Pennzoil team was able to pin on him the "$18 million dollar man" sobriquet, making him look like the epitome of greed. Lipton should have been the ultimate authority on what it takes to form a binding contract in a corporate merger, but Jamail was able to make him look foolish. It's impossible to tell whether Miller's team made the best of the hand they were dealt or whether they could have done better with more careful witness selection and more thorough witness preparation. It clear, however, that the dismal performance of Texaco's key witnesses contributed greatly to Texaco's disaster.

Jamail's skill as a lawyer certainly played a part. At every turn, he seems to have made the right move. But luck may have been a factor as well. If Judge Farris had remained for the whole trial, might he have given the jury a more even-handed charge? While Jim Shannon says his role in the jury deliberations was not as important as some claim, it is clear that he was an early and forceful proponent of the verdict. He had originally been an alternate and was only involved in the deliberations because another juror had to be excused.

The Impact of the Case

The *Pennzoil v. Texaco* jury sent a message to corporate America, but it wasn't the message they intended.

One thing corporate America learned was to make sure no one could claim there was a contract before all the details had been negotiated and the final documents signed. After *Pennzoil*, it became a common practice to begin negotiations by having all parties sign statements like the following, taken from a letter memorializing an "agreement in principle" a few years after the *Pennzoil* decision:

> Notwithstanding the foregoing ... or any other past, present or future written or oral indications of assent or indications of results of negotiation or agreement to some or all matters then under negotiation, it is agreed that no party to the proposed transaction (and no person or entity related to any such party) will be under any legal obligation with respect to the proposed transaction or any similar transaction, and no offer, commitment, estoppel undertaking or obligation of any nature whatsoever shall be implied in fact, law, or equity, unless and until a formal agreement providing for the transaction containing in detailed legal form terms, conditions, representations and warranties (secured by an appropriate escrow)

has been executed and delivered by all parties intended to be bound.... This paragraph may be amended, modified, superseded or canceled only by a written instrument which specifically states that it amends this paragraph, executed by an authorized officer of each entity to be bound thereby.[74]

Corporate America also learned to beware of juries, particularly hometown juries. *Pennzoil* provided an additional incentive for the use of arbitration clauses, jury waivers, and choice of forum clauses. These provisions, coupled with the added propensity to settle because of the possibility of a huge verdict like the one in *Pennzoil*, have contributed to the supposed vanishing of the civil jury trial.

Note on Sources and Further Reading

Three full-length books have been written about the Getty Oil takeover and the resulting lawsuit. James Shannon's *Texaco and the $10 Billion Jury* is particularly useful for students of advocacy. It concentrates on the trial from the perspective of a juror and contains extensive quotations from the transcript. *Oil and Honor* by Thomas Petzinger, Jr. gives detailed accounts of both the deal and the trial. Steve Coll's *The Taking of Getty Oil* concentrates on the deal. Its description of the trial is short on details but nevertheless gives valuable insights. In addition, Joe Jamail's memoir *Lawyer: My Trials and Jubilations* devotes nearly a hundred pages to the trial.

In writing this chapter, I drew heavily on all four of these sources as well as on the trial transcripts, which are available at the Center for American History in Austin, Texas. I would like to thank the staff of the Center for American History and the staff of the Tarleton Law Library at the University of Texas, particularly Jeanne Price, for the help they gave me when I was doing the research for this chapter.

The Characters in the Melodrama

The Getty Interests

(Getty Oil Company, The Sarah C. Getty Trust, J. Paul Getty Museum)

Berg, Harold–Director, Getty Oil and Chairman of the Board of Trustees, J. Paul Getty Museum. Berg had formerly been Chairman of Getty Oil Company.

Boisi, Geoffrey T. ("Geoff")—Partner, Goldman, Sachs & Company, investment bankers for Getty Oil Company. Boisi was head of his firm's

---

[74] Quoted at W.R. Grace & Co. v. Taco Tico Acquisition Corp., 454 S.E.2d 789, 790 (Ga. Ct. App. 1995).

mergers and acquisitions department and a witness for Texaco at the trial.

Cohler, Charles ("Tim")—Partner in Lasky, Haas, Cohler & Munter, attorneys for Gordon Getty and the Sarah C. Getty Trust.

Copely, Ralph David ("Dave")—Vice President and General Counsel, Getty Oil Company.

Getty, Gordon—son of J. Paul Getty, director of Getty Oil Company, and sole trustee of the Sarah C. Getty Trust.

Getty, J. Paul—founder of Getty Oil Company and the J. Paul Getty Museum.

Hays, Lansing—Attorney and confidant of J. Paul Getty. From Getty's death in 1976 until his own death in 1982, he dominated Getty Oil Company and the Sarah C. Getty Trust.

Lasky, Moses—Senior partner of Lasky, Haas, Cohler & Munter, attorneys for Gordon Getty and the Sarah C. Getty Trust.

Lipton, Martin ("Marty")—Partner, Wachtell, Lipton, Rosen & Katz, attorneys for the J. Paul Getty Museum.

Medberry, Chauncey—Retired chairman of Bank of America, Getty Oil Company director.

Petersen, Sidney ("Sid")—Chairman, Getty Oil Company.

Siegel, Martin ("Marty")—Partner, Kidder, Peabody & Company, investment banker for the Sarah C. Getty Trust. Siegel later went to jail for supplying inside information to arbitrageur Ivan Boesky.

Tisch, Laurence—Chairman, Loew's Corporation; Director, Getty Oil Company; witness for Texaco at trial.

Vlahakis, Patricia—Associate, Wachtell, Lipton, Rosen & Katz, attorneys for the J. Paul Getty Museum.

Wendt, Henry—Chairman and CEO, SmithKline Beckman Corporation, Getty Oil Company director, witness for Texaco.

Williams, Harold—President of the J. Paul Getty Museum, owner of 12% of the stock of Getty Oil Company.

Winokur, Barton J. ("Bart")—Partner in Dechert, Price & Rhoads, outside counsel to Getty Oil Company. Winokur was given the name "Back Door Bart" by the Pennzoil litigation team because of his involvement in secret Getty Oil Company board action against Gordon.

Pennzoil Company

Jamail, Joseph D. ("Joe")—Lead trial counsel for Pennzoil.

Jeffers, John—Partner in Baker & Botts, counsel for Pennzoil

Kerr, Baine—President, Pennzoil Company.

Liedtke, Hugh—Chairman, Pennzoil Company.

Liman, Arthur—Partner, Paul, Weiss, Rifkind, Wharton & Garrison, New York attorneys representing Pennzoil in the Getty Oil takeover.

Terrell, G. Irvin ("Irv")—Partner in Baker & Botts, counsel for Pennzoil.

Texaco, Inc.

DeCrane, Alfred ("Al")—President, Texaco, Inc.

Kinnear, James ("Jim")—Vice Chairman, Texaco, Inc.

McKinley, John—Chairman, Texaco, Inc.

Miller, Richard ("Dick")—Lead trial counsel for Texaco, partner in Miller, Keeton, Bristow & Brown.

Nickens, J.C.—partner in Miller, Keeton, Bristow & Brown, trial counsel for Texaco.

Perella, Joseph—Partner in First Boston Corporation, investment bankers for Texaco.

Wasserstein, Bruce—partner in First Boston Corporation, investment bankers for Texaco.

Weitzel, William ("Bill")—General Counsel, Texaco, Inc.

Others

Casseb, Judge Solomon C.—Judge who presided over the trial after Judge Farris became ill.

Farris, Judge Anthony J.P.—Judge who presided over the trial until he became ill.

Shannon, James ("Jim")—Juror, author of *Texaco and the $10 Billion Dollar Jury* (Prentice Hall 1988).

7

Angela J. Davis[1]

The People v. Orenthal James Simpson: Race and Trial Advocacy

Introduction

On the evening of June 12, 1994, Nicole Brown Simpson had dinner with her family at the Mezzaluna restaurant in Los Angeles. At around 10 p.m. that evening, Ron Goldman, a waiter at the restaurant, delivered a pair of prescription sunglasses that had been left at Nicole's table to her home. At some point between 10 and 10:30 p.m., someone brutally stabbed and killed Nicole Simpson and Ron Goldman in the courtyard in front of her home.

Nicole Simpson was the ex-wife of O.J. Simpson. Their relationship was volatile—before and after the divorce. There were allegations that O.J. had physically and psychologically abused Nicole. Nicole had called the Los Angeles Police Department ("LAPD") for help on several occasions during their marriage. The LAPD, enthralled with O.J. and insensitive to domestic violence, did little or nothing. One report resulted in O.J. pleading "no contest" to a charge that he assaulted Nicole.

Not surprisingly, attention quickly focused on Simpson as the prime suspect in the killings. In the early morning hours of June 13th, Detectives Philip Vannater and Mark Fuhrman went to O.J.'s home, allegedly to inform him in person of his ex-wife's death. Fuhrman reported finding a glove on the ground outside O.J.'s home that appeared to match a glove found at the scene of the homicide. Fuhrman also reported seeing what appeared to be blood on O.J.'s Ford Bronco parked in front of his home. Ultimately, police reported a DNA match between

---

[1] Professor of Law, American University Washington College of Law.

blood recovered on various items at O.J.'s residence and the blood of both Nicole and Ron Goldman. They also reported a match between blood found at the homicide scene and O.J.'s blood. O.J. was arrested on June 17th after a bizarre televised "slow speed" chase during which a caravan of police and television helicopters followed him in his Ford Bronco, driven by his friend, Al Cowlings.

The trial of O. J. Simpson was, at its core, about a famous ex-football player turned "B movie" actor charged with killing his ex-wife and her friend. There was nothing about the people involved or the facts of the case that warranted its ultimate ranking among the most significant trials of the century. O.J. Simpson was not the most famous football player in history, and he certainly was not the most famous or talented actor. In fact, he was more well-known for his orange juice and rental car commercials than his mediocre to bad films. Nicole Brown Simpson was known to the public only as Simpson's ex-wife. Her friend, Ron Goldman, was an unknown waiter in a Los Angeles restaurant. The alleged facts of the case were not particularly interesting or unusual. Nonetheless, this run-of-the-mill celebrity trial emerged as one of the most important trials of the century.

The Simpson trial will maintain its ranking in the history of American trials because it focused attention on some of the most important issues in the criminal justice system, including race and class disparities, race discrimination, domestic violence, police perjury, and DNA evidence. These issues certainly were not discovered during the Simpson case, but the ubiquitous television, radio, and print media coverage of the trial informed the American public and the world about them as never before, although not always accurately. Countless articles in newspapers, magazines, and scholarly journals were written about every aspect of the Simpson trial.[2] All of the prosecutors,[3] most of the defense attorneys,[4] and several jurors wrote books about the trial, as

---

[2] *See generally* Isabelle R. Gunning, *An Essay on Teaching Race Issues in the Required Evidence Course: Lessons from the O. J. Simpson Case*, 28 Sw. U. L. Rev. 355 (1999); Peter Charles Hoffer, *Invisible Worlds and Criminal Trials: The Cases of John Proctor and O. J. Simpson*, 41 Am. J. Legal Hist. 287 (1997); George Fisher, *The O. J. Simpson Corpus*, 49 Stan. L. Rev. 971 (1997); Keith Marder, *O. J. Simpson Trial Verdict Top TV Moment of Year*, Albany Times Union H1 (Dec. 31, 1995); Christopher Goodwin, *In a Prison Without Bars: O. J. Simpson*, The Sunday Times (United Kingdom) 9 (Nov. 26, 1995).

[3] *See* Marcia Clark, Without a Doubt (The Penguin Group 1997); Christopher Darden, In Contempt (HarperCollins Publishers, Inc. 1996).

[4] *See* Alan M. Dershowitz, Reasonable Doubts (Simon & Schuster 1996); Robert L. Shapiro, The Search for Justice: A Defense Attorney's Brief on the O. J. Simpson Case (Warner Books 1996); Gerald F. Uelmen, The O.J. Files: Evidentiary Issues in a Tactical Context (West Group 1998).

have numerous scholars and individuals with no connection to the case.[5]

This chapter will focus on how the issue of race affected the trial advocacy in the Simpson trial. No issue defined the Simpson case or had a greater effect on the trial strategies and advocacy than race. The issue was laid bare by the allegations themselves—a famous African American ex-football player charged with killing his white ex-wife. The accusations brought to mind images from America's shameful history of lynching black men believed to be associated in any way with white women and stirred up lingering conscious and unconscious views about these inter-racial relationships by people of all races. These views are ingrained in the psyche of most Americans as a consequence of this country's tortured history involving race. And no individual involved in the case—witnesses, prosecutors, defense lawyers, jurors, or the judge—could escape them. Race was juxtaposed against and complicated by the class and power dynamic between Simpson and his ex-wife—a former waitress who Simpson began dating shortly after her eighteenth birthday. The past allegations of Simpson physically and psychologically abusing his ex-wife added another layer of complexity to the racial dynamics of the case.

In light of the obvious dominant role that race played in the Simpson trial, it is astonishing that so many commentators and scholars have accused the defense team of "playing the race card"—a phrase that suggested that the defense lawyers somehow "injected" the issue of race into the case. Those who made this accusation suggested that the defense inappropriately focused attention on the issue of race throughout the trial to gain an advantage with a predominantly African American jury. However, those who expressed this view clearly did not understand the fundamentals of trial advocacy. Advocacy is about persuasion—specifically the persuasion of the twelve jurors chosen to find the facts and render the verdict in a trial. Any lawyer who ignores one of the most pivotal issues in a case and its effect on the jurors fails as an advocate. Most of the defense attorneys in the Simpson case understood that race was just such an issue. The prosecution team did not. Ultimately, each side's approach to the race issue helped to determine the outcome of the case.

The issue of race profoundly influenced many key decisions in the Simpson case, including jury selection, the substance and style of witness examinations, and closing arguments. Each of these decisions helped to shape the trial advocacy in the case and determine the outcome of the trial. Although unconscious views about race affected the actions and decisions of all the participants in the trial as it does whenever there is an obvious racial issue in a case, race also was openly discussed through-

---

[5] *See, e.g.* AMANDA COOLEY ET AL., MADAME FOREMAN (Newstar Press 1996); JEFFREY TOOBIN, THE RUN OF HIS LIFE (Random House 1996).

out the trial. Race was central to the direct and cross-examination of perhaps the most significant witness in the case—Detective Mark Fuhrman, the witness who regularly used the word "nigger" and harbored clear racial bias against African Americans, who comprised nine of the twelve jurors ultimately selected to decide the case. And race featured largely in the closing argument of Johnnie Cochran, the lead attorney on the defense team.

Although race permeated almost every aspect of the Simpson case, and the trial lasted for over a year, I will focus on key parts in which race most affected the trial advocacy. Trial advocacy begins not with the opening statements but with every decision that will ultimately persuade the twelve individuals chosen to deliver the verdict. Thus, in this chapter, I will discuss the choice of lawyers on both sides and how their approach to the race issue affected the case; the jury selection; the direct and cross-examination of Detective Mark Fuhrman; and the closing arguments.

The Lawyers

The choice of lawyers in the Simpson case was key to the trial's outcome. Although both sides made mistakes, Simpson was represented much more ably than the State of California. Simpson's team was, overall, much more experienced and talented. Most criminal defendants in the United States are indigent and are represented by whomever the court appoints. They have no choice in the matter. Simpson could afford to choose his lawyers, and his team included some of the best defense attorneys in the country. The prosecution team, however, proved to be embarrassingly inept in its performance and overall trial strategy. The prosecution's approach to the race issue was perhaps its most crucial failing.

For the Prosecution

Marcia Clark

Although a number of prosecutors worked on the Simpson case, the two attorneys who emerged as the lead prosecutors were Marcia Clark and Christopher Darden. Because the Simpson case was by far the most noteworthy handled by the Los Angeles District Attorney's Office, one would expect District Attorney Gil Garcetti to choose his most experienced and talented prosecutors. Yet Clark and Darden emerged as the lead attorneys on the team, not so much by choice, but by happenstance.

Marcia Clark was an experienced prosecutor when Simpson was arrested. She had 13 years of experience as a prosecutor and had handled several high profile murder cases, some involving complex forensic evidence and domestic violence. Yet there were more experienced and talented lawyers in the D.A.'s office at that time, and Garcetti didn't choose Clark. She ended up on the case because of a phone call made by Detective Vannater when he was investigating Simpson. Out of an abundance of caution, Vannater called Clark to get her advice on whether there was sufficient evidence to secure a search warrant for Simpson's residence. He called her because he had just worked with her on another murder case involving forensic evidence. From that point on, Clark stayed with the case. She brought the charges and held a press conference on June 20th. At that point, she had become the public face of the prosecution. It would have been difficult for Garcetti to remove her at that point, even if he thought someone else would be more appropriate as lead counsel.

There certainly were reasons for choosing someone other than Clark. She had a reputation for being an overly zealous prosecutor with an acerbic style. Clark approached her cases with an almost unprofessional disdain for the accused and a passionate, very personal attachment to the victims in her cases. For example, when Clark prosecuted an obsessive fan of an actress in 1989, she wrote a letter to the actress's mother that included the following:

> If all goes well the miserable, slimy piece of cow dung will be convicted of everything. . . . I will do everything in my power to see that her loss is avenged—I cannot promise justice because to me justice would mean Rebecca is alive and her murderer is dead. . . . The one thing I can promise you is that when this is all over I will honestly be able to tell you that I gave it my all, my very best, without reservation. Beyond that you have my love and empathy forever.[6]

She used the same kind of aggressive rhetoric at the June 20th press conference:

> It was premeditated murder. It was done with deliberation and premeditation. That is precisely what he was charged with because that is what we will prove.[7]

That statement was not only incredibly brash and inappropriate, especially at this early stage of the case, but it was also foolhardy. Clark clearly did not have evidence of premeditation. Even under the government's theory of the case—that Simpson was a batterer who finally killed his ex-wife—manslaughter or second degree murder were at least as reasonable predictions than first degree premeditated murder. From a strategic point of view, it was certainly risky to commit the government to proving premeditated murder at this stage of the proceeding. Yet Clark was willing to take that risk, presumably to influence the potential

---

[6] TOOBIN, *supra* note 5, at 77.

[7] *Id.* at 114.

jury pool. Even Jeffrey Toobin, the journalist and former prosecutor who was convinced of Simpson's guilt, stated that "Clark did not even pay lip service to such legal niceties as the presumption of innocence."[8]

Clark may have tried to influence the jury pool, but she clearly didn't understand the racial dynamics. Garcetti chose to try the case in downtown Los Angeles rather than Santa Barbara, for a variety of reasons. The jury pool in downtown Los Angeles would certainly have significant representation from the African American community and Santa Barbara would likely produce a predominantly, if not entirely, white jury. Garcetti believed that he had support in the African American community and thought that a guilty verdict from a predominantly African American jury would have more credibility and seem more just.[9] But Garcetti and Clark underestimated the African American community's mistrust of the LAPD. The government's circumstantial case depended on the jury trusting the police, and the LAPD had a long and sordid history of racism and brutality against African Americans. The Christopher Commission, formed to study the aftermath of the Rodney King beating, reached the following conclusion about the LAPD:

> The problem of excessive force is aggravated by racism and bias within the LAPD. These attitudes of prejudice and intolerance are translated into unacceptable behavior in the field.[10]

Even though Simpson lived in a largely white world and was married to a white woman, most African Americans supported him, before and after the verdict. The African American community in Los Angeles saw his arrest as yet another example of the LAPD treating an African American man unfairly. Crowds of African Americans cheered Simpson on as he passed them in the Bronco during the "slow speed" chase and the African American press and African American organizations supported him overwhelmingly. Clark's decision to go after him with such zeal in an early press conference rather than taking a more measured approach was the first in a series of missteps and misjudgments about the role of race in this case.

Clark's anger and fever pitch diatribes continued throughout the trial. Her style may have appealed to some, but it clearly turned off many of the jurors who ultimately acquitted Simpson. She came across as shrill and angry almost all of the time. Later, during trial preparation, a well-respected jury consultant volunteered his services to the prosecution team. During one survey of a group of mock jurors, the consultant asked them to comment on the lawyers in the case. All of the African

---

[8] *Id.* at 114.

[9] *Id.* at 118. *See infra* pp. 16–17 for a discussion of the choice of venue.

[10] *Id.* at 30.

American jurors, especially the women, reacted very negatively to Clark. She ignored the jury consultant's advice and dismissed him. Clark probably wasn't the best choice as lead counsel for the prosecution.

Chris Darden

Like Marcia Clark, Chris Darden was not initially chosen to join the prosecution team. Garcetti had assigned Bill Hodgman to serve as Marcia Clark's co-counsel. Hodgman was a very experienced prosecutor with a calm and understated style—the "anti-Clark." Hodgman was assigned to handle the scientific evidence and Clark would focus on the events leading up to the murder. As the responsibilities of the case grew, Clark asked Garcetti to allow Chris Darden to join the team. Darden was initially assigned to handle the grand jury investigation of the Bronco chase. He did not have a good reputation as a trial lawyer but he was Clark's friend so she convinced Garcetti to allow Darden to handle the domestic violence issues in the case. Darden had the additional advantage of being African American. The prosecutors certainly understood that an all-white prosecution team would present the wrong image in this racially-charged case.

Although Darden started out as a junior member of the team, he rose to replace Hodgman as the second chair when Hodgman suddenly became ill the day of Johnnie Cochran's opening statement. During a meeting with Garcetti and Clark at the end of the day, Hodgman felt a tightening in his chest and had to be rushed to the hospital by ambulance. His doctors suggested that his continued participation in the trial would threaten his health. So Darden took his place as second chair.

Unfortunately, like Clark, Darden was quick-tempered and had a tendency to fly off the handle about the most trivial issues. Furthermore, he lacked judgment and trial experience and often ignored the advice of senior lawyers. Darden made the single biggest mistake in the trial—asking Simpson to try on the glove that ultimately didn't fit, providing one of the themes for Cochran's closing argument. Darden made this decision off the cuff, after the prosecution team had decided that he should not do it. In addition, it was analogous to a violation of one of the most basic rules of cross-examination—"never ask a question if you don't know the answer." Darden asked Simpson to try on the glove without knowing whether it would fit. It was probably the second most influential decision in the trial that caused Simpson's acquittal, second only to the prosecution's decision to vouch for the credibility of Mark Fuhrman, the racist detective who committed perjury about his racism.

Darden simply was not a trial lawyer. He spent most of his fifteen years in the D.A.'s office in the Special Investigations Division investigating and prosecuting police officers in the LAPD. He had only one major trial and in that case, all of the officers were acquitted. His lack of experience was obvious. In addition to the embarrassing glove incident, Darden fumbled throughout the trial.

The other ongoing problem for the prosecution was that Darden was inevitably and consistently compared to his African American counterpart on the defense team, Johnnie Cochran. And there was no comparison. Cochran was a skilled trial attorney who was well-respected in the African American community and known for his success in high profile civil and criminal cases against the LAPD. Even when Cochran was a prosecutor, he worked in the division that prosecuted rogue cops. He was a passionate but measured trial lawyer and projected the image of experience and credibility. Darden projected the opposite image and his behavior during the trial didn't help. He alternatively battled with and apologized to Cochran during bench conferences. Cochran often scolded Darden as if he were a child and Darden fell into the role, pouting and stomping his feet rather than conducting himself as a skilled trial lawyer. Sometimes he made statements that bordered on the bizarre, such as the following—a profession of admiration for Cochran in the middle of his argument requesting sanctions after Cochran's opening statement:

> And I'm always proud of Mr. Cochran whenever I see him in court, Your Honor. I love him. I just don't like to go up against him.[11]

One of the most heated exchanges between the two men came during the argument about the extent to which the defense would be allowed to cross-examine Mark Fuhrman about his use of the word "nigger." Darden argued passionately that the cross-examination should not be allowed. The gist of his argument was that merely hearing the word, regardless of who said it or in what context, would so inflame the jury that they would not be able to fairly evaluate the evidence.

> It is a dirty, filthy word.... It is not a word that I allow people to use in my household. I'm sure Mr. Cochran doesn't. And the reason we don't is because it is an extremely derogatory and denigrating term, because it is so prejudicial and so extremely inflammatory that to use that word in any situation will evoke some type of emotional response from any African–American within earshot of that word.... It will upset the black jurors. It will issue a test ... and the test will be, Whose side are you on? The side of the white prosecutors and the white policemen, or on the side of the black defendant and his very prominent black lawyer? That is what it is going to do: Either you are with the Man or you are with the Brothers.... Mr. Cochran and the defense, they have a purpose in going into that area, and the purpose is to inflame the passions of the jury and to ask them to pick sides not on the basis of the

[11] *Id.* at 261.

evidence in this case.... We are not running around or talking about or seeking to introduce to the jury the notion that this defendant has a fetish for blond-haired white women. That would be inappropriate. That would inflame the passions of the jury. It would be outrageous.[12]

Cochran's response was equally dramatic and passionate:

His remarks this morning are perhaps the most incredible remarks I've heard in a court of law in the thirty-two years I have been practicing law. His remarks are demeaning to African–Americans as a group. And so I want ... to apologize to African–Americans across this country.... It is demeaning to our jurors to say that African–Americans who have lived under oppression for 200–plus years in this country cannot work within the mainstream, cannot hear these offensive words.... I am ashamed that Mr. Darden would allow himself to become an apologist for this man [referring to Fuhrman].... All across America today, believe me, black people are offended at this very moment, and so I have to say this was uncalled for, it is unwarranted, and most unfortunate for somebody that I have a lot of respect for—and perhaps he has become too emotional about this.[13]

The exchange between the two men was about so much more than the cross-examination of Mark Fuhrman. Darden's comments about the jurors being asked to pick sides was undoubtedly an expression of his frustration over his role in the entire trial—he was on the side of the white cops, including a racist cop who regularly used one of the most inflammatory racial slurs in the English language. He knew who the black jurors sided with, regardless of the judge's ruling on Fuhrman's cross-examination. Darden's presence on the prosecution team was not enough to deliver the black jurors, especially with Cochran on Simpson's team.

Cochran's response highlighted the contrast between the men and was just one example of how Cochran maintained his role as the authority on race who spoke for African Americans. He was older, wiser, smarter, and a more talented lawyer. When Cochran took it upon himself to apologize to all African Americans for the foolish remarks of the young, brash black prosecutor, it was akin to a public spanking—one of many throughout the course of the trial.

For the Defense

Like the prosecution, the defense had a team of lawyers, but it was a bigger, stronger, more talented team. The press called them "the dream

---

[12] *Id.* at 292–93.

[13] *Id.* at 293–94.

team." It was ironic that in the most widely televised trial in American history, the public was getting a distorted view of how the criminal justice system ordinarily works. Most criminal defendants are indigent and usually represented by overworked, underpaid public defenders or other court appointed attorneys.[14] The opposite was true in the Simpson case.

The dream team consisted of, alphabetically, F. Lee Bailey, Johnnie Cochran, Alan Dershowitz, Peter Neufeld, Barry Scheck, Robert Shapiro, and Gerald Uelmen. Shawn Chapman and Carl Douglas had less visible roles as junior associates in Cochran's law firm. Several lawyers on the defense team had national reputations as trial lawyers and others were less well known. However, as with the prosecution team, the Simpson trial brought fame to all, whether deserved or not.

One of the biggest problems with the defense team was its size. The Simpson team proved that it is possible to have too many lawyers, specifically too many lawyers who were accustomed to being in charge. At various points in the trial, it was clear that there was in-fighting on the defense team, an unfortunate experience for Simpson. Another problem was the tendency of several defense attorneys to talk about the case—on television talk shows, on the radio, at press conferences, or anywhere they could get a public audience. Sometimes these public statements were made with the purpose of assisting the defense case, even if they didn't always succeed in doing so. Unfortunately, oftentimes members of the defense team made appearances in the media to promote themselves, and, as in the case of Robert Shapiro, these appearances sometimes caused direct harm to Mr. Simpson's case.

Several of the attorneys played roles that had a direct effect on the issue of race in the trial. These lawyers included Shapiro, Cochran, Bailey, and Scheck. Each of these lawyers, in their own way, played a role in how race impacted the jurors and the ultimate outcome of the case.

Robert Shapiro

Robert Shapiro was not the first lawyer to represent Simpson after the LAPD focused on him as the prime suspect in the murders. Simpson's business manager and personal attorney at the time was Leroy "Skip" Taft. Taft was not a criminal lawyer so he called Howard Weitzman, the lawyer who had represented Simpson in the spousal abuse case. Weitzman, however, had very little experience as a criminal defense attorney as evidenced by a crucial mistake he made shortly after

---

[14] U.S. DEPT. OF JUSTICE OFFICE OF JUSTICE PROGRAMS, BUREAU OF JUSTICE STATISTICS, Indigent Defense Statistics, *available at* http://www.ojp.usdoj.gov/bjs/id.htm (finding that 66% of federal defendants in 1998 and 82% of felony defendants in the 100 most populous counties were represented by publicly financed counsel).

he was asked to advise Simpson. He left Simpson at the police station to be interviewed by Detective Vannatter. It doesn't take experience as a criminal defense attorney to know that a person suspected of a double homicide gains nothing by agreeing to give a statement to the police. Rarely, if ever, will an exculpatory statement convince the police that the person is innocent, and the statement will almost always be used against the person, even if it is exculpatory.

Weitzman has never explained the reasons for his decision, but others have speculated that Simpson must have insisted on giving the interview.[15] Nonetheless, most criminal defense attorneys would be confident in their ability to convince even the most adamant client not to talk to the police. At any rate, Roger King, a friend of Simpson's and a powerful businessman in Los Angeles, asked Shapiro to represent Simpson, and he agreed.

Shapiro was the public face of the Simpson defense team and for some time, maintained his status as the lead attorney in the case. He eventually lost this status when Cochran joined the team and the case proceeded to trial. Robert Shapiro did not have a reputation as an outstanding trial attorney. A former prosecutor, Shapiro had handled a number of criminal cases, including high profile cases involving celebrities or athletes. However, he had a reputation as a plea lawyer. He arranged excellent deals for his clients that involved pleas to a lesser offense and very little or no jail time. Shapiro also had a reputation for talking to the media and even wrote an article entitled "Using the Media to Your Advantage" for *The Champion*, the premier magazine for criminal defense attorneys published by the National Association for Criminal Defense Lawyers.

In addition to lacking criminal trial experience, Shapiro lacked something else that is critical to the successful representation of a client in a criminal case—a strong, client-centered criminal defense ethic. From the very beginning, Shapiro's public and private behavior suggested that he cared more about his own image and future than that of his client's. Shapiro appropriately agreed to turn Simpson in when the police secured a warrant for his arrest. But when Simpson could not be found at the agreed-upon delivery time, Shapiro seemed more worried about unfounded rumors that he was harboring a fugitive than about what was best for his client. Nothing else can possibly explain the press conference he called when the police were looking for Simpson. Without knowing where his client was or why he couldn't be found, Shapiro held a huge live press conference in which he could not have done more to make his

---

[15] SHAPIRO, *supra* note 4, at 10; *but see*, CNN television broadcast, Mar. 17, 1995 (reporting that Howard Weitzman stated that he was opposed to O.J. Simpson giving a statement to Detective Vannatter).

client look guilty. Amazingly, he revealed to the press (and to the world) everything that had transpired during that day, including the fact that he had informed Simpson that he had to turn himself in that day and that Simpson had disappeared shortly thereafter. Shapiro's sole purpose in making these extraordinarily damaging statements about his client seemed to be to clear his own name. As Shapiro stated, "the police were all but calling me a felon."[16] He made a point of informing the press of his history of cooperation with the LAPD:

> I have on numerous occasions in the past twenty-five years made similar arrangements with the Los Angeles Police Department and the district attorney's office and have always kept my word to them. In fact, I arranged the surrender of Erik Menendez from Israel on a similar basis. We are all shocked by this sudden turn of events.[17]

Shapiro didn't stop there. He then had Simpson's close friend Robert Kardashian read Simpson's so-called "suicide note" to the press. Simpson didn't confess in the letter, but it sounded as much like a note of a fugitive on the run as it did a suicide note. It made Simpson sound guilty and it made Shapiro look as if he was doing everything he could to cooperate with law enforcement officers. Shapiro's statements and actions arguably violated the attorney-client privilege and were contrary to the instincts of any true criminal defense attorney.

A defense attorney should never reveal confidential or incriminating information about her client. Even if a judge directly asks a defense attorney for such information in open court, she must not reveal it. For example, if a client does not appear for a hearing and the judge asks the defense attorney where the client is, unless the answer is helpful, she should not provide one. If the client told her that he wasn't going to show up or even if she has no idea where the client is, she should not reveal those facts. At worse, the response should be, "I have no representations to make at this time, Your Honor." Such a response would neither violate the attorney's duty of candor to the tribunal nor her duty to her client.

The astounding thing about Shapiro's press conference was that no judge ordered him to reveal anything about his client, nor was he in any real danger of being charged with harboring a fugitive. He simply chose to do so for his own selfish purposes. Shapiro had no idea where Simpson was, but just in case he was doing something illegal, Shapiro wanted to distance himself from that possible illegality. Instead of standing as a shield between his client and the government, he tossed Simpson right

---

[16] *Id.* at 45.

[17] TOOBIN, *supra* note 5, at 95.

into the lion's den. Many a defense attorney has withstood contempt citations and even jail to protect their clients, but not Shapiro.

Shapiro's lack of criminal defense ethics was further demonstrated by his ongoing desire to ingratiate himself with the LAPD and the district attorney's office. After hiring experts to assist in the case, Shapiro called and faxed members of the police department, offering his experts to "assist" in the investigation. Even if his goal was to have his experts influence the government's experts, at this early stage of the process it was not a wise move since he didn't know what their findings would be.

Shapiro's most shocking behavior came during the trial. The case was fraught with police misconduct—from the warrantless search of Simpson's property to Fuhrman's perjury. Understandably, one of the main defense themes was to attack the credibility of the LAPD. At one point during the trial, law enforcement officers began to wear blue ribbon lapel pins to show solidarity with the police force. Amazingly, Shapiro wore one of the blue ribbon pins to court during the trial.

Shapiro also opposed Johnnie Cochran attacking the police during his closing argument—not only an inappropriate demonstration of his alliance with cops but a clear demonstration of his lack of ability as an advocate. A failure to attack the police in a case fraught with evidence of police corruption would have been ineffective assistance of counsel, yet Shapiro wanted Cochran to back down:

> While there were certainly valid questions we could voice about the conduct of a couple of investigating detectives and the police lab personnel, I was against launching our relationship with this jury using a charge of blanket police corruption. "Just lay it out the way it actually happened, and let the jury draw their own conclusions," I suggested.[18]

This was Shapiro's best judgment in a case with nine black jurors, despite former Secretary of State Warren Christopher's accusations of racism against the LAPD in a report issued by the commission that bore his name.

In addition to Shapiro's lack of trial and criminal defense experience, he neither understood the complex role that race played in the case nor how to deal with it. Like so many others who become uncomfortable at the mention of the word "race," Shapiro seemed to think the best course of action was to ignore it. His naiveté was illustrated by one exchange with Cochran during jury selection:

> Shapiro: There's something happening that I don't like. Race shouldn't be an issue here.

---

[18] *Id.* at 229.

Cochran: It's always an issue, Bob. It's an issue in everything in life.

Shapiro: But I hoped it wouldn't be. I *believed* it wouldn't be.

Cochran: That's because you're not black.[19]

Shapiro did the unthinkable after the verdict. He went on The Larry King Show and the Barbara Walters show after the verdict and criticized Cochran for addressing the issue of race in his closing argument. Amazingly, he seemed to think the Simpson trial, and particularly the defense decision to address the racial issues head on, somehow set the country back in its efforts to overcome racial prejudice:

> Our country has experienced a great deal of growth in race relations since the Civil Rights movement. . . . But whatever gains we've made have been more than set back by the polarization that grew out of this case.

Despite his shortcomings, Shapiro performed a great service for Simpson—he invited a number of outstanding lawyers and experts to join the defense team. Shapiro was smart enough to know that he could not handle the case on his own. Soon after he was retained he brought on Harvard law professor and trial lawyer Alan Dershowitz and Santa Clara law professor and former dean Gerald Uelmen to handle the complex legal issues in the case. Their encyclopedic knowledge and skills were key to several defense victories in the case, most noticeably their motion to disband the grand jury.[20] Shapiro hired Barry Scheck and Peter Neufeld because of their expertise in analyzing DNA evidence. This was perhaps Shapiro's wisest decision. Scheck's analysis of the government's DNA evidence and his masterful cross-examination of their experts were key to Simpson's acquittal. Shapiro brought on F. Lee Bailey, who ultimately was not particularly helpful to the defense. Interestingly, Cochran was not Shapiro's choice. Simpson wanted Cochran, but Shapiro preferred Gerry Spence over Cochran. Cochran was invited to join the team when Spence's schedule did not permit him to join the team at that time. After inviting a powerful group of lawyers to join the team, Shapiro ultimately was forced to take a back seat in the trial. Not surprisingly, he resented losing his role as lead counsel.

Johnnie Cochran

Johnnie Cochran emerged as the lead attorney in the Simpson case soon after he joined the team. Cochran, who died in 2005 after battling prostate cancer, was a skilled trial attorney, although probably not the most skilled in the country. Nonetheless, he was the perfect attorney to lead the defense team. Like Shapiro, Cochran had served as a district

---

[19] *Id.* at 192.

[20] DERSHOWITZ, *supra* note 3, at 28.

attorney for a few years early in his career. But unlike Shapiro, Cochran
had a strong criminal defense ethic. This was somewhat surprising
considering the fact that Cochran did not have extensive trial experience
as a criminal defense attorney when he joined the Simpson case. What
he did have, however, was experience fighting the government, specifically the LAPD. Cochran had successfully sued the city and the LAPD in a
number of high profile cases involving police brutality in the African
American community. He was well-known and well-respected in the
community that would comprise a significant presence in the jury pool.

Cochran also understood that race was an important issue—if not
the important issue—in the Simpson case. He understood the role of
race, not just because he was an African American, but because he knew
better than anyone the long and shameful history of abuse inflicted upon
members of the African American community by the LAPD. He knew
that among many African American jurors, white police officers would
have to overcome the reputation that the department had earned for
lying, cheating, and abusing African Americans. Cochran knew that
African American jurors were aware of the fact that African Americans
have been treated unfairly in the criminal justice system—as defendants
and as victims—from the time of the Black Codes to the present. The
Rodney King Simi Valley verdict and the ensuing Christopher Commission were fresh in everyone's memory. Cochran understood all of this
long before the Mark Fuhrman tapes were discovered.

Unlike Clark and Darden (and Shapiro), Cochran chose not to ignore
race. He wisely and appropriately took it on. The press (and others)
called this "playing the race card"—a demeaning and insulting phrase
that trivialized the issue of race, treating it as if it were some kind of
magic elixir that could control a black jury regardless of the evidence,
the facts, or the law. If Cochran had chosen to ignore race, it still would
have played a role in the verdict. A true advocate who understands the
role that jurors play and how their life experiences legally and appropriately influence their verdict would never ignore race in a case where it
featured so dominantly. Judges tell jurors in their instructions to use
their common sense and their life experiences to help them reach a
verdict. Racism is an indelible part of the life experience of most African
Americans. Yet Cochran was criticized for taking this fact into account
in his examinations of witnesses and his closing argument. His critics
wanted him to ignore race, either because it made them uncomfortable
or because his advocacy played a role in acquitting a man that the
majority of white Americans thought was guilty.

Interestingly, Cochran was the primary target of most of the criticism of the defense team, even though everyone on the team except
Shapiro understood and supported the defense strategy to take on the
issue of race. Yet, perhaps because he emerged as the lead attorney or

because he clearly galvanized members of the African American community during his many speaking engagements and media appearances, Cochran was denounced more than others.

Many believe that Cochran's race played a role in his ability to connect with and persuade the jury. It undoubtedly played some part, but clearly it was not the deciding factor. After all, Christopher Darden was also an African American male. Cochran's trial advocacy skills made the difference. Black jurors convict black defendants in criminal cases across the country at the request of white prosecutors, frequently in cases involving black defense attorneys. In fact, Marcia Clark had a record of securing convictions from predominantly black jurors. And white defense attorneys who are skilled advocates can and do convince black jurors to acquit in cases involving black defendants and black victims, even when the prosecutor is black. In the District of Columbia, white lawyers at the Public Defender Service frequently secure acquittals from predominantly black jurors in cases involving black victims and black prosecutors because they are excellent advocates and understand how to persuade jurors. Some black jurors may identify with a black lawyer or prosecutor, particularly older black jurors who take pride in seeing an African American in a prominent role. However, if the lawyer is sloppy or incompetent, that pride fades in the face of the evidence. Cochran's status as an African American would never have convinced the jurors to acquit if he did not have the power of persuasion.

Cochran, like Shapiro, did his share of media appearances. Before he was asked to join the team, he was a commentator on the case for NBC, and after he joined the team, he held press conferences. Talking about a pending criminal case in the media is almost always inappropriate—for both the prosecution and the defense. However one might criticize Cochran for talking to the press, it was clear that every appearance and statement had the goal of furthering the interests of his client. When Ito forbade the introduction of all but two small segments of the tapes on which Fuhrman demonstrated his racial prejudice against African Americans, Cochran held a press conference decrying the judge's ruling:

> The cover-up continues.... This inexplicable, indefensible ruling lends credence to all those who say the criminal justice system is corrupt.[21]

Cochran should not have held a press conference to criticize the trial judge, but unlike Shapiro's statements to the media, Cochran at least appeared to have a pure motive—advocating for his client rather than himself.

---

[21] TOOBIN, *supra* note 4, at 406.

F. Lee Bailey

F. Lee Bailey had the most recognizable name on the defense team. He had more trial experience than anyone on the defense team and had represented numerous famous clients, including Sam Sheppard and Patty Hearst. Everyone knew who F. Lee Bailey was and his name became a metaphor for outstanding trial lawyering. If someone said, "He's no F. Lee Bailey" or "He thinks he's F. Lee Bailey," everyone knew what it meant.

Shapiro had known Bailey for many years. He called Bailey for advice early in the case and ended up asking him to join the defense team. It was an awkward situation since it seemed strange for someone of Bailey's stature to take anything other than a leading role in a criminal trial. Yet, Bailey was brought on to work on the "Shapiro team," and he claimed to understand and accept that role early in the case. Not surprisingly, the two men clashed and were not speaking to each other by the end of the case—a fact that was important only because their in-fighting must have been as obvious to the jurors as it was to everyone else.

As Shapiro became more alienated from the defense team, Bailey's role in the trial became more prominent. The cross-examination of Detective Mark Fuhrman was one of the most important in the trial. The defense theory was that Fuhrman had planted incriminating evidence to frame Simpson, and they had corroborating evidence to show that Fuhrman had a motive to do so. At the time of Fuhrman's testimony, the defense had not yet discovered the tapes of Fuhrman admitting his racial bias against African Americans. However, they had interviewed several witnesses who were prepared to testify that they had heard him use the word "nigger" and otherwise speak disparagingly about African Americans. The defense team decided that Cochran should not do this cross-examination (in hindsight, perhaps not the correct decision). Scheck was an excellent cross-examiner but he was already handling the government's DNA witnesses. Shapiro was clearly not an option. Not only did Shapiro have limited experience and skill in cross-examination, but he was not even committed to the defense theory. Bailey was the obvious choice, especially since he had a reputation as a master cross-examiner.

As will be demonstrated below, Bailey's cross-examination of Fuhrman will not go down in history as one of the greatest. In fact, his performance and behavior during the entire trial was troubling. Most of Bailey's cross-examinations rambled and went nowhere. He talked to the press constantly, at times bragging about his own performance. Sadly, after the trial, Bailey was incarcerated in a federal detention center when he failed to turn over a client's assets pursuant to a plea agreement. Ironically, Shapiro, who represented the client with him, was the government's main witness against Bailey. Bailey was later disbarred.

Barry Scheck

Scheck was different from all of the lawyers in the case. He didn't give press conferences or talk to the press at all. He didn't wear fancy suits. He didn't make jokes at counsel table or anywhere else. Scheck worked—probably harder than any lawyer on the case. He was smart, skilled and deeply committed to the client. These facts were apparent without an announcement at a press conference. Scheck stood out because of what he did, not what he said. He didn't talk the talk. He walked the walk.

Barry Scheck was trained as a Legal Aid lawyer in the Bronx and then went on to become a clinical professor at Cardozo Law School where he taught and tried criminal cases. A lawyer friend asked him to help with a murder case based on DNA evidence, and the rest is history. Peter Neufeld worked on the case with him and they went on to become the top expert lawyers in the country on DNA evidence, later establishing The Innocence Project, which uses DNA evidence to free individuals wrongfully convicted of crimes.

It is highly unlikely that Simpson would have been acquitted without Scheck's cross-examination of Dennis Fung, the government's criminologist, and his presentation of the expert testimony of Dr. Henry Lee, the defense forensic expert. Through these examinations, Scheck effectively demonstrated that the crime scene was severely compromised by cross-contamination. Scheck was able to extract admission after admission from Fung about how evidence was mishandled at the crime scene. By the time Scheck finished questioning Fung, it was clear that Simpson's hair and blood could very well have ended up at the crime scene because of either the negligence or purposeful behavior of members of the LAPD and the forensic staff. Scheck created reasonable doubt after reasonable doubt. When Fung left the witness stand, he looked worn out. In one of the many bizarre occurrences of the trial, as Fung walked past the defense table, Cochran and Simpson shook his hand, and Shapiro hugged him!

When Dr. Lee testified in the defense case, Scheck skillfully directed him through testimony that explained complex forensic evidence in a way that was understandable and at times, even entertaining. Lee had an impeccable resume as the chief criminologist for the state of Connecticut. Although he was a paid expert, he seemed totally unbiased—a scientist only interested in the facts. Lee was measured in his opinions and seemed apologetic for criticizing the government's expert. In fact, he testified that 95% of his experience as an expert witness had been for the prosecution. Lee corroborated Fung's concessions of a contaminated crime scene and explained, in laymen's terms, how the evidence should have been collected. Lee's simple statement "something is wrong" was repeated in Scheck's portion of the closing argument. Between the cross of Fung and the direct of Lee, Scheck reduced the government's mountain of DNA evidence to a pile of contaminated rubble.

It's fair to say that the defense theory would have had little currency without Scheck's examination of these two witnesses. Scheck demonstrated—through the government's own witness and a credible defense expert—that the crime scene had been contaminated. He raised doubt that alone could have provided a reasonable basis for an acquittal. However, when combined with indisputable evidence of Fuhrman's extreme bias and perjury, the government was hit with a one-two punch from which it could not recover.

Cochran and Scheck were clearly the two most effective courtroom advocates on the defense team. The legal work of Dershowitz, Uelmen, Neufeld, and Blazier (another DNA expert) was important and essential. However, the courtroom trial advocacy could have been carried by Cochran and Scheck alone. They each brought skills that were essential to the acquittal. Bailey's cross of Fuhrman could have been done, arguably more effectively, by Scheck or Cochran. Shapiro's work was over when he hired the other lawyers. The "Dream Team" could have been streamlined considerably.

Jury Selection

No part of a jury trial is more important than the voir dire. The theory is that twelve individuals, free of bias against either side, will decide the case based on the evidence alone. Yet no juror is free of bias or preconceived notions about any variety of issues that may come up in a trial, complicated by the fact that judges tell jurors that they should draw on their common sense and life experiences to help them judge the case. Their life experiences undoubtedly help to form biases of some type.

Of course, in a criminal trial, the reality is that, regardless of bias, the defense wants a jury that will acquit and the prosecution wants one that will convict. Peremptory strikes and strikes for cause provide each side with some limited control over who sits on the final jury. Since there are a limited number of peremptory strikes and no limit on strikes for cause, the voir dire can provide the basis for a "for cause" strike by revealing impermissible bias. Voir dire has another important purpose. If the judge allows the lawyers to do the voir dire themselves, or at least to participate by communicating directly with the potential jurors, voir dire gives the lawyers the opportunity to connect with the jurors and build the kind of good will and credibility that will help to persuade jurors later in the trial.

The Venue

Gil Garcetti had a choice of venues for the Simpson trial—Santa Monica or Los Angeles. He chose Los Angeles for a variety of reasons. First, because of the high profile nature of the case, it was clear that there would be a need for lots of security and other accommodations that were simply not available in the Santa Monica courthouse. Second, Garcetti stated that he did not want to bring the case in predominantly white Santa Monica. Before the Simpson case, Garcetti enjoyed a fair amount of support from the African American community and he did not want to leave the impression that he was trying to secure an all-white jury in what was clearly going to be a racially charged case. Garcetti was well aware of the criticism of his predecessor for moving the trial of the police officers who beat Rodney King to Simi Valley. As Gerald Uelmen noted, Garcetti "did not want to risk the criticism he would have gotten in the black community if he physically moved the case to Van Nuys or Santa Monica."[22]

Nonetheless, some critics lambasted Garcetti for bringing the case in Los Angeles,[23] suggesting that he should have avoided the city's racial diversity and brought the case in Santa Monica to secure a predominantly white jury. It is unconstitutional to exclude any juror during jury selection because of his or her race or gender.[24] Although the Supreme Court has not specifically addressed this issue in the context of jury pools, bringing the case in a predominantly white community for the sole purpose of excluding black jurors would have subjected Garcetti to well-deserved criticism. As it turns out, the Los Angeles jury pool from which the jury was ultimately selected was by no means predominantly African American. In fact, African Americans were in the minority with 40% white, 28% black, 17% Hispanic, and 15% Asian.[25]

Garcetti's decision not to seek the death penalty also had a great impact on the diversity of the jury. Had he done so, the jury would have been much less diverse. In death penalty cases, jurors who have a conscientious objection to the death penalty that would prevent them from voting for execution are excused for cause. Studies have shown that there is a lower rate of support for the death penalty among minorities, so minorities are excused from jury service in these cases at a much

---

[22] GERALD F. UELMAN, LESSONS FROM THE TRIAL—THE PEOPLE V. O. J. SIMPSON (Andrews and McMeel 1996) at 81–82.

[23] *See, e.g.,* VINCENT BUGLIOSI, OUTRAGE: FIVE REASONS WHY O. J. SIMPSON GOT AWAY WITH MURDER (W. W. Norton & Co. 1996).

[24] Batson v. Kentucky, 476 U.S. 79 (1986); J.E.B. v. Alabama *ex rel.* T.B., 511 U.S. 127 (1994).

[25] UNIVERSITY OF MISSOURI-KANSAS CITY LAW SCHOOL, FAMOUS AMERICAN TRIALS, *available at* http://www.law.umkc.edu/faculty/projects/ftrials/Simpson/Jurypage.html.

higher rate than whites.[26] Gerald Uelman was surprised when Garcetti passed up the advantage that the death penalty would have provided the prosecution in jury selection and praised him for making what Uelman believes was a principled decision.[27]

Jury Consultants

The defense hired Jo–Ellan Dimitrius, a well-known jury consultant, to assist them during the process. Ms. Dimitrius submitted her research to the defense team. She informed them that the best defense jurors were young, African American, and less educated. Judge Ito introduced Dimitrius to the jury pool during voir dire and she consulted with Cochran and Shapiro about every jury decision.

The prosecution had a jury consultant as well, but they didn't follow his advice. In fact, Marcia Clark fought him every step of the way. Don Vinson, the head of DecisionQuest, a jury consulting firm, volunteered his services to the prosecution team free of charge. He was no stranger to Garcetti's office, having volunteered to assist during the retrial of the Menendez case. Garcetti wanted to accept his offer but Clark did not. She didn't think she needed help picking a jury. Clark had won the vast majority of her trials before the Simpson case and had picked her own jury in each of them. Also, she liked the image of two lone prosecutors going against a team of well-paid attorneys and consultants. Nonetheless, Garcetti insisted that she and Bill Hodgman meet with Vinson.

Like Dimitrius, Vinson did mock jury studies and focus groups. His recommendations were consistent with those of Dimitrius. African American jurors would favor the defense. The mock juries always split along racial lines with African Americans voting for acquittal and whites and jurors of other races voting to convict. He also made another observation that the prosecution ignored—the African American jurors, particularly the women, were much less inclined to find the domestic violence issues relevant. Finally, the black women in Vinson's focus group reacted very negatively to Clark. They described her as "shifty" and "strident" and called her a "bitch."[28] She was hurt by their comments (which she observed on a TV monitor in the next room) and offered to step down as counsel. Garcetti kept her on the case, and she dismissed Vinson.

The Selection Process

The voir dire was a long and arduous process that lasted two months. The initial pool of 900 jurors filled out brief questionnaires designed to determine whether sitting through the trial would pose a

---

[26] UELMAN, supra note 21, at 84.

[27] *Id.* at 95.

[28] TOOBIN, *supra* note 4, at 193.

hardship for them. The judge released many jurors who claimed hardship. The pool was narrowed to 304 potential jurors from which 12 jurors and 12 alternates would be picked. These jurors were required to complete a questionnaire with 294 questions that included questions proposed by the prosecution and the defense. The lawyers actively participated in the process with individual questioning of prospective jurors.

Since race was clearly such a big issue in the case, it made sense to deal with it in voir dire. The question was "how?" There were so many complex and sometimes conflicting considerations. From the defense perspective, they had to be concerned about Simpson's marriage to Nicole. There were people of all races who had negative views about interracial relationships—perhaps as many African Americans (particularly women) as whites. Would some black women jurors resent Simpson for being married to this woman? What about the fact that Simpson seemed to live in a predominantly white world? He appeared to have very few black friends nor did he live anywhere near African Americans. Yet Dimitrius' research indicated that these issues would not pose a problem for the defense. African Americans generally admired Simpson and certainly favored him over the LAPD which they viewed as racist and abusive.

The primary issue involving race was Mark Fuhrman's bias against African Americans, particularly African Americans like Simpson who had relationships with white women. The defense had very strong proof of that bias and they planned to use it to destroy Fuhrman's credibility. There was nothing they should have done with this information in voir dire. After all, who, regardless of his or her race, would not question the credibility of someone with this kind of racial hatred in a case brought against an African American?

The prosecution, on the other hand, had a problem. Was there anything they could do or say during voir dire to assure that the jurors would not hold Fuhrman's racist statements against him or against the government? Probably not. Their mistake was not in failing to deal with Fuhrman during voir dire; it was the decision to sponsor him as a witness in the first place that lost the case for them.

The lawyers on both sides did deal with the race issue to a certain degree. Their purpose was more to secure promises from the jury that they would not allow racial favoritism or bias to affect their consideration of the evidence. For example, the following questions of one of the jurors seem to have this purpose:

Mr. Cochran: Now, you were asked in the questionnaire a series of questions about race. And around courtrooms and around courts of law we like to think that—have you ever seen a picture or a statue of the Lady Justice?

Prospective Juror No. 1118: Yes.

Mr. Cochran: And you know if you can picture that in your mind's eye, we like to think, you know, she is blindfolded. We like to think that one of the things is she is colorblind. That race, other than points of identification, are irrelevant and immaterial regarding an individual. Do you believe that, basically?

Prospective Juror No. 1118: Yes.

Mr. Cochran: In other words, Mr. Simpson's race is not going to count for him or against him in this case. Is that a fair statement?

Prospective Juror No. 1118: That's correct.

Mr. Cochran: If ever the question of race ever came up in this case, you would of course bring that to the Court's attention in any negative

Prospective Juror No. 1118: That's correct.

Mr. Cochran: Because you understand everything we are trying to do here is to get a fair trial for both sides of this lawsuit. Do you understand that?

Prospective Juror No. 1118: Yes, Sir.[29]

Ms. Clark: Now, with respect to race, you understand that the color of a person's skin is just as irrelevant when it comes to the victims? Do you understand that?

Prospective Juror No. 1118: That's correct.

Ms. Clark: We don't view them any differently than any other person who is killed just because of the color of their skin?

Prospective Juror No. 1118: That's correct.

Ms. Clark: Would you agree that if we focus on what color people are that we are going to be distracted from looking at the evidence?

Prospective Juror No. 1118: That's correct.

Ms. Clark: A trial is meant to be a search for the truth and that is why we are all here and we are all here to do justice, for the people of the State of California and for the Defendant. Do you understand that?

Prospective Juror No. 1118: That's correct.[30]

---

[29] 1994 WL 557335 at 12.

[30] *Id*. at 21.

In the following interchange, Cochran seemed to be assuring himself that a juror understood the nature of racial prejudice while protecting the juror from a strike for cause:

Mr. Cochran: You were asked a question about the issue of racial discrimination in this community and I think you had described— you answered that you didn't think there was a serious racial problem in this community. Was that your response?

Prospective Juror No. 321: Yes.

Mr. Cochran: And you believe that based upon what you've observed on a daily basis in this community.

Prospective Juror No. 321: I haven't had any problems. I know that there are—and there are a lot of people—they have their own opinions on things, but I've worked with people. I lived—I don't know if you know. I lived back in New York, and I've been in the service. I met everybody and anybody over the years, and I know people and I make my own judgments and I don't have a problem with race conflict.

Mr. Cochran: I appreciate that. So what you are telling us is that you accept people for whom they are, not based upon their race or their age or their religion?

Prospective Juror No. 321: Yes. Exactly. Yes.

Mr. Cochran: And that's what we want in a perfect world. But you do appreciate there is in this country, although we don't like to think about it, racism; is that correct?

Prospective Juror No. 321: Of course.

Mr. Cochran: Racial discrimination.

Prospective Juror No. 321: Yes.

Mr. Cochran: By your answer, I just wanted to ascertain from you that you understood that those concepts exist, even thought you have not been subjected to racial discrimination in your life. Is that what you are saying to us?

Prospective Juror No. 321: Oh, yes, I have.

Mr. Cochran: You have?

Prospective Juror No. 321: Yes. Oh, no. I've seen both ends of the coin.

Mr. Cochran: So you've seen it and you know it does exist.

Prospective Juror No. 321: I know what it is, yes.

Mr. Cochran: If you ever saw racial discrimination or the issue of race creep into this case in any way from the standpoint of jury deliberations or whatever, would you again have the courage to bring that to the Court's attention and to say that's wrong, that should not be in this case?

Prospective Juror No. 321: You can bet on it. Yes.

Mr. Cochran: We have your assurance regarding that?

Prospective Juror No. 321: Positively.[31]

In the following exchange, Cochran bonded with another juror while again protecting him from a strike for cause. Hodgman tries to respond:

Mr. Cochran: Now, you are an African American?

Prospective Juror No. 620: This is true.

Mr. Cochran: And you understand that people from all races and background should be able to sit on this jury?

Prospective Juror No. 620: Right.

Mr. Cochran: And the fact that you are an African American and Mr. Simpson is an African American is not going to make you favor him; is that correct?

Prospective Juror No. 620: Not one way or another.

Mr. Cochran: His color—we have your assurance that his color and your color will not affect your ability to be a fair and impartial juror and decide this case based upon the evidence that emanates from that witness stand?

Prospective Juror No. 620: I think I indicated that on the questionnaire. I think the bottom line in this case will be the evidence. That is what we have to go with.

Mr. Cochran: And if you are a juror, you believe that you can be one who can try and see that justice is done?

Prospective Juror No. 620: Absolutely.[32]

Mr. Hodgman: Mr. Cochran asked you some questions a moment ago and he acknowledged you are an African American and he—do you—sir, do you feel that race has anything to do with this double murder case?

Prospective Juror No. 620: No, I don't.

Mr. Hodgman: Can you figure out any way that race is an issue in this case where we've got a young woman and a young man who were murdered? How does race figure in? Can you tell us.

Prospective Juror No. 620: Doesn't figure in to me.

---

[31] *Id.* at 32–33.

[32] 1994 WL 586412 at 42.

Mr. Hodgman: Okay.[33]

Clark and Hodgman clearly alienated some of the potential jurors when they made some crucial mistakes during voir dire. On one occasion, during a hearing on the record when the jurors were not present, Clark accused many of them of lying during the voir dire just to get on the jury:

> Many, if not most, are lying to the detriment of the People because they are sitting there as fans of this defendant saying, "We want to get on this jury . . . so we can acquit this man, no matter what." . . . I wish that we could only put all the jurors on polygraph, because if the People could get just twelve fair-minded, impartial jurors to listen to the evidence, then we know what the outcome will be.[34]

After she spoke, she realized the mistake that she had made and asked the judge to seal the transcript but he refused to do so. It was reported in the news the next day. Bill Hodgman, in an attempt to find out whether the remaining potential jurors had read it, made things even worse. He asked one older black man if he knew what a polygraph was and his tone was slow and condescending.[35] The juror was offended and responded angrily. Later a black woman responded to Hodgman's questions with "You make me feel like I'm on trial here."[36]

Clark, to her credit, tried to address the issue of race head on, but she just didn't have the credibility to pull it off. Towards the end of voir dire when the panel had been reduced to less than 50 potential jurors, Judge Ito gave each side 75 minutes to do a final round of questioning. Clark proceeded as follows:

> We've all seen Naked Gun. He made us laugh. . . . We've had him referred to as the all-American hero. . . . And that's why it's so very difficult to have to present to you that someone of this image can do a crime so terrible. He's such a famous guy. He's such a popular guy that there's going to be a real temptation to do something different than what the law requires. This is a horrible situation, none of us like it, but that doesn't mean we suspend the rules of evidence. Just like in a football game—it's always a hundred-yard game no matter who's playing it. It doesn't matter if Mr. Simpson's on the team, it's still a hundred-yard game. It doesn't become an eighty-yard game,

---

[33] *Id.* at 45.

[34] CLARK, *supra* note 2, at 209.

[35] SHAPIRO, *supra* note 3, at 190–91.

[36] CLARK, *supra* note 2, at 211; 1994 WL 595261 at 22.

and it doesn't become a hundred-and-twenty-yard game, either. Rules are rules.[37]

After pointing out a number of the issues in the case—interracial marriage, a black defendant, white victims, spousal abuse—she asked them whether any of these issues would affect them:

> Which one of these do I have to worry about with you? Are you guys going to try and even some score you've got in mind? You all agree with me that that would be wrong? That the place to even the score is the ballot box, not in this courtroom? Is there anyone here ... rooting for one side or the other? I don't care which side it is. If you are sitting there rooting for "guilty" right now, I want you to get up and have the honor and the decency to excuse yourself from this panel.... If you've decided how this case should end, then you cannot be fair. And how about all these conspiracy theories? The Mafia did it. A Columbian cartel did it. A crew of white burglars did it. Are you going to make me shoot down these screwball theories before you'll listen to the evidence? How many trials do I have to do here? You could make the evidence fit anything, but that's not justice.[38]

Then Clark went on to reference the Rodney King trial:

> That case was in trouble from the very start, wasn't it? Because it had an all-white jury in a police community. And with a videotape, the most slam-dunk case you could possibly imagine. Our office lost that case, and we all know why.
>
> Do you know that had something to do with the fact that they were being tried ... by a jury that was all white? That it was tried in a community where a lot of police officers lived? ...
>
> That's what happens when you don't listen to the evidence, when you vote on the basis of some private agenda.[39]

Shapiro objected at this point, calling her statements "unprofessional conduct" and requested that she be sanctioned. The canon of ethics forbids a prosecutor from commenting on a verdict to a potential juror. Clark apologized to the court and to the potential jurors, asking, "I hope I did not offend you with any of the comments I made concerning the Rodney King verdict...." The jurors responded "No" in unison.

It was a crude attempt to secure a promise from these potential jurors that they would not let anything other than the facts of the case govern their decision. But Clark couldn't deliver the message. She didn't

---

[37] CLARK, *supra* note 2, at 212–13; 1994 WL 600993 at 33–34.

[38] 1994 WL 600993 at 39–42.

[39] CLARK, *supra* note 2, at 213.

have the credibility with the potential jurors, she didn't express the message well, and the message itself went too far. Clark's comparison to the Rodney King trial was off base. There was no videotape in the Simpson case and it was far from a "slam dunk." And Shapiro was correct to object to her comments about the case. Yet, she could have made the point in a more subtle way without referring to the case by name.

The main problem, however, was the messenger, not the message itself. Clark was angry, off-putting, and so obviously hostile to Simpson. And she had called the potential jurors "liars." The prosecution not only failed to fulfill one of the main purposes of voir dire—building good will and credibility with the jurors—they made things worse by digging a hole for themselves that they were never able to climb out of.

Direct and Cross-examination of Fuhrman

Mark Fuhrman was the one witness singly most responsible for the acquittal in the Simpson case. He was a racist cop who committed perjury in the presence of the jury—perjury that was proven to them when they heard an audiotape of his voice uttering one of the worse racial slurs in the English language after he swore under oath that he had not used the word in the prior ten years. Fuhrman had a clear, admitted bias against African Americans, especially African Americans who married whites. This bias was proven with concrete evidence—his statements in his personnel records, the testimony of several disinterested witnesses, and audio tapes of his own voice. How could any juror, regardless of her race, believe anything Fuhrman said?

Yet when Simpson's lawyers appropriately pointed out Fuhrman's extreme racial bias, through their cross-examination of him and through very strong extrinsic evidence, they were accused of "playing the race card." Did the critics believe that they should have ignored the bias? To do so would have been malpractice—at least ineffective assistance of counsel.

What makes the criticisms of the defense team even more astonishing is that the defense did not bring Fuhrman into the case—the prosecution did. The prosecution called him as a witness, and until his perjury was revealed to the jury, sponsored him and vouched for his credibility. They put him on the witness stand, and he testified about what he observed as one of the first cops on the crime scene. Most significantly, he testified about a glove that he found when he searched Simpson's property later that same night—a bloody glove that matched the glove that was found at the crime scene. The prosecution wanted the jury to believe him.

A primary purpose of cross-examination is to attack the credibility of the witness to demonstrate that the witness is not telling the truth, either because he is lying or because he is mistaken. Of course, there are times when cross-examination can be used to bring out helpful information from a witness, and in those cases, the cross-examiner wants the jury to believe the witness. But Fuhrman was not one of those witnesses. He was a witness who offered very damaging, incriminating evidence against Simpson. So of course the defense had the responsibility of convincing the jury that he should not be believed.

There are many ways to attack a witness's credibility. For example, the cross-examiner can show that a witness is mistaken because his vision or hearing was impaired or obstructed, his memory has faded, or because he only observed the incident for a brief period of time. However, if the witness is lying, the cross-examination is very different in style and substance. There are many different reasons why a witness might lie—because he has made a deal with the prosecution to testify in exchange for a reduced sentence, because he is guilty of the crime and he's trying to protect himself, because he is trying to protect someone else who is guilty of the crime, or because he is biased—either against the defendant or towards the prosecution or victim of the crime.

Bias is always relevant.[40] It goes to the core of a witness's credibility. And there is no bias more intense than racial bias. If a witness is biased against a particular racial group and the defendant is a member of that group, the defense has the duty and the right to cross-examine that witness about his racial bias.[41]

Evidence of Fuhrman's racial bias emerged early in the case. He filed a disability claim in the early 1980s and when it was denied, he filed a lawsuit against the city. The file was a public record and available in the archives of the Los Angeles County Courthouse. The file contained ample evidence of racial bias. For example, there was a report from a psychiatrist who had examined Fuhrman. Fuhrman told the doctor that he had left the Marines because "there were these Mexicans and niggers, volunteers, and they would tell me they weren't going to do something."[42]

There were other allegations of Fuhrman's racism. A man named Michael Landa who had served in the Marines with Fuhrman remembered Fuhrman saying that he "hated fucking niggers." And perhaps the most damning of all, allegations by a woman named Kathleen Bell who met Fuhrman. Ms. Bell said that Fuhrman told her that he would pull

---

[40] Davis v. Alaska, 415 U.S. 308 (1974).

[41] Delaware v. Van Arsdall, 475 U.S. 673 (1986).

[42] TOOBIN, *supra* note 5, at 148.

over any car that contained a black man and a white woman. She described their conversation as follows:

> I then asked him, "What if you don't have a good reason to pull them over?" Mr. Fuhrman stated, "I'd make one up." I then asked Fuhrman, "What if the two people are in love?" Fuhrman then appeared to get disgusted with me and stated, "If I had my way, they would take all the niggers, put them together in a big group and burn them."[43]

There were other potential witnesses who corroborated Fuhrman's racism, including an LAPD detective named Andy Purdy who stated that Fuhrman had painted swastikas on his police locker after Purdy married a Jewish woman.[44]

The prosecution team knew about all of this evidence of racial bias early in the case, but they decided to put him on the witness stand anyway. Their reasons for doing so are baffling. There were other witnesses, including Vannater and Lange, who had seen the glove on Simpson's property. Yet they stubbornly proceeded with Fuhrman.

In many ways, the decision to put Fuhrman on the stand was typical of the arrogant, immature behavior of the prosecution throughout the pendency of the case. Both Clark and Darden were guilty of making rash, illogical decisions in the case, but Clark was responsible for this one. Fuhrman himself warned Clark early on that there was information in his personnel file that the press might discover and that they would "smear me to kingdom come."[45] Clark insisted that anything in his personnel file was privileged and that the press would never be able to find it. Instead of immediately getting the file to find out what was there, Clark just asked Fuhrman whether there was anything in the file that would affect the truth of his testimony. When Fuhrman responded in the negative and told her that the information in the file had nothing to do with the case, she accepted his answer and did nothing else to follow up. According to Clark, "In hindsight, of course, I should have requested the file immediately. But in the heat of the moment, I just made a mental note to check it out."[46] She never did. This was an unbelievable oversight, especially since the allegations of Fuhrman's racism kept coming up. Clark dismissed them all. One of her own colleagues at the DA's office, Lucienne Coleman, told her about the swastikas and other reports about Fuhrman. Clark's response was,

[43] DARDEN, *supra* note 3, at 193.

[44] TOOBIN, *supra* note 5, at 315.

[45] CLARK, *supra* note 3, at 110.

[46] *Id*. at 110–11.

"This is bullshit being put out by the defense!"[47] Clark's investigation of all of these allegations was to ask Fuhrman if they were true. When he denied them, that was good enough for Clark.

To his credit, Darden was never comfortable with Fuhrman. Darden never believed Fuhrman's denials. The prosecution team originally asked Darden to put Fuhrman on the stand, but in the course of preparing him to testify, Darden was convinced that Fuhrman was lying. He ultimately refused to put him on, leaving the task to Clark.

The prosecution's reasons for using Fuhrman as a witness were weak. According to Darden and Clark, they didn't want to appear as if they were hiding Fuhrman. They had already put him on the stand during the preliminary hearing and if they didn't use him at trial, the defense would make a big deal of it. But could that have been worse than opening the door to all of the extrinsic evidence of his racism? Of course, at the time, neither side knew about the incriminating audiotapes, but the testimonial evidence from Kathleen Bell and others was bad enough. The decision to sponsor Fuhrman was just another example of the prosecution's incompetence and their insistence on ignoring sound advice—about the jury, about the glove, about talking to the press, and the list goes on.

Fuhrman's racial bias was just one of his problems. The other was perjury. In addition to its probative value as evidence of bias, F. Lee Bailey's cross-examination of Fuhrman about his use of the word "nigger" also laid the foundation to demonstrate his lack of credibility on another level. A witness may always be cross-examined on his prior inconsistent statements to show lack of credibility. Either the witness has lied or can't remember—either way, prior inconsistent statements damage the credibility of a witness. However, Bailey's cross-examination went further. It laid the foundation for presenting evidence that proved that Fuhrman was a perjurer. It is hard to imagine evidence more probative of a witness' lack of credibility than evidence that he has committed perjury.

The prosecution certainly had evidence that Fuhrman would commit perjury at the trial. There was abundant evidence that he had made racist statements and used racial slurs. The evidence was too widespread and from too many unrelated sources to ignore. They knew that the defense planned to cross-examine Fuhrman on this evidence and that he planned to deny everything. It was not until the famous audiotapes were produced that they conceded that Fuhrman had committed perjury. Prosecutors bring perjury prosecutions on far less evidence all of the time. After the tapes were played and the whole world knew that

---

[47] Toobin, *supra* note 5, at 315.

Fuhrman committed perjury, the prosecutors had no choice but to prosecute him. He later pled no contest.

The Direct Examination

There was not much Clark could have done to make Fuhrman's direct examination successful. Fuhrman was tainted beyond repair, and Clark should not have called him as a witness. There was no direct examination strategy that could have prevented the defense from cross-examining him on his despicable racial bias. If he admitted the bias, of course it would have been devastating to the prosecution's case. The prosecution knew that he would deny it, permitting the defense to present evidence that he was lying. At the time Clark put Fuhrman on the stand, no one knew about the tapes, but she knew that there were several witnesses who would impeach him. Clark obviously believed that the jury would ignore the testimony of these witnesses.

If a lawyer knows that her witness will be cross-examined about information that is harmful to her case, it is always best to bring the information out on direct examination. Sometimes called "pulling the sting," this practice serves several purposes. First, it allows the lawyer to present the issue in a manner that is least damaging to her case and permits the witness to explain the issue in his own words. Second, the damaging information will have less impact on cross-examination if the jury has already heard it. Finally, if the jury hears the information for the first time on cross-examination, it may believe that the presenting lawyer was trying to hide information about her witness.

Clark obviously knew that she should attempt to "pull the sting" of Bailey's cross-examination in some way. She began the direct examination as follows:

Q: Detective Fuhrman, can you tell us how you feel about testifying today?

A: Nervous.

Q: Okay.

A: Reluctant.

Q: Can you tell us why?

A: Throughout—since June 13, it seems that I have seen a lot of the evidence ignored and a lot of personal issues come to the forefront. I think that is too bad.

Q: Okay. Heard a lot about yourself in the press, have you?

A: Daily.

Q: In light of that fact, sir, you have indicated that you feel nervous about testifying. Have you gone over your testimony in

the presence of several district attorneys in order to prepare
yourself or court and the allegations that you may hear from
the defense?

A: Yes.

Q: And in the course of that particular examination, sir, was the
topic of your testimony concerning the work you did in this
case, the actual visitation to Bundy and Rockingham, was that
discussed?

A: No.

Q: It dealt with side issues, sir?

A: Yes, it was.

Q: All right. Now, what was the purpose of that exercise?

Mr. Bailey: Objection, irrelevant.

The Court: Overruled.

The Witness: I have never been confronted with a criminal proceeding such as this, so I was—I think it was a concern that some of
these issues have never been breached before.

Q: When you say you have never been confronted with a criminal
proceeding such as this, you have testified before, haven't you?

A: Yes

Q: In criminal cases?

A: Yes.

Q: Homicide?

A: Yes.

Q: So what do you mean when you say "A situation like this?"

A: Well, it seems that the issues we were concerned with weren't
evidentiary in nature or about the crime; mostly of a personal
nature.

Q: All right, sir.[48]

It is unclear what purpose this series of questions and answers was
meant to serve. Bailey's objection on relevance grounds could have been
made much earlier. Fuhrman's feelings about testifying and his opinion
that a lot of the evidence had been ignored and "personal issues" were
coming to the forefront was surely irrelevant. This part of Clark's direct
was also very leading. Bailey may not have objected more because the
substance of the examination was not harmful to the defense. In fact, it
is likely that the jury had no idea what Fuhrman was talking about. His

---

[48] 1995 WL 97332 at 35–36.

vague reference to "personal issues" coming into the case must have been baffling to this sequestered jury if they were following Judge Ito's orders to refrain from reading newspaper articles or watching television shows about the case. Even if the jurors understood the testimony, the message was that Fuhrman was nervous and reluctant to testify because something personal was going to come out in his testimony. The exchange did not "pull the sting" of the cross-examination nor did it make him appear sympathetic or likable.

After this brief, confusing reference to Fuhrman's problems, Clark then asked him where he was assigned on June 12, 1994, and inexplicably jumped back to 1985, asking him about an incident of domestic violence involving Simpson and his ex-wife, the decedent. Clark asked a series of questions that elicited a detailed description of that incident and then suddenly, with no transition, asked Fuhrman if he knew a woman named Kathleen Bell (one of the witnesses who heard Fuhrman use racial slurs).

Q: Now, back in 1985 and 1986, sir, can you tell us whether you knew someone or met someone by the name of Kathleen Bell?

A: Yes, I can tell you that I did not.

Q: But you do recognize the name, don't you sir?

A: Yes.

Q: When was the first time that you heard that name?

A: It was in '94, I believe in the fall of '94. I don't know exactly what month.

Q: By the fall you mean September, October?

A: September, October.

Q: And do you recall when you testified in the preliminary hearing in this matter?

A: Yes, I do.

Q: And when was that, sir?

A: I believe July 5th and 6th, 1994.

Q: Okay. So you first heard her name after you testified at the preliminary hearing?

A: Yes.

Q: And how was it that you heard her name in connection with what?

A: In connection with allegations of statements I made to her at a date some time in '85 or '86.

Q: And where did you hear those allegations, sir?

A: In the news.

Q: And were you informed about a letter she had written in July of 1994 after the preliminary hearing to Johnnie Cochran?

A: Yes, I did.

. . .

Q: So you are presently very familiar with the contents of the letter that this woman wrote to Mr. Cochran?

A: Oh, yes.

Ms. Clark: I'm going to ask that this letter be marked as people's

The Court: 102.

Ms. Clark: Thank you, your Honor.[49]

* * *

Q: I'm going to ask you, sir, when we left off, I asked you if you had seen a copy of the letter written by the woman named Kathleen Bell that she wrote in July of 1994 to Mr. Cochran. I believe it was July 19th of 1994 and I was about to ask you to read that letter on the monitor. Could you now do so, sir?

A: Yes.

* * *

Q: First of all, sir, with respect to this paragraph, did you visit a Marine recruiting office located in Redondo Beach in 1985 to— between 1985 and 1986?

A: Yes

Q: Do you remember meeting a woman named Kathleen Bell at that Marine recruiting office between1985 and 1986?

A: No.

Q: Did one of the district attorneys on this case ask you to watch Larry King Live on television?

A: Yes, they did.

Q: And do you recall approximately when that was?

A: I believe it was in the last month. I think it was the—the program she was on just before the most recent. So I think it would be about a month.

Q: So about a month ago?

A: A month, yes.

---

[49] *Id.* at 38–39.

Q: And for what purpose were you watching Larry King Live?

A: They asked me to just look at the show and see if looking at the woman jogged my memory.

Q: And did you then look at the show, sir?

A: Yes.

Q: Did you see a woman who called herself Kathleen Bell?

A: Yes.

Q: And did you recognize her?

A: No, I did not.

* * *

Q: Did the conversation Kathleen Bell describes in this letter occur?

A: No, it did not.

Q: At the beginning of your testimony, we referred to a practice session in which there were several district attorneys we referred to at the beginning of your testimony. That practice or mock cross-examination, did that deal with the anticipated cross-examination on this subject of Kathleen Bell?

A: Yes it did.

Q: Did it deal with your actual work on this case as a police detective?

A: No, it didn't.

Q: And how long did that examination take place for?

A: 20 to 30 minutes.

Q: And that conversation that is described in this letter from Kathleen Bell, did that occur, sir?

A: No, it didn't.

These two exchanges were the extent of Clark's questions about the racial bias allegations that would be raised during cross-examination. The rest of her direct examination consisted of routine questions about Fuhrman's involvement in the case, including his arrival at the crime scene, the visit to Simpson's home, and the discovery of the glove.

The Cross-Examination

The cross-examination of Mark Fuhrman was critical to the defense. The defense theory was that Mark Fuhrman was a racist and dishonest cop who had planted evidence in order to frame O.J. Simpson. According to the defense, Fuhrman was motivated by his deep racial prejudice against African Americans, particularly African Americans who dated or married whites. There was also a sub-theme that Fuhrman wanted to elevate his importance in the case by presenting himself as the person who discovered the most incriminating evidence against Simpson.

At the time of the Fuhrman cross-examination, the defense team had not yet discovered the damning tapes with Fuhrman repeatedly uttering the word "nigger." However, there were several witnesses who were prepared to testify about Fuhrman's hatred of African Americans. Fuhrman was the government's "star" witness, and the defense needed to destroy his credibility. Bailey had the ammunition to do just that, but unfortunately, despite his reputation as a master cross-examiner, his performance was disappointing.

Bailey seemed to break every basic rule of cross-examination. Unfortunately, his decision to break with traditional wisdom did not appear to be innovative risk-taking by a seasoned trial lawyer but the last swan song of a once great lawyer whose best days had come and gone. Instead of asking short, leading questions with one point per question, Bailey's questions were often long, open-ended, and compound. Instead of starting and finishing with strong points, his examination started weak and ended even weaker. Instead of asking questions only to establish certain facts or make points through leading questions, Bailey often appeared to be fishing for answers, leaving the jury unsure of why he was asking the question in the first place. To make matters worse, he frequently repeated himself, and then on issues of relative unimportance, Bailey's cross-examination was painfully long, rambling, repetitive, and disorganized. It lasted for three and a half days, interrupted only by occasional legal arguments about various evidentiary issues.

Bailey started his cross-examination with a series of open-ended questions on a relatively unimportant point—the lack of significance of a plastic cover found in the back of Simpson's car:

Q: Good morning, Detective Fuhrman.

A: Good morning, Mr. Bailey.

Q: Could you tell us when it was that you were enlightened as to the fact that the plastic you saw in Mr. Simpson's Bronco comes with the car, when you learned that?

A: Yes. I believe it was Saturday.

Q: Saturday.

A: Yes.

Q: So that after nine months of investigation, you discovered on Saturday that this important piece of evidence was perfectly innocuous; is that right?

Ms. Clark: Objection. Assumes a fact not in evidence.

The Court: Sustained. It's argumentative.

Q by Mr. Bailey: Okay. Now, when you first saw the shovel in Mr. Simpson's Bronco, did you think that a significant find?

A: I don't think "significant" was the word I would use.

Q: Do you have any experience in digging, Detective Fuhrman?

A: Yes, sir.

Q: Do you know the difference between the kind of shovel used to dig a hole and the kind of shovel you might use as a scooper for instance?

A: Yes, I do.

Q: Okay. And what kind of shovel is this?

A: Well, that's the type of shovel you use to muck a barn.

Q: Or scoop out doggie-do maybe?

A: It's a little large for that, but I think I see what you mean.

Q: It would work, wouldn't it?

A: Yes, sir.

Q: Okay. Now, as I understand it, your colleagues, Detectives Vannatter and Lange, on the 13th day of June 1994 had a total of some three hours in the company of Mr. Simpson, correct? Did you learn that?

A: I had never heard that time, no.

Q: You know they talked though?

A: Yes, I understand.

Q: You know that part of what they exchanged—

Ms. Clark: Objection.

Q by Mr. Bailey:—with Mr. Simpson was taped, don't you?

Ms. Clark: Objection. Irrelevant, beyond the scope, hearsay.

The Court: Overruled. The fact there was—they had a taped conversation is a fact. It's not contact.

Q by Mr. Bailey: Part was taped, part was not. Was that your understanding?

Ms. Clark: Objection, Your Honor.

The Court: Sustained. That's assuming facts not in evidence.

Mr. Bailey: Okay.

Ms. Clark: Beyond the scope.

Q by Mr. Bailey: Do you know if a formal statement was taken at some point on that day, just yes or no?

Ms. Clark: Objection. Would be speculation. This witness has nothing to do with it.

The Court: Overruled. You can answer the question.

The Witness: I can only say that through other sources, I assumed and I heard, but I had never seen anything or heard anything.

Q by Mr. Bailey: You never talked to Detectives Vannatter and Lange about what the suspect had said during three hours of conversation?

A: No, I didn't.

Q: Never did?

Ms. Clark: Objection.

The Court: Sustained. The jury is to disregard that. Mr. Bailey— Hold on. Be careful, Mr. Bailey. Proceed.

Q by Mr. Bailey: Did you ever learn if Mr. Simpson was ever asked any questions about a shovel?

The Court: Sustained. I am going to sustain the Court's own objection. That's hearsay.

Q by Mr. Bailey: All right. Did you ever ask Mr. Simpson any questions about a shovel?

A: I never asked—

Ms. Clark: Objection. Assumes he ever asked anything.

The Court: Overruled.

Q by Mr. Bailey: Did you?

A: I've never asked Mr. Simpson any questions.

Q: Okay.[50]

Bailey then inexplicably invited Fuhrman to explain his education and background in great detail:

Would you share with us, Detective Fuhrman, some of your educational background, high school, college, that sort of thing?[51]

This question led to a long series of questions about Fuhrman's education, training and experience that ultimately led to Bailey's apparent point—that Fuhrman knew that delaying the investigation of a homicide scene can compromise the evidence.

---

[50] 1995 WL 103849 at 20–21.

[51] Id. at 21.

Bailey moved on to make an important point about how there were potentially latent footprints on the grounds of Nicole Simpson's home that were not properly protected. However, before making this point, Bailey took Fuhrman through every step of his whereabouts from his home to the scene in excruciating detail and then repeated the line of questioning. When Bailey finally got to the important questions about Kathleen Bell—one of the witnesses to whom Fuhrman related his hatred of African Americans—his questions were so convoluted that they were barely comprehensible:

Q: Now, Detective Fuhrman, are you as satisfied with the quality of the trust of your denial of knowing Kathleen Bell as you are of your claim that you found the right-handed glove on Mr. Simpson's property? Is the quality of the truth of those two statements the same or is one stronger than the other, if you know?

A: I don't understand any of that.

Q: You don't understand that question?

A: No.

Q: Are you as certain that you've never met Kathleen Bell on any occasion as you are that you in fact found the right-hand leather glove we've been discussing on Mr. Simpson's property?

Ms. Clark: Objection. That misstates the testimony. The testimony was, he had no memory as with respect to Kathleen Bell, not—

The Court: Miss Clark, I can barely hear your. Is that—

Ms. Clark: I don't want to—

The Court: Objection, what?

Ms. Clark: Objection. Misstates the testimony.

The Court: All right. Overruled on that ground. Proceed.

Ms. Clark: Objection. Vague.

The Court: Sustained.[52]

The examination frequently rambled, and Bailey often abruptly jumped around from topic to topic, frequently going over the same points repeatedly. The point about the latent footprints was repeated so many times that Judge Ito interrupted Bailey at one point and scolded him in front of the jury, commenting that he was going over this information for the third time. One unimportant line of questioning about Fuhrman interrupting witness Kato Kaelin when he was questioning him on the

_____

[52] *Id.* at 40–41.

scene proved to be ironic in light of Bailey's own constant interruption of Fuhrman's answers:

Q: Did you ever ask him what a limo was doing there at 11:00 p.m.

A: No. I cut his conversation off and brought him into the house.

Q: As a matter of fact, you asked him if he had heard anything unusual and then you cut him off and said, "Who drives that Bronco," didn't you?

A: I believe I did.

Q: Why did you cut him off?

A: I don't know, sir.

Q: You interrupted an answer to get a different answer? Was this an important question, who drives that Bronco?

A: No. He answered that question.

Q: Hum?

A: He answered that question.

Q: I know that. In order to get that answer you cut him off from answering the previous question which was did something unusual happen tonight or anything unusual. Do you remember that?

A: Yes.

Q: Okay. Why was who drives the Bronco so important as to interrupt a witness?[53]

Later in the cross-examination, Judge Ito chastised Bailey for repeatedly interrupting Fuhrman's answers to his questions—answers which he provoked by asking open-ended questions. Ironically, Bailey asked Fuhrman about interrupting Kato Kaelin's answers, prompting Marcia Clark to make an inappropriate but painfully true comment about Bailey himself frequently interrupting witnesses:

Q: Well, do you normally ask somebody a question and then before they have a fair chance to answer you cut them off with another one?

Ms. Clark: Somebody does.[54]

In one of his more important lines of cross-examination, Bailey attempted to make the point that Fuhrman arranged to be alone behind Simpson's estate so that he could pretend to "find" the glove that the

---

[53] 1995 WL 103850 at 18.

[54] 1995 WL 106322 at 20.

defense accused him of planting. Bailey ultimately made the point, but the path was tortuous:

Q: Well, why would you instruct him to sit on a bar stool?

A: Because I wanted him to sit there.

Q: Why did you want him to sit there, Detective Fuhrman?

A: So Detective Vannatter or another detective could talk to him.

Q: That would take care of two of them, wouldn't it?

A: Two of who?

Q: If you instruct Vannatter to go and talk to Kaelin, that ties up two of the four people that were with you in the house, or the five, doesn't it, having a conversation?

Ms. Clark: Objection. That calls for speculation.

The Court: Overruled.

Q by Mr. Bailey: Do you understand my question?

A: No.

Q: All right. Would you agree with me, Detective Fuhrman, that everybody has got to be someplace?

A: I agree.

Q: And that one person can't be in two places?

A: Agreed.

Q: So that if you caused two people to join together in a conversation at a specific place, it is unlikely that they will be any other place until the conversation is over?

A: I would agree with that.

Q: Okay. Now, I will ask you one more time. Did you use words of instruction to Phil Vannatter telling him, without suggesting any subject matter, go talk to Kaelin?

A: Not in that manner, but yes, I did.

Q: All right. You had already formulated a plan that you were going to look out behind the building in the darkness for something, correct?

A: No.

Q: You had not?

A: I didn't even know if that was accessible from the front of the residence.

Q: Didn't you tell us that as you walked from the bungalow to the house you had made a decision that you would go look at the source of the noise?

A: I wasn't even—

Q: I'm sorry, did you say that?

A: Yes.

Q: Okay. Well, then at the time you said, "Phil, go talk to Mr. Kaelin," you were on your way, weren't you?

A: Yes.

Q: You didn't hesitate at all? Once that utterance was out of your mouth you kept right on moving?

A: Yes.

Q: You saw Phillips on the telephone?

A: Yes, I believe so.

Q: And did you see Detective Lange?

A: I don't recall if I saw him.

Q: Was he in the proximity of Arnelle Simpson apparently engaged in conversation of some sort?

A: He could have been.

Q: All right. That is five people in the house, correct?

A: Yes.

Q: Now, take us back, if you will, to your initial training about the buddy system, both military and police. Did you not say that it is axiomatic that you don't go in alone if danger could possibly be present?

A: Well, considering certain situations, that would be desirable, yes.

Q: Let's look at this situation. You were investigating, what you have called from your own testimony, an extremely significant homicide, weren't you?

A: Yes.

Q: Okay. Probably the most serious that you had encountered among the eleven on which you had worked? Is that a fair statement?

A: Yes, sir.

Q: Okay. You had seen evidence that somebody, either psychotic or psychopathic, had brutalized two human bodies with something, correct?

A: Yes.

Q: And you knew that that someone could be unpredictable and deadly if you were to encounter them, correct?

A: I don't think we knew anything about the killer at that time, but I would say that they would be dangerous, considering the scene.

Q: Wouldn't you draw an inference that somebody capable of that kind of murder might not hesitate to take you down?

A: Yes.

Q: Okay. So as you leave the building you left three guns behind, didn't you?

A: Three detectives, yes.

Q: Three detectives, each of whom was carrying the same sidearm that you are wearing today, correct?

A: Yes.

Q: That is a glock automatic pistol, is it?

A: No.

Q: What is it?

A: I believe all three of those detectives, one was carrying a two-inch .38 model 36, one was carrying a Smith and Wesson stainless steel, and Detective Vannatter, I don't recall what he was carrying. I was carrying a Beretta.

Q: All automatic?

A: Yes.

Q: Each capable of firing several shots in quick succession?

A: Yes.

Q: Now, had you thought about asking one of those fellows to go with you, maybe someone who had a grown-up flashlight?

A: No.

Q: You never considered that for a moment?

A: No.

Q: All right. Now, I will ask you once again: was it not your purpose to be in the area along the south wall alone?

A: No, it wasn't.

Q: It just worked out that way? Is that it?

A: I didn't even know the south wall was accessible.

Q: No. It just worked out that you left the house and made your investigation for fifteen minutes or more alone?

A: That is how it worked out.

Q: That is how it worked out.[55]

Bailey could have made this point so much more effectively, in a variety of ways. At a minimum, short, leading questions would have been an improvement. For example, the line of questioning could have been as follows:

Detective Fuhrman, you were alone when you supposedly "found" this glove, correct?

You decided to walk around in the dark behind Mr. Simpson's house by yourself?

Even though you knew that there could very well have been dangerous individuals in that area?

And you are aware of the buddy system from your police and military training, right?

You were trained never to go into an area alone if there could be danger, correct?

And there were two armed detectives at the Simpson residence, right?

Vannatter and Lange?

You could have asked either one of them to go with you to search the area?

But instead you asked Vannater to talk to Kato Kaelin?

And you saw that Lange was talking to Arnelle Simpson?

So everyone was occupied in the house?

And it was at that point that you chose to go out into the dark alone?

And as luck would have it, that's when you supposedly found this glove?

When no one else was around?

Fuhrman would have answered each of these questions with a simple "yes," and if the questions were asked with the right tone and a touch of

---

[55] *Id.* at 23–24.

sarcasm at appropriate times, the point would have been clear to the jury.

The most dramatic and important part of the cross-examination was about Fuhrman's use of the word "nigger." It is this line of cross-examination that raises the question of whether Bailey was the appropriate member of the defense team to handle this witness, even if he had been at his best. Any time a white person says the word "nigger," even if it is not being used as a slur and regardless of the context, there is a risk that it may be offensive or at least somewhat uncomfortable for African Americans who hear it. For that reason, many individuals, regardless of their race, refer to the word as "the 'N' word." There has even been a recent movement to ban the word in some communities.[56] Interestingly, even Johnnie Cochran seemed to avoid using the word in his closing argument. Although he used it a couple of times when quoting Bailey's cross-examination, most of the time, even when quoting Fuhrman or Bailey, he referred to the word as "the 'N' word."

Nonetheless, whoever cross-examined Fuhrman had to use the word—both for clarity's sake and to dramatize to the jury the intensity of Fuhrman's bigotry towards African Americans. Might Johnnie Cochran have been able to execute this task better? Probably. There is no question that the word does not have the same effect when used by an African American, regardless of the context and the way it is being used. Although Bailey's use of the word ultimately did not hurt Simpson's defense, it was a risk for Bailey to repeatedly say the word in his powerful, thunderous voice.

> Q: Okay. Did you say while in the recruiting station at any time during those years that when you see a Nigger driving with a white woman, you pull them over?
>
> A: No.
>
> Q: Do you recall anyone asking you if you didn't have a reason to pull them over, what would you do?
>
> A: I don't recall anybody ever asking me that question, sir.
>
> Q: Did you ever make a statement that if you needed a reason, you would find one?

---

[56] *See, e.g.*, Erika Hayaski, *N–Word is Still Spoken in N.Y.*, LOS ANGELES TIMES, Mar. 5, 2007 (reporting on the New York City Council's ban on the use of the "n-word" and the adoption of similar bans in Westchester County and Nyack, New York); Alllen Salkin, *Comedy On the Hot Seat*, NEW YORK TIMES, Dec. 3, 2006, § 9 (reporting on politicians and activists including Rev. Jesse Jackson and Rep. Maxine Waters (D., CA) calling for a ban on the "n-word.") This movement was largely born out of the response to an incident by comedian Michael Richards in which he repeatedly used the word in an attack on several African American members of the audience during one of his nightclub performances.

A: No.

Q: Okay. ... Did you say at any time in that recruiting station in the presence of any female including Kathleen Bell that you'd like nothing more than to see all Niggers gathered together and killed?

A: No.[57]

...

Q: Did you have a conversation in '85 and '86 in Hennessey's Tavern with a tall woman wherein you said that black men who have white women in their company are violating an act of nature?

A: No.

Q: And that you would arrest them whenever you saw that occur?

A: No.[58]

Later in the cross-examination, he returned to the issue:

Q by Mr. Bailey: Do you use the word "nigger" in describing people?

Ms. Clark: Same objection.

The Court: Presently?

Mr. Bailey: Yes.

The Court: Overruled.

The Witness: No, sir.

Q by Mr. Bailey: Have you used that word in the past ten years?

A: Not that I recall, no.

Q: You mean if you called someone a nigger you have forgotten it?

A: I'm not sure I can answer the question the way you phrased it, sir.

Q: You have difficulty understanding the question?

A: Yes.

Q: I will rephrase it. I want you to assume that perhaps at some time, since 1985 or 6, you addressed a member of the African American race as a nigger. Is it possible that you have forgotten that act on your part?

A: No, it is not possible.

---

[57] 1995 WL 106323 at 22.

[58] *Id.* at 23.

Q: Are you therefore saying that you have not used that word in the past ten years, Detective Fuhrman?

A: Yes, that is what I'm saying.

Q: And you say under oath that you have not addressed any black person as a nigger or spoken about black people as niggers in the past ten years, Detective Fuhrman?

A: That's what I'm saying, sir.

Q: So that anyone who comes to this Court and quotes you as using that word in dealing with African Americans would be a liar, would they not, Detective Fuhrman?

A: Yes, they would.

Q: All of them, correct?

A: All of them.

Q: All right. Thank you.[59]

Fuhrman was not going to admit to using the word at this point, regardless of the form or substance of the cross-examination. The audiotapes had not yet been discovered so he was obviously relying on the jury believing him over the witnesses who presumably would impeach his testimony. However, in addition to the open-ended and wordy nature of his questions, it may have been more effective to start the cross-examination with this line of questioning. Effective cross-examinations start strong and finish strong. Since Fuhrman would never admit to using the word, it would probably be best to cross on this issue at the beginning of the examination. It would get the jurors' attention and possibly cause them to discredit Fuhrman from the beginning if they believed he was lying.

Although Bailey's technique was less than stellar, he was certainly successful in laying the groundwork for Fuhrman's impeachment. What he lacked in technique, he made up for in persistence. By eliciting Fuhrman's repeated denials that he had used the "N" word, Bailey set him up perfectly for the dramatic impeachment with the audiotapes of his own voice uttering the vile word.

After cross-examining Fuhrman about his racial slurs, Bailey embarked on a bizarre line of cross-examination. He decided to question Fuhrman about why Clark chose to ask him certain questions on direct examination. The questions seemed to serve no useful purpose for the defense, and objections to most of the questions were sustained:

Q: All right. Do you recall Miss Clark then caused to be displayed to you parts of a letter allegedly written by Kathleen Bell to

[59] 1995 WL 109035 at 23.

Johnnie Cochran and invited you to examine the text of that letter? Do you remember that?

A: Yes, sir.

Q: Okay. Had you discussed the fact that this was going to happen before you ever came into the courtroom?

A: Yes. That letter, yes.

Q: This was no surprise to you, was it?

A: No, sir.

Q: And were you not advised that the effort in doing so was to steal the thunder from the inevitable cross-examination?

Ms. Clark: Objection, your Honor. That is speculation, it is irrelevant.

The Court: Sustained.

Q by Mr. Bailey: Was it explained to you that this was an effort to diffuse the impact of any accusations that might later be made against you?

Ms. Clark: Same objection. Same objection.

The Court: Sustained.

Q by Mr. Bailey: Why—if there was an explanation, was it explained to you that this method of introducing your testimony was to be used in this case?

A: It wasn't explained to me, no.

Q: Well, in other words, as I understand it, you were simply told here is what we are going to do, Detective Fuhrman, here is the order in which things will happen when you hit the witness stand, and we are not going to tell you why?

A: I am not the prosecutor, sir.

Q: I know that you are not the prosecutor; you are the witness.

A: That was—

Q: Did you have any comprehension as to why this tact was taken by the prosecution?

A: Yes.

Q: Did you understand that it related to possible experiences you might have on cross-examination?

A: No.

Q: Okay. What was your understanding as to why this letter was surfaced at the outset of your testimony?

Ms. Clark: Objection, that is irrelevant.

The Court: I think his frame of mind is irrelevant. Overruled.

Ms. Clark: As to the reason for the manner in which I understand him—

Mr. Cochran: Speaking objection.

The Court: No. I have ruled, counsel. It is relevant, his frame of mind. Overruled.

Q by Mr. Bailey: Give us your understanding of why this was done in this case.

A: Because that is why Miss Clark—the way she wanted to litigate this case.

Q: Okay. And beyond that, you had no comprehension as to why it was done; is that right?

A: No.[60]

Bailey's last line of cross-examination was also puzzling. Not only was it on an extremely drab subject, but it wasn't at all clear why Bailey chose to question on this issue at all:

Q: Okay. Detective Fuhrman, how did you call in the license plate of the vehicle that turned out to be Kaelin's on the morning of the 13th?

A: Police radio.

Q: Is that called a rover?

A: Yes, sir.

Q: Is that something you carry on your belt?

A: No. You could, but in plain clothes it is very difficult, so you usually just take it out of the car and hold it.

Q: Okay. Did you have it with you that morning?

A: At different times I did, yes.

Q: All right. Did you have it with you when you were in talking to Kato in his bungalow?

A: I don't believe so, no.

Q: Did you have it with you when you were out to look for the source of the noise?

A: No.

Q: Did you have any communications equipment with you at that time?

---

[60] *Id.* at 34–35.

A: No.

Mr. Bailey: Okay.

(Discussion held off the record between defense counsel.)

Q by Mr. Bailey: Detective Fuhrman, is there a police radio code where certain words are used to indicate letters of the alphabet as there is in aviation in the military, for instance?

A: Yes, sir.

Q: What is the police word for "N"?

A: Nora.

Q: "V?"

A: Victor.

Q: "N?"

A: Nora.

Q: "H?"

A: Henry.

Q: "I?"

A: Put me on the spot. It is Idaho in the military. I'm having a— Ida.

Q: Okay. Does "NVN" have a meaning to you?

A: No, sir.

Q: Do you use that on the radio at all?

A: No, sir.

Q: I mean the phonetic letters, Nora, et cetera?

A: Oh, the phonetics, if I'm running a license plate, such as that?

Q: No, no. You said "V" was represented by?

A: Victor.

Q: All right. Do you ever use the term Nora Victor Nora when talking to other officers on the radio?

A: Why would I do that?

Q: Do you ever use the term Nora Victor Nora talking to officers on the radio?

A: No, sir.

Ms. Clark: Objection.

Mr. Bailey: All right. Thank you. That's all I have, your Honor, until the other matters are settled.[61]

With that, the cross-examination of one of the most important witnesses in the case ended with a thud.

The Closing Arguments

The closing arguments in the Simpson case began a year after the trial began. The arguments lasted four days—from September 26th through September 29th. Marcia Clark and Christopher Darden did the initial closing argument for the government, with Clark beginning and Darden concluding with a focus on domestic violence and the race issue. Johnnie Cochran began the closing argument for the defense, with Barry Scheck discussing the scientific evidence and Cochran concluding. Darden started the government's rebuttal argument, and Clark finished it.

The lawyers dealt with the issue of race in the closing arguments much as they did throughout the trial—the defense addressed the issue head on, and the prosecution was on the defense. Johnnie Cochran argued that Mark Fuhrman was a racist whose extreme bias against African Americans in general and hatred for Simpson in particular motivated him to plant evidence and lie. The prosecution argued that Fuhrman's racism had nothing to do with the case and that the defense was using race to inappropriately appeal to the passions and emotions of the jurors.

By the time the case reached closing arguments, there wasn't much the prosecution could do about Fuhrman. The defense put on witness after witness to impeach him. Several uninterested witnesses with no connection to each other took the stand and swore under oath that Fuhrman had used the word "nigger" and had made additional statements expressing his hatred and disdain for African Americans. The most powerful witness was Laura McKinney, the writer who had interviewed Fuhrman for a screenplay she was writing about police officers. McKinney kept the audio tapes of the interviews and Judge Ito allowed the defense to play a portion of the tapes with Fuhrman's unmistakable voice describing African Americans as "niggers."

The prosecution's mistake was sponsoring Fuhrman as a witness in the first place after ignoring all of the evidence that he had repeatedly used racial slurs against African Americans and had expressed his prejudice against them and other ethnic and racial groups on numerous occasions. Only when they were confronted with actual audio tapes did they concede, and at that point it was too late. The only strategy left was to ask the jury to ignore all the evidence of his bias. They could not

---

[61] 1995 WL 111188 at 4–5.

abandon him as a witness at that point because he was so central to their case, having testified about much of the physical evidence found at the scene of the murders and allegedly at Simpson's home. So they ended up arguing that the jury should believe everything he said except the part about him not using racial slurs—an argument that ultimately rang hollow.

Although all of the lawyers touched on the issue of race to a certain degree, it was certainly no coincidence that it was more central to the arguments of Cochran and Darden. It made sense that the two African American lawyers would talk about the sensitive issue of race to a predominantly African American jury. Certainly a persuasive and skilled lawyer of any race could have done so as well, but the decision to divide the arguments as they did was a logical one under the circumstances.

Marcia Clark

Although Clark's job was to discuss the evidence in support of the murders, including the scientific evidence, she wisely chose to address Fuhrman's perjury and bias early in her argument. After all, he was the witness through which much of the crucial physical evidence was introduced. And the jury undoubtedly had Fuhrman on their minds. Clark addressed the issue as follows:

> On the other hand, although it would be completely understandable if you were to feel angry and disgusted with Mark Fuhrman, as we all are, still it would be wrong to find the Defendant guilty—not guilty just because of that anger and disgust.

> So as you listen to the arguments of counsel, please remember when you weigh the evidence and you consider all of the evidence, remember that appeal to passion and emotion is an invitation to ignore your responsibility as a juror. To be fair we must examine all of the evidence in a calm and a rationale and a logical way.

> Let me come back to Mark Fuhrman for a minute. Just so it is clear. Did he lie when he testified here in this courtroom saying that he did not say racial epithets in the last ten years? Yes. Is he a racist? Yes. Is he the worst LAPD has to offer? Yes. Do we wish that this person was never hired by LAPD? Yes. Should LAPD have ever hired him? No. Should such a person be a police officer? No. In fact, do we wish there were no such person on the planet? Yes.

> But the fact that Mark Fuhrman is a racist and lied about it on the witness stand does not mean that we haven't proven the Defendant guilty beyond a reasonable doubt.

> And it would be a tragedy if with such overwhelming evidence, ladies and gentlemen, as we have presented to you, you found the

Defendant not guilty in spite of all that, because of the racist attitudes of one police officer.[62]

The flaw of this argument is that it ignores the legitimate reasons why the jury was allowed to consider Fuhrman's racial slurs—namely his bias. Clark was probably right that his invectives inflamed the passions of the African Americans on the jury. But by focusing entirely on this issue, she left herself open for the criticism she ultimately received from Cochran—that it was insulting to suggest that African Americans would lose their ability to be "calm and rational" because of Fuhrman's racial slurs.

Chris Darden

Chris Darden addressed the bias issue at least to some degree in his initial closing:

> And there are some people that think because Fuhrman is a racist, that we ought to chuck the law out of the window, perhaps it shouldn't be applied in this case.

> But even though there are a lot of small issues, a lot of other issues, a lot of little distractions here and there, you're here to address a single issue. This is a single case, one issue: Did the Defendant kill these two people. One Defendant, O. J. Simpson. You heard from the defense in this case and they presented testimony about slurs, epithets as they call them, a bunch of nasty, hateful, low-down language used by Mark Fuhrman. And I'm not even going to call him Detective Fuhrman if I can help it because he doesn't deserve that title. He doesn't warrant that kind of respect, not from me. But this isn't the case of Mark Fuhrman. This is the case of O. J. Simpson.

> And let me say this to you, if you will allow me to. And I don't mean to offend you or demean you, and I hope that you don't feel that I am. But this is the case of O. J. Simpson, not Mark Fuhrman. The case of Mark Fuhrman, if there's to be a case, that's a case for another forum, not necessarily a case for another day, because today may be the day. But it is a case for another forum, another jury perhaps.

> This case is about this Defendant, O. J. Simpson, and the "M" word, murder; not about Mark Fuhrman and the "N" word. And you know what that is.

> I am going to ask you to consider the fact of his misstatements or lies or untruths, however you want to term it, because you have to consider that. That's the law. You have to consider everything

---

[62] 1995 WL 672670 at 18–19.

Fuhrman said on the witness stand because that's evidence in this case.

And I want you to consider it. I want you to consider all the evidence. So don't think that I'm saying, hey, just overlook it, just overlook what he said, just overlook the fact that he lied about having used that slur in the past 10 years. But I am asking you to put it in the proper perspective. You decide what it's worth. You decide what it means. If it helps you in assessing his credibility—and it should, or his lack of credibility, I don't know—then you use it.

But please just remember, Fuhrman isn't the only issue in this case and his use of that word is not the only issue in this case. And you have to be concerned about that. I have to be concerned about it as a lawyer for the prosecution in this case because it apparently was a very, very significant event for the defense.

I mean, you saw all those people that came up to testify about Fuhrman's use of this word and then at one point, you heard a tape of Fuhrman. And that was Fuhrman by the way, okay, no doubt about that, using those slurs.

And you heard a tape of him using those slurs, and it had to make you angry to hear him say that. Made us angry. But that wasn't enough. Not only did you get to hear the words, you were given—the transcript was scrolled across the Elmo. Remember?

So you could hear it and you could see it. But that wasn't enough. You had to have a transcript for some reason of the words as well. A lot of emphasis on that. I don't know why. I know you do.

This evidence, just like all the other evidence in this case, attach whatever value you think is appropriate. I would say use it to assess his credibility, and other use you want to put to it, look to the law, look to the instructions that the Judge gives you.[63]

Darden recognized that the jury was allowed to use the Fuhrman evidence to assess his credibility but argued that Fuhrman wasn't the entire prosecution case. This was probably the best argument that he could have made at this point.

Johnnie Cochran

Cochran's closing argument was the most memorable of all, for a variety of reasons. His famous phrase "If it doesn't fit, you must acquit" was quoted liberally in the press. Newspapers published photographs of him wearing the knit skull cap during parts of the closing. And predictably, pundits in the media criticized him for legitimately arguing the significance of Fuhrman's racist views.

---

[63] *Id.* at 64–65.

THE PEOPLE v. ORENTHAL JAMES SIMPSON

Cochran spoke to the jurors as if he knew them personally. He had credibility with them because he connected to them as someone from their community who knew them and the Los Angeles police department. Cochran was persuasive in his use of words and images, and he delivered the closing in a way that convinced the jurors and everyone who heard it that he truly believed every word he said. This was personal to Cochran—the LAPD was destroying another black man—an innocent one—and it was the jury's responsibility to stop them. It was a message that made a lot of sense to these jurors, and they were more than willing to do what Cochran asked them to do. Early on, he reminded them of their duty:

> But your verdict in this case will go far beyond the walls of Department 102 because your verdict talks about justice in America and it talks about the police and whether they're above the law and it looks at the police perhaps as though they haven't been looked at very recently. Remember, I told you this is not for the naïve, the faint of heart or the timid.[64]

Cochran discussed the evidence in meticulous detail. After discussing the timeline, the physical evidence, and comparing the credibility of the prosecution and the defense witnesses, he reminded them of their duty before embarking on a theme that crystallized the relevance of Fuhrman's racial animus:

> And Mr. Darden said something very interesting today. He said, "I'm just the messenger." Now, how many times have you heard that; "I'm the messenger. Don't blame me, I'm just doing my job?"
>
> There's no way out. He's a fine lawyer, but he can't hide behind just being a messenger. Well, whose message is he sending? Who is he representing in this message? He's a man of integrity. That statement is not going to fly; "I'm just the messenger." He's not any messenger. He's the prosecutor with all the power of the State of California in this case.
>
> We are not going to let them get their way. We're not going to turn the Constitution on its head in this case. We are not going to allow it. And so now we bring you to a segment of this discussion where we talk about, if you can't trust the messengers, watch out for their messages.[65]

In addition to bonding with the jury and reminding them of their duty—"we're not going to allow it"—Cochran used a most effective technique—taking the words of opposing counsel and using them against him. "If you can't trust the messenger, you can't trust the message"

---

[64] 1995 WL 686429 at 10.

[65] *Id*. at 68.

became a recurring theme which succinctly and accurately explained why the jury should dismiss Fuhrman's testimony. Fuhrman was not a credible witness because he had an admitted extreme bias against African Americans and because he committed perjury right before the jurors' eyes.

Later, Cochran directly addressed Fuhrman and explained in detail why the jury should totally disregard all of his testimony:

> Let me tell you why you're going to know that. They want to talk a lot about 1985, but he missed the whole point. 1985, something interesting happened in this case. In 1985, Mark Fuhrman responded to a call on Rockingham. Mark Fuhrman is a lying, purging, genocidal racist, and from that moment on, any time he could get on O. J. Simpson, he would do it. That's when it started, in '85.

* * *

> It all comes back to Fuhrman when he says in that letter, "If I see an interracial couple, I'll stop them. If I don't have a reason, I'll make up a reason." This man thinks he's above the law ...

* * *

> And who would know Mark Fuhrman better in this case, his lack of credibility, his lying, racist views than Ron Phillips, his supervisor, who apparently chose to look the other way. And I am sure he is as embarrassed as anybody else by this disgrace, Fuhrman.

* * *

> Now, can you imagine this? Fuhrman with his views, genocidal views, was going to go over to give notice to O. J. Simpson, to help O. J. Simpson in his time of need. Can you imagine that? He's going over there to help him, help him with his kids. That is ludicrous.

> So from Riske to Bushey, you've seen and are seeing part of this code of silence, this cover-up, the cover-up that Laura McKinny talks about. The male officers get together to cover up for each other, don't tell the truth, hide, turn their head, cover. You can't trust this evidence. You can't trust the messenger. You can't trust the message.

> When Fuhrman gets on the witness stand and says, "I haven't used this 'N' word for 10 years," you think Phillips knows he's lying? Some of you probably knew he was lying. It took those tapes to make those of you who didn't believe these kind of things exist to take place.

> Didn't he have an obligation to come forward under those circumstances? For—if Fuhrman speaks so candidly to this lady he met in a restaurant in West L.A., you think he talks like that to the guys on

the Force? She talked about he said those words in police administration, police procedures, that's the way he talks. That's the way he
is. Nobody came forward to reveal this. We revealed it for you.

And let me just take a moment. This whole thing about the police
and what they've done in this case is extremely painful to us and I
think to all right-thinking citizens because you see, we live in Los
Angeles and we love this place. But all we want is a good and honest
police force where people are treated fairly no matter what part of
the city they're in. That's all you want. So in talking to you about
this, understand, there is no personal pride. But I told you when we
started, this is not for the weak or the faint of heart.

* * *

Then we come, before we end the day, to Detective Mark Fuhrman.
This man is an unspeakable disgrace. He's been unmasked for the
whole world for what he is, and that's hopefully positive. His
misdeeds go far beyond this case because he speaks of culture that's
not tolerable in America.

But let's talk about this case. People worry about, this is not the
case of Mark Fuhrman. Well, it's not the case of Mark Fuhrman.
Mark Fuhrman is not in custody. He's no—that's the man who
they're trying to put away with witnesses like this, a corrupt police
officer who is a liar and a perjurer.

You know, they were talking yesterday in their argument about,
"Well, gee, you think he would commit a felony?" What do you
think it was when he was asked the questions by F. Lee Bailey so
well put?

And we'll talk about that at the very end, about whether he ever
used the "N" word in 10 years and he swore to tell the truth and he
lied and others knew he lied. But what I find particularly troubling
is that they all knew about Mark Fuhrman and they weren't going
to tell you. They tried to ease him by.

Of all the witnesses who've testified in this case, how many were
taken up to the grand jury room where they have this prep session
to ask him all these questions? Miss Clark—I went back and I read
again her introduction of Mark Fuhrman. How many witnesses did
they do that with, where they took him up there and prepared him
for this?

Because you see, they knew about the Kathleen Bell letter, but she
didn't fit. She didn't fit what they wanted. They didn't want her.
They'd rather malign her and believe this lying police officer. So
they knew. Make no mistake about it.

And so when they try to prepare him, talk to him and get him ready and make him seem like a choir boy and make him come in here and raise his right hand as though he's going to tell the truth and give you a true story here, they knew he was a liar and a racist.[66]

In the following passage, Cochran starts out with a biblical reference to good vs. evil and quotes a well known phrase from William Cullen Bryant's poem "The Battlefield" that is frequently used in sermons and speeches. He then goes on to mock and chide Clark for coddling Fuhrman during her direct examination and does so in a way that puts her clearly in the "evil" camp that tried to "crush the truth."

There's something about good versus evil. There's something about truth. The truth crushed to earth will rise again. You can always count on that. So when Miss Clark so gently puts him on the stand and talks to him about, "Tell us how you feel about testifying today," "Nervous," okay, "Reluctant" and all the things about this bad lady Kathleen Bell—they brought it out at the beginning. "This bad Kathleen Bell saying all these mean things about you. Oh, and you don't—you don't know her even, do you? When we asked you to look at her on the Larry King Show and you couldn't recognize her. You don't know her. Oh, well, it's just terrible, all these bad things happening to you, Detective Fuhrman."

Go back and you look at your notes of how the testimony was as they tried to bring him in here and pass him off. These things were all happening. Kathleen Bell's letter was in '85 and '86, the same time he went out to O. J. Simpson's house in '85 they want to talk so much about.

What they are talking about is not even relevant. What we are talking about now is what happened in this case. It's so, after having made all these denials, been adopted and accepted by the prosecution. And they put him on the stand and you saw it. You saw it. It was sickening.[67]

Cochran explains Bailey's cross-examination to the jury:

And then my colleague, Lee Bailey, who can't be with us today, but God bless him, wherever he is, did his cross-examination of this individual and he asked some interesting questions. Some of you probably wondered, "I wonder why he's asking that." He asked this man whether or not he ever met Kathleen Bell. Of course, he lied about that.

* * *

---

[66] *Id.* at 70–76.

[67] *Id.* at 76.

And they try to tell you it's not important. Let's remember this man. This is the man who was off this case shortly after 2:00 o'clock in the morning right after he got on it. This is the man who didn't want to be off this case. This is the man, when they're ringing the door bell at Ashford, who goes for a walk. And he describes how he's strolling.

* * *

And that's when he walks down and he's the one who says the Bronco was parked askew and he sees some spot on the door. He makes all of the discoveries.

He's got to be the big man because he's had it in for O.J. because of his views since '85. This is the man, he's the guy who climbs over the fence. He's the guy who goes in and talks to Kato Kaelin while the other detectives are talking to the family. He's the guy who's shining a light in Kato Kaelin's eyes. He's the guy looking at shoes and looking for suspects. He's the guy who's doing these things.

He's the guy who says, "I don't tell anybody about the thumps on the wall." He's the guy who's off this case who's supposedly there to help this man, our client, O.J. Simpson, who then goes out all by himself, all by himself.

Now, he's worried about bodies or suspects or whatever. He doesn't even take out his gun. He goes around the side of the house, and lo and behold, he claims he finds this glove and he says the glove is still moist and sticky.

Now, under their theory, at 10:40, 10:45, that glove is dropped. How many hours is that? It's now after 6:00 o'clock. So what is that? Seven and a half hours. The testimony about drying time around here, no dew point that night. Why would it be moist and sticky unless he brought it over there and planted it there to try to make this case? And there is a Caucasian hair on that glove.

This man cannot be trusted. He is sinful to the prosecution, and for them to say he's not important is untrue and you will not fall for it, because as guardians of justice here, we can't let it happen.[68]

* * *

Throughout his closing argument, Cochran hammers away at his theme of the big cover-up, including not just the police department, but the prosecution team as well. He successfully paints the picture of a corrupt police officer and police department, and by extension, he includes the prosecution team.

---

[68] *Id.* at 76–77.

Why did they then all try to cover for this man Fuhrman? Why would this man who is not only Los Angeles' worst nightmare, but America's worse nightmare, why would they all turn their heads and try to cover for them? Why would you do that if you are sworn to uphold the law?

There is something about corruption. There is something about a rotten apple that will ultimately infect the entire barrel, because if the others don't have the courage that we have asked you to have in this case, people sit sadly by.[69]

* * *

Credibility doesn't attach to a title or position; it attaches to the person, so the person who may have a job where he makes two dollars an hour can have more integrity than the highest person. It is something from within. It is in your heart. It is what the Lord has put there. That is what we are talking about in this case.[70]

* * *

Cochran again quotes the key jury instruction that gives the jurors the permission to discard all of Fuhrman's testimony:

"A witness willfully false in one material part of his or her testimony is to be distrusted in others. You may reject the whole testimony of a witness who willfully has testified falsely to a material point unless from all the evidence you believe the probability of truth favors his or her testimony in other particulars."

Why is this instruction so important?

First of all, both prosecutors have now agreed that we have convinced them beyond a reasonable doubt, by the way, that he is a lying perjuring genocidal racist and he has testified falsely in this case on a number of scores. That is what his big lies tell you.

And when you go back in the jury room, some of you may want to say, well, gee, you know, boys will be boys. This is just like police talk. This is the way they talk. That is not acceptable as the consciences of this community if you adopt that attitude. That is why we have this, because nobody has had the courage to say it is wrong. You are empowered to say we are not going to take that any more. I'm sure you will do the right thing about that.

So that what then it says we must do is you have the authority, you may reject the whole testimony, you can then wipe out everything

---

[69] 1995 WL 697928 at 8.

[70] Id.

that Fuhrman told you, including the glove and all the things that he recovered with the glove.

That is why they are so worried. That is why when people say Fuhrman is not central, they are wearing blinds. They have lost their objectivity. They don't understand what they are talking about.

It is embarrassing for learned people to say that, but they are entitled to their opinions, but we are going to speak the truth. In a courtroom you are supposed to speak the truth. A witness who walks through those doors, who raises his or her hand, swears to tell the truth.

You've heard lie after lie after lie that has been exposed and when a witness lies in a material part of his testimony, you can wipe out all of his testimony as a judge of the facts.

That is your decision again. Nobody can tell you about that.

Lest you feel that a greater probability of truth lies in something else, they said wipe it out. This applies not only to Fuhrman, it applies to Vannatter and then you see what trouble their case is in, because they lied to get in there to do these when Vannatter carries that blood. They can't explain to you why he did that, because they were setting this man up, and that glove, anybody among you think that glove was just sitting there, just placed there, moist and sticky after six and a half hours?

* * *

Witnesses willfully false in one material part, distrusted in others. These two form basically the cornerstone of the prosecution's case.

Now, you know people talk all the time, well, you know, you are being conspiratorial and whatever. Gee, how would all these police officers set up O.J. Simpson? Why would they do that?

I will answer that question for you.

They believed he was guilty. They wanted to win. They didn't want to lose another big case. That is why. They believed that he was guilty.

These actions rose from what their belief was, but they can't make that—the prosecutors can't make that judgment. Nobody but you can make that judgment.

So when they take the law into their own hands, they become worse than the people who break the law, because they are the protectors of the law.[71]

---

[71] *Id.* at 9–10.

After establishing the corruption and the cover-up, Cochran makes it clear to the jurors that they are the only people on earth that can put an end to it. He lays a heavy responsibility at their feet and he does it in a way that makes them almost heroes in the following passage that has been quoted repeatedly:

> Who then polices the police? You police the police. You police them by your verdict. You are the ones to send the message. Nobody else is going to do it in this society. They don't have the courage nobody has the courage.[72]

* * *

Have we proved that? Have we proved that it was compromised, contaminated and corrupted? And yes, even something more sinister—I think you will believe we do, but there is something else about this man Fuhrman that I have to say before I am going to terminate this part of my opening argument and relinquish the floor to my learned colleague Mr. Barry Scheck, is something that Fuhrman said.

And I'm going to ask Mr. Douglas and Mr. Harris to put that Kathleen Bell letter. You know, it is one thing, and I dare say that most of you, when you heard Fuhrman said he hadn't used the "N" word, that you probably thought, well, he is lying, we know that is not true. That is just part of it. That is just want the prosecutors want to do, just talk about that part of it.

That is not the part that bothers us on the defense. I live in America. I understand. I know about slights everyday of my life.

But I want to tell you about what is troubling, what is frightening, what is chilling about that Kathleen Bell letter.

* * *

You will recall that God is good and he always brings you a way to see light when there is a lot of darkness around, and just through chance this lady had tried to reach Shapiro's office, couldn't reach it, and in July of 1994 she sent this fax to my office, and my good, loyal and wonderful staff got that letter to me early on.

She says some interesting things. And she wasn't a fan of O.J. Simpson. What does she say?

"I'm writing to you in regards to a story I saw on the news last night. I thought it ridiculous that the Simpson defense team would even suggest that there might be racial motivation involved in the trial against Mr. Simpson."

---

[72] *Id.* at 10.

Yes, there are a lot of people out there who thought that at that time, and you know, you can't fault people for being naïve, but once they know, if they continue to be naïve, then you can fault them. That is what it is and this is why this case is important.

Don't ever say again in this county or in this country that you don't know things like this exist. Don't pretend to be naïve any more. Don't turn your heads. Stand up, show some integrity.

* * *

And so Fuhrman, Fuhrman wants to take all black people now and burn them or bomb them. That is genocidal racism. Is that ethnic purity? What is that? What is that? We are paying this man's salary to espouse these views? Do you think he only told Kathleen Bell whom he just had met? Do you think he talked to his partners about it? Do you think commanders knew about it? Do you think everybody knew about it and turned their heads? Nobody did anything about it. Things happen for a reason in you life.

* * *

You cannot believe these people. You can't trust the message. You can't trust the messengers. It is frightening. It is quite, frankly frightening, and it is not enough for the prosecutors now to stand up and say, oh, well, let's just back off.

The point I was trying to make, they didn't understand that it is not just using the "N" word. Forget that. We knew he was lying about that. Forget that. It is about the lengths to which he would go to get somebody black and also white if they are associated with black.

That is pretty frightening. It is not just African Americans, it is white people who would associate or deign to go out with a black man or marry one. You are free in America to love whoever you want, so it infects all of us, doesn't it, this one rotten apple, and yet they cover for him. Yet they cover for him.

* * *

Can you imagine the gall about that that you have racist views and yet would you put it on tape? Thank God he put it on tape. And so Kathleen Bell came in here and told you the same things in those letters...

* * *

But this man, Fuhrman, does it with immunity and his partner sat there and heard it and didn't report it. There is something rotten about this kind of conduct, that it is going on too long.

* * *

I started off talking to you a little bit about Frederick Douglas and what he said more than a hundred years ago, for there are still the Mark Fuhrmans in this world, in this country, who hate and are yet embraced by people in power.[73]

Finally, he makes it clear that they are working together as a team—Cochran and the jury—fighting together to preserve the basic values of the Constitution that Fuhrman, the police department, and the prosecution team tried to destroy:

But you and I, fighting for freedom and ideals and for justice for all, must continue to fight to expose hate and genocidal racism and these tendencies.

We then become the guardians of the Constitution, as I told you yesterday, for if we as the people don't continue to hold a mirror up to the face of America and say this is what you promised, this is what you delivered, if you don't speak out, if you don't stand up, if you don't do what's right, this kind of conduct will continue on forever and we will never have an ideal society, one that lives out the true meaning of the creed of the Constitution or of life, liberty and justice for all.

I'm going to take my seat, but I get one last time to address you, as I said before.

This is a case about an innocent man wrongfully accused. You have seen him now for a year and two days. You observed him during good times and the bad times.

Soon it will be your turn. You have the keys to his future. You have the evidence by which you can acquit this man. You have not only the patience, but the integrity and the courage to do the right thing.

We believe you will do the right thing, and the right thing is to find this man not guilty on both of these charges.[74]

Barry Scheck then delivered his part of the closing argument, which explained the scientific evidence to the jury in detail and demonstrated how the scientific evidence supported the defense theory of a plant and coverup. After Scheck's part, Cochran concluded the argument and finished with a final reference to their duty as jurors that was heavily-laden with references from the Bible:

In times like these we often turn to the Bible for some answers to try to figure out when you've got situations like this and you want to get an answer and you want to try to understand.

---

[73] Id. at 10–14.

[74] Id. at 16–17.

I happen to really like the Book of Proverbs and in Proverbs it talks a lot about false witnesses. It says that a false witness shall not be unpunished and he that speaketh lies shall not escape. That meant a lot to me in this case because there was Mark Fuhrman acting like a choirboy, making you believe he was the best witness that walked in here, generally applauded for his wonderful performance.

It turns out he was the biggest liar in this courtroom during this process, for the Bible had already told us the answer, that a false witness shall not be unpunished and he that speaketh lies shall not escape.

In that same book it tells us that a faithful witness will not lie but a false witness will utter lies.

Finally in Proverbs it says that he that speaketh the truth showeth the forthrightfulness but a false witness shows deceit.

* * *

You know when things are at the darkest there is always light the next day. In your life, in all of our lives, you have the capacity to transform Mr. O. J. Simpson's dark yesterday into bright tomorrow. You have that capacity. You have that power in your hand.

And James Russell Lowell said it best about wrong and evil. He said that truth forever on the scaffold, wrong forever on the throne, yet that scaffold sways the future and beyond the dim unknown standeth God within the shadows, keeping watch above His own.

You walk with that everyday, you carry that with you and things will come to you and you will be able to reveal people who come to you in uniforms and high positions who lie and are corrupt.

That is what happened in this case and so the truth is now out. It is now up to you. We are going to pass this baton to you soon.

You will do the right thing. You have made a commitment for justice. You will do the right thing.

I will some day go on to other cases, no doubt as will Miss Clark and Mr. Darden. Judge Ito will try another case some day, I hope, but this is O. J. Simpson's one day in Court.

By your decision you control his very life your hands. Treat it carefully. Treat it fairly. Be fair.

Don't be part of this continuing cover-up. Do the right thing remembering that if it doesn't fit, you must acquit, that if these messengers have lied to you, you can't trust their message, that this has been a search for truth.

That no matter how bad it looks, if truth is out there on a scaffold and wrong is in here on the throne, when that scaffold sways the future and beyond the dim unknown standeth the same God for all people keeping watch above His own.

He watches all of us and He will watch you in your decision. Thank you for your attention. God bless you.[75]

Cochran's frequent references to the Bible and his oratorical style were extremely effective with this jury. He believed in his message and he delivered it with passion and eloquence. It would be difficult for any lawyer to rebut, and it was especially difficult for Darden.

Darden's Rebuttal

Darden's rebuttal was reminiscent of his behavior towards Cochran throughout the trial. He did his best to show the jury that he could relate to them as much as Cochran, but his efforts fell short, and at times, were rather bizarre. After urging the jury not to rely on their emotion and accusing Cochran of injecting race into the case, Darden then made the following odd statement:

I heard the words they spoke yesterday about the Constitution. I read the Constitution. I'm a lawyer, I am a student of the Constitution. I know what it means and what it doesn't mean. I know what it is.

And Gil Scott–Heron said that the Constitution was just a notebook piece of paper. You remember that?[76]

Darden's strange statement about his knowledge of the constitution once again sounded like a little kid protesting that he was just as smart as Cochran. His reference to Gil Scott–Heron is baffling. Scott–Heron is a rather obscure African American poet/singer who was popular during the late sixties and seventies. He was as well known for his heroin addiction as he was for his poetry and music. It is doubtful that any of the jurors even knew who Scott–Heron was, but if they did, it was quite risky for Darden to assume that the jurors were fans. Furthermore, the quote about the Constitution didn't make any sense in the context of what Darden was saying. He went on to take quite a bit of poetic license with the constitution:

I also looked back at the Constitution last night, I sent my clerk to go get it for me, and I looked through the Constitution, and you know what I saw? I saw some stuff in the Constitution about Ron and about Nicole and the Constitution said that Ron and Nicole had the right to liberty. It said that they had the right to life. It said that

---

[75] 1995 WL 697930 at 49–50.

[76] 1995 WL 704342 at 5.

they had a right to the pursuit of happiness. It said that Nicole didn't have to stay with him if she didn't want to stay with him. That is what the Constitution said.

And I looked further and I looked in the Constitution to see if it said anything about O. J. Simpson. You know what it said? It said he doesn't have the right to take those lives. He did not have the right to do what he did.[77]

Darden decided to tell a story about Martin Luther King, but it was clearly an attempt to connect to the black jurors because it didn't help to illustrate any point that was important to the prosecution case. He told the story of how someone stabbed Dr. King in a book store in Harlem and left the knife in his chest. After the stabbing, Dr. King kept telling those around him to be calm and wait for the ambulance. Later, the surgeon who saved his life told Dr. King that the blade was next to his aorta and if he had not remained calm and had moved suddenly, he would have drowned in his own blood. After telling this story, Darden then said:

Some folks would like to get you all riled up and get you so upset that you move suddenly and so that you drown in the minutia, so that you choke on the smoke. Some people want to make you mad and angry and bitter.

King once wrote that we should never succumb to the temptation of bitterness and that the one thing about bitterness is its blindness. So don't be blinded by all of this; just do your job. I know what your job is. I know you know what to do.[78]

This analogy was at best a stretch and at worse, a not-so-veiled attempt to impress the black jurors with his knowledge of a great black leader.

Later in his rebuttal, Darden again referred to Dr. King and also to Malcolm X in another strange and obvious attempt to invoke the names of black leaders:

I will go back to Martin because I feel comfortable with Martin Luther King. Actually I have some Malcolm X, but I'm not going to drop that today. I don't want to get that deep.

* * *

Read along with me what Martin Luther King said about justice. "Justice is the same for all issues. It cannot be categorized. It is not possible to be in favor of justice for some people and not be in favor of justice for all people. Justice cannot be divided. Justice is indivisible."

---

[77] Id.

[78] Id. at 7.

Darden concluded his part of the rebuttal argument with a discussion of the crime scene, the timeline, and the glove demonstration. Clark finished with more discussion of the scientific evidence and the domestic violence evidence that was largely repetitive.

The Verdict

On October 2nd, the jury reached a verdict of "Not Guilty" after only four hours of deliberation. The verdict was announced on October 3rd, and media outlets all over the world were poised to capture the moment. The contrast in the reactions to the verdict along racial lines could not have been starker. Some television networks showed split screens with all black audiences and all white audiences when the verdict was announced. The black audiences cheered and celebrated while the white audiences expressed shock, sadness and anger.[79] The Simpson verdict, more than any other in modern history, demonstrated the deep racial divide in America.

Not all African Americans were happy about the Simpson verdict, but polls demonstrated that the overwhelming majority of African Americans supported the verdict.[80] Simpson was certainly not the most popular figure among African Americans. In fact, he was not very connected to the African American community. Nonetheless, the support for the verdict was not surprising. It was more an expression of relief and joy that a black man could be treated fairly in the criminal justice system than an expression of happiness for Simpson. African Americans have been treated unfairly in the criminal justice system from the time of the Black Codes to lynching to the present day—both as defendants and as victims of crime.[81] Thus, for most African Americans, the Simpson verdict was about so much more than Simpson.

There was widespread criticism of the verdict from pundits and legal commentators in the mainstream media. The jurors were called every-

---

[79] KATHERYN RUSSELL-BROWN, PROTECTING OUR OWN—RACE, CRIME, AND AFRICAN AMERICANS (Rowman & Littlefield Publishers, Inc., 2006), 11.

[80] GALLUP POLL, Oct. 5–7, 1995 (reporting that 78% of African Americans polled stated that they believed the verdict was right), *available at http://www.law.umkc.edu/faculty/projects/ftrials/Simpson/polls.html*.

[81] *See generally*, A. LEON HIGGINBOTHAM, IN THE MATTER OF COLOR: THE COLONIAL PERIOD (Oxford University Press, 1978) (tracing the black experience in colonial America); RANDALL KENNEDY, RACE, CRIME, AND LAW (Pantheon Books 1997) (exploring the history of race discrimination in the criminal justice system); KATHRYN RUSSELL-BROWN, THE COLOR OF CRIME: RACIAL HOAXES, WHITE FEAR, BLACK PROTECTIONISM, POLICE HARASSMENT, AND OTHER MACROAGGRESSIONS (New York University Press 1998) (noting that racism continues to undermine society's criminal justice system and skews the public's perception of its black citizens and crime).

thing from lazy to stupid.[82] Very few commentators acknowledged that it was reasonable for the jury to conclude that the government did not prove its case beyond a reasonable doubt. Yet most trial lawyers understood the verdict and believed that it made sense in light of the evidence and the advocacy.

If verdicts could be predicted by the quality of the trial advocacy, the Simpson verdict was predictable. Although neither side was perfect, the prosecutors made too many mistakes that were fundamental and that permanently damaged their case. From the decision to ignore all the clear warning signs about Fuhrman to the glove demonstration, the prosecution did more to create reasonable doubt than the defense. Although members of the defense team made mistakes as well, ultimately they made smarter decisions—from voir dire to closing arguments. Most importantly, the lawyers on the defense team understood the art of persuasion and were better advocates.

One of the most important differences in the trial advocacy of the prosecution and defense teams was the way each side handled the issue of race. Race was a central issue in the case, and the prosecutors largely chose to ignore it. That decision was not only unwise but costly. On the other hand, with the exception of Shapiro, the defense attorneys understood that race had to be a consideration in every decision from voir dire to closing arguments. The decisions about race probably affected the verdict more than all others.

Race is a constant and deep-seated influence on almost every issue in American life. Whether consciously or unconsciously, it is the lens through which Americans view, think about, and evaluate almost everything around us. Of the many lessons of the Simpson case, surely one of the greatest is the power and influence of race and its impact on trials in America.

---

[82] *See* Russell–Brown, *supra* note 79, at 53–55.

8

Barbara Bergman[1]

The Sweet Trials

On September 9, 1925, as a white mob surrounded the home of Dr. Ossian Sweet in Detroit, Michigan, a shot rang out killing Leon Breiner. The police arrested the eleven black occupants of the Sweet home, including Dr. Sweet, his wife Gladys, his brothers Henry and Otis, and seven friends, charging them all with Breiner's murder. Seven weeks later, on October 30, 1925, the murder trial began with Clarence Darrow representing all eleven defendants.

The events leading to the trial were symptomatic of the racial tensions that existed in Detroit and many other northern cities at the time. In 1910, approximately six thousand blacks lived in Detroit. As the demand for more workers mushroomed with the growth of the automobile industry, manufacturers began recruiting poor whites and blacks, particularly from the South, with the lure of higher wages and a better life. The great northward migration had begun. By 1924, the black population in Detroit totaled approximately seventy thousand people—most of whom lived in segregated housing in an area of the city known as Black Bottom.[2] Living conditions in Black Bottom were deplorable but demand for housing by the blacks moving to Detroit was so great that the landlords could charge exorbitant rents and had little incentive to make repairs.[3]

At the same time, the Ku Klux Klan had become a powerful political force in Detroit. In 1923, the Klan had twenty-two thousand Detroit

---

[1] Professor of Law, University of New Mexico School of Law.

[2] KEVIN BOYLE, ARC OF JUSTICE 108–13 (2004). Professor Boyle's book, a winner of the National Book Award which is cited often in this chapter, is an exhaustively researched and masterful discussion of the history and people who were an integral part of this case. Anyone wishing a detailed, historical analysis should read this book.

[3] *Id.* at 109–13.

members,[4] and by 1924 that number had grown to thirty-five thousand.[5] In November 1924, the Klan had tried to get Charles Bowles, one of its members, elected mayor in a special election held to fill the position of the previous mayor who had resigned due to illness. Although Bowles initially won the election by seven thousand votes, the election commission eventually threw out seventeen thousand of Bowles' ballots giving the election to his opponent, John Smith.[6] Because Smith was only filling out the unexpired term of the previous mayor, he had to run for re-election in November 1925, and the Klan was gearing up for a vicious campaign. In July 1925, the Klan held a rally on Detroit's west side which was attended by ten thousand members in white robes illuminated by a burning cross.[7] One of the ways the Klan sought to stir up the fears and anger of the Detroit voters was "to raise the specter of the Negro masses pouring across the color line into white man's land."[8]

Even before this electoral campaign, when blacks tried to move out of Black Bottom into white neighborhoods, they were often met with open opposition from the Klan as well as whites who, while not supportive of the Klan, still wanted to maintain segregated housing. In the early 1920s, restrictive covenants preventing the sale of property to blacks had become a common practice.[9] When blacks were successful in purchasing property in white neighborhoods, white mobs often attacked them. In the summer of 1925, five such mobs attacked black families in Detroit forcing them from their homes. Dr. Sweet was personally acquainted with one of the victims, Dr. Alexander Turner, chief of surgery at Dunbar Memorial Hospital. Dr. Turner had purchased a home on Spokane Avenue, an all-white neighborhood on Detroit's west side. Only five hours after he had moved in, a white mob attacked and, after gaining entry, ransacked the home. Barely escaping with his life, Dr. Turner later that night signed over the deed to the house to the "neighborhood improvement society" that had stirred up the mob.[10] During that summer, Dr. Sweet had listened to Dr. Turner describe in detail the horrors of that night.[11]

---

[4] *Id.* at 140.

[5] *Id.* at 8.

[6] *Id.* at 140–43.

[7] *Id.* at 24.

[8] *Id.* at 143.

[9] *Id.* at 144.

[10] *Id.* at 25.

[11] *Id.*

Racial violence was not new to Dr. Sweet. He was born in 1895 to a hard-working farm family in central Florida, the second of ten children.[12] As a youngster, he claimed to have witnessed the death of Fred Rochelle, a sixteen-year-old black who had confessed to raping and murdering a white woman. Dr. Sweet later described how he had seen a white mob place the young man on a hogshead of flammable material and then chain him to a tree. They stacked dry wood around the base and poured gasoline on the pile. The victim's husband struck the match. Dr. Sweet would "recount with frightening specificity: the smell of the kerosene, Rochelle's screams as he was engulfed in flames, the crowd's picking off pieces of charred flesh to take home as souvenirs."[13]

When he was thirteen, Ossian's parents put him on a northbound train to Xenia, Ohio, to attend Wilberforce University to obtain the education that would help him escape the hard-scrabble life they had lived. He spent eight years at Wilberforce, graduating in 1917. His poor eyesight disqualified him from military service in the World War I so he moved to Washington, D.C. to attend Howard University's College of Medicine.[14] Racial tension had been building in Washington after the end of the war, and in July of 1919, it exploded. A white mob roamed the streets of the city looking for black victims. Some of the worst fighting took place a few blocks south of the Howard campus. It took four days to eventually bring the mob under control. During the riot, Dr. Sweet saw the mob pull a black passenger from a passing street car and savagely beat him.[15]

Dr. Sweet graduated from Howard Medical School in 1921 and moved back to Detroit where he had spent summers working to earn money to pay for his college education. He received his medical license in November 1921, the only black man to qualify that year, and opened his medical practice in Black Bottom.[16] During this time Dr. Sweet began to take a more active interest in racial issues. He subscribed to all the major black newspapers and publications, reading about the lynching of black men throughout the country as well as the race riots in Tulsa, Oklahoma and Rosewood, Florida.[17]

By 1922, Dr. Sweet's practice was doing well. He met Gladys Mitchell, and they married in December of that year. His new wife was

---

[12] *Id.* at 59–62.

[13] *Id.* at 67–69.

[14] *Id.* at 87.

[15] *Id.* at 95–97.

[16] *Id.* at 113.

[17] *Id.* at 121–24.

too cultured and sheltered to live in Black Bottom so the newlyweds moved in with her mother and stepfather who lived in a working class primarily white neighborhood.[18] On October 6, 1923, the couple left for Europe. They spent the first three months in Vienna while Dr. Sweet attended lectures given by a leading surgeon, Anton von Eiselsberg, at the University of Vienna. They then moved to Paris for the winter and spring where Marie Curie was teaching at the Sorbonne and Dr. Sweet could attend her lectures on radium therapy's curative powers.[19]

While in Paris, Gladys gave birth to their daughter, Marguerite. Dr. Sweet had hoped that their child could be delivered at the American Hospital, a private institution providing care for American expatriates living in Paris. Despite making a donation to the hospital, when it came time for her delivery, the hospital refused to accept Gladys because she was black. Luckily, Gladys and the child did not need any special medical attention, but Dr. Sweet was deeply insulted by the hospital's action.[20]

Upon their return to Detroit, the Sweets again moved in with Mrs. Sweet's family but began the search for a home of their own. On three occasions, they found promising houses but each time they were turned away because they were black. Finally, in May 1925, they found a home at 2905 Garland that was for sale. It was located in a white, working class neighborhood; and its owner was willing to sell to the Sweets, although she increased her asking price to $18,500, substantially more than it would have cost if sold to a white family. Despite the usurious terms of sale, the Sweets signed the purchase agreement on June 7 1925.[21] The owners agreed to vacate the home by August 1.

Word spread through the neighborhood that a black family had purchased the Garland property. Those who objected to the Sweets moving into the home created the Waterworks Park Improvement Association, an organization committed to keeping blacks generally—and the Sweets in particular—out of the community. The Association adopted a constitution and bylaws and began a campaign to impose restrictive covenants on property in the area.[22] A public rally held on July 14th attracted seven hundred people.[23] A few days later a committee from the Association visited Marie Smith, who had sold the house to the Sweets, in an effort to convince her to revoke the deal. She refused unless the

---

[18] *Id*. at 124–27.

[19] *Id*. at 127–31.

[20] *Id*. at 132.

[21] *Id*. at 145–46.

[22] *Id*. at 158–60.

[23] *Id*. at 134.

Association was willing to pay her new asking price of $30,000, which they were not.[24]

The Sweets had postponed moving into the Garland property because of concerns about their safety. Finally, on September 8, 1925, the family moved into the home, leaving their infant daughter with her grandmother. Aware of the hostility in the neighborhood, the police had made arrangements, at Dr. Sweet's request, to provide around-the-clock protection for the family until the neighborhood quieted down. Despite the promised police presence, when moving into the house, Dr. Sweet had brought a shotgun, two rifles, six pistols and four hundred rounds of ammunition in case they needed to protect themselves.[25]

That afternoon, Gladys and Ossian were in the home along with Joe Mack, their chauffeur, Norris Murray, a hired handyman, Otis and Henry, the doctor's two brothers, and John Latting, Henry's friend and classmate. Later in the day, Edna Butler, a seamstress, and Serena Rochelle, an interior decorator, who were friends of Mrs. Sweet's arrived to help plan the decorating of the new home.[26] Gladys insisted upon fixing dinner for everyone and they lost track of time. It had gotten dark before Mack, Murray, Butler and Rochelle thought about leaving, and by then it was too late. When Dr. Sweet looked out, he realized that a white crowd of several hundred had gathered across the street from his home and in a nearby school yard. The police were keeping the crowd off the sidewalk directly in front of the house.[27] Dr. Sweet took the men upstairs and distributed the guns. With the lights extinguished, the men stood guard at the upstairs windows with their weapons in hand. Everyone remained in the house and most spent a sleepless night. Hours passed but nothing of consequence happened. The next morning Gladys' friends as well as Murray, Otis and Davis left. Henry and Latting stayed at the house to keep watch, while Mack drove Dr. Sweet and Gladys out to run errands.[28]

The next night Dr. Sweet, his wife, and his two brothers as well as seven friends who had offered to help the doctor were in the home. As they looked out, they saw that an even larger crowd had gathered outside—hundreds of whites were milling about. This time, shortly after eight, the mob began to throw stones and chunks of coal at the house shattering several windows. Suddenly, at around 8:25 p.m.,[29] Dr. Sweet

---

[24] *Id.* at 165–66.

[25] *Id.* at 27.

[26] *Id.* at 27–28.

[27] *Id.* at 27–29.

[28] *Id.* at 30.

[29] Arthur Garfield Hays, Let Freedom Ring 195 (1937).

heard two volleys of gunshots being fired from the upstairs bedrooms. In the second volley, one of the shots struck Leon Breiner in the back. The shot was fatal.[30]

Realizing that a bystander had been shot and probably killed, the police called for reinforcements to help control the mob. They then went into the Sweet home and placed everyone under arrest. The police managed to get all eleven suspects in a paddy wagon despite the presence of the enraged mob around the Garland home that police later estimated grew to four or five thousand people.[31] The police kept the mob from destroying the home. By midnight, passions had cooled, and only a few hundred people remained outside the Sweet residence.

At that point, Inspector Norman Schuknecht, the commanding officer on the scene, invited a newspaper reporter into the Sweet home. As they toured the house, Schuknecht gave the reporter his version of what had happened. According to Schuknecht, he had been on the street right before the shooting. He insisted that there had not been any mob threatening the home and no stones had been thrown. Instead, the street was peaceful when the occupants opened fire for no discernible reason. That was the version printed in the Detroit papers the next morning, and that was the story provided to the public.[32]

While Inspector Schuknecht was talking to the reporter, other officers took the eleven suspects to police headquarters where Ted Kennedy, an assistant prosecutor, interrogated them. During the interviews, each of the men initially told an unbelievable story that they had been at the Sweet home for a variety of reasons unrelated to any possible mob attack. The three insurance agents were there to correct an error on the doctor's policy. The chauffeur was just there doing his job. The handyman had come by to get paid for some previous work, and the remaining two were potential boarders who had come to look at the rooms. All insisted there had been no discussion about a possible mob or any efforts to protect the home and no guns had been distributed. These stories did not hold up very long under Kennedy's questioning.[33]

Mrs. Sweet was somewhat more forthcoming stating that they had been informed that there might be trouble. She admitted the presence of the guns and the fact that they had talked about using them, if necessary; but that was all she would say.[34] When Kennedy asked Dr.

---

[30] BOYLE, ARC OF JUSTICE 33–40.

[31] Id. at 182.

[32] Id. at 182–85.

[33] Id. at 174–75.

[34] Id. at 176–77.

Sweet why he had moved into the neighborhood, Dr. Sweet responded, "Because I bought the house and it was my house and I felt I had a right to live in it."[35] During those interrogations, the only one who admitted firing a shot was Henry Sweet, Dr. Sweet's twenty-one-year-old brother, who stated that he fired his rifle from an upstairs window to protect himself. The first time, he fired into the air. The second time he fired into the crowd. Although he had not aimed at anyone in particular, he claimed to have tried to fire a foot or two above the mob to frighten them off.[36] By 3:30 a.m. the interrogations were completed, and the prisoners were taken to the Wayne County Jail to await further proceedings.[37]

News about what had happened at the Sweet home spread quickly through the black community. Eventually, Dr. Sweet called his friend Julian Perry, a local black attorney. Perry in turn contacted Cecil Rowlette, a more experienced criminal defense attorney, for help. Hewitt Watson, one of the eleven under arrest, called Charles Mahoney, another local black attorney, requesting his assistance. When Perry, Rowlette and Mahoney tried to speak to their clients, the police refused them access.[38] Not until more than forty years later when the Supreme Court decided the *Miranda* case did the courts recognize a defendant's right to have an attorney present during questioning.[39] As a result, the Detroit police at this point were not willing to let the defense attorneys speak to their clients.

By the morning of September 10, the three attorneys had agreed to form a joint defense team. They promptly filed a habeas corpus petition. The first judge to whom they presented the petition denied it, but the attorneys eventually got the writ from a circuit court judge. Although the attorneys did not expect that this tactic would secure the release of their clients, they were hopeful that the writ would force the prosecution to file formal charges and they could then convince the court to dismiss the charges on the grounds that the defendants had acted in self-defense.

Thirty-eight year old Robert Toms was the Wayne County chief prosecutor. He was generally known as a "decent man," but he was also a man with political ambition, who quickly realized that if he wished to have any political future, he would have to prosecute these eleven

---

[35] *Id.* at 172–74.

[36] *Id.* at 177–78.

[37] *Id.* at 38–43; 170–79.

[38] *Id.* at 179–81.

[39] Miranda v. Arizona, 384 U.S. 436 (1966); *but see* Moran v. Burbine, 475 U.S. 412 (1986) (holding that *Miranda* was not violated when a suspect waived his rights and police refused to allow an attorney hired by the suspect's sister to see him while he was in custody).

suspects. Based on the versions provided by the police and eyewitnesses at the scene, his strategy was to argue that the occupants of the house had no reason to be afraid since there was no mob outside the home.[40] Thus, the shooting was not justified. At that point, Toms presented warrants to Frank Murphy, the criminal court's presiding judge, charging the defendants with the first degree murder of Leon Breiner and assault with intent to commit murder for wounding a second bystander. Judge Murphy took the warrants under advisement. Now that charges had been filed, the defense attorneys were permitted to meet with their clients almost three days after the shooting.

That night the Waterworks Park Improvement Association held a mass meeting with a thousand people in attendance. The secretary of the Association was joined on the podium by two Klansmen. Later that same night, the Klan held its own rally. The city was in turmoil. The next day the defense attorneys' hopes were dashed when Judge Murphy handed down the signed warrants and scheduled a bail hearing for the following Saturday.[41] The prosecution was moving forward.

While the attorneys were developing their legal strategy, the local NAACP Detroit branch had gone into action trying to raise funds and assuring the defendants that it would pay for the entire cost of the defense.[42] At the NAACP office in New York, James Weldon Johnson, the executive secretary of the organization, saw a newspaper article about the Sweet case and thought it looked promising as a vehicle for attacking segregation. Beginning in 1917, the NAACP had been challenging segregated housing practices in the courts. It had been successful in getting the Supreme Court to strike down a city ordinance in Louisville, Kentucky, which "prevent[ed] the occupancy of a lot in the city of Louisville by a person of color in a block where the greater number of residences [were] occupied by white persons."[43] Finding such statutory restrictions closed to them, segregationists had turned to other methods to achieve the same outcome. Restrictive covenants preventing white homeowners from selling to blacks and discriminatory mortgage practices proved equally effective at creating black urban ghettos. In 1923, the NAACP became involved in another court case—this time challenging restrictive covenants.[44] Johnson hoped to rally national support for these challenges

---

[40] BOYLE, ARC OF JUSTICE at 185–87.

[41] Id. at 192–94.

[42] Id. at 194.

[43] Buchanan v. Warley, 245 U.S. 60, 73 (1917) (striking down the ordinance on the grounds that the Fourteenth Amendment prevented such state interference with private property rights).

[44] In May 1926, the United States Supreme Court dismissed that case on the grounds that, because it did not present a substantial constitutional question, the Court lacked

and also hoped to be able to use the publicity they generated to raise money to finance the continued work of the NAACP.

The NAACP coffers had been badly depleted. Johnson saw the issue of segregation as one which had the potential to bring together a coalition of many different ethnic minorities—all of whom were subject to such practices. His efforts to use this issue to raise money initially proved unsuccessful. Then in the fall of 1925, Johnson came up with the idea of creating an NAACP Legal Defense Fund, which would request money from the American Fund for Public Service, a philanthropic organization created by Charles Garland with a million dollar inheritance from his father. Johnson proposed seeking $25,000 from the Fund and then matching it with an additional $25,000 of private contributions. To raise the $25,000 in private contributions, Johnson knew that he needed a cause that would capture the attention of the black community and encourage them to donate money.[45]

After reading the newspaper article about the Sweet case, Johnson thought he may have found what he needed. He contacted the local Detroit NAACP branch asking for more information and then offering "all cooperation possible." At first, the local branch wanted to handle the case on its own, but within a few days, W. Hayes McKinney from the Detroit branch asked the New York office to send Walter White, Johnson's assistant secretary, to Detroit as soon as possible in the hope that he could slip by the police guards and search the Sweet home for evidence.[46] White arrived in Detroit on Tuesday morning, September

---

jurisdiction. The Court noted: "It is obvious that none of these [constitutional] amendments prohibited private individuals from entering into contracts respecting the control and disposition of their own property. . . ." Corrigan v. Buckley, 271 U.S. 323, 330 (1926).

[45] BOYLE, ARC OF JUSTICE at 203–06.

[46] White once wrote: "I am a Negro. My skin is white, my eyes are blue, my hair is blond. The traits of my race are nowhere visible upon me." WALTER WHITE, A MAN CALLED WHITE: THE AUTOBIOGRAPHY OF WALTER WHITE 3 (1948). In his work for the NAACP, White's appearance gave him access to people, places, and information that he would not have had if viewed as black.

Over the next few years after he started working for the NAACP, White exposed lynch mobs across the South, walked the streets of riot-torn South Chicago, uncovered the perfidy behind the 1919 pogrom in Phillips County Arkansas, exposed electoral violence in 1920 in Florida, and revealed the gruesome details of the infamous 1921 race riot in Tulsa, where he went so far as to join a white posse patrolling the burned-out black section of town. It was extremely dangerous work. As he was gathering information in the tiny town of Helena, Arkansas, in 1919, a colored man took him aside to say that whites had discovered his identity. Walter raced to the nearby depot and leapt onto the first train heading north. The conductor couldn't understand why he was in such a rush to get out of town. "But you're leaving, mister, just when the fun is going to start," the man said. "There's a damn yellow nigger down here passing for white and the boys are going to get him." "What will they do to him?" White

15th with other plans. He met with Ira Jayne, a circuit court judge who was a member of the NAACP executive board. Jayne explained to him that Detroit had split straight down the color line and he was worried that there would be additional rioting. He was also convinced that as long as black lawyers were in charge of the defense, any jury would convict the defendants. He advised White to hire the most prestigious white lawyer the NAACP could find to take over the case. When White told the local counsel that they were to be demoted, they strongly objected. They had a preliminary hearing scheduled the next day,[47] and they refused to be replaced by any white lawyer.

At the preliminary hearing, Lester Moll, an assistant prosecutor who was to try to case with Toms, did not directly prove that there was a conspiracy to shoot into the crowd, for which he had little, if any, evidence. Instead, he focused on the evidence that the neighborhood was peaceful; and, therefore, the defendants—whoever fired the shots—had no justification for doing so. The logic of his argument was that if the defendants were in no danger, then they must have moved into the neighborhood to provoke a confrontation. Such motivation supposedly showed a conspiracy by implication.[48] Although the defense attorneys on cross-examination tried to get the state's witnesses to concede that there was a large mob throwing rocks at the house before the shots were fired, the witnesses refused to change their testimony. Perhaps because of the strong emotions the case had generated in the city, despite the weaknesses in the state's presentation, Judge Faust found probable cause and bound the case over for trial.[49]

Shortly after the ruling in the preliminary hearing, White returned to Rowlette's office to continue the discussion about the need for a lead counsel who was white. White had compiled a list of the best white defense attorneys in Detroit and only needed to get the current defense attorneys to agree to the plan. Rowlette grudgingly agreed to add a white attorney to the team, but refused to resign and insisted that the only acceptable white attorney was Thomas Chawke, who would receive $5,000 for handling the case. He also insisted that the three black attorneys split an additional $5,000 between them. White was not prepared to pay them such a fee, and he simply could not approve of

asked, all innocence. "When they get through with him," said the conductor, "he won't pass for white no more!"

BOYLE, ARC OF JUSTICE at 209; *see also* WHITE, A MAN CALLED WHITE at 50–51.

[47] BOYLE, ARC OF JUSTICE at 212–13.

[48] *Id.* at 215.

[49] *Id.* at 214–17.

Chawke who had a reputation for being on retainer to the mob. White boarded a train back to New York.[50]

Once arriving in New York, White assured Johnson that the Sweets "were the symbols he was looking for."[51] That was all Johnson needed to know and he immediately began to publicize the Sweet's plight and the importance of their cause. His appeals then moved on to requesting financial support in their defense. Unfortunately, large sums of money did not appear.[52]

White continued to work on finding a new white lead counsel for the trial. When word got out in Detroit about the pressure that White was bringing to bear on the black counsel on behalf of the national office, the local black community reacted with anger. They created their own local Sweet Defense Fund that began competing for donations to the national fund.[53] Rowlette used that development to undermine White's efforts. He insisted that he be permitted to handle the upcoming arraignment and to argue that the charges should be dropped.[54] The struggle over who would represent the defendants continued. On September 29, Otis Sweet wrote two letters to the national NAACP office on behalf of himself and three other defendants. He demanded that the national office take over responsibility for their defense given the importance of the case to all black Americans. The four defendants also arranged to have a telegram conveying those sentiments sent to the national office. That was all White needed to know. He made arrangements to return to Detroit with an ultimatum. When doing so, however, he was aware that all the attorneys who had been on his original list to take over the case had already been contacted and for various reasons had refused.

Meanwhile, back in Detroit, the presiding judge, Frank Murphy, had decided to keep the trial on his own calendar.[55] In many ways, the defendants were fortunate that the trial judge was to be Frank Murphy. In his 1923 campaign for the judgeship, Murphy had run on a liberal platform appealing to ethnic minorities and black voters arguing that they were entitled to equal rights under the law. The business community railed against Murphy, but on election day the voters, particularly on the east side, which was highly populated by the poor, blacks, and ethnic

---

[50] *Id.* at 217–18.

[51] *Id.* at 219.

[52] *Id.* at 219–21.

[53] *Id.* at 223, 240.

[54] *Id.* at 222–23.

[55] *Id.* at 214–17.

minorities, voted overwhelmingly for Murphy.[56] Once on the bench Murphy generally lived up to his campaign promises. A devout Catholic, he was so sympathetic to the poor and downtrodden that the court personnel began to call him "Father Murphy" behind his back.[57] Despite those views, Murphy was also an astute politician.[58]

Rowlette handled the arraignment on Saturday, October 3, and moved to quash the charges. He argued that the state—without an identified shooter and evidence of a conspiracy—lacked sufficient evidence to charge first degree murder. Judge Murphy took the motion under advisement and considered it over the weekend. Attuned to the political winds in the city, on Monday, October 5, he denied the motion, but granted bail for Gladys Sweet in the amount of $10,000. He then

---

[56] *Id.* at 138–40.

[57] *Id.* at 193.

[58] After leaving the circuit court bench, Frank Murphy was elected mayor of Detroit. That proved to be just the beginning of his illustrious career. "[H]e served as governor-general of the Philippines, governor of Michigan, and attorney general of the United States." *Id.* at 341. Then in 1940, President Roosevelt appointed him an Associate Justice of the United States Supreme Court. He served on the Court for nine years and during that time continued to champion the rights of the poor and victims of discrimination.

> [He] defend[ed] the right of Jehovah's Witnesses not to salute the flag, of Communist Party members to speak their minds without fear of reprisal, of protesters to picket peacefully, of accused criminals to receive fair trials. He abhorred "the ugly abyss of racism," he wrote in a searing dissent condemning the internment of Japanese Americans during World War II. And when the NAACP lawyers came before the court, as they did in several critically important cases during his tenure, Murphy always gave them his vote.

Id. at 341–42. *See, e.g.*, West Virginia State Bd. of Education v. Barnette, 319 U.S. 624, 646 (1943) (Murphy, J., concurring) ("I am unable to agree that the benefits that may accrue to society from the compulsory flag salute are sufficiently definite and tangible to justify the invasion of freedom and privacy that it entailed or to compensate for a restraint on the freedom of the individual to be vocal or silent according to his conscience or personal inclination."); Haley v. Ohio, 332 U.S. 596 (1948) (Murphy, J., joining in plurality opinion finding that confession given by "a Negro boy age 15" was involuntary); Screws v. U.S., 325 U.S. 91, 134–35 (1945) (Murphy, J., dissenting) ("Robert Hall, a Negro citizen, has been deprived not only of the right to be tried by a court rather than by ordeal. He has been deprived of the right of life itself. That right belonged to him not because he was a Negro or a member of any particular race or creed. That right was his because he was an American citizen, because he was a human being. As such, he was entitled to all the respect and fair treatment that befits the dignity of man, a dignity that is recognized and guaranteed by the Constitution. Yet not even the semblance of due process has been accorded him. He has been cruelly and unjustifiably beaten to death by local police officers acting under color of authority derived from the state."); Korematsu v. U.S., 323 U.S. 214, 233 (1944) (Murphy, J., dissenting) ("This exclusion of 'all persons of Japanese ancestry, both alien and non-alien,' from the Pacific Coast area on a plea of military necessity in the absence of martial law ought not to be approved. Such exclusion goes over 'the very brink of constitutional power' and falls into the ugly abyss of racism.").

scheduled trial to begin in two weeks on October 19.[59] Gladys Sweet was released from jail on October 6, after friends of her parents posted her bail.[60]

At that point, fate intervened. On October 2, 1925, a Chicago attorney who served as general counsel for the *Chicago Defender*[61] wrote to the national NAACP office with an intriguing suggestion.[62] He stated that he had "free access to such minds as Mr. Darrow's and other great lawyers here and it may be that we could use their knowledge and experience without actually paying the regular fee that they charge in such cases."[63] White did not read the letter until October 6 and even then appeared to be more concerned with getting additional publicity for the case in the Chicago paper than in following up on the suggestion that Darrow might be available. But by the next day, someone in the New York office had realized the implications of the suggestion.

At that time, Clarence Darrow was the most famous criminal defense attorney in the United States. Among others, he had already represented Eugene Debs,[64] Wild Bill Haywood,[65] Leopold and Loeb,[66] and

---

[59] BOYLE, ARC OF JUSTICE at 226–27.

[60] *Id.* at 243.

[61] The *Chicago Defender* was a black newspaper published in Chicago. *Id.* at 1.

[62] *Id.* at 227–28.

[63] *Id.* at 227–28; Letter from N.K. McGill to Walter White, Oct. 2, 1925, frame 1114, reel 2, part 5, NAACP Papers.

[64] Before he had become known as an attorney who represented the working man and criminal defendants, Darrow had worked for the City of Chicago's legal department and for the Chicago and North–Western Railway Company. Then in 1894, the workers who made Pullman railroad cars went on strike. Eugene Debs, the president of the American Railway Union, convinced members of his union to boycott work on any train that contained a Pullman car. Realizing that he sided more with the union than the railroads, Darrow quit his job with the Chicago and North–Western and became one of the attorneys for Debs. A federal court had issued an injunction ordering all the railroad workers to return to work. When the workers refused, the court cited Debs for contempt for violating the injunction. BOYLE, ARC OF JUSTICE at 233. Eventually, Darrow and S.S. Gregory defended Debs on this charge. Although Debs' first trial resulted in a mistrial, the jury at the second trial convicted him and he was sentenced to six months in prison. The conviction was affirmed by the United States Supreme Court in In re Debs, 158 U.S. 564 (1895). *See* CLARENCE DARROW, THE STORY OF MY LIFE (1932) at 57–73.

[65] In 1906, Wild Bill Haywood, a well-known radical labor organizer for the Western Federation of Miners, had been charged with the murder of Frank R. Steunenberg, a former governor of Idaho who was killed by a bomb blast in front of his home in 1905. A man named Harry Orchard was arrested for the killing but he claimed that Haywood and another union official had hired him to kill the former governor in retaliation for Steunenberg's asking President McKinley to sent federal troops to crush a strike of miners in the Coeur d'Alene region. Darrow was lead counsel in the murder trial which resulted in an acquittal. *See* DARROW, THE STORY OF MY LIFE at 127–56; *see also* J. ANTHONY LUKAS, BIG TROUBLE: A MURDER IN A SMALL WESTERN TOWN SETS OFF A STRUGGLE FOR THE SOUL OF AMERICA (1997) (a narrative of the murder, trial, and social tapestry of the time).

[66] In 1924, Nathan Leopold and Richard Loeb were charged with the murder of fourteen-year-old Bobby Franks in Chicago. The evidence was overwhelming and Darrow

John Scopes in the "Monkey Trial."[67] Johnson immediately saw the
possibilities in exploring whether Darrow might be willing to represent
the Detroit defendants. On October 7, Johnson sent a telegram to
Darrow's office in Chicago, which after briefly describing the Sweet case
stated:

> Case is dramatic high point of nationwide issue of segregation in
> which National Association for Advancement of Colored People has
> case now pending in United States Supreme Court. Stop. This issue
> constitutes a supreme test of the constitutional guarantees of Ameri-
> can Negro citizens. Stop. Defense requires ablest attorney of nation-
> al prestige that we can possibly secure who would be willing to
> undertake such a case. Stop. Please wire us collect if you would
> consider favorably request that you assume charge of the case.
> Stop.[68]

The next day Darrow's secretary informed Johnson that Darrow was in
New York City visiting his friend Arthur Garfield Hays, with whom he
had tried the Scopes trial three months before. Johnson immediately
made arrangements to meet with Darrow later that day at Hays' home
in Manhattan.

Johnson, White, Arthur Spingarn, chair of the NAACP's legal committee, and Charles Studin, Spingarn's law partner, arrived at Hays'
home with the hope that they could convince the sixty-eight year old
Darrow to take over the case.[69] Spingarn eloquently set out the facts of
the case and its importance. Darrow later described his reaction to
Spingarn as follows:

> I made the usual excuses that I was tired, and growing old, and was
> not physically or mentally fit. I knew that I would go when I was
> making the excuses. I had always been interested in the colored

---

represented both clients when on the morning trial was to begin, they entered guilty pleas
to the murder. The focus of Darrow's defense was on convincing Judge Caverly to spare his
clients' lives and sentence them to life imprisonment. He was successful in doing so. His
masterful argument to the court can be found in ATTORNEY FOR THE DAMNED, edited by
Arthur Weinberg (1957) at 19–87. See also DARROW, THE STORY OF MY LIFE at 226–43.

[67] In 1925 in the Scopes "Monkey Trial," Darrow and Hays defended John Scopes, a
high school biology teacher charged with illegally teaching the theory of evolution. William
Jennings Bryan, a three time Presidential candidate, prosecuted the case. See DARROW, THE
STORY OF MY LIFE at 256–78.

[68] BOYLE, ARC OF JUSTICE at 229.

[69] ARTHUR GARFIELD HAYS, LET FREEDOM RING 196 (1937).

people. I had lived in America because I wanted to. Many others came here from choice to better their conditions. The ancestors of the negroes came here because they were captured in Africa and brought to America in slave ships, and had been obliged to toil for three hundred years without reward. When they were finally freed from slavery they were lynched in court and out of court, burned at the stake, and driven into mean, squalid outskirts and shanties because they were black, or had a drop of negro blood in their bodies somewhere. I realized that defending negroes, even in the North, was no boy's job, although boys usually were given that responsibility.[70]

By the end of the meeting both Darrow and Hays had agreed to represent Ossian Sweet and the other defendants as long as the local defense attorneys wanted them in the case.[71] It took another week to work out the financial details.[72] Meanwhile White had returned to Detroit to discuss the situation with the local counsel, who agreed to remain on the defense team but give up control of the case to Darrow.[73]

To announce that Darrow was taking over the case, on Thursday, October 15, Johnson issued a one-page press release that described the case as a shooting in self-defense against a white mob and then linked the issues in the trial with the upcoming Supreme Court case on restrictive covenants. This time, with Darrow's high profile, the national press picked up the story.[74] White then orchestrated Darrow's "surprise appearance" at the courthouse to file a routine motion seeking a two-week continuance of the trial. His physical presence at the courthouse triggered additional news stories as the attorneys, judges, clerks, and courthouse staff all flocked to Judge Murphy's courtroom to see the famous Mr. Darrow. Judge Murphy granted Darrow's motion and gave the defense until October 30 to prepare for trial.[75] After this favorable publicity, Johnson let it be known that the NAACP was in dire need of money to fund the defense; and this time, it "came pouring in."[76]

---

[70] DARROW, THE STORY OF MY LIFE at 302.

[71] WHITE, A MAN CALLED WHITE at 76.

[72] Darrow agreed to take the case for five thousand dollars and expenses (one tenth of what he typically charged in murder cases) and Hays signed on for three thousand dollars and expenses. BOYLE, ARC OF JUSTICE at 239.

[73] Two additional defense attorneys were eventually added to the team—Walter Nelson, a white Detroit lawyer, and Herbert Freidman, a Chicago attorney and one of Darrow's colleagues. BOYLE, ARC OF JUSTICE at 254; PHYLLIS VINE, ONE MAN'S CASTLE: CLARENCE DARROW IN DEFENSE OF THE AMERICAN DREAM 166 (2004).

[74] BOYLE, ARC OF JUSTICE at 241–43.

[75] Id. at 242–43.

[76] Id. at 246.

The political climate in Detroit had also begun to change. The mayoral election was scheduled for November 3, and the Klan had mounted a vicious campaign against the current mayor, John Smith. In response, Smith "made the Klan his target"[77] and structured his campaign to appeal to the immigrants, blacks, and factory workers. They began to respond when he attacked the Klan's preaching of hatred and prejudice.[78]

On October 16, Darrow met for the first time with his clients. He had already spent some time with White learning the facts of the case. At one point, Darrow had asked White, "Did the defendants shoot into that mob?" White had initially hedged his answer, but ultimately conceded that he thought they had. Worried that Darrow might reconsider taking the case, White was relieved when Darrow not only was not concerned but responded, "If they had not had the courage to shoot back in defense of their own lives, I wouldn't think they were worth defending."[79]

During the meeting with his clients, Darrow listened carefully as they described what had happened that night at the Sweet home. He "gently press[ed] them to admit the shooting rather than cling to the unlikely stories they had concocted the night of the police interrogation, quietly reassuring them that the case could be won even if they had fired into the crowd, bridging the chasm between the famous white lawyer and ten desperately afraid colored men with his remarkable gift for empathy."[80] It was already apparent that Darrow and Hays planned to abandon what Rowlette had considered his strongest argument—that the prosecution could not prove who fired the fatal shot. Instead, they shifted their attention to the argument that regardless who fired the fatal shot the occupants of the house were justified in firing to defend themselves from the mob.[81]

---

[77] *Id.* at 251.

[78] *Id.* at 249–53.

[79] WHITE, A MAN CALLED WHITE at 76–77.

[80] BOYLE, ARC OF JUSTICE at 244.

[81] *Id.* at 254–55. In his autobiography, Hays described the meeting as follows:

We had concluded that the only defense lay in making a clean breast of the whole matter, and said so flatly. But our clients seemed evasive. None was inclined to talk. We took their stories one by one and they didn't wholly jibe. For some time Joe Mack insisted that during the excitement he had locked himself in the bathroom and was taking a bath. That seemed unlikely. Again, each claimed to have no knowledge of where any one else had been, or what he had been doing. There were the statements made to the police. Our clients had a very human desire to support their original and inept stories. Then they seemed to feel that in spite of our expostulations, we might be just as well pleased if we did not know too much.... But finally, little by little, we

Having only two weeks to prepare for a first degree murder case would have been daunting to any criminal defense attorney—unless perhaps you were Clarence Darrow. During that time Darrow received a crash course from White on racial violence in America. Included among the documents that White gave Darrow was Johnson's summary of the 1919 riot in Washington, White's own description of the Tulsa riot, and the NAACP's report of lynchings in 1924. White also educated Darrow about the NAACP's battle against segregation and the pending challenge to restrictive covenants. He gave Darrow Louis Marshall's brief in that case as well as W.E.B. DuBois's article on the interplay between racial prejudice and the powerful real estate interests who controlled the housing market.[82]

Meanwhile, Hays oversaw the legal research and crafted the strategic legal issues—considering if they should demand separate trials for each defendant and how to keep separate the charges of conspiracy and first degree murder. Starting with Rowlette's earlier motion to dismiss, Hays also focused upon the Michigan Supreme Court's 1860 decision in Pond v. People, which held that a person could defend his life and home from a mob even if he did not accurately understand the mob's intentions. A reasonable fear was all that was required.[83] Thus, Darrow had strong legal precedent to support his defense theory.

---

managed to impress upon them that we actually wanted the truth, the whole truth and nothing but the truth, and that there lay the only hope of the defense.

HAYS, LET FREEDOM RING at 199.

[82] BOYLE, ARC OF JUSTICE at 255.

[83] Pond v. People, 8 Mich. 150, 1860 WL 2630 (1860). First, the Court noted that "[r]easonable apprehension, however, is sufficient here, precisely as in all other cases." 1860 WL at *16. It then went on to explain:

It has also been laid down by the authorities, that private persons may forcibly interfere to suppress a riot or resist rioters, although a riot is not necessarily a felony in itself. This is owing to the nature of the offense, which requires the combination of three or more persons, assembling together and actually accomplishing some object calculated to terrify others. Private persons who can not otherwise suppress them, or defend themselves from them, may justify homicide in killing them, as it is their right and duty to aid in preserving the peace. And perhaps no case can arise where a felonious attempt by a single individual will be as likely to inspire terror as the turbulent acts of rioters. And a very limited knowledge of human nature is sufficient to inform us, that when men combine to do an injury to the person or property of others, of such a nature as to involve excitement and provoke resistance, they are not likely to stop at half-way measures, or to scan closely the dividing line between felonies and misdemeanors. But when the act they meditate is in itself felonious, and of a violent character, it is manifest that strong measures will generally be required for their effectual suppression, and a man who defends himself, his family or his property, under such circumstances, is justified in making as complete a defense as is necessary.

Id. at *16.

Darrow's personal style of pretrial preparation was not the methodical, logical analysis employed by many successful attorneys.

> [Darrow] did not see the need for painstaking preparation, not when he had at his command forty years' worth of words and images that he was sure could hold a courtroom transfixed, not when he knew that there was always a way to make a jury want nothing more than to set his clients free, not when he intended to transform the trial into yet another engagement in his life-long battle against the established order. It was enough to have a feel for the case and its context, and to rely on wit, manipulation and his incomparable persuasive powers to do the rest.[84]

Most attorneys—even after forty years of experience—do not have the skill and charisma to successfully adopt Darrow's approach. In addition, Darrow usually had co-counsel, such as Hays, who was more detail oriented and prepared more carefully.

Trial began on Friday, October 30, 1925, with jury selection.[85] Because Judge Murphy was committed to giving the defendants a fair trial, he was generous in granting defense requests to excuse jurors for cause.[86] In addition, under Michigan law, every defendant charged with murder was entitled to exercise thirty peremptory challenges—challenges which at that time counsel could exercise at their discretion. Because Darrow represented all eleven defendants, he had an astonishing 330 peremptories at his disposal.[87]

Judge Murphy had initially summoned a panel of 120 jurors of which 65 showed up.[88] The courtroom was packed with spectators as lead prosecutor, Robert Toms,[89] began the voir dire. The afternoon dragged

---

[84] BOYLE, ARC OF JUSTICE at 256.

[85] Just before the trial began, White had learned that Charles Garland's American Fund for Public Service had decided to provide the initial funding for the permanent NAACP Legal Defense Fund that Johnson had proposed. The Fund had agreed to provide $5,000 for the costs of the Sweet defense and would provide an additional $15,000 for the Legal Defense Fund as soon as the NAACP raised an additional $30,000 on its own. BOYLE, ARC OF JUSTICE at 257.

[86] If it appears that a potential juror cannot be fair in a particular case, either side may ask the court to excuse the juror "for cause." The court has a great deal of discretion when deciding whether to grant those requests. See, e.g., Mu'Min v. Virginia, 500 U.S. 415, 428 (1991) (noting that a trial court's findings of juror impartiality may be overturned only for "manifest error").

[87] BOYLE, ARC OF JUSTICE at 261.

[88] Eventually Judge Murphy summoned an additional panel of sixty-five. Id. at 260.

[89] Toms tried the case for the State with the assistance of Lester Moll and Ted Kennedy.

on as Toms slowly and carefully asked the jurors questions. By three o'clock, he announced that he was satisfied with the twelve in the box. Then it was Darrow's turn. Speaking in a soft voice and intimate style, Darrow asked the jurors about their backgrounds and beliefs. He inquired if they owned their own homes and how they would feel if blacks moved into their neighborhood.[90] He also asked if they thought that a man was entitled to defend his home from the attack of a mob. And finally, Darrow asked if they were members of any secret societies such as the Ku Klux Klan.[91] Needless to say any juror who answered "yes" to that question was struck for cause.

Darrow continued the voir dire through the remainder of Friday and all day on Saturday. By Monday, with 307 peremptories still remaining, Darrow announced that he was satisfied with the jurors who had been seated. Toms then spent the rest of Monday getting rid of fifteen jurors for cause and another nine using his peremptories. Tuesday was election day and 250,000 voters turned out, giving John Smith a substantial margin of victory over the Klan candidate. On Wednesday morning, Toms continued his voir dire. By the time he was done, Darrow struck only one juror (who also admitted membership in the Klan) for cause and then announced that he was satisfied with the jury.[92] The final panel consisted of twelve white men.[93] As the oath was being administered to the jury, Darrow supposedly said: "The case is won or lost now. The rest is window dressing."[94]

---

[90] Hays later wrote:

The difficulty of securing an impartial jury was clearly evident when one asked how the talesman would feel if property in his neighborhood was bought by a negro. Without exception, the talesman said they recognized the negro's right of free residence as well as his right of self-defense. But they seemed to question the wisdom of the exercise of such rights. Generally they seemed to agree with the philosophy later expressed by the Prosecutor, that people have many rights which they voluntarily waive. One has a right to grab a seat in a street car before a woman gets to it. One has a right to attend a dance (particularly if he is the host) in a bathing suit. One has the right to put his feet on the table, or take off his shoes in the parlor. But we don't do it. It doesn't conform to practice. The talesman did not seem to realize, nor did the Prosecutor, that there are some rights which one cannot waive and remain free, such as the right to live, and the right to refuse to be intimidated, whatever the cost.

HAYS, LET FREEDOM RING at 200–01.

[91] BOYLE, ARC OF JUSTICE at 259.

[92] Id. at 260–66.

[93] The jurors consisted of two men who were retired, one who could not seem to hold a job, and nine who were working men, including factory workers, a housepainter, an electrician and a street car conductor. While most were not immigrants, each was related in some way to an immigrant. Id. at 266–67.

[94] IRVING STONE, CLARENCE DARROW FOR THE DEFENSE 478 (1941).

Aware of how Darrow had handled his bombastic opponents in the Haywood and Scopes trials, Toms was not going to engage in any of the histrionics that Darrow knew how to handle so effectively. Instead, he chose to carefully and methodically present his case while showing Darrow the "utmost deference."[95] That was probably a wise tactic given how everyone seemed to be reacting to Darrow.

> "[H]e is the most amazing figure I've ever seen," Walter White wrote, one master manipulator admiring the work of another: "He's got the ... judge, clerk, [and] attendants all with him. Most of the jurors are eager—too eager in view of the strength of the Klan here—to serve, and he every so often makes some droll remark that sets the entire court to laughing and instantly all tension is relieved."[96]

In his opening statement it became clear that Toms planned to present the same theory that the state had presented at the preliminary hearing: there was no mob around the Garland house when the shots were fired and, thus, the shooting was unjustified. According to Hays:

> The picture painted by the prosecution showed a warm summer evening in a quiet, neighborly community. The Sweet house stood on a corner. Diagonally across was the high school with a spacious yard. Opposite and along the street were small frame houses owned and occupied by simple, kindly people—the men mostly mechanics, the women housewives, dutifully caring for broods of children. People were sitting on their porches enjoying the cool air after dusk, visiting and chatting. A few sauntered casually along the street. Some were on their way to a corner grocery. Here and there a car was parked. Of course, the fact that negroes had moved into the corner house was of interest, but peace and quiet was assured by half a dozen policemen who stood guard at various places, keeping the people away from the sidewalk in front and on the side of the Sweet house. Suddenly, unexpectedly and without provocation, a fusillade of shots rang out from the rear, sides and front of the house, and Leo[n] Breiner, chatting with a group on the porch of the Dove home opposite was killed. His pipe was still in his mouth when he was carried away.[97]

To prove that, Toms planned to call twenty police officers and forty-one people who lived in the neighborhood, who had been carefully selected and were prepared to deny the existence of the mob.[98]

---

[95] BOYLE, ARC OF JUSTICE at 268.

[96] Id. at 265–66.

[97] HAYS, LET FREEDOM RING at 201–02.

[98] BOYLE, ARC OF JUSTICE at 267–68.

Before the prosecution called any witnesses, however, Hays demanded that the state provide a bill of particulars insisting that the prosecution set out precisely what it intended to prove. Toms firmly committed to proving the existence of a conspiracy among the eleven defendants in which they all agreed that one or more of them would shoot to kill. In addition he told the court, Breiner died as a result of a bullet fired by one of the defendants aided and abetted by the others.[99] By doing so, Hays put in place his strategy to set up the prosecution for a later defense motion.

Although the defense was entitled to give its opening statement immediately after the state gave its opening, for some unknown reason, the defense had decided to wait and give its opening after the state presented its evidence. As a tactical matter, in most cases deferring the defense opening to after the prosecution's case is not wise. The jury will have heard the prosecution theory and then all its evidence before the defense is able to explain its theory and theme to the jury in a persuasive and coherent way. A strong defense opening can let the jury know that there is another side to the case and, by knowing the defense theory, hopefully the jurors will consider the testimony of the government witnesses with that perspective in mind.

Toms began to put on his witnesses immediately after his opening statement. He started with a neighbor who had identified Breiner's body at the morgue followed by the coroner who testified that Breiner had been killed by a bullet that went from back to front. He then called Inspector Schuknecht who testified that he had ten police officers with him at the Sweet home on the evening of September 9th. Toms then asked:

Q. There was no one there when you got there? The time of your arrival is about 7:30?

A. There were people on the street, but they were walking up and down and there was no congregating.

. . .

Q. Did you see any one armed with clubs or other weapons?

A. Not at any time.

Q. What happened at around 8:15?

A. Suddenly a volley of shots was fired from the windows of Dr. Sweet's home.

Q. What could you see?

A. I saw flashes of guns.

[99] HAYS, LET FREEDOM RING at 202–03.

Q. How many shots?

A. About fifteen or twenty.[100]

He went on to describe that after the shooting he had gone into the
Sweet house. No lights were on, and he found the rifles and pistols.
According to Schuknecht, the house contained very little furniture, just
some chairs, a small table and some mattresses.[101] "It was an ominous
image—eleven heavily armed Negroes hidden away in an all but empty
house, waiting for the opportunity to commit evil acts—and Toms let it
linger as he turned from Schuknecht and stepped back toward the
lawyers' table ..."[102] On cross-examination, Darrow asked Schuknecht
whether he had gone up to any of the bystanders outside the Sweet
home to ask them why they were there? Had he tried to determine the
real intentions of the Waterworks Improvement Association? He finally
got Schuknecht to admit that he had found a small stone in the front
bedroom of the house and some broken glass on the floor. Schnuknecht
also admitted that it appeared that the stone had been thrown through
the window from the outside.[103]

The other police officers who testified confirmed that they had told
the Sweets that they were there to protect them and if the Sweets saw
anything suspicious to let them know. They also described the barely
furnished rooms to make sure that the image remained in the jurors'
minds.[104] On cross-examination, these officers refused to give Darrow any
significant concessions like Schnuknecht had done.

The lay witnesses repeated much the same story as the police
officers although occasionally some of them faltered. For example,
Dwight Hubbard, when asked what had happened, initially forgot the
script. He began, "Well, there were a great number of people and the
officers ..." He paused and then corrected himself, "I won't say a great
number—there were a large—" Stopping again, he finally went on,
"There were a few people there, and the officers were keeping them
moving; suddenly there was a volley of shots."[105] On cross-examination,
Darrow made sure to emphasize how this witness had been coached.

---

[100] Id. at 204–05.

[101] BOYLE, ARC OF JUSTICE at 269.

[102] Id.

[103] Id. at 275.

[104] Id. at 269–70. What the prosecution failed to mention was that the Sweets had been
furniture shopping that very day, purchasing a dining room set, several armchairs, and two
bedroom sets for their boarders. Id. at 30.

[105] Id. at 271; Hubbard testimony, November 11, 1925.

Q: When you first started to answer the question, you started to say you saw a great crowd there, didn't you?

A: Yes, sir.

Q: Then you modified to say a large crowd, didn't you?

A: Yes, sir.

Q: Then you said a few people after that?

A: Yes, sir.

Q: Do you know how you happened to change your mind and whittle it down so fast?

A: No, sir.

Q: You have talked to a great deal about it, haven't you?

A: No, sir.

Q: Any officers talk with you about it?

A: Just Lieutenant Johnson, if you consider him an officer.[106]

Q: Well, I suppose he does, and I haven't any reason to think otherwise ... How many times did he talk with you about it?

A: Once.

Q: And you kind of forgot you were to say a few people, didn't you, when you started in?

[Objection by Toms; overruled by Judge Murphy]

Q: When you started to answer [Toms'] question, you forgot to say a few people, instead of a great many?

A: Yes, sir.[107]

Edward Wettlaufer, who lived around the corner from the Sweets, testified that he was outside the Sweet home when the shots were fired and he saw Breiner fall to the ground. He let slip that he had heard breaking glass before the shooting.[108] Except for a few such missteps, however, witness after witness for the prosecution repeated essentially the same story.

On cross-examination of these lay witnesses, Darrow made some important points. For example, when examining Eben Draper, who was a member of the Waterworks Improvement Association, Darrow was able to give the jury a sense of the real purpose of the Association and its size.

Q: When was the club started?

---

[106] Johnson was the detective in charge of the investigation.

[107] BOYLE, ARC OF JUSTICE at 277–78.

[108] *Id.* at 272–73.

A: A long time ago.

Q: When did you first hear that a colored family was moving into the neighborhood?

A: That was a long time ago, too.

Q: Did that have anything to do with your joining the club?

A: Possibly.

Q: Did it?

A: Yes.

Q: You joined the club to aid in keeping that a white district?

A: Yes.

Q: At the meeting in the school was any reference made to keeping the district free from colored people?

A: Yes.

Q: How many people were present at that meeting?

A: Seven hundred.[109]

When cross-examining Alfred Andrews about the meeting held by the Waterworks Improvement Association, Darrow questioned him about the speech given at that meeting.

Q: Did he tell you about the riot trouble they had in his neighborhood?

A: Yes, he told us about a Negro named Dr. Turner who had bought a house on Spokane Avenue.

Q: Did he say his organization made Turner leave?

A: Yes. He said his organization wouldn't have Negroes in their neighborhood and they would cooperate with us in keeping them out of ours.

Q: Did the crowd applaud him?

A: Yes.

Q: Did you applaud?

A: Yes.

Q: You feel that way now?

A: Yes, I haven't changed.

Q: You know a colored person has certain rights?

A: Yes, I was in favor of keeping the Sweets out by legal means.

---

[109] Transcript of testimony of Eben Draper; *available* at http://www.law.umkc.edu/faculty/projects/ftrials/sweet/transcriptexcerpts.HTM.

Q: Did the speaker talk of legal means?

A: No, he was a radical. I myself do not believe in violence.

Q: Did anybody in the audience of five hundred or more people protest against the speaker's advocacy of violence?

A: I don't know.[110]

Ray Dove lived directly across the street from the Sweet home and had testified that more women and children than men were outside the Sweet home the evening of September 9. On cross-examination, Darrow got him to admit the following:

Q: Did you make any estimate of the number of women and children in a crowd before?

A: No, I can't say that I have.

Q: As long as the question was asked by the State, you thought you were safe in answering it the way that you did?

A: No, not exactly.

Q: Was there a crowd?

A: No.

Q: Was there any disturbance?

A: No.

Q: Do you belong to any organization or club?

A: [No answer.]

Q: Have you any reason for not answering that question?

. . .

Q: When did you hear that Dr. Sweet had bought the place?

A: Quite a while before he moved in I heard rumors from the neighbors.

Q: Quite a discussion?

A: Yes, I guess so.

Q: How long before [he] moved in?

A: Six weeks or two months.

Q: You heard it from all the neighbors?

A: Yes, two, three, or four of them.

Q: You discussed it with your wife?

---

[110] Transcript of testimony of Alfred Andrews; *available* at http://www.law.umkc.edu/faculty/projects/ftrials/sweet/transcriptexcerpts.HTM.

A: Yes. Q: You didn't want him there?

A: I am not prejudiced against them, but I don't believe in mixing whites and blacks.

Q: So you didn't want him there?

A: No, I guess not....[111]

Darrow was able to get George Suppus and Ulric Arthur, both thirteen-years old, to concede that four or five kids had been throwing stones at the Sweet home. They had heard the sound of breaking glass and the shots were fired shortly after that.[112] Other witnesses also admitted hearing the sound of pebbles being thrown against the house. As Hays later described:

> [O]ne witness had heard a number of rat-tat-tats, as though pebbles had been thrown against the house just before the firing, and a crash of window glass. The size of the pebbles? Perhaps two inches in diameter—like those on the table (referring to exhibits)—stones and lumps of cement picked from the roof and yard the next day. Darrow dropped one of the pebbles as he was about to hand it to the witness. It resounded loudly as it bumped along the floor.[113]

By the end of the prosecution's case, Darrow had shown the contradictions between the witnesses and demonstrated that the prosecution's version of what had happened contravened common sense. He later wrote in his autobiography: "[Jurors] do not have much confidence in a lawyer if he asks them to believe strange or preposterous things. This is not complimentary to their mentality; most of the men in the panel have some sense . . ."[114]

On Saturday, November 14, Toms rested the prosecution's case. At that point, Hays moved to dismiss the charges.[115] At the beginning of the trial, in response to the defense request for a bill of particulars, Toms had committed the prosecution to a conspiracy theory. The defense now argued (outside the presence of the jury) that the prosecution had failed to present any evidence that the defendants had conspired together to kill Leon Breiner. Hays also argued that all the evidence the state had presented, including the number of people inside the house, the lack of furniture, and the arsenal of guns, was consistent with innocence.

---

[111] Transcript of testimony of Ray Dove; *available* at http://www.law.umkc.edu/faculty/projects/ftrials/sweet/transcriptexcerpts.HTM.

[112] BOYLE, ARC OF JUSTICE at 278–79.

[113] HAYS, LET FREEDOM RING at 211.

[114] DARROW, THE STORY OF MY LIFE at 427.

[115] BOYLE, ARC OF JUSTICE at 282–84.

During Hays' argument a baby in the courtroom began to cry. Judge Murphy demanded: "Who brought that child in here?" The defense answered: "That is the Sweet baby. We had her brought here as an illustration. Had she been in that house that night, she might well have been arrested and tried and the evidence here would condemn her to the same extent that it does the defendants."[116] Later that day, despite the defense's theatrical flourish and impassioned arguments, Judge Murphy denied the defense motion for dismissal of the charges and called for the jury to be brought back into the courtroom.[117] The persuasiveness of the defense arguments, however, seemed to have had some effect on the prosecution because on Monday morning, Toms quietly told Darrow and Hays that he was willing to drop the charges against Mrs. Sweet. When informed of that conversation, Mrs. Sweet protested that she did not want any favorable treatment. Although the prosecution can choose to dismiss any charges either before or during trial and does not need a defendant's consent, apparently Toms was not willing to do so over Mrs. Sweet's objection.[118]

Hays then rose to give the defense's opening statement. He began forcefully.

> The defense in this case faces and admits facts which are sometimes subject to equivocation and avoidance. We are not ashamed of our clients and we shall not apologize for them. We are American citizens; you men of the jury are American citizens; they are American citizens. Each juryman said that he conceded equal rights to all Americans. On the basis of the legal rights of the defendants we make our defense. We say this with the full realization of the sacredness of human life and having quite as much sympathy for the bereaved family of the deceased as has the prosecution.[119]

He then moved on set out the historical framework of the right of self-defense.

> The right of self-defense in Anglo–Saxon history is centuries old and is well expressed in the old phraseology of Lord Chatham:
>
>> The poorest man may in his cottage bid defiance to all the forces of the Crown; it may be frail, its roof may shake, the wind may blow through it; the storm may enter, the ram may enter; but

---

116 HAYS, LET FREEDOM RING at 212–14.

117 BOYLE, ARC OF JUSTICE at 286.

118 *Id.* at 286; Hays, *Let Freedom Ring* at 214.

119 HAYS, LET FREEDOM RING at 214.

the King of England cannot enter; all his forces dare not cross the threshold of that ruined tenement.[120]

He then got to the heart of the defense case:

You, gentlemen of the jury, have had told you a part of the story of September 9th, as it appeared from the outside, and it will be our duty and pleasure to show you the facts as they appeared from inside that little house on Garland Street and Charlevoix Avenue— the facts as they appeared to eleven people of the black race who had behind them a history, who were affected by knowledge of the appalling and almost uncivilized treatment of their race by those who should be their brothers and protectors. In other words, we shall show not only what happened in the house, but we shall attempt a far more difficult task—that of reproducing in the cool atmosphere of a courtroom, a state of mind—the state of mind of these defendants, worried, distrustful, tortured and apparently trapped—a state of mind induced by what has happened to others of their race, not only in the South where their ancestors were once slaves, but even in the North in the States which once fought for their freedom.

We conceive the law to be this—that a man is not justified in shooting merely because he is fearful—but that a man is justified if he has reasonable ground for fear. In other words, one must put himself in a position of a reasonable man. But the reasonable man is not a fiction. He is a man with a background, with a color, with the color with which he has been endowed. The question is not what a white man in a city of whites would do under certain circumstances. The question is what a colored man, a reasonable colored man, with his knowledge of the prejudice against him because of his color; with his knowledge that people had threatened to bomb his home and kill him if he moved into the neighborhood; with his knowledge that there was a society of men (also-called Improvement Association) formed for the purpose of ejecting him from his home; with his knowledge of what mobs do and have done to colored people when they have the power; with his knowledge of history, his knowledge of psychology; with his apprehension and fear from the facts as they appear to him.[121]

Hays then told the story of Ossian Sweet[122] and what had happened that night from the perspective of those who had been inside the house. He

---

[120] *Id.* at 214–15.

[121] *Id.* at 215–16.

[122] The one jarring note in Hays' opening was when he asked Dr. Ossian Sweet to "stand up so the jury can look you over"—words far too reminiscent of slavery. *Id.* at 217

described what Dr. Sweet had been thinking as the mob gathered outside his home with his thoughts turning to what he had personally seen and heard in his own life as well as what he had read about mob violence against blacks in the United States.[123]

The defense then began to call its witnesses.[124] Gladys' friends, Serena Rochelle and Edna Butler, described the night before the shooting that they had spent in the Sweet home, including the threatening crowd outside. Philip Adler, a white reporter for the *Detroit News*, estimated that the crowd in the intersection in front of the Sweet home a few minutes before the shooting contained "between four and five hundred people."[125] The Spauldings, a black couple driving down a nearby street shortly before the shooting, described the crowd they saw outside the Sweet house. James Smith, a black man who with his uncle had been out for an evening drive and had come upon the police roadblock shortly after the shooting, testified about how a "considerable mob" had stormed his car, shattering his windshield. Another black man, Charles Shauffner, described how when he drove into the neighborhood a mob had swarmed his car and someone hit him in the head with a brick before he was able to get the car started and drive away. He said that it seemed like "five thousand" people were there.[126]

Having established the existence and nature of the mob, Hays then called Dr. Ossian Sweet to the stand. While Dr. Sweet had a constitutional right to refuse to testify, given the defense theory and Hays' opening statement, his testimony was absolutely critical. In his opening statement, Hays had described the thoughts of Dr. Sweet in the moments leading up to the shooting. The only witness who could effectively testify to that was Dr. Sweet. Once a party tells the jury in opening statement that it will present certain evidence in the trial, counsel should do so if they wish to maintain credibility with the jury. That is one reason why it is important for counsel to be sure that there will be evidence of every important point they discuss in the opening statement. If such evidence is not presented, at a minimum, counsel will need to provide an explanation in the closing argument. In addition, opposing

---

[123] BOYLE, ARC OF JUSTICE at 287.

[124] When appropriate Darrow was masterful at lightening the mood in the courtroom. For example, the defense called witnesses to testify about the character of Mrs. Sweet. At the time, such testimony could only be based on a person's reputation in the community. One such witness testified "that he had never heard any one say anything about her reputation." When the prosecutor moved to strike his testimony, "[t]he interjection of the defense that that was one way of proving a woman's reputation aroused considerable amusement." HAYS, LET FREEDOM RING at 229.

[125] BOYLE, ARC OF JUSTICE at 287.

[126] *Id*. at 287–88.

counsel is likely to remind the jury of any unkept promises made during opening statement.[127]

As an educated medical doctor, Dr. Sweet was the most articulate and credible of the defendants. How well he performed on the witness stand was likely to determine the outcome of the trial and Dr. Sweet had to know that. Hays carefully developed the story Dr. Sweet had to tell. He took him through his life history, laying out the facts that Hays had described in his opening statement.[128] He then asked Dr. Sweet to describe "the racial incidents that scarred him most."[129] As Dr. Sweet recounted the killing of Fred Rochelle, the beating he had witnessed during the Washington riot, and all the stories of racial violence that he had heard, Toms objected. Darrow responded that it was relevant because "everything known to a race affects it actions."[130] Judge Murphy overruled the objection and permitted Dr. Sweet to answer.[131]

After a lengthy and detailed description of these atrocities, Hays began to take Dr. Sweet to 2905 Garland on the night of the shooting. He had Dr. Sweet describe how the lady who sold him the house had called to warn him that she had received a telephone call that if the sale went forward, she would be killed, Dr. Sweet would be killed, and the

---

[127] Of course, in a criminal case, the prosecutor must be very careful when making such arguments so as not to engage in "burden-shifting." It is improper and often reversible error for the government to make arguments which suggest that the defendant has the burden of proving his innocence in a criminal case. *See generally* In re Winship, 397 U.S. 358, 364 (1970) ("[T]he Due Process Clause protects the accused against conviction except upon proof [by the government] beyond a reasonable doubt of every fact necessary to constitute the crime with which he is charged."). The risk of reversible error is also implicated when the prosecution comments on a defendant's failure to testify in a criminal case. Every defendant has a Fifth Amendment privilege against self-incrimination, which means that a defendant has a constitutional right not to testify. As a result, any comment by the prosecution that can be interpreted to suggest that the jury should draw an adverse inference based upon the defendant's failure to testify also usually constitutes reversible error. *See* Griffin v. California, 380 U.S. 609, 614 (1965) (holding that the Fifth Amendment forbids either comment by the prosecution on the accused's silence or instructions by the court that such silence is evidence of guilt); *see also* Chapman v. California, 386 U.S. 18, 24 (1967) (applying constitutional harmless error standard to prosecution's comment on defendant's failure to testify; "before a federal constitutional error can be held harmless, the court must be able to declare a belief that it was harmless beyond a reasonable doubt").

[128] HAYS, LET FREEDOM RING at 218–20.

[129] BOYLE, ARC OF JUSTICE at 288; HAYS, LET FREEDOM RING at 220–22.

[130] BOYLE, ARC OF JUSTICE at 289. Although the modern practice is to limit all questioning, responding to objections, and making of objections to one attorney per side for each witness, that did not appear to be the rule at this trial.

[131] HAYS, LET FREEDOM RING at 226–28.

house would be blown up.[132] Dr. Sweet then described how he had moved into the house on September 8. He admitted bringing arms and ammunition. He told the jury that some of the weapons had been given to him and he had bought the remaining three guns with money he had saved to use to attend a medical convention.[133] Hays asked Dr. Sweet to talk about the men who were in the house on the night of the shooting and then summarized Dr. Sweet's testimony as follows:

> They were John Latting and Henry Sweet. Both were seniors at Wilberforce University; they had lived in the Mitchell house. These boys expected to stay four or five days with the Doctor, after which they would return to college. Both were in the Reserve Officers Training Corps. There was also Morris Murray, who had done odd jobs around the Doctor's house and painted his office. Joe Mack who had been driving the Doctor's car, likewise came. Another brother, Dr. O[tis].O. Sweet, the dentist, who had been staying at Mrs. Mitchell's,[134] also intended to live with the Doctor, and William Davis, a Federal narcotic officer, had arranged for a room. Davis and Dr. O.O. Sweet had been college mates at Howard University. Davis had fought in France as a captain in the Argonne.[135]

The final three men were insurance agents who were friends of Dr. Sweet and were willing to come help protect him.[136]

Hays then had Dr. Sweet describe what happened when he arrived home on the evening of September 9, 1925.

Q: What did you do when you got home on the evening of September 9th?

A: First thing I remember is my wife telling me about a phone conversation she had with Mrs. Butler, in which the latter told her of overhearing a conversation between the motorman of a street car and a woman passenger, to the effect that Negro family had moved into the neighborhood and they would be out before the next night.

Q: When did you first observe anything outside?

A: We were playing cards; it was about eight o'clock when something hit the roof of the house.

Q: What happened after that?

---

[132] Id. at 222.

[133] Id. at 223.

[134] Mrs. Mitchell was Gladys Sweet's mother.

[135] HAYS, LET FREEDOM RING at 223.

[136] Id. at 224.

A: Somebody went to the window and then I heard the remark, "The people, the people."

Q: And then?

A: I ran out to the kitchen where my wife was. There were several lights burning. I turned them out and opened the door. I heard someone yell, "Go and raise hell in front, I'm going back." I was frightened, and after getting a gun, ran upstairs. Stones kept hitting our house intermittently. I threw myself on the bed and lay there a short while. Perhaps fifteen minutes, when a stone came through the window. Part of the glass hit me.

Q: What happened then?

A: Pandemonium—I guess that's the best way of describing it— broke loose. Everyone was running from room to room. There was a general uproar. Somebody yelled, "There's someone coming!" They said, "That's your brother." A car had pulled up to the curb. My brother and Mr. Davis got out. The mob yelled, "Here's niggers! Get them, get them!" As they rushed in, the mob surged forward fifteen or twenty feet. It looked like a human sea. Stones kept coming faster. I ran downstairs. Another window was smashed. Then one shot. Then eight or ten from upstairs; then it was all over. . . .

Q: State your mind at the time of the shooting.

A: When I opened the door and saw the mob, I realized I was facing the same mob that had hounded my people throughout its entire history. In my mind, I was pretty confident of what I was up against, with my back against the wall. I was filled with a peculiar fear, the kind no one could feel unless they had [known] the history of our race. I knew what mobs had done to my people before.[137]

Not surprisingly, Toms went after Dr. Sweet with "uncharacteristically aggressive cross-examination." Dr. Sweet responded "with a dignity so fierce it was inspiring."[138] For example, on cross-examination, Toms confronted Dr. Sweet with the fact that his testimony at trial differed substantially from what he had told the police after his arrest. In response, Dr. Sweet testified: "I am under oath now. I was very excited then and afraid that what I said might be misinterpreted. . . ."[139] Ultimately, Toms made little headway against Dr. Sweet's testimony.

---

[137] Testimony of Dr. Ossian Sweet; *available* at http://www.law.umkc.edu/faculty/projects/ftrials/sweet/transcriptexcerpts.HTM.

[138] BOYLE, ARC OF JUSTICE at 290.

[139] Testimony of Dr. Ossian Sweet; *available* at http://www.law.umkc.edu/faculty/projects/ftrials/sweet/transcriptexcerpts.HTM.

None of the remaining witnesses were that important to the case. Over defense objection, the prosecution was permitted to introduce Henry Sweet's statement at the police station that he had fired his gun at the crowd. The defense then called Lieutenant William Johnson and grilled him about the interrogation methods used against the defendants, which the defense argued were designed to get the suspects to confess to a crime they had not committed. The defense also called Walter White to describe "his extensive research into mob violence, a threat so pervasive, he explained, every Negro lived in terror of it."[140] Testimony ended on Monday, November 23.

Closing arguments began the next morning. Lester Moll presented the prosecution's initial closing argument. He spent two and one-half hours going through the facts of the case and disparaging the defense theory, calling it "poppycock" and "bunk."[141] Then after lunch the defense attorneys began their closings. Hays went first "with a slashing, sometimes rambling attack on the state's argument, complemented by the recitation of yet another Harlem Renaissance poem—a piece by Countee Cullen this time[142]—and a final, soaring appeal to principle."[143] Given the composition of the jury, it is unlikely that his closing was particularly effective. "It was Hays' weakest performance of the trial, too highbrow for a jury full of workmen ... and too convoluted to be convincing."[144]

Then Darrow began his closing—which lasted for a total of seven hours and which at times seemed to meander back and forth between different topics. He began by talking about the problems of "race and

---

[140] BOYLE, ARC OF JUSTICE at 290.

[141] *Id*. at 291.

[142] Hays read the following poem to the jury:

"Once riding in old Baltimore,
Heart full, head full of glee,
I saw a Baltmorean
Stand gazing there at me.

"Now, I was eight and very small,
And he was no whit bigger,
And so I smiled, but he stuck out
His tongue and called me 'nigger.'

"I saw the whole of Baltimore
From April till December,
Of all the things that I saw there
That's all that I remember."

HAYS, LET FREEDOM RING at 230.

[143] *Id*.

[144] BOYLE, ARC OF JUSTICE at 291–92.

color and creed that have always worked their evil in human institutions."[145] Then he focused more directly on prejudice.

> If I thought any of you had an opinion against my clients, I would not worry about it because I might convince you; it is not so hard to show men that their opinions are wrong, but it is the next thing to impossible to take away their prejudices. Prejudices do not rest upon facts; they rest upon the ideas that have been taught to us and that began coming to us almost with our mothers' milk, and they stick almost as the color of the skin sticks. It is not the opinion of anyone of these twelve men that I am worrying about; much less is it the evidence in this case, for I know just as well as I know that you twelve men are here at this minute that if this had been a white crowd defending their homes, who killed a member of a colored mob, you would not leave your box. I don't need to say that no one would have been arrested, no one would have been on trial, and I would not have worried, and you know it, too. My clients are here charged with murder; but they are really here because they are black.

He talked about how it was unlikely that any of the jurors socialized with anyone who was black, and he blamed that on prejudice.

When Darrow turned to the specific testimony at trial—particularly that of the prosecution witnesses—his sorrow was tinged with anger. Darrow accused every prosecution witness of lying on the stand. "[T]here isn't any human being who knows anything about this case that does not know now why it happened, not one; there isn't any human being, whether he be a policeman, a neighbor, a prosecutor, a juror, a mere spectator, that does not know what happened ..." He talked about how the witnesses had been coached to testify that only a "few" people were on the street and cited to Dwight Hubbard's testimony.

When he got to the evening of September 9, he asked the jurors to put themselves in the shoes of the defendants—not as white men—but as black men. He went through the creation of the Waterworks Improvement Association and why it was formed.

> They had a meeting of six or seven hundred and got together just after Dr. Sweet bought that house. I asked him whether anybody said anything about the colored people at the meeting. "No, no." "What did you sign it for?" "For general improvement." "Did it have anything to do with keeping the district free from colored

---

[145] The text of this closing originally came from the complete trial transcript on microfilm in the Bentley Historical Library at the University of Michigan. This text is also *available* on the internet at http://www.law.umkc.edu/faculty/projects/ftrials/sweet/Darrow summ1.html. Unless otherwise noted, all quotations from Darrow's closing come from that text.

people?" A fellow will lie a certain distance; he does not like to go too far, and every single witness admitted in this way they joined, every one of them, and in that neighborhood they had a meeting so big that they had to adjourn from the auditorium of the school into the yard because Dr. Sweet had purchased a house across the street adjoining a neighborhood where he was not wanted.

He denigrated the role of the police. If "nothing was wrong," then why did the police even need to be there and why did they call for additional police to come to the scene? As a practical matter, they did nothing to disperse the mob. And there wasn't really any question that the mob was throwing stones and concrete at the house. Even the state's witnesses admitted that.

Another theme that Darrow developed throughout the closing was that the people whom the white working-class citizens of the neighborhood sought to exclude were more intelligent, more educated, and more cultured, than they. "For the testimony proved that the ignoble Nordics of Garland Avenue were determined to purge from their neighborhood— 'not especially a high-toned neighborhood at that, nothing swell about it'—people who were clearly their betters."[146]

Darrow came back to the overall defense theme when he talked about the history of the mob and racial violence.

Any reason to expect trouble? Yes. Imagine your face is black, would you have expected trouble? Why, why? He is an intelligent man, he knew the history of his race, he knew that looking back to the terrible years that have marked their history he could see his answer; loaded like sardines in a box in the mid-decks of steamers and brought forcibly from their African homes, half of them dying in the voyage; he knew they were sold like chattels as slaves and were compelled to work without pay; he knew that families were separated when it paid the master to sell them; he knew that even after he had got liberty under the Constitution and the law, he knew that the bodies of dead Negroes were hanging from the limbs of trees of every state in the Union where they had been killed by the mob; he knew that in every state of the Union telegraph poles had been decorated by the bodies of Negroes dangling to ropes on account of race hatred and nothing else; he knew they had been tied to stakes in free America and a fire built around living human beings until they roasted to death; he knew they had been driven from their homes in the north and in great cities and here in Detroit, and he was there not only to defend himself and his home and his friends, but to stand for the integrity and independence of the abused race to which he belonged, and I say, gentlemen, you may send him to

---

146 BOYLE, ARC OF JUSTICE at 293.

prison if you like, but you will only crown him as a hero who fought a brave fight against fearful odds, a fight for the right, for justice, for freedom, and his name will live and be honored when most of us are forgotten.

Throughout much of this closing Darrow seemed to be appealing to the jurors to take the higher moral ground and acquit these defendants because the jurors were capable of putting any prejudice they might have aside. In addition, he occasionally, seemed to back off from taking what he perhaps feared would be unpopular positions. For example, when he talked about segregation, he toned down his true beliefs. He did not say that segregation was wrong, but if it were "right, then it should be embodied in the law, shouldn't it?" And at the end, he asked the jurors

to use all of your judgment, all of your understanding, all of your sympathy in the decision of this case. I speak not only for these eleven people, but for a race that in spite of what you may do will go on and on and on to heights that it has never known before. I speak to you not only in behalf of them, but in behalf of the millions of blacks who look to these twelve white faces for confidence and trust and hope in the institutions of our land, and in the guarantees that the laws have made to them, those blacks who live up and down the length and breadth of our land, and whose ancestors we brought here in chains, I speak to you for those black people of Detroit who have come to work in your factories and your mills by the invitation of your men of business, and who must live or they cannot work. I speak to you in behalf of those faces that have haunted this court room from the beginning of this case, and whose lives and whose hearts and whose hopes and whose fears are centered upon these 12 men before you. I ask you gentlemen in behalf of my clients, I ask you more than everything else, I ask you in behalf of justice, often maligned and down-trodden, hard to protect and hard to maintain, I ask you in behalf of yourselves, in behalf of our race, to see that no harm comes to them. I ask you gentlemen in the name of the future, the future which will one day solve these sore problems, and the future which is theirs as well as ours, I ask you in the name of the future to do justice in this case.

Gentlemen, you twelve whites, with such intellects as have been given you, with such prejudices as have been forced upon you, with such sympathies as you have, and with such judgment as I can urge upon you, I ask you to understand my clients, and I ask in the name of the race, in the name of the past and the hope of the future, in justice to black and white alike, that you shall render a verdict of not guilty in this case.

At that point, Darrow sat down.

Toms gave the state's final two-hour rebuttal. He came back to Leon Breiner. "How little attention is paid to poor Breiner. Poor Breiner? Breiner? Oh yes, yes Breiner: Why yes, oh yes, he is the man who was killed. I had forgotten about him. We have gone to Orlando, we have gone to Tulsa, we have gone to Washington, we have gone to Vienna, we have gone to Paris. . . . And we have left poor Breiner dead here in Detroit."[147]

After the closing arguments, Judge Murphy read the instructions on the law to the jury. Hays later described the impact of those instructions:

> A fair and impartial judiciary has never been better represented than by Judge Frank Murphy at this trial. . . . [I]n his charge to the jury Judge Murphy left no word unsaid to indicate clearly that a man's home is his castle and that no one has a right to assail or invade it. He left no question of the right to shoot when one has reasonable ground to fear that his life or property is in danger. In spite of the general attitude of the community, he made it clear that these rights belong to negroes as well as to white men.[148]

The jury then retired to deliberate. Hour followed hour and day followed day. Finally, on Friday afternoon after forty-six hours of deliberations, Judge Murphy concluded that the jury was hopelessly deadlocked and declared a mistrial.[149]

Before leaving Detroit, Darrow and Hays moved for (and got) bail for the ten defendants who had remained incarcerated[150] and told Judge Murphy that next time they wanted separate trials for each defendant.[151] Overall, Darrow's initial reaction was that this first trial had gone as well as the defense could have hoped. The prosecution's witnesses had not held up well. By and large the defense witnesses generally had done well, and Dr. Sweet had been an excellent witness. Finally, the judge had been sympathetic and fair. But a retrial would give the defense the opportunity to correct some mistakes they had made.

Walter White was not thrilled at the thought of paying for eleven separate trials, but the rallies held during the first trial had brought the NAACP close to raising the $30,000 it needed to establish the Legal

---

147 *Id.* at 296.

148 HAYS, LET FREEDOM RING at 231.

149 BOYLE, ARC OF JUSTICE at 299. During one of the polls in the jury room, all of the jurors had agreed that eight of the defendants should be acquitted, but they had disagreed about Dr. Ossian Sweet, Henry Sweet, and, for some unexplained reason, one of the insurance salesmen.

150 DARROW, THE STORY OF MY LIFE at 310.

151 HAYS, LET FREEDOM RING at 232.

Defense Fund.[152] A strategic concern also surfaced about the separate trials. By trying them all together, the prosecution had had to deal with the conspiracy charge for which the evidence was weak, if it existed at all. In a separate trial with the government likely to select the most vulnerable defendant—which was probably Henry Sweet, since he had admitted to firing into the crowd—the prosecution might have an easier case to prove and a conviction for any of the defendants would have been a disaster for the NAACP. On the other hand, Darrow was convinced that by trying all eleven defendants together, the jurors were free "to divide their votes in any number of ways. . . . Better to present a jury with a single defendant and a simple choice: send him to prison or let him go free."[153] Not surprisingly, in February 1926, Toms announced that he would proceed first against Henry Sweet.[154]

Trial was initially set to begin on March 22. In the meantime, the defense team began to encounter problems. White wanted to force the black lawyers off the case to save money. Then on March 13, Arthur Garfield Hays informed the NAACP that he would not be able to co-counsel the second trial with Darrow because he was tied up in New York on another case. Although White waited until March 21 to tell Darrow, Darrow may have already known that Hays was not going to be available because he had already decided which lawyer he wanted to replace Hays. He told White that he wanted Thomas Chawke, a choice that did not please White. Chawke had been the white Detroit attorney the three black lawyers had wanted early on in the case, but White did not think he was an appropriate representative for the defense since he was widely known to be on retainer to the mob. But Darrow insisted.[155] To Chawke this case, like any other, was not about any cause. It was just business. He eventually agreed to co-counsel the case if it was properly handled, and he also asked for more money than Darrow was being paid. Despite those demands, an agreement was reached a week before trial.[156] Meanwhile, the trial date had been postponed to Monday, April 19.

Once the trial began, it became obvious that the prosecution intended to try precisely the same case—with the same witnesses and making the same arguments. With Darrow having had time to think about the first trial and now with Chawke as co-counsel, the defense took a different approach. During jury selection both Darrow and Chawke asked over and over again about prejudice. Gone was the Darrow who

---

[152] BOYLE, ARC OF JUSTICE at 302.

[153] Id. at 313.

[154] Id. at 311.

[155] Id. at 314–15.

[156] Id. at 315.

had selected jurors based on "instinct and assumption; this was a disciplined defense transforming jury selection into a prolonged opening statement, repeatedly presenting its central argument for all the jurors to hear, winnowing out those least likely to listen."[157]

By the following Monday, a jury—again of twelve white men—had been selected. The prosecuting attorneys came into court that morning and put all the weapons seized from the Sweet home on their table—a sight that was impossible for the jury to ignore. The prosecution then gave its opening statement describing the same evidence that had been introduced at the first trial, but focusing on Henry Sweet's admission the night of the shooting that he had shot into the crowd.

The prosecution expected the defense to defer its opening until after the state had presented its case as it had in the first trial. As a result, Toms planned to immediately start calling the state's witnesses after telling the jury about the state's evidence. Once the prosecution completed its opening, however, Darrow stood up and gave the defense opening. He told the jurors that it was likely that the shot that killed Breiner came from the Sweet home and it was possible that Henry Sweet pulled the trigger. But that did not make Henry Sweet guilty of murder. Rather the true villains were those who drove him to pull the trigger and who now were about to testify for the prosecution.[158]

Only then was the state permitted to call its witnesses. The defense had the advantage of having all the sworn testimony of the prosecution witnesses from the first trial, so any time they deviated from what they had said before they were subject to a withering cross-examination.[159] In addition, the manner in which Darrow and Chawke conducted the cross-examinations differed substantially from the first trial.

> Except when children took the stand, there would be no gentle buildup, no attempt to beguile witnesses into saying something damaging, the way the defense had sometimes done during the first trial. The questions would come hard and fast, ... Darrow's typically gentle voice dripping with sarcasm, Chawke's deep bass raised in anger; the two men daring Toms' witnesses to hold their ground, pressing them to crack.[160]

---

[157] *Id.* at 317.

[158] *Id.* at 319.

[159] Technically, both sides had this advantage when cross-examining their opponent's witnesses, but having the transcripts from the first trial appeared to have given the defense the opportunity to plan and develop areas that had not been thoroughly examined in the first trial. *See* BOYLE, ARC OF JUSTICE at 319–26.

[160] *Id.*

By the time Darrow and Chawke were done cross-examining the state's witnesses, the prejudice that had been rampant in the Garland neighborhood was obvious.

The defense called many of the same witnesses it had called at the first trial, including Ossian Sweet, but added at least one surprise witness—Theresa Hinties. She was Chawke's cleaning lady who lived just across the alley from the Sweet's home. She had not come forward in the first trial but this time she testified that when she tried to walk her dog on the night of the shooting she could not get through the mob of at least three hundred people on the sidewalks around the Sweet home.

Lester Moll in the state's closing again focused on Leon Breiner and made fun of Darrow's and Chawke's efforts to misdirect the jury by focusing on the rights of blacks to live where they choose. Chawke responded by bringing the case back to the issue of prejudice. "I was amazed to think that a public prosecutor at this eventual hour should go the burial place of Leon Breiner and drag his helpless body before you in order that you might send Henry Sweet to jail because Leon Breiner is dead and Henry Sweet is black instead of white."[161]

The next morning Darrow gave his closing argument and this time he gave it with a passion and eloquence that had been missing from his closing the first time. In the first trial, he had been somewhat cautious about offending the jurors by calling them prejudiced. In this trial, he did precisely that.

> I shall begin about where my friend Mr. Moll began yesterday. He says lightly, gentlemen, that this isn't a race question. This is a murder case. We don't want any prejudice; we don't want the other side to have any. Race and color have nothing to do with this case. This is a case of murder.
>
> ... I insist that there is nothing but prejudice in this case; that if it was reversed and eleven white men had shot and killed a black while protecting their home and their lives against a mob of blacks, nobody would have dreamed of having them indicted. I know what I am talking about, and so do you. They would have been given medals instead.
>
> ... Every one of you are white, aren't you? At least you all think so. We haven't one colored man on this jury. We couldn't get one. One was called and he was disqualified. You twelve white men are trying a colored man on race prejudice.... I want to put this square to you, gentlemen. I haven't any doubt but that every one of you are prejudiced against colored people.

---

[161] *Id.* at 329.

... Now, gentlemen, I say you are prejudiced. I fancy everyone of you are, otherwise you would have some companions amongst these colored people. You will overcome it, I believe, in the trial of this case. But they tell me there is no race prejudice, and it is plain nonsense, and nothing else. Who are we, anyway? A child is born into this world without any knowledge of any sort. He has a brain which is a piece of putty; he inherits nothing in the way of knowledge or of ideas. If he is white, he knows nothing about color. He has no antipathy to the black.

The black and the white both will live together and play together, but as soon as the baby is born we begin giving him ideas. We begin planting seeds in his mind. We begin telling him he must do this and he must not do that. We tell him about race and social equality and the thousands of things that men talk about until he grows up. It has been trained into us, and you, gentlemen, bring that feeling into this jury box, and that feeling which is a part of your life long training.

You need not tell me you are not prejudiced. I know better. We are not very much but a bundle of prejudices anyhow. We are prejudiced against other peoples' color. Prejudiced against other men's religion; prejudiced against other peoples' politics. Prejudiced against peoples' looks. Prejudiced about the way they dress. We are full of prejudices. You can teach a man anything beginning with the child; you can make anything out of him, and we are not responsible for it....

All I hope for, gentlemen of the jury, is this: That you are strong enough, and honest enough, and decent enough to lay it aside in this case and decide it as you ought to.[162]

Darrow did not mince words in this closing. He argued that Leon Breiner was not an innocent bystander.

Was Breiner innocent? If he was every other man there was innocent. He left his home. He had gone two or three times down to the corner and back. He had come to Dove's steps where a crowd had collected and peacefully pulled out his pipe and begun to smoke until the curtain should be raised. You know it. Why was he there? He was there just the same as the Roman populace were wont to gather at the Colosseum where they brought out the slaves and the gladiators and waited for the lions to be unloosed. That is why he was there. He was there waiting to see these black men driven from their homes, and you know it; peacefully smoking his pipe, and as

---

[162] The text of this transcript was published in 1927 by the NAACP. It is *available* at http://www.law.umkc.edu/faculty/projects/ftrials/sweet/darrowsummation.html. Unless otherwise noted, all quotations from Mr. Darrow's closing are from that transcript. *See also* ARTHUR WEINBERG, ed., ATTORNEY FOR THE DAMNED 233–263 (1957).

innocent a man as ever scuttled a ship. No innocent people were there. What else did Breiner do? He sat there while boys came and stood in front of him not five feet away, and stoned these black people's homes, didn't he? Did he raise his hand? Did he try to protect any of them? No, no. He was not there for that. He was there waiting for the circus to begin.

Darrow used some of the concepts from his first closing, but he had reworked them so they were much more effective. For example, in refuting the state's claim that his clients were cowards, he shot back:

Who are the cowards in this case? Cowards, gentlemen! Eleven people with black skins, eleven people, gentlemen, whose ancestors did not come to America because they wanted to, but were brought here in slave ships, to toil for nothing, for the whites—whose lives have been taken in nearly every state in the Union,—they have been victims of riots all over this land of the free. They have had to take what is left after everybody else has grabbed what he wanted. The only place where he has been put in front is on the battle field. When we are fighting we give him a chance to die, and the best chance. But, everywhere else, he has been food for the flames, and the ropes, and the knives, and the guns and hate of the white, regardless of law and liberty, and the common sentiments of justice that should move men. Were they cowards? No, gentlemen, they may have been gun men. They may have tried to murder, but they were not cowards.

Eleven people, knowing what it meant, with the history of the race behind them, with the picture of Detroit in front of them; . . . with the knowledge of shootings and killings and insult and injury without end, eleven of them go into a house, gentlemen, with no police protection, in the face of a mob, and the hatred of a community, and take guns and ammunition and fight for their rights, and for your rights and for mine, and for the rights of every being that lives. They went in and faced a mob seeking to tear them to bits. Call them something besides cowards.

The cowardly curs were in the mob gathered there with the backing of the law. A lot of children went in front and threw the stones. They stayed for two days and two nights in front of this home and by their threats and assault were trying to drive the Negroes out. Those were the cowardly curs, and you know it. I suppose there isn't any ten of them that would come out in the open daylight against those ten. Oh, no, gentlemen, their blood is too pure for that. They can only act like a band of coyotes baying some victim who has no chance.

And then my clients are called cowards. All right, gentlemen, call them something else. These blacks have been called many names along down through the ages, but there have been those through the sad years who believed in justice and mercy and charity and love and kindliness, and there have been those who believed that a black man should have some rights, even in a country where he was brought in chains. There are those even crazy enough to hope and to dream that sometime he will come from under this cloud and take his place amongst the people of the world. If he does, it will be through his courage and his culture. It will be by his intelligence and his scholarship and his effort, and I say, gentlemen of the jury, no honest, right feeling man, whether on a jury, or anywhere else, would place anything in his way in this great struggle behind him and before him.

Darrow had totally reorganized this closing. It no longer meandered from one topic and back to another the way the first had. In this closing, Darrow found his stride. It had cadence and power and it was compelling. He knew where he was going and what he needed to say. He turned to the state's claim that there was no mob that night.

[The mob] violated the constitution and the law, they violated every human feeling, and threw justice and mercy and humanity to the winds, and they made a murderous attack upon their neighbor because his face was black. Which is the worse, to do that or lie about it? In describing this mob, I heard the word "few" from the State's witnesses so many times that I could hear it in my sleep, and I presume that when I am dying I will hear that "few," "few," "few" stuff that I heard in Detroit from people who lied and lied and lied.

In an effort to explain why they had done what they did, he argued:

Are the people who live around the corner of Charlevoix and Garland worse than other people? There isn't one of you who doesn't know that they lied. There isn't one of you who does not know that they tried to drive those people out and now are trying to send them to the penitentiary so that they can't move back; all in violation of the law, and are trying to get you to do the job. Are they worse than other people? I don't know as they are. How much do you know about prejudice? Race prejudice. Religious prejudice. These feelings that have divided men and caused them to do the most terrible things. Prejudices have burned men at the stake, broken them on the rack, torn every joint apart, destroyed people by the million. Men have done this on account of some terrible prejudice which even now is reaching out to undermine this republic of ours and to destroy the freedom that has been the most cherished part of our institutions.

These witnesses honestly believe that they are better than blacks. I do not. They honestly believe that it is their duty to keep colored people out. They honestly believe that the blacks are an inferior race ... They are possessed with that idea and that fanaticism, and when people are possessed with that they are terribly cruel. They don't stand alone. Others have done the same thing. Others will do the same thing so long as this weary old world shall last. They may do it again, but, gentlemen, they ought not to ask you to do it for them....

Darrow then went through the testimony and the government's evidence in the case systematically and scathingly reducing it to absurdity.[163] In response to the state's argument that they took the guns to Garland to commit murder, Darrow disagreed:

They went there to live. They knew the dangers. Why do you suppose they took these guns and this ammunition and these men there? Because they wanted to kill somebody? It is utterly absurd and crazy. They took them there because they thought it might be necessary to defend their home with their lives and they were determined to do it. They took guns there that in case of need they might fight, fight even to death for their home, and for each other, for their people, for their race, for their rights under the Constitution and the laws under which all of us live; and unless men and women will do that, we will soon be a race of slaves, whether we are black or white. "Eternal vigilance is the price of liberty," and it has always been so and always will be. Do you suppose they were in there for any other purpose? Gentlemen, there isn't a chance that they took arms there for anything else.

As Darrow came to the end of his closing, he took a few minutes to remind the jurors of history.

Let us take a little glance at the history of the Negro race.... These men, the defendants, are here because they could not help it. Their ancestors were captured in the jungles and on the plains of Africa,

---

[163] Darrow's belittling of many of the state's witnesses and personal attacks at times seems harsh but there was no question of his outrage at what they had done. Throughout his closing, Darrow heaped scorn upon the ignorant people who lived in the Garland neighborhood. For example, he made fun of the witnesses who could not properly pronounce the name of Goethe Street. In one instance, when talking about Miss Stowell, he said: "Miss Stowell,—Miss Stowell—do you see her? I do. S-t-o-w-e-l-l. You remember, gentlemen, that she spelled it for us. I can spell that in my sleep, too. I can spell it backwards. Well, let me recall her to you. She teaches school at the corner of Garland and 'Gother' Street; fifteen years a high school teacher, and, in common with all the other people in the community, she called it 'Gother' Street."

captured as you capture wild beasts, torn from their homes and their kindred; loaded into slave ships, packed like sardines in a box, half of them dying on the ocean passage; some jumping into the sea in their frenzy, when they had a chance to choose death in place of slavery. They were captured and brought here. They could not help it. They were bought and sold as slaves, to work without pay, because they were black.

They were subjected to all of this for generations, until finally they were given their liberty, so far as the law goes,—and that is only a little way, because, after all, every human being's life in this world is inevitably mixed with every other life and, no matter what laws we pass, no matter what precautions we take, unless the people we meet are kindly and decent and human and liberty-loving, then there is no liberty. Freedom comes from human beings, rather than from laws and institutions.

Now, that is their history. These people are the children of slavery. If the race that we belong to owes anything to any human being, or to any power in this Universe, they owe it to these black men. Above all other men, they owe an obligation and a duty to these black men which can never be repaid. I never see one of them, that I do not feel I ought to pay part of the debt of my race,—and if you gentlemen feel as you should feel in this case, your emotions will be like mine.

Having spoken again for almost seven hours, Darrow ended his closing with a powerful plea:

Now, gentlemen, just one more word, and I am through with this case. I do not live in Detroit. But I have no feeling against this city. In fact, I shall always have the kindest remembrance of it, especially if this case results as I think and feel that it will. I am the last one to come here to stir up race hatred, or any other hatred. I do not believe in the law of hate. I may not be true to my ideals always, but I believe in the law of love, and I believe you can do nothing with hatred. I would like to see a time when man loves his fellow man, and forgets his color or his creed. We will never be civilized until that time comes.

I know the Negro race has a long road to go. I believe the life of the Negro race has been a life of tragedy, of injustice, of oppression. The law has made him equal, but man has not. And, after all, the last analysis is, what has man done?—and not what has the law done? I know there is a long road ahead of him, before he can take the place which I believe he should take. I know that before him there is suffering, sorrow, tribulation and death among the blacks, and perhaps the whites. I am sorry. I would do what I could to avert it. I would advise patience; I would advise toleration; I would advise understanding; I would advise all of those things which are necessary for men who live together.

Gentlemen, what do you think is your duty in this case? I have watched, day after day, these black, tense faces that have crowded this court. These black faces that now are looking to you twelve whites, feeling that the hopes and fears of a race are in your keeping.

This case is about to end, gentlemen. To them, it is life. Not one of their color sits on this jury. Their fate is in the hands of twelve whites. Their eyes are fixed on you, their hearts go out to you, and their hopes hang on your verdict.

This is all. I ask you, on behalf of this defendant, on behalf of these helpless ones who turn to you, and more than that,—on behalf of this great state, and this great city which must face this problem, and face it fairly,—I ask you, in the name of progress and of the human race, to return a verdict of not guilty in this case!

When Darrow ended, the courtroom was silent. No one moved and "[t]hen the crowd began to surge around him."[164] James Weldon Johnson later wrote: "He closed his argument with a plea that left no eye dry. When he finished, I walked over to him to express my appreciation and thanks. His eyes were wet. He placed his hands on my shoulders. I tried to stammer out a few words, but broke down and wept."[165]

Toms' rebuttal argument for the state the next morning, while competently done, could not compare to Darrow's oration from the day before.[166] This time the jury deliberated for three hours and twenty-seven minutes before returning a verdict of "not guilty".[167]

After Henry Sweet's acquittal none of the other defendants were ever retried for Leon Breiner's murder. It took Toms over a year—until July 25, 1927—to dismiss all the charges against the remaining defendants but he finally did so and the case was over.[168]

---

[164] Boyle, Arc of Justice at 334.

[165] James Weldon Johnson, Along This Way 384 (1933).

[166] Boyle, Arc of Justice at 334–35.

[167] White, A Man Called White at 79.

[168] Years after the trials were over, with the support of Darrow, Toms became a circuit court judge and a staunch advocate of civil rights. He even later joined the Detroit branch of the NAACP. Eventually, he prosecuted Nazi war criminals at the Nuremberg trials. Boyle, Arc of Justice at 341.

9

Michael E. Tigar[1]

The Vioxx Litigation: Two Case Studies

In 1999, pharmaceutical giant Merck released a new drug, Vioxx, to treat chronic pain. Vioxx and the competitor drug Celebrex, marketed by Pfizer, seemed like good news for arthritis sufferers. Vioxx was sold in more than 80 countries. In 2003, Vioxx sales were $2.5 billion. Most arthritis pain sufferers had been taking some form of NSAID, or non-steroidal anti-inflammatory drug, such as ibuprofen or aspirin. The problem with most NSAIDs is that they cause stomach bleeding. The incidence of stomach bleeding is higher among elderly people who take NSAIDs. The effects on the stomach can include bleeding to death, puncture of the stomach wall, and other fatal events.

The chemical and physiological explanation for these side-effects is something called Cox-inhibition. Before the research work that led to Vioxx, it was believed that there was one "Cox enzyme," which did two things: It sent signals to pain receptors and it also helped to curb inflammation of the stomach wall. NSAIDs were thought to suppress this enzyme, which was why they both treated pain and caused gastric bleeding. Drug company scientists discovered that in fact there were two enzymes at work, COX–1, which protected the stomach, and COX–2, which aided communication with pain receptors. Vioxx was claimed to be revolutionary because it suppressed or inhibited the COX–2 enzyme while leaving the COX–1 enzyme alone.

However, physicians began to question the safety of Vioxx. Within six months of Vioxx entering the market, initial results of a study that compared Vioxx to an NSAID known as Naproxen—marketed as Aleve among other names—showed that those taking Vioxx had a greater risk

[1] Research Professor of Law, Washington College of Law, Visiting Professor of Law, Duke Law School.

of cardiac episodes connected with blood clots than those taking Naprox-
en. Merck evaluated the results and made the claim that the difference
was due to the anti-clotting, cardio-protective effects of Naproxen rather
than to any increased danger from taking Vioxx. One might think that
the best way to see for sure would be to do a trial where some patients
took Vioxx and the others a placebo or sugar pill. Such an approach was
not considered feasible because all candidates for the study were people
suffering pain and it would be unfair to insist that sufferers give up
medication for the six months to a year that a study would take. This
study, which has played a central role in all Merck litigation, is known
by the acronym VIGOR.[2] Plaintiffs' counsel and Merck see the VIGOR
results from opposite ends: did Vioxx cause more heart attacks, or did
Naproxen lower the risk?

Some cardiologists disagreed with the way that Merck interpreted
the VIGOR data. One of these was Dr. Eric Topol, head of the Cleveland
Cardiology Clinic. He published his findings in the August 2001 New
England Journal of Medicine. Dr. Topol became an important figure in
the Vioxx litigation. He refused to accept employment by either side of
the dispute. He also refused to accept service of process for court
appearances outside his home state and the 100 miles provided for in
Federal Rule of Civil Procedure 45(b)(2) and its state counterparts.
Therefore, the parties have taken his deposition, which is played for
juries. The New York Times has described Dr. Topol as "a Naderesque
crusader against drugs he deems dangerous, as well as their makers."[3]

From this controversy emerged a central issue that is common to
every Vioxx story and every Vioxx trial: What effect does Vioxx have on
the patient's blood? To see this issue, we might begin by noting that
many adult males take a small daily dose of aspirin because medical
research shows that aspirin has an effect on red blood cells. It seems to
make the cells more "slippery," and therefore inhibits the formation of
clots that cause heart attack and stroke. Aspirin is a nonselective Cox-
inhibitor—there is pain relief but clotting is impeded. As noted above,
too much aspirin can actually cause gastrointestinal bleeding. Did the
Merck scientists do enough studies for long enough to see if their
product would have an effect on the blood that would promote clotting?
When they had "early warnings" that there was such an effect, did they
take steps to warn physicians, or did their interest in marketing Vioxx
overcome any thoughts of doing that?

---

[2] Vioxx GI Outcomes Research.

[3] See Ties to Industry cloud a Clinic's Mission, NEW YORK TIMES, December 17, 2005,
online edition, http://www.nytimes.com/2005/12/17/business/17clinic.html?ex=1292475600
&en=d44d70e27af8c3e5&ei=5090&partner=rssuserland&emc=rss. In October 2006, Dr.
Topol announced that he will be leaving the Cleveland Clinic to join a medical school
faculty in California.

As the controversy continued and some lawsuits were filed, Merck scientists were conducting a clinical trial to evaluate whether Vioxx was helpful in preventing a recurrence of colon and rectal polyps. This trial, known by the acronym APPROVe,[4] produced some disturbing information. As a Merck press release of September 30, 2004 announced:

> In [the APPROVe] study, there was an increased relative risk for confirmed cardiovascular events, such as heart attack and stroke, beginning after 18 months of treatment in the patients taking Vioxx compared to those taking placebo. The results for the first 18 months of the APPROVe study did not show any increased risk of confirmed cardiovascular events on Vioxx, and in this respect, are similar to the results of two placebo-controlled studies described in the current U.S. labeling for Vioxx.

In the same press release, Merck announced that it was withdrawing Vioxx from the market worldwide. Because Merck is a public company, and Vioxx was so important to its financial performance, there is a great deal of information in the public domain about the legal decisions that Merck faced in responding to the inevitable large number of lawsuits claiming that Vioxx had caused injury or death. As of September 30, 2006, on which date the statute of limitations would have run for a large number of potential plaintiffs in two-year statute jurisdictions, there were about 17,000 Vioxx lawsuits on file. Some of these are class actions. The federal lawsuits have been consolidated for pretrial purposes as a multi-district litigation under 28 U.S.C. § 1407.

Merck's general counsel is Kenneth C. Frazier, formerly a litigation partner in the Philadelphia law firm of Drinker Biddle. With the advice of outside counsel, Merck announced that it would defend all the lawsuits, and as of October 2006 had resisted efforts to engage in large-scale alternative dispute resolution procedures that would acknowledge liability and set up mechanisms for payment.

The Vioxx damages suits are being tried one by one, in different forums. In 2005–06, there were a total of about a dozen trials in Texas and New Jersey state courts, and in federal courts in Houston, Texas and New Orleans, Louisiana. The trial results were about evenly divided between plaintiff and defense verdicts.

Writers on tort policy have wondered whether the civil justice trial system is an appropriate mechanism to deal with large scale product liability cases of this kind. In this book, the focus is on advocacy decisions. I have chosen two Vioxx cases as illustrative. One is Ernst v. Merck, tried in Brazoria County, Texas state court. The plaintiff was

---

[4] Ademantous Polyp Prevention On Vioxx, a study of the drug's effect on colorectal polyps.

Carol Ernst, widow of Bob Ernst, who died in May 2001. Bob Ernst's doctor had prescribed Vioxx for him, and he had taken it for about a year before he died. The exact cause of his death was the subject of intense dispute at trial. Opening statements took place on July 14, 2005, and the jury returned its verdict on August 19, 2005: compensatory damages of $24 million and punitive damages of $229 million. Under Texas law, the jury's punitive damage award must be capped at $26.1 million. Merck announced that it would appeal.

In Ernst, tried under Texas law, the jurors' verdict was in the form of answers to questions. First,

> was there a defect in the marketing of Vioxx at the time it left the possession of Merck and Company, Inc., that was a producing cause of the death of Bob Ernst? A marketing defect includes a failure to give adequate warnings. A producing cause is "an efficient, exciting, or contributing cause that, in a natural sequence, produces the injury." There may be more than one producing cause.

Second,

> was there a design defect in Vioxx at the time it left the possession of Merck and Company, Inc., that was a producing cause of the death of Bob Ernst? A design defect renders the product unreasonably dangerous. The jury must consider and weigh the risks and benefits of the product, and the plaintiff must show that there was a safer alternative design.

Third,

> did the negligence, if any, of Merck and Company, Inc., proximately cause the death of Bob Ernst? A proximate cause is "that cause which in a natural and continuous sequence produces an event and, without which cause, such event would not have occurred." In order to be a proximate cause, the act or omission complained of must be such that a person using the ordinary care would have foreseen that event or some similar event might reasonably result therefrom. There maybe more than one proximate cause of an event.

The Ernst jurors were instructed that compensatory damages would include pecuniary loss, loss of companionship, and mental anguish. They were told that they could award exemplary damages by way of punishment based on culpability.

For purposes of contrast, I selected Plunkett v. Merck, which was tried to a federal jury in Houston, Texas. The case was moved to Houston from New Orleans because the federal courthouse there had been damaged in Hurricane Katrina. The plaintiff was Evelyn Plunkett, widow of Richard "Dicky" Irvin, for herself and on behalf of the minor children Richey and Ashley. She alleged that Mr. Irvin's death was due to Vioxx. Mr. Irvin had taken Vioxx for about 30 days. The jury failed to reach a verdict and was discharged. On retrial, the jury returned a verdict for Merck.

The Plunkett case was tried under Florida law. The plaintiff's three claims were first, failure to warn, as to which the plaintiff must prove that Merck knew or should have known that Vioxx was or was likely to be unreasonably dangerous; second, Merck failed to exercise reasonable care in warning Dr. Schirmer [Irvin's prescribing physician] of Vioxx's dangerous condition; and, third, Merck's failure to warn was a legal cause of the plaintiff's injury. Legal cause is the same as proximate cause under Texas law.

The second claim was "defective design," under which the plaintiff must prove that "Vioxx was a defective product due to a defective design," and that "Vioxx's defective design was a legal cause of the plaintiff's injury. . . . A product is unreasonably dangerous if the risk of danger in the design outweighs the benefits."

The third claim was negligence, and under Florida law the jury was asked to consider the potential comparative negligence of Merck, Dr. Schirmer and the decedent.[5]

The nine-person Plunkett jury was unable to reach a verdict. On a retrial, Merck won. Given the scant evidence of causation in Plunkett, why did at least one juror hold out for the plaintiffs? The answer probably lies in the very damaging evidence of internal Merck documents and attitudes about drug development and safety issues. The trial excerpts will allow you, the reader, to judge for yourself.

The two cases present sharply contrasting lawyer styles and strategies. The different results are due in large measure to the differences in the way the advocates approached their cases. Of course, other elements are also important, such as choice of forum, federal v. state procedure, and the different factual scenarios of the two cases. For example, in Texas state court, cross-examination is not limited to the scope of the direct, as it is under Federal Rule of Evidence 611(b). This distinction makes a big difference in trial strategy. However, I believe that studying the two cases side by side yields important insights. The combined trial transcripts of the two cases run to almost 7,000 pages. It is thus a challenge to tell the trial stories and to present some insights about the trial process.

ERNST v. MERCK IN ANGLETON, TEXAS STATE COURT

The plaintiff's lawyer in Ernst was Mark Lanier, of Brazoria County, Texas, which is near Houston. Lanier is a part-time preacher and a

---

[5] Plaintiff withdrew two additional claims, based on fraud and breach of warranty, at the close of her case-in-chief.

powerful and charismatic jury lawyer. His law office has many Vioxx cases, and it appears at this writing that he will try them all in state court, if possible. Also on the plaintiff team was Dallas lawyer Lisa Blue, a veteran of many plaintiffs' cases and a partner at Baron & Budd.

The Merck defense team for Ernst was drawn from Williams & Connolly of Washington, and Fulbright & Jaworski of Houston, among other firms. The Merck team included two lawyers who also hold M.D. degrees.

Lanier's strategy for the first week of the Ernst trial put him in control of the trial issues and process and put his story of the case powerfully before the jury. The trial transcript suggests that Merck was never able to catch up, and this conclusion is echoed by several experienced trial observers including members of the trial teams speaking off the record.

Lanier's opening began with the theme of Merck as an irresponsible profit-seeking corporate entity. He moved from there to a vivid description of the warning signs he said one could find in Merck's studies concerning Vioxx. These were Lanier's strongest points. He discussed the alleged causal link between Vioxx and Bob Ernst's death, but not in great detail. As the trial evidence unfolded, it became clear that causation was the weakest part of Lanier's case, and he waited until the jurors had heard much evidence about Merck and Vioxx safety in general before fully unfolding the theory that a Vioxx-induced clot caused Bob Ernst's death, even though no clot was found during the autopsy.

Lanier began by talking about Bob and Carol Ernst. Bob had been married before he met Carol, and she had been married and divorced. Lanier talked about their lives together, focusing on how they were active and engaged in many forms of outdoor exercise together. The unspoken focus here was that Bob Ernst was not a candidate for a coronary event. He then turned to the themes of his case. Read how he empowered the jurors, acknowledged and embraced his burden of persuasion, and outlined the 1–2–3 of his proposed proof:

> He was 59 years old when he died. And what you've got to do is basically be the detectives here. You've got to figure out why he died. That's your job: figure out whether or not, of the reasons he died, Vioxx is one of those causes. And that's your job. This is—if we were going to put it into a TV show, this would be "CSI Angleton" because this is your chance.
>
> And I think the way you do it is going to be real easy. What you're going to do is, you're going to follow the evidence, like any good detective would. You follow the evidence. And the evidence is going to lead you to one place. It's going to leave you—lead you to Merck. It's going to lead you to Merck, one of the largest pharma-

ceutical companies in the world. And when you got anything big, there are lots of different ways it can be painted.

You were told yesterday [during voir dire] by Ms. Lowry, Merck is a good company with good people. I have no doubt there are good people at that company. But you're going to hear a tale where it's not just an e-mail that she was referencing of, gee—do you understand sometimes you put things in e-mails they wish they hadn't put. You're going to see the evidence. And not just from somebody. You're going to see it from the head of science as he cusses out the FDA and says what he really thinks about it.

You're going to hear all of this evidence because what you've got—your job to do is to get us to justice. There isn't anybody else. The way our country is set up, there is no one else, no one else that can find out whether or not Merck is a cause but you. That's it. That's the calling. This is what's on your life right now. Nobody else has this power. A judge can't do it. This is not a bench trial. Judge can't do it. Politicians can't do it. Nobody else can do it. This is something you've got. This is where you can make a difference in the world, absolutely can.

How are you going to do it? My suggestion to you is, again, you've got to follow the evidence. First of all, I'm going to show you a motive. I'm going to show you the means. I'm going to show you the death. And I'm going to show you ultimately the alibis and how the alibis don't fly.

I'm going to show you the motive, and I'll prove it to you. And my burden is to prove it by 51 percent, but I got to tell you, I'll prove it to you. There's not going to be that doubt in your mind. You're going to see the motive. You're going to see it clear.

The means, I'm going to show you Vioxx was a cause. That's my burden of proof. That's what the Judge makes me do. That's what I'm glad to do. I'm going to show you the death and that the Vioxx— the motive and the means combined to cause the death of Carol's husband, Bob.

And then we'll walk through their alibis, at least the ones, I'm guessing, based on what I heard yesterday and what I've been reading in the papers and what I've been hearing. We'll look at their alibis. We'll show that those excuses don't work.

Let's start with motive. Merck had the motive. What was the motive? The motive was money. Don't get me wrong. I think it's fine for a corporation to exist to make money. That's how we have jobs. That's how we have products. I think that's a good thing. But what companies have to do is, they have to watch to make sure that money doesn't take a priority position over health and safety.

Merck had new management that came into play in 1994, and this new management took the company and they tried to turn Merck into an ATM machine, a machine that's spitting out the money, a machine where they could punch the buttons and they could draw out all the cash they want and need. This is 1994.

Let me tell you about it. This is a new direction for the company. Merck—you heard the expression, "The changing of the guard"? That's what happened here. The guard changes. Okay? Merck flip-flops.

See, the historical company Merck had been a family-run company. It had been a good company. I'm going to tell you, the history of Merck before this is a good history. Founded by George Merck. They put out real nice books on it (indicating). This was a company that was really working hard to find good drugs over the years.

This is a company that stumbled upon[6] a drug that cured an African blindness, River blindness, and the people who could be cured with the drug. They didn't have money to buy it. They didn't have insurance. And so Merck gives it to them to try and take care— all right. They did get tax benefits and all that kind of stuff. It wasn't totally gratuitous. But Merck gives it to them, and I applaud them for that.

They had been a good company run by scientists. There was this fella. In fact, he wrote the foreword to this book, Dr. Vagelos or Vagelos. And I don't know how to pronounce it. I've never met him, but I've read about him. And he was a good scientist, a doctor, one of the best doctors in the country, running this drug company, and he did a good job. But what happened?

It is in 1994—in 1994, Merck broke with tradition and they hired a new CEO. This is the fella right here (indicating), Ray Gilmartin. That's the new CEO hired in 1994. I say they broke with tradition because, historically, Merck had always had the guy running the company—they brought him up through the ranks so he understood the company values. He understood how the company worked. He was one of their top scientists. He was one of their top doctors. But in 1994, the family is not running the company any more. That's over. This is now this big international concern. And what the board did is, they chose to be a new kind of company in 1994. They hired Ray Gilmartin.

---

[6] Careful choice of words. Not "through scientific research that cost a lot of money," but "stumbled upon."

Now, you might be thinking, "All right. I wonder what kind of a guy Ray Gilmartin is. Was he a top-flight doctor? Was he another— like Dr. Vagelos, was he one of the best doctors in the country?" No, he wasn't. Well, if the board didn't turn to a doctor, maybe they turned to a chemist, because they're doing chemistry, right? Maybe they turned to a chemist and got one of the best chemists in the world to help this company develop good chemicals. No, they didn't hire a chemist either. Maybe they hired a pharmacist. It's a pharmacy company. Maybe they hired a pill expert, a drug expert. Maybe that's who Ray Gilmartin is.

No, Ray Gilmartin is not any of those things. And those were not the priorities Ray Gilmartin brought to the company when he came. What the company did is, they went and they hired Ray Gilmartin, and Ray Gilmartin is a Harvard-trained businessman, not a scientist. There's nothing wrong with a businessman running the company if he runs it right, but you're going to see what he did. If a Boy Scout has a compass or a Girl Scout has a compass and the needle is supposed to always point north, Ray Gilmartin took this company and made the needle always point to the dollar sign, and that's how they chose their direction.

Ray Gilmartin made it not science first like it had always been, not health first, not medicine first, not drugs first. Ray Gilmartin made it profit first. He turned a good drug company into a business-first company.

Studded with exhibits that the trial judge had found admissible during pretrial proceedings, Lanier went through the elements of his case. In the Ernst case, the plaintiffs were allowed more leeway than in the Plunkett case in presenting evidence of Merck's disputes with the FDA over labeling of drugs other than Vioxx. This difference illustrates the role and value of pretrial motion in limine practice.

On the issue of motive, Lanier pointed to evidence that in 2000 and 2001 a number of Merck drugs were coming off patent and that there was pressure to get Vioxx to market.

Defense counsel's opening statement poses a special challenge. Defense counsel must seize the jurors' attention and pose an alternative story to the one presented by the plaintiff. Jurors come to see the case as a story. They take a tentative view of what happened and more readily accept evidence that tends to support that view. Jurors need guidance, so that they can see the most important issues in the case, and what significance they should attach to items of evidence they will hear or see. It seems obvious, but bears repeating that, in opening statement, a lawyer must acknowledge unfavorable evidence and must focus on the case-winning issues. When, as here, plaintiff's counsel portrays the case as presenting a significant moral and social issue, defense counsel must choose the response carefully.

In the Ernst case, Merck's counsel's opening was disappointing. Merck had powerful evidence that Vioxx did not cause Bob Ernst's heart attack. Their lawyers also knew that there would be a lot of evidence about Merck's actions and attitudes that a jury might find unsettling. But all of that would be irrelevant if Merck could win on causation. Defense counsel in criminal cases are familiar with the problem that Merck's counsel faced: the defendant may not be a sympathetic person, but he or she did not commit the charged conduct, or at least the proof falls short on that score. Of course, counsel seeks to portray the defendant in the best light. But there is a time and place for that work.

Merck's counsel's opening began with

Good afternoon, ladies and gentlemen. My name is David Kiernan, and I'm pleased to speak with you this afternoon on behalf of Merck. As you might imagine, we wouldn't be here today if there weren't two sides to this story. If it were an open and shut case, as plaintiffs have suggested, this case would have been over long ago. As Judge Hardin mentioned during jury selection, this will be a somewhat lengthy case, lots of evidence to be presented, documents, and witnesses, some live, and some who gave their sworn testimony before trial and videotape. You'll see both during this trial.

We appreciate the important job that each of you have ahead of you. It's a tough job to sort through and weigh all of the evidence, to tell the difference between allegations and proof; and we appreciate you undertaking that responsibility here. We believe that at the end of this case you will see that the scientists and leaders at Merck conducted themselves prudently and responsibly. I don't ask you at this early stage to take my word for it. At this juncture, all I ask is that you keep an open mind until all of the evidence is in.

This case comes down to four issues. First: Was Merck responsible in its development of Vioxx? What you will learn in this case is that Vioxx was one of the most carefully and extensively studied pain relievers in history, not only before the medicine was put on the market, but after, as well. Merck continuously monitored the safety of Vioxx.

Second: Did Merck share, or as plaintiffs have suggested, hide, the scientific information on Vioxx? The evidence will show that Merck's safety studies were supplied and analyzed by the United States Food and Drug Administration, the FDA, that reported adverse reactions, including cardiovascular events, were monitored by Merck and noted right on the label for doctors to review and that Merck made public the results of its studies.

The third issue: Did the people at Merck, like Mr. Gilmartin,[7] make their decisions based on science? The evidence will show that at the time Mr. Ernst started taking Vioxx, around October of 2000, scores of studies involving thousands of patients had shown that Vioxx presented no more risk of heart attacks or strokes than taking a sugar pill. Even today, after a recent break-through in the science, the evidence is that Vioxx presents no risk until after continuous, day-in, day-out, long-term use for as much as 30 months or longer. And even then, the risk is very small and about the same as other pain relievers that you can buy at your local drug store, like Advil, Motrin, or Ibuprofen. We now know that the risk that we've talked about this morning is roughly the same with all of the medicines in this class. This will prove important because you will hear that before Mr. Ernst was taking Vioxx, he was—he was, in fact, taking one of those pain relievers; and it was Advil, or Ibuprofen, and he was taking 16 pills a day.

The fourth issue—and I ask you not to lose sight of this point—did Vioxx cause Mr. Ernst's death? After all is said and done, this issue should decide the case. I feel for Mrs. Ernst. She lost her husband. I do. But the evidence will show you, no matter what you think about Vioxx at the end of the case, it had nothing to do with Mr. Ernst's death. Mr. Ernst died from an arrhythmia, which is an irregular heartbeat. He did not have a heart attack, which occurs when a clot interrupts the flow of blood to the heart. The two are entirely different. Be wary, please, of attempts to blur the distinction between the two. And no one, not any study or legitimate scientist anywhere, suggests that Vioxx increases the risk of arrhythmia. It doesn't.

These are the four issues that we will ask you to focus on during this trial. We will avoid presenting to you snippets or tidbits of data so we won't mislead you about what the science clearly says. Please watch out for that. We will show you all of the data so that you can make a judgment about what it tells you and whether Merck's scientists were making reasonable decisions. We will avoid trying to suggest that ten years of scientific investigation can be explained with a handful of e-mails taken out of ten million e-mails amongst 62,000 employees.

---

[7] Counsel spent five minutes of a one-hour opening defending Ray Gilmartin's character, with references to his background, public service, church-going and family life. Gilmartin would not appear at the trial as a live witness, but rather by deposition. It is arguable that the issue is not Mr. Gilmartin's personal characteristics, but whether he ran Merck efficiently and effectively, and whether in fact science-based decisions were made by people qualified to make them.

What's wrong with this picture? The opening statement lacks drama. The lawyer doesn't talk about his strongest point—causation—until the end. The lawyer tells us little or nothing about why Vioxx was a revolutionary drug, how Merck is science-driven, or how risks and benefits are a part of every drug profile.

One good way to see the missed opportunities in this opening is to look at Phil Beck's opening for Merck in the Plunkett case. Mr. Beck began:

> Thank you, your honor. Mr. Birchfield [plaintiff's counsel] talked for about 60 minutes. While he was talking, about 60 people across the United States died from exactly the same thing that caused Mr. Irvin's death and not a single one of them was taking Vioxx. I'm going to talk for about 60 minutes, and while I'm talking another 60 people across the United States will die of the same thing that caused Mr. Irvin's death, and not a single one of them is taking Vioxx. The reason is that the thing that caused Mr. Irvin's death is the leading cause of death in the United States of America. That was true before Vioxx ever came on the market, and that's true today after Vioxx is no longer being sold. Several-hundred-thousand people a year die from having arteries that are clogged up with plaque, then having a rupture in the plaque, and then having a blood clot form in the artery so that not enough blood gets to the heart. It's the leading cause of death in the United States.
>
> Lots of people who die from this cause are people like Mr. Irvin: men in their 50s; men who are a little overweight; men who don't get enough of the kind of cardiac exercise that doctors say you should get in order to protect your heart. Meanwhile, Mr. Irvin only took Vioxx for less than 30 days. Just for less than 30 days. Now, you saw a lot of Vioxx studies, and you'll hear about them during the trial. With most of the studies that were done on Vioxx, there is no indication of a higher risk of any sort of cardiac problem no matter how long anybody takes Vioxx. There was one study that showed that there may be a higher risk taking Vioxx, but that was only for people who took it every day for a long period of time, for at least 18 months, and the risk did not become what they call "medically significant" until people had been taking it for over 30 months. That study showed no difference at all for people who were taking Vioxx for short periods of time, certainly for something like one month. In fact, there were lots and lots of studies done on Vioxx, and not a single one of them—not a single one—shows an increased risk of any heart attack problems for somebody who uses it for only a month or so.

Now, that brings us to the two things that the evidence is going to show in this case, and these are going to be the two focuses of our presentation of evidence. The first one is that Vioxx did not cause Mr. Irvin's death. The second one is that Merck acted responsibly when developing and testing Vioxx.

Actually, I'm going to come back to number 1 a little bit later. I'm going to start with number 2. What did Merck do when developing and testing Vioxx? To start with the development of Vioxx, it's important to understand what Vioxx was developed to do. Vioxx is medicine that was researched and developed in order to treat pain. You heard a little bit about that from Mr. Birchfield. Now, all of us have experienced pain in our lives, and most of us have experienced severe pain, the kind of pain where it hurts so bad that it's hard to concentrate on anything else. It's hard even to be around other people. Happily, for most of us, that kind of pain passes. In fact, the knowledge that that pain is going to pass is the thing that makes the pain bearable for most of us. To some people, they have that kind of real bad pain, but it doesn't pass, and they know it's not going to pass. They have it minute after minute, day after day, night after night, week after week, and it never goes away. It interferes with their ability to lead a normal life—just simple things like going for a walk, picking up the grandkid, writing a "thank you" note. The pain that people have who have severe arthritis and other conditions can be so severe that they can't lead a normal life. This kind of chronic pain is a big problem in the United States. There are, the estimates are, 70 million people in America suffer from osteoarthritis, one of the kinds of conditions that have this kind of pain. So people need relief. Lots of people in America need relief from serious pain. I would like to spend a little bit of time talking about how our bodies work, how it is that you feel pain, and how it is that medicines and—including Vioxx—go about relieving that pain, and the example that I'm going to use is just somebody jamming their finger.

Beck then discussed the uses of morphine, aspirin and ibuprofen as pain relievers. For aspirin and ibuprofen, he set out the risks of stomach bleeds from continued use, and outlined how Vioxx suppressed the pain transmitter enzyme but did not interfere with the stomach protective enzyme.

Let us return our focus to Ernst. When a corporate or other entity is a party to litigation, it can designate a representative to sit at counsel table. Merck chose Dr. Nancy Santanello for the Ernst case. She is a physician who worked on the development of Vioxx. She no longer practices medicine. Lanier called her as as an adverse witness immediately after opening statements, and examined her as though on cross-

examination.[8] He began with questions that established that Ms. Santanello was chosen by Merck from among 62,000 employees to be the
corporate representative and that she was not a senior executive of
Merck or any of its divisions.

Lanier then went after Merck's opening statement. Ms. Santanello
said that she had been in the courtroom for both openings. Merck
counsel had chosen to reply to Lanier's claims that Merck misled the
public, and that the FDA had sent warning letters. Merck counsel put up
an FDA letter that complained about the type size and type face of a
disclaimer on a Merck ad for a high blood pressure medication. With Ms.
Santanello on the stand, Lanier showed her another warning letter,
concerning Vioxx and addressed to Mr. Gilmartin.[9]

Q. Well, let's look at the letter and see if it's about the use of color
    or the spacing or the headlines or see if it is, in fact, from
    scientists at the FDA. Do you have the letter in front of you?

A. Are we looking at the letter to Mr. Gilmartin, the one that's the
    warning letter?

Q. Yes, ma'am, the one that we started with.

A. Okay.

Q. Okay. You got it in front of you?

A. I do.

Q. It says on the second paragraph, "You have engaged in a
    promotional campaign for Vioxx that minimizes"—do you see
    the word "minimizes" there?

A. I do.

Q. —"minimizes the potential serious cardiovascular findings."
    Let's stop for a minute. "Cardiovascular findings." That's your
    heart and your blood system, right?

A. That's correct.

Q. That includes heart attacks, right?

A. It does, uh-huh.

---

[8] On the use of adverse witnesses, *see* Michael E. Tigar, EXAMINING WITNESSES, ch. 7 (2d
ed. 2003)(hereinafter "Examining Witnesses").

[9] These warning letters had been either pre-admitted in evidence or their admissibility
ruled upon or agreed. Counsel is entitled to considerable leeway in "publishing" to the jury
the contents of admitted exhibits. Counsel can generally read from the exhibit, subject to
the opponent's right to require other portions to be read if necessary to put matters in
context. Counsel can ask a witness to read the exhibit. With the court's permission, counsel
can display portions of the exhibit on an enlargement or, in a courtroom equipped with
video monitors, on a screen. *See* Examining Witnesses 156–84.

Q. It includes sudden cardiac death, doesn't it?

A. Yes, it does.

Q. Just like Mr. Ernst had a sudden cardiac death, right?

A. That's my understanding, yes.

All right. So you've "engaged in a promotional campaign for Vioxx that minimizes the potentially serious cardiovascular findings that were observed in the Vioxx gastrointestinal outcomes research." You-all nicknamed that VIGOR, right?

A. That's right.

Q. That was your VIGOR study. "And, thus, you've misrepresented the safety profile for Vioxx." Is that what it says?

A. Yes, sir, you're reading that correctly.

Q. Now, ma'am, this is not just a concern over the use of the color or the spacing or the headlines, this is pretty serious stuff, isn't it?

A. This, sir, is a warning letter.

Q. Yeah, they're warning you you're violating the law, right?

A. But the issue was that you were portraying all the letters as if they were warning letters, and they were not, sir. This is a warning letter.

Q. No, ma'am. And if you go back and look at my opening—you can read it word for word—I said very clearly what these things were—

A. Okay.

Q. —with great exactitude. I'm just going from what Mr. Kiernan said that these are about color and spacing. Just so we're clear, this isn't about color or spacing, this is something very serious, isn't it?

A. This is a warning letter, and Merck certainly takes warning letters very seriously. I think that Mr. Kiernan also pointed out that Merck has a very, very well-known reputation for not receiving warning letters. This is not anything that Merck is used to receiving, and we took it very seriously.

Q. It's not your only warning letter from the FDA. You've gotten others, haven't you?

A. I don't know.

MR. LANIER [to an assistant]: Pull the other warning letter, please.

What is going on here? Lanier used part of his opening to display and refer to a series of FDA warning letters that Merck had received over the years on various issues, including relatively minor issues such as type face in advertisements. The court had ruled that these warnings, most of which did not refer to Vioxx, were admissible. Kiernan, opening for Merck, directly attacked Lanier's opening and displayed the letter that complained about the type face. He did not significantly address the more serious warning letters. It is always risky for defense counsel to make a direct reference to part of the plaintiff's opening. The gambit might be seen as a personal attack on opposing counsel, thus inviting a rebuke from the court or retaliation, as happened here. The personal credibility of the lawyers becomes an issue. Some judges outright refuse to let counsel start down that road.

Also, the defendant's opening is an opportunity to tell the defendant's story, based on careful preparation. Turning the opening into a defensive response to the other side foregoes the opportunity. Also, the responses that a lawyer crafts "on the spot" may turn out to have flaws, or provide additional ammunition to the opponent. The advocate should hesitate before abandoning a solid and well-considered case theory and trial plan. Some opponents will be provocative in an effort to force tactical misjudgments. Rising to their bait can be dangerous.

Ms. Santanello had not been prepared to deal with Merck's business decisions, its relationships with the FDA, or with the broad policy issues that Merck faced in deciding to bring Vioxx to market and eventually to withdraw it. Like many long-time employees of large organizations, she was a loyalist, accustomed to thinking well of her company and her colleagues, and very defensive when it or they were under attack. Her defensiveness might come across as hostility, anger or even lack of candor. Merck did not anticipate well in advance that Ms. Santanello would be called as the first plaintiffs' witness, nor prepare her well for that experience.

Lanier continued to focus on the VIGOR study, using the FDA warning letter:

Q. You started selling the drug before you finished the VIGOR test; am I correct?

A. Well, the drug was on the marketplace while VIGOR was ongoing.

Q. In other words, yes, Mr. Lanier, we started selling the drugs before we got the final results of VIGOR, true?[10]

---

[10] What has happened here? Lanier has asked a leading question, seeking a yes answer. The witness has seemed to him to waffle a bit. To impose his control of the cross-examination, he insists on getting the answer he seeks.

A.   That's true.

Q.   Okay. Now, the VIGOR study came back and had some pretty shocking findings. Would you agree with that?

A.   Well, it depends on who you talk to as to whether or not the findings were shocking.

Q.   Okay. Because y'all suspected these findings might actually occur, so maybe you-all weren't shocked. Is that fair to say?

A.   Well, it's very consistent with the mechanism of Naproxen to be cardioprotective.

Q.   Well, now, ma'am, that's the very kind of statement that the FDA got on to you-all for making, and you're still making it today. Did you read the bottom paragraph of this letter?

A.   Well, I personally believe Naproxen has a cardioprotective effect, so—

Q.   Ma'am, if you read—my question was: Did you read the bottom part of this letter where the FDA says quit saying that kind of stuff?

A.   So it says—the part where it says the exact reason for the increased rates of MIs—

Q.   Yeah.

A.   —observed in Vioxx treatment is unknown?

Q.   Let's do it this way. Let's get there gradually. But let's first explain why it's important.[11] Okay? If you look at what the FDA said, they said that your promotional campaign on this study up there that we put on the board misrepresents the safety profile. It discounts the fact that in that VIGOR study patients on Vioxx had four to five times as many heart attacks as those that were on VIGOR, right? That's what it says, doesn't it?

A.   Yes, it does.

Q.   So you've got four to five times as many heart attacks happening in the group taking your drug as the group that's taking Naproxen, true?

A.   Yes.

Q.   And the FDA warning your company because you-all are misrepresenting that truth?

---

[11] He now has the FDA letter before the witness, but wants to ask his questions in an order and at a pace that makes the jury aware of the reason he is exploring this subject. It is easy for a lawyer who is very familiar with the case to skip steps or "start in the middle." Lanier is reminding himself and the witness to slow down.

A. Well—

Q. That's what it says, doesn't it?

A. Yeah. But I think you have to look at what actually makes up that misrepresentation.

Q. All right. That's the next paragraph. "Although the exact reason for the increased rate of MIs"—and, again, that's the heart attacks we're talking about, right?

A. Those are heart attacks, correct, yes.

Q. "Although the exact reason for the increased rates of MIs observed in the Vioxx group"—that's the far part of my tablet, right?

A. Yes.

Q. —"is unknown, your promotional campaign selectively presents the following"—what's that word after following?

A. Hypothetical.

Q. Yeah, "hypothetical." That means it's not anything anybody has proven. It's a hypothetical. It's an idea, right?

A. It's a hypothesis.

Q. Okay. "Your promotional campaign selectively presents the following hypothetical explanation for the increase in heart attacks: You assert Vioxx doesn't increase the risk of heart attacks. The VIGOR finding is consistent with Naproxen's ability to block platelet aggregation like aspirin." That's what it says, isn't it?

A. That's correct.

Q. And that's what you just told this jury just now. You said, well, we don't—I am personally of the opinion that it's the Naproxen was helping the heart instead of Vioxx was hurting it, right?

A. Yes, correct.

Q. The FDA warned you about that and they said that's a possible explanation but you failed to disclose that it's hypothetical, that it's not been demonstrated by substantial evidence and there's another reasonable explanation.

Lanier kept Santanello on the stand from the afternoon of July 18, all day July 19, and most of July 20. There was a break to present two plaintiff's witnesses, then Lanier recalled her for another two days of testimony. Using plaintiff's exhibits, he led her from the FDA warnings, through the studies of Vioxx problems, memoranda showing sales and marketing techniques used by Merck, and the profitability of Vioxx. He concluded the examination with a series of questions that brought out that Bob Ernst had few of the risk factors associated with fatal cardiac events.

Merck counsel David Kiernan had concluded his opening statement by saying:

> One final point: Let me conclude with the allegation that the leaders and scientists at Merck were knowingly letting people die from heart attacks and hiding their knowledge to make more money. Here are some of the people at Merck who took Vioxx before it was withdrawn from the market. These are folks at Merck who took Vioxx personally. Dr. Ed Scolnick, the head of all science and research at Merck; David Anstice, the head of marketing and U.S. sales that Counsel referred to this morning; Dr. Alan Nies, who was head of the Vioxx development program; Jeffrey Mason, one of the reps who actually saw Dr. Wallace and detailed, as they say, Dr. Wallace, the prescriber in this case; Dr. Louis Sherwood, the physician that was accused of trying to—you know, the Merck physician who was accused of trying to intimidate people who were criticizing Vioxx; Dr. Peter Kim, the current head of all science at Merck; Dr. Nancy Santanello, who's with us here today. All of these folks took Vioxx before withdrawal. And I leave you with that thought.

One may question whether restating the "allegation" is effective, even to rebut it, and whether it was wise for counsel to end the opening with this claim. In the end, however, it was perhaps unwise to make the claim at all. Lanier brought out towards the end of the adverse examination that Dr. Santanello had taken Vioxx over a period of many months, but only sporadically—once or twice a month for specific conditions.

Merck's counsel Gerry Lowry conducted the cross-examination, which for an adverse witness is like a direct examination in the sense that the examiner may not use leading questions. After some introductory questions, Lowry began by asking who had worked on the development of Vioxx, eliciting a list of people with their various titles and roles. I invite the reader to imagine the situation at this trial juncture. Lanier had used Santanello to go over almost every aspect of the plaintiff's case. When Merck's counsel stood up, it was important to give the jury a sense of direction.

I have written of the use in direct examination of loops, prologues, and transitions:

> A loop is a repetition of a part of a previous answer to underscore the answer and to help guide the witness to the next event. A prologue sets out themes in advance. A transition is a statement or question that signals a change in subject matter. All three devices can be used in direct and cross-examination—and with any type of

witness. They are among the most important devices for focusing on important elements of proof and providing context.[12]

Lowry's examination of Santanello came at a crucial trial stage. Lanier had seized the advantage of primacy. Merck needed to recapture the momentum of the case, and to reassert its story of events. Santanello had the experience and knowledge to assist in that undertaking. Lowry might therefore have introduced the examination with a prologue that stated the themes she was going to explore. Her examination should have been driven by exhibits that she would show the witness, to make Santanello comfortable with the process and to provide a basis to remind jurors of where Santanello's testimony had taken them. Instead, the friendly cross was broken up by the testimony of other witnesses. Counsel took the witness through some important areas but seemingly without an overall plan.

Of course, one might contend that Santanello was so shaken by the adverse examination that she would not be able to fulfill Merck's expectations. The point, however, is that the trial was then in plaintiff's case, and examining Santanello was virtually the only option available in the search to regain control.

After Santanello's testimony, the plaintiffs turned to Dr. David Egilman, a medical doctor who teaches, lectures and practices in the fields of internal medicine and preventive medicine. He is noticed as an expert in hundreds of asbestos and pharmaceutical cases being handled by Lanier's firm, and has testified for several hundred trials in the past 25 years. Lanier used a chart contrasting Egilman's qualifications with Santanello's, as a basis for arguing that Egilman was more qualified.

Lanier's direct examination on Dr. Egilman's qualifications took about two hours, and by the end of it, the jurors were ready to listen. Here is a sample of the questioning:

Q. Let's talk about your educational background. Did you go to college?

A. Yes.

Q. When did you graduate from college?

A. 1974.

Q. What was the name of your college?

A. Brown University.

Q. Where is that?

A. Providence, Rhode Island.

Q. Is that one of those Ivy League schools?

---

[12] Examining Witnesses 61–63.

A. Yes, sir. . . .

Q. What did you get your college degree in?[13]

A. I got a bachelor of science in molecular biology.

Q. In molecular biology.[14] Would you please explain to the jury what your college degree means to us, especially in terms of a case like this? What does it mean?

A. Okay. My—basically what I did was study how substances—let's use drugs as an example—get into the blood, how do they get from the blood into the cells, how do they change the cells and have effects on the cells, so that kind of process.

Q. And you have a college degree in that?

A. Yes.

Q. In addition to that college degree, you got any other college degrees?

A. That's it.

Q. Okay. What's your next schooling then? I thought you had, like, a medical degree. Isn't that a college?

A. It's—medical school is a postgraduate.

Q. But it's still college, isn't it?

A. I'm willing to go with you on that.

Q. All right. I just mean—all right. Give me your next educational thing.

A. Okay. I went to medical school, graduated in 1978.

Q. All right. College was—you said '74?

A. Yes.

Q. Then you went straight into med school?

A. No.

Q. What did you do first?

A. I was a Vista volunteer, which was the domestic part of the Peace Corps.

---

[13] Notice how Lanier breaks down the information into small pieces, rather than having the witness say "I got a degree in molecular biology from Brown University in Providence, Rhode Island in 1974." The witness is prepared to answer each question with just the information requested and let the examiner ask the next one. The witness has been prepared to listen carefully to each question, a trait that stands him in good stead on cross-examination.

[14] Lanier has used a "loop," repeating the answer as a prelude to the next question to emphasize this item of information.

Q.   How long did you do that?

A.   A year.

Q.   Then a year later did you go to med school?

A.   Yes.

Q.   What did you do as a Vista volunteer?

A.   I worked in community clinics in Providence.

Q.   When you went to med school, where did you go?

A.   I went to Brown.

Some judges require that the qualification process be brief. That was the case in the Plunkett trial, where the trial judge directed that each expert could prepare and read to the jury a three-page summary of background and qualifications at the start of the direct examination.

Dr. Egilman's qualification to testify as an expert witness had already been ruled on before he took the stand. Therefore, Lanier could begin the examination—even before getting to qualifications—by letting the jury know the main point that Egilman would be making:

Q.   Dr. Egilman, is it important for drug companies to tell us what they know about their drugs?

A.   Absolutely. . . .

Q.   . . . Why is it important that the drug companies give us the information that they have about their product safety?

A.   Well, first, the—the first question is, who has the information? And the drug companies do the testing.

Q.   Does the FDA do the testing?

A.   No, sir. Nor can private doctors or academic doctors, on their own, do the testing unless they're part of a company-sponsored trial. Before a drug comes to market, the company that owns the drug controls the drug, how it's tested and where it's tested. They get all the test results first.

On the failure to warn claim, Lanier would eventually present the testimony of the prescribing physician, Dr. Brent Wallace, and he had explored with Dr. Santanello the way in which pharmaceutical salespeople call on doctors and use incentives to get doctors to prescribe particular products. Dr. Egilman had personal experience with Merck sales representatives:

Q.   . . . Did Merck send salespeople into your office?

A.   Yes.

Q.   Salesmen and saleswomen?

A. Yes.

Q. All right. Did they try to talk you into writing Vioxx prescriptions?

A. Absolutely.

Q. Did they tell you Vioxx was safe?

A. Absolutely.

Q. Did they tell you Vioxx was safe on the heart?

A. Yes.

Q. Did they send you a letter about this?

A. Yes, because I was disputing that fact. . . .

Q. Why were you disputing the fact?

A. Well, actually, around the time—this is 2001—there was another drug company selling Celebrex, which you've heard of. And there was a large story about how Celebrex had done a one-year study to try to prove that their drug saved people from getting ulcers. And they published that study after six months. And at the six-month time frame, it looked like their drug prevented ulcers, and that's the results that were published. But at the time they published those results, they had their 12–month results. And the 12–month results, which they did not publish and hid, showed the opposite. So the analogy I use for my students is, it's like wanting to know if falling off a tall building will kill you, and you count people at the seventh floor, saying "So far, so good. Nobody dies from falling off this building." And so when they had done that, that had keyed me into, all of these drugs may have problems. And so I didn't want to use any of them.

Because Dr. Egilman was not qualified as an expert in clinical trials, he was not permitted to give his complete critique of the Merck studies, but his main points came through. He focused on the disturbing aspects of the VIGOR study. Then, he turned to a discussion of causation. The jury had not yet seen the autopsy results on Bob Ernst, which are seriously debatable on the issue of causation. Rather, Lanier put the plaintiff's theory out first. This tactic may have gained effectiveness considering that the Merck opening had not made causation the centerpiece of the discussion.

Dr. Egilman provided an overview of his theory about Vioxx causing heart attacks like the one sustained by Bob Ernst:

Q. Okay. Do you believe Vioxx can cause a heart attack?

A. Yes.

Q. How can Vioxx be a cause of a heart attack, sir? . . .

A. Well, I'm going to give you a—I guess the abbreviated fast
    version. [Witness draws a picture.] We have plaque in here, and
    you have platelets. Those are the things that cause your blood
    to clot and they cause—so, if you cut yourself on your arm, it's
    the platelets that get in there and close it up and make it a
    thrombus clot in your forearm. Same thing can happen in your
    heart. Basically a heart attack means that the supply of oxygen
    is not enough to feed the work of the heart. You can get there
    two ways or both. That means that you can have too little
    oxygen or you can start beating your heart fast and you don't
    get enough because your heart's working too hard and the work
    outstrips the oxygen supply. That—you've heard, you know,
    people are exercising—that's an example of somebody who's
    exercising—and they have a heart attack. If they were just
    walking, they wouldn't have had a heart attack. When your
    heart works harder, it needs more oxygen. And if you have
    plaque in here, enough plaque, then the blood can't get by to get
    enough oxygen to the heart. So, that's how a heart attack
    happens. That's how—that's a—that's basically a supply and
    demand problem.

    Now, your platelets are always circulating around in your blood.
    Sometimes a platelet may come by; and if a platelet goes by and you
    get a cut in your finger, the platelet says, "Okay. We've got a cut."

    And what a platelet does then is it puts—it activates a COX–1
    enzyme, and that activities a bunch of other things. And it basically
    says, "Okay," calls for all the friendly platelets in the neighborhood.
    "We've got a cut here. We've got to stop it. We've got to put a
    thrombus in there. We've got to clot it off." And there's a bunch of
    enzymes that do that.

    Now, that thrombus stops eventually because, otherwise, every
    time you've got a clot that clotted a cut off, you'd just clot your
    whole body off. So, the body has another mechanism that says,
    "Okay. That cut's fixed. We can stop now." Okay? And that enzyme
    is prostacyclin, and actually it works as a feedback cycle.[15]

Q. Time out. Is that one that says "stop the clotting"—the prosta-
    cyclin, is that the same prostacyclin that Dr. Santanello told us
    Vioxx reduces in your body?

A. That's right. So, that brake—let's think about it like an acceler-
    ator and a brake in a car. The accelerator is the platelet

---

[15] Many judges would not permit such a long narrative answer on direct, but there was
no objection.

> producing that thromboxane, saying "Let's get all clotting going." But this—instead of it being a car that you've got to put the brake on, the brake is automatic. So, if you're going too fast, that brake puts it—it does it itself, and it stops the clot from forming. And then eventually you get thrombolysis, which means the clot breaks away. That's why you don't have your permanent—every time you get a cut, the clot goes away. Same thing if you clotted a vein off, it would eventually go away, because you've got your own body system corrections to rechannel the veins and arteries if you get a clot.

This formulation supported the theory that there might have been a clot that caused Bob Ernst's heart attack, but this witness has not yet explained why the autopsy did not reveal any evidence of a clot. However, Dr. Egilman set out his conclusion with the last question and answer that the jurors heard on a Friday afternoon:

> Q. Okay. Dr. Egilman, based upon your analysis and the studies, scientific liability—I mean, scientific plausibility, the epidemiology, all of the different things that you've looked at, do you have an opinion, based upon reasonable medical probability, as to whether or not Vioxx was a cause of Bob Ernst having a heart attack?
>
> A. Yes, sir. . . .
>
> Q. And what is your opinion, sir?
>
> A. That his taking Vioxx caused and contributed to—and/or contributed to his heart attack.

On the following trial day, a Monday, Lanier got permission to put on Dr. Isaac Wiener, out of order. Dr. Wiener is a cardiologist and cardiac electrophysiologist. He is an expert in the installation of pacemakers. Lanier spent an hour or so going through Dr. Wiener's relevant qualifications, focusing on his work with patients and on his publications related to arrhythmias. Dr. Wiener then used a model of a heart[16] to show the jury the heart structure and the blood vessels that surround it. Dr. Wiener is not an epidemiologist, and had not read all the studies relating to Vioxx and its potential side-effects. The trial judge overruled defense objections to opinions based on epidemiological considerations.

However, Dr. Wiener had read Bob Ernst's chart and the coroner's report. First, he said that Vioxx could cause the type of cardiac event that Bob Ernst experienced, specifically that "the heart suddenly doesn't get enough blood." Vioxx was "a significant contributing factor in causing this event."

---

[16] The model was one that Merck supplies to physicians.

Given that there was no autopsy evidence of a clot that cut off blood supply, Dr. Wiener reasoned that since statistically most sudden cardiac events in situations like Bob Ernst's are caused by clotting, it is therefore likely that there was a clot. Dr. Wiener disagreed with Dr. Santanello's testimony that a clot would have been found had it been there. He thought it might have broken up—"lysed" is the word he used—and not been found.

If there was a clot, then the diagnosis would have been a myocardial infarction, or MI. On cross-examination, Merck lawyer David Kiernan first established the standard medical criteria for MI, including chest pain, pain radiating down the arm and so on. Then, he asked the crucial question:

Q. In fact, the criteria for diagnosing a myocardial infarction or heart attack, were not present at the time of Mr. Ernst's death; isn't that correct, Dr. Wiener?

A. My answer is the same that, yes, the criteria were not present, but on the other hand, there are limitations to the criteria in this setting. And, therefore, I think we cannot say one way or the other whether he had a myocardial infarction.

Q. You can't say?

A. I think it's possible, but it's also may not be. We just cannot say.

Q. You were actually provided with [the tissue] slides [prepared during the autopsy] in this case, weren't you?

A. They sent me the slides, yes.

Q. But you didn't even look at them?

A. I didn't have a place to look at them, and I wouldn't know what I was looking at.

Q. All right. So you don't specialize in pathology?

A. I've answered that. No, I don't—I don't even have a sub—you know a minor interest in pathology. I work with some great pathologists.

Q. Okay.

A. And they're very, very useful and very, very helpful, and I defer to them.

Q. All right. The microscopic examination was done by the coroner, and here, again, there was no evidence of recent or remote infarction, correct?

A. The report says there's no evidence of recent or remote infarction. And, again, I think the information about remote infarction is very, very important. The evidence of recent infarction is not something we can rely on.

Q. Okay. In this case, at least, both in looking at the heart grossly, as you did this morning in front of the jury, and looking at the tissue under the microscope using both examinations, the coroner did not find any evidence of an old or new myocardial infarction, correct?

A. That's what the report says.

Q. Okay. And there's also no indication anywhere in the report that there was any evidence of a thrombus or a clot, correct?

A. I did not see mention of a thrombus.

And later:

Q. Now, just so we're clear, there are drugs that can be used to dissolve clots in patients who had heart attacks or strokes, correct?

A. There are several drugs.

Q. And they were not used with Mr. Ernst, correct?

A. No.

Q. There's no evidence he received any kind of clot dissolving medications of any kind, correct?

A. He did not receive thrombolysis.

Q. And based upon all of the evidence that we've discussed here this morning, Dr. Wiener, you are not able to say to this jury to a reasonable degree of medical probability that Mr. Ernst, in fact, had a myocardial infarction, correct?

A. Again, as I said, I think the traditional ways of diagnosing myocardial infarction do not apply in sudden cardiac death. Because the patient dies too soon, we cannot rule it in or rule it out.

Q. Let me ask the question one more time, Dr. Wiener. Based upon all the evidence that you've talked about here today, you are not able to tell this jury to a reasonable degree of medical probability that Mr. Ernst, in fact, had a myocardial infarction, correct, sir?

A. Okay.

Q. You agree with that?

A. Yes, I would agree with that.

Dr. Wiener also conceded that Mr. Ernst had coronary artery blockage, which would have put him at risk for a cardiac event.

After Dr. Wiener's half-day appearance, Dr. Santanello took the stand again for more examination by Merck's counsel. She discussed Merck's position with respect to the studies performed on Vioxx and the various FDA concerns that Lanier had raised. Merck's counsel also asked her to review and rebut some of the medical conclusions that had been offered by plaintiff's witness Dr. Egilman. This of course opened up more adverse examination, during which Lanier compared Santanello's views to those of Dr. Egilman. Egilman's testimony was to resume after Santanello's had finished.

In all, the interruptions in Dr. Santanello's testimony, and Merck's effort to use her against the plaintiff's case, were harmful to Merck's case. Given the trial schedule, she could not have been well-prepared to present a comprehensive rebuttal to the plaintiff's theory. She did not have the qualifications in cardiology or pathology of the other Merck witnesses that appeared in the defense case-in-chief. The jurors' impression of her based on the initial adverse examination was probably not favorable. Merck would have done better to insist on the plaintiff's case going in one witness at a time, with cross-examination to follow direct and then the witness being excused.

After Santanello's testimony,[17] plaintiff called three physicians as experts, and presented the videotaped deposition of Merck CEO Raymond Gilmartin, and the testimony of Carol Ernst's daughter and of Mrs. Ernst herself. In addition, and over objection, plaintiff presented Dr. Maria Araneta, the pathologist who performed the autopsy on Mr. Ernst.

When Dr. Egilman took the stand, Lanier spent more time with him discussing the various studies of Vioxx. During her reappearance after interruption, Santanello had characterized Dr. Egilman's analysis in these words:

> It's mixing apples and oranges and peaches and blueberries and strawberries. It's mixing everything together into the fruit salad.

When he reappeared, Dr. Egilman seized that metaphor in several answers, characterizing documented adverse effects in the Vioxx studies as various kinds of rotten fruit. Figures of speech can be effective in trial advocacy, but in litigation as in life they can also be punctured, or turned against the person who invokes them.

---

[17] As noted, Santanello's testimony was interrupted while plaintiff put on two experts. This accommodation of schedules probably worked to plaintiff's advantage by bringing Santanello back. A trial judge more concerned with courtroom control might have insisted on finishing one witness before another one was sworn, and limited repetitious questioning.

Merck lawyer David Kiernan began his cross-examination by seeking to portray Dr. Egilman as a "professional expert" who mainly supports plaintiffs. Egilman sought to turn Kiernan's questions against him:

Q. Now, over the course of your career as a testifying expert, you've criticized a number of companies and government agencies; isn't that correct?

A. That's correct.

Q. You've accused the petroleum industry and epidemiologists they hired of misclassifying workers, correct?

A. That's correct.

Q. You've accused IBM and Computer and Business Equipment Manufacturers Association of covering up information concerning musculoskeletal disorders associated with keyboards?

A. That's correct.

Q. You've accused the Chemical Manufacturers Association of a conspiracy to hide the health effects of chemicals?

A. I don't think conspiracy, but they've certainly together worked to do that, that's correct.

Q. March 12, 1999, you testified as an expert that General Refractories was engaged in a conspiracy with other companies to increase profits at the expense of workers?

A. I don't think I used the word "conspiracy," but it's certainly true they acted together with other companies to do that.

Q. You've accused the American College of Chest Physicians as being a front for asbestos companies to hide the harmful affects of asbestos, correct?

A. On one particular issue, that's correct.

Q. You've also criticized the United States Environmental Protection Agency, the Occupational Health and Safety Agency, and the Food and Drug Administration, correct?

A. That's correct.

One might ask how these questions were impeaching. The questions do not suggest, nor the answers tend to show, that Dr. Egilman was doing anything improper or that his opinions in those cases were somehow invalid. He begins to look like a public-spirited person, at least to a jury that by this time has been tuned in to a basically populist, anti-corporate, anti-bureaucratic message.

Kiernan continued the cross-examination by reading parts of an adverse student evaluation from one of Dr. Egilman's courses, criticizing his anti-corporate bias, and by mentioning that "courts" had criticized Dr. Egilman's testimony. Although Lanier did not object, these questions raise hearsay issues. More significantly, it may be that Kiernan was trying to use cross-examination to do more than it can. Cross-examination is about immanence,[18] that is, what is inherent in the witness-lawyer exchange. If Dr. Egilman has a bad reputation, witnesses in the defense case can comment on his lack of credentials and the unreliability of his conclusions.[19]

Kiernan then moved on, eliciting that Dr. Egilman had never participated in designing a major clinical trial or designing a label for a pharmaceutical product, or in several other areas relevant to the opinions he offered. Kiernan brought out that American Medical Association ethical standards limit expert testifying to subjects on which the witness is qualified. He continued:

Q. Now, let me ask you about your experience with NSAIDs and pharmaceuticals. You've never published an article on Vioxx in a peer-reviewed medical journal, correct?

A. Published? That's correct.

Q. You've never published an article on NSAIDs or non-steroidals in a peer-reviewed medical journal, correct?[20]

A. That's correct.

Q. You've never published an article on any pharmaceutical drug in any peer-reviewed medical journal; isn't that correct, sir?

A. That's correct.

Q. You're not a practicing pathologist?

A. That's correct.

Q. You're not a practicing cardiologist?

A. That's correct.

Q. In fact, you don't have a regular clinical practice of any kind?

---

[18] On the idea of immanence, see EXAMINING WITNESSES 200.

[19] Kiernan also asked questions about Dr. Egilman's standard fees for expert services. Egilman said he was not getting a fee in this case, and Lanier brought out on redirect that Egilman had directed that any fee to which he was entitled be donated to a local cardiac care facility. This is the sort of thing that a lawyer opposing an expert must be careful to learn from pretrial discovery, so that questions about compensation do not backfire.

[20] It might have been helpful to use a series of leading questions to describe for the jurors the role of peer-reviewed publications in the medical profession. Alternatively, one can discuss this issue in opening statement and then use defense experts to talk about it. Kiernan would also have been entitled to elicit from Dr. Egilman that Baylor College of Medicine, from whence the defense experts come, is a leading teaching and research facility.

A. That's correct.

Kiernan turned to the issue of causation:

Q. According to the death certificate, the immediate cause of Mr. Ernst's death was cardiac arrythmia, correct?

A. That is correct.

Q. And this occurred, according to the death certificate, minutes before his death, correct?

A. That is correct.

Q. According to the death certificate, sir, cardiac arrythmia was due to coronary atherosclerosis, correct, sir?

A. That is correct.

Q. And according to the death certificate, Mr. Ernst's coronary atherosclerosis had been present for several years, correct?

A. That is correct.

Q. The death certificate does not say that Mr. Ernst died from a heart attack, correct, sir?

A. That's correct.

Q. In fact, the death certificate states that Mr. Ernst died of an arrhythmia, correct?

A. That's correct. . . .

Q. You were provided with a set of pathology slides to look at in this case; isn't that true, sir?

A. That's correct.

Q. But you didn't look at them?[21]

A. That's correct.

There were other areas of cross-examination, directed to Dr. Egilman making conclusions and agreeing to be an expert witness even before he had looked at all the documents. It is clear from the trial record that Dr. Egilman works closely with the Lanier firm on a number of lawsuits, and is a sort of "all-purpose" medical expert.[22] In any jurisdiction, there would be a serious admissibility issue, both as to some

---

[21] These are all good leading questions. What's missing here is one or two leading questions on each item to define and explain "atherosclerosis" and "arrhythmia." Granted, they have heard these terms throughout the trial, but what's important here for the defense is that the autopsy supports the idea of death being caused by events that antedate and are irrelevant to Vioxx usage. One would not ask those "conclusion" questions, but those objective facts can be brought out.

[22] Merck also accused Dr. Egilman of violating pretrial protective orders by sharing Merck discovery documents with government agencies.

of his conclusions in fields where he lacks education and experience, as well as based on his meager record of relevant peer-reviewed publications.

The plaintiffs then presented, by videotape deposition, Dr. Maria Araneta, who I,n her capacity as assistant medical examiner for Johnson County, Texas performed the autopsy on Bob Ernst. She had no independent memory of the autopsy, and could testify only from the autopsy report and the other information in the autopsy file. Her primary function as medical examiner was to rule out foul play and suicide. She did see an indication on the emergency room record that Ernst might have had a myocardial infarction. She examined his heart and the associated blood vessels. She noted her autopsy report conclusion on the cause of death: "cardiac arrhythmia secondary to coronary atherosclerosis." Nothing in her report suggested a myocardial infarction because "it wasn't there to be seen."

Dr. Araneta then delivered the opinion that supported the Ernst case:

> So, in this case the logical situation is an acute ischemic event. Something blocked that artery that was already narrowed, either a clot, a fissure, block, a ruptured atheroma, none of which I saw, but it—these things could be dissolved. He was resuscitated very vigorously. Emboli could have been dislodged, you know. And they fractured his ribs. They were pounding on his chest. The MI could be before me, but I can't see it. So, how can I put it down?

In short, there could have been a clot that either "dissolved" or was dislodged in the resuscitation efforts. Under examination by Lanier, Dr. Araneta stated categorically that Ernst died from a myocardial infarction, that is, from a clot that set off the chain of events that led to his death. Whether this possibility and Dr. Araneta's qualifications to opine on it, have enough scientific support to sustain the Ernst verdict will be debated on appeal. The trial judge allowed the Araneta testimony and that of plaintiff's experts who supported this view.[23]

Lanier presented the video deposition of David Anstice, president of the Merck Human Health division for Canada, Latin America, Japan, Australia and New Zealand.[24] Anstice had been president of Merck North America. He has a business background, and Lanier focused on Vioxx

---

[23] When Merck learned of Bob Ernst's death, a Merck employee spoke with Dr. Araneta and made a memorandum of the conversation. In that memorandum, Dr. Araneta is quoted as saying that she felt that Ernst's death was not related to Vioxx, although Mrs. Ernst was concerned about that possibility. Dr. Araneta did not remember that conversation, and Merck lawyers did not call as a witness the employee who had the conversation.

[24] Merck objected to the broad-ranging inquiry into sales and marketing practices as irrelevant and as repetitious of other evidence.

sales and marketing issues. One can get the flavor of this adverse examination from the following exchange:

Q. ... I understand you're the president of some part of Merck. What part are you the president of?

A. Human Health for Canada, Latin America, Japan, Australia, New Zealand.

Q. At some point, were you the president of Merck America or something like that?

A. Yes, I was.

Q. When was that?

A. From the period late '94 through to the end of 2002.

Q. You're the president of Human Health, and you don't have a medical degree?

A. I do not.

Q. Well, did you go to any medical school at all?

A. No, I did not.

Q. Well, as the president of Human Health, what kind of human health schooling do you have?

A. I—I'm responsible for sales and marketing activities, and I have the training and skills developed—in 31 years at Merck.

Q. Okay. That wasn't my question, sir. What kind of schooling do you have in human health if you're going to be the president of the Human Health division?

A. I have schooling—I have tertiary education in economics. And I joined Merck and—typical with many people on the business side, I do not have a medical degree or a medical background.

Q. So, the president of Human Health is a salesman?

Lanier again brought out, through Anstice, that in the 1999–2000 period, several important Merck drug patents were running out and the company needed new products to maintain growth. Anstice also admitted that he was aware of allegations that Merck scientists and others were attempting to block information about potential Vioxx safety issues from becoming public, and that there were discussions among Merck employees about how to discredit or silence critics.

To support the theory that cardio-pulmonary resuscitation (CPR) might have dislodged a clot, Lanier called Dr. Benedict Lucchesi, a professor of pharmacology at the University of Michigan. Dr. Lucchesi has M.D. and Ph.D. degrees. He had never engaged in the clinical practice of medicine, and had no personal experience with CPR since the

1960s or 1970s. Merck counsel David Kiernan conducted a voir dire examination out of the jury's presence as the basis for moving to prevent Dr. Lucchesi from expressing any opinion about the clot-dislodging effect of CPR. The examination concluded:

Q. Okay. Are you aware of any published literature suggesting that CPR can dislodge or move clots, sir?

A. No, I'm not.

Q. Are you aware of any case reports that would suggest CPR can dislodge or move clots, sir?

A. No, I'm not.

Q. Okay. Are you aware of any publication anywhere in the world that would suggest that CPR can dislodge or move a clot?

A. No, I'm not.

Q. In any recorded human history at any point in any language?

A. No.

The trial judge ruled that Dr. Lucchesi could not offer an opinion about the potential effect of CPR on a clot. However, he could and did testify in support of the theory put forward by Dr. Egilman. Dr. Lucchesi had for many years studied the clotting propensities of drugs that affect Cox inhibitors. He had published on this issue. He also believed that a dangerous clot that caused a blockage could dissolve or be broken up by electrical charges during defibrillation. He summarized his conclusions:

Q. All right. Now, would you please put this all together within the realm of Bob Ernst taking 25 milligrams once a day of Vioxx—let me first ask it this way: Do you have an opinion, based upon reasonable medical probability, of whether or not Vioxx was a cause of the death of Bob Ernst?

A. Well, I reviewed—

MR. KIERNAN: Same objection.

THE COURT: Overruled.

THE WITNESS:—the Ernst documents very carefully. And my final conclusion, based on reasonable medical probability, is that he died of an arrhythmia, precipitated by a transient ischemic event[25] leading to ventricular fibrillation.

Q. (By Mr. Lanier) Was Vioxx a cause in that process?

A. In view of the fact that he was taking Vioxx and in view of the fact I know that Vioxx blocks COX–2 and in view of the fact that he had underlying vascular disease, which makes him a

---

[25] The ischemic event referred to here is a blockage.

candidate, along with Vioxx, for such a serious event, my only conclusion would be that Vioxx contributed significantly to this. And that's beyond any probability. The probability there is in favor of Vioxx having contributed to this. And he's not the only one, because there are many other instances where we've seen similar cases.

Q. Without Vioxx, based upon reasonable medical probability, would Bob Ernst be here today?

A. That's hard to say. He may have been crossing the street at the wrong time or something. But looking at his medical history where he had no symptoms, I don't see why he would not be here today.

On cross-examination, Merck lawyer David Kiernan established that Dr. Lucchesi had conceded publicly that Vioxx should remain on the market, provided adequate warnings were given, and provided that it was used for patients with a high risk of stomach bleeds. He also conceded that some of the literature on which he relied for his conclusions about the clotting effect were based on studies of Celebrex, not Vioxx. He also conceded that there was a substantial debate in medical literature about the proposition that COX–2 inhibitors have an effect on clotting. Turning to the controversial VIGOR study, Kiernan asked:

Q. Okay. In your view, sir, the naproxen group in the VIGOR study probably benefited from some degree from the platelet inhibition, correct, sir?

A. Well, that's a possibility.

Q. Okay. Do you know Dr. Carlo Patrono?[26]

A. Very well.

Q. Okay. You respect him?

A. Pardon me?

Q. You respect him, sir, correct?

A. I did.

Q. Okay. You think he's a good scientist?

A. He is.

Q. Okay. You're familiar with a journal Circulation, correct, sir?

A. I think I am, yes.

---

[26] It is permissible, in examining an expert, to ask him or her to comment on the conclusions of another expert, and to refer to learned articles and treatises. EXAMINING WITNESSES 424–28.

Q. You were on the editorial board? You may be on the editorial board today, correct, sir?

A. Yes, I am. . . .

MR. KIERNAN: If we can pull up—do you have Defendant's 454? I think this is already in evidence. Hold on one second. Is 454 in evidence? If it's not, we offer it as a demonstrative, Your Honor. It's an article from Circulation.

MR. LANIER: I don't have any objection to using it, Judge.

THE COURT: It's admitted as a learned treatise.

(Exhibit D–454 admitted.) . . .

Q. (By Mr. Kiernan) This is an article in Circulation by Dr. Capone and Dr. Carlo Patrono. That's the gentleman we've just been talking about, correct, sir?

A. Yes. . . .

Q. (By Mr. Kiernan) Circulation is the journal you mentioned here today, correct, sir? 2004. . . . According to Dr. Patrono, he states that "We found that the chronic administration of a therapeutic anti-inflammatory dose of naproxen, 500 milligrams, twice a day to healthy subjects caused persistent and almost complete suppression of platelet thromboxane production throughout the 12–hour dosing interval that was indistinguishable from that of low-dose aspirin." Did I read that correctly, sir?

A. Yeah. So what?

Q. That happens to be Dr. Patrono's views on the topic, correct, sir?

A. Okay.

Q. Okay. If you could go to the next quote. It says, "In conclusion, the present study demonstrates the pharmacodynamic plausibility of a COX–1 dependent cardioprotective effect of naproxen and contributes to the interpretation of the VIGOR cardiovascular findings." Did I read that correctly?

A. Yes.

Q. Okay. You agree with that, don't you, sir?

A. I know it to be true, yes. I did not need Dr. Patrono to tell me that. . . .

Q. Okay. Thank you. And on Page 245, . . . "While the cause of the apparent excess risk of MI in the Vioxx GI outcomes research trial cannot be conclusively established, a combination of some cardioprotective effect of naproxen and the play of chance does seem to offer a plausible explanation for these unexpected findings. While other mechanisms cannot be discounted, there is currently little evidence in humans to support a pro-thrombotic effect for Coxibs." Did I read that correctly, sir?

A. You did.[27]

When I finished a draft of this chapter, my research assistant Natalie Hirt read it and made a note next to the excerpt quoted above, "This seems difficult for a lay-person to understand." She is right. Kiernan failed to restate the key points and get the witness to agree to an understandable version of matters.

After Dr. Lucchesi's testimony, the plaintiff presented Bob Ernst's daughter Shawna Sherrill to talk about her mother and stepfather's close and loving relationship. Lanier then played brief excerpts from the video deposition of Bob Ernst's treating physician, Dr. Brent Wallace.[28] Because Dr. Wallace had originally been named as a defendant, Lanier could examine him with leading questions. Dr. Wallace was not uncooperative, however. He said that the Merck sales representatives did not inform him of FDA warnings and of possible adverse effects from Vioxx. Had he been fully informed, he would not have prescribed Vioxx for Bob Ernst.

On cross-examination by Merck counsel, Dr. Wallace conceded that many drugs have side effects. Sometimes these effects are serious. Dr. Wallace said that he became aware of the VIGOR study and that Merck representatives visited him to present the view that the study results were accounted for by the cardioprotective effect of Naproxen. Dr. Wallace said that he not only prescribed Vioxx after the VIGOR study, but used it himself.

Plaintiff's next witness was Ken McCoin, an actuarial accountant who presented financial figures projecting what Bob Ernst's financial contribution to the Ernst household would have been if he had lived out his natural life span. The trial judge limited cross-examination that would have pointed out that Bob Ernst had been married five times before marrying his widow and that this fact created some doubt as to

---

[27] Kiernan's cross-examination of Dr. Lucchesi showed a grasp of the epidemiological issues, and was effective and controlled. Looking at the cross renews the sense that Kiernan's opening statement was a missed opportunity to lay out a story of the case that was positive and not defensive, and that gave the jury a preview of what they would be hearing from Merck. A defendant's opening says to the jury that the defense case begins with cross-examination of defense witnesses. That cross-examination, in turn, keeps the opening statement promises.

[28] Although Dr. Wallace practices in Texas, he was outside the territorial limit of effective subpoena service and could not be compelled to testify in person in Brazoria County, Texas, where the trial was held.

whether he would have stayed married to Mrs. Ernst. These financial projections are based on the number of years that Mr. Ernst would probably have stayed in the work force, and what his probable income would have been.

Finally, Mrs. Ernst took the stand. Her direct examination was conducted by Lisa Blue, a prominent Texas trial lawyer and partner in the firm of Baron & Budd. Mrs. Ernst described how she met, fell in love with, married and lived with Bob, and then recited the events surrounding his death. The direct examination was organized and effective, as a few excerpts will show:

Q.   I have six areas to ask you about. All right?

A.   Okay. . . .

* * *

Q.   Next subject. Bob Ernst is not able to testify in this trial, so you have to be his voice for a little bit. Okay?

A.   Okay.

* * *

Q.   Two down. Four to go.

A.   Okay.

Q.   We've already done some of this next subject, because I want to talk about you and Bob together. Okay? You told us how you met.

* * *

Q.   Okay. Ms. Ernst, I want to talk now about what life has been like after Bob died. You—I'm assuming this was in the middle of the night?

A.   Yeah.

Merck counsel Gerry Lowry cross-examined. Reporters who covered the trial have said that Ms. Lowry's tone and manner appeared to alienate the jury. The transcript bears out this observation. Ms. Lowry posed many questions about Ms. Ernst's background and education. She asked questions designed to show that Ms. Ernst was not particularly close to Mr. Ernst's children by a former marriage. She brought out that when Ms. Ernst first met her husband-to-be, he was not single but was getting a divorce. She had Ms. Ernst admit that Mr. Ernst's salary had declined over the couple of years before his death, when he lost his job managing a pizza restaurant and then went to work for Wal–Mart. If, as occurred, Merck were to be held liable in this trial for a large compensatory damage verdict, most of these questions could serve only to reduce a relatively small portion of that verdict—the portion dealing the loss of support and companionship. The potential "savings" in damages does not seem to outweigh the substantial risk of alienating the jury and adding fuel to juror anger that might drive up other parts of the award.

After the plaintiff rested her case, Merck presented four live witnesses and the video deposition of Raymond Gilmartin, CEO of Merck from 1994 to 2005. In order, the witnesses were Dr. Alan Nies, who had supervised development of Vioxx at Merck, pathologist Dr. Thomas Wheeler, Mr. Gilmartin, Dr. Alise Reicin, who worked on clinical trials and other studies of Vioxx at Merck, and Dr. Craig Pratt, a cardiologist.

Dr. Nies discussed the atmosphere at Merck and in the pharmaceutical industry in which Vioxx was developed. He defended the development process. On cross-examination, Lanier confronted him with Merck marketing documents about the importance of Vioxx, showing that, at the time Nies was directing the Vioxx effort, Merck was concerned that Searle would get to market first with a Cox-inhibitor—which turned out to be Celebrex—and that Merck expected significant financial benefits from Vioxx:

Q. ... Sir, when you tell this jury we're not under any race, we're not under any pressure, we didn't have a clue where Searle was in their drug, you-all knew two years earlier or at least suspected that Celebrex, your competitors, would be filing in the fourth quarter of '98, didn't you?

A. That's what it says.

Q. And because of this you-all were under pressure and decided you were going to proceed, let's see, aggressively on developing Vioxx—"The development of Vioxx must proceed aggressively."

A. That's true. We wanted to get this drug out.

Q. Because of the money, right?

A. We felt this would be a major advance to patients.

Q. No, sir. You wanted to get the drug out because of the money?

A. Not me.

Q. This is your development plan, this is your company and your company wanted to get the drug to market first for the almighty dollar, right?

A. We want to put out drugs that will sell, yes. There's no question about that.

Q. No, sir, that wasn't my question. The reason you-all wanted to get to market first—[quoting from a Merck document] "The development of Vioxx must proceed aggressively to meet this challenge. The primary objective is to achieve the same filing date." Do you see the same filing date?

A. A 4Q '98 filing. That was our objective, yes.

Q. And the reason why, if we go to the end of the document, is because it will make you-all an extra 600 and some odd million dollars if you're first, right?

A. I don't know about that.

Q. Well, let's look.

A. That's not my expertise.

Q. Well, it's in your program, it's in your document and here's what it says on Page 64. It says the best case scenario of Vioxx first to market means you're going to make 889 million. Do you see that?

A. Yes.

Q. In the event Vioxx is second to market, you get beat, however, you're only going to make 278 million. Do you see that?

This brief excerpt reveals once again the inherent contradiction faced by defendants in many product liability cases. The company is in business to make a profit, and its internal corporate documents and public reports to shareholders and regulators will interpret plans, activities and results in terms of profit and potential growth. Employee evaluations will focus on contributions to "the bottom line." At the same time, management will have many reasons to insist that products be safe, effective and well-made. Potential lawsuits, regulatory controls, shareholder dissatisfaction, and reputation in the marketplace are among these reasons. But management can also choose to create and foster an internal culture around certain values. A given management may even have public service goals. One of Lanier's strong points in this trial was his portrayal of a change in Merck corporate philosophy. The contradiction with which Lanier confronted Dr. Nies, though inherent in Merck's position, should also have been clear to Merck lawyers. In their story of the case, they had the responsibility to acknowledge and even to embrace the contradiction.

Dr. Thomas Wheeler is a Baylor College of Medicine professor and a noted pathologist. He looked at the autopsy report, Ernst's medical records and the slides of coronary artery tissue made in connection with the autopsy. He described Bob Ernst's coronary artery as so affected by calcification that one could not cut it with a scalpel. It had to be soaked in a chemical bath to soften it enough so that microscope slides could be prepared from transverse slices of it. He directly contradicted the Egilman, Araneta and Lucchesi theories about cause of death. Dr. Wheeler told the jury the figures about sudden cardiac death in America, particularly among older men. He showed the jury the autopsy slides:

Q. And how do those—are those the arteries where there's most calcification?

A. In this gentleman, yes.

Q. Okay. All right. Is there anything else of significance on here that you'd like to point out to us that we haven't discussed?

A. There are several pieces of tissue. This is one of three.

Q. Okay. You can go ahead and show us.

A. And they all show basically similar findings. Here you can actually see the calcification even better. Here's the thick fibrous cap here, the purple—I mean the pink. It would be like leather, the consistency of leather. And then this is the big rock of calcium. And this actually shows up. . . .

Q. What else did you see on here that would be important to us?

A. Well, what's significant is what we don't see. We don't see a lipid rich cholesterol plaque which are the ones more vulnerable to rupture, particularly the ones that have a thin cap. This had very little cholesterol, had mainly calcium, had a thick fibrous cap. That's the type of atherosclerotic plaque that is less likely to rupture to initiate the blood clot formation.

Q. Okay. So what does that tell us in this case bottom line?

A. Well, it tells us that we wouldn't have expected a thrombus to form here.

With respect to Dr. Lucchesi's theory:

Q. And so when Dr. Lucchesi told us that the clot would continue to dissolve after death; is that true?

A. No, it's absolutely false.

And specifically on Dr. Araneta:

Q. Now, there's also been some testimony by Dr. Araneta that even though she didn't find a clot that maybe there possibly was a clot that got dissolved or dislodged by CPR. Do you remember that testimony?

A. Yes.

Q. Could EMTs have dislodged or broken up a clot when they were doing CPR on Mr. Ernst?

A. I don't mean to be disrespectful, but it's a preposterous notion for several reasons.

Q. Go ahead and explain.

In sum, Dr. Wheeler's presentation was an orderly and illustrated discussion of the defense theory and a reply to the plaintiff's experts. By that time in the trial, however, it may have been too late. David Kiernan had referred to the Ernst autopsy report near the end of his opening statement. He mentioned Dr. Wheeler and cardiologist Dr. Craig Pratt only briefly, and did not give the jury a complete look at their qualifications nor a detailed preview of their conclusions. He therefore missed the opportunity to put the vital causation evidence into perspective before the plaintiff's parade of witnesses, and to make causation the central theme of the defense story.

On cross-examination, Lanier stressed that Dr. Wheeler's pathology experience had focused a great deal on prostate pathology rather than cardiac pathology. He presented evidence that contradicted some of Dr. Wheeler's use of terminology to describe Bob Ernst's extent of coronary artery disease. Lanier's cross-examination was no doubt structured based on learned treatise materials that plaintiff's own experts had found and put together.

The issue of Merck scientist credibility arose again during Dr. Reicin's testimony. She came across in her direct examination as a committed and concerned scientist. She disagreed with plaintiff experts and discussed the research that preceded and followed introduction of Vioxx to market:

Q. Dr. Reicin, I'd like to go right to Vioxx and talk about that a little bit if we could. The jury has heard a fair amount about the early studies on Vioxx, and I want to touch upon those as we move forward. But today I'd like to ask you questions primarily as we move from VIGOR forward. Is it possible for you to give us an estimate of the total number of clinical trials or clinical studies that were performed on Vioxx starting from the very beginning up to the present?

A. There have been a lot of clinical trials. Before we submitted the NDA, that's the new drug application which is our regulatory filing, I think there were approximately 58 clinical trials including close to 10,000 patients. That was either the biggest or one of the biggest new drug applications in terms of number of trials in patients that Merck had ever filed. And once we filed it, we didn't stop. The number of trials that we've done post filing have been enormous, again, one of the largest programs that Merck or probably any other pharmaceutical company has performed. I think post filing we've had over 70 studies or approximately 70 studies in close to 40,000 patients. So we are talking about an enormous, enormous database and program for the study of both the efficacy and the safety of Vioxx.

Q. If my math is right, that's over 125 clinical trials on Vioxx?

A. I think it's something like that; that's correct.

And later:

Q. We heard from an expert witness called by the plaintiffs, a Dr. Egilman, that the studies leading up to the new drug application were too few. Do you agree with that?

A. I do not agree with that, and the regulatory agencies did not agree with that.

Q. We heard from Dr. Egilman that the studies were too short. Do you agree with that?

A. Again, I don't agree with that. I think we had extensive long-term data for a new drug application, as I said, several fold more than regulatory guidelines call for.

Dr. Reicin referred to the Patrono study, about which Merck lawyer David Kiernan had asked Dr. Lucchesi, concerning the cardioprotective properties of naproxen. Kiernan's questions went issue by issue over the development and testing of Vioxx, in a structured and measured direct examination that addressed each of the plaintiff's issues. Dr. Reicin is a vice-president of clinical research at Merck and has a distinguished academic and professional record. She is also a poised and carefully-prepared witness. She knows the science and has a good grasp of the drug development process. She also appeared in the Plunkett case. The direct examination concluded:

Q. A couple of final questions. Mr. Ernst passed away from a ventricular arrhythmia. Are there any studies that conclude that Vioxx causes ventricular arrhythmias?

A. No.

Q. Does Vioxx cause ventricular arrhythmias?

A. No.

Q. The plaintiffs in this case claim that Mr. Ernst may have had a blood clot that led to a heart attack and sudden death. And I want you to assume that Mr. Ernst took Vioxx for six to eight months. Are there any clinical trials against placebo or sugar pill that show a statistically significant relationship between the use of Vioxx milligrams for six to eight months and myocardial infarction or heart attack?

A. No.

Q. Are there any clinical trials against placebo or sugar pill that show a statistically significant relationship between the use of Vioxx 25 milligrams and sudden death in patients while they were taking Vioxx?

A. No.

Q. Finally, have you used Vioxx yourself?

A. Yes, I have.

Q. For how long a period of time?

A. I have lower back problems. And sometimes for a couple days, but I've taken it for prolonged periods of time as well; for, on average, several months, several months.

Q. Did you take it up through withdrawal?

A. Yes, I did.

Q. Looking back, Dr. Reicin, is there anything different you would have done with respect to Vioxx?

A. I think we did the right thing. We thought the drug was safe. I thought the drug was safe. I took the drug. We continued to study the drug. Doing otherwise would have been against the core of who I am. It would have been against the whole reason I went into medicine. And it would have been against the core of the colleagues I work with at Merck.

On cross-examination, Lanier's attack began with excerpts from Dr. Reicin's personnel records, showing that her superiors at Merck praised her for "defending the Vioxx franchise" and "building the scientific base for a COX–2 business." Lanier showed her an e-mail on which she was copied, referring to Vioxx critics as "barbarians at the gate." He then explored in detail her role in damping internal and external criticism of Vioxx. Recalling that Dr. Reicin had been asked to comment directly on Bob Ernst, Lanier asked a question about Ernst's health history:

A. I really can't comment on the details of Mr. Ernst's case because I'm not aware of them.

Q. Did you not—you have not looked at the medical records?

Q. So before you came in and testified to this jury that Vioxx wasn't linked up to anything he had or any problems he had, you hadn't even read his medical records?

A. I have not been asked to read his medical records.

The trial judge allowed, over objection, questions about marketing and labeling disputes of which Dr. Reicin had no personal knowledge or professional connection. Lanier kept Reicin on cross-examination for more than a full trial day, more than twice the time she spent on direct examination.

Cardiologist Dr. Craig Pratt was Merck's final witness. He is a well-respected Houston, Texas practitioner and teacher. He is also an electrophysiologist, and serves as chair of his hospital committee on pharmaceuticals. Merck lawyer Gerry Lowry took Dr. Pratt through his qualifications, and then asked him a series of questions about the plaintiff's experts. Pratt fairly but pointedly compared his own qualifications to theirs. He mentioned that Dr. Lucchesi is "a brilliant basic scientist" whose "primary work is in animal models."

Dr. Pratt deconstructed the plaintiff's experts' theories, while offering his own view of Bob Ernst's death as unrelated to any condition that Vioxx might have caused or contributed to.

Lanier's cross focused on Dr. Pratt's professional connections to pharmaceutical companies and the proportion of his income derived from being an expert witness. These were areas of cross-examination that might better have been anticipated in the direct examination.

Over defense objection, the trial judge permitted the plaintiff to recall Dr. Lucchesi as a rebuttal witness, once again to put forward his theory about a clot being responsible for the events leading to Bob Ernst's death. The judge also allowed Lucchesi to give some opinion concerning the possible effect of vigorous CPR in dislodging any clot that might have been present. Lucchesi also said that because the clot might have been in a small peripheral vessel, it might have been too small to detect during the autopsy. On cross-examination, Merck lawyer David Kiernan focused on Dr. Lucchesi's lack of publishing and research experience on human blood that would have permitted him to form scientifically-valid opinions on the subjects of his rebuttal testimony.

The summations in Ernst did not seek high drama. Lanier focused on the questions the jurors were to answer, and on Merck's alleged misconduct. The defense began its summation with a discussion of causation then ranged over the various scientific and marketing issues. Gerry Lowry summed up for awhile, then David Kiernan, then Ms. Lowry again. Whether it is a good idea to divide summation in this way is open to debate.

Towards the end of her final appearance, Ms. Lowry made an argument that trial observers claimed was a tactical error:

Now, Mrs. Ernst, when she testified, told you that she feels tremendous guilt because she recommended that her husband go and ask about Vioxx. And I'm sure that guilt hasn't been lessened in this case by all these lawyers telling her that Vioxx killed her husband. But you have a chance to do the right thing, and that is to release

Mrs. Ernst from that guilt, to tell her the truth, which is that Vioxx had nothing to do with her husband's death. What caused her husband's death was something that started long before she ever even met Mr. Ernst, and you have a chance in this case to tell her that and send her that message and relieve her of that guilt that she feels so she can go on with her life. Don't let her continue to carry this wrong impression with her.

This argument led Lanier to launch his rebuttal in this way:

I do want to take your attention away from what's been said for just a moment because it bothers me. I'm bothered by a lot that's been said over the last—I think they used an extra ten minutes, but over the last two hours and 50 minutes. I'm bothered because we've hit a point now where it's not just discredit the doctors. And Dr. Egilman, you can handle this. You've had them at your doorstep before. Dr. Lucchesi, he can handle it. I got really miffed when they went after Mrs. Ernst, and I got miffed when they did it again today because that's not right. For them to have the audacity to stand up here and say, please vote for Merck for Carol Ernst's sake, so Carol Ernst can go away from here knowing she's guilt free, that's bad. That's bad.

As mentioned at the outset of this essay, the jurors voted for the plaintiff.

PLUNKETT v. MERCK IN FEDERAL COURT, HOUSTON, TEXAS

The trial judge in Plunkett, Eldon Fallon of the U.S. District Court for the Eastern District of Louisiana, is also the judge conducting the federal multi-district litigation pretrial proceedings. He has a nearly encyclopedic view of the issues and personalities that are common to Vioxx cases, including many of the expert and fact witnesses who will make appearances in more than one trial.

Judge Fallon's trial style shows a keen understanding of the Federal Rules of Evidence. He is also a judge who keeps the trial moving, by imposing time limits on lawyer argument, discouraging speaking objections, and reminding lawyers not to be repetitious. Judge Fallon excluded some evidence of events after Mr. Irvin's death, although he did allow mention of the 2004 Merck withdrawal of Vioxx from the market. He limited sales and marketing evidence. As noted above, he applied Federal Rule of Evidence 611(b), limiting cross-examination to the scope of the direct. The Rule 611(b) limitation does permit parties more control over the content of their respective cases, and arguably sets up a more coherent adversary process. All of these factors contributed to Plunkett being a shorter trial than Ernst, some 9 trial days[29] as opposed to more than 20 for Ernst.

Plaintiff's lead counsel in Plunkett were Jere Beasley, Andy Birchfield, and Paul Sizemore of Montgomery, Alabama. Merck counsel were Philip Beck and Tarel Ismail of Chicago. We have already seen a sample of Mr. Beck's opening. Mr. Birchfield began:

> If Merck had warned of heart attack risks, we wouldn't be here. You heard judge Fallon talk about a failure to warn claim. You'll hear at the end of the case an instruction a drug company has a responsibility—a duty—to warn about risks of its drug, and all drugs have risks. So who bears the responsibility when those risks turn into serious injury or death? It depends. If a drug company warns, then that responsibility shifts from the company to the doctor or patient. If the drug company doesn't warn, the responsibility remains with the company. In this case, Merck made a deliberate premeditated financial decision not to warn. Why would a company do that? If they could shift responsibility by simply warning, why would they not do that? You're going to hear the evidence in this case that answers that question of motive. Here is Ms. Evelyn Irvin Plunkett. She remarried about three years after his death. She had been married for 31 years. Together, through thick and thin, they raised four children together. At the time of his death, their marriage was as good and as strong as it had ever been.

Birchfield set out his themes:

> Now, I want to talk to you about the evidence, and I think it would help at this point if we divide it up into four categories. We want to look at first the medicine, then the man, then the marketing, then the motive.
>
> Dicky Irvin was 53 at the time he died. He worked for a seafood shop, loading and unloading boxes delivered to his workplace and from there to restaurants and stores. He suffered a back injury while working. His son-in-law, Dr. Chris Schirmer, is an emergency room physician. He prescribed 30 days worth of Vioxx. Dicky Irvin took 22 Vioxx tablets in 24 days and had what Mr. Birchfield called "a Vioxx heart attack." The case therefore raised not only autopsy-based cause of death issues, but the epidemiological issue of whether Vioxx taken for such a short time raised a realistic probability of adverse effects. Despite the evidently weaker Irvin facts, the Houston jury failed to reach a verdict. On retrial in New Orleans, there was a Merck verdict.

---

[29] Excluding voir dire.

Plaintiff began with Dr. Benedict Lucchesi. In Judge Fallon's court, an expert begins by reading to the jury a short statement of background, qualifications and experience. Counsel is not given the chance to spend time on these issues in question and answer form. However, opposing counsel has the right to take the witness on what is known as a "voir dire" to inquire about qualifications. A lawyer will often take advantage of this opportunity, even knowing that the witness is going to be accepted as an expert, as a way of undercutting the value of the proposed testimony.[30]

> Mr. Beasley: We tender him as an expert ... in the area of cardiovascular pharmacology; physiology; and pharmaceutical research and development, including clinical trials.
>
> The Court: you may cross-examine him.
>
> Q. (by Mr. Beck). Doctor, how long ago as it that you graduated from medical school?
>
> A. 1964.
>
> Q. After finishing medical school, did you enter a formal residency program?
>
> A. No, sir.
>
> Q. Have you ever been licensed to practice medicine?
>
> A. No, sir.
>
> Q. Are you allowed to prescribe medicine?
>
> A. No, sir.
>
> Q. Are you aware that the FDA had an advisory committee, committees that were appointed to look at Vioxx and other COX–2 inhibitors?
>
> A. Yes.
>
> Q. Did the FDA ask you to be on the 2002 advisory committee?
>
> A. No, sir.
>
> Q. Did they ask you to be on the 2005 advisory committee?
>
> A. No.
>
> Q. Has the FDA ever asked you to be on any FDA advisory committee for any drug?
>
> A. No.
>
> Q. On the subject of labeling, have you ever written a drug label?

---

[30] Dr. Lucchesi had given a deposition in the Merck litigation, so counsel knew the answer to all of these questions before asking them.

A. No.

Q. Have you ever participated in drafting a label for a prescription drug?

A. No, I have not.

Q. Have you ever even read the regulations from the FDA on labeling?

A. Not that I recall.

Q. And you don't consider yourself to have any expertise in that area, do you, sir?

A. No, sir.

Q. Also, on consumer advertising of prescription medicines, have you ever reviewed the FDA regulations on that subject?

A. No.

Q. Have you ever reviewed Merck's submission to the FDA concerning direct-to-consumer advertising?

A. No.

Q. Have you ever reviewed the FDA's response to Merck concerning consumer ads?

A. I have read the letters in which the FDA has reprimanded Merck on some of their ads.

Q. Did you read the response from Merck to that letter and then the FDA's resolution of that issue?

A. I recall reading it, but I don't recall the detailed response from Merck.

Q. When you were doing your work for this case, did you review the backup material that Merck submitted to the FDA when it made its new drug application, the NDA?

A. I don't recall.

After a few more questions of this nature, and some redirect examination, Judge Fallon accepted Dr. Lucchesi as an expert in "his chosen field."[31]

---

[31] Judge Fallon follows the general practice of saying that the witness may testify as an "expert." He does remind the jurors that they are the ultimate judges of whether to accept his opinion and whether the opinion has a sound factual basis. Judge Richard P. Matsch, of the District of Colorado, has a different practice. He does not tell the jury that the witness is an "expert," but rather says that the witness may offer "opinion" testimony. Judge Matsch believes that the judge unduly interferes with the jury function by using the word "expert."

Dr. Lucchesi's theory about Vioxx was the centerpiece of plaintiff's case. Irvin had a clot. The clot killed him. Dr. Lucchesi provided an answer to the question whether short-term low dose use of Vioxx could plausibly be the cause or a contributing "but for" cause of this event. It would be up to a pathologist to say whether Vioxx was in fact the cause. Given that Dr. Lucchesi's views are very controversial in the scientific community, would the plaintiffs have been better advised to begin with one of the anti-Merck witnesses who appeared later?

Dr. Lucchesi began with an overview of his conclusions:

Q. Specifically, I want you to tell the jury what your opinions are, then we're going to go back to—

A. The first thing I said, I believe COX–2 inhibitors, Vioxx, can produce blood clots. Secondly, I believe that Merck either was aware or should have been aware that the potential for this existed. In literature, it's well documented the fact that this could occur, if you interfered with a COX–2. I'm of the opinion that the hypothesis that Merck came up with to defend their position on the VIGOR study, that the drug Naproxen, which was the drug that was used as the comparative drug against which they compared Vioxx, they compared that Naproxen was cardio-protective. And thus it made it look as if Vioxx was cardio-damaging. I don't agree with that opinion, and I don't agree with the fact that Naproxen is cardio-protective. I think Merck—my opinion is that Merck should have invested more in basic studies as well as designing some specific clinical trials in which it specifically tests this hypothesis whether or not blood clots were potential in this situation. Overall, I think a drug like Vioxx carries a specific risk in a very select group of patients. Patients who are at risk of cardiovascular disease, although they may not be aware of the fact that they have an underlying cardiovascular disease, I think a drug like Vioxx poses a danger.

Q. Specifically, did you form an opinion as to whether or not Vioxx would be unreasonably dangerous for that segment of the population that would be at risk?

A. That is right.

Q. What is that opinion? . . .

A. Patients who have cardiovascular risks, underlying cardiovascular risks, are going to be a greater risk of having a thrombo-involving event in the presence of Vioxx.

Q. That would be the formation of clots?

A. The formation of clots, yes, sir.

Q. And do you have an opinion specifically whether or not Vioxx can cause a heart attack?

A. Oh, yes, I do.

Q. And what is that opinion?

A. I believe that—I believe it has that potential to do that, yes.

Dr. Lucchesi's theory is that when the blood platelets become agitated, there is a potential for clotting, and that Vioxx inhibits prostacyclin and this causes clot formation or prevents dissolution of clots that have already formed. This phenomenon can produce a heart attack even without arterial plaque rupturing. Another way to see it, Dr. Lucchesi says, is with a teeter-totter analogy, reflecting the natural bodily balance between prostacyclin, which inhibits clot formation, and thomboxane, which encourages it. Aspirin and ibuprofen inhibit the two substances equally, Vioxx does not. So a patient taking Vioxx is upsetting that balance and encountering increased clotting risk.

Two plaintiff experts had examined the Irvin autopsy slides. One of them concluded there was plaque rupture, and the other said there might have been; plaque rupture could cause a heart attack independent of any effect from Vioxx. Dr. Lucchesi is not a pathologist., and he had to concede that he did not have the qualifications in examining autopsy slides that a pathologist would have.

Dr. Lucchesi is discursive. Judge Fallon called counsel to the bench and complained, "We're going to have to go a little faster. You're asking him a question and he's making a speech for ten minutes. If we do that, you'll never get through. You'll be out of time and you'll still have him on."

This exchange provides an insight into Judge Fallon's trial management technique. Judges have different means of expediting trials, including as here the use of time limits on lawyer argument and witness presentation. A trial judge who, like Judge Fallon, had extensive experience as a trial lawyer, can craft rules that save juror time and yet not interfere with effective advocacy. A common juror complaint is that lawyers waste time being repetitious. However, some trial judge limits on lawyer presentation undervalue the role of advocacy and undermine the advocate's role in choosing how best to persuade the jurors. Trial speed is not an end in itself.

A little later, when it appeared Dr. Lucchesi had not heeded the message, Judge Fallon said to him in the jury's presence:

Okay, doctor, you're still under direct. Doctor, we're going to try to finish your testimony today, and I really need your cooperation. So if you'll listen to the questions and focus on the questions, just answer the question, please.

The cross-examination focused on the two main issues—evidence of harm from short-term use, and the risks of clotting.[32] Excerpts from the examination show Beck's technique:

Q. Now, out of the hundreds of peer-reviewed articles that you've authored, have you ever written one on the subject of whether Vioxx can cause heart attacks in short-term use?

A. No, sir.

Q. And before you talk about how you looked at some other COX–2 inhibitors such as Celebrex, have you ever written a peer-reviewed article on whether Celebrex can cause heart attacks in short-term use?

A. Yes, I have.

Q. And the one article, I think you've written about Celebrex ... that article doesn't have any conclusions whatsoever about whether Celebrex can cause heart attacks in human beings in short-term use, does it, sir?

A. That article was done in an animal model. It's the same model that Merck used to test their drug.

Q. Does your article contain any sentence that somebody could read that talks about whether Celebrex can cause heart attacks in human beings in short-term use?

A. My article describes the biology which applies in human as well as to the animal. And one comes to, by deductive reasoning, could make that assumption.

Mr. Beck: I would like an answer to the question, Your Honor.

The Court: Doctor, you're going to have to help us out here. Listen to the question and try to answer the question. If you need to explain yourself, I'll let you explain it.

The Witness: Thank you. I'm sorry.[33]

Later in the cross-examination:

Q. Would you agree with this statement that for the vast majority of people, Vioxx is perfectly safe?

A. Yes.

---

[32] Merck witnesses would address the reasons why the clotting issue was not the subject of more studies than were conducted.

[33] By this point, Dr. Lucchesi has been corrected often enough for discursive and unresponsive answers that he is apologizing. The imagery of this turn of events will not be lost on the jury. This is the plaintiff's first witness.

Q. And would you—and I think you've testified before that, as far as you're concerned, it's—Vioxx has a place on the market; is that right?

A. Yes.

And still later:

Q. But I asked a different question and I really would appreciate an answer to it. My question is, is there a single piece of peer-reviewed literature in the world that actually demonstrates that Vioxx contributes to plaque rupture in the coronary artery?

A. An animal study or human studies or both?

Q. Let's start with human studies.

A. I don't know of any human studies that have been done. I don't know of any, any clinical trial that could be designed to address this particular hypothesis. How do you test it? How do you put together an informed consent that the patient has to sign in which it says we're determining whether or not the—

The Court: Doctor, what's your answer to the question?

The Witness: The answer is, you cannot do such a study.

Q. But you could do such a study on animals if you wanted, right?

A. Yes, sir.

Q. And isn't it also true that there is not a single piece of peer-reviewed literature in the world that demonstrates that in an animal model Vioxx contributes to plaque rupture?

A. You can demonstrate that Vioxx, well, not Vioxx, but you can demonstrate that COX–2 inhibition leads to enhancement of atherogenesis in an animal. Dr. Fitzgerald has done that.

Q. Was your deposition taken in this case on October 18, 2005?
   . . .

Q. And you were under oath just as you are today, correct?

A. Yes, sir. Yes.

Q. At page 331, line 21, through page 332, line one, were you asked this question and did you give this answer under oath: "Question: Would you agree, sir, that there is not a single piece of peer-reviewed medical literature that demonstrates even in an animal model that Vioxx contributes to plaque rupture in the coronary artery?" "Answer: There may not be today." Is that your sworn testimony?

A. If you're referring specifically to Vioxx, the answer is what I gave last time. That would be the answer today. But—

Q. That's all I've been asking you about for the last 15 minutes, doctor.

To testify on the cause of Dicky Irvin's heart attack, plaintiffs called Dr. Colin Mercer Bloor, a well-qualified pathologist and emeritus professor at the University of California, San Diego, Medical School. Plaintiffs counsel began by asking Dr. Bloor to give a summary of his opinions, to orient the jury on what was to follow.[34]

Dr. Bloor concluded that Vioxx was a contributing factor to forming the clot that caused Dicky Irvin's fatal heart attack. On cross-examination, Beck confronted Bloor with the expert report that the doctor had furnished in discovery.[35]

Q. I am also showing defendant's exhibit 1029 up on the screen here. I would just like to walk through a chronology here to look at what work you did. First of all, the report that you have up there, your expert report, what's the date of that expert report?

A. That is dated the 24th of September, 2005. . . .

Q. Okay. So are your notes—and am I right that you were first contacted in this case or at least signed a retainer agreement in this case in August of 2005?

A. That's correct.

Q. And that was with a lawyer named John Restaino?

A. Yes.

Q. And then the next thing that happened is you had a phone conversation with Mr. Restaino, right?

A. That's correct.

Q. But then the first real work you did was when you met with Mr. Restaino in September, right?

A. Yes.

Q. And the first real work that you did in the case was on September 24, 2005; is that right?

A. That's correct.

Q. And that is the same day that you submitted an expert report was the very first day you started working on the case, right?

---

[34] Plaintiff's counsel objected to a defense expert being in the courtroom when Dr. Bloor testified and asked the court to impose "the rule" under Federal Rule of Evidence 615. The judge pointed out that experts are exempt from the rule, and in fact that one expert may comment on another's testimony.

[35] This is a good example of examination technique for an expert who is retained and quickly supplies an initial opinion with a lawyer's assistance.

A. Actually, I had some preliminary material on the report because I knew the format it needed to be put in. The reason the work was not done before this date is that I was out of state for a period of about three weeks during September, and that was the first that we could get together.

Q. But the first time that you ever looked at any of the materials that you talked about this morning concerning Mr. Irvin, and you looked at the coroner's report, that sort of thing, that was on September 24, 2005. Right?

A. Yes.

Q. And on that very same day, you submitted an expert report in the case, right?

A. Yes.

Q. And the reason that you submitted an expert report on the very same day that was the first day you ever looked at anything was because you understood that the expert reports were due in the case just two days later, right?

A. That's correct.

Q. So you really only had one day to spend on it, right?

A. I spent quite a bit of time on it that day, as a matter of fact.

Q. Six hours or so, I think you testified to before?

A. Yes....

Q. Now, in your report—your report itself is 18 pages long, right?

A. That's correct.

Q. And am I correct, sir, that of the 18 pages on your report, only two of them actually have anything to do with this case?

A. In regard to the materials that he brought down that day for me to review and the like, that would be true.

Beck took Dr. Bloor through the first fifteen pages of the report, noting that they deal with the doctor's qualifications and with general issues about pathology and heart disease.[36]

A. I used as a template or format for this report essentially the—I believe you call this a Rule 26 in federal court, or this type of report that I had done before, and so I knew that certain parts of this are necessary to include.

---

[36] This rather extensive excerpt shows a method for cross-examining on omissions or inconsistencies in a prior statement, and that sometimes it is useful to restate the direct examination as a prelude to attacking it. Note that at one point, Beck actually uses a whiteboard to write down key points for emphasis.

Q. So when you talk about a template, basically what that means is that the first 15 pages were cut and paste from other reports you've done in other cases, and you've just dropped it in as the first 15 pages in the case. Right?

A. They were not simply cut and pasted. I mean, they were also brought up-to-date too.

Q. Cut and pasted and brought up-to-date?

A. Yes.

Q. And then we finally get to two paragraphs about Mr. Irvin in your expert report, right? . . .

Q. Then the first paragraph that you talked about, paragraph 35, that's just a list of the stuff that the lawyer brought for you to look at. Right?

A. That was the materials that I reviewed at that time in preparing this, yes. . . .

Q. And so, then, it's two paragraphs that actually talk about Mr. Irvin, right?

A. 36 and 37, yes.

Q. Now, tell me if I am getting sort of the headlines correct of the opinion that you expressed today. As I listened, you said that Vioxx contributed to Mr. Irvin's death. That's what you testified to today, right?

A. Yes. I think it's a substantial contributory factor.

Q. And as part of your analysis, you said, I think—did you say that there was no plaque rupture?

A. In the slides that I have looked at, there is no plaque rupture. Definitely in the location where the acute thrombus is.

Q. And you said that since there—in your opinion that you expressed today—is no plaque rupture, something else must have caused the clot, right? We know there was a clot.

A. Yes.

Q. And the opinion that you're giving today is that, since there was no plaque rupture, the something else that caused the plaque must have been Vioxx. Right?

A. Well, since there is no plaque rupture at the site where this nonattached thrombus is located, I considered what other factors may be. And knowing that the patient was on Vioxx and on the assumption, the basis for which I've stated before, that it's a prothrombotic agent, that this is why I've considered it to be a substantial contributory factor to the cause of death.

Q. So is that a long way of saying, yes, what you're saying today is that, since there was no plaque rupture, according to you today, there must have been something else, and the something else was Vioxx?

A. Well, when you say it that generally. Again, I said, "at the site where this nonattached thrombus is located."

Q. And in your 18–page report, how many times do you mention Vioxx?

A. I didn't mention it at that time.

Q. So the expert report that you filed two days before the expert reports were due, after having spent all this time with the—Mr. Restaino, you didn't make one mention of Vioxx anywhere in your report, did you?

A. At that particular time, I became aware there was another set of slides that I had not yet seen.

Q. Did you, in your report, mention Vioxx anywhere?

A. No, I did not.

Q. And in your notes that I handed you, that report on work that you did, is there any mention in your notes of Vioxx?

A. No.

Q. You said that Vioxx is a prothrombotic agent. Does prothrombotic mean something that can cause or accelerate a blood clot, a thrombus?

A. The formation of that, yes. Another term that is sometimes used is "thrombogenic."

Q. And in your report, when you talk about Mr. Irvin in those two—two paragraphs, is there anything in your actual expert report that says that there was some prothrombotic agent at work?

A. No, there is not.

Q. And in your notes that you've prepared when you spent that day with Mr. Restaino going over the materials, is there any mention that there is some prothrombotic agent at work?

A. There is not at that time.

Q. And is there any mention in either your report or your notes that there is a COX–2 inhibitor—even though you wouldn't know which one that was—at work?

A. No.

Q. In your report, do you say that there was no plaque rupture?

A. Can you phrase that again, please.

Q. In your report, do you say there was no plaque rupture?

A. No, I did not say that.

Mr. Beck: If I may, can I step up here to the board?

The Court: Yes.

By Mr. Beck:

Q. I just want to contrast what you put in your expert report with what you're testifying to today. And in your report you do not say no plaque rupture, right?

A. Yes.

Q. And, in fact, you don't take a position in your report on whether there was plaque rupture or not, right?

A. That's correct. Because I was aware that there was another set of slides that I had not seen.

Q. You didn't say that in your report, though, did you?

A. No.

Beck then focused on Dr. Bloor's reliance on Dr. Lucchesi:

Q. When you come to that conclusion, you are assuming, are you not, that using low-dose Vioxx, 25 milligrams, somehow increases the risk of blood clots even if the duration of use or length of time is less than a month. That's one of your assumptions, right?

A. Yes.

Q. Because you know that from everything we understand from Mr. Irvin's family, that he took Vioxx for less than a month, right?

A. That's what I'm aware of, yes.

Q. And the low dose, the 25–milligram version, right?

A. Yes.

Q. But the truth is you don't really know anything yourself about Vioxx, do you?

A. I have not studied Vioxx, and so the assumptions I made in arriving at that opinion, as I've already stated, are based on Dr. Lucchesi's expertise and his testimony in deposition and in his report and also on what statements are made in the APPROVe

study. And going beyond that, I would defer to an epidemiologist about what he would have to say about the duration
required.

Q.   So just so that we're clear, then, you're kind of standing on the
     shoulders of Dr. Lucchesi, right?

A.   I think I can stand on his shoulders because, as I recall, he still
     is very strong, although maybe not that tall.

Q.   Analytically, when it comes to your opinion, for your opinion to
     have any validity at all, Dr. Lucchesi's opinion has to be
     accepted, right?

A.   For that part of it, yes.

Q.   So for your opinion to have any validity about the cause of
     death, Dr. Lucchesi, his opinion has to be correct that low-dose
     Vioxx taken for a short period of time causes blood clots, right?

A.   I cannot comment on that specific nature. I am talking about
     his statements on the prothrombotic activity of Vioxx in
     terms—but you also used the term "cause of death." If we go
     back to my cause of death, I am saying that it was the acute
     nonattached thrombus that occurred at the site, where he
     already had significant narrowing by a plaque, led to an acute
     ischemic state that, in turn, introduced the fatal arrhythmia.
     And then the next step is what potentially caused that acute
     thrombosis, and that's where I looked at Vioxx as having a
     substantially contributory factor.

Q.   Have you ever prescribed Vioxx?

A.   No, I have not.

Q.   And you've done practically nothing to familiarize yourself with
     the scientific evidence that addresses this question about wheth-
     er Vioxx could cause clotting when used at low doses for short
     periods of time, right?

A.   No, I have not.

After Dr. Bloor, plaintiff's counsel called Dicky Irvin's daughter
Lesley. She and her older sister Allesha were over 21 at the time of Mr.
Irvin's death. Lesley talked about the family. She also provided information about her father's back pain. The next witness, Richey Irvin, was a
minor when his father died. By the time of the trial, he had gone to work
in the seafood business where his father worked.

Plaintiff then played a video deposition of David Anstice, this one
taken by California lawyer Mark Robinson. Robinson was co-counsel in
Plunkett, though he did not play a major role. In 2006, he was lead
counsel in another Vioxx case in New Orleans, and obtained a substan-

tial plaintiff's verdict. His approach to Anstice was similar to that used by Mark Lanier in the Ernst case.

In the continuing effort to establish a relationship between Vioxx and fatal clots, plaintiffs called Dr. Thomas Frederick Baldwin, a well-qualified cardiologist. Merck challenged his credentials to offer the opinion that the plaintiffs were seeking. Merck lawyer Tarek Ismail took him on voir dire and brought out that he has never diagnosed a patient as having a Vioxx-related thrombosis, is not an expert in epidemiology, and has not since 1988 done any clinical research into sudden cardiac death. Based on this questioning, Judge Fallon allowed Dr. Baldwin to testify as an expert, but said he would be open to objections as to specific areas of inquiry.

Later in the direct examination, Judge Fallon ruled during a bench conference that Dr. Baldwin could not testify about the specific alleged relationship between Vioxx and Dicky Irvin's death. Using the Federal Rules of Evidence standards, the judge ruled that Dr. Baldwin's methodology in coming to a Vioxx-related conclusion was adequate, in that the doctor had read medical journals and other materials about Vioxx. However, the doctor was not "qualified" within the meaning of Federal Rule of Evidence 702 (which Judge Fallon called "the first hurdle") to give an opinion because he has no personal experience with Vioxx, is not an epidemiologist, and "knows nothing about COX-2 inhibitors other than what he has read." The plaintiff argued that the doctor was qualified by "knowledge" and this is an alternative basis for accepting his expertise. Judge Fallon disagreed. This ruling came as a surprise to the plaintiff's lawyers and they took a break to let the doctor know not to talk about Vioxx.[37]

Dr. Baldwin looked at the autopsy slides and said that Irvin's 60% coronary artery blockage was not "flow-limiting," thus suggesting that by itself it would not be a significant contributor to Irvin's death. Judge Fallon did permit Dr. Baldwin to testify that he had, on a consulting basis, seen about 100 patients who were taking Vioxx and that he had generally counseled the referring physician to find alternatives to Vioxx, based on a "risk-benefit analysis." This testimony was, Judge Fallon said, related to the doctor's own experience. Dr. Baldwin also said that Mr. Irvin did not have significant risk factors for a heart attack.

The defense, having succeeded in blunting Dr. Baldwin's direct testimony, did not cross-examine him. They no doubt felt that his limited testimony had not badly hurt them, and that they risked "opening the door" to areas held inadmissible if the cross-examination for some reason strayed too far.

---

[37] One wonders why Dr. Baldwin did not simply say, as had Dr. Bloor, that he was relying on Dr. Lucchesi's expertise.

The plaintiff then called Dr. Alan Nies, a retired Merck scientists who played a leading role in Vioxx development. They could subpoena Dr. Nies because the trial was being held in Houston, within subpoena range of Nies's home. His direct examination—by leading questions as an adverse witness—and cross-examination went over the ground that he covered in the Ernst trial.[38] In Ernst, the defense had called Dr. Nies, and Mark Lanier did an effective job of cross-examination in an effort to tear down the image of science-driven research at Merck. It is an open question whether the plaintiff calling him as an adverse witness was worth the risk. Certainly Irvin's lawyers were able to introduce a great deal of good evidence through Dr. Nies. However, the "friendly" cross-examination gave the defense a chance to go step by step through the development and testing of Vioxx, and Dr. Nies comfortably talked about this material.

To support the theory that Merck knew Vioxx was dangerous and that its risks outweighed its benefits, the plaintiffs called Dr. Wayne Allen Ray. Dr. Ray holds a Ph.D. degree in computer science. He is a pharmacoepidemiologist, a specialty he described:

> Pharmacoepidemiology is the study of the risks and the benefits of medications, particularly after they have been marketed and with respect to outcomes that affect patients' health. So, for example, a pharmacologist might study what effect a drug like Lipitor has on your blood, what it does to the cholesterol in your blood. A pharma-coepidemiologist might study is the drug likely or actually prevents heart attacks or if it, as some people think, has other benefits. That's kind of, in a nutshell, what we do. We study the risks and benefits of medications in real human users of the drugs in terms of the health outcomes that are tangible like heart attacks and ulcers.

Dr. Ray had never before testified in litigation. He is a tenured professor at Vanderbilt Medical School, and has taught at several other universities. He is a reviewer for more than a dozen leading medical journals, has been a consultant to the FDA and to leading pharmaceutical companies—including Merck, and has specifically focused on NSAIDs, including Vioxx. From the standpoint of a first impression on the jury, he is an ideal witness. He has none of the "professional witness" baggage, and no apparent stake in whether Merck wins or

---

[38] For cross-examination, defense counsel gave Dr. Nies two binders containing the exhibits to which counsel would refer in the examination. This technique has several advantages. First, it eliminates the need for counsel to traipse back and forth between the lectern and witness box with each exhibit. Second, in a courtroom equipped with video monitors for exhibits, it lets the witness focus on counsel and the jury more easily than if the witness is constantly turning to a video monitor in the witness box. Third, it gives the jurors a visual picture of a witness handling paper exhibits just as they will be handling them in the jury room during deliberations.

loses. The defense did not ask him any questions on voir dire about his qualifications.

In November 2000, Merck asked Dr. Ray to comment on the VIGOR trial, which compared Vioxx to Naproxen. Plaintiff's counsel Jere Beasley led up to this testimony by questioning Dr. Nies on redirect about Naproxen.

Q. So has Merck actually sought your assistance as a consultant?

A. In the past, yes.

Q. In what specific areas?

A. The occasion was a meeting that I was invited to discuss the cardiovascular outcomes of the VIGOR trial. That would be in November of 2000.

Q. Who actually invited you, from Merck, to attend the meeting about the cardiovascular outcomes of the VIGOR trial?

A. Dr. Harry Guess.

Q. What happened in this meeting, doctor?

A. The results of the VIGOR trial, particularly with respect to the cardiovascular results—that is, the effect on heart attacks— were presented and the various explanations for those results were put forth and the persons at the meeting were asked to comment on those explanations.

Q. Did Merck scientists or Merck employees ask your opinions or your conclusions about the VIGOR study?

A. Yes, they did.

Q. What were your opinions at that time, doctor?

A. My opinion was that the theory that naproxen was a very effective drug for preventing heart attacks, the theory that that explained the VIGOR findings, I thought that was speculative. I said that it was speculative and dangerous to assume that that explained the results of the VIGOR trial.

After this disclosure and a discussion of qualifications and experience, plaintiff's counsel Paul Sizemore asked Dr. Ray for a summary of his opinions.[39]

---

[39] Doing this at the outset of an expert examination, and indeed in other contexts as well, helps the jury prepare to receive what is to follow. In the excerpt above, there was an interruption as the defense sought to limit the scope of Dr. Ray's opinions on causation. The quoted response on that issue was tailored to the judge's ruling, which forbade Dr. Ray from giving an opinion on what caused Dicky Irvin's heart attack.

Q. Doctor, I want to move on to your opinions in this case while we are here. Have you developed expert opinions in reference to this case, doctor?

A. Yes, I have. . . .

Q. Having reviewed the medical and scientific literature, doctor, and then having conducted studies in this area, are you prepared to offer your opinions to a reasonable degree of scientific certainty today?

A. Yes, sir, I am.

Q. Did you develop your opinions utilizing the same care and diligence that you ordinarily exercise while practicing in the field of pharmacoepidemiology?

A. I certainly did my very best, sir.

Q. Doctor, would you, then, tell us what opinions you do have in this case in a summary fashion so we can, therefore, move on.

A. Yes. My first opinion is that Vioxx causes heart attacks. . . . My second opinion is that the benefits of Vioxx, with regard to preventing ulcers, are less than the excess risks of heart attack and other serious cardiovascular disease. My third opinion is that the increased risk of Vioxx for heart attacks is present for people who use it between one and 30 days. My fourth opinion is that even people who already are at risk for heart attack because they have something we call risk factors will have their risk of heart attacks increased by Vioxx.

Q. Any others, doctor?

A. My final opinion . . ., that is, in patients who are taking Vioxx and have a heart attack, the Vioxx is more likely than not the cause of their heart attack.

Dr. Ray then worked through the various clinical studies of Vioxx and evaluated the results. Merck lawyer Philip Beck's cross-examination dwelt to some extent on Dr. Ray's having consulted for Merck competitors and on Dr. Ray having at one time written that low dosages of Vioxx did not seem to contribute to cardiac events.

However, Beck focused more at length on an area where Dr. Ray would be sure to support Merck's position: the dangers of stomach bleeding from the traditional NSAIDs such as ibuprofen and aspirin, the nonselective Cox inhibitors, and the deaths that resulted from NSAID use by the elderly. Beck then questioned Dr. Ray about studies showing relative risk assessments between Vioxx and Celebrex on the one hand and traditional NSAIDs on the other. Dr. Ray did not become defensive under cross-examination. However, he would not be moved from his principal conclusion, as the first questions on redirect showed:

Q.   Doctor, Mr. Beck talked to you about the risk and benefits of Vioxx. Have you examined this issue?

A.   Yes. There is one clinical trial, the VIGOR study, where you can compare the clinical benefits to the clinical risks, and I've examined those findings.

Q.   Do you have an opinion whether the risks of Vioxx in causing heart attacks and death outweighs the GI [gastrointestinal] benefits?

Mr. Beck: I object, Your Honor.

The Court: I overrule the objection.

The Witness: The findings of the VIGOR study clearly show that it was. There were 9.4 extra cases of serious cardiovascular disease per thousand patients, and 7.8 serious ulcer complications prevented. So it's more serious heart disease caused than ulcers prevented. And that's pretty clear-cut.

Q.   Let me ask you a simple question, doctor. Is Vioxx a cure for NSAID-related deaths?

A.   No. It's not, really. And you know, we have to be sure that—and I as much as anyone would love to see a pain medication that, you know, is freer of side effects than the old NSAIDS. And everybody thought that Vioxx might be, but unfortunately, it causes more cardiovascular disease than ulcers prevented. so those are the facts.

Dicky Irvin took Vioxx prescribed for him by his son-in-law, Dr. Christopher Schirmer. The plaintiff offered Dr. Schirmer's testimony by deposition. Dr. Schirmer's wife Allesha, who was Irvin's daughter, told Dr. Schirmer of her father's back pain and asked him to phone a prescription from his Florida office to the pharmacy nearest the Irvin home in Alabama. Mrs. Schirmer is a cardiopulmonary technician. Irvin was not Dr. Schirmer's patient. The two men saw each other perhaps twice or three times a year. Dr. Schirmer's testimony was essential to establishing how Irvin came into contact with a regular supply of Vioxx. Dr. Schirmer testified that he did not see any warnings connected with Vioxx that would lead him to avoid prescribing it. However, he was not an expert on the subject. The only medical "conference" he had ever attended on COX–2 inhibitors was a steak and "twelve year old Scotch" dinner given by Pfizer to discuss the merits of Celebrex. He received most of his information about Irvin's physical condition from Mrs. Schirmer. He had not reviewed Irvin's medical records.

However, Dr. Schirmer did say that as a treating physician specializing in emergency medicine, he relies on the pharmaceutical companies to give him complete and accurate information so that he can evaluate the risks and benefits of drugs.

Plaintiff's counsel decided to wind up their battle of the experts with two video depositions from Dr. Eric Topol, the cardiologist who has been active in criticizing Vioxx and Merck,[40] and Merck scientist Dr. Edward Scolnick, who also appeared by deposition in the Ernst trial.[41]

Dr. Topol testified that when Merck looked at the VIGOR study results, its scientists should have seen the risk that Vioxx was contributing to clotting and therefore to cardiac events. He drafted an article setting out his concerns, and gave a copy of it to some Merck scientists, including Dr. Alise Reicin. Dr. Topol has criticized Merck and the FDA for failing to appreciate Vioxx risks for patients with cardiovascular problems. He summarized his central concern:

A. Well, in 1999, in May, the FDA approved Vioxx for commercial use, so that is an important time, time line. That was also at the time when the FDA had a formal review of the medicine, where the primary reviewer already had expressed in her document,

---

[40] The medical journal discussions of Vioxx include articles co-authored by Dr. Topol, e.g., E.J. Topol, Failing the Public Health: Rofecoxib, Merck and the FDA, New England Journal of Medicine, vol. 351, p. 1707 (2004); E.J. Topol, et al., Risk of cardiovascular events associated with selective COX-2 inhibitors, Journal of the American Medical Association, vol. 286, p. 954 (2001). The Merck results were reported in Reicin, et al., Comparison of gastrointestinal toxicity of rofecoxib and naproxen in patients with rheumatoid arthritis, New England Journal of Medicine, vol. 343, p. 1520 (2000).

[41] By this time in the trial, the jury had heard many hours of video deposition, as had the Ernst jurors. Because of territorial limits of subpoena service, most federal and state civil cases that involve complex facts require the lawyers to present deposition testimony. Before the days of video, lawyers or paralegals would read deposition testimony, with the "witness" on the stand and the interrogator reading the questions. This is still the practice with testimony that has not been preserved on video. One must ask, however, whether jurors will truly pay attention to video monitors that feature a "talking head" for more than twenty or thirty minutes. Most video depositions focus only on the witness. The jury misses the chance to evaluate the interplay between witness and examiner. Anecdotal evidence suggests that juror attention flags after awhile. Trial lawyers should consider editing video depositions down to preserve the important answers, and some of the questions, and offering edited versions that compress the examination. In oral testimony at trial, the witness is not permitted to narrate. The examination must proceed with questions and answers, if only to permit the trial judge to exercise control and prevent inadmissible matter from reaching the jury. That risk is gone when the deposition has been concluded and the parties have chosen the parts they want the jury to hear. Dr. Topol's testimony provides an example of what "might have been." His video deposition took an entire trial day, yet the "meat" of it was perhaps a couple of hours. On the other hand, one might argue that the information he is presenting is difficult to put into perspective and a slower pace aids understanding.

Dr. Villalba, that there was a concern regarding clotting events with Vioxx even at the time of approval in May 1999.

Q. You write here that, "the approval was based on data from trials lasting three to six months and involving patients at low risk for cardiovascular illness." Do you see that?

A. That's right.

Q. What is the significance of that fact?

A. Well, this is one of the most significant parts of the whole clinical development of the Vioxx medicine, and that is that patients with heart disease were not tested in any meaningful way, and we know from multiple databases and surveys that at least 40 to 50 percent of the patients who actually took this medicine when it was in clinical use actually did have known heart disease.

In response to Dr. Topol's draft paper speaking of the VIGOR study results, Dr. Reicin wrote an e-mail note to her Merck colleagues, saying "We prefer to flip the data and say it was reduced on Naproxen" and another saying "Conclusion needs to be toned down.[42]" Dr. Reicin and other Merck scientists came to Cleveland to meet with Dr. Topol and his colleagues. Dr. Topol testified that he believed they were not really concerned about the science but were trying to influence him to change his conclusions. They suggested to Dr. Topol that his publishing his paper would be "an embarrassment" to the clinic he heads.

The deposition cross-examination of Dr. Topol did little to blunt the force of his comments. He did say that he had taken Vioxx over a period of time for knee arthritis, and acknowledged that he sent a note to a Merck scientist thanking the Merck people for "insightful" comments on his draft paper, and that he would incorporate some of those in the final version.

Plaintiff concluded the battle of experts with the video deposition of Dr. Edward Scolnick, who was president of Merck Research laboratories during the Vioxx development period. On adverse examination, plaintiff's counsel Birchfield confronted Scolnick with damaging e-mail communications about Vioxx. On June 1, 1998, Dr. Scolnick sent an e-mail to a number of Merck employees saying that he would resign if Merck did not beat the competition to market with a COX–2 inhibitor.

Scolnick was aware that a potential Vioxx study focusing on cardiac events—the very point that Dr. Topol raised—was talked about but

---

[42] In this as in many recent cases involving corporate or other organizations, hastily-drafted and ill-considered e-mails come back to haunt their authors and the organization.

never done. Birchfield then confronted him with a March 2000 e-mail, in which Scolnick reacted to the VIGOR study:

Q. As of March 2000 you, Edward Scolnick, knew that the CV events—the heart attacks and strokes—were clearly there; and you, Edward Scolnick, knew that they were mechanism-based with Vioxx, true?

A. That was my very first reaction when I saw the data from the VIGOR trial.

Q. You knew it from the get-go; it was your first reaction, right?

A. It was my first reaction before other data was available.

And to follow it up:

Q. So after you studied the data, you went through it, you sent a memo out to everybody—even though you hold yourself to a high standard—telling everybody that the CV events are clearly there, and that was in March of 2000, wasn't it?

A. Yes, it is.

Q. You never sent out an order at that point in time for a CV outcomes study, did you?

A. I did not send out an order for a CV outcomes study. We took many immediate actions to try to understand the cardiovascular events since we couldn't conclude what was going on in the trial because there was no placebo in the trial.

Indeed, within 18 days of his first reaction to the VIGOR study, Scolnick had changed his mind and adopted the view that Naproxen's cardioprotective effect accounted for the VIGOR results and that Merck should put out a press release saying so. Birchfield also showed Dr. Scolnick an e-mail in which he wrote "the FDA, they are bastards," referring to a proposal to put a cardiac warning on Vioxx.

Birchfield's adverse examination continued for almost an entire trial day. While there is no doubt that Dr. Scolnick is a distinguished scientist who has had a productive career, his manner of expression and his company loyalty made him good material for the plaintiff's case.

The defense cross of Scolnick was brief. Counsel went over his qualifications and experience, and then had Scolnick discuss the risks and benefits of Vioxx. The cross-examination was perhaps designed to show Scolnick in a more favorable light. It would not have been tactically sound to end his appearance with the plaintiff's questions.

Evelyn Irvin Plunkett appeared as the final plaintiff's witness, to talk about her close and loving relationship with her husband, his athletic activities, and his good health. During cross-examination, Merck counsel Beck made one of those rare—for him—missteps that sometimes come from insufficient preparation. He brought out that the Irvins had lived apart for a time, perhaps to suggest that their relationship was not as close as Mrs. Irvin had claimed. It turns out that in 1996 Mr. Irvin lost his job and the family could not afford to keep their home, so Mrs. Irvin moved in with her mom to take care of the kids and Mr. Irvin would live closer to his place of work. The family continued to work as a unit and pursue all its regular activities.

The defense case consisted of four live witnesses:

- Dr. David Silver, a rheumatologist who practices and teaches in Los Angeles. Rheumatologists, Dr. Silver explained, deal with "diseases involving pain, inflammation such as arthritis, diseases of the joints, muscles, bones, and autoimmune diseases." Dr. Silver is also board-certified in internal medicine. He is associate medical director of a nonprofit center that conducts clinical trials of new medicines, and is on the staff of hospitals as well as a faculty member at UCLA Medical School. He has written peer-reviewed articles and a popular book on coping with arthritis.

- Dr. Briggs Morrison, a Merck vice president who had some oversight responsibility for Vioxx development. He had been at counsel table during the trial as Merck corporate representative and testified as a fact witness rather than as an expert.

- Dr. Alise Reicin, who appeared in the Ernst case, discussed Vioxx development and responded specifically to Dr. Topol's statements about his draft article and to his claim that Merck ought to have conducted a clinical trial with patients with cardiovascular problems.

- Dr. Thomas Wheeler, the pathologist who also testified in Ernst, who spoke about the cause of Dicky Irvin's fatal heart attack.

Dr. Silver was a good choice. He is involved in patient care. He understands how to communicate his views. He is not a Merck insider. He has written thousands of prescriptions for selective and nonselective NSAIDs, and has given dozens of medical school lectures on Cox inhibitors. In contrast to the witnesses in the Ernst case, he presented graphic testimony about the benefits of Vioxx and why it represented an important advance in medical research.

Granted, as plaintiff's counsel brought out on the voir dire, Dr. Silver is not a cardiologist, hematologist, pathologist epidemiologist, or pharmacologist; he is not an expert in drug label warnings, except that he works with those warnings when deciding what to prescribe for patients. He was, Judge Fallon ruled, qualified to give opinions in his areas of practice with specific reference to the risks and benefits of COX–2 inhibitors.

Beck introduced the subjects of Dr. Silver's direct:

Q. Have we asked you to come here today—and it looks like tomorrow, as well—to discuss with the jury the subject of the importance of treating chronic pain and inflammation?

A. Yes.

Q. Have we also asked you to come here and discuss with the jury the subject of the contribution that Vioxx and other COX–2 inhibitors have made to treating pain and inflation (sic)?

A. Yes.

Q. Inflammation. I'm sorry. I guess inflation you really can't do much about.

A. No. I don't proffer myself as an expert in that, no.

Q. Then we asked you to come and discuss with the jury the subject that we have alluded to here of whether the benefits of Vioxx, in your professional judgment, outweigh the risk?

A. Yes.

Dr. Silver described the consequences of stomach bleeding that can be caused by ibuprofen and other nonselective NSAIDs, when patients take enough of them to get the pain relief they need:

Q. So explain, then, what happens.

A. What happens is this ulcer erodes into this blood vessel, goes down, and the blood vessel starts bleeding. This is usually an artery which is under high pressure, and blood just starts spilling out. Unfortunately, usually patients don't have a warning sign. In the majority of cases, there's nothing to tell them that this ulcer is going to occur until they just start vomiting blood or having blood coming out their other end, and this can happen very quickly and they can hemorrhage and bleed enormously.

Q. Have you seen this, yourself, with your own eyes?

A. Unfortunately, I have. Even back in times when I was a medical student and a resident, I recall seeing patients in the intensive care unit who would be just basically bleeding out, bleeding to death, from these horrible ulcers. I've actually seen, unfortunately, patients die from this. I've looked at them with the gastroenterologist, looked through one of these scopes. You can put a scope down through the mouth and the stomach called an endoscope and you can see these ulcers that are bleeding. You can just see the blood sort of shooting out. It's almost like a faucet. It's coming out and it's a horrible sight, it really is.

Q. You said there were two main problems. One of them is if the acid starts to eat through the wall and hits one of these arteries. What's the other most significant problem that can come with these nonselective NSAIDs?

A. The other serious problem is something called a perforation. Basically, the ulcer goes completely through the entire wall of the stomach and the stomach perforates. What happens is all the contents of the stomach go into your abdominal cavity—that's your abdominal area—and cause a condition called peritonitis, which is a horrible life-threatening infection.

Then, said Dr. Silver, came the COX–2 inhibitors:

When the COX–2 inhibitors came around, this opened a whole new opportunity of treatment to our patients who were suffering with this chronic, terrible pain from a number of different causes, including arthritis, and now we were able to treat them.

For the remainder of Dr. Silver's direct examination, Beck used a chart that he had shown the jury in opening statement about the risks and benefits of Vioxx compared with other pain relievers, ticking off points on the chart as the examination proceeded. This was an excellent way to remind the jury of the first things they had heard from the defense.

Dr. Silver described a physician's role as reviewing all the available literature on a product and assessing the risks as to each patient. He said he assessed cardiovascular risks as to Vioxx.

Q. As a treating physician, a medical researcher, and a professor who teaches both doctors and medical students, do you have an opinion as to whether the disclosure of the cardiovascular risks was adequate for folks like you to make the risk-benefit analysis?

A. Yes, I do believe it was appropriate.

Q. Why is that?

A. Because it sums up what the opinions were at that time. It basically states, here is the results, you know, you can make your interpretation, but that the feeling at that time in the medical community is that the significance of those results was unknown.

Dr. Silver was aware of the basic hypothesis that Dr. Lucchesi embraces, which in this trial was sometimes called the Fitzgerald hypothesis, but he did not agree with it. Here is how he put the matter:

Q. Have you heard of the—something called the Fitzgerald hypothesis?

A. Yes.

Q. That COX–2 inhibitors may cause some sort of an imbalance between thromboxane and prostacyclin?

A. Yes.

Q. When did you first become aware of the Fitzgerald hypothesis?

A. In the late 1990s.

Q. How did you become aware of it?

A. It was talked about in the literature, in published papers, I believe starting back in 1999, as well as it was discussed at, you know, scientific meetings and other venues.

Q. In the world of medicine, what does the word "hypothesis" mean?

A. Hypothesis is basically a theory that someone—we hear about these all the time—that somebody will say, "I believe based on what I'm looking at that this may occur." We hear theories all over the place. There are theories that COX–2 actually, because of their anti-inflammatory effects, lower the rate of heart attack. We heard about the Fitzgerald hypothesis and a number of other things that were floating around.

Q. Does the fact that something is out there with the phrase "hypothesis" attached to it; does that mean that it's been proven or supported by any actual medical data?

A. Not necessarily, no.

Q. Does an unproven hypothesis affect how you practice medicine?

A. Absolutely not. I mean, the problem is, if we looked at every hypothesis that was available and just accepted it, our hands would be tied as a doctor. We would never be able to practice medicine. We have to look at all the clinical data, what all the clinical data is, and make a decision whether or not this hypothesis applies to my patients when I'm looking at the individual patient in my office.

Q. Did your knowledge of the existence of the hypothesis, of the Fitzgerald hypothesis, cause you not to prescribe Vioxx or Celebrex to the patients who needed pain relief?

A. No.[43]

---

[43] This is a good approach when the other side has the burden of proof—to characterize the opponent's theory as an unproven hypothesis.

Dr. Silver also reviewed, for the jury, literature showing that the FDA doubts Dr. Lucchesi's hypothesis, and work by other researchers casting doubt on it. In doing the examination, Beck did not himself take on the role of an expert talking to a colleague, but was seeking to be the jurors' surrogate, asking the questions he thought they would want to ask.

The cross-examination confronted Dr. Silver with the opinions of plaintiffs' experts. Counsel Mathews also focused on Dr. Silver not being a cardiologist, to which Dr. Silver replied that he understood that Mr. Irvin had severe pain and that was something within his specialty and with which he deals regularly in his practice, where he sees patients with pain symptoms who also have cardiovascular issues.

Dr. Morrison began by talking about his parallel professional interests, ever since medical school, in both patient care and laboratory research. In addition to talking about aspects of risk and benefit, Dr. Morrison directly addressed reasons why Merck did not do a specific cardiac risk Vioxx study, and why he had himself counseled against such a study. He said that a principal reason was that such a study would have to include people at high risk for cardiac events, and that in order to isolate any potential effect of Vioxx, the study group could not be taking low-dose aspirin. If that were done, Dr. Morrison said, it would pose an unacceptable risk to that patient population. In addition, in the group that was deprived of aspirin, there might well be an increase in cardiac events and that result might unjustly be blamed on Vioxx. Dr. Morrison held up well on cross-examination that focused on the issues that all Merck witnesses faced.

Dr. Alise Reicin[44] was the next-to-last witness. Beck conducted the direct examination. Reicin used an analogy to show how she viewed the VIGOR results:

Q. Now, just to back up a bit, you said that one of your first projects with respect to Vioxx was setting up or designing a GI outcomes trial with respect to the drug?

A. That's correct. One of the serious toxicity of NSAIDs, traditional NSAIDs, is that they cause serious gastrointestinal side effects. We were trying to prove that Vioxx, a COX–2 inhibitor,

---

[44] There was also the issue, which has continued to resonate in Vioxx litigation, of whether Merck scientists' article in the New England Journal of Medicine about the VIGOR study was misleading because it left out some of the results of that study. When the omissions were discovered, the New England Journal reacted with harsh criticism of Merck. Dr. Reicin, in the Plunkett case, said that the omissions were caused by late data reporting and would not have altered the significance of the Merck conclusions. Based on this controversy, a New Jersey judge awarded a new trial in a case that Merck won. *New Jersey Judge Vacates Merck Vioxx Trial Win*, http://jurist.law.pitt.edu/paperchase/2006/08/new-jersey-judge-vacates-merck-vioxx.php

would have a significant reduction in those serious GI side
effects compared to traditional NSAIDs.

Q. What I want to talk about, doctor, is what the state of science
was at the time that you were designing this GI outcomes trial
in around 1997. If there was a clinical trial that put on the one
arm placebo and the other arm aspirin, what would you expect
the cardiovascular data from that trial to show?

A. You would see fewer serious cardiovascular events, such as
heart attack, in patients who were taking aspirin—I assume
we're talking about low-dose aspirin—compared with placebo.

Q. Would it be appropriate in such a trial to conclude that a
placebo, a sugar pill, was causing an increased amount of
cardiovascular events?

A. I think you would assume that the placebo was neutral and that
the aspirin was reducing the incidence of heart attacks. It would
not be appropriate to assume that placebo was increasing the
rate.

Dr. Reicin also discussed the reasons for not conducting a cardiac
events study that took potential cardiac patients off of low-dose aspirin.
She agreed with an e-mail that Dr. Morrison had sent, saying that if you
deprive patients of their aspirin while they are taking Vioxx, there would
be more clotting events and this might unfairly be blamed on Vioxx.

Reicin portrayed her meeting with Dr. Topol as collegial. She said
that they had a good discussion of the hypothesis that Vioxx might have
a clotting effect—the "Fitzgerald hypothesis" that Dr. Lucchesi had
embraced.

At the end of that, he actually told me that he found the data to be
quite reassuring, but that he still felt that the question of Vioxx
cardiovascular safety needed to be further investigated. He also
went out of his way to tell me that he took Vioxx for his knee—
apparently, he is an avid basketball player—and found it to be a
quite effective drug.

Dr. Reicin then described the APPROVe study and the events that led
Merck to withdraw Vioxx from the market.

On cross-examination, Birchfield addressed Reicin's opposition to a
change in the Vioxx label following some of the early studies. She fielded
the question, concluding with a well-crafted statement about how to
decide what to put on a drug warning label:

Q. Did you know that adding a CV risk to the product label would
have a major impact on sales, correct?

A. It certainly may have had an impact on sales. But as I said before, I didn't care if there was an impact on sales. I was going to do what was right for patients. I didn't believe that it—that it belonged in the warning section.

Q. You didn't believe that a CV risk belonged in the product label for Vioxx?

A. I didn't believe it belonged in the warning section. I believe that the VIGOR cardiovascular results should be in the label.

Q. Well, you would agree that a heart attack is a substantial, serious risk; right?

A. Yes, I do, but we did not believe that Vioxx was causing heart attacks. I still don't believe that, with short-term use, it causes heart attacks.

Q. But if the rule is first do no harm, wouldn't you advise doctors of any potential risks that is so serious as a heart attack?

A. In drug development, overwarning is just as dangerous as underwarning.

Dr. Wheeler was the final Merck witness. He took the autopsy report on Dicky Irvin and sentence by sentence discussed the autopsy findings. He used the autopsy slides to illustrate his points. He commented on the paucity of Irvin's medical records, making it difficult to assess some issues. However, he was sure that given Irvin's arterial blockage and the evidence of clotting caused by plaque rupture, these events accounted for his death. At the end of his examination, Dr. Wheeler specifically commented on Drs. Bloor and Lucchesi. A part of that exchange is worth quoting because it illustrates how one expert can comment on another and still maintain a professional attitude:

Q. Was there anything unusual about Mr. Irvin's plaque rupture, clot forming, and the sudden cardiac death?

A. No. Again, this is really the most common cause of death in the United States. This is the top major health problem in the western world. There's nothing unusual. This whole sequence of events is what we teach medical students about in terms of the beginning basis of—pathologic basis of disease for the first-year medical student.

Q. Were you here during Dr. Bloor's testimony?

A. Yes, I was. . . .

Q. Why is it that you wanted to be here when their pathologist testified?

Plaintiff's counsel objected to Dr. Wheeler commenting on Dr. Bloor's testimony. Judge Fallon overruled the objection, noting that "fact witnesses are generally not allowed to comment on fact witnesses' testimony, but experts are."

Q. Doctor, I believe my question was why is it that you wanted to be here and be here physically present to see Dr. Bloor's testimony?

A. Well, Dr. Bloor is a pathologist, like I am, and whenever there's a disagreement, I would like to reconcile that and give the opportunity for him to explain what he sees and correlate it with what I see. So I had hoped that he would show some slides and maybe make that explanation, but it turns out there were no slides demonstrated.

Q. Did you hear Dr. Bloor testify that if, in fact, there was plaque rupture, that that is what lead to the clot and, thus, to the death of Mr. Irvin? Did you hear his testimony on that?

A. I did, yes.

Q. Do you agree with Dr. Bloor that if, in fact, there was plaque rupture, that's what caused the clot and ultimately Mr. Irvin's death?

A. Yes.

Q. Did you read Dr. Lucchesi's testimony?

A. Yes.

Q. Did you read where Dr. Lucchesi said that if, in fact, plaque rupture takes place, the normal response of the body is, when this lipid goo comes into contact with the blood, to form a clot?

A. Yes, I remember that.

Q. That that would happen in somebody who never took Vioxx in their life?

A. Yes.

Cross-examination was brief and focused to some extent on what Dr. Wheeler was being paid. On redirect, Beck brought out that the plaintiff's experts were also paid. When Dr. Wheeler finished, Beck at first said Merck had another witness and then changed his mind and rested.

Plaintiff's counsel in this civil case delivered an opening and a rebuttal summation. The trial judge limited summation time to about one and one-half hours total per side. The plaintiff reserved about 40 minutes for rebuttal.

Andy Birchfield gave the first plaintiff summation. His initial theme was to count the scientists who "stood up" to Merck. He counted off Dr.

Topol and Dr. Ray, and identified them as whistle-blowers, people who raised responsible questions without expectation of reward and at some professional risk. He then took jurors through the special issues on the verdict form, suggesting what evidence supported positive answers to each question. He concluded by returning to the "stood up" theme:

> I want you to know that this family has suffered a loss, but this case is more than just about the money. This is about standing up and making a difference. You'll have to answer those questions about the appropriate amount to compensate them and make them whole, the same questions for Richard Irvin and Ashley Irvin. They stood up. Now it is your turn.... You've heard the Vioxx story. You have heard about how Merck, in search of a blockbuster drug to fill their coffers, they were losing patents and they needed a blockbuster drug to fill the gap. That's Dr. Scolnick's testimony. What did they do in pursuit of that blockbuster drug? They ignored serious cardiovascular events. They ignored those heart attack risks. They didn't stop and do a CV outcomes study before they went to market with this drug. They didn't stop when VIGOR, their big first study, showed a fivefold increase in heart attacks. They didn't stop. They kept pushing forward with an aggressive marketing campaign, all at the expense of the public. You can make a difference. Dr. Topol stood up. He stood up for public health. Dr. Wayne Ray, another whistle-blower, stood up for public health. Now, it's your turn. Thank you.

Phil Beck began with causation, as he had in opening:

> Good morning. Was there plaque rupture? That's a big important question in the case. The reason it's such an important question is that if there is plaque rupture, then the damage case is over. The reason is because the plaintiff's experts agree that if, in fact, there was plaque rupture, then Vioxx did not play any role in the death of Mr. Irvin. Both of them agree to that.
>
> Dr. Lucchesi, you remember him. He was the first witness in the case, an elderly gentleman from the University of Michigan. He's the one who believes in the Fitzgerald hypothesis about the imbalance, and he described that for you. What he also said, when I was asking him questions, was that if there is plaque rupture—and I'm going to use a term that's not very scientific, "goo." I said, "if it's the kind of plaque that's got that lipid core"—that has that goo—"and if there is plaque rupture and the blood comes into contact with the goo"—with the lipid core—"what's the body going to do whether somebody has ever seen Vioxx or not?" He said, "That's going to start the clotting cascade." He agreed that if there is plaque rupture, then the body's natural reaction is going to form that kind of clot that we saw; and that clot is going to cut off the

blood to the heart, and that can result in sudden cardiac death. Dr. Lucchesi said that's been happening since time immemorial, happening before Vioxx was ever around. It's been happening after we stopped selling Vioxx. He said it has nothing to do with Vioxx if, in fact, there is plaque rupture.

Dr. Bloor was even more direct. Now, Mr. Birchfield said that Dr. Bloor testified that Vioxx contributed to Mr. Irvin's death. He did say that; but, of course, he said, that based on his assumption that there was no plaque rupture. Remember, we went back and forth, Dr. Bloor and I did, on that. He said that if there was plaque rupture, Vioxx played no role. . . . He said that several times. I liked that answer, so I kept asking the same question over and over and over again, and he kept saying over and over and over again, "You're right. If there was plaque rupture, Vioxx played no role."

Beck went on to spend perhaps half of his summation on the pathologist evidence about why Dicky Irvin had a fatal heart attack.

For summation, Beck used the same visual aid he had used in opening statement and with some of the witnesses. It was a magnetic board with refrigerator magnets showing each of the significant issues in the case. A chart of this kind, with or without magnets, can be a significant help. In opening, one makes a first impression and a promise of evidence to come. In the trial, one keeps the promise with cross-examination and by calling witnesses. In summation, it is helpful to look back and say, here are the promises I made to you and here is how I kept them.

Beck's summation also illustrated one of the dangers a party can court with overstatement. Recall that Dr. Topol had said that the Merck scientists had treated him disrespectfully, in their writings and in a meeting. In his direct examination on video deposition, he was quite exercised about this. Beck picked up on this issue and went after Topol for exaggerating about the meeting. And, the reasoning would be, if Dr. Topol would exaggerate about that, one might question his scientific conclusions. This is always the problem with the "believer" witness—a tone and manner that creates a negative impression that can influence evaluation of the witness's underlying message. See how Beck addresses it:

I know you were paying close attention. You know, I listened to Dr. Topol and he's so vehement. I think he said he's written more articles than anybody in America. He's the kind of guy who not only counts how many articles he writes, he counts how many articles other people write beside his articles. He knows it off of the top of his head. He's an important guy and he thinks of himself that way, but he kept contradicting himself during the testimony. He kept contradicting in his sworn testimony today what he actually wrote down back in 2001 when he was talking about the VIGOR study. I talked about the e-mails. They are not the biggest deal in the world, but they reflect a little bit on Dr. Topol. You know, he set up the meeting. He said, "This mean Dr. Reicin came in and tried to intimidate me, scare me off of writing my article." You saw Alise Reicin. You saw Dr. Topol on the screen. Do you think Alise Reicin, 98 pounds sopping wet, is going to intimidate Dr. Topol when he's sitting there in his big office at the Cleveland Clinic? Of course, while he said that it was very unpleasant, his e-mails said, "It was very nice to meet you. Thank you for coming." My pal, Andy Goldman, was the guy who was asking the questions. He said, "Well, didn't you later say, 'Thanks for the suggestions. They were helpful, and I'll see if I can incorporate this,' " he said, "Absolutely not. I never got any suggestions in the first place; and if I did, they weren't helpful." He got angry at the very thought that he received suggestions. Andy said, "But here is your e-mail where you say, 'Thanks for the suggestions. The helpful ones, I'm going to try to put them in the manuscript,' " and he got angry at Andy for showing him an e-mail that contradicted what he said under oath. So the e-mails, as I said, not the biggest deal in the world, but interesting insight into the guy.

Beck addressed questions about Merck's conduct. He ticked off the names and accomplishments of the Merck scientists who worked on Vioxx, the outside experts Merck had called in, and the Merck analysis that eventually led to withdrawing Vioxx from the market because of some possible risk among patients who took it for 36 months.

As noted above, the jury failed to agree and on retrial Merck got a verdict.

On November 9, 2007, Merck announced that it will create a fund to settle many if not most of the Vioxx cases. This step reflects the experience that plaintiffs and defendant lawyers gained in the initial round of litigation cases. One value of trials such as those chronicled in this chapter is to permit the parties to evaluate settlement prospects in related litigation. Litigation experience is often far more valuable than estimates of probabilities that do not draw upon real-life trial results.

Author Biographies

Michael E. Tigar is Research Professor of Law at the American University Washington College of Law and Visiting Professor of Law at Duke Law School. He has been a lawyer, author and law teacher for more than 40 years, and has tried cases and argued appeals in many forums across the United States. His clients have included Terry Lynn Nichols, John Connally, Sen. Kay Bailey Hutchison, Fernando Chavez, Lynne Stewart and Dominic Gentile. Professor Tigar is the author of many works on advocacy, including *Examining Witnesses* (2d ed. 2003) and *Persuasion: The Litigator's Art* (1999).

Angela J. Davis is a Professor of Law at the American University Washington College of Law where she teaches Criminal Law, Criminal Procedure, and Criminal Defense: Theory and Practice. She is the author of *Arbitrary Justice: The Power of the American Prosecutor* (Oxford University Press, 2007) and a co-author of the 4th edition of *Basic Criminal Procedure* (West Thomson, 4th Ed. 2005). Professor Davis received the American University Faculty Award for Outstanding Teaching in a Full–Time Appointment in 2002 and the Washington College of Law's Pauline Ruyle Moore award for scholarly contribution in the area of public law in 2000. Professor Davis was a Soros Senior Justice Fellow in 2004. A graduate of Howard University and Harvard Law School, Professor Davis is a member of the visiting faculty of the Harvard Law School Trial Advocacy Workshop and is a former staff attorney and executive director of the Public Defender Service for the District of Columbia.

Barbara Bergman is a Professor of Law at the University of New Mexico School of Law where she teaches courses on Evidence, Trial Practice, Criminal Law, and Criminal Procedure. Before turning to teaching fulltime in 1987, she was a staff attorney at the Public Defender Service for the District of Columbia. Professor Bergman has served on the faculty at the National Criminal Defense College and the Institute for Criminal Defense Advocacy and is the co-director of the Southwest Regional NITA Trial Practice Program. She is also the co-author of the *EveryTrial Criminal Defense Resource Book* as well as the fifteenth edition of *Wharton's Criminal Evidence* and the fourteenth edition of

Wharton's Criminal Procedure. Professor Bergman is a past-president of the National Association of Criminal Defense Lawyers ("NACDL") and is a co-chair of the NACDL Amicus Committee.

Paul Bergman is Professor of Law Emeritus at UCLA School of Law. His books (authored or co-authored) include: *Reel Justice: The Courtroom Goes to the Movies* (2d ed. 2006); *Evidence Law and Practice* (3d ed. 2007); *Trial Advocacy in a Nutshell* (4th ed. 2007); *Lawyers as Counselors: A Client Centered Approach* (2nd ed. 2004); *Represent Yourself in Court* (6th ed. 2007); *Trial Advocacy: Inferences, Arguments, Techniques* (1996); *The Criminal Law Handbook* (9th ed. 2007); *Nolo's Deposition Handbook* (3d ed. 2006); *Deposition Questioning Strategies and Techniques* (2001); *Fact Investigation: From Hypothesis to Proof* (1984). Articles include: The Movie Lawyers' Guide to Redemptive Law Practice, in Lawyers' Ethics and the Pursuit of Social Justice. (NYU Press 2005), reprinted from 48 U.C.L.A. L. Rev. 1393 (2001); Emergency! Send a TV Show to Rescue Paramedic Services, Current Legal Issues 2004, Oxford Univ. Press; Teaching Evidence the Reel Way, 21 Quinnipiac L. R. 973 (2003); Taking Lawyering Skills Training Seriously, 10 Clin. L. Rev. 191 (2003); A Bunch of Circumstantial Evidence, 30 U.S.F. L. Rev. 985 (1996); Pranks for the Memory, 30 U.S.F. L. Rev. 1235 (1996); Mistrial By Likelihood Ratio: Bayesian Analysis Meets the F–Word, 13 Cardozo L. Rev. 589–619 (l991); Learning from Experience: Non–Legally Specific Role Plays, 38 J. of Legal Ed. 535–53 (1987).

James E. Coleman is the Professor of the Practice of Law at Duke Law School where he teaches criminal law, legal ethics, negotiation and mediation, capital punishment, and wrongful convictions. His prior legal experience includes serving as Chief Counsel for the U.S. House of Representatives ethics investigation of Pennsylvania Representatives Joshua Eilberg and Daniel Flood and as the Deputy General Counsel of the Department of Education. Professor Coleman also was Assistant General Counsel of the Legal Services Corporation and a partner at the law firm of Wilmer, Cutler and Pickering. In private practice, he specialized in federal court and administrative litigation and represented criminal defendants in capital collateral proceedings. Professor Coleman is a graduate of Harvard College and Columbia Law School.

Robert A. Ferguson is the George Edward Woodberry Professor of Law, Literature, and Criticism at Columbia University. He teaches in both the Law School and the Department of English and Comparative Literature at Columbia University and is the author of *Law and Letters in American Culture* (1987), *The American Enlightenment, 1750–1820* (1997), *Reading the Early Republic* (2004), an edited addition of *The Federalist* (2006), and *The Trial in American Life* (2007). He is currently writing on the novel of generational conflict.

Robert M. Lloyd is the Lindsay Young Distinguished Professor at the University of Tennessee College of Law, where he was the founding Director of the Clayton Center for Entrepreneurial Law. He holds a B.S.E. in Aerospace Engineering from Princeton University and a J.D. from the University of Michigan. Prior to coming to Tennessee, Professor Lloyd served in the United States Marine Corps and practiced law in Los Angeles. Professor Lloyd is the author of numerous publications in the fields of contracts, commercial law, and damages. His primary research interest is damages in business litigation.

Carol Steiker is the Howard J. and Katherine W. Aibel Professor of Law at Harvard Law School. Professor Steiker attended Harvard–Radcliffe Colleges and Harvard Law School, where she served as president of the Harvard Law Review. After clerking for Judge J. Skelly Wright of the D.C. Circuit Court of Appeals and Justice Thurgood Marshall of the U.S. Supreme Court, she worked as a staff attorney for the Public Defender Service for the District of Columbia, where she represented indigent defendants at all stages of the criminal process. She has been a member of the Harvard Law School faculty since 1992, where she was Associate Dean for Academic Affairs from 1998–2001 and where she currently serves as the Dean's Special Advisor for Public Service. Professor Steiker is the author of numerous scholarly works in the fields of criminal law, criminal procedure, and capital punishment. She recently has joined as co-author the Kadish, Schulhofer & Steiker casebook, *Criminal Law and Its Processes* (8th ed. 2007), she is the editor of *Criminal Procedure Stories* (Foundation Press 2006), and she served on the Board of Editors of the *Encyclopedia of Crime and Justice* (2nd ed. Macmillan, 2002). In addition to her scholarly work, Professor Steiker has worked on pro bono litigation projects on behalf of indigent criminal defendants and has served as a consultant and an expert witness on issues of criminal justice for non-profit organizations and federal and state legislatures.

Marianne Wesson, known to friends as Mimi, has been a law professor at the University of Colorado at Boulder since 1976, where she teaches Evidence, Trial Practice, Criminal Law, and a seminar in Law and Literature. In the past she has been a federal prosecutor, university administrator, acting dean, and best-selling novelist. Her three novels about Boulder lawyer Cinda Hayes, RENDER UP THE BODY, A SUGGESTION OF DEATH, and CHILLING EFFECT, have been national bestsellers and won prizes in this country and overseas. Professor Wesson has been designated a President's Teaching Scholar, the University of Colorado's highest form of recognition for excellence in teaching. Her other awards include the Mary Lathrop Award, bestowed by the Colorado Women's Bar Association, and Elizabeth Gee Memorial Lectureship at the University of Colorado. Professor Wesson is also a regular legal correspondent for National Public Radio. She is working on a book about the Hillmon case.

Ellen Yaroshefsky is a Clinical Professor of Law, Executive Director of the Jacob Burns Ethics Center and Co–Director the Intensive Trial Advocacy Program at the Benjamin N. Cardozo Law School in New York City. She is also Of Counsel to Clayman and Rosenberg, a criminal defense firm. A former Seattle–King County Public Defender, an attorney for the New York-based Center for Constitutional Rights in New York and a private practitioner, she has litigated civil rights, criminal and international human rights cases. Professor Yaroshefsky serves as an ethics consultant and expert and is a frequent lecturer on ethics topics and criminal advocacy. The recipient of teaching and litigation awards, she is the Chair of the National Association of Criminal Defense Lawyers Ethics Committee and co-chairs the American Bar Association's Committee on Ethics, Gideon and Professionalism. Professor Yaroshefsky writes in the area of criminal defense and prosecution ethics.

†